Souwesto Lives

Souwesto Lives:
John Hair and Alice Runnalls

Donald S. Hair

Rock's Mills Press
Rock's Mills, Ontario • Oakville, Ontario
2022

Published by
Rock's Mills Press
www.rocksmillspress.com

Copyright © 2022, 2017 Donald S. Hair
All rights reserved. Published by arrangement with the author.

First Rock's Mills Press hardcover edition: November 2017
First Rock's Mills Press paperback edition (with corrections): November 2022

For information, contact the publisher at customer.service@rocksmillspress.com
or visit us online at www.rocksmillspress.com.

In memory of

John Alexander Hair
Born 21 July 1902 – Died 9 July 1983

and

Alice Maud Runnalls
Born 10 May 1908 – Died 2 February 1982

CONTENTS

ACKNOWLEDGEMENTS ... *ix*
INTRODUCTION ... *xiii*

1. My Father's Birth (1902), his Forebears, and Early Life in Brooke Township ... *1*
2. My Mother's Birth (1908), her Forebears, and Early Life in Dawn and Caradoc Townships ... *36*
3. John Hair's Early Life: 1902–1926 ... *59*
4. Alice Runnalls's Early Life: 1908–1926 ... *98*
5. My Father's Life: 1927–1935 ... *126*
6. My Mother's Life: 1926–1935 ... *144*
7. Wedding and Early Married Life: 1935–1939 ... *167*
8. The War Years and After: 1940–1947 ... *184*
9. The Post-War Years: 1948–1954 ... *218*
10. The Watford Years: 1954–1960 ... *247*
11. The 1960s and Early '70s ... *268*
12. The Final Decade: 1972–1983 ... *288*

REFERENCES AND SOURCES ... *311*
INDEX ... *317*

ACKNOWLEDGEMENTS

Many sources underpin this narrative, and I am grateful to a host of people—librarians, archivists, genealogists, and family members—for access to the records, documents, notes, family trees, and memoirs that make this story possible. I had been collecting such materials for years, but sustained work began in the D.B. Weldon Library and its ARCC (Archives and Research Collections Centre) at Western University, with their microfilm copies of the Watford *Guide-Advocate* and the Strathroy *Age-Dispatch*. Western's holdings of the *Guide* end in 1927, and I am grateful to Laurie McBeth, curator of the Lambton County Archives in Wyoming, for generously lending me microfilm of subsequent issues. And where numbers were missing in both libraries' holdings, the staff of the *Guide* itself allowed me to use bound copies of the paper, still stored, at that time, above the century-old office on the main street in Watford. When I needed particular issues of the *Age*, the staff at the Middlesex County Library in Strathroy cheerfully found them for me. And thanks to Darlene Wiltsie, Archival and Special Collections librarian, University of Guelph, for photocopies of my grandfather's academic records from 1898–9, and for relevant sections of the *O.A.C. Review*.

I am grateful to Hilary and Peter Neary for their interest in this project, for their guidance in finding materials, and for their extensive knowledge of sources relating to the cultural history of Ontario. They led me, among other places, to the war records at Library and Archives Canada, which supplied me with photocopies documenting the wartime experiences and deaths of Roy Runnalls and Billy Wilson.

A book like this inevitably includes family stories and memories that do not have supporting documentary evidence, but while facts may be missing, the stories themselves are true to their time and place. And I am grateful to everyone who did commit to paper names and dates and facts: to our cousin Catherine Watson for all her work on the Watson, Campbell and Smith families, on the history of Salem Church, and on school sections 10 and 5, Brooke Township; to Betty Searson-Anderson for information on St. James Cemetery, Brooke Township; to Bill Dolbear for a letter about his Aunt Edna; to the Reverend Jim Breen of Hope United Church, Alvinston, for facts about the closing of Walnut Church; to Aunt Mima Thompson for her recollections of the Runnallses in Dawn Township; to Thompson and McCracken descendants in

Mount Brydges for gathering together notes on their family; to Uncle Frank Runnalls for his memoirs and to his daughter Dr. Donna Runnalls for publishing them; to Jean Runnalls for preparing a Runnalls family history; and to Lynn Runnalls for sending me a typescript documenting in a thorough way the family and descendants of Richard Runnalls and Hannah Dykeman, as well as a family tree I knew about but had never seen, one compiled by Lawrence Runnalls in 1941. I inherited papers from both my parents: their autograph manuscripts with memories of their early lives; my mother's family tree for the Runnalls and Thompson families, an invaluable factual record of names and dates and relationships; my father's volumes of newspaper clippings about his career in municipal politics and as a county administrator; photograph albums, many of them frustrating for the family historian, for very few pictures have names, dates or places attached to them; some few letters out of the many that must have been received and written; many postcards, preserved in albums not for their messages but for their pictures; newspaper clippings (too often without source or date) and birth and death notices pasted in haphazard ways in school notebooks; wedding invitations and funeral cards; even a 1935 fine for a parking violation in Montreal. A scattered, miscellaneous collection, like pieces in a jigsaw puzzle, waiting to be assembled into a coherent narrative.

My greatest debts are to my cousin, Helen Annett Zavitz Clark, and to my sister, Marjorie Hale.

More than thirty years ago, Helen prepared the first comprehensive history of the Hair(e) family, gathering together (before the age of the internet) names and dates and facts from family members, from wills and newspapers, from census and land records. Since then, she has generously shared with me a great deal of additional information not only about our ancestors, but about people in Brooke Township, the community of Walnut, and the village of Watford; and her research skills turned up suppressed or ignored information about our great-great-grandfather, Richard Carter.

To my sister I am indebted for much of the material I include about our Irish roots: for information from census records in the UK and army records at the National Archives in Kew; for on-the-spot investigations in County Monaghan, Ireland, that yielded material about the Presbyterian churches in Clontibret; for sharing with me facts and stories from Clontibret's local historian and genealogist, Jack Storey. Marjorie also did research in databases such as the Canada-USA border crossings and in the story of early settlement in King and East and West Gwillimbury Townships. She found Uncle Charlie Bateman's estate papers in the Archives of Ontario; and she obtained regimental histories, including one—Sargent's *The Colonial Garrison*, published in Australia— that made it possible to tell a fuller story about William Haire (Hare). We conferred regularly while this project was in progress, and I am very grateful for her interest, input and support.

My sister and I consider ourselves lucky to have had loving parents and a happy childhood, and our greatest debt is to the two people at the centre of this story.

David Stover—one of my best students and now a longtime friend—expressed an interest in this book for which I am very grateful: he had faith in the broader social and cultural appeal of a family story, and in a telling about a region which, as Northop Frye said sixty years ago, is "surely one of the most inarticulate communities in human culture" (*Bush Garden* 91). (My narrative counters that comment: Frye was unaware of the storytelling that was part of every family and social gathering.) David and I share a

Souwesto background, and he brought to the copy-editing of this book an instinctive sense of the terms and references that needed explanation. I am grateful for his careful work and for his publishing expertise.

INTRODUCTION

This is a family history, but a family history with a context. At its centre are the lives of John Hair and Alice Runnalls, my parents; the context is the society and culture of Souwesto where they lived.

When my parents died, I was acutely aware of how much died with them: memories, primarily, but also facts about their lives and their families, and all the remembered details about their experiences and ways of life that disappeared with them. So this book began as an act of filial piety: its purpose was not only to record the facts about their lives, but also to preserve those memories, insofar as I knew them.

My father was a great story-teller, and one purpose of this narrative is to preserve as many of those stories as I remember. From my earliest childhood, when I was with him at the barn or back at the bush, mending fences or driving to the feed mill in town, he would tell me about grandparents and great-grandparents, relatives and neighbours, ministers and local officials, stories about his childhood and school days and young adulthood in Brooke Township, so I grew up with a strong sense of place and time, now in danger of disappearing when my own memory is no more. For I am mindful of Sir Thomas Browne, that wise seventeenth-century English physician, and his saying, in his meditation upon burial urns discovered in an English field, that there is no antidote against time: "Our Fathers finde their graves in our short memories, and sadly tell us how we may be buried in our Survivors."

My father was not the only story-teller; my mother, too, had stories, stories about growing up in Caradoc Township in Middlesex County. When I started putting her stories and my father's stories together with a factual narrative of my parents' lives, I soon began to realize how much their experiences reflected the social, political and religious concerns of the first half of the twentieth century, the ways of thinking and ways of doing things that made up the culture of southwestern Ontario at that time. So this book is more than just a family history: it is an attempt to record what life was like from the days of first immigration to the early 1980s.

My parents lived in that part of the province of Ontario called, by Greg Curnoe, James Reaney, and others, "Souwesto"—southwestern Ontario, that is, that great stretch of fertile land between Lakes Huron and Erie. I attempt to define the character of that region and of its people—the same kinds of people James Reaney has as his forebears and Alice Munro writes about in her short stories, people mostly of Scots-Irish descent; Protestant; practical, hard-working people attached to the land, defining their community as their school section and their social milieu as their rural Methodist or Presbyterian church. My mother and father were part of that great shift in Canadian demographics, from the family farm and a predominantly rural society to a mostly urban setting and lifestyle, for my father left farming when he was in his forties and my parents eventually became city-dwellers. My story is also an attempt to set my parents' lives in their historical context: the opening up of the West, the introduction of the rural telephone and rural mail delivery, the First World War, the shift from the horse-and-buggy to the automobile, the Great Depression, the Second World War, and the great economic expansion following that conflict. That context includes politics, for my father and mother, while mainly Liberal in their political sympathies, both had links with the United Farmers of Ontario, and later my father was deeply involved in political affairs at the municipal level. That historical context also includes religion, for the Hairs came out of a strongly Methodist tradition; and while my Runnalls grandparents were Presbyterians, the rest of Grandad Runnalls' family, like many Cornish people, was Methodist. It is no surprise that my parents were members of the United Church of Canada.

The word "Souwesto" first appeared in the 1960s, popularized, as I have already said, by the artist Greg Curnoe and by James Reaney. At that time Reaney was doing the archival research for his trilogy of plays, *The Donnellys,* and, to gain a firm documentary sense of life in Biddulph Township in the 1860s and '70s, he read straight through the issues of the London *Free Press* and the London *Advertiser* as if they were novels: novels with a large cast of characters and with a fragmented and discontinuous narrative, but novels, nonetheless, with an instinctive sense of place, novels that reflected the nature of the community where they were written simply because they could not tell their stories in any other way. For me, the Watford *Guide-Advocate* and the Strathroy *Age-Dispatch* have been the same kind of novel, and my narrative, as the reader will see, owes a great deal to those small-town weekly newspapers.

But the *Guide* and the *Age* are not my only sources. Though my parents destroyed most letters (like many people in Souwesto, they thought there was something vaguely disgraceful about any personal revelation), my mother did construct a family tree, and both she and my father, at my urging, wrote accounts of their early lives. Aunt Mima Thompson, having passed her one-hundredth birthday, reminisced about the early life of the Runnallses in Dawn Township, and her daughters circulated the typescript to other family members. Catherine Watson brought together a great deal of material on our Watson and Campbell ancestors. And my cousin Helen Clark wrote and published the first complete history of the Hair(e) family, and did subsequent research not only on Brooke Township, Walnut and Watford, but also on missing bits and pieces in an earlier history, W.H. Johnson's 1940 account of the descendants of our ancestor Eliza England. Finally, my sister's memories have been invaluable, both as a supplement and a corrective to mine.

I have tried to integrate all that material into a continuous narrative.

Chapter One tells the story of my father's family before his birth in 1902. It includes an account of his forebears, Hairs from Ireland and Watsons and Campbells from Scotland, plus the Smiths, who were German (Schmid) and from New York State. But my focus is on our Irish roots. Bruce Elliott's concept of "chain migration" explains the number of Irish Protestant families from Monaghan and North Tipperary—among them the Hairs and McLellans, Woodses and Roanes—who settled in the northeast part of Brooke Township. I tell the story of the pioneer experiences of those people, the three generations preceding my father's, and that story is also about early life in Brooke Township, with its one-room country schools and rural churches, its drainage problems and its lumber industry, its pathmasters and poundkeepers, its tea meetings and box socials, its "boodlers" and tramps. The family farm was the basic social unit; agriculture was the main economic activity; and for progressive people like my grandparents, that involved not only farming itself, but training at the Ontario College of Agriculture (for my grandfather) and membership in the Women's Institute (for my grandmother). The story also involves Methodism, for the Hairs and Watsons all attended Salem Methodist Episcopal Church, and I attempt to define its thinking and attitudes and its influence on the ways people conducted their lives. There is also a wider context. Passed down in our family were a muzzle-loading British Army rifle from the beginning of the nineteenth century, a bullet mold, and an army discharge paper dated 1838. The story of those items is the story of British imperialism from the point of view of an ordinary soldier, William Haire: recruitment in Armagh, service in New South Wales, service in India, and a return to Ireland.

Chapter Two begins with my mother's premature birth in 1908 and tells the story of her forebears and their early lives in Souwesto. The Runnallses were Cornish people; the Thompsons and McCrackens were Irish Protestants; and the Dykemans were Loyalists of Dutch descent. This chapter has two major narratives. One is the story of the Runnalls' and Dykemans' twenty-year stay in Dawn Township, Lambton County, a story of pioneer life recorded, as I have already said, by one of Grandad Runnalls's sisters, Jemima, who lived to be over one hundred. The other is the history of our Loyalist ancestors. Their story begins in Manhattan in the middle of the seventeenth century, continues through their fleeing the United States as refugees in 1783, and takes them on to New Brunswick and then Ontario. Runnallses, Thompsons and McCrackens all eventually settled in Caradoc Township, where they lived most of their lives.

Chapter Three is an account of the first twenty-five years of my father's life, from his boyhood on a Brooke Township farm until his return from a brief period of working in Detroit. It includes my father's account of the neighbours in our school section, S.S. No. 10 Brooke; there are sections on Salem Methodist church, its "socials" and picnics and garden parties, and on card playing and dancing, both frowned upon by an earlier generation of Methodists; on "Northwest fever" and on family members who went "out West"; on the coming of the telephone and of rural mail delivery; on my grandparents' involvement in literary societies and the Women's Institute; on the issue of temperance and on the United Farmers of Ontario, the political party my father supported when he was first old enough to vote. The Great War was the chief international event of my father's boyhood, and I try to define local attitudes and effects; and there is a section on a contemporary play performed in Salem Church, *The Minister's Bride*, written by the wife of a Presbyterian minister in Ottawa and focusing on the New Woman of the new century—women like my grandmother and her sister Eva, both of whom had roles in the production.

My mother's own account of "My Home and School Years" is the basis of my fourth chapter, which is about her life up to the point when she graduated from the Strathroy

Collegiate Institute in 1926. She herself tells what it was like to grow up on a Caradoc Township farm at the beginning of the twentieth century, and to go to a rural school and the local Continuation School. Her father was an elder and choir leader in the Presbyterian church (and twice a delegate to the Church's General Assembly) and her mother a faithful worker in the Women's Missionary Society and the Ladies' Aid. Public speaking was a large part of the school curriculum at the time, and my mother was successful in a number of competitions, winning a gold medal during her last year in high school. She, like my father, had stories about neighbours, about accidents and deaths, about the First World War and about migration to the West. Alice's first cousin, Roy Runnalls, was killed in France in September 1917, after having survived "that scrap" (his word) at Vimy Ridge, and her brother Frank's best friend died at Passchendaele.

Chapter Five brings the story of my father's life down to 1935, the year he and my mother were married. Municipal politics figure in a large way at this time: in 1927 John's father became a township councillor. I tell about the duties and remuneration of councillors, and about his involvement in local issues, which in Brooke Township always centred on drains and roads. Sherman Hair successfully opposed the reintroduction of statute labour for the maintaining of roads in the township, but his successes in the annual elections varied: in 1929 he topped the polls for councillor; but in 1930, when he ran for deputy-reeve for the first time, he lost by one vote. His early death at the age of sixty brought his political career to an end. The other major story at this time is the coming of the Great Depression. I tell how township and county councils responded to it with cuts in tax rates and expenditures. And I tell how, in the midst of the Depression, my father courted my mother.

In Chapter Six I pick up the story of my mother's life in 1926, when she attended Normal School in London and then, at the age of nineteen, started teaching in a one-room country school in Caradoc Township, where she would stay for eight years. Through the people she boarded with, the Crawfords, she was deeply involved in the life of her school section and in the activities of the North Caradoc Presbyterian Church; and she continued to be deeply involved in the activities of her home church in Mount Brydges, as president of the Young People's Society, as part of the dramatic club, and as church organist. She gave papers and readings; she acted in plays; she coached her pupils in oratorical contests. The chapter ends with my mother's resignation as teacher and with the school and church gatherings in her honour before her marriage.

My parents were married on 5 October 1935, and Chapter Seven tells about their wedding, their wedding trip to Montreal and Quebec City, and their early married life in Brooke Township and in Walnut Church. There my mother became active in the Women's Association, and my father was choir leader: he had a fine tenor voice, and was often invited as guest soloist at church anniversaries and garden parties. This was also the time of my father's first involvement in municipal politics, first as assessor of Brooke Township, and then—unexpectedly—as councillor. The story of how he became councillor is part of the story of one of the most sensational events in Sarnia's history: the 1936 shoot-out at the liquor store that killed the country's most notorious criminal, "Red" Ryan.

The war years and after are the subject of Chapter Eight. From the early 1940s on, there was rationing of meat and gas; my parents made maple syrup when sugar was scarce; and school kids collected milkweed floss for use as insulation in airmen's jackets and in flotation devices. I tell about three "boys" from Watford who lost their lives in the war; and I tell about my father's two years as reeve of Brooke Township, when council approved a scheme for the rehabilitation of returning servicemen. My father's last full year of farming was 1946, the only year for which I have facts about the economics of farm life at that time. In 1947, as a result of his decade of experience on township and county councils, my father was appointed treasurer of Lambton County, and our transition from a rural to an urban lifestyle began: Dad held a clearing auction sale of farm equipment; and (in his first new car in twenty years) he started to commute daily to Sarnia.

Chapter Nine deals with the post-war years, between 1948 and 1954. Consumer goods were once again available; motor trips for pleasure could be undertaken, since my father now had summer holidays and no daily "chores." I tell about travel in those days, with motels and two-lane highways and meals cooked on a Coleman stove at roadside tables. My father was an avid and venturesome traveller, taking us "round the Gaspé" when the route was only a gravel road; and taking us to Florida before any interstates had been built. In the early 1950s my parents made their final break with farm life: they bought a house in Watford and sold the farm. They continued to attend a rural church, however, and continued to be active in the church's music and in its Sunday School. Late in 1954, John Huey, the long-time clerk of the county, died, and council appointed my father as clerk-treasurer.

Chapter Ten describes my father's duties as clerk-treasurer, his relations with the wardens (there was a new one every year), and his handling of sensitive issues. His early years in office coincided with two of the county's major construction projects in the 1960s: the home for the aged, Twilight Haven in Petrolia, and the new county buildings, court house and gaol in Sarnia. The latter were opened by Prime Minister Diefenbaker, and his visit to Sarnia was a red-letter day for my parents. Meanwhile, my mother was deeply involved in Christian education in Watford. In 1960, the high school board expropriated my parents' house and demolished it to make room for an addition to the school, and my parents bought a house in Sarnia. They had been there only a month or so when our grandmother had a fall that led to her death.

Chapter Eleven tells the story of my father's last ten years as clerk-treasurer, up to his retirement in 1970. The Ontario Municipal Association's conventions were part of my parents' lives at this time, and attending them meant travelling to many different cities around the province. One trip to Ottawa resulted in a chance meeting with Prime Minister Trudeau. This decade saw the last of our family trips by car (the most ambitious was to Mexico), the marriages of my sister and myself, and the first grandchildren. It also saw the emergence of health problems that would eventually claim my parents' lives.

Chapter Twelve is "the final decade." My parents had a good ten years in retirement, filled with projects in which they were interested, with excursions by car, and with visits to and from family and relatives. My father brought up to date a history of Lambton County Officials and saw it published. The last sections of this chapter are sad ones: they tell of our parents' deteriorating health, their last illnesses, their final stay in the North Lambton Rest Home (my father had been a member of its building committee), and their deaths.

My epigraph is a sentence I once heard on a CBC Radio One program: "Perhaps, when we die, we all become a story, told and retold by those who love us." For my parents, this is that story.

Souwesto Lives

CHAPTER ONE
MY FATHER'S BIRTH (1902), HIS FOREBEARS, AND EARLY LIFE IN BROOKE TOWNSHIP

My father's birth

John Alexander Hair—he always hated his second name and never used it except on official documents—was born on 21 July 1902, ten months after the wedding of his parents, Sherman Hair and Dessa Watson. As was the custom in those days, his birth took place at home, in a farmhouse in Lambton County's Brooke Township, a white frame house on the east one-half of lot 26, concession 13, on the road everyone knew as "The Twelfth Line." Sherman Hair had bought the farm from Thomas Roane two and a half years earlier, and even at that relatively late date, according to my father, "almost a third of it was in heavy timber." That July was an unusual one: "The summer I was born, my parents told me, was a very wet one. The fields were so soft that the binders would sink into the mud and it was very difficult to harvest the grain. Sam McLellan (Chester's father) had six acres of wheat in a field on the corner of 27 Sideroad and the Twelfth Line, and he had to cut it with a cradle."

The summer of 1902: throughout the season the Watford paper carried stories of rain and wind, storms and floods, and of the difficulties they created for farmers. The bad weather began in June and carried on into mid-July, when crops were half-grown and haying ought to have been in progress. A week or so before John was born, there was "a terrific rain and windstorm …. The rain fell in torrents …. Out in the country the grain fields were damaged …. It was one of the fiercest storms witnessed here for some years" (*Guide* 11 July 1902). Hay was particularly affected. "Ontario never before had such a hay crop as this year, but, unfortunately, the weather has been the worst possible for the cutting, curing and stocking of it. For four weeks or more now it has rained more or less nearly every day…. While the crop has been very satisfactory in every respect, the opportunities for harvesting it has [sic] been of the poorest" (*Guide* 11 July 1902). For hay could not be stored in barns unless it was perfectly dry; if damp, it would overheat (because of a chemical reaction within the hay), and the temperature could become hot enough to start a barn fire. The rain flooded fields of potatoes, corn, and sugar beets; and the winds flattened large swathes of oats, wheat, and barley, delaying the ripening of the grain and making it difficult for the binders to cut. Mosquitoes flourished and burdock and other weeds grew rank. But the most unusual effect of the wet weather was the finding of fish in the fields. That happened in Moore Township, where fish made their way up watercourses draining into Bear Creek and the Sydenham River: when the flood subsided, they were stranded on farmland.

A short period of good weather at the end of August made the harvest possible, and in spite of fears of grain sprouting in the sheaves and potatoes rotting in the fields, the quality of the farm produce was much better than expected. At that time, the technology for harvesting was far in advance of the cradles the pioneers had used. The cradles were a type of scythe wielded by hand, but by the end of the nineteenth century there was a machine, the horse-drawn binder, which cut the grain and tied it into sheaves, which were then set up in stooks in the fields. The stooks were later loaded on wagons and drawn into the farm yard for threshing. For that, a farmer would hire threshers and a machine, and the threshing itself was a neighbourhood event, typically lasting one day: the men worked in hot and dusty conditions, and then would stop at noon for "dinner" (always the mid-day meal), washing hands and faces at a pump before sitting down to a large meal prepared by the farm wives.

Beyond that brief respite, the fall of 1902 was, like the summer, wet, too wet for plowing or for the sowing of fall wheat, and the grain which the farmers had not yet been able to thresh was spoiling in the stooks.

Such was the world into which my father was born.

John was an only child. My parents and grandparents were always reticent when it came to saying anything about human reproduction, so I have only a vague memory of my father mentioning a little brother who died at or shortly after birth, and who was buried in the churchyard of St. James' Anglican church on the Sixth Line, where his Hair ancestors lay under a tall gray stone with an urn on top. The cemetery board has no record of the interment, but in such cases, Betty Searson-Anderson told me, "families could go to the cemetery and inter the body without involving the clergy." (The Searsons were long-time neighbours of ours on the Twelfth Line, and they too were an Irish Protestant family, from Roscrea in County Tipperary.)

Giving birth in those days could be difficult and dangerous for both mother and child. Our grandmother suffered from what was then called "milk leg," a painful swelling occurring in women after childbirth as a result of a thrombosis of the femoral vein, and during the time when my sister and I were growing up, she continued to have an ulcer on her lower left leg which would never completely heal, even after she had spent weeks in bed.

Brooke Township

John was born in that part of the township where both his Hair and Watson forebears had been pioneer settlers: the Watsons had moved to Brooke from Chippewa, near Niagara Falls, in 1853; and the Hairs had emigrated from the townland of Bryanlitter in the parish of Clontibret, County Monaghan, Ireland, in the 1860s. While the western half of the township was low-lying and flat, with heavy (but rich) clay soil left after the draining of the great Brooke-Enniskillen swamp, the northeastern part, where the Hairs and Watsons lived, was more elevated (though still flat), had clay-loam soil, and was scarred by various tributaries of the Sydenham River, the nearest one (half a mile to the west) being known to everyone simply as "the creek." The Sydenham itself, which meanders from Poplar Hill and Strathroy through Napier and Alvinston, along the townline between Lambton and Middlesex counties and south into Euphemia township on its way to Wallaceburg, was simply "the river."

The township itself was laid out in the usual grid pattern, with the concessions running east and west and the sideroads north and south. There were fourteen concessions, numbered from south to north, while the sideroads, which divided units of three two-hundred-acre lots, were numbered from west to east. The only interruption in this neat layout was on Brooke's eastern boundary, where Mosa Township in Middlesex County and the Sydenham River itself forced the roads to angle and curve. The "peak of Mosa" was a sharp-pointed triangular section of that neighbouring municipality that thrust itself up into Brooke Township. People who didn't know the area often got lost when faced with roads angling off in unexpected directions. James Reaney makes a surveyor's blunder of that kind, which happened in most townships, a metaphor for a state of mind: "it pushes the country people crooked where they might have gone straight" (*Box Social* 75). So it is, in literary terms, an emblem of "Ontario Gothic," bits and pieces of which are part of my story.

European settlement of Brooke Township was recent. The township had not been surveyed until 1832-3, and the farms that John's father owned were granted by the Crown to their original owners in 1835 and 1836. "The farm across the road"—that was how we always referred to our second one hundred acres, the east one-half of lot 26 in concession 12—was first occupied by a Vincent Jackson who, according to the original parchment document granting him the land and signed by Sir John Colborne, was the son of a United Empire Loyalist from the Frontenac district. Between 1835 and 1864 that land changed hands ten times, and my guess is that not much of it was cleared in those early years. In 1876 "Old Tom" Roane bought it, and in 1889 he sold it to his son, "Young Tom," for $5000. My father remembered "Young Tom" well. "Tom Roane was fat," he said, "and had difficulty breathing." John's parents were always amused by him: "He would come in from doing the chores, puffing and wheezing, and lie down; Mrs. Roane would administer a damp towel. In a few minutes Tom would be sitting up, doing what he loved best: talking and telling stories." In that he was like his father, who was "a very entertaining companion." Because "Old Tom" had first come to the township in 1850 and had helped clear some three hundred acres of it, he had plenty of stories to tell. "His accounts of the early pioneer days were worthy of publication, and he was often called upon to recount his experiences" (Beers 42). None of those stories has survived, so far as I know. "Old Tom" died in 1905; "Young Tom" sold the farm to my grandfather in 1920, moved to Petrolia, and died there in 1946, at the age of eighty-one.

Our home farm—the one hundred acres of the east one-half of lot 26, concession 13—had been first granted by the Crown in 1836 to a Godfrey Mason, about whom I know nothing. My father had all the deeds and land transfer documents for the farm across the road but none for the land on which we actually lived. I know only that "Old Tom" Roane, who was an immigrant from King's County, Ireland, bought that farm in 1878; that when his wife died in 1890 he and his daughter Elizabeth continued to live there; and that Sherman Hair bought the farm from father and daughter at the end of the century. The bill of sale is dated 6 January 1900; the price was $4500, and Sherman took out a $2000 mortgage.

John was born surrounded by family. His grandparents and his aunts and uncles all lived on neighbouring farms, and the centre of their world was the corner of the Twelfth Line and 27 Sideroad. For their church—Salem Methodist Episcopal church—stood on the northeast side of that intersection; Grandad Watson's farm was on the southwest, and Grandad Hair's on the southeast. (The McLellan farm was on the northwest.)

In 1902 "Grandad Watson" (so my father always referred to his maternal grandfather, R.—for Roderick—David Watson) was living on fifty acres with his second wife, Ella Reid, and his second family, a daughter christened Ada Evelyn but always called "Eva," and Ella's nephew, George W. Green, whom he raised as his son and whom everyone called "George Watson." There were more Watsons close by. Two of Grandad Watson's younger brothers, Harry and Pete, lived on adjacent farms a little further to the east, close to the townline with Metcalfe Township. Their properties were parts of lot 28, the original Watson farm.

"Grandad Hair"—so John called his paternal grandfather—lived across the road on a one-hundred-acre farm with his wife Ann Carter and their children. John's father Sherman was the first of that family to marry, but his brother and his five sisters were all still living at home at that time. James, the oldest son, had inherited the original Hair farm (the west one-half of lot 27, concession 13) where James and Nancy (Leathem or Latham) Hair had lived from the time they left Ireland in 1868 until their deaths in the 1890s. There James lived after his marriage in 1904, and there his first three children, Amy, Elsie, and Harold, were born. My father was the oldest of the many cousins he would have on the Hair side of the family.

My father had a strong sense of family history, at least insofar as he knew it, and some of the most vivid memories I retain from my boyhood are the bits and pieces he told me when I was out with him doing chores. So I was always aware of the fact that the farm next to ours—the one where Uncle Ches and Aunt Ruth McLellan lived—had been the farm the Hairs bought when they first came out from Ireland. And those bits and pieces fostered in me a strong desire to fill out the family history and so make our sense of identity as precise and detailed as possible.

The Hairs always identified themselves as Irish (though we were, like most people, a mixed bag, with ancestors from Scotland and Germany as well as Ireland). "Scots-Irish," however, would be a more accurate label, for the early nineteenth-century Hairs were Presbyterians, probably originated in Scotland, and may have first settled in Ireland as part of the Scottish colonisation of Ulster after the Tudor conquest of the province at the end of the sixteenth century. According to Black's dictionary of the surnames of Scotland, Hair is from the Irish *O'hIr*, "descendant of Ir," and was a common name in Ayrshire and the Lowlands. "Ir" ("Aichear") means "fierce" or "sharp." But MacLysaght does not even list "Hair" or "Haire" in his comprehensive account of "The Surnames of Ireland," though he does include Hehir, Hegher, Haier, and Haher. His omission makes the Scottish origin of the Hairs that much more likely.

But for my father and the generations immediately preceding his, the "old country" was Ireland. For John Hair—my father's "Grandad Hair"—had been born (according to his obituary) in Armagh, in September 1846, and grew up in County Monaghan, on the townland of Bryanlitter, at Clontibret. He was "a lad of seventeen" when he emigrated to Canada in 1863. It was not until 1868 that his parents, James and Nancy (Latham or Leathem) followed him. I once asked my father if his grandfather had reminisced about Ireland or about his crossing the Atlantic: what ship did he travel on? where did he land? how did he happen to choose this area as his destination? No one thought to ask him those questions, my father said. He knew only that his grandfather had come by steamer (whereas Grandmother Hair—Ann Carter—had come by sailing ship, on a voyage that took six weeks). The stories about Grandad Hair in the 1860s were few and thin; between that time and his boyhood in "the old country" there was an impenetrable mist, as if the Atlantic had been Lethe. Two tales about Grandad Hair's early experiences in this country were all my father had to offer. He was apprenticed to a harness-maker in Strathroy, and the difference in idiom between the English of the "old country" and the English of Canada led to his being laughed at. His master told him to see to the fire because it was "out"; John looked all around, and finally said, perplexed, "I don't see where it's got out." The other story was about his working at a sawmill in Port Huron, Michigan: he did that in the wintertime, and he got there by crossing the St. Clair River on the ice.

Grandad Hair's parents are the earliest generation of our Hair ancestors about which any information survives. What do I know about my great-great grandfather, James Hair? Only that he was born in the spring of 1816 and he was fifty-two years old when he emigrated in 1868. He was a Presbyterian. At that time there were two Clontibret Presbyterian churches, one (at a crossroads called Legnacreeve) established in 1715-25, and a second at a crossroads half a mile away, Braddox, which had split from the first in 1779. According to Jack Storey, a local historian in Clontibret, the first congregation was "mainline Presbyterians" and the second "Seceder Presbyterians (much stricter)." A Haire descendant who remained in Ireland—Ernest Haire—says that the family belonged to the stricter congregation, as did the McLellans, who lived on the adjoining townland: "Calvinistic church goers they were—no organ, no hymns. The precentor with a tuning fork gave the congregation the note and we sang metrical Psalms. ... When the second prayer arrived, it usually lasted ten minutes. ... The sermon lasted anywhere from 50 minutes to an hour..." (Clark, *Hair(e)* 148). As for Clontibret itself, it was only a tiny hamlet on the main road halfway between Castleblayney, "a fair size market town," and Monaghan, the county seat. It had a post office, an Episcopal Church, a Roman Catholic chapel, a few houses, and three pubs. "This county of Monaghan was beautiful, rolling undulating country," Ernest writes. "Away from the main roads, little country lanes, high hedges, outcrops of smooth rock on the road, very small fields, some only two or three acres, and the largest only ten or twelve, little trout streams, small mills with water wheels and a general air of peace and serenity. ... The border between Ulster and the Republic of Ireland (Eire) runs through what was formerly our land..." (Clark, *Hair(e)* 148).

What do I know about my great-great grandmother, Nancy ("Ann") Hair? Even less than I know about my great-great grandfather. She was born in 1812, and her maiden name was Latham or Leathem. I do not know when she and James were married. The only document we have is an entry in the marriage and baptismal register of the First Clontibret Church (Presbyterian), which records the baptism of her youngest son in 1849. It reads "Thos. son of James Hair & Nancy Leathem of Bryanlitter born 16th July & baptised 4 August 1849" (Clark, *Hair(e)* 80). A photograph taken late in life shows her in a black dress and patterned shawl; she is wearing a black cap, the frilly white fringe of which outlines her face. She was known to her family not as "Nancy" but as "Ann": that is how her name appears in the census of 1871. She was four years older than her husband, and she outlived him by a year and a half, dying on 16 February 1896. She was buried in the churchyard of St. James.

William Hair (Hare, Haire), soldier

Some relics of the Hair emigration have been passed down in our family: a muzzle-loading British army rifle from the early part of the nineteenth century (with ramrod but without bayonet), a bullet mold, and a parchment certificate for a "William Hare," whose relation to our ancestors I do not know (though my father told me, late in his life, that William Hair was a brother of my great-great-grandfather, James Hair). It is an army discharge paper dated 1838, and the words "48th Regiment of Foot" head it. It reads as follows: "These are to certify that William Hare Private born in the Parish of Clontibret in or near the Town of Monaghan was enlisted at Armagh for the foresaid Corps on the 26 November 1816 at the age of Seventeen Years. That he has served in the Army for 25 Years and 261 Days. Was in New South Wales Seven Years and [line illegible because of fold] That he is discharged in consequence of being unfit for further service." The signature of the commanding officer is illegible; "Dated at Athlone 18 June 1838." Under "character" is the sentence "William Hare has been a well conducted soldier."

British Army Service records and a history of the 48th Foot make it possible to construct a narrative of William's military life. After the Peninsular War ended in 1814, the 48th had moved from Spain to Ireland, for "garrison duty" and recruitment. William, whose trade at that time was "weaver," enlisted at Armagh in November 1816, and spent the next twenty-five years of his life in the army. His service took him to the far reaches of the empire in a progress which was typical of military life at the time: home, New South Wales, India, and, after many years, home again.

William embarked at Cork in March 1817, on a ship transporting convicts to New South Wales: members of the 48th served as guards. The voyage took four months. Their route was south to Madeira and Rio de Janeiro, then across the south Atlantic and Indian Oceans to Australia, to "Port Jackson and Sydney Cove." There the 48th became one of several colonial garrison regiments whose duties were to protect fortifications and government installations, to guard convict working gangs, and to pursue escapees and bushrangers, who at that time were usually escaped convicts. William was a private in No. 8 Company, under the command of a Captain Francis Allman, who seems to have been a wise and compassionate man. Early in 1821 No. 8 Company was chosen for service at Port MacQuarie, a new settlement on the coast some two hundred and fifty miles north of Sydney. The new settlements provided hope for convicts who volunteered for them because, if their work was satisfactory after eighteen months, they were given tickets of leave or conditional pardons. But there were dangers to both convicts and soldiers from the aborigines. On the coast, relations between them and the settlers were good, but parties who ventured up river to cut timber met with hostilities. In October 1821, for instance, natives attacked the wood cutters with spears, killing one convict, wounding another.

It would have been such an incident that left William with a mark he carried with him for the rest of his life. Here is how the doctor who examined him on his discharge in 1838 described it: "In the right hypochondrium there is the cicatrix of a Wound which, he says, was inflicted by a Spear while in the discharge of his duty." (And, in spite of the commendation of being "a well conducted soldier," the doctor also noted that "Back shows traces of corporal punishment.")

When the time came for the regiment's transfer to India, there was considerable apprehension among the soldiers: they feared service in the tropics and knew of the high mortality rate there. Their fears were justified. When they arrived in Madras in the late spring of 1824, cholera was everywhere, and within days one in ten of the company died. They quickly moved outside the city, and settled in Trichinopoly, where they remained for three years, until they moved to Cannanore. William survived, but the doctor in 1838 noted that he had "suffered from Bowel complaint with Fever while in India." (The doctor also observed that he "has taken mercury." At the time, mercury was the standard treatment of syphilis.)

In November and December, 1834, two detachments of the 48th embarked for England in two ships, both arriving in March, 1835; a third ship arrived a month later. The men were stationed at various places in England for the next two years. The final stage of their tour of duty was in 1837, when they travelled from Manchester to Ireland. They did so on the country's first railroad, the Manchester to Liverpool line, the home of Stephenson's "Rocket." By March 1838 they were at Athlone, and that is the station at which William Hair underwent a medical assessment and was honorably discharged from the army. At the time of his discharge, he was thirty-eight years old. He was five feet eight inches tall, and had brown hair, grey eyes, and a complexion described as "dark." The main focus of the hearing on 18 June 1838 was William's medical condition. The surgeon of the 48th, describing William as "an Irishman & a laborer," confirmed that he was unable "to march any distance, or to perform duty efficiently." The Board concurred with this assessment, but also noted that William's "conduct and character have been that of a good and efficient soldier." A month later, on July 27, came confirmation of the decision: "William Hare was this day examined by a Medical Board in Dublin, of which said Regiment was found unfit for Service from Chronic Rheumatism, varicose veins of legs and carcocele of left testis."

And with that, William Hair disappears from all documents. How and where did he live the rest of his life? When did he die? What exactly was his relation to our Hair ancestors? Those questions remain unanswered, and are perhaps unanswerable.

Clontibret immigrants in Brooke Township

I have often wondered why my Hair ancestors headed for this part of the country and ended up in the northeast part of Brooke Township. The answer seems to be that other families from Clontibret had already come here, and while large parts of the township were settled by the "Scotch" (as we called them), other parts became home to the Irish. (One school section—not ours—was called "Little Ireland.") In fact, the Irish were "the largest ethnic group in Upper Canada (Ontario) in the nineteenth century" (Elliott 116), and two-thirds of them were Protestant. In his study of North Tipperary Protestants and their migration to Canada, Bruce Elliott uses the term "chain migration, in which one emigrant is followed by another, who is followed by others in turn" (4), leaving "a common overseas place of origin" (4) and clustering in areas in Ontario where they were linked (as they had been in Ireland) by proximity or kinship. All of our Irish Protestant ancestors were, so far as I know, farmers, and brought their preference for a rural way of life to this country. The basic economic and social unit was the one-hundred-acre family farm, and their basic goal in coming to Canada was "a farm for every son" (Elliott, 214).

The earliest immigrant from Monaghan to the Twelfth Line seems to have been William Kelly, who came to Canada in 1837 (according to his obituary) or 1836 (according to Sara Campbell's Brooke Township History) and settled on the east one-half of lot 13 in concession 12. That farm was still occupied by Kelly descendants when my sister and I were in public school, and one of the daughters of that family, Nina Kelly, was my second public school teacher in the 1940s. Nina had a sister and two brothers and, in a pattern not untypical of rural Protestant Irish families in those days, none of them married. The four lived together in the big old white frame farmhouse set back from the Twelfth Line, at the end of a broad laneway lined with maples.

The Kellys were followed in the 1840s by the McLellans, who were neighbours of the Haires in Clontibret. Samuel McLellan, Uncle Ches's father, had been born there in 1838 and emigrated in 1845; he settled in Brooke in 1861. His mother and father—another Samuel—also emigrated, and all would eventually be buried in the churchyard of St. James. Other immigrants from Clontibret were James Henderson and the Fosters. They both lived "back 27 sideroad," in the far northeast corner of Brooke. James Henderson died in 1909, and our great-grandfather, David Watson, was among the pallbearers at his funeral. Among James's children was William, whom we knew as Billy, a bachelor who lived alone in the (by the 1940s) dilapidated farm house, a small unpainted frame building, not much more than a shack. Our parents would speak of "Billy Henderson" when we drove back 27 Sideroad; I do not remember ever seeing him, and I think he must have died when we were very small. Directly across the sideroad from the Henderson farm was the Foster farm. Leander and Mabel Foster and their only daughter, Doris, lived there, on land which Leander had inherited from his father Isaac. Leander's grandmother, Margaret Foster, had been born in County Monaghan in 1819, and lived to be 103; she died in June, 1922.

So the settlement in our section mirrored the Protestant population of a small area in County Monaghan, even as late as the 1940s, when I was a boy. Our neighbours had the same surnames as the Haires' neighbours in Clontibret a hundred years earlier: McLellan and Kelly, Henderson and Foster, Higgins and Hastings.

The first Hairs in Brooke Township

Immigration narratives are few, and there is none for the Haires, but there is substantially more information about their early life in this country. In 1869 James Hair bought for $800 a one-hundred-acre farm in Brooke Township, the west one-half of lot 27 in concession 13, and he farmed there until his death in 1894. He and his wife, Nancy or "Anne," attended St. Andrew's Presbyterian Church in Napier, then a substantial village on the Sydenham River in Metcalfe Township. They had three sons, all born in Ireland: my great-grandfather, John Hair (born 1846), and his brothers Robert (born 1843) and Thomas (born 1849).

The railway which was crucial in opening up our part of the country for settlement was not in Brooke Township at all, but ran in an east-west direction across Warwick Township, just north of Brooke's fourteenth concession (which we called "The Sixth Line"). It was the Great Western (later the Grand Trunk, and later still the Canadian National), and it had been built between London and Sarnia in 1857-58, running from Komoka through Strathroy and Kerwood to Watford, the Haires' principal market town, and on through Wanstead, Wyoming, and Mandaumin to Sarnia. That line was officially opened on 28 December 1858. It brought a major change of pace and scale to the sixty-mile trip between London and Sarnia: fifteen hours by stage coach before the railway, eighty-five minutes afterwards (*Guide* 18 February 1887). It also played a role in the first major task the Haires faced: clearing the land. Before the coming of the railroad, the whole area around Watford "was dense growth of unbroken wilderness," and for many years afterwards there was "excellent timber in great abundance, as yet untouched by the wood-man's axe" (*Guide* 13 August 1880). In my father's account of his early life, he tells how his great-grandparents, James and "Anne" Hair, cleared the bush and were connected with the railroad: "The winter before they settled on this farm ... a large amount of oak timber had been taken out to ship to England to build ships. As only the very choicest timber was shipped, there was a large amount left lying on the ground. They cut this timber in the required lengths and split it to make spokes. There was a good demand for oak to make buggy and wagon spokes and they were able to sell it all." They also sold wood to the railway. "At that time," my father continued, "the steam engines burned wood. [My great-grandparents] cut wood and drew it out along the 27 sideroad to the railroad and piled it beside the track. A railway representative would come and measure the wood and pay for it. The trains would stop beside the woodpiles and quite often passengers on the train would get off and help load the wood on the engine tender. The selling of spokes and wood to the railway perhaps gave [my great-grandparents] the first money they were able to make."

It is possible to piece together a picture of the James Hair farm as it was at the end of the 1860s and the beginning of the 1870s, from census records and from an insurance policy which James took out in 1870, and which has somehow survived family moves and clearings-out. The policy lists "his barn (log)," "shed (log)," "stable (log)," "threshing machine therein," and "ordinary contents" of barn, shed, and stable. The house, apparently, was not insured, and no description or photograph of it is extant. The census of 1871 fills out the picture of the farm, noting wagons and sleds, ploughs and cultivators, and a fanning mill as some of the "contents," and listing crops and livestock. The livestock included two horses, one colt, five milk cows, fourteen "horned cattle," twelve sheep, and nineteen pigs. The crops consisted of wheat (thirty bushels), barley (fifty bushels), oats (150 bushels), peas (forty bushels), and potatoes (eighty bushels), plus thirty tons of hay, one hundred pounds of maple syrup, four hundred pounds of butter, fifty pounds of wool, sixty pounds of flannel, thirty spruce logs, 150,000 staves, and twenty cords of firewood. All this from a farm with sixty-five "improved acres," sixteen acres of pasture, and two acres of "garden or orchard."

James retired from farming in 1887, and had an auction sale of "farm stock" in November of that year. He died in August 1894, at the age of seventy-eight, after having been "in feeble health for some time," according to the Watford paper, and was buried in "the English cemetery, 6th line"—the churchyard of St. James Anglican church, where so many other early settlers in our part of the township are buried. James left the farm to his grandson and namesake, apparently because his son John—Grandad Hair—had left the Presbyterian church and decided to attend Salem Methodist Church close to home. James's other two sons had much earlier purchased, with their father's help, one-hundred-acre farms in Moore Township, and he made no further provision for them. "Providing for their children was the most important goal these settlers shared and their achievement of this aim should be the major measure of their success or failure" (Elliott 231).

Our great-grandparents, John Hair and Ann Carter

I turn now to the next generation: my great-grandfather, John Hair, and great-grandmother, Ann Carter. We know a great deal about Grandmother Hair's background, thanks to a family history compiled in 1940 by William H. Johnston of Exeter. He titled it "A Brief History of the Descendants of the late Eliza England of Mountrath, Queen's County, Ireland." Eliza England was Grandmother Hair's mother, who was born in 1806 to James England and Mary Davis, and they lived on a farm named Clonohill, near Mountrath. Eliza was twice married and had six daughters. Her second husband was William Carter of Ballytarsna, Queen's County, and Ann—Grandmother Hair—was the second daughter of that union. William Carter emigrated in 1849. Ann, her four sisters, and their mother followed in 1853 (according to the 1901 census) or 1854 (according to Johnston's history). They settled near Kettleby in King Township and there, according to Johnston, "in 1861 Mrs. Carter [Eliza England] died and was buried in the old Church of England cemetery west of Newmarket on Eagle Street."

Our Irish Protestant ancestors from North Tipperary and vicinity

Our Haire ancestors were, as I have already said, from Monaghan, and probably originated in Scotland, but the Carters and Englands were from North Tipperary and nearby areas in King's County and Queen's County. "The Protestant population of the North Tipperary region was of predominantly English descent" (Elliott 13), as their surnames indicate. They were likely seventeenth- and eighteenth-century migrants into Ireland, which was under English control following the Cromwellian invasion of the 1640s and the subsequent seizing of property for English settlers. Estate owners, given land taken from Irish Catholics, wanted Protestant tenants, and from the 1660s on encouraged immigration from England. Our Carter, England, and Davis ancestors may well have been among those families. Bruce Elliott, whose study of Irish migrants focuses on North Tipperary, twice mentions the Carter name among Protestant tenants, one from a 1776 list of freeholders in Modreeny parish, and the other in a 1806 list for the Castle Otway estate. There is an even earlier list, this one from the seventeenth century, of "Adventurers for Lands in Ireland," English subscribers who, between 1642 and 1646, paid for property (which was not actually taken up until much later). The name Carter appears three times in that list, and Davis twice (Prendergast 403-48).

Our ancestors from North Tipperary were clustered around Roscrea, a garrison town in the nineteenth century, but of ancient origins. The Civil Survey of 1654 describes it as having "a large stronge castle with sixty cottages & thatcht houses" (qtd. by Elliott 18), but our ancestors were country people, not town-dwellers, and faced increasing difficulties in the nineteenth century. The rural population grew quickly in the century's first four decades; subdividing farms among family members put pressure on the availability of land; there were very few jobs outside agriculture; and "small and middling farmers" were caught between the gentry and large commercial farmers on the one hand, and small-holders and labourers on the other (Elliott 37). Moreover, the Protestants were a "declining minority increasingly at odds with a disgruntled and assertive Catholic majority" (Elliott 31). Defending one's right to land became the root cause of "the disturbances and 'outrages' that typified North Tipperary more than any other part of Ireland in the 1840s" (Elliott 58). Upper Canada was attractive because, as Francis Evans explains in his 1833 *Emigrants' Directory and Guide to Obtain Lands and Effect a Settlement in the Canadas*, "When [a settler] becomes the proprietor of a piece of land, all his work is for his own benefit, no rent or taxes being to be paid: he has the full produce of the soil for his support; and the surplus he can send to market, when and how he pleases as he is not in dread of the agent coming to distrain him for *the rent* ... (qtd. by Elliott 69).

The first organized emigration of North Tipperary Protestants was in 1818, and subsequent movement established two main areas of settlement in Upper Canada: the Ottawa Valley and London Township. Others included areas north of Toronto—King Township; East, North, and West Gwillimbury—and Brooke Township. These all grew by "chain migration" and "kinship links" (80). One has only to look at the names on the gravestones in St. James Anglican cemetery on the "Sixth Line," the northern boundary of Brooke, to identify the Irish families linked by origin, experience, and blood: not only the Hairs, but Kellys, Woodses, Powells, McLellans, Searsons, Roanes, Hendersons, and Carter descendants. They determined the character of the township: "the Ontario descendants of North Tipperary Protestants were still at heart a rural people," and in their new home "retained a strong preference for a rural way of life" (Elliott 232, 241).

Two of the North Tipperary families who would have close connections with the Hairs in Brooke Township were the Woodses and the Roanes. The story of the Woods family begins with Gilbert Woods, who was born in Tipperary in 1797 and died at Roscrea in 1847. His widow, who had been Elizabeth Serson (a sister of Richard Serson, the first husband of our ancestor Eliza England), emigrated with her family, died in 1873, and was buried an ocean apart from her husband. The family felt a need to note on her gravestone in St. James cemetery that she was a "Native of Kings Co. Ireland where her husband died in 1847 and buried in Rose Cray Church Yard" ("Rose Cray" being the phonetic approximation of Roscrea). Two of their sons were Thomas (1833-1908) and William (1837-1907). The family had left Ireland in April 1850 and came to Toronto, where Tom had jobs making bricks in the summertime and cutting cordwood in the winter, and where Will worked first as a wick setter in a candle factory and then as a fireman on the Grand Trunk Railway between Toronto and Belleville, when the line was being built. In 1858 the brothers came to Brooke Township and purchased land. Kinship may have influenced the move, because their sister Floranna had married a Roane and was living on the land that would become our home farm. Tom bought property on the Twelfth Line: it was lot 28 in concession 12, the west half of which would eventually be owned by Grandad Hair. Will's farm was close by: it was the south part of lot 27 in Brooke's fourteenth concession, "back 27 sideroad," in our homely phrase, and halfway between the Twelfth Line and the "Sixth Line." That farm remained in the Woods family for some eighty years, all the time my father was growing up, when another Gilbert Woods, named for his grandfather, lived there. Will Woods was "a staunch Conservative and ... a consistent member of the Church of England" (*Guide* 21 Novembet 1907). Tom was a member of the Orange Lodge; he too "was a staunch Conservative and frequently remarked, 'A British subject I was born and a British subject I will die'" (*Guide* 1 January 1909). Sir John A. Macdonald had famously made that same profession of political faith eighteen years earlier, in 1891, during the last election he fought (Creighton 553).

The Roanes had emigrated in the same year as the Woodses: 1850. Tom Roane had been born in King's County, Ireland, in April 1824, "and just before leaving his native land was married to Floranna, daughter of Gilbert Woods, and their honeymoon was spent on the ocean. In 1858 he removed to Brooke Township, then a wilderness, locating ... on lot 26, con. 13" (*Guide* 10 November 1905). That lot became our home farm, and Tom Roane was largely responsible for cutting the bush both on that property and on others. According to his obituary, "he assisted in clearing off three hundred acres of timber land." By the time my grandfather, Sherman Hair, bought the Roane farm in 1900, about two-thirds of it had been cleared.

While the Woodses were moving to Souwesto in the late 1850s, some of the Carters were just arriving in the Toronto area. Eliza England's first husband, Richard Serson or Searson, had died in 1833, and his widow had married a man younger than she, William Carter, who had been born in 1811 (according to the census of 1861) or 1819 (according to his obituary). They had four daughters, one of whom, Ann, became our Grandmother Hair. In 1849 William Carter and one of his step-daughters sailed from Liverpool and arrived in New York on December 3. Their stated destination was Chicago but in fact they came to Toronto. William's wife Eliza and their remaining daughters emigrated in 1854, and the reunited family settled on a farm in King Township, near Kettleby. By 1861, one of the daughters, Jane, was living with a family named Platt in Toronto, and another, Ann, was with the family of Robert Graham near Burlington. How they came to be with these families we do not know, but all may have had a common origin in North Tipperary. About this same time, and somewhere in the same area, Jane Carter met William Woods; they were married in 1861, and settled on the Brooke Township farm that Will had bought three years earlier.

The marriage of Jane Carter and Will Woods led to the marriage of our great-grandparents, Jane's sister Ann Carter and John Hair. The family story is that Ann came to Watford to help her sister, and went to a tea meeting in the Methodist church. That is where she and John met. They were married in Watford on 11 March 1871. Two versions of the marriage certificate have survived, one in the possession of a grand-daughter, Dorothy (Delmage) Dolbear, and one in the Hair family Bible (in my possession). The two agree on one witness—Elizabeth Roane, the daughter of Floranna Woods Roane—but disagree on the other. According to the former, the second witness was Thomas Woods; according to the latter, he was Joseph Hair (a cousin who would move out west and die in Edmonton at the age of 105). The former is probably correct, since it has the actual signatures of the witnesses; the latter document is all in the same hand, and may have been filled in some time after the event, from memory (it gives the date of the marriage as April 11 rather than March 11). Nonetheless, the documents indicate the close relations of the Hair, Woods, and Roane families. While the couple were getting married, Jane Woods and Floranna Roane were preparing the wedding dinner at the Woods home. The guests included Hairs, Roanes, Thompsons and Searsons (who were Twelfth Line neighbours), and McLellans. According to a family story, Sam McLellan celebrated the wedding by dancing an Irish jig on the cellar door. (At that time, cellar doors, either slanted or flat with the ground, were typically outside the foundation of a house and covered the steps leading down to the storage space for fruits and vegetables.)

A note on our great-great-grandfather, William Carter: when William H. Johnston published his "brief history of the descendants of the late Eliza England" (his grandmother) in 1940, he gave little information about his step-grandfather, William Carter, from whom we are descended. No date of birth; no date of death or place of burial; not a word about his life after Eliza's passing. Thanks to Helen Clark's research, the "untold story" can now be told. William appears in the 1861 census for King Township, when he was recorded as being forty years old. 1861 was the year of Eliza's death. In 1864 Carter remarried. His second wife was Margaret Ann (Gibney) McWhirter, a widow living in East Gwillimbury Township, and they had one child, a son (Margaret had five children from her previous marriage). Sometime in the 1870s the Carters built a new home on their farm—now a heritage property in the regional municipality of Gwillimbury. William Carter died in January 1887, at the age of sixty-eight, and was buried in the Holt Free Methodist Cemetery. Helen Clark speculates that his second marriage did not sit well with his first family, and his step-grandson simply said as little as possible about him in the family history.

The "bush farm"

Many years later, when one of William and Jane Wood's sons, Dr. W.H. Woods of Mount Brydges, died, his obituary noted that his parents "came to Canada as young people, met in Toronto, married and moved to a bush farm in Lambton County" (*Guide* 29 January 1937). That label, "bush farm," is richly suggestive for anyone trying to define a Canadian sensibility. It can be read as an earlier version of the label coined by Margaret Atwood: the "bush garden." That appeared in Atwood's 1970 volume of poems, *The Journals of Susanna Moodie*, and it was "pilfered" (his word) by Northrop Frye for the title of his 1971 collection of "Essays on the Canadian Imagination." The oxymoron sums up the hopes and anxieties of the Canadian immigrant experience: the creation of a human and civilized space, and the stubborn resistance of a nature that remains threatening and will not be conquered. Its material existence in southwestern Ontario lay in the practice of never completely clearing the land and of leaving bush at the backs of farms. Mrs. Moodie, that early (1832) settler in Douro Township north of Peterborough, hated the word "bush," which for her represented everything dark and alien. For later immigrants the word "bush" did not carry such a weight of anxiety, but that psychological reaction never completely disappeared either. The uncleared land was always "the bush," rather than the less threatening "woods" or "forest." "Woods" and "forest" existed in England and Scotland; "bush" was Canadian. "Back at the bush" was a phrase my parents regularly used for the far reaches of our farm, and it designated something wild and untamed, lurking behind the orchard and the neat fields of wheat and oats and corn.

The family of John Hair and Ann Carter

The family Bible was at that time the usual place to record births, marriages and deaths. The Hair family Bible was a large heavy volume with a thick cover, illustrations, maps and glossary, ornamental borders, and elaborate capitals with scrolls and curlecues. Someone's careful cursive script preserves names and dates.

John and Ann's seven children—two boys and five girls—were born in the ten years between 1872 and 1882: James in 1872, Sherman, my grandfather, on 29 July 1873, Mary in 1875, Elizabeth (Liza) in 1877, Louise in 1878, Rebecca in 1880, and May in 1882. Sherman was christened not at Salem but at St. Mary's Anglican Church, Napier, on 7 December 1873, for Salem was a Methodist Episcopal Church, and members of that denomination were expected (following Wesley's practice) to seek the sacraments in the Church of England. St. Mary's is the oldest remaining Anglican church in Middlesex County, and is now a heritage building, dating from about 1840. It is a tiny white frame structure with a square tower at the front and a little pinnacle on each corner of the tower, and it is surrounded by an old cemetery where many of Napier's pioneers are buried.

There is one more fact about Ann (Carter) Hair, only recently discovered by Helen Clark: our great-grandmother was an accoucheur or midwife, and delivered a number of the neighbourhood children.

In 1884, Grandad Hair bought the Chittick house and farm on the Twelfth Line. Christopher Chittick was a brother of Emma, the wife of Samuel McLellan, Uncle Ches's parents, and he lived on lot 28, concession 12 in Brooke, across from the original Watson property. The farm was one hundred acres and, in addition to a barn and orchard and a dug well (into which, in later years, my father was always afraid my sister and I would fall), there was a handsome white frame house, big enough to have both front and back stairs to the four bedrooms on the second floor. The Chitticks had decided to move to Michigan, but the selling of the farm turned out badly for them. The purchase price was $6500, and John Hair made a down payment of $5000. "The following week," Helen Clark writes in her history of the Hair family, "the Fawcett Bank failed and Mr. Chittick lost this initial payment for the farm" (29). The Fawcett Bank was in Watford, and at that time it was, according to the Watford paper, "the most extensive private banking business in Ontario" (*Guide* 8 July 1887). Its failure "crippled and financially paralyzed" hundreds of people. For much of 1884 and 1885 the Watford paper carried stories about Fawcett's attempts to deal with his depositors. Tens of thousands of dollars had gone missing, as had books and records, and Fawcett himself eventually fled to the United States. When the bank's affairs were at last wound up in 1887, the final settlement was a miserable four and three-quarters cents on the dollar.

Boodlers

To disappear to escape creditors, as Fawcett did, was in those days called "to levant," meaning "to steal away, 'bolt' ... to abscond." People who "levanted" were "boodlers." In its issue of 30 September 1887 the *Guide* referred to "the great Canadian army of boodlers across the lines," the "lines" being the international border, and the paper labelled the United States "the land of the boodlers." One of my father's stories was about a farmer who went into town, bought on credit a new wagon and household items and provisions, and then he and his family simply disappeared during the night. They made for the American border, my father said, and I have a mental image of horse and wagon, laden with parents and children and goods, making their plodding way westwards, in the darkness and silence of a country night, along one of Lambton's concession roads, the parents knowing that, by the time their flight was discovered, they would be safely across the St. Clair River and beyond the reach of their creditors. Every once in a while the Watford paper carried a story about some indebted individual disappearing, only to be spotted boarding the ferry at Sarnia.

John and Ann Hair's farmhouse and barn

When Grandad Hair bought the Chittick farm, he built a new barn. The usual method in those days was a barn-raising, when men came from miles around to put up the frame of the building. Though Grandad Hair was a Methodist and did not touch alcohol, he knew that he would have to supply drink—"the men wouldn't work without it," my father said—and my grandfather Sherman was sent to Napier where, for twenty-five cents, he had a gallon jug filled with whisky. I have a vague memory of my father's saying that Sherman walked to Napier and back.

Some images associated with Grandad Hair's farm define the family's memory of it. On the roof of the back kitchen was a dinner bell, a large bell which Grandmother Hair had used to summon Grandfather in from the fields when dinner—the noon meal—was ready. It was a large heavy bell—the bottom measures almost twenty inches across—with a deep tone, and I suspect that my father always associated its sound with his grandparents' farm, for he removed the bell and kept it when the farm was sold. Then there were the trees. Grandad Hair had planted a row of maples on either side of the laneway leading back to the house, saying at the time that he wondered how long it would be before their branches met overhead. By the 1940s, when Marjorie and I were little but long after our great-grandfather's death, those trees provided a continuous canopy for the whole lane. And when Alice Cavanaugh (Aunt Mary (Hair) Galbraith's daughter) remembered her grandparents' farm, the trees were the defining feature. Alice once said to me that, when she walked through rustling leaves in the fall, "they remind me of Grandpa's lane." Finally, there was an etching or engraving in the spare bedroom upstairs, a room with a brass bed, a chest of drawers, a bevelled mirror—and a picture on the wall of "William Crossing the Boyne." This was probably a print of the well-known painting by Benjamin West, showing the king on his white horse, about to cross the river and leading the way with his sword. That picture is the sole bit of evidence that the family retained a sense of their place in Irish history (though Grandad Hair was not, so far as I know, ever a member of the Orange Lodge).

The education of the Hair brothers and sisters

My grandfather, Sherman, and his brother and sisters, were the third generation of Hairs in Canada, but they were the first generation whose education was a concern of their parents. Grandad and Grandmother Hair held advanced views for their time, thinking that their daughters needed an education just as much as their sons. The sons of a farming family usually became farmers themselves, and while it is true that the daughters often became farm wives, my great-grandparents provided their girls with the means to support themselves. Mary, the oldest daughter, became a seamstress in Watford; Liza and Lou became public school teachers; Beccie intended to become a nurse and was a care-giver; and May, the youngest (and a fun-loving redhead) became a hairdresser. All of them had a primary education in a one-room country school; four of them attended the high school in Watford when it first opened in the 1890s.

Courting on the Twelfth Line: Hairs and Kings

The 22 May 1891 issue of the *Guide* printed a cryptic account of courtship in its regular "Brooke" column: "The roads on the 12th concession have assumed a condition favorable for the exercising of the high-lifed roadsters in that vicinity. The distant neigh and prancing hoof tell only too plainly the keen competition to see which shall have the pleasure of carrying home the fair one on Sunday evening. Excitement has reached such a point that even the King himself indulges in the same pleasure. When the Hairs get back in the buggy you can bet there is no grass growing under his roadster."

My father's Hair relatives

The number of people who appear in this narrative, and their relation to each other, can be confusing. Here is a list of the children of John Hair and Ann Carter, with their spouses and children, my father's first cousins:

James Alexander Hair (born 15 April 1872; died 14 March 1928), who would marry (on 11 October 1904) Arabella Annett (born 18 February 1873; died 29 December 1939); they would have five children, Amy, Elsie, Harold, Clarence and James;

William Sherman Hair (born 29 July 1873; died 21 May 1934), who would marry (on 11 September 1901) Mary Fedicia Catherine Watson (born 4 June 1877; died 13 January 1961); they are John's parents and my grandparents;

Mary Ann Hair (born 4 January 1875; died 30 September 1970), who would marry (on 27 December 1910) Angus B. Galbraith (born 27 March 1873; died 26 February 1946); they would have two daughters, Alice and Marjorie;

Elizabeth Jane Hair (born 5 October 1877; died 27 August 1950), who would marry (on 29 March 1910) John Malcolm Mark (born 7 September 1878; died 4 April 1972); they would have three children, Anna, Eleanor, and Donald;

Sarah Louise Hair (born 27 November 1878; died 20 November, 1970), who would marry (on 25 October 1906) Robert Disney Roe Delmage (born 22 February 1875; died 22 December 1920); they would have three children, Dorothy, Horace, and Jessie;

Rebecca Hair (born 26 September 1880; died 24 February 1971); and Floranna May Hair (born 1 May 1882; died 19 April 1962).

The Watsons

John's mother, Dessa, was a Watson, and the Watsons were among the earliest settlers in Brooke Township. James and Mary Watson, my father's great-grandparents, had established themselves in Brooke in 1853, on lot 28, concession 13, at the eastern end of the Twelfth Line, and both of them died in the first decade of the twentieth century, James in 1907 and Mary in 1909. My father remembered his great-grandparents: he told me how his great-grandfather had a beard and gave him candy; and he told me about being taken to see his great-grandmother in her last illness—he remembered her moaning. The weather was so wet at her funeral, my father said, that planks had to be laid in the yard so that people could get to the house.

The early history of the Watsons is a matter of family tradition—stories handed down from generation to generation, without supporting documentation. According to this oral transmission, the Watsons from whom we are descended originated in Annan in the lowlands of Scotland and were sheep herders in the Cheviot Hills. At some point at the very end of the eighteenth century the family moved from Scotland to Ireland and, according to these family stories, their son William—the earliest named Watson ancestor for whom we have information—was born on the way across the Irish Sea. William Watson was a young man of twenty-one when he left Ireland, on his own, and ended up in Pennsylvania. His family followed him there but did not stay long, for in 1821 the Watsons came to Niagara and settled on the east one-third of lot 15, concession 4, in Willoughby Township. Aside from the land records, the earliest documentation of their presence is a marriage certificate, when William married the daughter of a neighbouring Irish family whose surname was Milligan. The document reads as follows: "This certifies that Wm. Watson and Jane Myligien of Woolibe Upper Canada were lawfully married on the 5th day of April 1825 by David M. Smith, Minister of the Presbyterian Congregation of Lewiston State of New York. David M. Smith Lewiston Apl 25th 1825."

William and Jane Watson had two children, James David, born 8 May 1826, and Mary Elizabeth, born 14 August 1832. James, our great-great grandfather, was, again according to the family's oral tradition as recorded by Catherine Watson, "a fresh-water sailor" and "one of the crew on the ferry below Niagara Falls." The ferry service had begun in 1846, but when the first suspension bridge was built, the ferry business dropped off. Then (I am quoting Catherine's narrative) "during the winter of 1851, the river ice took out the ferry landing on the Canadian side and sank the ferry. In the spring, it was recovered and was converted into a sight-seeing boat" which became famous as the *Maid of the Mist*. James Watson was one of her crew. And her captain (according to family tradition) was George Albert Smith, whose daughter, another Mary Elizabeth, James married. The wedding took place in Buffalo on 11 January 1850, before a Justice of the Peace.

The Smiths, in spite of their surname, brought German blood into our family. In the census of 1901, Mary Smith Watson identified herself as "German," because her father was of "Pennsylvania Dutch" stock, and her mother had been Mary Rosena Snively (1808–1883), that surname being a corruption of Schneelein, "little snow man," a German-Swiss name.

The Smiths were originally Schmids. They migrated from Philadelphia to New York State to the Niagara Peninsula, arriving in Willoughby Township in 1822 or 1823. George Albert Smith's father was Georg Peter Schmid, and his mother Maria Van Alstein or Alstyne. George Albert himself was born in New York state, in Brunswick, Rensselaer County, on the east bank of the Hudson River opposite Albany, on 7 April 1804, and he was christened in the Gilead Evangelical Lutheran Church in Brunswick, at the centre of a German colony dating from the early eighteenth century. He died in Brooke Township in May 1875, and was buried in the Alvinston cemetery, in a plot next to the Watson and Campbell plots, on a high bank above the valley of the Sydenham River.

"A howling wilderness"

Such was Brooke Township when the Watsons arrived. The label is Biblical (Deuteronomy 32: 10), from the song in which Moses celebrates God's providence, and when the early settlers used it—so often that it became a cliché—it may have been not only an expression of fear but also of hope for God's beneficent guidance amid the hardships and privations they endured. Certainly when it appears in James Watson's obituary in the Watford paper (April 1907), it is alongside an account of his hospitality, his beliefs and his conversion. "The late Mr. Watson was born in the township of Willoughby… He moved to Brooke in the year 1853, when it was a howling wilderness, and with the aid of his now sorrowing wife hewed out a comfortable home. Many a wayfaring person has found a comfortable shelter in his humble abode for he was never was [sic] known to turn away a hungry man from his door. Mr. Watson will be missed by a large circle of friends and especially in the church. Deceased was converted in a series of special meetings conducted by the Rev. F. W. Dighton and being a faithful follower of the Blessed Lord and Saviour Jesus Christ, leaning on his breast through all of his afflictions." Not mentioned in the obituary is the fact that James's parents, William and Jane Watson, donated the land for Salem Methodist Episcopal church. The congregation had been formed in 1860. On 28 March 1862 the Watsons deeded for one dollar a quarter acre of their property, on the northeast corner of the Twelfth Line and 27 Sideroad, and a log church was erected. It was known as "Watson's Meeting House," and served until 1880, when a new frame church was built—the one attended by my father when he was growing up.

How the Watsons came to the "howling wilderness" of Brooke is the subject of stories passed down to my father. In January 1853 James Watson's father, William Watson, sold his log house and farm in Willoughby Township for £212 and ten shillings, and on March 5 he bought the Brooke Township farm for £150. The journey from Chippewa to Brooke took six weeks, according to family tradition. Three generations, William and Jane, their son James and his wife Mary, and their two small sons travelled in a covered two-wheeled ox cart (the oxen were called "Buck" and "Bray") and led a milk cow. All their possessions, including a stove and a table, were in the cart. David Watson, James and Mary's second son (who would become my father's "Grandad Watson") described himself as "a babe in arms" at the time, and the cow provided milk for him and his older brother William. (David's birthday was 16 November 1852, and in later years he always said he "had been born four miles from Niagara Falls.") A twelve- or thirteen-year-old girl named Catherine Everson was with the Watsons and looked after their infant sons during the trip. She was apparently an orphan, and had lived with the family in Chippewa. The farm that William and Jane Watson bought was completely bush. There were so many pheasants and wild turkeys about that, years later, Peter, their youngest grandson (who was born in Brooke in 1871) referred to them as his "chickens."

The two hundred acres of lot 28, concession 13, were the original Watson farm, and there parents, children, and spouses all lived. The first house on the property was built by the parents, William and Jane Watson, and it was on the west section of the east half of lot 28. It was one of the first houses in Brooke, and the timber came from the bush on the farm. That house, about which we know only that it was "long" and "low," survived until 1916, when Peter Watson, their youngest grandson, then living on that portion of the farm, had the old house torn down and replaced by the distinctive hip-roof house that is still there. William and Jane's son James and his wife Mary built a two-storey house to the east of their parents' house. It was a frame structure when they first erected it in 1854, but it was eventually bricked, and when Marjorie and I were small that was where another of the grandsons, Uncle Harry Watson, lived. The west one-half of lot 28 was where William and Jane's daughter Mary and her husband Peter Smith built their house. That portion of the farm was eventually bought by Sam McLellan, Uncle Ches McLellan's oldest brother, and in 1916 he built the fine brick house which still stands, though altered and updated.

James and Mary Watson had eleven children in the twenty-three years between 1851 and 1874. The two oldest boys—William and David—were, as I have already said, born in Chippewa; Mary was just nineteen when William was born. Nancy, their first daughter, was the first of their children to be born in Brooke, in April 1856. Two more followed, a girl in 1858 and a boy in 1861, but neither survived childhood, the daughter dying at age three and the son at age nine. Henry (our "Uncle Harry Watson") was born in March 1863; Elcie in 1865; Ceilan in 1867, Mary in 1869, Peter in 1871, and Maggie in 1874, when her mother was forty-two. By that time William, the oldest son, was married. The second son, David—"Grandad Watson"—married a year later, and his first child, my grandmother Dessa, was born in 1877. Some of her Watson aunts and uncles were only a few years older than she was, and this was the cause of much puzzlement when I was a boy first taking notice of things and trying to sort out relationships. I could not quite comprehend the fact that the men we called "Uncle Harry" and "Uncle Pete" were not only my uncles and my father's uncles, but my grandmother's uncles as well.

The family's grandmother, Jane Watson, died in Brooke on 25 February 1880, "aged 86 years and 8 months," and William Watson died on 24 August 1883, "aged 83 years." Salem church did not have a cemetery attached to it, so both were buried in the churchyard of Mount Carmel Methodist Church, which was on the Twelfth Line west of the Nauvoo Road and west of 15 Sideroad. Although the church itself—a plain white frame building erected in 1880—has survived, the cemetery which surrounds it was allowed to deteriorate and the stones marking the earliest Watson graves disappeared. James and his wife Mary are also buried there, and James's son, Uncle Harry Watson, and his wife and son Vern. Their stones remain.

Here is the Watson side of my father's family. First, the three children of David—Grandad Watson—and Catherine ("Kate" Campbell) Watson:

Mary Catherine Fedicia ("Dessa") Watson, who married Sherman Hair;

David Oscar Alexander Watson (born 25 August 1882; died 24 July 1952), who married (on 20 April 1911) Jennie Munro (born 10 June 1878; died 21 February 1936) and (on 26 May 1945) Jean (Breckenridge) Stephens (born 7 April 1898; died 17 June 1977). Uncle Oscar had no children.

Guy Bernard Watson (born 27 October 1885; died 31 December 1920), who married (on 27 March 1907) Mary Emeline Hay (born 21 October 1879; died 18 January 1942); they would have one daughter, Catherine. Grandad Watson had one daughter by his second wife, Ella Reid:

Ada Margaret Evelyn ("Eva") Watson (born 14 July 1889; died 17 May 1976), who married (on 29 June 1916) William Gordon McNeil (born 17 November 1888; died 31 August 1968); they would have one son, John.

Our Scotch ancestors: the Campbells

Our descent from the Campbells is through Dessa (Watson) Hair's mother, who before her marriage had been Catherine ("Kate") Campbell (1853-85), and whose family had come to Brooke from Lobo Township in 1871. Lobo Township, which is northeast of Strathroy, had been settled in the 1820s, mainly by Highlanders from Argyleshire. Among them were so many Campbells, with so many names in common, that the settlers had to resort to nicknames to distinguish the men from each other. So our ancestor, Duncan Campbell, was Duncan "Hedley," after the creek which ran through his property. Duncan "Hedley" (1787-1846) was the son of John and Christine Campbell of the parish of Glassary, near Lochgilphead in Argyleshire, the fourth of nine children.

In 1809 he married Margaret Mitchell (1792–1871), and they had five children, all boys. Their home was "near Loch Fine."

I have elsewhere lamented the lack of immigration narratives among our ancestors, but we do have one for Duncan "Hedley" and Margaret Campbell. The story begins in 1830, with the decision to emigrate: the family took "a coasting boat" from Lochgilphead to Greenoch. From there they sailed on the "River of London" to Quebec, took a river boat to Montreal, and then proceeded by wagon to Marintown in Glengarry County, where they stayed for two years. In 1832 they sailed by lake boat the length of Lake Ontario, landed at Queenston, travelled by wagon to Port Colborne, and took another lake boat along the Lake Erie shoreline to Port Stanley. There they were met by Campbell cousins who conducted them overland to Lobo, crossing the Thames River at what is now Byron, where there was a bridge. They settled on lot 18, concession 9, and called their property "Spring Creek Farm." The nearest mill—always a concern of the early settlers—was at Duncrief.

Duncan "Hedley" died in November 1846, at the age of fifty-eight, and was buried in the old pioneer cemetery (the Hume Cemetery) at the corner of the Coldstream and Ilderton roads, but the stony subsoil and high water table led to the abandoning of that burial ground, and when Duncan's wife Margaret died, twenty-five years after her husband, she was buried in the Ivan cemetery on the Nairn Road.

We are descended from Duncan and Margaret's youngest son, also named Duncan (born in 1821 or 1822, died in 1892), who married Sarah McLellan (1830–1905). In 1871, as I have already said, Duncan and Sarah moved to Brooke Township, to a farm on the north side of the Tenth Line (lot 17, concession 11). That farm was directly south of Grandad Watson's farm on the Twelfth Line, so when my grandmother Dessa was a girl visiting her grandparents, she walked south along 27 Sideroad and then (because the sideroad did not go all the way through to the Tenth Line) through the bush to get to her grandparents' farm. The reason for the truncated sideroad was in the middle of the bush: it was a circular depression, an acre or more in size, reputed to be filled with quicksand and fenced to keep livestock out of it. Children were warned to stay away from it.

Duncan and Sarah (McLellan) Campbell had eight children, Dessa's mother Kate being the second. Their oldest son was yet another Duncan, who married Nancy Watson, a sister of Dessa's father David, and emigrated to Carson City, Michigan. One of my childhood memories is a visit from one of my grandmother's Michigan cousins, Orpha or Ilma (names which seemed exotic to me), and all I can remember about the visit is that she presented me with a shiny American penny.

Dessa's grandfather, Duncan Campbell, died in December 1892, at the age of seventy, and his "relic" (in the repellant diction of the day), Sarah, at seventy-five, in May 1905. Both are buried in Alvinston cemetery.

But the sad deaths at the time were the deaths of young women in childbirth or shortly after. Dessa's mother Kate, as we shall see, died in 1885, at the age of thirty-two, shortly after the birth of her son Guy. And Kate's sister Mary, who had married Alfred Clothier, died in 1890, also at the age of thirty-two, not long after the birth of her third child. Ten years later Mary Watson, Uncle Harry Watson's wife, would die at thirty-three, shortly after the birth of their son Vern. Perhaps the saddest death of this sort was that of Verna (Acton) Moffatt, the first wife of my father's cousin, Hiram Moffatt. She died in September 1927, in childbirth, at the age of twenty-seven. I have a vague memory of my father telling me the story which my cousin Helen (Annett) Clark told me years later, about the burial at St. James: "The infant died the day of the funeral and they opened the casket at the cemetery and placed her baby in her arms."

My father did not tell me much about these painful circumstances, and only once or twice did my grandmother mention the trauma of her mother's death (she was eight years old at the time). The stories my father did tell me were more likely to be comic, like the story of Alfred Clothier's second marriage: he had fourteen children by his second wife (in addition to the three by his first). So when Alfred emerged from the bedroom with a newborn in his arms, saying, "Well, what shall we name this one?" one of the women who were present snorted: "Name it? I'd start numbering them!"

The Campbells, like other Scots immigrants, retained a vaguely romanticized view of Scotland, but in fact their place in Scottish history is not a happy one. At Glen Coe in 1692, a regiment of Campbells, who were Protestant and loyal to William III, massacred thirty-seven men of the Macdonald clan, whose allegiance had been to the Jacobite cause. The deed made the Campbells outlaws among the Highlanders. Even now, apparently, there is in Glencoe a hotel and pub popular with climbers, with a sign on the door reading "No Hawkers or Campbells."

Brooke Township in the 1870s, '80s and '90s

The western half of Brooke Township was late in being settled because much of it was swamp. Not a wetland with great open stretches of marsh grasses and cattails, but a heavily timbered area, with ash and oak and beech, walnut and maple growing out of heavy clay soil for which there was no natural drainage, so that the trees stood in water for much of the year. Such was the great Brooke-Enniskillen Swamp, which extended into Dawn and Sombra Townships as well.

The Brooke portion of the swamp remained largely untouched until the early 1870s, when the provincial government promoted the draining of land and when the "municipal drain" became a familiar part of the landscape. It was typically a deep ditch alongside the road allowance, and material dug from the drain was used to build up the roadbed. Extensive drainage created the characteristic look of the western and southern parts of the township: flat open fields stretching away to the bush at the backs of farms and, alongside the concessions and sideroads, ditches deep enough and broad enough to swallow up a horse and buggy. Brooke, which in 1850 had been the most thinly populated area in the whole Western District, saw in the 1860s an influx of settlers (including the Hairs) to the higher ground in the eastern parts of the township and in the 1870s to the newly drained land in the west and southwest. In July 1905 the Watford paper, in its regular "Brooke" column, said of the "once despised" land in the west that "there are no better crops in Ontario this season than those produced on the old Brooke swamp," by that time considered the finest farmland in the township. But it was heavy clay, and an old joke circulated about it. Question: "what do you get when you mix a load of Brooke Township clay with a load of sand?" Answer: "two loads of Brooke Township clay." The poor drainage of much of the township continued to be a political and financial problem. In January 1908 the *Guide* noted that "Brooke has more trouble than any township in the West over ditches and watercourses, and the township Council that can get along without any friction in this regard has yet to be elected."

In prehistoric times the swamp had been the home of beasts now extinct: a Brooke farmer found (in 1893) the tusk of a mastodon, nearly four feet long and weighing twenty-five pounds. In the 1870s the swamp remained home to a great variety of wildlife: deer, partridge, wild turkeys, wild hogs ("more ferocious and subtile than any beast in the woods," said the Alvinston paper in 1878), bears, and wildcats. In January 1879 Grandad Hair's brother Robert, then living in Moore Township, killed "a very large wild cat," which he sold to "a gentleman from Petrolia," to be stuffed. And in July of that same year the paper complained that "the bear that inhabits the woods west of here [Alvinston] has not yet been captured."

Hunting in the great swamp was not, however, the chief activity: for several decades the area supported an extensive lumber industry which involved at least one member of our family: Uncle Harry Watson, Grandad Watson's younger brother. By this time, the first railway had been built across the township. It was the St. Clair branch of the Canada Southern, constructed in 1871–72 to serve the lumber business, and it ran from Glencoe across Mosa Township to a high-level bridge over the Sydenham, into Alvinston and on to Inwood and Courtright on the St. Clair River. Lumbering was seasonal: in the winter, the cutting of trees and the drawing out of logs; in the summer, sawing, cutting, and planing. In Sutorville and Inwood and now forgotten places like Wilsoncroft and Weidman there were saw-mills, stave-mills, and planing mills, which depended upon winter conditions for their supply of logs. In 1893 those conditions were so favourable that (as reported by the Watford paper) "this stock will furnish two years solid sawing, and means constant employment for a full staff of mill hands for that time. The getting out of the logs has, of course, afforded employment to a large number of men during the winter." Uncle Harry Watson was one of those men, and he must have told my father about his experiences. "The men who worked at drawing out the logs lived in shanties in the bush, and worked all winter with their teams," my father said. "The thick woods harboured not only partridge, quail, and deer, but even bears and wildcats. It was common to hear the wildcats screaming around the shanties at night." My father, who was mechanically-minded and practical, like most men of his generation, was primarily interested in the way in which the work was done: "the tramway by which the men hauled the logs out. It was constructed entirely of logs. Trees, selected for their length and straightness, were cut and laid end to end to form rails. The ends were mortised together. The underside of the logs was flattened at regular intervals, and ties, also logs, were laid at those points. The cars which ran on these tracks consisted of two axles fitted with wheels which had a wide flange. This permitted them to fit over the contour of the logs which were the rails. The carriages were built especially to carry logs and were drawn by a team of horses." The tramway ended at Wilkesport (where the logs could be floated on the north branch of the Sydenham River), and it extended miles back into the woods. "In the spring, when the frost began to come out, the tracks would heave or sag, and many spills meant long hours of extra work." My father also told me something about the economics of the enterprise: "Timber at that time was worth only two dollars for one thousand board feet in the log, and this was only for the best wood. The poorer wood was cut down and burned. Uncle Harry helped take out oak logs, which were hewn into square timbers. They were then shipped to England for the ship-building industry."

Cutting wood was not just work in the 1880s: it was also a competitive sport. In April 1886 the *Guide* reported that "Henry Watson and Sidney Smith sawed a cord of elm wood in 4 minutes and 51 sec. the other day, on the east half of lot 28, 13th con." The paper's comment on this feat: "Big time." "Henry" is Uncle Harry, at that time twenty-three years old, and he was a man with considerable physical strength and stamina. Competitions for the shortest time for sawing wood seem to have been commonplace, and one, in April 1887, enlivened the work on the farm of Dessa Watson's grandfather, Duncan Campbell: "Some very creditable work was done in the sawing line on Wednesday of last week, on the farm of Dun. Campbell, lot 27, con 11, Brooke. Messrs. G. Bowie and E. Sedwick cut a beach [sic] log 12 inches in diameter, in the short space of eight seconds; followed closely by Messrs. John Campbell and Jos. Miller, who finished in nine seconds. Mr. Jno. Brown, of this village, who held the regulator and acted as master of ceremonies, vouches for the above" (*Guide* 8 April 1887). Uncle Harry would have been no slouch in such competitions.

Threshing, too, was competitive. Uncle Harry's older brother William and his brother-in-law Silas Cook were threshers, and in January 1887 "threshed 36 bushels of clover seed for Mr. Wm. Shugg, lot 13, 10th concession, and 500 bushels of oats and 390 of wheat in nine and a half hours one day last week. Pretty lively work" (*Guide* 21 January 1887). Uncle Harry himself had a reputation for herculean efforts. "It must not be forgotten," the paper said in its issue of 13 September 1889, "that Harry Watson is on his old threshing route again able to contend with any others of the day. Last week he arrived at F. J. Sander's, of Brooke, at 1 o'clock p.m., and at 5:30 shut down with 515 bushels of assorted grain in the granary." And in October 1891 Uncle Harry did the threshing for Grandad Hair: "Mr. Henry Watson, one of the leading threshers in this vicinity, threshed with a McCloskey on the premises of Mr. John Hair, 164 bushels of wheat in 1 hour and 7 minutes." The correspondent's comment: "No flies on the employer's men" (*Guide* 2 October 1891). It was indeed "pretty lively work."

Uncle Harry was a horseman as well: he raced horses, and did not hesitate to pay considerable amounts of money for the best animals. In August 1889 he paid $130 for a horse called "Honest Tom." By 1892 he owned another named (either felicitously or hopefully) "Greyhound," placed it under the care of a leading horse trainer in the neighbourhood, and raced it regularly. Uncle Harry was not the only horseman on the Twelfth Line. In 1909 Grandad Hair sold "a McGregor colt" for "a good price": it had attracted a good deal of local attention because "the McGregors are always in demand by the best buyers" (*Guide* 5 February 1909).

With so much of the west of Brooke flat and low-lying, drains were an ongoing concern of and expense for the township council, but they were needed on the higher ground of the northeast part of the township as well. One such drain ran in a westerly direction across the back end of our farm, and it was deep enough and wide enough that my father had to construct a bridge across it, of logs and planks, to get a team of horses (and later tractor and combine) to the fields that were (in our homely phrase) "back at the bush." Years earlier, in July 1892, Grandad Hair had petitioned council to construct a drain between the Twelfth and Tenth Lines, and while "there were more than five interested in it," he "could not get a majority to sign the requisition." But no one appeared to oppose the drain, and so council voted in favour of it. Only two years later, the drain needed cleaning out, and again Grandad Hair asked council to authorize the work. The cost: $1,618. Clearing existing drains was a regular and ongoing expense for council: I have a vague memory of large machines at the back of our farm, lifting great bucketsful of heavy clay out of the bottom of the ditch and leaving it in muddy heaps on the banks.

Country churches in north Brooke

Presbyterians, Church of England people, and Methodists were the chief denominations in the northern part of the township. The Hairs and the Watsons were (with some exceptions) Methodists, and the "Brooke Circuit" was their division of the church. By the time my father was a boy, the term "circuit rider" seems to have disappeared, and preaching in homes and barns was replaced with services in new churches built in the '70s and '80s: Walnut, which the Hairs would attend after Salem closed, built in 1878; Salem, our home church, and Mount Carmel, both on the Twelfth Line and both built in 1880; and Chalmers, at the corner of the Tenth Line and the Nauvoo Road, built in 1891. The first three were Methodist; the last was Presbyterian. All were within a few miles of each other.

The community called Walnut, at the corner of the Tenth Line and 15 Sideroad, has wholly disappeared. Only a plaque on a stone on the northeast part of the intersection marks the spot where the church once stood—the church that our parents and grandparents, and Marjorie and I, all attended. But in the last decades of the nineteenth century Walnut boasted a post office (opened in 1875), the Methodist church, a school, and a cheese factory. The cheese factory, which was erected and operated by W. G. Willoughby, the long-time clerk of the township and the best known public figure in the area, was a thriving enterprise, receiving thousands of pounds of milk from neighbouring farms and shipping hundreds of boxes of cheese annually.

Walnut church, built (as I have said) in 1878, was a white-brick structure, very plain but with hints of Gothic: a pointed doorway at the front and pointed windows in the facade and along the sides. But no stained glass: the glazing was covered with a cream-coloured paint, which let light in but didn't let people see out. The ceiling inside was of dark wood, and looked like an inverted tray. There was a raised platform at the front of the church, with pulpit, chairs for the choir, and a pump organ. The arrangement indicated the primacy of the preaching of the Word: the pulpit, with its massive Bible, was elevated above the communion table, which stood on the floor of the auditorium.

The building was dedicated at the end of October 1878, and remained largely unchanged for the next forty-four years: in 1922 the church was raised and a basement excavated under it. Outside was a shed to shelter horses and buggies during services. The most curious item I've come across in the history of Walnut church is a single-sentence item in the 11 December 1896 issue of the Watford paper: "The miracle of casting out devils was performed at the Walnut church Sunday morning." Nothing more than that. But it was an exorcism, and one would like to know a great deal more about it.

Mount Carmel Methodist Church was, unlike Walnut's brick, a white frame structure, and it was located on the south side of the Twelfth Line west of 15 Sideroad . Of the four churches I am describing, it alone still stands, perhaps because it is the only one surrounded by a cemetery. That is where many of our Watson ancestors and relatives are buried.

We had less to do with Chalmers Presbyterian Church than with the other three, but I do remember being at services there, and I think my father must have been guest soloist on a number of occasions. The building occupied a prominent position on the Nauvoo Road, to the east of Walnut and at the corner of the Tenth Line. The church was formally opened in September 1891; there were morning and afternoon services, and at the afternoon service "the Rev. Archibald Stewart, of Mosa, preached in English and Gaelic" (*Guide* 2 October 1891).

Salem, the church attended by the Hairs and the Watsons, was built in 1880, the new frame structure being put up alongside the old log one, which was then torn down. The new building was never painted, so the boards weathered to a barn-like gray; it had four tall pointed windows along each side and a plain interior with wooden pews and a pulpit; the box stove from the old log church continued in use in the new one, and that was the stove my father used to light before services in cold weather. The new church was dedicated at the beginning of July 1880. The dedication, which took place over three days, was a marathon of sermons relieved by meals. On Friday 2 July there were three sermons (each by a different guest minister), at ten, two, and seven, with dinner at twelve and supper at six. On Sunday, there were three more sermons. When Salem celebrated its sixtieth anniversary in 1924, the minister at the time, the Reverend J. L. Foster, prepared a history of the church, and mentioned James Watson, our great-great grandfather, and both Grandad Hair and Grandad Watson: "Among the early trustees were Robert Edgar and James Watson, now long deceased…. John Hair, who was another of the early trustees who served in the old log church, is still living and takes a very active interest in the church and its work. David Watson was one of the first stewards of the church…."

The Salem congregation, like every congregation, had its differences of opinion and its divisions. I do not know how much input individual congregations had in choosing their pastor, but they must have had some, for in May 1895 Grandad Hair got up a petition to the London Conference, "for the purpose of securing the services of the Rev. J. P. Westman back on this circuit for the ensuing year…." At the time Westman was on the Napier circuit, and there seems to have been some controversy, for in early June the "stationing committee" of the London Conference named no one to the Brooke circuit, noting only that there was "one to be sent." In the event, the one who was sent was the Reverend R. W. Knowles, who had "come out" directly from Ireland to minister to this predominantly Irish congregation, and at the end of June the Reverend Westman left Napier. Knowles's successor, the Reverend H. E. Curry, was the subject of no such division in the congregation. When he left in June of 1900, "about three hundred of the members and congregation of the Brooke Methodist church assembled at the parsonage to say farewell" to a man described as "the popular and esteemed pastor of the church for the past three years" (*Guide* 29 June 1900).

The church was the centre not only of the religious life of the Hairs and the Watsons, but of their social activities as well. Those activities were nearly all fund-raising events for the church, and they are part of the cultural life of the time. The tea meeting was one of the church's standard fund-raising activities. What was it? The Watford paper for 13 October 1876 describes one such gathering, which took place in the old log church (still called, at that time. "Watson's Church"), and which was likely attended by the Hairs and Watsons of my great-grandparents' generation: "On the occasion Squire Shirley occupied the chair in his usual happy and able manner, and introduced the several speakers. The first was Rev. J. H. Kennedy, of Alvinston, who took for his subject 'Small things,' which he handled in his usual highly interesting and able style. Mr. F. Kearney also made an excellent speech, it being eminently practical, and delivered very acceptably. Rev. J. Drader, in a few apt words, explained the object of the meeting, and thanked those present for their attendance. Rev. G. C. Squire followed, who spoke upon the benefits to be derived from a Christian life. His address was a very able one indeed, and listened to with marked attention. The choir consisted of Misses Kearney, Holbrook and Watson, and furnished some very enjoyable music at intervals, adding much to the interest of the meeting. The committee who superintended the providing and serving of the edibles, which, by the way, were of the most excellent description and heartily enjoyed, consisted of the Misses Clothier, Miss Watson, Miss Smith and Miss McDonald, who did their duty nobly, and well deserved the hearty thanks of all present."

The tea-meeting was still going strong when my grandparents—Sherman Hair and Dessa Watson—married in 1901. When my father was not yet six months old, the church announced a "grand tea-meeting" for 19 December 1902, when the Ladies' Aid sponsored an evening's entertainment at the church, with "excellent music, vocal and instrumental, addresses, etc." Admission was 15 cents for children, 25 cents for adults.

Another, and more complex activity—because it was really a courtship ritual—was the "basket sociable," a practice which became the basis of James Reaney's notorious story from the late 1940s, "The Box Social." The basket sociable or box social (the terms are synonymous) originated in the 1880s, and the *Guide* (8 December 1882) described how it worked: "A new and rather novel style of entertainment is becoming popular in many places this winter. It is called a 'basket sociable,' and the mode of conducting it is as follows: The young ladies prepare a basket filled with an elaborate repast, place their cards therein, and then the baskets are sold to the gentlemen without the knowledge of the owners. Each gentleman then is expected to partake of the feast with the lady whose basket he has purchased. ... It would be difficult to devise a plan more likely to incite a worthy rivalry in the art of cooking. Let these entertainments become common, and the young ladies who cannot or will not learn to make good bread and digestible pastry, will be likely to be left in single blessedness." The sexist assumptions here are obvious enough; the social and sexual tensions of the practice can be guessed at. The box social, too, was still going strong when my father was a boy: in 1912, for instance, there were box socials for the benefit of the Napier Literary Society and the Kerwood Epworth League.

The social gatherings in the church fell into a predictable annual pattern: in June, the Sunday School picnic; in the early fall, "harvest home"; later, the "honey festival"; and in December, the Sunday School Christmas entertainment. The June picnic was usually held in "Mr. Hezekiah Lett's woods" or "Mr. Kearney's grove," and after races and various athletic games, there was a program of music and speeches, recitations by the children and, of course, abundant food. The "harvest home" was typically a dinner with entertainment. On the last day of August 1900, Salem offered a "first class fowl supper" to be followed by "an excellent program," and afterwards the Watford paper printed an enthusiastic report of the gathering: "The Harvest Home of the Salem Methodist church was a grand success. The evening was as fair and fine as the breath of the air, and the bright moon could make them. Between four and five hundred, we believe, enjoyed the very excellent supper and program following while one wonder was that the Salem friends could feed such a crowd and another wonder was that the crowd could talk so loud after all eating and being filled." There was music by the "Bethesda and Salem orchestras," and some of the young women gave recitations: "Sandy Lashen's Courtship," "Tene Wene Little Fellows." The "honey festival" or "honey social" was held in December in the early 1890s, and it too featured food and entertainment. One in December 1891 included speeches, vocal solos, selections by the choir, a recitation by

"J. Hair," and two recitations "illustrated by lime light views"; in December 1894 "the song entitled 'Remember Boy Your [sic] Irish' was sung in honor of Rev. Mr. Knowles." (Knowles had "just come straight from Old Ireland to accept the pastorate"; *Guide* 19 September 1924.) There were similar numbers at the Sunday School Christmas entertainment. The announcement for December 1889, for instance, said that "the program will consist of readings, recitations and speeches by gentlemen from Watford and vicinity. Music will be furnished by the Salem choir ..... Chair will be occupied by Dr. Harvey, of Watford. Doors open at 7 o'clock, admission 15c." " Among the vocal selections were "several" by the longtime teacher in our school section, Alma Hughes.

Rural schools in Brooke Township

There were twenty-one school sections in Brooke Township. Ours was S. S. No. 10, and directly to the west of it, across the Nauvoo Road, was S. S. No. 5. By the time Marjorie and I were small, our own school had closed for lack of pupils, and we were "transported" (that was the word at the time) to S. S. No. 5, but my father and my grandparents all attended S. S. No. 10, which would reopen in the late 1950s, in time for Marjorie to spend one year there before we moved into Watford. Defining one's community as a "section" was a common way of thinking. When my father wrote an account of his neighbours on the Twelfth Line, for instance, he used the boundaries of our section as the limits of his narrative.

The school building in S. S. No. 5 was much older than the one in our section: while S. S. No. 10 had a handsome new building, erected in 1907 in an English cottage style, S. S. No. 5 had been completed in November 1886, was plain and utilitarian in design, and was still in use in the 1940s and 1950s, when Marjorie and I attended it. It was typical of one-room rural schools in Ontario. There were two doors at the front, one for girls and one for boys, and inside each was a cloakroom, also segregated, with cubby-holes for lunch boxes and towels. The main room of the school had three large windows along each side, rows of desks, and a raised platform at the front for the teacher's desk. Behind it a blackboard ran from wall to wall, and on a side wall hung a map of the world, in Mercator's projection, with the British Empire in red and Canada at the top centre, the largest land mass on the map. In the 1940s photographs of the king and queen—the king in a naval uniform, the queen in an ivory satin evening dress—hung above the teacher's desk. The room was heated by a large wood-burning box stove, for which the winter's supply of fuel was kept in the woodshed, a kind of lean-to at the back of the school. Fred Watson, one of the Wallace Watson family whose farm was west of the school, came in each morning in cold weather, well before the pupils arrived, and lit the fire in the stove. There was no running water. Water had to be fetched from Alec Kelly's well—the Kellys lived next door to the school—and was kept in a big metal container at the back of the room, on a shelf beside a wash basin. Outdoor toilets were at the back of the schoolyard. There was a flagpole at the front, near the road, and the yard itself was marked off from the farm fields around it by a line of spruce trees on the west and south sides. To the east, at the bottom of a slope, was Alec Kelly's orchard. And still further east, beyond his farm, was the white rectangle of Mount Carmel Methodist church and the gray stones of the cemetery around it.

Pathmasters, pound keepers, and fence viewers

Township roads were maintained, not by salaried township employees, but by the ratepayers themselves, under a system called "statute labour," the statute being the Assessment Act which required, of every man in the township, two days of labour annually on the roads. Each year the township council appointed "pathmasters," whose duties were "keeping open township roads during the season of sleighing" and calling out residents to perform the work when it was needed. Grandad Hair's name as a pathmaster first appears in the list in the second-ever issue of *The Watford Advocate and East Lambton Reflector* on 25 February 1875, and it appears regularly after that (in 1880, 1882, 1892, and 1894, for instance). How well the system worked is open to question. In an editorial on 29 May 1891, the *Guide-Advocate* called statute labour "amateur bungling" and attacked such road work as a "farce" and a "failure." It should, the editorial said, "be abandoned everywhere." On 8 January 1909 the paper reported that "one hundred and fifty-three townships in Ontario have abandoned statute labor and adopted the system of cash payments for the maintenance of roads." Brooke was not one of them: it continued to rely on statute labour until 1921.

The township council controlled stray animals through poundkeepers, who were appointed annually. Their duty was to take legal custody of animals "running at large" or "trespassing or doing damage." The owner either paid "all costs, damages and poundage fees" or forfeited the animal, which the poundkeeper was then empowered to sell. Grandad Hair was a poundkeeper in eight years between 1894 and 1910. Not subject to the provisions of the Act were dogs. Dogs from various farms would habitually gather together at nights and run in packs, when they would attack and kill sheep and other farm animals. The township council reimbursed farmers for any losses from such attacks, and regular items in the council minutes were petitions giving details of the losses and asking for compensation. Grandad Hair was one such petitioner. The *Guide* reported on 27 February 1891 that "John Hair applied for renumeration [sic] for four sheep killed and two damaged by dogs, valued by Inspector Woods at $36.00. Two more badly injured but claim not put in till it was known whether they would live or not."

In addition to pathmasters and poundkeepers, the township council appointed fence-viewers, who resolved disputes over fences between adjacent landowners. At that time fences were a far more important part of the landscape then than they are now. Everyone then had livestock, and animals had to be kept from wandering. Every farm had "line fences," which marked the boundaries of the farm itself, and within those boundaries individual fields and pastures were fenced as well. So, often, was the lane that ran back through every farm. When Marjorie and I were small, the fences were all wire fences, with a strand of barbed wire on top, and the earliest ones—rail fences—had almost completely disappeared. My father once told me that his father had built a rail fence, and that there was a long one along the lane on the Roane farm. Like most men of his generation, my father was knowledgeable about the materials. The rails were black ash, he said, because, while black ash had no commercial value (unlike oak), it split easily and did not rot when exposed to the weather. Moreover, black ash was a readily available material in Lambton County because it grew well in swampy ground.

The disappearance of fences along the roads has been a major change in the appearance of the township. Things used to grow wild along the line fences: not only tall grasses and weeds—wild carrot, milkweed, chicory, teazle, burdock, goldenrod, gentian—but white clover, elderberry and hawthorn, wild grape and wild apple trees, wild raspberries, great clumps of asparagus, stands of sumac, and scrub trees of all kinds.

That exuberant growth choked the ditches and crowded the road allowance, with summertime greenery so close to the gravel that one could reach out from a car window and touch it. All that has disappeared. Farmers now often mow the boundaries of their properties, and what was once wild is now neat and orderly.

Sherman Hair's early life and education

My grandfather was the second child and second son of John and Ann (Carter) Hair, and he was born, as I have already said, in Brooke Township on 29 July 1873. I know very little about his boyhood and early education. He attended S. S. No. 10 when the school building was on the corner of James Annett's farm. At that time the practice of publishing student grades and standing in the local paper was just beginning, but Sherman's name appears only three times, in the "honor roll" for the months of March, April and May 1889, when he was in Class IV. He seems to have been good in school, for he stood first in all three months, ahead of all others, including Dessa Watson, whom he would eventually marry. There was an age difference of four years between Sherman and Dessa—in 1889 Sherman was fifteen while Dessa was eleven—yet they were only a year apart in school. For Sherman had been ill with rheumatic fever. That childhood disease can affect the heart valves and the heart muscle itself, and although Sherman apparently recovered, the underlying damage had been done and would lead to his early death at the age of sixty.

In June of 1889 Sherman wrote the Entrance Examinations, and was one of the "successful students" whose names were published in the Watford paper on 26 July 1889. My father told me a curious fact about his father's results, and that was that it was possible to receive more than one hundred marks for a perfect paper. Sherman received 105 marks on the mathematics examination: he answered all the questions correctly, and there were an additional five marks given for neatness.

There is no evidence that Sherman ever attended high school. He was a farm boy, and he intended to make farming his life's work, but he was the third generation of Hairs to farm in Brooke, and his outlook was more up-to-date than that of his pioneering father and grandfather. At that time the Ontario Agricultural College in Guelph offered farmers' sons courses in advanced farming methods: a two-year course which led to an "Associate" diploma, and a three-year course which led to the degree of B.S.A. (Bachelor of Science in Agriculture). Sherman enrolled in the former, in the fall of 1898, when he was twenty-five years old. The basis of his admission was the Entrance Examinations he had passed in 1889, plus the "practical experience" of farming.

The courses he took in his first year fell into four broad categories. The first was "Agriculture, Dairying, [and] Veterinary Science"; the second was "Botany, Bee-Keeping & Horticulture"; the third was a range of science courses, "Chemistry, Physics, Geology & Zoology"; and the fourth was English Literature, Mathematics, and Euclid (and included bookkeeping). His marks at Christmas 1898 were a mixture of seconds and thirds, and he stood twenty-sixth in a class of forty-three. By the end of his first year, and with the addition of courses in Farm Management and "Field Experiments," his standing in class rose to thirteenth. (But he must have had some talent as an artist: in Drawing he "tied for 1st rank.")

In his second year Sherman had courses in Livestock, Dairying, Horticulture, Organic Chemistry, Botany, Entomology, Veterinary Pathology, English Literature and Economics. At Christmas he stood eleventh in a class now reduced to twenty-nine men. The courses in the second term of that year took a more practical turn: "Judging Cattle," "Judging Sheep," "Practical Poultry," "Veterinary Obstetrics," "Practical Horse," "Agricultural Chemistry," "Engine and Boiler," and "Carpentering"—these in addition to Biology, Physics, Economics, and English Literature (in which he "tied for 1st rank"). His grades were all seconds and thirds, but when he completed the course his rank, under "proficiency for whole year," was tenth in the class.

I still have my grandfather's graduation certificate. It is headed "Ontario Agricultural College and Experimental Farm" and dated 15 April 1900. It certifies that William Sherman Hair, "having successfully pursued the studies and satisfactorily passed the Examinations," is admitted to "the status of Associate of the Ontario Agricultural College." The certificate is signed by the then Minister of Agriculture, John Dryden (in the cabinet of George W. Ross, the premier at the time, who was from Nairn in Middlesex County), and by the president of the college, James Mills, M.A.

I know only bits and pieces of my grandfather's life as a student. Some photographs of his fellow students have survived all the family moves and clearings-out, but my father was unable to identify any of them except one, a man named Waters—Benomi J. Waters—who seems to have been Sherman's best friend: one photograph shows the two of them together. Though Waters had come to the college from the farm of a cousin at Ivan (on the Nairn Road in Lobo Township) he was in fact from Keechi, Texas, a very small town about halfway between Dallas and Houston, and he was in the degree course. When Waters graduated in 1902 he, like my grandfather two years earlier and like nearly all other graduates of the college, returned to the Middlesex County farm where (according to the *O.A.C. Review* of 1908) he devoted himself to "the production of pure-bred stock" and, like my grandfather, served "on the provincial staff of expert judges." What the *Review* said of Waters in 1910 could have been said of Sherman Hair as well: he "is making good use of the training he received while at College, in the advancement of agricultural conditions in general." By 1930 Waters was back in the United States.

The only other fact I know about my grandfather's life at college was that he was a member of the championship tug-of-war team in 1899. A photograph of the team has survived, and he and his team mates are named in it.

As for my grandfather's character, I have always liked the description of him in William H. Johnston's 1940 family history, *The Descendants of the late Eliza England* (who was Sherman's grandmother): he was, Johnston wrote, "quiet, capable, and agreeable."

Dessa Watson's early life

My grandmother was born in Brooke Township on 4 June 1877. At that time her parents, David Watson and Catherine ("Kate") Campbell Watson, were living on a fifty-acre farm on the southwest corner of the Twelfth Line and 27 Sideroad, the east one-half of the east one-half of lot 27 in concession 12. She was christened Mary Catherine Fedicia (the spelling of her third name varies; it was sometimes Phidisa), but she was always known as "Dessa."

Dessa's parents had married on 3 November 1875, when David was twenty-three and Kate twenty-one. The witnesses at the wedding were Kate's sister Anne, and Alfred Clothier, whom Anne would later marry. David's parents, James and Mary Watson, lived on the Twelfth Line, "kitty-corner" from David's farm, and Kate's parents, Duncan and Sarah Campbell, lived on the Tenth after moving there from Lobo Township, on the farm immediately to the south of the farm of the newlyweds. The house in which my grandmother was born was a white frame house about one-third of the way back in the farm and facing onto 27 Sideroad. The north part was one storey, the south part two. The one-storey part was the kitchen, with a vine-covered verandah on the east side; the two-storey part had a parlour downstairs and three or four bedrooms upstairs. As was usual in those days, the parlour was used only on special or formal occasions. The kitchen was the centre of family and social life. "They always visited in the kitchen," a neighbour, Mary (Reid) Cooper remembered, and it "was a fairly good size. … There was a big table in the middle of the room and a cook stove," and "there might have been a pantry…."

Dessa, the first-born, had two brothers, Oscar Alexander, who arrived on 25 July 1882, and Guy Bernard, born 27 October 1885. But childbirth could be a dangerous thing in those days, and a month after Guy was born, Kate Watson died. She was thirty-two years old.

The Watford paper published an extended obituary on 4 December 1885:

> Died, on Saturday, Nov. 28th, Catherine, beloved wife of R.D. Watson, at their residence 12th line Brooke. The deceased passed away very suddenly on Saturday evening last. She had been seriously ill for some weeks past, but had so fully recovered that she had discontinued the doctor's treatment and medicine. The acquaintances of Mrs. Watson will regret to hear of her death as she was highly esteemed by all who knew her. The Rev. D. Pomeroy, her pastor, attended her in her sickness, to whom she gave satisfactory evidence of a lively faith in Christ, and also those who attended or visited her bedside saw her bear her illness with true Christian patience and fortitude, ever looking unto the strong for strength, bearing her pain and suffering as coming from the hand of a loving father, who "doeth all things well." Her age was 32 years, 2 months and 17 days. She leaves a husband and three children to mourn their loss. The children are a girl about eight years, a boy three, and an infant boy about five weeks old. While with us her kind and generous manner as a neighbor and friend, her consistent walks in life, in the home, the church, and Sabbath school, as a Christian, won the respect and love of her many friends and neighbors, who now realize they have met a loss, though her eternal gain. Her husband and family have the heartfelt sympathy of all in their bereavement, and we commend the husband to put his confidence in Christ, whom his beloved wife had learned to love and trust even unto the end. / Her remains were interred in the Alvinston cemetery on Monday the 30th ult., and notwithstanding the almost impassible state of the roads, almost thirty teams and a large concourse of friends attended the funeral. The funeral sermon will be preached (D[eo] V[olente, meaning "God willing"]) by Rev. D. Pomeroy in Salem church, on Sunday morning, 6th inst., at 10:30 o'clock.

My grandmother was, as the obituary says, eight years old when her mother died, and it was a loss that haunted her all her life. I can remember her saying to me how difficult it was to lose a mother, and I have vague memories of the difficulties she mentioned. Her father married again—it was on 21 June 1888 that he married Ella Reid, the daughter of a neighbour—and while there is nothing to suggest that Dessa's stepmother was anything but kind to her, Ella could not take the place of her own mother. Ella Reid's sister Ada married a man named Green, who lived in Stoney Creek, and I have another vague memory of my grandmother telling me about being sent to live with them—an unhappy time for her. I always had the impression that Dessa and her brothers were very close because of their loss, and—a telling fact about the success of her father's second marriage—Dessa was very close to her half-sister Eva, who was born on 14 July 1889. About that same time another child came into the Watson household. Ada (Reid) Green died an early death and left an infant son, George, whom Dessa's father and stepmother adopted as their own. By the 1890s then, there were five in David and Ella Watson's family: Dessa, Oscar, Guy, Eva, and George.

Dessa attended public school at S. S. No. 10, but how far she advanced I do not know. Her name appears in the school reports for S. S. No. 10 only in 1889 and 1890, when Alma Hughes from Napier was the teacher in our section. From that time until her marriage, Dessa's name does not appear in the paper, and I know nothing about that eleven-year period of her life.

Methodism

The Hairs and the Watsons were, as I have said, all Methodists, and by the 1870s theirs was the largest Protestant denomination in Canada. Decades earlier, the loyalty of Ontario Methodists had been suspect because of the church's ties with the Methodist Episcopal Church in the United States; and in later decades the Wesleyan Methodist Church in England claimed oversight of "church governance, missionary financing, [and] forms of worship" (Webb 28). Canadian Methodists eventually broke with both—an early expression of nationalist feelings—and their church, in Neil Semple's words, became "the most Canadian of all the churches" (Semple 443).

What did they believe? In his 1882 history of Canadian Methodism, Egerton Ryerson summarizes the doctrines preached in the nineteenth century: "the natural depravity of the human heart, the atonement made by Jesus Christ as a full and sufficient sacrifice for the sins of the whole world; the offering of salvation to every individual, on condition of repentance towards God and faith in our Lord Jesus Christ; justification by faith alone; but from the faith which justifies, good works proceed; the witness of the Spirit, which may be enjoyed by every believer attesting his sonship; and the pressing after 'holiness, without which no man can see the Lord'—followed by the doctrines of future rewards and punishments, together with the immortality of the soul and the resurrection of the body" (73–4).

This listing of beliefs, however, is not enough to define the culture and psychology of Methodism. It was primarily, in Ryerson's key adjective, an "inward" religion (96). It did not rely on the sacraments, and much less on "millinery costumes, genuflexions, and external ceremonies" (96). Methodists did celebrate the Lord's Supper, four times a year, and while it was a solemn occasion, it had no efficacy beyond memorializing: "Do this in remembrance of me." That injunction, intoned by the minister, punctuated the eating of bread and drinking of wine as I remember from the 1940s. The bread was only little cubes cut out of a white loaf, and the wine only grape juice, in glasses so small that they held no more than a swallow. With such minimal food and drink, there was never any question about the metaphors—"this is my body," "this is my blood"—being taken literally. There was no magic in those material things; the magic lay in the Word.

The preaching of the Word and the acceptance of it into the mind and heart of those who heard it was the central experience of Methodism. It began with the arrangements in Methodist churches: the pulpit was at the front of the church, centred on the centre aisle, and on the pulpit rested an oversize Bible, its heavy covers to be lifted ceremoniously and its thick pages spread and turned carefully to the text from which the sermon would be preached. The carrying of the Word into the mind and heart was thought to be the action of the Holy Spirit, not to be effected by ritual or by any external means. This internalizing of belief had its cultural consequences: affirmations of faith were an individual matter and a personal responsibility; in the early days they were to be confirmed verbally, to the minister after conversion, and to the minister on one's deathbed. Later, that internalizing would become more and more a private matter, and feelings of embarrassment and even shame inhibited public professions of faith. By the time I was attending to church practices in the 1940s, the confession of sin was a set text, repeated in unison by the congregation, and borrowed from the Anglican Book of Common Prayer. That general confession kept one's individual sins from being a public embarrassment.

In the 1880s the deathbed affirmation of faith was a conventional part of obituaries. "The dying were constantly observed and questioned as to their spiritual condition, and by their example and often their words of warning, they encouraged religion in others." Their "last hours reflected a proper fulfilment of a holy life" (Semple 60–1). So it was with my great-grandmother, whose obituary I quote again: "The Rev. D. Pomeroy, her pastor, attended her in her sickness, to whom she gave satisfactory evidence of a lively faith in Christ, and also those who attended or visited her bedside saw her bear her illness with true Christian patience and fortitude, ever looking unto the strong for strength, bearing her pain and suffering as coming from the hand of a loving father, who 'doeth all things well.' "

The social dimensions of Methodism are well known: they believed in hard work, in honesty in all one's dealings, and in a lively family life. They avoided card-playing and dancing and alcohol. Women "were counselled to avoid socializing with and especially marrying any man who drank" (Semple 69)—which explains why Aunt May broke off her relationship with a Brooke Township man in Saskatoon. Sunday was a day of rest, when work was set aside, and the day was devoted to church and Sunday School. My father had a story about one of our neighbours, Billy Powell, "a strict Methodist," Dad said: "In sugaring-off time, he would not collect the sap on Sunday, but would sit up until the clock struck twelve, and then go out with his lantern and work."

But it would be a mistake to think that Methodists never had any fun. Neil Semple argues that theirs "was not a joyless, puritanical retreat from the world. Rather, it was profoundly sociable and convivial, providing a warm, outgoing sense of fellowship which welcomed all to join" (56). They enjoyed good food and lots of it, animated conversation, music and laughter. One has only to look at the Watford paper's account of a 1900 "Harvest Home" supper, when Salem welcomed some four or five hundred people (I quote it again here): "one wonder was that the Salem friends could feed such a crowd and another wonder was that the crowd could talk so loud after all eating and being filled. ... The miracle was that they didn't bust" (*Guide* 7 September 1900). On that occasion there was music, both vocal and orchestral, and there were recitations of poetry that "charmed all" and humorous pieces that were "very pleasing." I have not come across any references to the "love feast," but its spirit pervaded every church gathering: the tea meeting, the church supper, the Sunday School picnic, the Christmas concert. Though frivolity and some amusements were frowned upon, Methodists were not Puritans: they did not distrust happiness, as did the Calvinists in English Canada and the Jansenists in Québec. But they didn't entirely trust it either. The characteristic Souwesto reaction to good weather—a sunny day, a mild spell in January, a warm spring—was to say "we'll pay for it."

The marriage of Sherman Hair and Dessa Watson

At the end of the summer of 1901 Salem Church held its annual "harvest home festival." The advertising said that "the entertainment promises to excel all previous years," and afterwards the paper reported that the evening has been "a great success." "There was a large crowd present and every one enjoyed the excellent program provided. An abundance of everything desired by the inner man was provided by the good ladies of the church. First class music was furnished by the Mt. Carmel Orchestra and Salem Pleasure Party .... The Rev. W. H. McTavish and others gave instructive addresses, and Dr. Wickett filled the duties of chairman in a most acceptable manner. The proceeds amounted to about ninety dollars" (*Guide* 6 September 1901). This particular harvest home was held on 30 August 1901. Twelve days later two young members of the church, Sherman Hair and Dessa Watson—my grandparents—were married.

They had known one another since childhood, and they attended the same church and school. My grandmother once told me that, when she was growing up, she didn't like Sherman. That obviously changed. By the time I was old enough to be aware of feelings and emotions in others, I sensed how devoted she was to his memory. She often told me that she wished my grandfather had lived to see me; and visiting his grave in Strathroy cemetery was something we did regularly. So I grew up thinking that their marriage was very much a love match. Dessa was a passionate woman with strong feelings and a will not to be denied; she responded to energy in others, and she had a temper: when roused, her dark eyes would snap with anger. Sherman was quiet and (I am guessing) even-tempered. Yet, in spite of their differences, I think their marriage was indeed a love match.

They were married on 11 September 1901, and the Watford paper noticed the wedding in its issue of September 20: "MARRIED — In Brooke, on September 11th, 1901, by Rev. A[ndrew]. W. McCulloch, Wm. Sherman Hair to Miss Fedicia Watson, daughter of David Watson, all of Brooke." No other details about the wedding itself survive, but the Watford paper did note, about that date, that "Wednesday was 'Cupid's Day' in Brooke, no less than six weddings being reported in the township" (*Guide* 13 September 1901). One of them was a union which would produce a daughter who, years later, played a part in my father's life: it was the marriage of "Mr. Wm. R. Dolbear, and Miss Nettie, daughter of Mr. and Mrs. George Annett, all of Brooke."

The early married life of Sherman and Dessa Hair

Sherman and Dessa began their married life on the farm that Sherman had bought the previous year: the east one-half of lot 26, concession 13. It had a white frame house on it, where Roanes had lived, plus a barn and granary (which had the date "1885" carved at the top of the south wall). My father had a few stories about the early married life of his parents: one of them was about tramps.

The tramp was one of two marginalized figures in rural society at that time (the other was the hired man). Tramps wandered the countryside, sleeping in barns or haystacks, and appearing at people's doors, asking for food. When they were mentioned in the Watford paper, it was always in a bad light: there are accounts of their stealing, and warnings about their not to be trusted when performing odd jobs. For instance, there was a robbery at Frank Powell's at New Year's, 1890: "On Sunday afternoon last, while the family were absent at church, some unknown parties entered the residence of Francis Powell, 13th con., Brooke, and stole fifty dollars in money and a gold watch. The crime is supposed to be the work of tramps, as two suspicious characters were seen in the neighbourhood about the time the robbery was committed. No arrests have yet been made" (*Guide* 3 January 1890). Tramps were often arrested for vagrancy, held for a time, and then released on the understanding that they would simply disappear. "Tramps are numerous," said the paper in a one-sentence item under "Home News" on 25 August 1893, but winter reduced their number: "The weather is now too cold for the tramp fraternity to roost in their favourite lodging, a hay stack or a hay mow" (*Guide* 8 December 1893). In the summer in which Sherman and Dessa were married, however, the number of tramps increased: they were drifting eastwards toward Buffalo, attracted by the Pan-American Exposition, a world's fair held in 1901. During the day Dessa was alone in the farmhouse, and as a new bride she must have been nervous about these strange men who appeared at her kitchen door, asking for a handout. But, my father told me, Grandad Hair had a large dog who was in the habit of coming every morning to our farm and spending the whole day there. Dessa would go to the door with the dog beside her, and the tramps, my father said, would be "awfully civil" at the sight of the dog. Dessa had them sit on the stoop while she made them a sandwich and she "never had any problem" with them.

Sherman and Dessa probably considered themselves very much a modern couple as they started their life together on the farm: Sherman because he was an associate of O.A.C. and had been educated in the latest and most advanced farming methods, and Dessa because she was soon to be involved in an organization that sought to make women as scientifically advanced in their work as men like my grandfather were in theirs: the Women's Institute. It had been founded in 1897 by Adelaide Hunter Hoodless, and gained legal status in 1902 in Ontario with the Agricultural and Arts Amendment Act, which brought the Women's Institutes under the aegis of the Minister of Agriculture, "for the purpose of improving rural home life, and of imparting information in regard to women's work upon the farm." In their first ten years (1897–1907) the Women's Institutes increased to 400 branches, and by 1914 had 30,000 members and 888 branches. Their purpose was to educate women in what was then called "domestic science" or "household science," and later referred to as "home economics." The Institute's constitution called for "a better understanding of the economic and hygienic value of foods," the "scientific care of children," and "any line of work for the uplifting of the home or the betterment of conditions surrounding community life." The Institute's motto: "For Home and Country." Dessa would play a leading role in the Brooke Women's Institute, which was organized in 1912.

But that was after the birth of my father. He came into this world in July 1902, and the paper carried a brief notice of the event under "Born": "In Brooke, on July 21st, the wife of S. Hair of a son."

CHAPTER TWO
MY MOTHER'S BIRTH (1908), HER FOREBEARS, AND EARLY LIFE IN DAWN AND CARADOC TOWNSHIPS

My mother's birth

My mother was born on 10 May 1908—the first Mother's Day, as she often told us. Alice's birth was notable for another reason as well: she was born prematurely (after seven months), and again she often told us the story of her appearance in this world. Her mother, then in her fortieth year, had had a fall. She had gone out to the barn and had slipped on some stone steps there; Grandad Runnalls had himself brought the stones for the barn's foundation from the bed of the Thames River at Kilworth. So Alice appeared unexpectedly, on that Sunday: her father had gone to church—St. Andrew's Presbyterian Church—where he was the choir leader (he had a good bass voice); he was summoned home quickly—and was criticized for leaving the service although, as our mother said to us, "Don't you think he had good reason?" For three months she was not expected to live, which explains why her birth was never registered: years later, when she wanted a birth certificate and a passport, she had to go through a number of complicated steps to obtain official documentation of her existence.

She was named Alice Maud—"Alice" she associated with *Alice in Wonderland*, a book she always loved, and "Maud" was the name of the midwife who attended her birth, which took place at home on the family farm. It was on what was referred to then as the Fourth Concession of Caradoc, though the farm's official designation was Lot 19, Concession 3, and from the back of the barn one could look out in a southerly direction across the gently sloping fields and past the bush to the village of Mount Brydges, strung out along the Adelaide Road (later Highway 81) about a mile away. The white frame house in which Alice was born was still standing at the beginning of the twenty-first century, when its official address was 8779 Falconbridge Drive.

Caradoc Township

The soil of Caradoc Township, in contrast to the clay of Brooke Township, is light and sandy, and while Brooke Township is largely flat, Caradoc is gently undulating. In the last ice age the township had been part of an extensive glacial lake called by geologists Lake Whittlesey, which left behind the Caradoc sand plains and many acres of wet lands—so much so that an employee on the CPR was heard to refer derisively to the Caradoc station as "Caradoc-in-the-Swamp." Large mammals had roamed there in the prehistoric period, and one of the permanent pieces on display in a science building at the University of Western Ontario is the lower jaw of a mastodon, "found by Mr. Hugh G. Forbes in the Lake Whittlesey sands in Caradoc township, Con. VII, lot 18, south half, in 1908," the year of Alice's birth; the bone, so the label tells the viewer, is approximately 13,000 years old. Also housed at the University of Western Ontario (and now in the Museum of Ontario Archeology on Attawandaron Road) were the Indian artefacts collected by Wilfrid Jury, a great many of them from Caradoc. The area was a favoured camping ground for the Attawondarons, and the dry sandy soil hid skeletons, tools and implements, and ornaments. Ploughs often turned up flint arrowheads and spears, awls and bone needles, stone axes and knives, amulets, beads, pipes and pottery shards in the fields, and Alice's brother Howard had an extensive collection of them.

When European settlers arrived, they laid out the township in the usual grid pattern, but tilted it, so that the line of the concessions was roughly parallel to the line of the Thames River, which forms the southern boundary and runs in a southwesterly direction toward Chatham and Lake St. Clair. The main road from Strathroy to Mount Brydges cuts across this grid, curving and winding in defiance of geometry: it angles south from Strathroy, curves between Mount Carmel church and cemetery, both on a sandy rise, straightens out to run in a leafy tunnel of maple trees, and slopes gently down between apple orchards to the CPR crossing. The country's two major railways at that time, the CPR and the Grand Trunk, both had main lines running across the township, parallel and about a mile apart. The CPR's Caradoc station, now long gone, was a dark red building of the railway's usual English-cottage design, and just beyond the crossing there was a water tower with a long arm that swung out over the steam engines—the trains always stopped there—and refilled their boilers. The school that Alice and her brothers and sisters attended was close by this crossing also, on an acre or so of land surrounded by tall spruce trees; the church the family attended was closer to the village, on the northwest corner of the Fourth Concession and the Adelaide Road; and the farm, about a mile to the east, was between the two railways, though some distance from both. The farm on the Fourth Concession, St. Andrew's Presbyterian Church, the CPR station, and S.S. No. 10 were the centre of Alice's world when she was a girl.

St. Andrew's Presbyterian Church

Alice's father, Joseph Runnalls, was deeply involved in both school and church. He was a member of the school board at the time in 1916 when a room was added to S. S. No. 10, and he was an elder and a member of the building committee of St. Andrew's church. When his son Frank received a copy of C. W. Middleton's 1978 history of the Presbyterian churches in Caradoc Township, Frank recalled, in a 1980 letter to his brother Howard, his father's role in organizing the congregation and renovating the building. "I remember," Frank wrote, "how much Dad was involved with the beginning of the church. There were originally three different kinds of Methodists in Canada and they all apparently had church buildings and congregations in Mt. Brydges. In 1884 the three churches came together to form the 'Methodist Church in Canada,' and sometime later the three congregations in Mt. Brydges came together, so two of the church buildings were no longer used. I seem to remember that when St. Andrew's was formed they wanted to get the old 'Mt. Olivet,' but the Methodists didn't want another church to start up, so the Presbyterians got Dan McEvoy to buy it privately. When it was re-opened as a Presbyterian church, the Methodists didn't like it and there was bad feeling. Grandad Runnalls [Richard Thomas Runnalls] was a Methodist, and you may remember him coming to visit us on Sundays. He walked over from his home on the 2nd concession. When we went to church on Sunday night in the democrat, he would ride with us as far as the church corner and then get out and walk to the Methodist church. I cannot remember that he ever came to our church." His grandfather, Frank wrote in his *Memoirs and Reflections*, "was a devout Methodist, and when he visited in our home Father always asked him to lead in family worship, a scripture reading and prayer. For the prayer we knelt on the floor with eyes closed and heads bowed over the seat of our chairs. Though I could not understand all the meaning of Grandfather's words, I sensed something of his fervour and eloquence" (5–6). "Our home," Uncle Frank wrote, "was a religious home" (23).

"I remember the old frame church," Frank continues in his letter to Uncle Howard, "—'St. Andrew's'—with the queen heater at the back. Then it was remodelled in 1906: raised and a basement built under it, and brick veneer built around it. Dad was deeply involved: I think he must have been the head of the building committee. He was called to go to the church many times to clear up some question. I remember one day when we were in the middle of harvest, he got an urgent call to settle some problem at the church, and had to drop everything to go. When he got the message to come, he uttered something like 'The Lord help us.' I am sure his thoughts were on stronger words that I shouldn't hear."

St. Andrew's was first organized in 1900 and developed in the context of an existing pastoral charge, Cook's Church on the Second Concession and the Presbyterian church in Delaware. In 1902, the congregation asked the Cook's Church session for permission to elect their own elders—a request that was granted—and three men were subsequently ordained as elders. One of them was Alice's father.

The Runnallses and the Thompsons

Alice was the youngest of five children. Her parents, Joseph Runnalls and Matilda ("Tillie") Thompson, had both been born the year after Confederation and had married in September, 1894. Alice's oldest brother, Frank, born the next year, was thirteen years older than she, and six years older than the next child, Ruth, born in 1901. There followed Eva (1903) and Howard (1906).

The Runnallses were Cornish in origin. Alice's great-grandfather, William Runnalls, had been the blacksmith in Burlawn, a tiny village near Bodmin in Cornwall. Alice's grandfather, Richard Thomas Runnalls, emigrated to Canada in 1853, according to his daughter, Aunt Mima Thompson, or in 1858, according to the 1901 census. Alice remembered him, since he lived to the age of eighty and died in 1915. He is buried in the cemetery in Mount Brydges, alongside his wife Hannah Dykeman, who had died of breast cancer twenty-four years earlier, at the age of forty-six.

Alice's other grandparents, the Thompsons, lived on the Second Concession of Caradoc (now Parkhouse Drive), next to Cook's Church; they had donated the land for the original building. Alice's grandfather, John Thompson, was, we were always told, a well-read man, especially in law, so that his neighbours went to him for legal advice. He was twice married, and his second wife—Tillie Runnalls' mother—was a McCracken, a daughter of a well-to-do family whose money had come from their estate at Bally Mena in County Antrim, Ireland. The McCracken family was a large one when in 1846 they emigrated to Canada—there were ten children—and our mother used to say that, through her grandmother, we were related to half the population of Caradoc.

But the McCracken connection was not the only reason for the large number of Alice's relatives. Her father was the third of eight children, and he had four brothers and three sisters, all of whom married and had offspring, so that Alice, like Sir Joseph Porter in *H.M.S. Pinafore*, had cousins whom she could reckon by the dozens. Twenty-nine of them, in fact, on the Runnalls side, and most of them lived in the Mount Brydges area, except for two families who, like so many Ontario people at the beginning of the twentieth century, had gone "out west" when the land was first opening up for settlement:

Richard (1864–1931) was the oldest of Joseph Runnalls' siblings. He lived in Dawn Township until 1903, when the family moved to Lot 14, Concession 6 (now Olde Drive) in Caradoc. Like so many Cornish people, the Runnallses were Methodists. Uncle Richard and his family attended Mount Carmel Methodist Church, about half way between Strathroy and Mount Brydges. They were two families, in fact, for Uncle Richard was twice married: by Margaret Jane Swedden he had five children, Leslie, Celecta, Edward, Ada, and Roy (who was killed in the First World War); by Mary Jane White he had three more, Percy, Una, and Maurice. Les was the oldest of Alice's first cousins (he was born in 1888); he married Eliza Snelgrove, and Les and Liza lived in a big white frame house on the western edge of Mount Brydges, where Les, who died in 1971, had an extensive garden on which my mother always commented when we drove by.

Mary (1866–1955), the second child of Richard and Hannah Runnalls, married Charles Ringrose—she was his second wife—and they went west, to Claresholme, Alberta. There were five children in that family: May, Ada, Mima (Jemima), Tom and Douglas. Celecta ("Aunt Lectie," 1870–1964), the fourth of the Runnalls children, and her husband Robert Heath farmed one road over from her brother Joseph, on what is now Glendon Drive, and they had five children (Earl, May, Willard, Hershel, and Lulu). The fifth child, Jemima ("Aunt Mima," 1873–1976) lived a remarkably long life: she was one hundred and three when she died. To her we owe an account of the family's early life in Dawn Township. She married John Thompson (a half-brother of Tillie, Alice's mother). The Thompsons moved west in 1906 and farmed near Stettler, Alberta. (Also in Stettler from 1906 on were the Griggs; John P. Grigg of Caradoc had married Alberta Margaret Thompson ("Aunt Bertie"), a half-sister of Alice's mother Tillie, and they had two children, Elsie and Morley.) Aunt Mima and Uncle John had three children (Robert, who died in infancy, Hazel, and Violet). Violet was the Alberta cousin best known to her relatives in the east, because she moved to Ontario and married Neil Campbell of Melbourne. John Runnalls (1875–1965) was the sixth child in the family. He married Sarah McCracken, and they had three children (Jennie, who died in infancy, Neil, and Kenneth). They lived on the Second Concession of Caradoc and attended Cook's Church. Lockwood (1878–1956), the seventh child, married Mabel Trott, and they had two children (Clifford and Evelyn). Finally, Edwin ("Uncle Ed," 1880–1980), the youngest sibling (who died just short of his one hundredth birthday), and his wife Lola Thomson would move, for a few years only, to the farm directly east of Grandad Runnalls' farm on the Fourth Concession, and their children, Helen, Lenna, and Ralph, were perhaps the closest of the Runnalls cousins. In the late 1940s, Uncle Ed and his son Ralph moved to a farm in Warwick Township, Lambton County, and made Watford their home town. But—with the exception of Lenna and Ralph—"we didn't really keep up with Dad's relatives," Aunt Ruth once said to me, perhaps because they were so many. The families of Aunt Mary Ringrose and of Uncle Lockwood Runnalls, in particular, were strangers to us.

The cousins on the Thompson side were fewer—thirteen only (or ten, if you don't count the double cousins)—though Alice's Grandfather Thompson had been twice married and had fathered thirteen children. There were seven by his first wife, Jane Hamilton. Infant mortality rates in those days were high, and three of their children died young, including one named Jane, listed by my mother in her family tree with the note, "I do not recall ever hearing of her." Another child, Margaret (1856–1936), spent much of her life in the McCormick Home in London. I do not know what disability she suffered from, but Alice remembered visiting her, mainly because that meant going on the train to London with her mother, always an adventure for a small girl. Three children in Grandfather Thompson's first family survived childhood: Alberta ("Bertie," 1851–1929) who, as I have already said, married John Grigg, moved to Alberta, and had two children, Elsie and Morley; Eliza (1858–1936), who married John McKee (his farm was on No. 2 highway just east of Melbourne) and had one son, Howard who, at the age of three, was killed in a farm accident; and John (1862–1940), who married Jemima Runnalls (Alice's "Aunt Mima"), also moved to Alberta, and had two daughters, Hazel and Violet.

There were six children in Grandfather Thompson's second family, by Sarah McCracken. One died at the age of seven; another—Frank (1874–1910)—"drowned in west" (according to my mother's terse note; she once said to me, "we never knew what really happened to him"). Tillie, Alice's mother (1868–1944), was the oldest child in that second family. Her sister Agnes (1872–1954) married Robert Irvine, lived in Toronto, and had one son, Robert Wilton. Her brother Stanley (1877–1965) lived on the home farm and was twice married (first, to Mary Sutherland, secondly to Sylvia Trott) but had no children. And her youngest sister, Edna (1878–1939), married Edwin Robinson and had three children, a boy, Wilfred, who died of tuberculosis, Honor, and Stanley. They lived on a farm in south Caradoc, near the Muncey reserve.

Our Cornish forebears: The Runnalls family

The Runnallses, as I have already said, lived at Burlawn, near Bodmin in Cornwall. Among my mother's papers was an undated photograph labelled "the old house": it showed a plain two-storey stone structure with a low stone wall in front and a stone outbuilding to the left, which I took to be the forge. The house was still standing when I saw it in 1992, at that time whitewashed and with blue trim, and it had an addition which doubled its size. By the twenty-first century it was being rented out to holidayers.

From family sources—plus records in the UK—it is possible to construct a history of our great-grandfather and of his parents. He was, as I have already said, Richard Thomas Runnalls, and he was born on 18 February 1835, in Burlawn. His father was the village blacksmith, Joseph William Runnalls—he was always known as William—who had been born in 1808 or 1809 in Cardinham, Cornwall, and lived all his life in Burlawn, where he died, in April 1888, and is buried. Richard's mother was Mary Thomas, whose parents, Jacob and Joanna Thomas, kept a hotel in Lanivet, another village close to Bodmin. She was born in 1805 or 1806, and she and William were married in St. Breock parish church on 22 October 1831. They had seven or eight or nine children (the number varies with the source of information). Mary predeceased her husband and died in the same year, 1888, at the age of eighty-four.

Richard's older brother William succeeded his father as blacksmith in Burlawn, and another brother, Jacob, also lived there, but two of Richard's brothers, John and Joseph, as well as Richard himself, emigrated to Canada. The date of Richard's emigration (as given in the 1901 census) is 1858. John and Joseph were millwrights, and came to Delaware where (according to Uncle Howard) they ran the Rocky Mill before moving on to Nebraska and losing all contact with the rest of the family. The RootsWeb web site says succinctly of John that he "went to Nebraska, disappeared."

Our great-grandfather Richard Thomas Runnalls came (according to Aunt Mima Thompson) to Baden, Ontario. How he met our great-grandmother I do not know: she was Hannah Elizabeth Dykeman, a descendant of United Empire Loyalists from New Brunswick, and they were married in Sheffield, Ontario on 12 November 1862. Sheffield is in Beverly Township, Wentworth County, and Hannah's grandparents, Jacob Dykeman and Satira Camp, who had migrated from New Brunswick, are buried in the Lamb Cemetery there. But our great-grandparents did not stay in that area. They moved to Middlesex County (perhaps because Richard's brothers were living in Delaware), and their first three children—their oldest son, Richard Thomas (1864), their oldest daughter, Mary Elizabeth (1866), and our grandfather, Joseph (27 March 1868)—were all born near Komoka. I remember riding in the car with my grandfather east on the Fourth Concession to (what locals called) "the diamond," where the main southern Ontario line of the CPR crosses the main line of the CNR, and my grandfather saying to me that he had been born close by.

At some point between our grandfather's birth and the birth of the next child, Celecta Jane (1870), the family moved to Dawn Township in Lambton County to take up fifty acres of Crown land. It was Lot 25, Concession 13 in Dawn, at a community called Oakdale, and when the Oakdale post office was established in 1887, it was on a corner of that same lot. There Richard and Hannah's next five children were born: Celecta (as already mentioned), Jemima Satirea (1873), John Wesley (1875), William Lockwood (1878), and James Edwin (1880). The 1881 Dawn Township census lists all eight children, ranging in age from Richard (seventeen) to Edwin (one), and gives their church affiliation as "Methodist Episcopal." By the time of the 1891 census (where the family is mistakenly listed as "Reynolds"), only son Richard and his wife Jane Swedden and their son Leslie, then three years old, remained in the township: the rest of the family had moved back to Caradoc. According to Aunt Mima Thompson, the moves took place in 1889 and 1890.

Grandad Runnalls, in Aunt Mima's narrative, "was to take over the Dawn place when we moved to Caradoc and Sister Lecta was to keep house for him, but she didn't want to so I went. He worked at Mawlams and came home nights. However, I got homesick and left. Brother Richard drove me to Newberry [sic] to catch the train home. Joe wasn't too satisfied and wanted to be at Mt. Brydges with the rest of the family so Mawlams took over Father's old farm."

Back in Caradoc, Grandad Runnalls' parents, Richard and Hannah Runnalls, settled on a farm on the Second Concession of Caradoc, Lot 20, Concession 2. There Hannah died an early death, of breast cancer, on 3 April 1891, at the age of forty-six. Her stone in Mount Brydges cemetery has a common nineteenth-century emblem in the medallion above her name—clasped hands—and below is a verse in which she speaks to her husband from beyond the grave:

> Dry up your tears and do not weep
> My sufferings now are past
> You gave to me your kindest aid
> As long as life did last.

Twenty-four years later, Richard died, on 10 May 1915. He had suffered from chronic nephritis for some time, and that kidney disease eventually killed him.

"Memories of my Dawn home"

Aunt Mima Thompson, one of Grandad Runnalls' younger sisters, is our sole source—except for some isolated bits and pieces— for information about the twenty years between 1869-70 and 1889-90 when the Runnalls family lived in Dawn Township. In 1974, when Aunt Mima was one hundred and one, her daughters, Hazel and Violet, encouraged her to write down her memories of her early life. They then circulated the typescript to other family members, including my mother.

Aunt Mima begins by mentioning Grandad Runnalls: "My brother Joseph was born when living at Komoka, I know I was born in the old log house in Dawn. When my father came to Dawn it was all bush. He built a log house and hollowed out logs for rain troughs." The "old log house" became a granary when the "new frame house" was erected. That was when "either Brother Lockwood or Brother Edwin were babies," so the date would be 1878 or 1880. Mima's Grandpa Dykeman was a carpenter and, along with his son Sydney, helped build the new house, for the Dykemans—Mima's mother's family—were also living in Dawn at this time.

Buttonwood trees, which were very large and hollow, grew in the flats of the Sydenham River close to the farm, and one of those big hollow trees became a smoke house: "it was big enough around to step inside, and meat was hung around the sides with fire on the ground to smoke it. There was a door with a sack hung inside to keep the smoke in." Cherry, peach, crabapple, plum and pear trees grew around and behind the house, and on the walls were grape and hop vines ("I helped Mother pick the hops off before frost to dry and put in a sack. They were steeped and the liquid used to make yeast"). "There was a big pit dug in the garden where potatoes were stored" in the wintertime; "another pit was dug for the apples" when the trees which Mima's father had planted started to bear.

Aunt Mima's account pictures their Dawn home as a kind of Eden, with fruits and vegetables in abundance, as well as wild fruits, nuts, edible fungi, and maple syrup. Tapping the hard maple trees was an annual spring task. "I remember going with Sister Mary to collect the sap. She had a wooden yoke over her shoulders, with a pail hung on either end. They boiled the sap down in a big kettle in the bush and brought it to the house for Mother to cleanse it. ... She put in a beaten egg which brought the impurities to the top to be skimmed off." In the summer, there were wild raspberries to be picked in the "slashing," which was an open area strewn with the debris of cut trees: "we walked a mile to get there, early in the morning, and home for dinner." The picking was a community affair: "the neighbours all went too." Wild berries served another purpose when Mima and her brother John "had the job of cutting bull thistles with the hoe where Father was clearing the bush. For lunch we picked berries, and made a sandwich of leaves." In the fall, there were hickory nuts, gathered after a rain because "the wet would open the burrs," but "we used to crack [the nuts] with our back teeth, and Mother warned us we'd suffer for it." Mother was right: "I lost my back teeth early." Also in the fall were mushrooms, picked "in Mr. Mawlam's field, where there were many sheep grazing," and then fried. Mima's oldest brother, Richard, shot black squirrels in the bush: they too were fried. So the family's diet was a varied one, but Aunt Mima recalled that "our supper was often a big pan of boiled bread and milk, or boiled rice with eggs in it."

"Mother kept a lot of geese and ducks. I can remember coming home from school and seeing Mother and Sister Mary picking geese. There was a tin with handles fitting down in the boiler, and the goose lay on it to steam and loosen the feathers. We all had feather beds."

Much of the land remained uncleared, and the "bush," that presence in the Canadian landscape so abhorred by Mrs. Moodie fifty years earlier in *Roughing It in the Bush*, was a pervasive part of the family's experiences. The Runnalls children were always going into the bush or walking through the bush or hunting in the bush, though without Mrs. Moodie's sense of revulsion and feelings of anxiety and horror. Aunt Mima remembered walking through "a big bush" to get to Mawlams' farm—Mawlams were their neighbours—and she remembered walking to school through the bush "where there were Indians but I never remember seeing any." That is one of only two passages where Aunt Mima mentions Canada's native peoples. "There were Indians in the bush," she writes, "who came around to the homes with baskets and bows and arrows to sell. One was called Ben Indian, and Mother said he was a good Indian."

The river flats were heavily wooded, and the Sydenham itself was a barrier that often had to be crossed. Sometimes the children "crossed a shallow part of the river by the island." But "I often went across in the canoe and I remember Brother Joe used to scare us by rocking the canoe." Then Mima continues: "One time he saw a deer coming down the river, quite a rare sight, and he was quite excited and shot it." Grandad Runnalls mounted the antlers of that deer on a little wooden plaque he made, and they hung in his Caradoc home for years. I still have them. But he took risks in getting them: he was told that he could have been drowned. One of the Mawlam children, a boy three years old and "brother of Henry," had, some time in the mid-1880s, drowned in the river, and that tragedy was fresh in their memories.

"I walked to school," Mima writes. "It was about two miles to the old log school," but later there was a frame school a quarter-mile away, "so we went home for dinner." Mima's first teacher was a Mr. Berdan, about whom the pupils used to sing:

Mr. Berdan is a very fine man,
He tries to teach us all he can.
Writing and reading and 'rithmetic,
But he don't forget to use his stick.

For corporal punishment was an accepted practice at that time. Such beatings were the reason Grandad Runnalls left school so early: after "the Second Reader (the equivalent of grade two or three today)," according to Uncle Frank, or in the middle of Grade Four, according to my mother. Aunt Mima explains the circumstances: "One lady teacher we had was a big fat woman and cross, and people where she boarded said she drank. One morning she got mad at Brother John and I was scared. Brother Joe said 'Run, John, run!' and Brother John ran." Neither ever returned to school. But Grandad realized that he had made a mistake, my mother said in telling me this story, and he was determined that all of his children would have a good education—in spite of attitudes such as that of the hired man, who told my grandfather, with a drawl, "You're makin' fools out of your children with all that schoolin'." Aunt Mima herself left school in 1888, when she was fifteen, but Uncle John came to resent his brother's imperative, and on his deathbed blamed Grandad for his not having an education.

Methodist church services which the family first attended were held in the old log schoolhouse. "Preacher Kelty had only one leg, and drove around in a horse-drawn gig. He often stopped at our house for supper." Later the services were "moved to Florence, four miles away, so then we walked to the Presbyterian Church at Oakdale, only about two miles. I remember walking there with Mother many times …. The women sat on one side, and the men on the other, unless they were married. They sat down to sing and stood up to pray. The preaching was an hour long. Sometimes prayers were so long, we stood first on one foot then on the other…. There was a second service held after, in Gaelic, for an old lady, a Mrs. McDonald, who couldn't understand English." A standard method of raising money was the tea meeting: "Everyone sat in a seat, and plates of food were passed around. There were all kinds of cakes and pies and other things. Mother was considered a good fruit-cake maker. The people paid to get in, and the church was always full." Music was a major part of the church services. "Mother was a good singer and always led the singing in the old log school. The Dykemans were all good singers," Aunt Mima says, and Grandad Runnalls inherited that ability: he had a good bass voice and was, much later in his life, choir leader at St. Andrew's Church in Mount Brydges. There is an intriguing sentence in Aunt Mima's memoirs: "One winter Sister Celecta, Brother Joseph and I went to singing school." Nothing more than that about the school: Aunt Mima says only that "I always wanted to get out places."

Other religious observances provided more drama and excitement. "Father sometimes drove us to Florence to hear the Salvation Army. They marched on the street and sang, and one, Happy Mattie, played the tambourine." Other occasions shaded into the Gothic. "At Shetland the Free Methodists held camp meetings in a big tent. The young folks used to go for something to do, enjoying the visiting. I remember once going with Sister Mary. There was shouting and praying, and one of my schoolmates was up in the front. She was crying and they were praying over her, trying to convert her. Anyway, I cried and Sister Mary took me out. The girl's father was one of the leaders, and she later lost her reason and died."

Illness, injuries, accidents and deaths appear in a matter-of-fact way in Aunt Mima's narrative. The family's physician, a Dr. Campbell, lived in Florence: he "lost two little girls with diphtheria, and had one left." When the Campbells moved away, they "gave me a little wooden trunk with doll clothes. I still have the trunk." Mima's sister Mary was attacked by a neighbour's dog, who bit her leg. "I remember seeing her in the kitchen and Mr. and Mrs. Mawlam were there doctoring her leg, putting on red salve. She always carried a big white scar after that. The dog disappeared and I always had a feeling father knew where it went." Then there is the story of Mima's aunt, Prudence Jane Runnalls, who emigrated from Cornwall, came to Dawn, and married a Mr. Cox.

"Her wedding dress was red," Aunt Mima writes, "and the old saying was 'Married in red, you will see blood shed.'" Cox was killed in a mill accident, and his widow subsequently married a Mr. Hart. One of her sons from her first marriage, Jack Cox, was also involved in an accident which affected the Runnalls family deeply. "One day when they were hauling logs from our bush Jack Cox somehow cut his thigh badly on an axe on the load. Father carried him to the house on his back. My sister Mary ran to the school to get my oldest brother Richard who went for Auntie Hart and the doctor. When Uncle Will came in and when he saw the blood he collapsed on the doorstep in a faint. My sister Mary used to take epoleptive [sic] fits after that for some time but some doctor cured her. They said it was from the shock."

The most prominent family among the neighbours in Dawn was the Mawlams. English, and originally from County Durham, Thomas Mawlam and his son Henry arrived in Dawn in 1827 and settled on four hundred acres on the banks of the Sydenham River: Lots 23 and 24 in the 14th Concession. The Mawlams were well-to-do, affluent enough to hire help. "Father used to work for Mr. Mawlam a lot during the summer, as he needed money," Aunt Mima writes, "and Mawlams had a lot of land." By this time the third generation of Mawlams in Canada was living on the property: another Henry, born in 1858, and his wife Rachel Currie, whom Henry married in 1884. They had five children, born between 1885 and 1897. Mima's oldest brother, Richard, "worked for Mawlams by the day," and continued to do so even after he was married, while her sister Lecta "worked for Rachel Mawlam when her boys were born." The first time Mima was in the Mawlam house, "when Mother sent us over for something," she and her brother John "were too shy to say anything." She remembered chiefly the Mawlams' two big dogs, Nero and Prim, who always "came running out and barking, but not cross."

Events in the Mawlam household were always matters to be noted and talked over: "I remember the night Mr. Mawlam died," Mima begins one segment of her narrative. And everything about the "big brick house" itself—its setting above the river, its garden sloping down to the water, the hollyhocks at its back door, its "big kitchen" with its "big fireplace" above which hung "a long row of iron cooking kettles"— was as familiar to Mima and her brothers and sisters as their own house.

The Mawlams played a large role in the young life of Grandad Runnalls. "Brother Joe worked for them as soon as he was old enough and came home some weekends," his sister Mima records. The Mawlams "had big barns, mostly open sheds. They kept cattle and lots of sheep." Henry Mawlam "provided board and lodging" for Grandad Runnalls, according to Uncle Frank, "but not much money." And my mother told me that her father had lots of stories about working at the Mawlams', though only one has survived. He slept in a huge upstairs room or attic, and tramps who appeared asking for food and shelter were also lodged there. Grandad slept with a pistol under his pillow.

By the time the Runnallses were moving away from Dawn, twenty years after they had arrived, their first boy, Richard, was married and had a son, Leslie, the oldest of my mother's first cousins: he was born in 1888. Richard's sister Mary was also married in Dawn, but her daughter May was born in Caradoc. One by one the brothers and sisters moved away from their childhood home, leaving only their oldest brother and his family. "Brother Richard lived in the old Dawn home, for a time, until he too moved to Caradoc." So ends Aunt Mima's narrative.

Joseph Runnalls acquires a farm and marries Tillie Thompson

By the time he was twenty, Grandad Runnalls "had accumulated a few hundred dollars … with the hope that he might some day acquire a farm of his own," Uncle Frank writes (7). There was a cheap but not guaranteed way of doing that, and that was by buying land sold for unpaid taxes. The "tax sale" was one of the annual events my father had to administer when he was clerk-treasurer of Lambton County, and that led to his discovery, in 1971, of a record my mother knew nothing about: in the old tax sale book for October 1890 was an entry which showed that Joseph Runnalls (who gave his address as Florence) had bought a farm at the sale, one hundred acres in Dawn Township. His hopes were dashed when the property was "redeemed"; that is, the owner paid the back taxes in full, plus penalty and interest.

There was another source of land at the time, and it was in the west. Farm land around Brandon was being advertised, and Grandad travelled to Manitoba to see it. He returned after going no farther than Winnipeg—because (in Uncle Frank's words in his memoirs) there "he met some other young men returning from Brandon and quite disillusioned with what they had seen. They said the prairies were only fit for Indians and buffalo and advised him to return to Ontario" (7).

The farm Grandad Runnalls eventually bought was in Caradoc, Lot 19, Concession 3. It had "about thirty acres broken and tilled, for which he made a small down payment, and carried a mortgage for the balance, with interest at four percent. The total cost of the farm was only about four thousand dollars, but I remember," Uncle Frank writes, "how Father struggled for a good many years to pay off that mortgage" (8). The mortgage was held initially by Archie Waters and his wife, the same people from whom Grandad bought the farm, and it dated from February 1893. After 1898 a number of other people held the mortgage, its principal diminishing with Grandad's payments until, in December 1926, he finally paid it off in full.

How did Grandad Runnalls meet our grandmother, Tillie Thompson? The Thompsons lived on the Second Concession of Caradoc and attended Cook's Church, at that time a Presbyterian congregation. Uncle Frank tells the story which was passed down in the family: "Father and Mother first met in her church. Father, a Methodist, decided to see what the Presbyterian Church was like. As Mother told it, she saw this strange young man in an adjoining pew without a hymnbook. She gave him her book and he turned to the cover page to find her name. That was the introduction" (8). I know nothing about their courtship, but they were married in 1894. My mother kept her parents' wedding invitation: "Mr. & Mrs. John Thompson / request the pleasure of your company at the / Marriage of their daughter / Tillie / to Joseph Runnalls / Wednesday, Twelfth of September / Eighteen hundred and ninety-four / at 3 p.m. / at their residence." Bride and groom were both twenty-six years old. And although Grandad had been brought up a Methodist, and although denominational lines were strong at the time, he became a Presbyterian when he married my grandmother.

The Thompson family

The Thompsons were a Scots-Irish family, and came from County Down. The first Thompson about whom we have any information—Robert H. Thompson—lived in Downpatrick, where he was born in 1793. Family stories about him are vague: he was either a military man ("we think," according to one family historian) or a sailor (according to his grand daughter Agnes (Grammie Runnalls' younger sister). "I never seemed curious as to where he sailed," Aunt Agnes wrote many years later, "but he taught my Father a lot of sailor lore like splicing rope and tying sailor's knots." This Robert Thompson married Mary Ross, whose father was indeed a military man: he was a sergeant-major of the 42nd Highlanders in Dundurn, County Down. When Robert and Mary emigrated in 1820, they came to Burlington, Ontario, and settled on land in Nelson Township. There Mary died in 1830, and she and her parents, John and Jeanne Ross, are buried in the Mount Vernon Pioneer Cemetery at Appleby, in what is now the Golden Horseshoe.

Robert and Mary Thompson had four children, their first being our great-grandfather, John Hamilton Thompson, who was born in 1823. In 1837 Father Robert and son John, then about fourteen years old, came to Caradoc to claim land that had come into Robert's possession in 1835: Lots 11 and 12 in Concession 2. That move was the result of a land swap: Robert had had a grant of Crown land in Nelson Township, two hundred acres, and a man named David Springer had had a grant of Crown land in Caradoc, also two hundred acres. Robert deeded his Nelson Township land to Springer on 12 December 1835, and on that same day Springer transferred the Caradoc Township land to Robert Thompson.

The first task facing father and son was the same as that of other pioneer families: clearing the land and providing shelter. Aunt Agnes remembered a few details about that period: "My father started living in a log cabin with a loft where they slept, and I have heard him tell of the wolves howling round at night and the bears getting in and licking the fat in the frying pan. Of course they cooked on a fireplace and mostly made baking soda biscuits," but they also had maple sugar and maple syrup. Meanwhile, the others in the motherless family stayed with relatives in Burlington until 1844, when the girls, Margaret and Mary, then about sixteen and fourteen respectively, walked all the way from Burlington to Delaware, and then along a trail blazed with an axe through the bush to their father's home.

Robert Thompson died in 1859, and his two hundred acres were divided between his two sons, John (our great-grandfather) getting Lot 11, and his brother Francis Lot 12. Between the two properties there was a sandy knoll, and as early as 1860 it was the location of a number of burials. That was the beginning of the Cook's Church cemetery.

The early immigrants not only faced the task of clearing the land and building a home, but also felt it their duty to establish a church with the same denominational affiliation as the congregations they had left behind in Ireland. In 1862 fourteen south Caradoc families, among them the Thompsons and McCrackens, came together as the "Caradoc Presbyterian congregation," associated first with the Presbyterian Church in Delaware, and then recognized by presbytery as an independent congregation in 1865. In October 1867 they determined to build a new church, "erected at the site of the old frame." Does this mean that there was an earlier church building there? No one seems to know for sure. What we do know is that the site was on the Thompson farm. Our great-grandfather, John Thompson, deeded three-quarters of an acre to the Presbyterian Church in Canada, and construction proceeded immediately. The building opened in December 1867. The preacher at the opening service was asked to name the new church, and he chose "Cook's," to honour a well-known minister in Belfast, the Reverend Henry Cooke, sometime moderator of the church in Ireland. Cooke, by this time an old man, died just about the time the new congregation was holding its first services.

Those services were like those in the church in Dawn: the women sat on one side, the men on the other; the congregation sat while singing and stood for prayer. There was no organ in the early church, but there was a choir, and two of the Thompson girls—Alberta ("Bertie") and her first cousin Tamar—sang in it.

The old white frame church stood for almost forty years. It was where our grandparents, Tillie Thompson and Joseph Runnalls, first met in the early 1890s. In 1906, the congregation built a new church on the opposite side of the Second Concession, one of the prettiest of all the rural churches in Southwestern Ontario. That church still stands in the twenty-first century.

Cook's became famous for its garden parties. They were one of the principal fund-raising activities of all churches, summer's night's entertainments typically held out-of-doors in fine weather, and offering varied programs: music, ranging from solos and duets and choirs to instrumentals and band selections; comedy acts; juggling and acrobatics; speeches and patriotic displays—and crafts, cool drinks, and food. Cook's held its first garden party in 1891, and from 1896 on it was an annual event. The 1896 gathering, which was held not at the church but rather in the school yard, attracted an immense crowd. "Special trains stopped at the crossing on the 12th sideroad, bringing people from London and Strathroy," the church historian says. "The roadside for half a mile from the school yard was lined with horses and buggies." The lighting arrangements were ingenious: "platforms, four feet square, were erected on posts four feet above the ground. On these, sods were placed and fires of pine knots were kept burning for hours, lighting the entire school yard."

When the Thompsons replaced the old log house, they built a fine brick house with an ornate front verandah. That was in 1885. The house with its patterned brickwork—a style popular in the late Victorian period—was still standing when my mother and I visited Uncle Stanley Thompson there, in the early 1960s. It has since been demolished.

Our Thompson great-grandparents both died in 1909, when our mother was about a year old. John Thompson died in the summer-time, on August 12. Though he had donated land for the Presbyterian Church, he had been (what Uncle Frank calls) a "Hard-shell" Baptist, and they were conservative and Calvinist in their beliefs and opposed to missions. And though his second wife—our great-grandmother—remained a Presbyterian all her life, John Thompson (so the Strathroy paper reported in his obituary) "had been for over forty years a consistent member of the Old School Baptist church," and "died in the sure hope of entering upon the saints' inheritance." Our great-grandmother died in the winter-time, on January 14. On January 7, the paper noted that "Mrs. John Thompson is on the sick list"; two weeks later it reported her death and printed a conventional obituary, beginning with the sentence "One by one the ranks of the old pioneers are becoming thinned." What the paper does not give is the cause of death, which is disturbing: "strangulation / suicide by hanging." The official record (preserved by the province) is signed by Dr. W. H. Woods, the doctor in Mount Brydges at the time (brother of Gilbert Woods on 27 Sideroad in Brooke Township, and a first cousin of Sherman Hair). What on earth would cause a seventy-four-year-old woman to kill herself? No one—not our mother, not anyone in her family—ever mentioned this death, and my sister and I wonder if our mother even knew that her grandmother had committed suicide. Perhaps she did, and thought some family secrets are best never revealed. But Marjorie remembers a visit from Aunt Agnes when we were on the farm, and our mother's wanting to have a private conversation with her aunt. Marjorie, who was lurking nearby, was shooed out of earshot. She remembers Aunt Agnes saying, "Little pitchers have big ears."

The McCrackens

My mother's maternal grandmother, Sarah Jane Thompson, had been a McCracken before her marriage to John Thompson, and the McCrackens were, as I have already said, a well-to-do family from Bally Mena, County Antrim, near Belfast in Ireland. Squire John McCracken "had inherited an estate of five hundred acres with six tenant houses for the families who did the farm labour and provided house service as maids," according to Uncle Frank (*Memoirs* 6). The parents and their family of ten children emigrated in 1846 and settled in Caradoc Township. Aunt Lizzie Bateman, the second youngest in that family of ten, remembered that they made the voyage across the Atlantic in a sail boat, that the journey took nine weeks, and that they travelled up the St. Lawrence and on to Toronto "in a leisurely manner" (*Age* 14 May 1936). "From Toronto the family made their way by boat to Buffalo and Cleveland, and a year from landing at Quebec they arrived at their homestead on the second concession of Caradoc.... A rude shelter was put up in the heart of the forest until Mr. McCracken could cut down trees enough to make a log house. This land was chosen by the father since even then there was talk of a railway going through from Detroit to Niagara Falls, and a few years later this dream became a reality when the Great Western was built and passed through the McCracken farm." The construction of the line in 1854 gave John McCracken an early opportunity to make money: he sold vegetables, butter and eggs to the men engaged in the work (*Age* 14 May 1936).

Aunt Lizzie told the Strathroy paper in 1936 that, when she "was but seven years old, her mother died, and that same year her elder sister married, leaving all the duties of mothering the family to the second daughter, then nineteen years old" (*Age* 14 May 1936). Their mother, whose name before her marriage had been Elizabeth Smiley, died in 1855 and was buried in the "English Church" graveyard in Delaware. Their father, Squire John McCracken, would live on until 1883.

In the mid-1970s my mother told me a few more details about the McCracken immigration. They brought with them furniture and glass, and sixty thousand dollars—"a fortune in those days," my mother said. The children attended the Livingston Academy on the Longwoods Road. Aunt Lizzie Bateman was the last surviving of the ten children, dying at the age of ninety-seven in 1941. My mother wanted to know if I remembered her, saying I had been taken to see her—but I have no recollection of her whatsoever. She was a tiny woman, my mother said, and weighed only sixty pounds when she died.

The Dykemans: Our Loyalist ancestors

There was a time in Ontario when being able to claim Loyalist descent was considered a mark of social and political superiority. That was in the late nineteenth century, one hundred years after the principal exodus from the United States, but no one in the Runnalls family seems to have made such a claim or have cared much about it. Yes, our great-grandmother, Hannah (Dykeman) Runnalls, was, the family knew, somehow linked with Loyalists, but memories of that link had faded, to be replaced by the story that she had been born in Pennsylvania and came to Upper Canada "riding all the way by horseback." Uncle Frank, who recounts this tale, writes that "someone has said that she was a United Empire Loyalist, but they belonged to the previous century" (5)—and leaves it at that.

Yet the Dykemans, who are a very large family, retained a strong sense of family connections, mainly through their annual reunion, held every summer between 1927 and 1941, usually in Springbank Park in London. It was a large gathering, and my mother and Uncle Howard were, in 1933 and 1934, two of the organizers. For the 1934 reunion Uncle Howard wrote a poem by way of invitation, ending with this quatrain:

> So plan now to be present,
>   It will please us all so much,
> For a day of real enjoyment,
>   You cannot beat the Dutch.

He titled his poem "Gou Men, Oude Vrienden Vergeten?" ("Good Folk, Forget Old Friends?"). At least the memory of the Dykemans as Dutch was alive, and for anyone who wanted more detail, "the family tree will be on display." I have never seen that family tree.

The program for the fifteenth reunion in 1941 included a photograph of a good-looking elderly couple, identified as "G.J.H. Dykeman 1814–1894" and "Matilda Main Dykeman 1825–1912." My mother did not know their relation to us, nor did Uncle Frank, who supposed (without having any evidence) that they were the parents of his grandmother, Hannah (Dykeman) Runnalls.

Forgotten relationships! To fill in the gaps, I begin with the fact that the Dykemans lived in Dawn, at Oakdale, about the same time as the Runnallses. A son of the family remembered, many years later, that "G.J.H. Dykeman, with wife and family of seven children, came to Dawn from near Galt on October 31, 1877, coming to Newbury by train, with household effects." They then travelled by team and wagon, and settled on the northeast quarter of lot 24 in the 13th concession. Mr. Dykeman was a carpenter, and found plenty of work adding to and improving the houses and barns first put up by the early settlers. At the time of the 1881 census, George Joseph Hatfield Dykeman—for that was his full name—was sixty-seven years old, and gave his ethnic origin not as "Dutch" but as "German." Three of his children were still living at home.

As we now know, the very size of his family obscured his relation to our great-grandmother, Hannah, who was indeed his daughter. For G.J.H. Dykeman was twice married, and had thirteen children by his second wife, Matilda Main. That family overshadowed his first, two boys and a girl, who was Hannah, born in June 1844. They lived "near Galt," at a village called Sheffield, in Beverly Township, Wentworth County, and there, in October 1839, G.J.H. Dykeman had married Elizabeth Flock. She is a shadowy figure: apparently a Dutch woman born in 1816; we know only that she died an early death, in November 1846. The family continued to live in Beverly Township after G.J.H.'s second marriage, and there his oldest daughter, Hannah, met and married Richard Runnalls. Both the Runnallses and the Dykemans moved to Dawn Township, as I have already said, but just when G.J.H. Dykeman moved away again is not clear. His son says he returned to "near Galt" in 1880, but he died in Chatham, Ontario, in 1894, and was buried in the cemetery of the Methodist Church in Shetland, on the east bank of the Sydenham River and close to the Runnalls and Dykeman farms in Dawn.

He might have been buried "near Galt." For there is a pioneer cemetery close to Sheffield—the Lamb Cemetery—now a well-kept grove of trees on the edge of Highway 8 a mile or so east of the village. The few surviving gravestones have been gathered in a semi-circle at the centre of the property, and we are fortunate that one of the most legible is that of G.J.H. Dykeman's parents, Jacob Wiggins Dykeman, who died in Sheffield in April 1855, and his wife Satira Camp, who died in February 1858. Both had come to Ontario from New Brunswick; both had been born in the United States; and both came of Loyalist families. It is time now to go back to those beginnings.

The Dutch had established a fort and a settlement at the tip of Manhattan Island in the early part of the seventeenth century, and by the 1650s were expanding northwards. While the west side of Manhattan is rocky and steep, the east side is flat and fertile, with woods and meadows stretching out to salt marshes. There the Dutch laid out the town of New Harlem, and by 1661 thirty-two families had homes and farms there. They were the "Patentees," the first landowners in Harlem—"patentees" because they were the recipients of patents or grants of land—and the patent issued by Governor Dongan in 1686—the third such document—named all the original freeholders. There are twenty-three names on Governor Dongan's list: we are descended from five of those men.

They were a diverse lot. Not just Dutch, but French, Danes, Walloons, Swedes and Germans. Our ancestors were Resolved Waldron, Joost Van Oblinus, Daniel Tourneur, Johannes Vermilje, and Jan Dyckman (as the spelling was then).

The Waldrons originated in England, but Resolved Waldron was born in the Netherlands, emigrated to New Amsterdam in 1654, and owned a house and lot on Broadway, near (what is now) Wall Street, before moving to Harlem, where he was a prominent citizen and held a number of public offices. Joost Van Oblinus was a Dutchman, a magistrate, deacon and elder in the Dutch Reform Church which the early settlers built in Harlem.

Daniel Tourneur was French—the Tourneurs were a Huguenot family from Picardy—and he is the only one of our ancestors who might be considered a murderer. Tourneur was attending the funeral of a Huguenot friend in his home town, Amiens; the king's (Catholic) troops tried to stop the Protestant service and arrest Tourneur; he drew his rapier, killed the officer of the guard, and put the other soldiers to flight. Tourneur was charged with the death of the officer, one Tilie Maire, and (in the words of the family historian) "found it best to take a sudden leave." He fled to Leyden, where he married a Walloon woman, and then in 1652, he, his wife and infant son, left Holland for New Amsterdam. But the charge of murder followed him to the New World and became the issue in a long-continuing court case. For though Tourneur held responsible positions in New Harlem—*schepen* (magistrate), deputy sheriff, overseer—and though, according to the historian Riker, the new town owed much of its success to Tourneur's energy and organizing abilities, at the same time he seems to have been a hot-tempered man, rashly provoking quarrels with his neighbours (including our ancestor Resolved Waldron) and belligerently prolonging litigation. The early settlers could be a quarrelsome lot, and the quarrels involved not only words and legal proceedings but fisticuffs and weapons as well. The early history of New Harlem is full of stories of beatings with sticks and battles with knives, and of the court's attempts to counter the settlers' "mutual disposition to vex one another" so that they would "live hereafter in all charity, friendship and peace" (Riker 319, 284–5).

Johannes Vermilje, another of the original patentees from whom we are descended, was from a Walloon family and was a figure of some importance in colonial New York. He was by trade a brewer, and he held the positions of constable and magistrate in Harlem, but it was as the commander of a military company that he figures in early histories of the city. In 1674 the English permanently replaced the Dutch as the colonial rulers of Manhattan, but the transition had been preceded by ten years of Anglo-Dutch conflict, for in 1688—the year of the "Glorious Revolution" in Britain—there was a popular uprising against the English of Dutch laborers and artisans, led by a well-to-do merchant named Jacob Leisler. The historian Charles Howard McCormick tells the full story of Leisler's Rebellion, which ended with Leisler being hanged for treason in 1691. Johannes Vermilje had been a supporter of Leisler and a member of his Council. He too was charged with treason and sentenced to death. But the political situation was fluid and changing, and in 1692 the Queen, responding to a petition, pardoned Vermilje and set him free.

The fifth of the patentees from whom we are descended is Jan Dyckman, the remote ancestor of our great-great grandfather, G.J.H. Dykeman, and Jan's origins make it possible for his descendants to claim either German or Dutch ancestry. Dyckman came from Bentheim in Westphalia, but that town is on the Dutch border near Oberyssel, and when he emigrated to the New World in 1660, he fitted easily into a Dutch settlement. In 1666 he obtained farmland along the East River, in the newly established town of New Harlem, and he eventually became one of the largest and wealthiest landowners among the patentees: at the time of his death in 1715 he controlled about three hundred acres. The centre of his landholdings was at Spuyten Duyvil, on the Harlem River near what is now 210th Street. Among the present sights in Manhattan is the Dyckman Farmhouse Museum, on Broadway at 204th Street, but this house dates from 1785 and was built by the Dyckmans who were "Patriots" during the American Revolution. We are descended from the Loyalist branch of the family, and have no connection with that building, but the house serves at least to mark the area where our first ancestor lived. That was at the south end of the King's Bridge, a toll bridge built in 1693 to connect Manhattan with the mainland on the east bank of the Hudson.

Jan Dyckman was chiefly responsible for developing the northern end of Manhattan Island as farm land. He was an energetic man, clearing much of the land himself, establishing pastures and planting crops. Dyckman and "honest Jan Nagel" leased some of their lands and meadows for a period of twelve years, after which time he and Nagel regained possession of the land, plus the houses, barns, and stables built by the lessors, and half an orchard of "fifty fruit trees, both apple and pear." It was "the first successful effort to make improvements in that section of Manhattan Island, on which as yet there was not another white man's hearthstone north of Harlem village" (Riker 344).

Jan Dyckman had a long career as an official in Harlem and as a leading supporter of the Dutch Reform Church. He was appointed a *schepen* or magistrate of the local Dutch court, and was for many years an overseer, assessor, and constable. He contributed to the *voorleser's* salary (the *voorleser* was lay reader, town clerk, and schoolteacher); he contributed both money—a hundred florins— and labour to the construction of the new church, which opened in 1686. Others contributed materials: stone "broken and drawn to the church," timber "cut," shingles "delivered at the church," lath and lime. Resolved Waldron laid the cornerstone on 29 March 1685.

Jan Dyckman was twice married. His first wife was Magdalena Tourneur, daughter of Daniel Tourneur, and his second was Jan Nagel's widow, Rebecca Waldron. We are descended from Jan's first marriage, and from their third child, Gerrit, who was baptized in March 1678 and died in 1729. He lived on the west side of Manhattan Island, on a farm given to him by his father, but he also had a trade, as wheelwright. Gerrit's second son was named Jacob, and our line of descent is through him.

Jacob Dyckman, the third generation of Dyckmans in America, was the first of his family to leave Harlem and move north to Philipsborough Manor, where he was a tenant farmer. The manor had been established on the English model, in which the lord rented land in return for money or services. Philipsborough Manor was a large one—it extended north from Kingsbridge along the east bank of the Hudson for twenty-four miles and included some 156,000 acres. The landowner was Frederick Philipse, who was a Loyalist, and who would pay dearly for his loyalty at the time of the American Revolution: his lands would be confiscated and he himself was threatened with death if he ever tried to return.

Frederick Philipse built the Reformed Dutch Church, now a National Historic Landmark, in Sleepy Hollow, north of Tarrytown. It still stands on the Albany Post Road, and there Jacob Dyckman's second child and first son, named Gerrit after his grandfather, was baptized on 6 June 1741. (The church records of the baptism are still extant.) The church had been built in 1685. Its walls, of local fieldstone, are two feet thick; the gambrel roof supports an open-air steeple with a bell. Inside are wooden pews, a railing and communion table and, behind it, a pulpit to which one ascends on a winding staircase. The church figures in one of the best-known pieces of American literature, Washington Irving's "The Legend of Sleepy Hollow," which is the story of Ichabod Crane and the Headless Horseman. Here is Irving's description of the church in that sketch:

> it stands on a knoll, surrounded by locust trees and lofty elms, from among which its decent, whitewashed walls shine modestly forth, like Christian purity, beaming through the shades of retirement. A gentle slope descends from it to a silver sheet of water, bordered by high trees, between which, peeps may be caught at the blue hills of the Hudson. ... On one side of the church extends a wide woody dell, along which raves a large brook among broken rocks and trunks of fallen trees. Over a deep black part of the stream, not far from the church, was formerly thrown a wooden bridge; the road that led to it, and the bridge itself, were thickly shaded by overhanging trees, which cast a gloom about it, even in the day time; but occasioned a fearful darkness at night. Such was one of the favourite haunts of the headless horseman .... (*Complete Works* 8: 289–90)

The horseman is "the ghost of a Hessian trooper" whose body had allegedly been buried in the churchyard. The church was not only the setting for Irving's fiction: it was the real-life setting for the social and religious life of the Dyckmans. "Many Dyckmans worshipped within its gray weathered walls," say Romer and Hartman, "and its early registers contain many Dyckman and allied family names" (15).

Jacob Dyckman had been born in Harlem in March 1720, and died on Philipsburg Manor in February 1774. His marriage brought into the family more of the original Harlem patentees: his wife was Rebecca Vermilyea, daughter of Isaac Vermilyea and Josyntie Van Oblinus. Their son Gerrit, who was baptized in the church in Sleepy Hollow on 6 June 1741, became our Loyalist ancestor.

Gerrit grew up on the manor of a Loyalist; Westchester County was a predominantly Loyalist area; and Gerrit married into a Loyalist family, the Hatfields, who were originally from Yorkshire and lived in White Plains. His wife, Eunice Ann Hatfield, was the niece of Captain Abraham Hatfield, a veteran of the Siege of Louisbourg and an officer of the Westchester County militia. His tavern in White Plains was a gathering place for Tories. Its rival, commercially and politically, was the Isaac Oakley Inn. An incident in the spring of 1775 characterizes the conflict that the Americans call their "Revolution" but which was in fact their first civil war. The New York Assembly, with a majority of Loyalists, had refused to appoint delegates to the Second Continental Congress, which was to meet that summer in Philadelphia. The opposition decided to bypass the Assembly and, by a direct vote of freeholders, set up a new legislative body, a Provincial Convention. On 11 April 1775 men assembled at the Oakley Inn to elect deputies, but Captain Hatfield considered the gathering a "meeting of rebellion" (Hatfield 45), a group "unlawfully called together, and for an unlawful purpose." Men from the Hatfield Inn confronted men from the Oakley Inn at the courthouse and refused to take part in the election, showing "their detestation of all unlawful committees and congresses" and affirming "their allegiance to their gracious and merciful sovereign King George the Third" (Scharf 1: 250). Captain Hatfield's label for his political opponents—"rebels"—was accurate, and its replacement in American political myth—"patriots"—is a rewriting of history, as is usually done by the winners in any historical conflict. Gone from the collective memory of Americans, Thomas Allen writes, is "the fact that much of the fighting had been between Americans and Americans" rather than "between Americans and the British" (Allen 333). It was a civil war as much as a revolution.

New York was "the Loyal Province" and New York City "Torytown." At the beginning of the war, in the summer of 1776, Washington's army was defeated on Long Island and retreated northwards from Manhattan, "leaving New York City firmly in the hands of Loyalists and British soldiers, and making it a haven for Loyalists for the duration of the war." Loyalist regiments were recruited from the surrounding areas: "eventually New York would send more men into Loyalist regiments than into the Continental Army" (Allen 170). Many of the recruits were tenants on the great Hudson River Valley estates, lured by the promise of "postwar land-grant rewards to loyal subjects" (Allen 179).

Gerrit Dyckman was one such recruit, but we have no documentary evidence for his military service, and his name does not appear on any extant muster roll. According to Romer and Hartman, Gerrit Dyckman served in the First Regiment, Westchester County militia, a Loyalist regiment that would eventually be commanded by a prominent New York Loyalist, James DeLancey. Their role was to protect Westchester County from rebels who plundered crops and livestock, to secure the approaches to New York City, and to ensure the city's supplies. DeLancey's aim was to maintain, among the inhabitants of Westchester County, "the firm & general Attachment at least of such of them as were loyally disposed" (*Online Institute for Advanced Loyalist Studies*).

Those who were "loyally disposed" faced increasing difficulties. In New York—now a state rather than a province—the legislature in October 1779 passed "An Act for the Forfeiture and Sale of the Estates of Persons who have adhered to the enemies of this State," the notorious Act of Attainder, which confiscated Loyalist estates and legislated, for any Loyalists "ever found anywhere in New York again," "death, as in cases of felony." "Particularly named" were Frederick Philipse, "esquire," and his son Frederick, "gentleman." Tories were tarred and feathered, their lives threatened by mobs, their homes likely to be destroyed and their belongings confiscated. There are scenes of such harassment in Kenneth Roberts' *Oliver Wiswell* (1940), an historical novel that tells the story of the American Revolution from a Loyalist point of view (even though Roberts was from Kennebunkport, Maine). The eponymous narrator is an historian whose aim is to write a "true history" of the war. His title for it: *Civil War in America*.

We know nothing about Gerrit Dyckman's experiences during this period of upheaval. He now spelled his name Garret Dykeman, and he had left the Dutch Reform Church and became an Episcopalian. We do know that he was seized at his home in 1779 and imprisoned in Connecticut—a fact that suggests that he was prominent enough among the Loyalists to be considered a threat.

Garret and Eunice (Hatfield) Dykeman must have known, from witnessing the persecution of other Loyalists, that they had little choice but to emigrate. They were but a few out of a very large number of Americans who left the United States at that time as political refugees. How many were there? According to Maya Jasanoff in *Liberty's Exiles* (2011), 60,000 Loyalists, 15,000 slaves, for a total of 75,000 people, "or about one in forty members of the American population" (6). With the Treaty of Paris in 1783, the evacuation of Loyalists from New York began, under the direction of Sir Guy Carleton, and continued through much of that year—"the first important evacuation of political refugees in modern times" (Wright 67). In the early fall the Dykeman family gathered in New York, Garret coming from prison in Connecticut to join his wife and five children for the sailing of the "Fall Fleet." On 3 October 1783 they boarded the *Neptune*, a vessel of four hundred tons, with 163 passengers (Wright 92), and on 7 October the fleet set sail.

Its destination was St. John, New Brunswick—then called Parr Town. All who sailed had suffered materially, and the British government had set up a commission to inquire into the Loyalists' losses and to receive claims for compensation. Garret Dykeman estimated his loss at £149 in New York currency, but his claim for compensation was denied, as were most of the more than five thousand submissions. Not denied was the help given to every Loyalist family: passage to New Brunswick, provisions for the voyage, further provisions for a year, implements for trades and farming, and—most important—grants of land. The first grant to the Dykemans was in St. John itself: a lot on St. George's Street (now King Street East), recorded in Garret's name on 20 April 1784. The Dykemans also received lumber, shingles, and bricks, so they must have built a house, but they did not stay long in St. John. By April 1786 they were in Queen's County, on land on the east bank of the St. John River, but Garret's title was not firm, and in that same year he petitioned the Governor of New Brunswick for the grant due to him:

To his Excellency Thomas Carlton Esq., Governor of the Province of New Brunswick:

The memorial of Garret Dykeman of Queen's County humbly sheweth

That he being a Loyalist left New York when it was evacuated by the British, and he came to New Brunswick and set down with his family on land supposing it to have been crown lands which proved to be lot No 7 on Sprys Grant as it was called which your Memorialist is informed is now become forfet. That your memorialist has made considerable improvements since his settlement on the said Lot in building clearing &c and it is now become valuable.

Your memorialist has had no lands yet granted him in this Province or in Nova Scotia.

He therefore prays your Excellency would be pleased to grant him the said Lot No 7 and so in duty bound will ever Pray.

June 7th 1786　　　　　　　　　　　　　　　　　　　　　Garret Dykman [sic]

Garret's petition was successful; the settlement became Jemseg in Waterborough parish; and eventually Garret came into possession of adjoining lots. He prospered, so that when he died, he had land and money to leave to his sons, household furniture and money to bequeath to his daughters.

Garret and Eunice Dykeman were pew-holders in St. John's Church in Gagetown, on the west bank of the St. John River, and both are buried in the churchyard. Eunice died in November 1808, at the age of sixty-two, and Garret in June 1813, at the age of seventy-two. For years a broken stone lying on the ground marked Eunice's grave, while Garret's had only a "rough footstone." In the twenty-first century, Dykeman descendants have placed above the graves a block of rough fieldstone on which there is a plaque giving the names and dates of the father and mother of many of the Canadian Dykemans.

Garret and Eunice Dykeman's second son, Jacob Wiggins Dykeman, was born in Tarrytown, New York, in March 1771, but not christened until August 1792, in Gagetown, New Brunswick. Among the four sons in that family, Jacob was the only one to inherit from his father money but no land—which may account for the fact that he, his wife and family, moved from New Brunswick to Ontario sometime in the early nineteenth century. They came to Sheffield in Beverly Township, east of Galt, and there Jacob died in April 1855.

Jacob's wife, Satira Camp, was from Connecticut, where she had been born in either 1779 or 1783, and she brought into the family more Loyalist ancestors and stories of Loyalist activities that are more detailed than those of the Dykemans and Hatfields. For Satira's father was Abiather Camp, Jr., who had been born in Wallingford, Connecticut, in 1757 (and died in New Brunswick in 1841), and her grandfather was Abiather Camp, Sr., who had been born in 1732 in Durham, Connecticut (and died in New Brunswick in 1788). This Abiather Camp was a well-to-do merchant, trader, and shipowner, with homes in both Wallingford and New Haven, where he was an acquaintance of Benedict Arnold (he and Arnold happened to join the Masonic Lodge on the same night). He was a noted Tory, and an active one—with the result that, in September 1776, he was declared "an enemy of the State." He was arrested in New Haven but permitted to live in Wallingford, until the assembly there voted to send their selectmen to "go and warn said Abiather Camp immediately to depart said Town," where he "shall not dwell ... nor be an inhabitant." When the British arrived in New Haven in 1779, Camp went with them to New York, where he received from Sir Guy Carleton a house, rations, and stipend. In return, Camp aided the British expedition against New London in 1781. New London was at the time a patriot supply depot and a port for rebel vessels. The British commissioned Benedict Arnold to attack the town, since he had grown up nearby and knew the harbour. Five years later, Arnold would sign a document certifying that Abiathar Camp had "been always considered a loyalist, ... forced within the British lines on that account, and ... active in procuring guides and pilots for the expedition against New London." With the evacuation of New York in 1783, Camp sailed for St. John as part of the "Spring Fleet." His losses were the most substantial of those of all our Loyalist ancestors: he "claimed £3,872 sterling for his losses, and was paid £1,146 sterling" (Palmer 131).

In June 1783 Camp and part of his family moved up the St. John River, and then Camp himself returned to New York. There is a family tradition that he made two or three trips between New York and St. John in his own vessel, and that on his last trip he transported 203 Loyalists. In St. John Camp prospered. "He was a man of substance," Palmer writes, "owning several town lots and farms, a corn and saw mill, and a brew and malt house" (131). His wife was Rebecca Cook, and through her we are descended from Puritans who had come to Salem, Massachusetts in 1638. While our Dykeman roots are deep in Manhattan and in Westchester County, our Camp roots are deep in New England.

It is now possible to construct our Dykeman line of descent. Here it is:

First generation
Jan Dyckman, born in Bentheim, Westphalia, died 1715 in Harlem, New York; married (first wife) Magdalena Tourneur (daughter of Daniel Tourneur and Jacqueline de Parisis), born 1658 in Flatbush, King's County, New York; died about 1689 in Harlem, New York.

Second generation
Jan Dyckman and Magdalena Tourneur's third child was Gerrit Dyckman, baptized 6 April 1678 in Harlem, New York, died 1729 in Harlem; name of Gerrit's wife not known.

Third generation
Gerrit Dyckman's second son was Jacob Dyckman, born 12 March 1720 in Harlem, New York, died "about 1765" or 17 February 1774 in Philipsborough Manor, Tarrytown, New York; married Rebecca Vermilyea (daughter of Isaac Vermilyea and Josyntie Van Oblinus), born about 1721, died between 1760 and 1762.

Fourth generation
Jacob Dyckman and Rebecca Vermilyea's second child was Gerrit Dyckman (afterward Garret Dykeman, United Empire Loyalist), baptized 6 June 1741 in Sleepy Hollow, New York, died 13 June 1813 in Waterborough, Queen's County, New Brunswick; married Eunice Ann Hatfield (United Empire Loyalist, daughter of Gilbert Hatfield and Ann Tamar Brundage), born 9 November 1739 or 1740 in White Plains, New York, died 16 or 17 November 1808 in Queen's County, New Brunswick.

Fifth generation
One of Gerrit Dyckman and Eunice Hatfield's sons was Jacob Wiggins Dykeman, born

4 March 1770 or 1771 in Tarrytown, New York, died 16 April 1855 in Sheffield, Ontario; married Satira Camp (daughter of Abiather Camp, Jr. and Mary Fleet Chidester), born 9 July 1780 in Connecticut, died 13 February 1858 in Sheffield, Ontario.

Sixth generation
One of Jacob Dykeman and Satira Camp's sons was George Joseph Hatfield Dykeman, born 2 February 1814 in Gagetown, New Brunswick, died 11 April 1894 in Chatham, Ontario; married (first wife) Elizabeth Flock, born 19 December 1816 in Holland, died 22 November 1846 in Sheffield, Ontario.

Seventh generation
G. J. H. Dykeman and Elizabeth Flock's third child was Hannah S. Elizabeth Dykeman, born 2 June 1844 in Sheffield, Ontario, died 3 April 1891 in Mount Brydges, Ontario; married Richard Thomas Runnalls (son of Joseph William Runnalls and Mary Thomas), born 18 February 1835 in Cornwall, England, died 10 May 1915 in Caradoc Township, Middlesex County, Ontario.

Eighth generation
Hannah Dykeman and Richard Runnalls' third child was Joseph Runnalls, born 27 March 1868 in Caradoc Township, Middlesex County, Ontario, died 22 December 1949 in Strathroy, Ontario; married Matilda Caroline Thompson (daughter of John Thompson and Sarah Jane McCracken), born 22 September 1868 in Caradoc Township, Middlesex County, Ontario, died 3 May 1944 in Brooke Township, Lambton County, Ontario.

It was long after my mother died that I put together all of this material. I regret that she knew so little of this: she would have been fascinated with it.

CHAPTER THREE
JOHN HAIR'S EARLY LIFE 1902–1926

"Some of the events and happenings in my early years"

When my father was in his late seventies and having occasional bouts of heart trouble, I urged him to write down his memories of his childhood. He finally did so, in his sprawling longhand, and titled them "Some of the events and happenings in my early years." Then, because he was full of entertaining stories about life in Brooke Township, he wrote a second account which he titled "Our Neighbours."

"In trying to remember as far back as possible," my father writes, "my mind goes back to when we attended Watford Fair. The first fair that I can remember I think perhaps I would be four or five years old, and I wore a little sailor suit which I detested. I remember mother meeting a Mrs. Robbins, who before her marriage had been a Thompson; she and mother had gone to school together. She had a boy about my age and, would you believe it, he wore a sailor suit identical to mine. I hated the suit, I hated him, and we didn't get along together at all."

Every community in Southwestern Ontario had a fall fair, but "London Fair" was the big one, and my father remembered going to it by train from Watford. There was a huge crowd at the station, so many that not everyone could get on. The conductor assured people, "Don't worry; there'll be another train in twenty minutes." Once in London, they went to the fairgrounds by streetcar, an open car with benches running across it, and a narrow board on each side along which the conductor walked. The country people had a good laugh when the streetcar passed a dairy that had a sign featuring a cow's head with a full set of teeth, top as well as bottom. (Cows have no top front teeth.)

Going to a fall fair was not just an outing: Sherman Hair had an official role in the day's events. "During my early school days," John writes, "my father was sent by the Department of Agriculture to judge beef cattle and sheep at a number of fall fairs in Ontario. Of course there were no cars, and he had to depend on the trains. He attended a number of fairs in Huron, Bruce, and other counties," going as far away as Lion's Head in the Bruce Peninsula. "He caught the train in Watford and went to London, changing there to go north or wherever he might be going. One time he was sent to Chatham, so my mother decided she would like to go too, and of course took me. I think perhaps I would be about six at the time. The railway line from Petrolia via Kingscourt to Glencoe was in operation then," an extension of the Grand Trunk's main southwestern Ontario lines, and it ran diagonally southeast across Brooke township and through Alvinston. "We drove up the Twelfth Line to Sutorville to catch the train. Dad left the horse at Herb Holbrook's, who lived nearby, and we took the train to Glencoe. We had a long wait and caught the Chatham train about dark. We reached Chatham and went to a hotel and then to the fair the next day. I don't remember if we were able to get a train that evening or if we stayed over in Chatham. Anyway, if it were today you would drive to Chatham in an hour, do the work, and come home that evening."

Little documentary evidence remains of John's father's work as a judge at fall fairs, but one postcard has survived. It is addressed to John's mother and it is postmarked Toronto, 25 September 1913: "Dear Dessa: We are leaving Shelburne this morning at 8:30. There was a fine fair here and I had lots of work to do but got along pretty well. Will try and send a letter to-morrow. Sherman." When John's father travelled in the area northwest of Toronto, he would call at the home of a family named Kitchen, who lived in Schomberg. Mrs. Kitchen was a first cousin: Sherman's mother (Ann Carter Hair) and her mother (Rebecca Carter Lloyd) were sisters. How Sherman came to keep up with this one cousin out of all his Carter relatives I do not know. Nor do I know how a postcard addressed to Mrs. James Kitchen ended up at our place: "Dear Cousin, You will be surprised to get a card from me now. The reason is that I may be coming to New Market instead of Tottenham. Will try and get over to see you whichever way I come. Sherman Hair." The Kitchen house at Schomberg, which still survives, is a fine, unusually large nineteenth-century house, a variation on the classic design of Ontario farmhouses, with patterned brickwork (a characteristic late Victorian fashion) and, instead of the usual pointed window in the gable above the front entrance, a Gothic door opening out on a little balcony.

School days at S.S. No. 10, Brooke, 1908–16

When John was old enough to start to school, he walked half a mile west on the Twelfth Line to the new schoolhouse for our section, S. S. No. 10. It was a one-room country school, typical of schools in rural Ontario in those days, and one teacher taught all classes. A child usually started school at age six, and would remain for seven or eight years, though absences in spring and fall to work on the family farm were not only tolerated but expected. The schoolhouse was new.

"I think it must have been about the same year [as the episode at Watford Fair]," my father writes, "that the old schoolhouse closed. The school was just west of the creek on land off James Annett's farm. I remember being at the school to a party, and I think it must have been the last day that the old school was used. I do not know what became of [it]. The land is again part of the farm owned by Harold Hair. An acre of land on the corner of 24 Sideroad and the 13th Concession was purchased from William Powell and the new school was built there." The site was on the northwest corner of what is now the Lasalle Line and Hardy Creek Road. For years the house built on the site after the school was demolished incorporated in an outside wall the stone block which had been above the school's front door, the block inscribed "Brooke / S.S. No. 10 / 1907." Now that house has been replaced by another newer one, and all evidence of the school has disappeared.

"I started to school the second year the new school was in operation [September 1908]. The first teacher [in the new school] was Edith MacIntyre, who was also my first teacher as she stayed two years. I remember the first day walking the half mile to the school and looking back and seeing my mother standing on the road watching me."

My father, like most men of his generation, was of a practical mind, good with his hands, and always interested in how things worked. So his narrative continues: "This school had a unique heating and ventilating system. Of course the heater was a large cast-iron box stove that took a two-foot stick of wood. But the unique part was that, when the school was built, pipes were installed to carry fresh air from the outside to the main register under the stove. Over the stove was built a jacket of Galvanized with slides running down to the floor on either side and a screened opening around the stove pipe, about two feet square, to let the heat out. When the school was cold, the slides on the lower side of the jacket were opened and the register under the stove was closed. This drew the cold air from the room and heated it. When the school was heated, the register under the stove was opened and the slides on the side of the jacket were closed, and fresh air from outside was drawn and heated. Registers were adjusted at the ceiling to carry out the stale air. It was a very simple system and worked surprisingly well."

"We seemed to have a new teacher almost every year following Edith McIntyre. The next teacher was a married man by the name of Mills; I do not remember his first name, and he stayed two years. He lived on a sideroad west of Strathroy, in an old brick house beside the railway. He boarded at our place and always came back from the weekend on Sunday evening."

Finding teachers was an annual problem for the trustees, whose "teacher wanted" ads boasted a "new school and small attendance," but also noted that "duties ...[are] to include janitor work." After Mills left, "teachers were scarce," John writes, "and our school did not have a teacher at the first of September." Then someone turned up: he was Gordon McNeil, and although he had been born in Hancock in the "thumb" of Michigan, the McNeil farm was in Metcalfe Township, a few miles to the east of ours. Gordon, then in his twenty-first year, had been working for the summer with a railway survey crew in Northern Ontario; "he applied for the school about the first of October and of course was hired immediately.... He left at the end of the school year to attend Queen's University in Kingston." I think he may have boarded with John's parents, for his coming to our section had consequences: he met John's aunt, Eva Watson, and they were married in 1916.

"I am not sure in which order the next teachers came to our school," John continues. "There was Hazel Dolbear, a sister of Mrs. Russell Powell; she later married 'Zeb' Janes" who was for many years the Conservative MLA for our riding. "Stella McManus of Watford, a daughter of Jim McManus, a well-known cattle buyer at that time, stayed just one year. Then there was Lois Johnston, also of Watford, the daughter of Bob Johnston, a farm implement dealer"; she also stayed only one year. "The last two years I attended public school, Russell Woods [John's cousin] was the teacher. He lived at home [on 27 Sideroad north of the Twelfth Line] and came to school on a bicycle when the weather was good. Following his teaching he attended the University of Toronto and studied to become a dentist," establishing a practice first in Arkona and then from 1942 on in Watford.

In the 1890s local papers had started to publish the grades of pupils, and that practice continued well into the 1950s and '60s, on the assumptions, I think, that student progress was a matter of community concern, and student success a mark of the teacher's ability. The Watford paper printed monthly reports from the area's schools, though not all teachers submitted reports regularly, and the record is sporadic. My father's name first appears in December 1908, when he was in "Junior One," and too much a beginner to be assigned a grade. In subsequent years, his grades were unremarkable. His best was in November 1915, when he earned eighty per cent and stood first in his class, but all of his other grades were lower, and in June 1916—his last month in public school—he was behind everyone else in his class. Nonetheless, he passed the Junior High School Entrance Examinations (which were province-wide and written over three days in June 1916). Of the thirty-seven Watford candidates at that time, John earned a "Pass" and stood nineteenth among the twenty-eight on that list. His cousin, Norval Woods (who was the same age as my father) stood ninth.

Some of my father's classmates at S.S. No. 10 would be, decades later, our neighbours when my sister and I were small and still living on the farm. A few, like the Bowies and Clothiers, had moved away by that time, but others remained. Some, like George Reid, Alex McLean and his sister Rachel, and Ruby Atchison, we knew well; others were names my father often mentioned: Harry and Albert and May Reid, Cassie McLean, Pearl Powell, and Gordon, Charlie, and Henry Miller. And although my father was the oldest of all his Hair cousins, Uncle Jim Hair's children, Amy, Elsie and Harold, eventually joined him in the school. Also at S.S No. 10 and several years ahead of my father were two Barnardo boys: Norm Wilson and Clarence Lewis.

The Watford paper occasionally carried advertisements like this one: "BOYS FOR CANADA—Dr. Barnardo, of London, Eng., is sending out in the early spring, a party of boys ranging from 10 to 16 for farm and other employment. Those desirous of obtaining boys should apply early ..." (*Guide* 26 February 1886). And a month after my father was born in 1902, the paper reported that "Seven young boys from Dr. Barnardo's Home, London, England, passed through London on the G.T.R. on Monday on their way to different points in Western Ontario, where they will be placed with farmers. Their ages ranging from 11 to 18. Four went to Watford, two to Kerwood and two to Wyoming, and the other up the Huron & Bruce Railway" (*Guide* 8 August 1902). Norm Wilson was four years older than my father, and he was only eight when he left Liverpool and arrived in Canada in 1906; he was assigned to Dick Searson, whose farm was just west of ours on the Twelfth Line. Clarence Lewis was also born in 1898, but he was ten when he sailed from London in 1909, and came to live with Uncle Pete Watson. Some Barnardo boys were exploited and mistreated, but Norm and Clarence were not: both of them went to school, and both grew up to own their own farms and to establish their own families.

Norm's mistreatment was at the hands of his teacher at S.S. No. 10. My father had stories—Dickensian stories—about physical punishment of pupils, commonplace and accepted at that time but, Dad said, "men would be put in jail now for the things they did then." Norm was a hunchback and, perhaps because of his deformity, the teacher would go after him, taking his ear and twisting it, or pursuing him with a pointer or strap, so violently that Norm crawled beneath the desks to protect himself. It was Mills who did that, my father said, as he told that story with indignation. In after years, Norm owned Wilson's Shell station on the south side of Watford, pumping gas, selling ice cream and pop and cigarettes, and supplying licence plates when the fixed time for renewal came round each year. During the Depression he and his wife had eked out a living on fifty acres just east of our "farm across the road" but were unable to pay for the land; they fared better with the gas station, which they opened in 1946 and continued to operate until 1969, when Norm retired and his son Dave took over the business.

Clarence Lewis came to work for Uncle Pete and Aunt Net Watson who, having no children of their own, treated him as their son. Uncle Pete was the youngest boy in the Watson family, and he farmed that portion of the original Watson property that had belonged to his grandparents, William and Jane Watson: his distinctive hip-roof house stood where theirs had once been. In 1909 he married Minetta ("Net") Ferguson of the Eighth Line of Metcalfe; he was thirty-seven at the time, she forty-three. They gave Clarence a start in life, and he eventually bought two farms on the Twelfth Line. One was Grandad Watson's fifty acres at the corner of 27 Sideroad, where Clarence grew crops, pastured cattle, and maintained the barn—it was the only building left after the fire of 1918. Clarence also owned the farm directly to the west of ours. Over the years it had had quite a few owners and renters, including Uncle Oscar Watson, who lived there for a year or so when he was first married; and people by the name of Willer, whose family were all born there, but who lost the barn to fire and the farm itself to the mortgage company. The company moved a new barn onto the property; and Clarence bought it. He had married Annie Ferguson, and they had four sons: Ernie and Earl, who were older than I, and the twins John and Gene, who were younger. All went on to become elementary school teachers, and Gene would become head and general secretary of the Elementary Teachers' Federation of Ontario. (Clarence and Annie also adopted a girl, Anne.)

Salem Methodist Episcopal Church

The Hairs and the Watsons were all Methodists, and the centre of their lives, both religious and social, was Salem Methodist Church, which stood on the northeast corner of the Twelfth Line and 27 Sideroad, a weathered frame structure with four tall pointed windows along each side and a plain interior with wooden pews and a pulpit. John writes about it as follows: "We attended Salem Methodist Church on the corner of lot 28 concession 13. This was a small corner off the farm of Sam McLellan. I understand that the land was originally donated by William and Jane Watson (my great-grandparents)." My father's understanding was right: on 28 March 1862 his great-grandparents had deeded for one dollar a quarter acre of their property, and hence the church was known as "Watson's Meeting House." My father continues: "According to the Brooke Township History by Mrs. Mac Campbell, the first congregation was formed in 1860 and an old log building was used as a place of worship. Then in 1862 a log church was built and used until 1880. Then a new frame church was built, and this is the one that I attended when I was growing up. When I was in my teens it was my job to go to the church early Sunday morning and light the fire in the large box stove which heated the church. Sunday School was at ten o'clock and church at eleven. I had to hurry to get the fire on, then walk home and dress to be back at the church at ten o'clock. Needless to say, you were not paid in those days. Some years later the congregation became so small that the church had to close; this was in 1930. The building stood for a few years, and was finally sold [in 1940] to Davidson brothers for a honey house. It still stands on their farm," which is at the north end of Brooke's 27 Sideroad (now called Salem Road). One of my earliest memories is of looking out the window of our back kitchen and seeing, across the fields to the east, the dark bulk of the church being hauled slowly northwards along the line of maples on the sideroad.

Salem's minister when my father was born was A.M. McCulloch, who had married my grandparents, but the first minister whom my father remembered was Mr. Burton, who came to the Brooke Circuit in 1908.

"Our Neighbours"

My father's account of "Some of the events and happenings in my early years" stops at 1916, when he was fourteen, but he filled out the picture of that time with a second document, which he titled "Our Neighbours." People at that time referred to their community as a "section," and "our neighbours" were the people who lived in "our section"—our school section, that is, the boundaries of which set the limits of my father's narrative. The east end was the townline with Metcalfe Township in Middlesex County; the west end was Dick Searson's farm—his other farm—just east of the Nauvoo Road. Along that stretch of the Twelfth Line, Dad knew every farm and farm family, and he knew the peculiarities of the survey: the acreage, the divisions and consolidations when land was bought or sold, the gore that ran between the thirteenth and fourteenth concessions and added about twenty acres to each hundred, either to some of the thirteenth concession farms, or to others in the fourteenth.

He begins: "We lived on the East one-half of Lot 26 Concession 13, Brooke. Dad bought this farm from 'old Tom Roane,' as he was known, and in later years he bought the farm across the road from 'young Tom Roane,' the son. The first farm would be purchased about 1900 and the second farm about 1920."

"To the east was Uncle Jim Hair who ... sold to Ches McLellan [in 1911]. The McLellans lived on the west side of 27 sideroad, and the buildings were back the sideroad. Sam McLellan (Chester's father) died about the time I started to school [on 3 February 1910]. About all I can remember about him were his long red whiskers that came down to his waist. I understood that he had never shaved in his life."

The McLellans were longtime neighbours of the Hairs, both in Ireland and in Canada. Samuel McLellan, who had been born in Ireland in 1838 and left there at the age of seven, arrived in Brooke in 1861, two years before Grandad Hair. He married Emma Chittick in 1878, and they had four sons. Three of them married but none had any children, so there are no direct descendants. While the Hairs were Methodists, the McLellans were Anglicans, and attended St. James on the "Sixth Line," where the original members of both families are now buried; and while the Hairs were usually Liberal in their politics, the McLellans were Conservatives. There was one more tie between the families when (in 1930) Ruth, my mother's oldest sister, married the youngest of the McLellan sons, Chester, and Aunt Ruth and Uncle Ches farmed on the original Hair farm, next to ours on the Twelfth Line.

My father remembered that Samuel McLellan had received a medal for his part in repelling a threatened Fenian raid across the St. Clair River in 1870. Sam had volunteered, and had been a private in the No. 6 Company of the 27th Lambton Battalion. The medal—the Canada General Service Medal—was not authorized until January 1899, twenty-nine years after the event it commemorated, and those who were eligible had to apply for it. Samuel McLellan stated in his application that it was for "Frontier Service At Sarnia in 1870. Attack expected." The medal, with an image of Queen Victoria on it, had the recipient's name, service number, rank and unit engraved on the rim, while the clasp on the ribbon read "Fenian Raid (1870)." I have no idea where that medal is now. It was not among the (very few) McLellan family items when I cleared out Aunt Ruth's house in 1990.

"North on the sideroad back of McLellans lived Gilbert Woods and his family." That sentence is all my father wrote about the Woodses, though they were relatives and closely connected with the Hairs. Gilbert Woods's mother, Jane (who died on 17 February 1905), was an older sister of Grandmother Hair (who was Ann Carter before she married John Hair), and Jane had married a William Woods. The Woodses were from Bally Rickert, King's County, Ireland (now County Offaly) and, like the Hairs, emigrated to Brooke township. Jane Carter and William Woods had seven children, Gilbert being the second. The first was Elizabeth, who married a Moffatt, and through her we are related to another large family, including Elmer Moffat, who bought our "farm across the road" when Dad became clerk-treasurer; Elmer's son Glen Moffatt, the next-door neighbour of my parents on Webster Drive in Sarnia in the 1960s and 70s; and Keith Moffatt, partner in Moffatt and Powell, a lumber supply business which (at the beginning of the twenty-first century) had outlets in Lambton, Middlesex and Huron counties, and also manufactured roof trusses. (Melvin Powell, the other partner, was a neighbour of ours on the Twelfth Line.)

Gilbert Woods, who was born in 1865 and died in 1943, married Marion ("Minnie") Clothier (1888–1937), and they had four sons, of whom three played a part in our lives (the other son, Arthur, went out west). Will Woods was the oldest: he was born in 1889. He was a cattle dealer and, after Dad started working in Sarnia, rented our farm to pasture Herefords he brought down from the west to fatten up for market. The third son was Russell, one of my father's public school teachers and afterwards a dentist in Watford, and the fourth was Norval, who became a United Church minister. He was almost the same age as my father, having been born on 28 August 1902, five weeks after my father's birth.

Two of Gilbert Woods's brothers were doctors; another owned and operated the general store in Kerwood. The latter was Arthur Woods (1873–1937), whose son Fred (1914–1979) was still running the Kerwood store when Marjorie and I were small. The former had practices in Chelsea, Michigan, and Mount Brydges. The Michigan doctor was John T. (1868–1928), and he was an 1897 graduate of the Michigan College of Medicine in Detroit. The Mount Brydges doctor was William Henry (1871–1937), who attended the medical school at Western. I do not know if he was the Runnallses' family doctor, but he seems to have attended the Thompsons: he signed my great-grandmother's death certificate in 1909. Among the Hairs, Aunt Beck and Aunt May seem to have been particularly close to their Woods cousins. Aunt Beck travelled regularly to Chelsea, and our postcard albums were full of views of that Michigan town.

My father's narrative takes the reader along the north side of the Twelfth Line (Concession 13) east to the boundary with Metcalfe, and then back along the south side (Concession 12). Not included in his written account is a story he told me about a family who lived on the east side of the townline, outside our section. The family's name was Hardy, and the creek that ran along the townline was known as the Hardy Creek. One day, my father told me, Mrs. Hardy simply got tired of husband and family, and moved out to another smaller house elsewhere on the farm. Mr. Hardy moved another woman in (without benefit of clergy) and went on raising children. When his first wife walked by, Hardy would say to their kids, "There's your mother coming down the road. Run out and have a visit with her."

The first farm on the Brooke side of the townline was Clothiers', and the second Kings'. Jack King "was the same age as my father, and I was quite a big boy when he married Beccie Pollock" [in 1917]. "Next on the east side of 27 sideroad was my grandfather's (John Hair's) farm. When he retired, my father rented the farm; we grew crop on it and used to winter cattle in the barn. Later it was all turned into pasture. After my father died, I still rented it from my aunts [Beccie and May], who owned it after their father died, and I gave it up only when I was appointed County Treasurer" [in 1947].

Grandad Watson's farm was next, and then Bill Reid's. "When I first remember [the Reids], the grandparents were there too. They were old and died when I was quite small. The old man had been a coachman in London, England, but came to Canada when they were married." The family consisted of two sons and two daughters. One of the sons was Bill, who remained on the home farm; one of the daughters was "Mrs. R.D. Watson," Grandad Watson's second wife and Aunt Eva's mother: they lived on the adjacent farm.

Salem's minister in the early 1920s was a Mr. Steadman, "one of the Plympton family, and they were great horsemen," my father writes. "Bill Reid, who was an Anglican (though some of the kids went to Salem) despised most of the Salem ministers but he loved horses. Steadman would call on him and look over his horses and praise them. Bill grudgingly admitted that that 'd—b—is not too bad.'"

"Bill Reid had a large family," my father continues. "He died suddenly, being injured when his team of horses ran away." That was in 1927. He was driving a team and wagon when the tongue of the wagon suddenly dropped down, frightening the horses, who bolted. Reid was thrown from the wagon, suffered serious internal injuries, and died the next morning. He left behind four daughters and three sons. "Eventually all the family left except George. His mother lived with him for a while but, when she became unable to look after herself, she moved to London and was cared for by the daughters. She lived to be 105" and died in 1973, forty-six years after her husband.

When Marjorie and I were small, George Reid and his mother were still living in the old farmhouse. George had been overseas in the First World War, and he made a trip to England in 1950, when the neighbours thought he would return with a bride, but he remained a bachelor, and was rather awkward and formal in his manner with us kids. I do not remember ever seeing his mother.

I skip over my father's account of the Roane farm, which I have used in an earlier chapter, and move to the next property to the west, which we knew as "the Bowie farm," but which had an earlier history for my father. "The next farm to the west [of Roanes'] was owned by Joe Lightfoot. I can just barely remember him. He used to buy one shoe at a time. There was a shoemaker in Watford by the name of Sam Howden, and when Joe needed a shoe Sam would make one for him. One time during a thunder storm Joe was sitting with his feet on the front of the cook stove. The old stoves in those days had a front that protruded out from the stove perhaps a foot. I think it was to catch any coals that might fall out the front door that had a grate in it. Anyway, lightning struck the chimney and followed the stove pipe down to the stove and tore the sole off of one of Joe's shoes. Sam would have another job."

There were more, and worse, stories to be told about Joe Lightfoot than that one of my father's. In its issue of 29 April 1892, the *Guide-Advocate* printed the following item under the heading "Diary of a Week": "MR. AND MRS. JOSEPH LIGHTFOOT, of Brooke, were in town Wednesday. Old Joe is a cranky old customer and has been accused of ill-treating his wife more than once. Mrs. Lightfoot purchased a fifteen cent mop which Joseph considered the height of extravagance, and after driving out of town a short distance he proceeded to break that useful article across his wife's head, varying the proceedings by pulling her hair. No complaint has yet been made against the brute, but he well merits a taste of the lash and may get it sooner than he anticipates unless he reforms his ways." The paper subsequently carried more stories about Lightfoot, stories of assault, and one involving the mysterious disappearance of several hundred dollars he had withdrawn from the bank. Detectives "came to the conclusion that Lightfoot's wife and daughter had taken the money to prevent the old man from loaning it to a neighbour." A judge dismissed the case, ruling that "little credence was to be placed in the girl's evidence and the old lady was the party who probably took the money" (*Guide* 12 June 1896). The "old lady" died suddenly in October 1907, and in that same month her husband sold the farm to George Bowie. Lightfoot himself died in 1916, at the age of eighty-five.

My father had another story of spousal abuse, this one not about anyone in our section. It was about a township farmer who regularly got drunk in town and then came home and beat his wife. When the woman's brother found out about the abuse, he dressed up in her clothes one night and waited for the man's return. He came in, roaring drunk, and hit out as usual; the brother hit back, and proceeded to beat up the husband. That stopped the abuse—until, my father said, "the stupid woman confessed to the trick." Then the abuse began again.

West of the Bowie farm were the Dick Searson and Ed Thompson farms. Mrs. Dick Searson was a first cousin of John's mother Dessa: she had been Evelyn Clothier before her marriage, the daughter of Alfred Clothier and Mary Campbell, a sister of Dessa's mother. "The Thompson farm was a long narrow farm running south on the east side of 24 sideroad. Old Ed Thompson was still alive and Tommy and Lizzie, who were both a little slow, lived with him." Thompson died in 1926, in his one hundredth year.

"On the west side of 24 sideroad was a three-hundred-acre block owned by James Annett. ... This was the farm that was purchased by Uncle Jim Hair when Mr. Annett retired." So my father continues westward, to the Harrison farm ("Ivy Harrison was our first mail carrier") and the McDonald and McLean farms, to the McLachlans' farm, just beyond the boundary of our section. The McLachlans were all sailors and ships' masters on the Great Lakes, disappearing from the township during the shipping season and returning just before Christmas. Dad always referred to the farm as belonging to "Pilot McLachlan." The pilot's son, Nichol, then age twenty-three, was killed in action in July 1917. In November 1918, "on receipt of the news that Germany had capitulated, Pilot McLachlan, 12th line, at once threw to the breeze a thirty-foot 'whip,' to let all in seeing distance know that her Germans were whipped. These long pennants, called whips, are used on the lakes when a competing boat is whipped in a race" (*Guide* 22 November 1918).

On the north side of the Twelfth Line at the west end of our section were the Miller farm, the Paul Kingston farm, and "a small farm of perhaps 33 acres ... I can't remember who lived on it when I was going to school. Later Andy Spalding lived there and drove the school bus when our school was closed." The next farm to the east was the Hastings farm. "Isaac Hastings lived in Watford a number of years and was head of the Hastings wagon and sleigh company. After the company went bankrupt he still hand-made wagons and sleighs," and was a well-known figure around town. The Hastings were yet another family on the Twelfth Line who had immigrated from County Monaghan. Their farm subsequently had several owners, among them James Dempsey, "who used to play for all the school dances."

The Fred Atchison farm was next, and then the Thomas Saunders farm. "They had one son, Vern, who stayed on the farm when his parents passed away. [In 1915] he married an Oke girl from south of Alvinston. They had one daughter, Jessie [born in 1916], who married Glen McLachlan. Glen was a sailor, and used to ride with me in the winter to Sarnia where he was studying for his captain's papers. After becoming a captain, he commanded his own ship but was killed when he fell through an open hatch." That happened in November 1954. At the beginning of that year, Glen had become captain of the "Shelter Bay," owned by the Ontario Pulp and Paper Company, and his route extended from Killarney and Manitoulin to Anticosti Island. In November, the ship had an accident in one of the canals near Montreal, and workmen began immediately to repair the damage. Glen, anxious to get through the canal, was standing by an open hatch with the foreman, watching the workers. The ship was carrying flax, and the snow-covered deck was slushy and slippery. Somehow Glen lost his footing and plunged to his death. His body was brought back to Watford for burial in St. James. My mother was pianist at the funeral.

"The next farm was owned by the Pollocks. They had been a large family, but when I first remember them there were only John, Beccie, and Adeline. All the rest were married. Later Beccie married Jack King." Her brother John was the victim of yet another farm accident, when a bundle of sheaves of grain being drawn up to the mow in the barn fell on him. His injuries were severe, so that he had to give up farming. "He and Adeline moved to Strathroy where he had a farm implement agency."

"Next was a fifty-acre farm owned by William Powell. There was a good maple bush on this farm and the Powells had a modern sugar house with an evaporator." Billy Powell, my father told me, "was a strict Methodist. In sugaring-off time, he would not collect the sap on Sunday, but would sit up until the clock struck twelve, and then go out with his lantern and work." North on 24 Sideroad was another Powell family, that of Francis Powell. When my sister and I were small, the Powell farms were occupied by the next generations: Melvin Powell, Billy's grandson, lived on the farm at the corner of the Twelfth Line and 24 Sideroad, and north of him, "back the sideroad," was Ernest Powell. In 1908 Ernest Powell had married Annie Hay, who was a sister of Catherine Watson's mother, Mary (Hay) Watson. Catherine, who was a first cousin of my father, lost her mother to cancer in 1942, and would live with her Aunt Annie and Uncle Ernest while she was teaching school at S.S.No. 5. She was my first teacher.

"Do You Mind?"

"Do you mind?" That was the question with which people started to tell stories, "mind" meaning "remember." My father did not begin his stories that way, but Uncle Harry Watson did, and so did Uncle Ches McLellan and Sam McLellan. Story-telling was part of every get-together. I remember Sam McLellan being at our place, and trading animal stories with my father. I was just old enough to think that I ought to write them down, but not old enough to know how.

The earliest event in his life that my father told stories about was one that he could have learned only from others, for he was six months old when it happened. It was the great Wanstead wreck of 26 December 1902. By that time the St. Clair tunnel, an engineering marvel in its time, had been completed, and the Grank Trunk that ran through Watford was the main line between Toronto and Chicago. Much of it was double-tracked, but in 1902 the line across Middlesex and Lambton counties was still a single track. Wanstead was the next village to the west of Watford. In a blinding snow storm on Boxing Day night, 1902, "orders violated" by the Watford station agent sent a passenger train heading west toward an eastbound freight that ought to have entered the siding at Wanstead, but delays and a flurry of telegraph messages left it on the main line. The head-on crash was catastrophic. "The engines reared up against each other," my father said, and the momentum of the cars behind brought carriage after carriage into the pileup. Twenty-eight people were killed, thirty-two seriously injured. For years afterwards the Watford paper printed accounts of the wreck on the anniversary of the disaster, and published poems about it. One, which appeared in August 1948, used Tennyson's line, "Someone had blundered."

Another event that my father vividly remembered was the Great Lakes storm of November 1913. November gales were common on the Great Lakes, but this one was unusually severe, lasting for days (November 7 to 10). The worst of the storm was on Sunday, November 9, when high winds raised thirty-foot waves and sank eight ships in Lake Huron alone, all aboard being drowned. My father told me that his father, anticipating a major storm because of the high wind, went to the schoolhouse and brought John home to safety; the other pupils were all sent home. They were fortunate: the wind and a heavy fall of snow brought down trees and made the roads impassable.

Excursions by train

Railroads and trains always fascinated my father: they were the way to the world outside Brooke Township, to the excitement of travel and adventure. Excursions by train were a "big thing" when he was a boy and young man, Dad said: excursions to "London Fair," and excursions to Niagara Falls. The latter cost two dollars. The train left from the Kerwood station at seven o'clock in the morning, the coaches jammed with holidayers. Open windows let in cinders from the steam engine. People would spend all day at "The Falls," and the train stayed well into the evening, long enough for people to see the illuminations.

Sarnia was another destination. The train went directly to the old Northern Navigation dock, where my father and his parents boarded the "Tashmoo" and went off down the river for a picnic on Tashmoo Island. They could have gone on to Detroit for an hour's visit there.

"Northwest Fever"

Many of my father's stories were about friends and relatives who had gone "out west." It is hard for us now to recover the excitement and the promise and the longing packed in that phrase, but a 1911 headline in the Watford paper captured in metaphor some of those feelings: "Northwest Fever." Each week the paper listed those who were "off for the West" on the CPR, lured by reports such as that provided by John Grigg, then mayor of Stettler, Alberta (and married to my mother's "Aunt Bertie" Thompson, a half-sister of Grammie Runnalls). On a hurried trip east to his old home in Caradoc Township, he said that "the West will produce a banner harvest this year and all expect the grain yield to break the record. At present only about two per cent of the land in the great and vast west is yet under crop ...." So, not surprisingly, "the people of Brooke have always looked upon the Canadian Northwest as a country affording great opportunities to the young man of the east" (*Guide* 7 March 1913). Sherman Hair was one of those young men, but young women were just as likely to go: Sherman's sisters, Eliza and May, both went too.

Before Sherman was married, my father told me, he had gone west on a harvest excursion. The fare was ten dollars, and he rode "all the way to the prairies on seats that were only wooden slats." Like many men of his generation, Sherman "once thought of settling out there." He didn't, but his sisters did. According to my father, both Aunt Liza and Aunt May went west "about 1900"; the earliest documented evidence of their living in Saskatoon is in the rolls of the Third Avenue Methodist Church, which Aunt Liza joined in 1906, Aunt May in 1908. She had been in the west for some time before she returned "to her home at Salem last week"—this was in July 1911—and on going back her name appeared in the Watford paper among those "ticketed ... for the North-West" (*Guide* 21 July 1911; 25 August 1911). In Saskatchewan, Aunt Liza met a man named John Mark, married him in 1910, and settled on a farm at Warman. In Saskatoon, Aunt May was a business woman, providing "Hair Goods, Hairdressing, Manicuring, Chiropody & Swedish Massaging" with a partner, and then on her own, as sole proprietor first of the "May Hair" business and then of the Beauty Parlors in the Flanagan, a downtown luxury hotel built in 1907. As a member of the Third Avenue Methodist Church, she was involved in quilt making, and her name appears on one of the Canadian Red Cross quilts sewn by the church during the First World War. There is an undated photograph of Aunt May in Saskatoon: it is wintertime, and she is at an outdoor rink, on ice skates with a hockey stick in her hand—the very image of the new independent woman. But ties to her family were strong, resented but never broken. She was engaged to a man who, like her, was originally from Brooke Township, but broke it off under pressure from friends and relatives who felt he had a problem with alcohol. And she wanted to buy land in Saskatoon, but her father thought the price—three hundred dollars—was too high. It is "now valuable property," according to my father.

The west was the chief destination in everyone's mind at that time. In the summer of 1912, May's sister Beccie and her first cousin Gilbert Woods went west to see family, and in August 1915 Grandad Hair "left ... for Purdue, Sask. where he will spend several weeks visiting relatives" (*Guide* 13 August 1915). Aunt May came home regularly, but at the time of her mother's death in November 1919, she was listed as living in Saskatoon. I do not know how long she stayed: by the time of her father's death in 1927, she was, according to his obituary, "at home."

The Northwest also figured in the experiences of the Watson side of the family. In September of 1905 Dessa's brother Guy, not yet twenty years old, was in Souris, Manitoba, though what he was doing there I do not know. Perhaps he was on a harvest excursion. But the event which my father remembered and told about in after years was the accident that killed George Watson.

George Watson—born George Green—was the orphaned nephew whom Grandad Watson had raised as his own son and as a brother to his youngest daughter, Eva. In the spring of 1912, George went west to work as a fireman for the C.N.R.—the Canadian Northern Railway, not the Canadian National, which did not yet exist. On Sunday, 22 June 1913, "word was received here" in Brooke that he had been killed that day "in a railway wreck." He was twenty-one years old. In its issue of 11 July 1913 the Watford paper reprinted a report of the accident from the Kindersley, Saskatchewan, *Clarion*: "A sad fatality occurred last Sunday morning [June 22] at 8 a.m., six miles west of Alsask, when George Watson, a fireman on the C.N.R. was instantly killed. The engine was backing up when seven box cars and the engine left the track. The engineer warned Watson to hold fast to the engine, but he jumped and rolled down the embankment. He was just in the act of climbing up when the tender turned turtle, pinning Mr. Watson under. It is reported that death was instantaneous." The body was shipped back to Watford and, a week later, "on Sunday morning at 10 o'clock, service was held at the home of the father of deceased, Mr. David Watson, lot 27, con. 11 [sic], Brooke, by the Rev. S. V. R. Pentland, and the remains were followed to their last resting place in St. James' cemetery by a goodly number of friends and neighbors." There George was buried with his mother's family in the Reid plot.

Meanwhile, back in Ontario ...

While her brother and sisters were "out west," Aunt Beck travelled to Chelsea, Michigan, to stay with her cousin, Dr. John T. Woods, and to undertake training as a nurse. She crossed the border in April 1908. There is a postcard from her to her nephew John from this period, with an illegible postmark and date: "Hello John, how are you now? Heard you could go down to grandpa's all by yourself. You will go often now when Dorothy is there. This is the street I live on. You had better walk over to see me. But you will not have time as you will soon be haying. Auntie Beck." Her intention to become a nurse was never fulfilled. The Michigan census of 1910 lists her as a "servant" in Dr. Woods's household, but in 1916 her mother fell ill, and Aunt Beck came home to look after her. She did so until Grandmother Hair's death in 1919, but at a cost both to her health and to a possible career. As for her prospects of marrying, I have a vague memory of my father telling about Aunt Beck going to a Sunday School picnic with a young man: she was high-spirited and he was a stick-in-the-mud, and she ended up going home with someone else. That brought the relationship to an end, of course. "There were tears afterwards," my father said, but there was no repairing the breach, and Aunt Beck remained single all her life.

My grandfather, Sherman Hair, was, as I have said, the first of his family to marry, and it was not until 1904 that his older brother, Uncle Jim Hair, marrried Arabella Annett, the daughter of James Annett, who lived further west on the Twelfth Line. Uncle Jim and Aunt Arabella settled on the farm directly to the east of my grandparents, the original Hair farm, and there three of their five children were born: Amy, the oldest of my father's first cousins, on 5 October 1905; Elsie, on 15 August 1907; and Harold, on 1 April 1910. In 1911, Ches McLellan bought that farm, and Uncle Jim moved his family to his father-in-law's farm, Lot 24 in the 12th Concession. "James Annett was Aunt Arabella's father," my father explained, "and he was retiring." The creek ran through it and much of the floodplain land was not arable, but the farmhouse itself, a large and handsome white-brick structure built in 1889, had a wonderful setting, on a broad lawn surrounded by ancient trees, with a panoramic view of the winding course of the creek and its wooded banks, of the concession road itself, and of the iron bridge that carried the road over the creek. The move brought other changes. "In those days, Grandfather, Uncle Jim and Dad all worked together in haying and harvest," but that came to an end in 1911, when Uncle Jim moved away and Grandad Hair retired.

Then John's father relied on casual labour in the summer months. "There were a Pentland boy and a Burton boy who used to work at our place in the summer holidays" and that led to an accident. "We had a sliding door in the stable, and for some reason I had my hand up on the track when one of the boys suddenly slid the door back. Of course it caught me, tearing the nail of my first finger and bruising the rest. We had to make a trip to the doctor to have it dressed. It seemed a long way to go to Watford by horse and buggy just for a finger. I still have the mark where my finger was crushed."

"Another boy from Watford who worked in the summer was Ross Annett, a nephew of Aunt Arabella. He was a little older than I but we were together a great deal. Later he went to the First World War as a pilot in the Royal Air Force. Following the war he settled in the west and became a writer: many of his stories were published in the *Saturday Evening Post*. At that time the *Post* was a weekly magazine, and we always looked forward to reading his stories after having known him so well." Ross published his "Babe" stories between 1928 and 1960; combining humour and sentiment, they were about a farm family living in drought conditions on the prairies—Big Joe, Little Joe, Babe, and Old Pete. Ross Annett belongs with W. O Mitchell and Sinclair Ross in writing about the West during the Depression. For our family he was a personal connection to a part of the country to which my father had many ties but that he would never see.

A note on my father's reading: his favourite author was Jack London, but the bookcase at home was filled with novels by G.A. Henty and Ralph Connor. *The Sky Pilot* was there, and *Glengarry School Days*, Gilbert Parker's *The Seats of the Mighty*, histories of the First World War, and some of Walter Scott's novels. A favourite Henty novel was *With Lee in Virginia*.

The first decade of the twentieth century was the time when my father's Hair uncle and aunts married and established families of their own: Uncle Jim Hair in 1904, as I have already said; Aunt Lou in 1906; Aunt Mary and Aunt Liza, both in 1910. Aunt Lou had gone to the London Normal School, graduated with its first class (1899–1900), and taught in our home school, S. S. No. 10. She married Disney Delmage, who lived on the Lake Huron shoreline near Camlachie, on a farm they called Bonnie Doon. Their oldest child, Dorothy, was born on Christmas Day 1907, and their son Horace on 6 December 1911. My father had a funny story about that birth. A neighbourhood boy was at Delmages' when Horace was born, and when he returned home his parents asked him what the Delmages were calling the new baby. "Horsehair," he said. The boy stoutly maintained that that was what he had been told: for Aunt Lou and Uncle Disney had decided to call their son "Horace Hair."

Aunt Mary, the oldest of the Hair sisters, did not marry until 1910, when she and Angus Galbraith made their home in Napier.

Another memory from this time: pets. Every farm had a dog, of course; John had rabbits; and there were always cats around both barn and house. The door from the room at the very back of the house into the kitchen had a pull with a latch on it, and when one of the cats wanted in, John lifted it up and put its paw on the latch, teaching it to open the door for itself. One day the family had company for dinner, and everyone sitting round the table was startled when the back door suddenly opened—and the cat came swinging into the room, clinging to the pull. A great burst of laughter, and an amusing story to tell afterwards.

The coming of the telephone to the Twelfth Line: Summer 1912
"I was going to school when the telephone line was built. The telephone was a wonderful thing, as we could call anyone in Watford or elsewhere, as well as the neighbours. Before the telephone, if you needed a doctor, you had to drive to town to get one, and of course with the horse and buggy. We had a party line that took in all between the east townline and the Nauvoo Road, including the sideroads halfway through [to the next concessions]. Later this line was divided in two so it was not quite so busy." Each subscriber had his or her own ring; ours was one long and two shorts.

Brooke Township had its own municipal telephone system, which by the summer of 1911 had nearly one hundred subscribers who paid an annual rate of $11.35. There was then a proposal to extend the service to the north part of the township, the stipulation being "at least three subscribers to each mile of pole line before the work is undertaken" (*Guide* 12 April 1912). There was no difficulty in getting people to sign up, and lines were built along the tenth and twelfth concessions in the summer of 1912.

The coming of rural mail delivery: 1913
"Rural mail delivery was another thing that came about the same time as the telephone. Joseph Armstrong, M.P. for East Lambton, was called the Father of the Rural Mail Idea, and was credited with getting the system started. Before that we had a box in the Post Office in Watford and were lucky to get mail once a week."

The service was established in bits and pieces. In August of 1911 a petition for a mail route along the Twelfth Line was sent to the Post Office Department, "and it is to be hoped," the Watford paper opined, "the same will be granted as a mail service in this part of the township is very much desired" (*Guide* 25 August 1911). The new route would begin in Watford, and proceed "along the Nauvoo to 12th con., thence east to townline Brooke and Metcalfe, thence north to townline Brooke and Warwick and west to Watford" (*Guide* 16 February 1912). But it was October 1913 before the paper reported that "Rural Route No. 7, sixth line east to 27 sideroad, was commenced on Friday last; Miss Harrison is the courier" (*Guide* 24 October 1913). So our farm's address became R. R. 7, Watford.

"Our first carrier was Ivy Harrison. Of course, [the mail] was delivered by horse and buggy or, if in the winter, by cutter. The Harrisons had two horses, and in the morning Ivy drove one horse to Watford and picked up the mail." She then delivered to half of her route, arrived home about noon and had lunch, and then, in the afternoon, drove the other horse on the other half of R.R. 7.

"Dad subscribed to the *Mail and Empire*, a weekly paper published in Toronto. I remember being down at Grandfather's when someone brought the paper with the news about the sinking of the Titanic. That would be in 1912. I believe that, for years or so before mail delivery, Dad subscribed to the *Daily London Advertiser*, and it was brought from Kerwood every day by Joe Campbell, who drew milk to the factory in Kerwood."

"Drawing milk" to the Kerwood Creamery and Cheese Factory
"Joe Campbell had a wagon with a large flat top, and the milk was sent to the cheese factory in thirty-gallon cans. By the time he reached Kerwood he had a full load. On his return trip be brought back what was left from the cheese making; this was fed to the pigs. He also brought back butter and cheese for anyone that wanted some, and even a few groceries if someone needed them. Perhaps while on the subject of drawing

milk I should tell that everyone who sent milk had a milk stand [at the end of the farm lane, next to the road]. No one person could lift a thirty-gallon can of milk up on the wagon. These stands were built the same height as the top of Joe's wagon, with steps up the back. The milk can was wheeled or drawn to the stand and taken up the steps to the top. When Joe came along, he drove close to the stand and was able to roll the heavy can of milk onto the wagon. In later years people began to purchase cream separators and sent only cream to the factory to be made into butter. ... There were many cheese factories at that time, but I do not know of any in Lambton County today."

The Donnellys

The Donnelly massacre, which took place on 4 February 1880 on the Roman Line near Lucan, Ontario, was the major news story of the day, and its anniversary was regularly noted by the Watford paper, in 1916, for instance: "The Donnelly murder occurred in Biddulph Township 36 years ago ... Jas. Donnelly, his wife, Mrs. Donnelly, their sons, John and Thomas, and their niece, were murdered by a party of masked men who were never brought to justice. Johnny O'Connor, a boy visiting the Donnellys, escaped and was a witness in the famous trial that followed" (*Guide* 25 February 1916). For years after the murders, newspapers reported the doings of the surviving family members. Two of the sons moved away from Biddulph Township, Bob to Glencoe and Will to Appin, and the Watford *Guide* and the Alvinston *Free Press* mentioned them frequently. Will, the oldest son, who did more than anyone else to bring the killers of his parents and siblings to justice, ran the St. Nicholas Hotel in Appin. He died in March of 1897, and I don't suppose my father might have told me anything about him or his family had it not been for James Reaney and his *The Donnellys* trilogy, the plays that Jamie developed through workshops in University College at Western in the mid-1970s, after which his NDWT Company took them on a national tour. That spurred my father's memory. He said that when he was ten or eleven, his father sold cattle to a man in Appin, and arranged to deliver them to a point on the Appin Road south of Napier. But when they got there, they found that the people engaged to take the cattle on into Appin had not shown up. The purchaser paid my grandfather to drive the cattle on to town, and then bought him and my father dinner at the St. Nicholas Hotel. It was one p.m., after the dinner hour, and seated in the dining room was only one other group, the family who owned the place. My grandfather said quietly, "Those are the Donnellys." Will's wife and family, that is, Will having died years earlier. "What," I asked my father, "was the attitude toward the Donnellys then?" "It was all hearsay," my father said, "but they were known to have done dreadful things—burn barns, cut the tongues out of horses, etc." When Reaney staged the *St. Nicholas Hotel* in Western's Drama Workshop in October 1975, the backdrop was a stylized map of southwestern Ontario from St. Thomas to Exeter, and beside each place name Jamie wrote a sentence or two using reminiscences of local people. Beside Appin he wrote: "My father remembers driving cattle over to Appin with his father in 1912. They had dinner at the St. Nicholas Hotel, & someone said that there's the Donnelly family over there—Don Hair."

Church picnics and garden parties

Salem was part of the Brooke Circuit of the Methodist Church, which included Walnut on the Tenth Line and Bethesda on the Sixth Line, in the northwest corner of Brooke. When my father was small, the three congregations held fundraising activities that had not changed much since the nineteenth century: the oyster supper, with a program of speeches and other entertainments, and "socials" of various kinds, with music and games. But to these were added, in the summertime, a "big pic-nic" at the lake, at Hillsboro Beach northwest of Forest on Lake Huron. The excursion was an all-day event, with boating and bathing, everyone lingering well into "the shades of evening" (*Guide* 29 July 1910). There are photographs of my grandfather and other church members, in bathing costumes, seated in boats and holding oars, looking awkward, their arms and faces deeply tanned, their upper bodies white. Also in good weather was the garden party. In June 1911, the Watford paper announced that "the ladies of Salem church are giving a garden party at Sherman Hare's [sic], 12th line, Brooke, on Friday evening next [June 9]. Good program and choice refreshments. This will be a nice outing for those in town who enjoy a pleasant evening in the country" (*Guide* 2 June 1911). Afterwards the paper reported that the event was "well attended," the refreshments abundant, and the program "choice and entertaining." The paper gave no details of that particular program, but at other church-sponsored gatherings, my grandmother's sister Eva Watson and other young women of the congregation sang solos or played "instrumentals," and Russell Woods, my father's cousin, was gaining a reputation as an entertainer "with his humorous vocal selections which led to encores every time he sang" (*Guide* 8 September 1911).

My father's music lessons

At the centre of much of the artistic and musical activity in Watford at that time was the Jones family, one of whom—Jeddie (Geraldine)—became my father's music teacher. My father labelled them "English," perhaps because Jeddie's husband (whose surname was O'More) used to stroll around town in plus-fours, but in fact they were Irish, a mother, Mrs. Marsh Jones, and two daughters, Jeddie and Lulu. They made their living by taking in pupils for lessons in "Music and Fine Arts," which they gave in their "music rooms and studio" on Ontario Street, where Central United Church now stands. They laid claim to social, artistic and musical superiority, far above anything in Watford at the time. Mrs. Jones, who advertised that she had studied "under Signor DeVescovi, London, England," was an instrumentalist and composer, and we had at home two pieces of her sheet music, "Canada's Diamond Jubilee March," "dedicated by special permission to His Royal Highness Prince George Duke of York," and "Canada's Souvenir Coronation Waltzes for Piano," dedicated, also by "special permission," to "His Royal Highness Prince Arthur, Duke of Connaught," who had been appointed Governor-General in 1911 and was a son of Queen Victoria. One daughter, Lulu, became a "teacher of stringed instruments" at the Hellmuth Ladies' College in London, but her sister Jeddie remained in Watford, where the *Guide* occasionally noted her public performances. At a concert in January 1893, for instance, she played "a difficult operatic medley … with brilliancy of execution and precision of an accomplished pianist." I do not know when my father began to take music lessons, nor how long he continued with them, nor whether they included voice as well as piano, but Jeddie lived on in Watford until her death in 1948. When her sister Lulu died in 1940, Jeddie contributed an "In Memoriam" piece to the Watford paper, detailing the family's claims to social superiority: "the generations, as they came down," she wrote, "were all high up in the British army, navy and church and were all of noble and historic birth": "the Earl of Desart, and the Very Rev. Right Honourable Jeremy Taylor, and Narcissus Marsh, Lord primate of

Ireland" were forebears on her mother's side, while the Joneses were "founders of the famous college called 'Nutgrove'" (*Guide* 13 December 1940). "High up": that was the operative phrase, no doubt impressive in Watford in the early twentieth century, but far less impressive was the Jones's domestic life. They were not very good housekeepers, my father told me, and when, after a music lesson, my grandmother found a bedbug on the dining room curtains at home, she knew where it had come from.

Butter in the cistern

My father once told me that his parents bought butter from Mrs. Roane, who lived across the road. Why they needed to do so I don't know: one of my memories from childhood is of churning butter for my grandmother. She had a big stone crock which held several gallons of cream, and there was a wooden plunger which went down through a hole in the ceramic top, and which took all my boyish energy to move up and down, until I could feel the butter solidifying. Then my grandmother would scoop it out, add salt, and store it in a cool place until we used it. Mrs. Roane kept the butter cool, my father said, by putting it in a crock and lowering it into the cistern. We did not have a cistern, but many farmhouses did. It was a concrete tank in the basement where rainwater was collected from the eavestroughs. From it, a pipe ran up to a hand pump in the kitchen, above a sink, so one always had soft water for household use. Aunt Ruth and Uncle Ches had a cistern, and so did Grandad Runnalls in Mount Brydges.

The Farmers' Club and the Women's Institute 1911–16

The social and intellectual life of my grandparents was bound up not only with Salem Church but also with these two organizations. Sherman Hair was a regular participant in a literary and debating society formed by the farmers in the northeast part of the township, and Dessa Hair was active in the Brooke Women's Institute. First, the Farmers' Club.

The club was a "literary society" of the kind examined by Heather Murray in her 2002 book on such organizations in nineteenth-century Ontario: they were a crucial part of the province's culture at the time. Their purpose was, in Murray's words, "self- and mutual improvement, through literature" (xi), and they "characteristically combined with their rhetorical pursuits—reading, composition, declamation, and performance—a range of other cultural activities, such as musical interludes, current-events discussions" (7) and debates, as well as purely social gatherings such as picnics and oyster suppers. All of these were included in the catch-all term, "literary."

The Brooke organization called itself by various names. When it was formed in November 1911 it was the "North Brooke Literary Society"; by January 1912 it was the "North Brooke Debating Society," and it held regular meetings in the schoolhouse through that spring and through the winter of 1912–13, when the paper referred to it as the "East Brooke Farmers' Club." Its main activity seems to have been debates on the issues of the day. On New Year's Eve (31 December 1912) the subject was "Resolved that mixed farming is more profitable than special farming." Uncle Jim Hair was the leader on the affirmative side (*Guide* 10 January 1913). In January 1913, the resolution was "that the franchise should be extended to women." The six debaters were all women, and Eva Watson was one of three to speak on the negative side. "The judges, Mr. Howard Woods, Miss Mary Fisher and Miss Rebecca Hair, had a difficult task to decide the winners, but finally gave it to the affirmative side by a small margin" (*Guide* 7 February 1913). Not every gathering of the club, however, was devoted to a serious debate of current issues. In that same year the club held its first oyster supper, at the home of Paul Kingston. How the Kingstons managed the crowd I do not know, for the paper reported that "there were over ninety present." The "sumptuous supper" was followed by "an excellent program of speeches, songs, and recitations" (*Guide* 21 February 1913).

The oyster supper became an annual wintertime event, and it seems to have been a jolly occasion, with both food and entertainment. At the one held in February 1915, John's mother and his Aunt Eva played (or sang?) a duet; his Uncle Jim made a speech; and his father "occupied the chair and helped to make the evening a social success" (*Guide* 19 February 1915). Two years later the Watford paper concluded its account of another such supper with the sentence, "All returned to their homes feeling that the annual supper is one of the greatest benefits to the social life of the community" (*Guide* 23 February 1917).

Sherman Hair had been one of the judges of the East Brooke Farmers' Club debate on 25 February 1913 (*Guide* 7 March 1913), and at the club's next meeting, on March 18, he was the "leader of the affirmative side" on the resolution, "that the farmer is responsible for the high cost of living." He was, the paper reported, "ably assisted by Miss Eva Watson" [his sister-in-law], and while the three judges "had a difficult task to decide the winner," they "finally decided that the affirmative side won by a small margin" (*Guide* 28 March 1913). The club reorganized itself in October 1913 and seems to have changed direction, for in January 1914 they heard an address from Lambton's "ag rep" (representative of the Department of Agriculture), a man named Bramhill, who awarded prizes for varieties of corn. Chester McLellan was one of the winners. At the meeting of 23 November 1915, Sherman Hair made use of his O.A.C. training by giving a speech on the "Feeding of Cattle," and in May 1916 he hosted "an apiary demonstration" by an instructor from the Department of Agriculture, but he also continued as an active debater. The resolution at the February 1916 meeting was "that protection is preferable to free trade as a commercial policy for Canada." Sherman led the negative side, but the judges decided in favour of the affirmative (*Guide* 11 February 1916). The final debate for 1915–16 took place in March: "'Resolved that Education is of more benefit to mankind than money.' The affirmative side was led by Miss Kathleen Kingston assisted by Messrs Sherman Hair and Russell Woods, the negative being taken by Miss Belle McIntyre assisted by Mrs. Richard Searson and Mr. Russell Powell. The judges… decided the debate to be a tie" (*Guide* 11 February 1916).

Unlike her sister Eva, Dessa Hair seems not to have taken part in the debates sponsored by the farmers' club, but she was active in the Brooke Women's Institute in the second decade of the twentieth century, hosting meetings and giving papers. The November 1914 meeting was at her home, when the women of the Napier branch provided the program. It was typical of the Institute's meetings: "After singing 'The Maple Leaf' [then thought of, among English-speaking Canadians, as the country's unofficial national anthem], roll call was answered by favourite quotations. Excellent papers on 'The Life of Florence Nightingale' by Miss Lulu McLean; 'Getting the most out of life' by Mrs. Gardiner, and 'Training up the parents in the way they should go' by Miss Anna Bowie, were given and very much enjoyed. Miss Joan Beer sang in splendid voice 'What would the rose say,' and solos, 'Just across the bridge of years' by Mrs. G. Denning, and 'Love me as the Ivy loves the old oak tree' by Miss Irene Gough, were sung very acceptably. A splendid reading 'The bravest battle ever fought' was given by Miss Mabel Bowie. After singing 'Tipperary' and the 'National Anthem' [was it "O Canada"or "God Save the King"?] this part of the program was brought to a close. The hostess then served a very dainty lunch" (*Guide* 27 November 1914).

Dessa Hair was particularly active in the Women's Institute during the four years of the First World War, when the Institute expanded its usual activities to include the war effort. My grandparents had an apiary, and when Dessa gave a paper at the meeting of the Brooke Women's Institute on 11 February 1915, her subject was "Bee Culture and Financial Profits from Products," a paper which the *Guide-Advocate* described as "splendid" (19 February 1915). The roll call at that meeting was "different uses of honey," and Dessa's audience was not a small one: fifty women were present. They sang "The Maple Leaf" as "an opening chorus" and "God Save the King" to bring the meeting to a close; they voted to send some money to the Red Cross and decided to spend the balance in "purchasing supplies and comforts for the soldiers." There had been a new member contest, and Eva Watson was the winner: she and others had recruited a total of forty-three new members. At the May 1915 meeting, Eva was elected assistant secretary and pianist, while Dessa was one of six women "appointed to represent the branch at the district annual meeting" (*Guide* 21 May 1915). At the annual meeting three years later, Dessa was "formally elected" as district director for the Brooke branch (*Guide* 28 June 1918). In the spring of 1919, she was one of four women elected to the Institute's program committee (*Guide* 16 May 1919), and at the June meeting, held in the afternoon's "extreme heat" at the home of Mrs. Fred Atchison, Dessa gave a paper on the "Preparation of Vegetables for the Table" (*Guide* 20 June 1919).

Eva Watson hosted the June 1915 meeting of the Institute, and it is notable as the first recorded occasion on which John sang in public. When he was older, he would have a fine tenor voice and would be the soloist at many church services and garden parties, but in June 1915 he was just approaching his thirteenth birthday. The meeting featured two papers, one on "Teaching Our Children True Patriotism," and the other on "How to Plan Summer Menus," and after these, "John Hair sang a solo, which was quite amusing and very favorably received" (*Guide* 4 June 1915). John performed again in June 1916, this time with a "mouth organ selection" accompanied on the piano by his Aunt Eva (*Guide* 16 June 1916).

The Great War

The last two years of John's public schooling were also the first two years of the First World War. John was too young to fight in it—he was sixteen when the war ended—but the papers were full of patriotic stories, plus puzzles and cartoons directed at young people, and John kept scrapbooks full of such materials. A good deal of the war propaganda in the first heady months of the conflict was created for young people, and presented them with idealized images of adventure, heroism and sacrifice. I still have a rough booklet the twelve-year-old John made out of brown paper and stitched together with string: in its pages he pasted the "Daily War Puzzle" which started appearing in the London *Advertiser* on 16 November 1914 and ran for some sixty-six days. Each puzzle is a black-and-white drawing, and each drawing an image of an heroic figure, or a gun or battleship or aeroplane. The puzzle is to find heads or faces hidden in the surroundings, and the solution requires a shift in one's visual perspective, where meaningless background lines and shapes become recognizable foreground figures. The very first puzzle, "Joseph Leyssen, boy scout, slipping past the invaders' lines," presents an image of youthful heroism and "pluck" (a key word at the time). For Leyssen, now long forgotten, was a Belgian boy scout celebrated in his time for carrying messages (he is pictured with his bicycle) and for unmasking two Germans disguised as priests. The puzzle: "find a German soldier and a spy." Official educational policy at the time reinforced those popular images of heroism. John collected many issues of *The Children's Story of the War*, thin, pamphlet-like publications with dark green covers, "recommended by the Minister of Education for use in the Public and Separate Schools of Ontario."

The Watford paper carried items about local "boys" who were fighting "overseas," and published weekly stories about Lambton's own battalion, the 149th. The "boys" who signed up trained locally, and their training involved long marches outside town.

In January of 1916, the Watford company of the 149th marched south into Brooke and east along the Twelfth Line, where the Bowies and the Hairs provided a meal, and John, the young amateur photographer, took pictures of the soldiers. The *Guide-Advocate* reported that, "in spite of the fact that the roads were in such shape as would lead one to look for May 24th inside of a week, the quality and quantity of the meal provided at the end of the trip more than made up for the difficulties of the journey. Mr. Sherman Hair provided for some 15 or 20 of the company, the balance dining at Mr. Bowie's. After dinner a few songs were rendered by different members of the company and after photographs had been taken and cheers given for the host and hostess the boys started back for Watford, making the return trip in very good time. Friends along the road very kindly provided the boys with baskets of apples which were much appreciated" (*Guide* 28 January 1916). At that time Watford had a new Armory and Drill Hall, completed in 1913; Col. Sam Hughes, the Minister of Militia, had laid the cornerstone.

On 9 May 1916 John witnessed a full military funeral in Strathroy, and took photographs of it. The dead soldier was a Private Howard James, who had died of pneumonia before he could be sent overseas. There are pictures of the flag-draped coffin on a gun carriage (its wheels covered with black crepe), of the team of black horses and marching soldiers, of the cortege turning the post office corner off Frank Street on its way to the service in the Baptist Church.

There was a great deal of euphoria and an outpouring of patriotic spirit at the beginning of the war, my father said. Everyone expected the conflict to come to a speedy end. The Johnson brothers from Watford enlisted in 1914, and they hoped that "it wouldn't be over before they got there." They had no idea of its horrors, my father said, nor did anyone know what a turning point the war would be in our history. Old tactics were favoured: "the commanders still wanted to use cavalry." Then he told me the story of George Reid. He was the son of our neighbours on the Twelfth Line (and a first cousin of Aunt Eva, whose mother was a Reid). George ran away when he was fifteen, joined the army, and went overseas; he was one of the lucky ones, and survived. "The Reids never talked much about George running away from home," Dad said. And it was only years later, when the Watford Legion celebrated its fiftieth anniversary (in 1980) that George himself talked publicly about his experiences.

"Reid was a soldier in the 52nd battalion, joining the army when he was 15 years old in 1916. He recalls the gore of battles on Vimy Ridge and Passchendaele in France as if it were yesterday. He spent a year and a half on the front lines in France during 1917 and part of 1918. He was hit by fire twice and was gassed several times during that period, but 'you just took it and went on' said Reid. There were no facilities in the first war, just mud, mud, and more mud. The weather was the worst hardship. It was nothing for Reid and the other soldiers to walk 25 miles through the mud with 70 lbs. on their backs through the mud and trenches. There were no transport trucks, they walked everywhere" (*Guide* 4 June 1980).

Another wartime memory of my father's: he recalled seeing Sir Adam Beck in an open car at Alvinston Fair, there to buy horses for the army. He was in a big car with the top down, and the car had "real wire wheels," which caught Dad's attention. "But I don't suppose he knew much about horses," Dad said.

Ward Zavitz was another Brooke Township "boy" who enlisted in 1916. He was twenty-one years old then, and would later marry John's first cousin, Amy, and farm at Walnut on the Tenth Line. The community's send-off was an upbeat patriotic event; his actual departure was a foreshadowing of the realities of war. Flags and bunting decorated his parents' home for the gathering of friends and neighbours, who presented Ward with a wrist watch and fountain pen. "You have nobly responded to your country's call to fight under the proud folds of the Union Jack to assist in crushing the German despot and his murderous system of militarism"—so Clarence Dolbear read from the address: "we realize that by enlisting you offered to help protect us and our homes." At the actual departure from the Grand Trunk station in Alvinston, "the boys took their leave-taking in a matter-of-fact way yet one could see that they began to realize the grim business before them, and there was little cheering. Songs were started but they fell flat; some there were who had little to say" (*Guide* 28 April 1916). For the number of casualties was beginning to have an effect on attitudes toward the war, and the Watford paper regularly carried detailed stories on each local "boy" who was killed. Ward was one of the lucky ones. Though he went overseas, he never reached the Western Front. He fell ill in England, and was "invalided home" in October 1917.

The Women's Institute packed bales of supplies for the war effort. What did they include? A *Guide-Advocate* story of 22 October 1915 gives a list: "blankets, sheets, pillow-cases, towels, web of bandage cotton, 32 pr. sox, 20 surgical towels, 4 dressing gowns, 80 handkerchiefs, 18 packages chewing gum." In addition, the women held a "jam shower for the soldiers" and "a splendid collection of fruit, jam, honey and maple syrup was donated."

And then there were the Dumbells. They were a group of entertainers who put on shows for the troops, to bolster morale, and they continued as a touring company after the war. My father told me that they came every year to the Grand Theatre in London, and he saw them several times. Dad remembered one show in particular in which Ross Hamilton (the female impersonator) sang a song while swinging on a huge silver crescent representing the moon. "You couldn't tell he wasn't a woman, he was so good," Dad said.

The Minister's Bride

When my father was in his early teens he was an enthusiastic amateur photographer, and took pictures of family and friends, livestock, cars and buggies and farm machinery—and of local events. One set of pictures is of a production of a play mounted by the young people of Salem Church on 26 February 1915 (*Guide* 19 and 26 February 1915). It was called *The Minister's Bride*, it had been written by the wife of a Presbyterian minister in Ottawa, Clara E. Anderson, and the cast included many of our neighbours. My grandparents, Sherman and Dessa, were in it, and so were Will Woods, Russell Woods,

Beccie Hair, Beccie Pollock (who would marry Jack King, also in the cast), Annie and Ern Powell, Mae Atchison, Mary Harrison, and two of the Clothiers. The title role was taken by Aunt Eva Watson. The play is of some importance in the history of early feminism in the province, and the fact that the Salem young people chose to produce it is, perhaps, a recogntion of the evolving role of women in a society that was still largely patriarchal. The announcement of the performance, however, did not draw attention to the play's social significance, but instead described it as "a laughable character sketch." In my father's photograph album there are pictures of various female characters, in costume but unidentified, and there is a picture of the entire cast standing on the steps in front of the church, in the snow and the cold and the pale February sunlight. Aunt Eva is wearing a white gown which approximates Anderson's specifications: "muslin, frilled to the waist, tight bodice, hoops, bustle and fichu of net."

The play was a good one for "Young People's Societies, Bible Classes and Other Church Organizations" (Anderson's target groups, defined on the title page) because it had a large cast: there are multiple named characters, and the final scene has "a number of young people at a party in minister's house. As many as wish can attend the party" (35). Moreover, it is a comedy, always more appealing "entertainment" (Anderson's word) than a tragedy. It is a comedy in two senses. First, it is an outing of broad comic types (Anderson calls it a "character sketch"), and in the conventional characterization of comedy (as defined by Aristotle), the comic characters are an excess or defect of some virtue. The women of the church are the excess of the virtues indicated by their names: Mrs. Betterdays, Mrs. Sharpe, Mrs. Charity, and Mrs. Seegood; and (if crabbiness is the defect of charity) Mrs. Joe Crabbe. They set themselves up as the judges of their minister's new bride, who says less than she knows or thinks (a stance which is, in Aristotelian terms, the defect of truth-telling, but one which is more attractive than the women who say far too much, so that the reticent character is usually the heroine of comedy). The second sense in which the play is a comedy is in its structure. Comedy conventionally begins with a tragedy, with an older and repressive society and with a division or breaking apart of some sort, and it ends with a new and better social group forming around the newlyweds. Here the "deputation of women" (3) in the first and second scenes, all dressed in old fashions (Anderson is precise and detailed about costumes), is a repressive society claiming the right to help choose the minister's bride. Not one of them gives a thought to the wishes of the bride herself, but are set to determine "whether she is the woman for him or not" (3) and whether she suits the congregation. The party in the final scene is the formation of a young and better society with the minister and his bride at its centre, and it takes a form familiar to every churchgoer at the time: the program of a tea meeting. The minister appoints himself as chairman; he introduces a number of musical selections (chorus, solo, instrumental, duet, quartet) plus a recitation. Then "all form circle around the minister and his wife and sing closing chorus, 'Auld Lang Syne,' followed by 'God Save the King' " (38). That's the conventional comedy resolution translated into the early twentieth-century culture of Souwesto.

But there is another dimension to the characterization of the bride herself. When we first see her in the second scene, she is already asserting herself, changing the appearance of the parlour, and wanting to get rid of "those awful draped pictures" (13) of her husband's dead predecessors. To the deputation of women she serves tea and is unfailingly polite, but her repressed feelings are apparent at the end of the scene when she "has sunk into chair exhausted, puts handkerchief to eyes" (24). The stages of the Bride's evolving thinking toward that of the New Woman are marked by the appearance of two couples with contrasting courtships. The young man in the first couple has been promising marriage for ten years, and the young woman at last insists on his keeping his promise. The minister comments that perhaps the young woman "showed her preference for him in too marked a degree" (28), and the Bride exclaims, "Preference! Why, John, it is all a revelation to me. Why, I thought girls had to be coaxed and coaxed before they said Yes. Why, you remember I wouldn't even pretend to like you for fear you would think I was running after you" (28). The young man in the second couple is named Mr. Right, but in fact he is Mr. Wrong, pompous and self-satisfied. When the Bride expresses surprise at the young woman's interest in him, the minister says that it is no surprise at all: "a fine clever young man like that" (30). That evokes a spirited response from the Bride: "How like a man that sounds, as if girls were just setting around, waiting to be asked by any man at all; I am surprised to hear you talk that way" (30)—and she leaves the room in a huff.

But none of these nods toward social change and newly independent women would be upsetting to the audience. The marriage of the minister and his bride is a conventional one; the minister shows no signs of any changes in his attitude to the relations between the sexes; and the Bride, whatever the shifts in her thinking, willingly takes on the role of the minister's wife and even, in the last scene, plays the matchmaker.

The wedding of Eva Watson and Gordon McNeil: 29 June 1916

How much of the attitudes of *The Minister's Bride* entered into Aunt Eva's thinking I, of course, do not know, but she was, like my grandmother, one of the new women of the new century, new because they believed, however tentatively, in being as up-to-date and independent and self-determining as men, and yet, paradoxically, they supported a patriarchal society because they continued to think of marriage, home and family as the height of a woman's ambitions. Aunt Eva was, as I have already said, active in the Women's Institute, which aimed to make the household practices of women as scientific and modern as farming was becoming for their husbands.

Aunt Eva's choice of husband is an indication of her independent judgment. According to her niece, Catherine Watson, "Ches McLellan took Eva Watson out some, but she was not too fond of him." She liked Gordon McNeil. He was soft-spoken, had an engaging sense of humour, and was well-educated. After teaching in S.S.No.10, he had enrolled in Queen's University, where he won prizes in English and History, and graduated with honours. In June 1915 he was awarded an M.A. by the Faculty of Education and was then qualified to teach English and History in a collegiate institute. Much of his career would be at South Collegiate Institute in London, but his first teaching job was in Orillia. He and Aunt Eva were married after his first year there.

"At noon on Thursday, June 29th, a very pretty wedding took place at the home of Mr. and Mrs. R.D. Watson of the twelfth line, Brooke, when their daughter Eva was united in marriage to Mr. Gordon McNeil, of Orillia. The wedding march was played by Master John Hair, nephew of the bride." John also took pictures of the wedding party, lined up between the Presbyterian minister at one end of the group and Salem's minister (Mr. Snell) at the other. Uncle Gord's parents and sister and brother are there; Aunt Eva's parents and brothers and sister are there; and so is Aunt Eva's best friend, Mary Harrison. Aunt Eva is in a white dress, with long sleeves, a high neckline, and a broad sash around her waist. Cradled in her left arm is a bouquet. On the lawn in front of the wedding party two chickens are pecking in the grass.

I do not know how long the McNeils were in Orillia, but they were home for Christmas in 1916, and they were home again in Brooke for the birth of their son the following spring. He was John Grant, born on 17 April 1917. Aunt Eva called him "Little John" to distinguish him from his first cousin, "Big John." And like "Big John," "Little John" would be an only child.

John at Watford High School 1916–18
Watford had had a high school since 1891, and in the fall of 1916 it had 106 students, "with more expected," since they could delay starting classes at the usual time—the first week in September— to work on the family farm. John was one of thirty-five new students registered in Form I.

I do not know a great deal about my father's high school years. I have only a vague memory of his telling me that he had boarded in town, with a family named McCormick. He did not reminisce about his teachers, as he did about his public school teachers, and he did not have stories about the two years that he spent in High School. His name is absent from all of the *Guide-Advocate*'s reporting on high school activities between 1916 and 1918, nor does it appear in the regular reports of examination results and promotions. There was at the time a "'farm labor' option" for students, an option that was part of the war effort; anyone who completed three months of work on a farm could be promoted, and perhaps that is the option that John chose. In May 1917 the Watford paper reported, under "Local Happenings," that "A number of boys and girls, students of the Watford High School, are now out helping on farms, in response to the appeal of the Resources Committee. Most of them will be granted their promotion certificates" (*Guide* 11 May 1917). But when, in February of 1918, the Watford paper carried a story on the high school commencement exercises and listed the names of successful candidates, John's name was not among those from the "Lower School and Military Farm Service" (*Guide* 15 February 1918). I know only (from an inscription in a text book) that in 1917–18 he was in Second Form.

Did he finish Second Form? I simply do not know. The Watford paper in July 1918 provided a partial list of "Successful Lower School Candidates" and in August printed a "final report"; in May 1919 it named those who "last June ... received diplomas" and had passed the "departmental examinations" (*Guide* 2 May 1919). John's name does not appear on any of those lists. And I wonder what discussions he had with his parents about his future. Following his father to OAC was a possibility, and at some point during his two high school years his father took him on a visit to Guelph, where John photographed the college and its barns and farm. On an endpaper in his high school geography text there is a drawing labelled "Pig Pen Guelph Ontario." That seems to be all that came of the excursion. By the time John was sixteen, he had decided to leave school and farm with his father.

The Hairs' first car: 1918
"My father purchased his first car in 1918, a Ford touring car with an open top, that cost $650.00. Actually there had been a couple of cars in our neighbourhood bought the year before for $495.00. There were no paved roads, and the cars were not used in the winter."

In July 1909, the Hairs' cousin, Dr. J. T. Woods of Chelsea, Michigan, visited relatives in Brooke and "came over on a Ford touring car." The car was a novelty: "a number of old friends enjoyed a ride on his speedy motor" (*Guide*). My father told me that that car was the first he had ever seen. Dr. Woods had gone to the Michigan State Fair, where the first of Henry Ford's Model T's were being shown, and he bought one. Motoring to Brooke Township was a challenge. There were no gas stations in those days, Dad said, but drug stores kept some gasoline for cleaning purposes. By buying a bit here and a bit there, Dr. Woods was able to make the trip.

By 1918 cars were more common and the purchase of them no longer considered newsworthy. In June of that year the *Guide-Advocate* reported that "The fourth line of Warwick boasts of sixteen cars owned by farmers in one section of six miles. That's nothing. There are ten cars owned by farmers in only one mile on the twelfth line of Brooke" (*Guide* 28 June 1918). For the yield of farm crops was unusually good that season, and the prices for them were high: the war created a strong market for grains, my father told me. A good yield for wheat was forty bushels to the acre, and my grandfather had ten acres, the yield being even more than usual because he had used fertilizer for the first time. At harvest that year, wheat was selling for $3.75 a bushel (according to my father), and from those ten acres my grandfather earned enough to buy his first car. For fifty dollars he put up a garage, a substantial lean-to on the south end of the granary, which had been built by the Roanes thirty-three years earlier.

I still have the white-and-blue licence plates from that first car: long flat plates—no raising of letters or numbers—with "ONT 1918," the provincial coat of arms, and the number 102447. For years after that drivers purchased new plates annually, and my father nailed the old plates on the inside wall of the garage. By the time he moved from the farm in 1953, the wall was almost covered. He left all but the 1918 plates there.

Sherman and Dessa Hair host the Institute and an oyster supper: February 1918

On two successive days—Thursday 14 February and Friday 15 February 1918—my grandparents hosted large gatherings of friends and neighbours. The first was a meeting of the Women's Institute, "with a good attendance." "Two splendid papers were given, 'Effects of Woman Franchise' by Mrs. D. McDonald, and 'The Life of Kitchener' by Miss R. Clark. Mrs. Kingston and Miss Harrison gave several instrumental duets and Miss Bowie, a reading, all of which were much enjoyed. The hostess served a very dainty lunch and the meeting was closed by the National Anthem" (*Guide* 22 February 1918). That meeting was on a Thursday; the next evening, John's parents hosted another group, and it was a large one: "The annual oyster supper of the Hillsdale Farmers' Club was held at the home of Mr. W. S. Hair, on the 15th inst. There were about 90 present. After supper was served Mr. John Farrell was asked to act as chairman and a fine programme consisting of speeches, music and recitations was given and a very profitable evening was spent. The programme was brought to a close by singing the National Anthem after which all returned to their houses much pleased with the kind hospitality of Mr. and Mrs. Hair" (*Guide* 22 February 1918).

Grandad Watson's house is destroyed by fire: April 1918

If the frame houses in those days caught fire, they burned to the ground, the construction being such that a fire, once started, could spread quickly. For the outside walls, which were not insulated, had uprights which ran from ground level to the roof above the second floor, and a fire simply raced up in the open spaces between the inner and outer walls.

There is an eyewitness account of the fire that destroyed Grandad Watson's house by one of the Reid girls, Mary (afterwards Mary Cooper; the Reids lived on the next farm to the west, and their house was only a few hundred yards from Grandad Watson's). Catherine Watson wrote down what Mary said: "I remember really well the day the house burned down. We were having dinner at noon, of course. George was sitting where he could see out either the window or the open door. He called out 'Dave's house is on fire'—no time for 'uncle'—and they ran as hard as they could—Dad and Harry and George. Albert was in France. I think they got the piano and some other things out but Eva always regretted that they lost the pictures and many other things which could not be replaced." "It was a nice spring day," Mary recalled. The only story my father told about that disaster was one of people panicking and throwing things out the windows. "Those things were smashed," my father said, "and what good was that?"

After the fire, David and Ella Watson rented the house of Duncan Campbell on the Tenth Line for a few months, but in the fall of 1918 they moved to Strathroy, to a house on High Street. By that time Grandad Watson was sixty-five years old, and the fire must have hastened his decision to retire from farming. John's parents hosted a farewell gathering: "A large number of friends met at the home of Mr. Sherman Hair to bid farewell to Mr. and Mrs. David Watson who are leaving Brooke to live in their new home in Strathroy. They were presented with a set of beautiful dining-chairs and two lovely rugs." Frank Powell read an address. "Although taken completely by surprise Mr. Watson made a very suitable reply expressing his appreciation of the gifts and his regret at leaving old friends" (*Guide* 18 October 1918).

The Spanish flu epidemic 1918–19

In the fall of 1918 social gatherings grew fewer and then were prohibited altogether: the epidemic of Spanish influenza had come to Southwestern Ontario. In its issue of 13 December 1918, the *Guide-Advocate* had a front-page notice from the local Board of Health, forbidding "until after January 20th next, the holding of any public gathering for the purpose of amusement or entertainment." I do not know if anyone in our family contracted the flu; certainly no family member died of it. But one of the Miller boys—Henry—with whom John had gone to public school, fell ill in the spring of 1919, and when he died, John, along with some other schoolmates, was asked to be a pallbearer at his funeral. John was just sixteen at the time, the same age as the boy who died, and I think that death haunted him all his life.

Grandad Hair's windmill

My father was a practical man, mechanically minded and always interested in how things worked. Here is his account of his grandfather's use of wind power:

"One thing that always fascinated me was the power windmill. They were popular at that time but I doubt if you could find one any place in the country now. One of Grandfather's barns had been widened and as a result had a very steep roof, like a church. The windmill was mounted above this barn on the end of a very long heavy stick of timber that stood on the barn floor and protruded through the roof for perhaps fifteen or twenty feet. There was a trapdoor beside the timber in the roof so a person could climb up to oil the mill. It was a heavy piece of machinery and I would think that the wheel must have been at least ten feet across. There were heavy gears, and a driveshaft ran down the post to a pulley on the barn floor. It also connected to a grain grinder, and Grandfather ground all his own grain. Another attachment carried a jerker rod to the well at the other side of the barn yard and pumped all the water needed for the livestock. I well remember helping Grandfather to cut wood. He ran a belt from the drive pulley on the barn floor to the circular saw outside the door. On a windy day it sure could drive that saw, perhaps not at the same speed all the time, but you could cut a lot of wood."

Death of Grandmother Hair: 20 November 1919

She died at the age of seventy-seven, and John was a pall-bearer at her funeral. She had been ill with heart disease for several years, and Aunt Beck had been at home looking after her. The Watford paper described her as "an old and much loved resident of the twelfth line," and said that she "passed away peacefully." "Of a kindly disposition and a most exemplary christian character she had a wide circle of friends who sincerely mourn her demise" (*Guide* 28 November 1919). Grandad Hair was a quiet man, but Grandmother was vivacious, as her grandchildren remembered her, and enjoyed family gatherings. "She was a spiritually devout person and would ask her eldest son, James, to read a Bible passage" (Clark, "England-Searson-Carter Family," 43).

"The funeral was held Saturday afternoon from the family residence to St. James' cemetery. The service was conducted by her pastor the Rev. S. J. T. Fortner. The pall-bearers were her two sons, James A. and Sherman, two sons-in-law, A. Galbraith and R. D. Delmage; a grandson John Hair and a nephew, T. A. Woods. Among the many floral offerings was a beautiful wreath from Salem Church of which deceased was a member …" (*Guide* 28 November and 5 December 1919).

The United Farmers of Ontario 1919–23

I once asked my father if he had ever belonged to the Orange Lodge, and he said he never had, nor had his father. Grandfather Hair and Sherman Hair, he said, voted Conservative, until the Ontario election in which prohibition was an issue. I'm not quite sure which election he was referring to, 1911 or 1914, but he said the leaders were "Whisky" Whitney and "Righteous" Rowell. Whitney was a Conservative, and premier from 1905 to 1914; Rowell was a Liberal, leader of the opposition, and a prominent Methodist. One of my father's earliest memories was of hearing his father, and Uncle Jim and Aunt Lou, arguing "violently" (my father's word) over the issue. My grandfather and his brother voted for Rowell, Aunt Lou for Whitney. After that, the Hairs were mostly Liberal in their political leanings—except for a period just after the Great War.

When my father was eligible to vote for the first time in a provincial election, he told me, the party he voted for was the United Farmers of Ontario. That was the election of 25 June 1923, in which the U.F.O., which had formed the government in 1919, was defeated, and the Conservatives under G. Howard Ferguson took power. In our riding of East Lambton, however, Leslie Oke, the U.F.O. member of the provincial legislature, was re-elected by a large majority: in Brooke Township, he had 692 votes, as opposed to 482 for the Liberal candidate and 128 for the Conservative (who was Bill Connolly, at that time Reeve of Watford and, much later, one of the longtime county auditors when my father was clerk-treasurer).

But it was the election of October 1919 that my father often talked about. The U.F.O. had not expected to win, he said, and did not even have a leader. After the election they chose E. C. Drury, a farmer from the Barrie area who had been a classmate of Sherman Hair at Guelph. So Drury became premier, and forged an alliance in the legislature with the Independent Labour Party. The Drury administration established the provincial highway system, my father often reminded me, and they developed a policy for funding "small regional universities like Western" when previous funds had gone principally to the University of Toronto. That enabled Western to build its first two iconic buildings, called, at the time, the "Arts Building" (University College) and the "Science Building." In June 1923, less than a month before the election which would turn him out of office, Drury himself laid the cornerstone of University College, and thirty years later, in a formal act of gratitude, Western gave Drury an honorary degree.

The election of 1919 was notable for two reasons: it was the first provincial election in which women could vote, and a major issue was the Ontario Temperance Act, which severely limited the sale of alcoholic beverages. Public debates too often elided temperance and prohibition. A "Prohibitory Liquor Law" had gone into effect in the province in September 1916; it brought to an end all licences to sell liquor, but something called "local option beer" was still available (*Guide* 15 September 1916). The date of the election of 1919—20 October—was also the date of a referendum on the Ontario Temperance Act, and it was upheld by a two-to-one majority. "Local option beer" had a limited alcoholic content. My father once told me about his first taste of such beer, which was at a large gathering of the Campbell clan in Poplar Hill in the summer of 1922: he and a number of other young fellows went off to the local hotel; the beer, he said, "tasted awful." My father was not a drinker, and so far as I know he never again had a beer in his life. (Nor did he smoke, when many men of his generation did.)

I do not know how well my grandfather, Sherman Hair, knew Ernest Charles Drury. Drury had enrolled at the Ontario College of Agriculture in Guelph in 1898 and graduated in 1900, so he was there at the same time as my grandfather, and the student body was relatively small: about one hundred and fifty, according to Drury. But there were differences between them: Drury was in the three-year degree course (which he completed in two) and Sherman Hair was in the two-year course for an Associate diploma; Drury was active in campus life (he was one of the editors of the *O.A.C. Review*, for instance), and his writing and debating made him one of the more prominent students at the time, while my grandfather led a more ordinary student life (the only thing I know about that life is his being a member of the champion tug-of-war team in 1899).

Drury's memoirs are useful because they define how the O.A.C. shaped the lives of the young men who attended. "It was," Drury wrote, "essentially a farmers' college, and the great majority of its graduates went back to the farm. The President of the College, Dr. James Mills, believed in farming, its dignity and worth, and impressed upon us that our part was to go back to the farm and there to become leaders in our communities in the introduction of advanced farming practices" (43–4). My grandfather was, by all accounts, a quiet, gentle, and modest man, and would not have thought of himself as a "leader in his community," but he certainly played the part envisaged by Dr. Mills, judging livestock at fall fairs around Southwestern Ontario, hosting a teaching session on bee-keeping (as I have already recorded), giving papers to farmers' clubs and being active in their organization, and later serving as a member of the township and county councils.

The election of 1919 was in October; in August of that year the *Watford Guide-Advocate*, recognizing the growing social and political power of the U.F.O., published an extensive article on the movement. It had been first organized in 1914, and five years later "numbered over 775 clubs, and had a membership of over 30,000." "A voluntary democratic association of Ontario farmers organized for the advancement of rural interests" throughout the province, it was composed of "all local organizations, such as farmers' clubs, associations or granges," and it welcomed women as well as men. The United Farm Women of Ontario was formed in 1918, and there was a unit in Caradoc Township when my mother began teaching there in 1927, for she took part in some of their meetings, but there is no evidence that the U.F.W.O. had a branch in Brooke Township. The aims of the U.F.O. were in part the same as those of the literary societies, such as "promoting social intercourse and the study of economic and social questions through the holding of debates and lectures," but they also encouraged "studying and teaching the principles of co-operation," "promoting the establishment of co-operative organizations," and "endeavoring to suppress personal, local, sectional, national, political, partisan and class prejudices, and thereby to promote the best interests of Canada as a whole." The movement's ideals were a challenge to the established political order, the challenge lying not so much in specific policies but in the promotion of informed debate and the articulate expression of opinion. The U.F.W.O., for instance, aimed "to help train our members to train themselves to think intelligently and express their thoughts clearly to the end that they may be fully capable of taking their proper places in our democracy" (*Guide* 8 August 1919).

The vote in 1923 indicates that the U.F.O. enjoyed wide support in Brooke Township where, according to the minute book (preserved in the archives at Western), the East Lambton club was "one of the largest in point of membership in the riding." The party was successful in Brooke Township for longer than almost anywhere else. For ten years, between 1919 and 1929, Leslie Oke held the East Lambton seat in the legislature.

One aim of the U.F.O. was longer-lasting than the movement itself: "promoting the establishment of co-operative organizations." The "co-op" is now a familiar business in many Souwesto towns, and there was one in Watford, the "Watford Farmers' Co-Operative Association." It was formed in 1919, and Sherman Hair was a member and shareholder; he was appointed a director in 1927. The Watford "co-op" began as a feed business, and developed into a store selling groceries and footwear. The store was managed for many years by Thomas Coristine, who early in 1947 bought the business from the shareholders, and my father, who had inherited his father's share, benefited from the distribution of assets. When my sister and I were children, that store was still operating. We knew it then as "The Farmers' Store," one of several grocery stores on Watford's main street, and it was run by Thomas Coristine's daughter, Alice, and her husband, Chuck Way. We always shopped there.

Mrs. Thomas Coristine died in January 1939, and my father was one of the pallbearers at her funeral. Tom Coristine had a heart attack and died suddenly in September 1947, only a few months after he purchased the business. His funeral was, according to the Watford paper, one of the largest the community had seen in years, and he was buried in Mount Carmel cemetery. My father was again a pallbearer. He must have done something more—perhaps sing a solo—for in her card in the paper on 12 September 1947, Alice Coristine added "special thanks" to four people. "John Hair" was one of them.

The Harrisons' dog
"We had our first new car in 1918, and I suppose it would be two or three years later, as I could not drive until I was eighteen, that I was driving up the road. There was a fish pedlar stopped in front of Harrisons and as I came along their old dog suddenly stepped out from behind the pedlar's wagon. I couldn't stop in time and I hit the dog and killed it. As the Harrisons had the name of being a little short in the grain, I was scared and kept going. When I arrived home I told Dad, and he scolded me for not stopping and going in and telling them what happened. Anyway, he said, as soon as we had dinner I was to go back up and explain. During dinner the phone rang, mother answered, and it was Aunt Arabella. She said she had been talking to Mary Harrison and Mary had told her that someone had hit their dog and killed it. But Mary said they were really thankful because they had acquired a pup and they didn't know how they were going to get rid of the old dog. Needless to say, I didn't have to go up to the Harrisons, but I think Aunt Arabella had a good idea who killed the dog."

Card playing and dancing
"My grandfathers on both sides were Methodists; they did not believe in card playing or dancing, so I think it was a shock to my parents when I learned to play cards. Anyway, Dad said if you are going to play cards other places we will play them at home. When he went to Watford he purchased a deck of cards and both he and mother learned to play and enjoyed it."

"Again going back to when I first grew up—I think of the dances and we had some wonderful times. Most of the schools lifted their desks and put them on slides so that they could be readily moved to clear the floor. There were a few dances held in the homes but most were in the schools. One of the big dances I remember was held in a barn. Bobby Auld, who lived on the Second Line of Warwick Township, built a new barn, and the whole of the upper part above the stables was a good smooth floor. He threw a big dance to celebrate the finishing of his new barn. I do not know how many people were there, I imagine several hundred, and everyone had a good time."

That dance took place in the spring of 1932, but my father had happy memories of many earlier dances. "The school dances and dances in the homes were all by invitation and there never was any rowdyism. There were no open bars, so liquor was not a problem. I never missed a dance, no matter how bad the roads or the weather. I remember a dance in the Tenth Line school in the spring when the roads were terrible. That afternoon I had been at a woodcutting bee at McLellans and Norman McLellan wanted to go too, so he came over to our place early in the evening and we wore rubber boots and carried our shoes. We walked back through our farm on the south side of the road, then through the farms behind, and we knew where there was a bridge to cross the Hardy Creek. Then we got to the Tenth Concession and walked up the road to the school. I don't remember who had a car from the Twelfth Line, but we rode with them up to the Nauvoo and then down part way on the Twelfth Line to get home."

"Another time there was a dance in the Annett school up the Twelfth Line. It was impossible to get a car through, so I hitched up an old driver that had belonged to

Grandfather Hair. After he died we had taken the old horse home. I put the horse in Alex Kelly's barn and went to the dance. We danced till about 3 a.m. and I started for home. I remember crossing the Nauvoo Road but I went to sleep and the old horse must have walked every step of the way, for I woke up when the horse turned in home, as one wheel of the buggy went over the end of the culvert. It was broad daylight and Dad was just going out to the barn to do chores."

"Most of the music was supplied by local musicians. James Dempsey and his son Irvine played for most of the dances. They played all evening for $5.00, a far cry from the cost now. The girls brought cakes, and sometimes bread and salmon or ham were purchased and they made sandwiches there. The boys paid 25¢ apiece, so there was usually some money to pay any expenses. There was a chap by the name of Dell Coulter who lived on the Lakeshore Road and he played for an occasional dance. Then one time we had what was known as the Kansas Farmer. I think he came from some place in Huron County. I remember he and his partner came to our place for supper. Before the dance they presented a short program. They were quite popular in Western Ontario."

Driving Mr. Fortner

"Some of the ... [Salem] ministers I remember were Mr. Pentland, Mr. Burton, Mr. Fortner, Mr. Foster, and Mr. Steadman. ... One time Mr. Burton, who by this time was stationed in Warwick Village, was invited back to Bethesda for an Anniversary Service, and Mr. Fortner had to take his charge for the day. He did not have a car and asked if I would drive him. I think I would be nineteen or twenty. I drove him to the old Warwick church, which was on the sideroad that now leads to the conservation area. There was a service at 11:00 a.m., and after we went to Burtons' for lunch. In the afternoon we drove to Uttoxeter for the 3:00 p.m. service and then back to the Burtons' for supper. Then there was an evening service in the Warwick church. One of Mr. Burton's daughters married a Ferguson and they still reside on a farm near the Village."

Mr. Fortner was Salem's minister from 1917 to 1920. Mr. Burton had served earlier, from 1908 to 1912.

Two sad deaths in December 1920: Uncle Guy Watson and Uncle Disney Delmage

December 1920 was a sad month: John's Uncle Guy Watson, his mother's youngest brother, died of smallpox, and his Uncle Disney Delmage, who had married his Aunt Lou, one of his father's younger sisters, committed suicide.

In 1907 Guy Watson had married, at the age of twenty-one, Mary Hay, who was six years older than he. Eleven years would pass before they had a child, Catherine, who was born 17 March 1918. By that time they were living in a house on Metcalfe Street in Strathroy, and Guy, who had learned carpentry, had a thriving business not only selling steel barns and farm buildings of various kinds, but also erecting them, and manufacturing wooden doors and window frames. He was the agent for a company in Preston, the "Metal Shingle and Siding Company," and while he was on a business trip to Preston just prior to Christmas 1920 he had an appendectomy. He came home ill. His daughter recounts what happened after that: "At first his illness was not diagnosed as smallpox. He was isolated in the parlour of his home where a bed had been put up. A nurse was hired to look after him. Mary Watson opened the door into the den so that Guy could see his daughter, Catherine, whom Mary held in her arms. He died at home on 31 December 1920. There was no funeral as people were afraid of getting the smallpox. His body was taken out of the window at night and buried in the Watson plot in Strathroy cemetery." He was only thirty-five.

A week before Guy's death, and three days before Christmas, Disney Delmage hanged himself. The Sarnia paper published on its front page a sensational account of his death, describing him as a "prominent cattle buyer" despondent "over financial losses." He "had been uptown transacting business in the morning and had appeared to have nothing preying on his mind. He evidently, it appears, went to his home about noon, went to the barn a short distance from his house, tied a rope around his neck, making it fast to a beam, and jumped to his death. His wife discovered the body hanging there and cut it down" (*Sarnia Canadian Observer* 23 December 1920).

Aunt Lou left Bonnie Doon as soon as possible, and returned with her three children to live with her father on the Twelfth Line. Her two oldest children, Dorothy and Horace, attended S. S. No. 10. Horace may even have lived for a while with my grandparents, for I know that he remained grateful to them for the rest of his life, and Ferne MacGregor, whom Horace would eventually marry, once said to me that his Aunt Dessa and Uncle Sherman had been "very good" to him when he was small. As for the farm at Bonnie Doon, Aunt Lou sold it, only to become the owner of it again when the buyer defaulted on the mortgage. It would eventually become the home of Horace and his family, who would subdivide and develop the lakefront property.

A Gathering of the Campbell Clan: June 1922

By the 1920s the original pioneer families had become extended families, with children and their spouses and grandchildren and more spouses. When one spoke of one's relatives, they might number in the hundreds. It seemed important to remember one's roots and to "keep up" with one's relations, and one way of doing that was the family "reunion," a picnic held in a park like Springbank in London. The meal was usually "pot-luck." On 8 June 1922 one of the largest picnics the Hairs and Watsons ever attended was in the park in Poplar Hill, and it was a gathering of the Campbell Clan. A photograph survives, a long picture that unrolls like a scroll: there are 578 people in it.

Our descent from the Campbells is through Dessa Hair's mother, who was Kate Campbell. John and his parents, Sherman and Dessa, are in the picture, and Oscar Watson and his wife, Jennie Munro, Eva (Watson) McNeil, and many families from Lobo Township.

The *London Advertiser* carried a detailed story on the clan gathering, which was an all-day event. Each person had a name tag "surmounted by the Campbell tartan." Dinner was eaten in the open air, and featured a cake "seven stories in height," each person present receiving a portion. "When the picknickers were seated at dinner," there was an address of welcome, a toast to the king, the singing of the national anthem, a toast to Canada, and a toast to the clan. When this last was announced, "the music of the pipers was heard down near the orchard, and as the band approached their selection was recognized as 'The Campbells Are Coming.'" After dinner the crowd adjourned to the grandstand, where gifts were presented to the oldest family members present, and addresses were given on the Campbell family tree and on various branches of it. "The concluding feature of the platform program was the baby show." "The entire clan then posed for a panoramic picture, and the sports of the day were initiated": races, and, in the evening, a baseball game. "Supper was served in the open air at 6 p.m., and there was an abundance of those delicacies dear to the Campbell heart." What were those "delicacies"? The story does not say.

Dessa Hair and the Women's Institute 1920–5

In May 1921, at a meeting hosted by Aunt Beck, Dessa was elected second vice-president of the Institute, and might have been expected to proceed to first vice and then president, but she apparently did not do so. She did, however, continue to instruct (she was one of four ladies to present "demonstration of salads" in August 1920), to give papers, and to host meetings. In April 1921 her topic was "The Importance of Physical Development on the Young," a paper the *Watford Guide* described as "splendid." Dessa repeated that paper at the August meeting, but she prepared a new one, on "Household Management," for December 1922 (*Guide* 22 December 1922), and she was host for the April 1923 meeting which featured "competition button-holing" (*Guide* 6 April 1923) and "an instructive demonstration on hot supper dishes" (*Guide* 20 April 1923). Aunt Net Watson hosted the September 1924 meeting, when my grandmother "gave a very interesting paper on 'Social Side of Farm Life'" (*Guide* 19 September 1924). I would love to know that she said on that topic. Dessa hosted the December 1924 meeting, when the *Guide* ended its account of the gathering with a sentence that might be construed as suggesting that the women's activities were trivial: "A pleasant hour was spent over the teacups" (*Guide* 2 January 1925).

In the spring of 1925 the Women's Institutes marked the twenty-fifth anniversary of their work in Western Ontario, and that milestone included reflections on their history and purpose. Household matters had dominated the Institute's concerns in the early days but, twenty-five years later, "the real feminine public spirit was ... to be shown by a developing interest in community problems." The Institute's motto was "For Home and Country," but "Home" remained at the centre, on the assumption (voiced by an observant overseas visitor) that "without homes there is no country worth talking about" (*Guide* 20 March 1925).

The new house on the farm, 1922–3

Since my grandparents' wedding in 1901, they had been living in the white frame house that had belonged to "Old Tom" Roane, and they must have been finding it aging and out-of-date. For some time they had been thinking about building a new house, and had been making preparations for it. Three years before the actual construction, my grandfather cut beech logs out of our bush, stored them, and let them dry for all that time. They were cured still more at the furniture store in Strathroy. Then a man in Strathroy cut and planed them for the floors—and the boards were so hard, Dad said, that when Stephenson, the builder, came to lay the floor, he had to dip the nails in grease to drive them in. Dad took a team and wagon to Strathroy to pick up the flooring. He put the horses in the livery stable at Prangley's Hotel, and had a restaurant meal, which cost him twenty-five cents. The journey home was a difficult one because the boards were so slippery, and he had to keep stopping and binding them more tightly. There was another trip with horses and wagon to the railway station in Strathroy, to pick up materials, but the roads were breaking up because frost was coming out of the ground. My father stayed overnight with Aunt May and Aunt Beck, and returned home in the early morning, when the nighttime temperature had frozen the mud and gravel.

The red brick which gave our house its distinctive appearance came from Milton and cost twenty dollars a thousand; the house took 11,500 bricks.

The contractor was George Stephenson (1882–1952), born in Brooke but then living in Watford, and he had two men working for him, Johnny Hawes, who lived on the Tenth Line, and Stan Cowie. Cowie was an Englishman, Dad said, with no immediate relatives in Canada, but his name lived on for us: he carved it into a board in the haymow of our barn. In the fall of the same year that Hawes and Stephenson built our farmhouse—1922—they built a house in Watford for the Cokes. It was the same style as our place—red brick, two storeys, white-framed windows—and it was next door to the high school. When my parents moved into town in the early 1950s, that was the house they bought. Its general appearance was a familiar one.

My grandparents demolished only the front part of the old Roane house; they retained the back kitchen (and a pantry behind it), and that was our summer kitchen, where we lived during the hot months. There was a cream separator in the pantry, but that space was used mainly for washing clothes, which were then hung on lines in the back yard. The front part of the house was entirely new. It, like the old part, was raised on a cement foundation, so that there was a full basement under the whole structure, with a wood-burning furnace and a hot-air heating system. On the main floor there was a kitchen which faced west, with built-in cupboards and a counter, at the end of which was a door into a closet with a "dumb waiter." This was a device for keeping food cool in the days before refrigerators. It was a set of shelves attached to ropes and pulleys, and the shelves could be lowered into the basement, which was cool, and raised when food was wanted. The kitchen opened into the dining room on the east side of the house, and it, in turn, had double glass-panelled doors (called "French doors") into the living room at the front of the house. Beyond was a front hall, about half the size of the living room, with the front door on the south side, and on the other side three steps leading up to a landing and the stairs. (On the other side of the landing were three steps leading down into the kitchen.) Upstairs were four bedrooms, all with sloping ceilings because of the pitch of the roof, and between the two back bedrooms was a bathroom which was never finished, and which was used for storage: the house had no running water, nor was it wired for electricity. (We would not have hydro until after the Second World War.) Water was carried from a well some sixty feet or so to the rear of the back kitchen; and when one had to "go," there was a wooden privy or outhouse, which we called a "closet," in the back yard. Coal-oil lamps provided light.

The house presented a handsome appearance to the road. A broad verandah ran across the whole front of it, and wide steps led down between red-brick pillars to the lawn. Above, the broad roof sloped down to the level of the first floor, and jutting up through it was a gable with two windows and a door opening out onto a little porch. One of those upstairs windows and the door were in the master bedroom; the other window was in the second front bedroom, and it had a seat in a little alcove under the window. Under the seat was a storage space where back issues of the *Star Weekly* (with the "funny papers" or comics), the *Saturday Evening Post*, *Maclean's*, *Life*, and *Collier's* were kept. That window-seat was a wonderful place to curl up in on a cold or rainy day, and read for hours and hours.

Spirea and forsythia and red barberry bushes were planted around the foundation of the house, and lilacs and honeysuckle, and blue and yellow iris. On the west side of the house there was a long cedar hedge, running from the back yard out to the road. My father had gone to the Dorchester swamp, southeast of London, pulled up cedars bare-rooted, and brought them home—in those days, one could do that—and, he said, "they all grew." On the east side of the house, and to the east of the lane, he planted a double row of cedars, and they grew into a thick hedge some nine or ten feet high. When I was old enough, it was my job to trim that hedge once a year. He also planted a cedar hedge to separate the front yard from the back yard, and he planted a number of maple trees.

Since I am describing the house, I had better describe the rest of the farm buildings. The oldest structure on the property was the granary, which was on the east side of the lane, and it had the date "1885" carved in its gable. My father used it to store grain, of course, but he also stored a cutter on the rafters above, and on the main floor was a fanning mill, which separated the grain from the chaff. When the Hairs acquired a car, they built a lean-to on the south side of the granary, for a garage. Behind the granary was the henhouse, a long low building, and behind it was the barn. It was a typical Ontario barn, rectangular in shape, and faced with unpainted barnboard, which had weathered to gray. The main floor was the stable, and the cows and steers wintered there, as well as our two big Clydesdales, Pat and Mike. At some later date Dad kept pigs in some parts of the stable that he had modified to accommodate them. Above was the hay mow—two mows, actually, separated by the "barn floor" into which, during haying, one drove the wagonload; to get the hay into the mow, Dad lowered a big fork in the shape of an inverted "U," tipped with prongs that could be closed inward, and lifted the hay on a pulley, raising it up and then rolling it along a track above the mow, where he released the prongs and dropped the load into the pile. Because the mow was on the upper level of the barn, there was a "barn bridge," which started on the level as a graded slope, and then, for the last ten feet or so, was actually a bridge from a concrete abutment to the barn wall. The "barn bridge" was a fine place to toboggan in the wintertime, our farm being so flat that there were no other slopes close by. West of the barn and facing it was the "drive-shed," where Dad stored machinery, and on the south side of that structure was a kind of cabin which was his workshop. It had a workbench, and there he kept all his tools. The well was in the pumphouse attached to that workshop, and it supplied water for the farm animals—there was a pipe to the tank in the barnyard some sixty feet away—as well as the house. Dad built the pumphouse only after we had electricity; before that, we pumped water for household needs by hand, and relied on wind power to provide water for the cattle and horses. I have a vague memory of the windmill that preceded the pumphouse.

John as tenor soloist

In the early 1920s John's name begins to appear with some regularity in the Watford paper, as a soloist at garden parties and special church services. He had a fine tenor voice, and I have many boyhood memories of his singing, accompanied by my mother at the piano. Our piano bench was full of sheet music, not only religious pieces suitable for church services but also songs from the First World War era, such as "There's a long long trail," and songs popularized by the Dumbells and Sir Harry Lauder. Captain Plunkett's name was on the front of many of those pieces from the Dumbells' shows, and there was a whole book of Sir Harry Lauder's compositions, among them "Roamin' in the Gloamin'" and "The End of the Road" (music with a determined beat written after his son had been killed in action in the war), and comic songs, such as "Boss o' the Hoose." I do not know who my father's accompanist was in the 1920s: he had not yet met my mother.

When Walnut church celebrated its anniversary in May 1923 with a "splendid supper" and garden party, my father was one of the featured "artists" (*Guide* 18 May 1923). A month later, when Salem Church held its annual garden party at the home of Mr. and Mrs. Gilbert Woods, John was part of the "splendid program" (*Guide* 15 June 1923). The March 1925 meeting of the Women's Institute was a St. Patrick's Day celebration at the home of Mrs. W. S. Shugg (who was a cousin of my grandmother's), and John sang a solo there. In January 1926 the Institute sponsored a concert in Walnut Church (by that time a "United Church"), with a four-act play and "musical selections by the Watford High School Orchestra and Mr. John Hair" (*Guide* 29 January 1926). There was a similar concert in the spring of 1926 at Chalmers, the Presbyterian Church on the Nauvoo at the Tenth Line, when "the vocal numbers given by John Hair and Clarence Lewis were very much enjoyed" (*Guide* 30 April 1926). A few weeks later, John sang at a concert following the anniversary services at Walnut (*Guide* 4 June 1926).

Salem's sixtieth anniversary, 1924

In September 1924 Salem church celebrated its diamond jubilee. There were two services on Sunday and a fowl supper and entertainment on Monday. The Reverend J.L. Foster was the minister at that time, and he prepared a history of the church which was printed in the Watford paper two weeks later. I have already used parts of that history, but add here his references to the Hair, Watson, and Woods families: "Among the early trustees were Robert Edgar and James Watson, now long deceased. ... John Hair, who was another of the early trustees who served in the old log church, is still living and takes a very active interest in the church and its work. David Watson was one of the first stewards of the church ...."

"The present stewards ... are: James Hair and Gilbert Woods, and Sherman Hair is secretary-treasurer of the trustee board. Mrs. Fred Atchison is organist and choir leader. The officials of the Sunday School are: Superintendent, James Hair; secretary-treasurer, Miss Rebecca Hair; teachers, Mrs. Peter Watson, Mrs. Gilbert Woods, Mrs. James Hair and Norval Woods. The officials of the Ladies' Aid Society are: President, Mrs. Gilbert Woods; secretary-treasurer, Mrs. Sherman Hair" (*Guide* 19 September 1924). At the end of November 1924 the Salem ladies held a bake sale at the Farmers' Store in Watford as part of their fund-raising activities.

The Hairs' 1926 Pontiac

Sometime in 1926 John's father bought a new car, this time a Pontiac. I do not know the exact model: the paper advertised the "Pontiac Six Sedan" at $1035 and the "Landau Sedan" at $1125. I note this purchase only because my father would drive that car for the next twenty years. The coming of the Great Depression made everyone short of money, and in the 1930s a new car was out of the question. Then the Second World War made consumer goods scarce, so that 1926 Pontiac was the car my father was still driving in 1946 (though I have a vague memory that he had replaced the engine in it after the old one had become embarrassingly noisy). Its top speed was forty miles an hour.

The United Church conference of 1926

That same fall, the newly formed United Church held a large gathering in Toronto under the leadership of the church's second moderator, Dr. James Endicott. In its issue of 8 October 1926, the Watford paper informed its readers that "Messrs. A. B. Sisson, John Hair Jr., and Rev. F. J. Rutherford are representing Brooke circuit churches at the United Church Conference in Toronto this week."

The Toronto *Globe* for 6 October 1926 gave the gathering extensive coverage: "DOMINION AND WORLD SERVICE PROMOTED IN CHURCH SESSIONS. THREE-DAY CONFERENCE OF UNITED CHURCH ATTENDED BY 1,300 DELEGATES FROM QUEBEC AND ONTARIO AND MORE THAN 2,000 PEOPLE IN ATTENDANCE AT MASSEY HALL. STRIKING ADDRESS FROM MODERATOR." At this same time, John's cousin, Norval Woods, was in training for the ministry, and perhaps it was on this occasion that Norval took John to see the campus of the University of Toronto. They had lunch in Hart House. But what John chiefly remembered from the trip had nothing to do with the church at all: it was the automobile race on the way home, when Mr. Rutherford proved what his new car could do.

Here is my father's account of that event, part of his reminiscences of Salem's ministers: "The last minister was a Reverend Rutherford, and he had married a Richardson girl from Kerwood. One time there was a church convention in Toronto, and Rutherford invited one of the Sissons brothers from Bethesda and myself to go to Toronto with him. He had a new Star car made by the Durand company and this was the first year of production. We went to the convention and stayed at his sister's in Toronto. On the way home (gravel roads) a chap in a Chevrolet decided to pass, and the race was on. The Star car could really travel and was soon away ahead. Rutherford was in great spirits and laughed and joked all the rest of the way home."

A week or so after he returned from Toronto, John sang at anniversary services at Bethesda. He assisted the choir at the evening service, when the guest minister, the Reverend George Morley of Toronto, "gave a dramatic interpretation of several selections from *Ben Hur*" (*Guide* 22 October 1926).

Salem's Christmas bazaar 1926

Raising money for the church now took the form of a pre-Christmas bazaar, which was held in Watford in late November. It was first announced and then described. "Brooke Circuit Ladies' Aid will hold a Bazaar in the Armory, Saturday, November 20th, at two p.m. The main attraction will be a supply of beautiful needlework suitable for Christmas gifts. / A dainty afternoon tea 10¢, consisting of ham and chicken sandwiches, cake and tea, served in excellent style by the Salem ladies" (*Guide* 12 November 1926). No doubt my grandmother did a great deal of work for this event, and it paid off. "Brooke Circuit held a very successful bazaar in the Armory on Saturday last. The building presented a very attractive appearance. The various booths were decorated in white with trimmings of green, purple or patriotic colors. The display of needlework was appreciated by the visitors as was also the home cooking and candy, if one were to judge by the rapidity with which the tables were emptied. The tea room was well patronized and all were greatly impressed with the generosity of the Salem ladies when they undertook to serve a 10c lunch" (*Guide* 26 November 1926).

John goes to work in Detroit: November—December 1926

The bazaar was on a Saturday. Two days later, on Monday, 22 November 1926, John left home to go to work in Detroit. He was twenty-four years old, and (except for his boarding in Watford to go to high school) had never lived or worked away from home, nor had he ever set foot in the United States. But the seasonal work had been done on the farm, and his father did not need him as much in the winter as he did at other times of the year. So John and another Lambton boy, Art Minielly from Plympton Township, set out. They entered the United States at Port Huron, Michigan, having crossed the St. Clair River on the ferry (the Bluewater Bridge would not be constructed and opened until 1938), and there they filled out forms for immigration. Marjorie discovered our father's form in the Detroit Border Crossings and Passenger and Crew Lists 1905–1957 database. Physical description first: he was five feet, eleven inches tall, with "dark brown" hair, "blue" eyes, and a "ruddy" complexion. He declared that he had fifty-seven dollars with him, answered "no" to the question "ever in the US?" and said that his stay would be "indefinite." When asked the purpose of his entry into the United States, his answer was "seeking employment."

On that late November day in 1926, John travelled on the "inter-urban," a kind of trolley car that ran on a rail line in a southwesterly direction from Port Huron through Mount Clemens to Detroit itself. His first concern was to find a place to board and, with newspaper ads in hand, he asked the advice of a policeman, who recommended Highland Park as a good area. So John travelled up Woodward Avenue and arranged to board with a family at 34 Westminster Street, just off Woodward and just south of Highland Park. The family surname was DePadry, and they were Irish Catholics. John was always amused by his landlady saying to him that those who went to mass didn't need to go, while those who didn't should. And he was amused by another boarder, a school teacher, who asked him, "Do you have snow up at your place year round?"

His first job was in a lumber yard just off Grand River Avenue, six or seven miles from his boarding house, and he took the streetcar to work after having breakfast at a small restaurant on the corner of Woodward. The company was the Hurd Lumber Company, which made window sashes and other items that involved woodworking. John, however, was not hired for manufacturing, and the work he did was hard physical labour: unloading boxcars and piling lumber. The only relief from it came when the company had to make deliveries and John went out on their truck. He worked a ten-hour day and earned fifty cents an hour, which, he told me, he thought was "good money."

In the meantime, Art Minielly, who was selling insurance in Detroit, had a car, and when he was driving home in mid-December, he offered John a ride. They got to the end of the pavement on Highway 7, just east of Reece's Corners, when a tire went flat, and while they were fixing it, Art complained about a sore throat and swollen glands. "This was a Saturday, a week before Christmas," Dad said, and he went back to Detroit the next day, taking the train to Sarnia, the ferry to Port Huron, and the interurban to Detroit. But "times were already getting hard," Dad said, and he was laid off. For a day or so he worked on construction, on a new addition to the Dodge plant, but cold weather and snow halted that project, and he was laid off again. So he came home for Christmas without a job. It was then that he learned that Art Minielly had the mumps, and had exposed Dad to them. "Christmas was a time of parties and dances," Dad said, and he did not want to miss any of them. He did not fall ill until just after New Year's, 1927, on the day before he was to return to Detroit. Because he was an adult, the disease hit him severely, and days and weeks went by. He never did return to Detroit. But, he said, he had been accepted by immigration, and could in time have become an American citizen.

The road not taken.

CHAPTER FOUR
ALICE RUNNALLS'S EARLY LIFE 1908–1926

"My Home and School Years"
Three or four years before she died, my mother wrote an account of "My Home and School Years." In it she tells what it was like to grow up on a Caradoc Township farm at the beginning of the twentieth century, to go to a rural school, to witness her parents' activities in the Presbyterian church. And she records stories about neighbours, about accidents and deaths, about the First World War and about migration to the West, things that occupied people's minds at the time.

She begins: "I have been trying to think what may have been my first recollections, and they may well be when Dad built the addition to our house. The early house had two bedrooms upstairs, one bedroom downstairs, a dining room, a small room off it, a dining-room-kitchen-pantry & hall. [Behind the house was a drive shed where machinery was stored; it was, my mother wrote, "where we had lots of fun playing ball."] The addition was built in 1911 as both Frank & Howard recall, so I would be three years old. The new addition added a parlour, stairs, two large bedrooms upstairs, and a large bedroom downstairs as well as enlarging the basement, and it was in half of the basement that potatoes were later stored. Somehow I faintly recall building this addition. I should say too that there was a large closet in the bedroom downstairs. This was a real delight to me—a real fantasy place. Aunt Agnes was always sending clothing—coats, dresses, & things which she was discarding. We would just receive a phone call from the CPR stationmaster to say there was a parcel there. It contained marvellous things with labels like Holt Renfrew and so the materials were of high quality. Mother was a good dressmaker, so she was able to use them to remake into clothes for 3 daughters. Unfortunately Aunt Agnes had a habit of trying to remake some of the clothes for herself. She did not quite make it and when these arrived they were impossible to put back together and remake, and not of much use. Back to the closet. Mother used to store these things there until she could make use of them. The closet was dark, & I used to place the mirror from Dad's shaving outfit on the windowsill, adjust it that there was a reflection of the sun on the closet wall, & lo & behold the closet was lit and I could explore and try on all these wonderful things (hats included)."

In the same year as the building of the addition, 1911, Alice's father travelled in June to Ottawa as a delegate to the General Assembly of the Presbyterian Church in Canada. Union with the Methodist and Congregational churches was already in the air, and this General Assembly discussed the form in which the question was to be put to their congregations. From Ottawa, Grandad Runnalls wrote postcards home to each of his children. They give glimpses of the Runnalls family life when my mother was three years old, and I reproduce the messages exactly as her father (who had a limited education) wrote them:

"Ottawa June 9 Dear Eva how are you getting along I suppose trying to pass hard as ever I am getting along al fine we have three sessions a day here morning at 10 afternoon 2:30 & evg at 8 so I get home about 11 so you see we are busy last night the time was taken up with preachers from foran missions for 2 hrs so there is ministers here from all over say even that Mr Patterson that stopped at our place from india was on yesterday & I was going to hunt him up today at 2 the government gave time tables to us for dy & S love Pa"

"June 9. Dear Ruth how are you getting along I am getting along fine I was awful tired last night we had a long day yesterday the church is always crowded & in the evening there is as many women as men & it is a jam but I ha alway get a seat so far but we have a lot to do & a lot to see & a lot to hear love PA."

"July [a mistake for June] 9/11 Dear Alice how are you I suppose al wright Pa is fine I am bording across the st- from the convent where there is a lot of little children & they have lots of fun yesterday there was about 100 boys about the size of Ruth & Eva & nuns come out & march down the st & a half a dozen teachers I suppose of for a [word illegible] there is a little girl here whose name is Alice & a baby girl about the size of yourself whose name is Ethel & we have lots of fun if it were not for her I would be lonesome X from Pa."

"Ottawa June 10th/11 Dear wife this is for you & Alice as I have no more cards this morning I am well & I hope you are the same & not working to hard say we are having a good time but it is lonesome I wish you was here there is a lot of ladies with there husbands I get awful tired sitting so long but the evengs are taken up so far by speakers from Missions Prayers & songs & speakers there was 6 speakers last night and they only had 10 mins a piece & it was fine D D Buchanan was one I was pleased to hear al was well & al right this is for you & Alice X Xxxxxxxxx."

[addressed to Howard] "My Dear boy how is your ma & all the wrest I am on my way to the church I am boarding with an undertaker [at 223 Rideau] a fine place I wish mama was here to this is a fine place the sights is so new to me & I hope you are all well as I am well love to all Jo R."

"Ottawa June 10 Dear Frank how are you getting along dont work to hard & tell your grandpa to do the same for when I come home we will soon catch up to the work only look after every thing in shape & it will be al right I cross a bridg close to this seene 6 times a day Frank this is nice I wish you could see it Pa."

"Ottawa June 11/11. Howard my dear Boy how are you getting along without your Pa are you getting lonesome I am lonesome to see you is you & Alice old chums as ever I suppose you look after the Horses & the cows & hens & Pigs & how is coly & the cats I suppose you help your ma & do lots of things for her & I suppose ethel is not back yet I got a letter from home & a letter from all but frank now Howard it is Franks turn next xxxxxxxx Pa."

"Dear Ruth my little Daughter I got your letter & it was all right & I will goe down to your aunties on the way home so if you dont get those things it will not be my fault I suppose you have lots to do to help your mother & look after the house when your mother is now looking after other things I passed near these falls yesterday a party of us went down to see Eddies match works we were invited & the assembly let us of so they are good to us when I come home I will tell you how a match is made & how paper is made & [word illegible] paper Pa xxxxxxxxx."

"dear Little Eva I got your letter al right & I could read it fine how are you getting along at school I suppose ahead of al the wrest thats uright & if you stay there when you grow up to be a woman you will be ahead of the women then to wont that be swell think of it now I dont know when I will to home for we are so busy it took al day at one question yesterday so bye bye from PA xxxxxxxxxxx."

My mother told me that the General Assembly in Ottawa was not the only one that Grandad Runnalls attended. In 1908, the Presbyterians had gathered in Knox Church, Winnipeg, and Grandad Runnalls was a delegate. He went west once again, at Christmas 1912, to Stettler, Alberta, where his sister Jemima and her husband John Thompson were living, and where John Grigg (who had married Aunt Bertie Thompson, Grammie Runnalls' half-sister) was also living. Grandad was away over Christmas, and sent a postcard (stamped December 26) to Howard: "Dear Howard how are you getting along busy as a bee tell ma to give you an extra slice of turkey for me & be good to little Alice does this look like her Bye my dear boy Your Pa."

My mother continued: "It was a real challenge being a mother then, and as Mother was a dressmaker she made all our clothes, including everyday shirts for Dad & the boys. As well, most of the dresses required starching and ironing, and heating irons on a wood stove in the summer time was something I am sure no one would endure to-day."

"So Mother had to have help, and the girl who helped was Ethel Snelgrove. I recall her face yet, and she must have been very good to me as for many years after she sent me cards. ... Later she married a Joe Mawson and lived in London on Maple Street." Alice's mother had help from her mother and sister as well as Ethel Snelgrove. "After Eva was born Ruth went to Grandma Thompson's to live. They were trying to help Mother and Aunt Edna took care of her so Ruth had a great affection for her. As soon as it was time to start school, Ruth came home."

"I am so glad that I lived on a farm. You are really in tune with nature and learn to appreciate so many things. In the spring we would go to the bush when wild flowers grew in profusion: jack-in-the-pulpit, adder tongues, trilliums, marsh marigolds, & blue and white and yellow violets. Every spring we explored the whole bush and knew where all these grew best. Then there were the birds: bluebirds, red-winged blackbirds, killdeer, robins, mourning doves, etc. We found the nests in trees and in meadows, and left them alone, waiting for the wee birds. However, at one time Howard had a very large collection of birds' eggs, one of several varieties."

"Then in summer we went barefoot, and playing in the ditch was the thing. There were horrible crayfish, wee tadpoles, and green frogs."

"Well in the summer & fall there were apples. I remember where every variety grew and all the trees we could climb. There were woodpecker nests in some of the older trees. We had all kinds of fruit trees—cherry, peach, pear, plum—as well as strawberries, raspberries & black caps. Dad had also planted grape vines & they yielded great quantities. Mother always made the communion wine for the church as well as canning them. There were all kinds of nuts to gather—hazel nuts in the bushes along the rail fences, beech nuts and butternuts in the bush and of course the chestnuts which we gathered in abundance." In the spring, Alice's father made maple syrup. "The arch was in the yard behind the house so Dad drew the sap in 2 large barrels from the bush on a stoneboat."

"I must tell of one incident. It was in 1914 the year the silo was built. The men worked all week. It was a cement silo & when they went home for the weekend they left an old Ford car, without a top, sitting there. Frank decided that he just had to drive that car. So on Sunday afternoon Dad & Mother had gone away & Frank got us kids in the car, started going first round and round the orchard and then on to the road for half a mile and turned & came back. Then he made us kids go into the orchard and cover up the tracks. But we had had a car ride."

"There was one thing that I recall in my pre-school years and that was the train rides I was privileged to have. Aunt Margaret (Mother's half-sister) spent many years in the McCormick Home in London. Mother used to take me on the train to London to see her. We always travelled CPR as the hours were good as well as the accommodation. My one regret when I started to school was that I would have no more train rides."

Neighbours and Cautionary Tales

"Across the road lived the Buchanans; Ila was Howard's age & Laura was younger than me. The four of us played together all the time. In the Buchanan family there were Nelson (Frank's age), Herman, and Mary (Ruth's age). They also had a little boy who died from eating green apples."

He was Edward (1903–5), and the story of this event must have had a considerable impact on my mother, for it was one of her cautionary tales for us when we were small.

Another was about a little girl who, in my mother's blunt wording, "burned to death." This little girl was a pupil in the school where Aunt Agnes (Thompson) taught, in south Caradoc. One day, while Aunt Agnes was home having lunch, the pupils raked leaves in the schoolyard and, even though Aunt Agnes had warned them about playing with matches, set fire to the pile. This girl had long blonde hair, which was down to her waist; her hair caught fire, and instead of standing still and smothering the flames, she ran, hair and flames streaming out in her panic-stricken flight: "they said it was like a torch behind her," according to my mother's vivid account. She was burned so badly that she died.

That had happened years earlier. Aunt Agnes taught in her home school, Cook's (S.S. No.5, Caradoc) for two years (1895–7), and this tragedy occurred on 22 April

1897. The little girl was Emily Trott, and she was eleven years old at the time of her death. The newspaper account differs from my mother's: "Yesterday at noon the school children were playing in the school yard and carrying dry leaves and dropping them on the fire, which they had made, and instantly the little girl's clothes became ignited, and before they could be extinguished were burned off to the waist; only the shoes were left on." A neighbour carried her into the schoolhouse; her father carried her home; a doctor attended her, "to no avail"; she died early the next morning. I have often wondered about Aunt Agnes's liability in this case. She left the section at the end of the school year and went to teach in Orangeville, where she met (and subsequently married) Norman Irvine.

My mother had more stories about the Buchanans, stories that shade into Ontario Gothic: "Mr. Buchanan died of TB, and I have heard Dad tell so many times of the hard trip to the cemetery. It was winter time and they had to take the body to Nairn cemetery by sleigh. I think of it every time I see the sign to Nairn on Hwy. 22. It was a very cold day and Dad took the team & sleigh & had to drive to the cemetery & back." The date was March 1909, and Alice's father was one of the pallbearers. A few months later—on 15 July 1909—Mr. Buchanan's son Hugh died at the age of thirty-seven and was also buried at Nairn. Again, Joseph Runnalls was one of the pall-bearers.

Mrs. Buchanan eventually remarried, her second husband being a man named Milt Colvin. "He had come up from the southern states & was a questionable character. He started up a tile yard using sand from a pit at the side of the house. He had a large building where the tile were made. We used to think it lots of fun inside it. … Milt later started a tile yard in the swamp in Lobo Twp. & he moved there and lived by himself. The soil was black and he grew vegetables. One year he planted poppy seeds along the ditch in front of his place for a half mile. These made a great show… Then he went back south & Mrs. Buchanan seemed to be afraid of him and always kept the doors locked in her fear of him returning."

The farm directly east of the Runnalls farm belonged to people by the name of Sullivan. "Jack Sullivan and two unmarried sisters lived there. I remember Ellen very well. She used to give us bouquets of lily-of-the-valley and other flowers. She gave me a fountain pen when I passed Entrance." One of the sisters, Mary, had died in March 1909, and my mother had stories about her death. Neigbours offered to sit up with the corpse during the night, for the Sullivans were Catholic, my mother explained, and candles had to be kept burning. The brother checked on them periodically during the night. Ellen's reaction to her sister's death was dramatic. "When Mary died, Ellen went into deep mourning. She pulled down the blinds and had everything darkened for five years. Then she changed and had Smallman & Ingram's decorate the whole house and she bought new furniture. They were supposed to be really well off." Ellen died in August 1931. "When Jack died he willed everything to the Catholic church in Strathroy. He also never married." He died in 1937, and was "the last remaining member of the family" (*Age* 11 March 1937). And while he "spent his entire life in Caradoc" where he "farmed successfully," said the paper in noting his death, each year, my mother said, the priest came out and told Mr. Sullivan what to plant in each field. What Grandad Runnalls thought of all this I do not know. He was (I am sorry to say) a member of the Orange Lodge in Mount Brydges, and I think he must have had some anti-Catholic feeling, for Uncle Howard thought he would have some fun with his father when he was courting Aunt Eleanor and about to bring her to Mount Brydges to meet his parents for the first time: he told his father that Eleanor McEwen was a Catholic.

Uncle Ed, Grandad Runnalls' youngest brother, eventually bought the Sullivan farm and lived there until he and his son Ralph moved to Warwick Township in 1947.

Alice in public school, S.S. No. 10 ("McEvoy's School") Caradoc (1914–21)

"I started to school after Easter in [1914]. I had not been strong hence late starting but I spent only 7 years in Public School. The custom was for children to start after Easter and it gave them 2 months to prepare for a full year, almost equal to kindergarten now. I do not think there would be much time for play in school as the teacher had all classes to prepare for final exams and I think every class from Grade 1 to Grade 8 had examinations to pass. I do not recall the name of my first teacher but some of the teachers at that time were Miss Patterson, Miss Marsh and Miss Verna Coulton. She may have been my first teacher as I recall her quite well. She was from London. Miss Marsh was from Arkona. There were 80 pupils at the time and some of the teachers did not have enough discipline to control so many. So it was decided that a second classroom should be built. But before this was done, I hope I am recalling this correctly, two teachers were hired, one for the lower grades, one the upper, and they taught in one room. My teacher then was Marjorie Slater from Strathroy and I recall that she was very very pretty. I recall having to stand and read at the front of the class one day but that seems to be all I remember. The older classes had History and Geography lessons and my attention must have been on their lessons. When Sir Wilfrid Laurier died in 1919 I can still see the large picture that appeared on the front page of the London paper and the write-up took up all the page. The lessons must have been quite impressive as I recall how the older students had to write essays on his life."

"When the second room was built I was in it—I am not sure for one or two years—and my teacher then was Ella Collins from Strathroy (now Mrs. Herbert Davidson). Every Friday night she walked home to Strathroy and back again on Monday morning. She was a real talker and used to take a quick breath and shrug her shoulders a lot. But she used to have a reward—I do not know what you had to do to get it but on Saturdays she took a pupil to London on the train. One Saturday I was the lucky one. Saturday morning in London she took an organ lesson and in the afternoon we went to a show. I can still recall the thrill of that day and it surely made her tops with me."

"Most of our seat work was done on slates. There were Readers, Spellers, and arithmetic books for each class. The arithmetic book carried on for more than one class and we were to have covered the work to a certain page in order to enter the next class. The Library had Golden Rule Books—books for each class and if you finished your work in advance you were allowed to read the Golden Rule book at your seat. The Book had poems as well as stories."

"There were blackboards across the front of the schoolroom as well as at the sides. The trustees must have had to supply a lot of chalk and brushes but the pupils had to buy slates and slate pencils, any text books and later on note books pencils and pens. Ink was also supplied and there was a little well on each desk with a lid on it. These had to be refilled and there was many and many a spill. There were no lights except some coal oil lamps on the side walls. On very dull days it was sometimes very difficult to see the blackboard. But what a wealth of maps there were—certainly one for each continent and extra for Canada."

Christmas

"I do not recall too many specific Christmases as such but the time of preparation was one of great excitement. My Dad had planted a row of spruce trees along the lane. These grew very rapidly and every year he cut the top off one for a Christmas tree so we were never without a tree. Usually the tree was cut ahead of time and left on the side porch until it was time to be put up in a small room off the dining room. One year there must have been a severe ice-storm as the tree had to be put in the basement by the furnace to melt off the ice."

"It was our task to decorate the tree. This we did using tinsel, red and green crepe paper and strings of popcorn. There were no lights on it but there was always a star at the top made of silver or gold paper. For several days we worked making chocolate fudge and caramel candy and popcorn balls. These were made by pouring a syrup over the popcorn and with buttered hands very quickly forming the popcorn into balls."

"As for Christmas day itself for our meal we always had goose. I do not recall any turkey at the time. Mother had made a beet pickle which I especially liked and there were of course potatoes and gravy, vegetables and plum pudding."

"At one period there had come to our church as minister a Mr. Robertson. He and his wife had come from Scotland so had no close relatives here. They were very dignified and well-liked and I think there were at least 2 Christmas days Mother had invited them to our place. I do not know where they went after leaving Mt. Brydges but I shall always remember them because they brought me a most precious book of stories which I still have called *Cassell's Children's Annual*. The one story was about a little girl called Marjorie which was my inspiration for our name for Marjorie. The second book was the story of *Alice in Wonderland*. The Robertsons had 2 children—a girl Jean who became a nurse and later married a doctor, I believe, in Detroit. The boy enlisted in the First World War and later died from the effects of the poisonous gas which had been used in battle." (The Reverend Duncan Robertson was minister of St. Andrew's from 1913 to 1917. In 1913 St. Andrew's and North Caradoc had joined to form one pastoral charge, and Robertson was its first minister.)

"I remember getting up very early Christmas morning to see what Santa had left which was usually an orange, crayons, pencil, ruler etc. The coal-oil lamp on the kitchen table had to light the room at those early hours and I still recall how dark the morning seemed."

"I was six years old when Frank started to University in Toronto. He graduated the year that I finished Public School. So we always looked forward to him being home for Christmas. One year be brought me a silver watch. He had found it on the street in Toronto and advertised it in the paper but no one claimed it. He took it to a Jeweler who valued it at $20."

"Christmas seemed to be a time for concerts. I do not recall a concert at Public School because I think the teacher had plenty of work without. Miss Coulton, who was an excellent teacher, had 8 grades and 80 pupils. But there was the concert which the Sunday School put on and it was held in the town hall in Mt. Brydges on New Year's. This meant practising every day of holidays at the church. There was a large stage at the hall and as I recall there was a stairway up at the back which led to the dressing room. It was crowded and we dressed for our numbers there. Looking back I think what a fire trap it could have been. The concert consisted of recitations, choruses, dialogues, drills—I remember a star drill, wand drill, soldier drill, flag drill etc. and the final number was always a cantata. This was put on by the senior girls. They wore long white dresses made of cheese cloth and trimmed with tinsel. They also wore tinsel in their hair. A soloist at the back sang a carol. I particularly remember 'Hark the Herald Angels sing' and the girls did motions appropriate to the words. The lights were dimmed and there were just the footlights on the stage. It all made a very effective ending for the concert. There was a large decorated tree on the stage and gifts were distributed—mostly books. I remember receiving books by Mrs. Meade which I read and re-read, also Bible Story Books."

"At this time Frank attended High School in Strathroy as it was the only one close. He drove every day, horse & buggy in the spring & fall & the cutter in the winter. Billy Wilson went with him for five years. I used to wait for him to come home to see if he had left anything in his lunch pail." For Alice's oldest brother had decided to train for the Presbyterian ministry, and so had Billy Wilson, who was five years older than Frank and was his Sunday School teacher at St. Andrew's. The two of them commuted to the collegiate in Strathroy, first to the old school for four years, and then to the new building on the hill above the Sydenham River: it was built in 1913–14 and opened to its first pupils in January 1914.

"This was the period of the war years and the mothers baked cake and cookies and knit warm socks which they packed in boxes and sent to the boys overseas for Christmas. They had to be packed very carefully to carry well."

The War Years (1914–18), Roy Runnalls, and Billy Wilson

One of my mother's many first cousins was killed in the First World War. He was Roy Runnalls, the son of Grandad Runnalls' oldest brother, Uncle Richard. He had been born in August 1897, when the family was still living in Dawn Township, and his mother had died when he was only a year old. Roy's father moved to Caradoc, married again, and had a second family.

On 7 February 1916 Roy, who was then five months beyond his eighteenth birthday, went into Strathroy and enlisted in the Canadian Over-Seas Expeditionary Force. His attestation paper provides details of his physical condition: he was five feet eight inches tall, with blue eyes and brown hair, and a complexion described as "dark." He weighed 145 pounds, and both his "physical development" and "habits" were judged to be "good."

My mother, who was only nine years old when Roy was killed, knew very little about his wartime experiences, but various sources—a regimental history, Roy's file with Library and Archives Canada, and the war diaries for Roy's unit (the 15th Infantry Battalion with the 48th Highlanders)—make it possible to construct a narrative about him.

Roy embarked from Halifax on 22 August 1916 and landed in Liverpool eight days later. In southern England, he was stationed at two of the three camps set up by the Canadian Army—Witley and Bramshott—until early December, when he was "taken on strength" with his unit in northeastern France. There his first instructions were in the use of gas helmets; his first duties—a route march and an inspection parade—were cancelled because of wet weather. It was not until after Christmas that Roy first moved "up the line"; that is, forward to the Front, where they relieved another battalion. Such was the pattern of troop movements: to the Front until relieved, away from the Front until ordered forward again. Roy's first months at the Front—January and February 1917—

were generally uneventful: "Casualties were light, days quiet and nights comparatively peaceful" (Beattie 201). The usual retreat away from the Front was at Bully-Grenay, and it became so familiar that it had the feeling of a refuge. Horace Partridge, a 48th Highlander who survived the war, wrote these verses which were published years later in the Strathroy paper:

> Though I've taken a tour through the trenches of France
> And a musketry course on the Marne,
> Though I've been there and back with a ninety-pound pack
> And snored with the pigs in a barn—
>
> Though I've eaten in chateaux and shaved in a church,
> Though I'm blessed by a priest every day,
> I shall never be right till I get back tonight
> To my billet in Bully Grenay.
>
> For the straw in the barn is as soft as a bed
> (It must be nigh twenty feet deep)
> And the rats on the shelves keep to themselves
> And allow a poor soldier to sleep.
>
> Stout Madame Yvonne fries bacon tres bon
> While I'm sipping her cafe au lait—
> And I'll never be right till I get back tonight
> To my billet in Bully Grenay.
>
> Oh! I know every cottage in Bully Grenay
> And I know ev'ry shell hole by sight.
> Just over the way there an old staminet
> There'll be drinks round in Bully tonight!
>
> So hurry up train, get a move on again
> And drive! Don't doss on the way!
> There are cups to be filled and a calf to be killed
> In my billet in Bully Grenay.

Two words require explanation. One is "staminet"—"estaminet," that is—which was a small café, bar, or bistro, especially a shabby one; the word apparently comes from "staminet," manger. The other word needing explanation is "doss": slang for sleeping, or passing the time aimlessly.

In mid-March 1917 the battalion moved to a new sector, facing Vimy Ridge, amid rumors of "The Big Push" and with growing evidence of preparations for it. Early in the morning of Easter Monday, April 9, in darkness and in "a thin, cold, driving rain" with traces of snow (Berton 217), the Canadian attack on Vimy Ridge began. Roy's regiment was part of the 1st Canadian Division, which was assigned to the southernmost part of the ridge. The commander was Arthur Currie, whose childhood home was just west of Strathroy. Currie had planned the attack meticulously, and his preparations brought him success where others had failed. For the victory he was knighted by the king; Roy survived the battle, unscathed; and "Vimy Ridge" became a defining name in Canada's sense of itself as a nation.

A month later, Roy wrote home to his parents about (in his words) "that scrap on Easter Monday": "No doubt you have been thinking or rather wondering about me this past month as I haven't been able to write except drop a whiz-bang through from which you were able to understand I was still alive and well and came through that scrap on Easter Monday, April 9th. This leaves me feeling fine, except my poor stomach and it's a wonder it held as much as it did yesterday. You see our parcels came night before and believe me, they were a blessing after such hard times. Haven't seen Leonard for a few days and am going to hunt him up. Sorry to say Charlie was killed the morning of the advance with machine gun fire. The last I saw of him was when we were standing together in our front line just before the fray started. I miss him terribly as we were like brothers ever since we left the dear old shores of Canada and made up our minds to stick together as long as possible, which we sure did. Tell Moses Mitchell I have his ring which he left with a corporal and said to send it to him, should anything happen, so I am waiting for a chance to send it. Received both of your boxes and enjoyed the contents very, very much and must say [words illegible] Oh, that marmalade! It's too good to eat! Of course you know we can eat anything nowadays whether poor or good. Hope you send another box later on. April VIth—and here I am again. I ate so much it made me sick, after having hardly anything and then "filling" ourselves so full of sweets and cake. We are all complaining of the same trouble, but you can bet a working party will use it all. Leonard is well. Was talking to him yesterday. Did I tell you I met Wes Leitch a few days ago? He is cook for the sergeants of the A.M.C. One night we went to see him and he gave us a lot of good stuff to eat. I intend to send a few souvenirs to you, along with Charlie's ring, which you kindly give to Mr. Mitchell." "Drop a whizbang through" needs some explanation. It was soldier slang for sending a postcard printed with standard sentences, and the sender simply ticked off those that applied to him, such as "I am quite well" or "I hope to be home soon." The actual whiz-bang was a small high-velocity shell that made a whizzing sound in the air and a bang when it hit.

By mid-July preparations were under way for the next major offensive: the taking of Hill 70. Currie directed the whole operation, and it was successful. Afterwards, on August 27, the Commander-in-Chief, Field Marshall Sir Douglas Haig, inspected the battalion, "never … looking better" in spite of the pouring rain. After a brief break at the beginning of September, the battalion was moved to Cité St. Pierre, where conditions were as difficult as any they had so far encountered. There was constant shell fire, and constant use of mustard gas. By the end of the month, the sound of trench mortar-fire was getting on the men's nerves, and they were exhausted, the unrelenting shelling making sleep impossible.

Such was the situation when Roy was wounded. It happened on Friday, 21 September. His file indicates only that he suffered a "Shell Wound, Head, Legs & Ankle," and that he was evacuated to "6CCS"—No. 6 Casualty Clearing Station—which at that time was located at Bruay-la-Bussière (Nord-Pas-de-Calais). A "casualty clearing station," as the name indicates, was designed to provide initial assessment and treatment of wounds but became in practice a field hospital. Roy was assessed as "dangerously wounded"; there is a rubber-stamped notation which reads "Wounded to hospital" dated 29 September, and then, on 30 September 1917, at "6CCS," "died of wounds suffered in action." Roy was buried in the Barlin Communal Cemetery Extension, Pas de Calais, France, his grave now marked by the standard stone with a maple leaf above and a cross below. He was just twenty years old.

In its issue of 11 October 1917 the Strathroy *Age* reported Roy's death in the language of the day: "Another native Caradoc boy has laid his life on the altar of sacrifice for his country's safety and honour. Mr. and Mrs. Richard Runnalls, of this township, received sad news a few days ago .... The deceased soldier was born and raised to young man in this township and the announcement of his death has cast a gloom among the legion of friends and relatives around his old home." A memorial service, described by the paper as "impressive," was held in the Mount Carmel Methodist Church on Sunday, 14 October. "Glowing tribute was paid the deceased soldier for his courage and prowess by the pastor, Rev. Mr. Reycraft, who preached an appropriate sermon from the words: 'One shall be taken, and one left.' The church was filled to its capacity and there were suitable decorations for the sad occasion."

How is Roy remembered? His name appears in the Book of Remembrance in the Memorial Chamber in the Peace Tower in Ottawa; and his name is on both the cenotaph in Mount Brydges and the memorial plaque in the Middlesex Tower at Western University. It also appears in one other spot. Not at the gravesite of his father, who died in 1931, or of his stepmother, who died in 1944, both of them buried in Mount Brydges Cemetery, but on the gravestone of his mother in Shetland Cemetery. The inscription reads: "RUNNALLS / Margaret Jane Swedden 1865—1898 / Beloved Wife of / Richard T. Runnalls / Private Roy Runnalls / 1897—1917 / Died in France." The local legion has placed an aluminum maple leaf at the foot of the stone.

Another war death that affected the Runnalls family deeply was that of Billy Wilson. Billy's father was the mail carrier in Mount Brydges, and the Wilsons were members of St. Andrew's Church. In those days, saying that "they go to our church" meant that families felt a close connection with one another, and the Runnalls-Wilson connection was even closer, in the friendship of their two oldest sons, Billy Wilson and Frank Runnalls. Billy was five years older than Frank and, according to the Strathroy paper, "an enthusiastic worker among the young people" of the church: "he had been my Sunday School teacher," Uncle Frank writes, "and I was greatly attached to him." As I have already said, both had made up their minds to train for the Presbyterian ministry. For five years they drove together to the collegiate in Strathroy, and in the fall of 1914 they went together to Toronto and Knox College, the Presbyterian theological school. In March 1915, before completing his first year, Billy enlisted in the Canadian Over-Seas Expeditionary Force. St. Andrew's held a farewell gathering for him, and though my mother was only six years old at the time, she remembered Billy saying, "Well, goodbye Mrs. Runnalls—and goodbye, Alice." For my mother, as the youngest in the family (and thirteen years younger than Uncle Frank), had been the pet of her oldest brother and his best friend. Letters and postcards were often addressed to her though really intended for her parents; and she kept the Christmas card that Billy sent from England. By that time—Christmas 1915—he was at a training camp at Westenhanger in Kent. The Christmas card was followed by a postcard to my grandfather: "Westenhanger Jan 12/16, Hello Mr. Runnalls,— I have been intending to write you people a letter ever since I came here but have failed to do so so I am writing this card instead. Hope this finds you all well as it leaves me. Am getting along fine—hope to be soon on the firing line. Remember me to Mrs. Runnalls and children. W. T. Wilson." Four days after Billy sent that postcard, he embarked for France. His wish to be "on the firing line" would soon be realized.

The Battle of the Somme, that long-drawn-out offensive in which neither side gained much ground and where the cost was many casualties, filled the summer and fall of 1916. During that time, Billy was writing regular letters home, and they were occasionally reported in the Strathroy paper. For instance, on 10 August 1916 the *Age* noted that "In a letter received last week from Corp. Wm. Wilson, now in Belgium, son of Mr. and Mrs. R. Wilson, the former expressed the belief that he would spend Christmas at his home here. Corp. Wilson is with the artillery, and he voices his discontent that he sees so little of the enemy and actual trench fighting."

In February 1917 Billy was sent to England for officer training, and when he returned to France in August of that year, it was as a lieutenant in the Canadian Field Artillery. At Passchendaele his wish to be involved in "actual ... fighting" was realized as he witnessed the "intense shell fire & awful mud" (War Diaries). Then comes the War Diaries' sad entry for 1 November 1917: "Lieut. W.T. Wilson ... was killed this morning. This officer had just returned from England, where he had undergone a cadet course and received his commission." His battery had been answering an S.O.S. call.

Billy Wilson was buried in the New Military Cemetery at Vlamertinghe, Belgium, a village about five kilometers west of Ypres. The Strathroy paper, in reporting his death, added a sad detail: "His mother received a letter from him last Saturday telling her all was well."

And what about Frank Runnalls? Uncle Frank writes in his memoirs that "by 1915 World War I was claiming more and more men for military service." He does not say anything about being "claimed" himself, but my mother told me that Uncle Frank was rejected for military service because he had flat feet, and in those days when long marches were routine, flat feet made a recruit unfit. The news came as a great relief to my grandparents. When Uncle Frank's letter arrived, my grandmother and mother went out to the barn at once, to tell my grandfather: "It was a serious thing," my mother said when she told that story. When conscription was introduced in 1917, Uncle Frank was called up, only to be rejected again, this time because the army doctor found that he had a slight curvature of the spine.

The churches were heavily involved in the war effort, both materially and psychologically. By June 1916 fifteen members of St. Andrew's were on active service—"a splendid record indeed," in the words of the Strathroy paper (22 June 1916), and one that encouraged enlisting. In November of that year, the ladies of St. Andrew's met in the basement of the church and packed fourteen boxes of Christmas gifts to send to the "boys" overseas. The packing of boxes continued throughout the war years. What was sent? Many items of clothing—socks, scarves, "trench caps," "pyjama suits," and flannel shirts; feather pillows; "trench-lights"—and candies and cakes.

On 22 November 1916 there was a "grand patriotic entertainment in aid of the Red Cross" in the town hall in Mount Brydges. It was under the auspices of the Ladies' Aid Society of St. Andrew's, in which my grandmother was an active member, and it was announced as a special event: "The occasion will be unique in view of the presence of several returned soldiers (who have been wounded in action ...Come out and ... hear our boys who have returned with honorable wounds from the firing line" (*Age* 16 November 1916). The concert, the paper reported two weeks later, "was a decided success," and raised fifty-two dollars for the Red Cross. "About 35 soldiers came out [from London] in autos and proceeded to St. Andrew's Presbyterian Church, where they were treated to a hot fowl supper with all the other delicacies which go to make up a good meal. After supper they thanked and cheered the ladies"—and then drove them to the town hall in their autos, a gesture that was "much appreciated" at a time when the horse-and-buggy was still the usual means of getting around. (My grandparents did not own a car until 1920, when Grandad bought a Model T Ford.)

Caradoc Township was among the earliest of all municipalities to set up a war memorial. Early in 1919 council initiated planning for it, and it was dedicated on 16 June 1920. Like many such memorials in Canadian villages and towns, it had a soldier carved in stone standing on top of a square granite shaft. The unveiling of the memorial was a public holiday; three thousand people were present; and hundreds of school children, led by a band, marched to the park adjacent to the town hall, placed wreaths on the monument, and sang "The Maple Leaf Forever." My mother was likely one of those school children. The *Age*, ignoring the lyrics which celebrate British supremacy in this country, labelled "The Maple Leaf" "Canada's National Anthem." It was still being sung in the 1940s when I was in public school.

St. Andrew's Presbyterian Church: Socials, suppers, and garden parties

The centre of my grandparents' religious and social life was St. Andrew's Presbyterian Church. Grandad Runnalls had served continuously as elder and clerk of session from 1902 on, and he was the choir leader. Grammie Runnalls was a worker in the Ladies' Aid and the Women's Missionary Society. Some of their activities, such as the annual picnic in Springbank Park in London, were purely social, but most were to raise money for the church. The chief fundraisers were "socials," garden parties, and church suppers.

In the spring of 1916, for instance, the Ladies' Aid held, in the basement of the church, a "pie social," which included "entertainment" as well: "games of all kinds, and an interesting contest." Admission was ten cents for children, fifteen for adults. That summer the church held "a grand garden party" on its grounds, which were lit for the occasion with electric lights. The "talent engaged for the evening" included a "comic vocalist," an elocutionist, the Strathroy Male Quartette, and the Kerwood Brass Band. Garden parties always had a chairman, usually a prominent local figure, and the chairman for this event was Duncan Ross, M.P., Strathroy lawyer and son of former Ontario premier George Ross. The accompanist for the evening was Edna Ramsay, the church organist and my mother's first music teacher.

The garden party at St. Andrew's was one of the smaller ones in Caradoc Township. The big ones were at Cook's and at North Caradoc. The 1916 event at Cook's was announced as a "mammoth electric light garden party" with "monster ice cream and lemonade booths," while the North Caradoc event was advertised as "a colossal moonlight entertainment and promenade concert." My mother remembered the huge crowds—in the thousands, she said. Special trains ran out from London, and the 1917 attendance at North Caradoc, when "the evening was ideal, and the roads … in good condition," set a record, about 1500 people. Cook's was even bigger. The announcement for the 1919 garden party boasted of "ample accommodation for twelve thousand people," with an added attraction: "automobiles and aeroplanes parked free of charge, at owner's risk" (*Age* 24 July 1919).

St. Andrew's sponsored various kinds of "socials," among them the "box social" and the "tea meeting," which was by this time considered old-fashioned, and was presented for its nostalgic value: "There will be songs your mother used to sing; tunes your father used to play; recitations of long ago. Come and let us take you back to childhood days" (*Age* 6 March 1919). But St. Andrew's was inventive in the kinds of "socials" it put on. In the spring of 1918 and again in 1919, for instance, the Ladies' Aid held a "poverty social," and it was an occasion to dress down: "Come in rags, come in tags, but not in velvet gowns, or you will be fined. Every woman must wear a poverty dress and apron. ... No gentleman with a boiled shirt or white collar will be allowed to come unless he pays a fine of 5 cents." Almost any occasion was an excuse for a "social": St. Andrew's had a St. Patrick social (which featured Irish stew), a Hallowe'en social, and, in June, a "lawn social."

Church suppers were another common fund-raising activity, and St. Andrew's regularly held "fowl suppers" and "oyster suppers," both of which must have meant a lot of work for my grandmother. The oysters were cooked in milk, and on one occasion Grammie discovered, just in time, that a container of milk that someone had brought was sour. Oyster suppers were always in February; fowl suppers went along with "anniversary." That word had a special weight of meaning for every church in Souwesto, for "anniversary" marked the date of the congregation's first service, which at St. Andrew's was in late September or early October. On Sunday, "anniversary" would be two services, with guest ministers and special music; on Monday, there would be "a grand fowl supper and entertainment." In 1917 the "entertainment" consisted of speeches by ministers and returned soldiers, musical numbers, and "recitations." On that occasion, the church raised fifty-one dollars.

The Women's Missionary Society

Though my grandmother seems to have been mainly a biblical Martha, devoting her energies and organizing skills to the Ladies' Aid, she was a biblical Mary in her involvement in the Women's Missionary Society (see Luke 10: 38–42). The attraction of the Ladies' Aid is easy to understand: it raised funds for the church through suppers, "socials," and entertainments of various sorts. The appeal of the Women's Missionary Society is more complex, and while I know nothing of Grammie Runnalls' attitudes, I do know that the missionary movement had a profound effect on my mother's thinking: it shaped her concepts of the religious and heroic life.

The Presbyterian Church sponsored more overseas missions than any other Canadian Protestant denomination (Brouwer 5–6), and the missionary movement was at its height when my mother was a girl. Home support for foreign missions was the special responsibility of the Women's Missionary Societies because, in the sexist attitude of the day, "matters of religious and moral responsibility" were considered to be "ones for which women had a special affinity" (Brouwer 4–5). Missions had the authority of Christ himself ("Go ye into all the world, and preach the gospel to every creature" Mark 16: 15); that injunction fused with an imperialist impulse; and both mixed with the romance of foreign lands and the appeal of a heroic life that one could live there, actually for missionaries, vicariously for those at home.

The St. Andrew's Women's Missionary Society was organized in June 1915 (*Age* 19 June 1941). Grammie Runnalls was its first vice-president, and then president. In June 1941 the auxiliary celebrated its twenty-sixth year with a luncheon and tea, which was "poured at a long table centred with the lovely birthday cake," cut by "the only one of the first executive present" (*Age* 19 June 1941). Grammie Runnalls, by that time seventy-three years old, and in spite of her long years of faithful work, was not there.

I have some sense of how hard my grandmother worked as a farm wife and mother of five, and how circumscribed her life was. The missionary society must have given her a sense of a wider world and of her ability to claim a place, however modest, in it. At the January 1924 meeting of the W.M.S., for instance, "Mrs. Runnalls read a letter from Miss Stuart, of India, giving an account of a wedding she attended" (*Age* 17 January 1924). In August 1925, when Grammie hosted a meeting, the speaker was a woman from Chicago who told "of the difficulties in church work in the large cities, where there is so much attraction to places of amusement" (*Age* 27 August 1925). The August 1926 meeting was typical of W.M.S. gatherings: it was "held at the home of Mrs. J. Runnalls, with a large attendance of members and visitors, the president, Mrs. Brown, presiding. The Scripture lesson was read by Miss A. Courtis. Miss Campbell led in prayer. Mrs. Frank gave a very able paper on 'Time, Talents and Money—How we ought to use them for the Master's work.' Miss Honor Robinson [my mother's first cousin] gave an instrumental selection, which was much appreciated. Mrs. T. Colvin gave a reading, 'How we can help the missionaries in our suitable selection of articles to send in the bales.' Roll call was answered by verses of Scripture having the word 'prayer.' Mrs. A. Toles sang 'Face to Face' in her usual excellent style. … At the close of the meeting, refreshments were served by the lunch committee and a social time spent" (*Age* 19 August 1926). Grammie hosted the meeting again in August 1927, when there was "an attendance of over fifty members and visitors." On that occasion, "Miss Eva Runnalls [my mother's sister] rendered a beautiful solo, 'One Sweetly Solemn Thought.'" "After the meeting, everyone adjourned to the lawn, where tables were set for a ten-cent tea, the proceeds of which amounted to over five dollars" (*Age* 18 August 1927). It was in the Ladies' Aid, however, that Grammie Runnalls showed her leadership abilities: she became president in 1927, and "took the chair" for the planning of "socials," suppers, bake sales, and anniversaries.

The Presbyterians' "most celebrated missionary" (Brouwer 23) was George Leslie Mackay. He was from nearby Oxford County, and he had a long (and controversial) career in distant Formosa (as the name was then). He was the subject of a paper my mother gave in 1934. For my mother's reading—then, and when I was growing up—was often the lives of missionaries and ministers. I can remember books at home on David Livingstone and Robert Moffatt, among others. They embodied her idea of the heroic life.

Church union and the "continuing Presbyterians"
When Grandad Runnalls attended the Presbyterian Church's General Assembly at Knox Church in Ottawa in 1911, church union was the major topic of discussion. The Assembly considered, among other matters, "the form in which the mind of the people is to be learned on the great question of organic union with the Methodist and Congregational churches." They decided on a ballot with three questions (*Guide* 23 June 1911). The issue had been on the church's agenda for some time—since 1904, in fact, when official discussions had got under way among the three denominations. Five years after Ottawa, the General Assembly of 1916 voted to merge with the Methodists and Congregationalists. The aim was admirable: to create a national Protestant church, "part of a Christian commonwealth in which the church was the conscience of the country,

its evangelizer and moral exemplar" (Cahill). The leadership of the church was, for the most part, in favour of union, and those leaders were a powerful influence at the annual General Assemblies, but almost from the beginning of the movement there was opposition to it. The opposition was a "conservative lay movement" and "most of its members [were] located in Ontario" (Clifford 3). In his 1985 book Keith Clifford gives a full account of "the resistance to church union in Canada" (his title) in the years between 1904 and 1939. In Mount Brydges the matter came to a head late in 1920.

"Mt. Brydges is Divided on Union," said the headline in the Strathroy paper (2 December 1920); "Presbyterian Congregations Will Have None of it—Methodists Favor It." The story continues: "The congregation of St. Andrew's Presbyterian Church, Mt. Brydges, on Sunday evening rejected the proposal for co-operative union with the Methodists in the district. Rev. J. D. Byrnes delivered an address explaining the plan, after which the following motion was introduced: 'While we believe that co-operation may be useful in some localities, we feel that we know our church and people better than any outsider can, and believing that any move in that direction would not be for the best interest of Christianity in this community, we as St. Andrew's people positively and absolutely refuse to have anything to do with it or take any steps in that direction.' A standing vote of the congregation resulted in 57 in favor of the motion and four against." My grandparents voted with the majority. The tone of the main clause of the motion indicates the depth of feeling on the issue.

The *Age* continued with the story: "A similar meeting was held at North Caradoc Presbyterian Church on Friday evening. ... A vote taken at the close of the meeting was unanimous in opposition to the proposed co-operative union. / Notwithstanding this action, the Methodist congregation in Mt. Brydges Tuesday night voted unanimously in favor of co-operative union, and it was even agreed to give up the morning service in favor of the Presbyterian if desired."

Uncle Frank had graduated from Knox College in 1921 and was ordained in the Presbyterian Church, where he favoured union, perhaps under the influence of Knox's principal at the time, Alfred Gandier, one of the leaders of the movement. He began his ministry in British Columbia, and his second church there, in Grand Forks, called itself "united" because it "had just formed a local union church in anticipation of the official and formal union that would establish the United Church of Canada in 1925" (*Memoirs* 92). In spite of that earlier vote, the Grand Forks congregation did break into opposing factions, and that kind of break affected families as well. "At the time of church union in Canada in 1925," Uncle Frank writes, "I chose to enter the United Church but my parents and family chose to remain Presbyterian. This controversy divided many families, but it did not divide ours. The attitude of my parents toward me never changed and for this I have been forever grateful" (*Memoirs* 23). So my grandparents were "continuing Presbyterians," but among my mother's brothers and sisters, only Uncle Howard stayed with the church he had grown up in: he and Aunt Eleanor were lifelong Presbyterians.

Many years later, I heard a sermon on the subject of church union preached in Knox College chapel. The minister's text was "Keep your hearts together but your tents separate." I assumed at the time that that text was biblical and had therefore a certain authority. It wasn't and it didn't, but it could have been the motto of the "continuing Presbyterians."

The Orangemen of Mount Brydges

Grandad Runnalls was, as I have already said, a member of the Orange Lodge in Mount Brydges. It was L.O.L. No. 1186, and while it occasionally opposed legislation which seemed to favour Catholics, its usual activities were more social in nature. There was an annual church service and, of course, the celebration of the "Glorious Twelfth," which in 1916 took the form of a picnic in Kidd's grove. But in Strathroy the Twelfth was a notable event: in 1919 over six thousand people watched the parade of "brethren of the great order, with their scarfs and sashes, fife and drum bands playing, and banners waving." "Three beautiful white horses carried the marshalls of the assembled lodges." The spectacle was a brilliant one, white, orange and royal blue being the dominant colours (*Age*). The membership of the Mount Brydges lodge was about one hundred, but there is no evidence that Grandad Runnalls ever held office in the Lodge. I still have his ribbons, with their brass clasps and bright colours, which he must have worn on ceremonial occasions.

Caradoc Township potatoes

Caradoc Township was known for its potatoes. The soil—"a deep rich sand loam, with a clay subsoil" (*Age* 15 February 1917)—was especially suited to the tubers, and in a good year—as 1918 was—an acre could yield up to 320 bushels (*Watford Guide-Advocate* 29 November 1918). Each year Grandad Runnalls grew potatoes, stored them in the basement of the house, and sold them by the bag in the Covent Garden Market in London. The Paul Peel painting of 1883, now in Museum London, shows what Covent Garden looked like at the time: a market square, dating from 1845, and a brick market building erected in 1853. Grandad Runnalls travelled the fifteen miles to London with a wagon and a team of horses. According to Uncle Frank, Grandad asked fifty cents for a one-hundred-pound-bag of potatoes (20). The price included delivery, so after he had sold all the bags, he still had to take them to purchasers around the city before he could head home.

Alice at the Mount Brydges Continuation School (1921–5)

There was no high school in Caradoc Township, and any pupil who wanted a secondary school education had to commute to Strathroy, like Frank Runnalls and Billy Wilson. But in 1917 several school sections united to establish a continuation school in Mount Brydges—it offered four years of high school—and in the summer of 1919 they bought a property on the main street to be remodelled into a school building. It was an old hotel, known both as the "American Hotel" and the "Commercial Hotel," and by December 1919 it was ready. It had two classrooms, a laboratory, a library, and cloakrooms. A purchase of an additional three acres made room for a schoolyard, and for a shed for horses and buggies. The building, closed as a school in 1954, still stands, remodelled once again into apartments.

My mother passed her entrance examinations in June 1921, and started at the continuation school that fall. She was a good pupil. I still have her reports, issued from the Department of Education in Toronto; and I have her grades as published in the Strathroy *Age*. (Province-wide examinations and publication of student grades in the local newspaper are practices long since abandoned.) In the first two months of the fall of 1921, for instance, she earned 82 per cent (when honours was 75), and she was competing for top marks with her cousins Lenna (Uncle Ed Runnalls's daughter) and Neil

(Uncle John Runnalls's son). She wrote only three papers in the Lower School Examinations in June 1922—Geography, Canadian History, Botany—and a letter from one of her teachers, Georgia Davidson, perhaps explains why: "Dear Alice, I am pleased to enclose your certificate which will show that you passed in everything, which was very good considering how much school you missed." For she was "never that strong," as she used to say, and her health was never robust—the lingering effects, I think, of her premature birth. Still, she entered into the work and activities of the school with surprising energy and enthusiasm.

The curriculum at the school ranged widely: Literature, British History, Ancient History, Canadian History, Latin, French, Geometry, Physics, Chemistry, Algebra, Agriculture and Horticulture. Though Alice's grades were not always firsts and varied from year to year, she earned a final average of 79 in Form III in June 1924, and at the end of her final year she earned firsts in French and Latin, and seconds in her other papers.

The chief school activities in which Alice participated were debates, public speaking, and basketball.

Alice was an enthusiastic member of the school's basketball team. She once told me that she had ruined her singing voice by cheering too much and too loudly at games. The team's most successful season was in 1923–4, when the girls won the district trophy in competition against the Delaware, Melbourne and Lambeth schools. The Strathroy paper named the members of the team: in addition to Alice, they were Shirley Wyatt, Mabel Wilton, Maryn Miles, Helen Wilton, Mary Campbell, Marie Gough, and Katie Veale (*Age* 24 January 1924). Those girls were Alice's friends, as were Wynne Kincaid, Helen McEvoy, Dorothy Wyatt, and Bernice Wilcox—all of whom, I assume, are in the many pictures in my mother's photograph albums. To the frustration of the family historian, none of the pictures is dated, and no girl is identified. Only a photograph of the championship team in the Strathroy paper (24 January 1924) matches names and faces.

In addition to athletic competitions, there were "oratorical contests." Their value, as defined by the Strathroy paper, was the development of the ability to "stand up, without notes, and without hesitation discourse fluently and well on a given subject for a period of fifteen minutes" (*Age* 7 February 1924). Speakers prepared a paper on a subject of their own choosing, but there was some debate about how best to develop the ability to "discourse fluently and well" since (I think) speakers often memorized their papers word for word, and that did not encourage thinking on one's feet, as the debate did. But Alice was a good speaker, and she was a debater as well. In an "oratorical contest" held in the Community Hall in Mount Brydges at the begining of January 1924, "The first honours of the girls' contest were won by Alice Runnalls, who spoke on the subject of 'Peace' in a most pleasing manner" (*Age* 3 January 1924). Her subject, my mother told me years later, indicated just now much people in the 1920s wanted no more wars. In the previous spring, Alice had been one half of a debating team in an event held under the auspices of the Caradoc Literary Society. The resolution was "that the girls of today will be of more benefit to Canada than the boys of today." Alice and her partner Jean McGregor upheld the affirmative, but "the judges after a lengthy consideration decided in favor of the negative" (*Age* 3 May 1923).

The interest in literary societies and in debating had first developed in the previous century, and those societies were a large part of Ontario culture at the time. Their initial purpose was "improvement"—"the quest for self- and mutual improvement, through literature," in Heather Murray's words (xi)—and the spoken word was at the centre of all their activities. The Caradoc Literary Society was a late development of the movement. It first met in the fall of 1922; its first meeting was held "to organize a literary or debating society and develop a wholesome community spirit"; its first program consisted of "a debate, music and literary numbers" (*Age* 2 November 1922).

During Alice's fourth and final year at the continuation school (1924–5), public speaking continued to be one of her principal activities, but her name does not appear in any of the reports on oratorical contests which appeared regularly in the Strathroy paper. Nonetheless, she must have been successful in at least one competition, a volume of the complete works of Shakespeare being the evidence. It is a handsome volume from Oxford University Press, with tooled leather binding and gold lettering, and it is inscribed "Awarded to Miss Alice M. Runnalls by the Caradoc Literary Society for Oratory / April 1925."

Georgia Davidson had taught in the continuation school for seven and one-half years, and was principal when she resigned at the end of Alice's last year—June 1925. The school held a day of events for her at the beginning of August, with softball games in the afternoon, followed by a "sumptuous repast," more sports, and then an evening program of readings, music, and speeches. The pupils presented Miss Davidson with silverware, and Alice was one of those who signed the address. She also read a paper she had prepared, "Reminiscences of the Mt. Brydges High School during Miss Davidson's Teaching Term," a paper which was subsequently published in the Strathroy *Age* (13 August 1925). Alice provides a history of the school, names and thanks the trustees, lists the various teachers, and tells about examination results, achievements in sports, and the Literary and Athletic Societies. She concludes with a poem which begins "'Tis perseverance, constant toil, / That gains the highest stand" and which ends with the assurance that, "Where great deeds are recorded," "will and earnestness / Are in the end rewarded."

Alice's brothers and sisters in the early 1920s

The decade's first summer was the last summer that Alice's oldest brother, Frank, spent at home. He graduated from Knox College, Toronto, in 1921, and was ordained at the beginning of November. He had "dreamed of seeing the Rocky Mountains and British Columbia almost since childhood" (*Memoirs* 75), had earlier served in a mission field in McBride in the province's interior, and wanted to return: his first appointment as a full-fledged minister was in McBride. There he met Nellie Oliver. She was teaching school, and her presence was much noted, because she was the daughter of John Oliver, at that time the premier of the province. When she and Uncle Frank were married, on 17 October 1923 in Victoria, the story was front-page news in the Strathroy *Age*, which published a detailed account of the wedding. Two days later, Uncle Frank was inducted as the minister of the United Church in Grand Forks.

No one in the Runnalls family attended the wedding. At that time, the only way to get to the west coast was by train, a journey of several days. And much as Uncle Frank loved British Columbia, the distance from home must have been in his mind, especially when there were events that might have involved his family. Aunt Ruth once told me that, when she and Aunt Eva went west in the summer of 1926, Uncle Frank begged her to stay. The birth of the first Runnalls grandchild—Jean—was one event which might have involved my grandparents in a more immediate way than was possible. Jean was born on 17 August 1925, and Uncle Frank and Aunt Nellie would have four more children: Dorina (1929), Bruce (1931), Donna (1933) and Joyce (1935).

Ruth, my mother's oldest sister, was not so good in school as her siblings. I do not know how long she was at the continuation school, but when she left (before my mother even started), she went to Toronto and stayed with Aunt Agnes. She told me that this was during the First World War. She was there—still there?— in September 1921, but later that fall she went into training to be a nurse at the Strathroy Hospital School of Nursing. At that time the hospital was on the west side of Carrie Street (opposite its present location), and it was in a large old home that had been built by a private banker in Strathroy. The town council constructed a new wing and a nurses' residence in 1923–4, and in June 1924 the Strathroy paper published photographs of the new buildings. One of them shows the nurses-in-training, a "pretty lineup" that includes Ruth and her best friend, Marion Grogan. The graduation exercises for the class of 1924 were held in St. Andrew's Presbyterian Church (in Strathroy) the following February, and the ceremony was "impressive," said the paper: "the graduating nurses were veritably showered with flowers and other remembrances" (*Age* 12 February 1925). I still have the hospital's pin presented to Aunt Ruth on that occasion, in a little green velvet jewel box. And I remember a story she told about her time in training: an old, old lady was brought in to the hospital, swathed in layers of clothing, unkempt, unwashed, unable to move without assistance. When the student nurses helped to undress her, a mouse jumped out of her clothing.

In the same year that Ruth was starting her nurse's training (1921–2), the next sister, Eva, was at the Normal School in London. She had always done well academically, and when she passed her final examinations, she was "now qualified to teach in public schools throughout the province" (*Age* 20 July 1922). Her first teaching job was close to Mount Brydges. I know that because a postcard she wrote to a fellow student somehow ended up among my mother's papers. In it she laughs about one of her instructors ("We showed Fleming that we knew something after all (ha ha)") and then asks, "Have you a school? Mine is near Melbourne." She would also teach in Hagersville and at Golspie in Oxford County.

Brother Howard, who was closest in age to my mother, was with her at the continuation school only during her first year there, after which he went on to the collegiate in Strathroy. At the continuation school's commencement exercises in the fall of 1922, someone read a poem about the pupils who had graduated, a poem entitled "Gone But Not Forgotten." It included these lines about Uncle Howard, who was a tall good-looking man:

> Howard Runnalls fair as could be
>> With permament wave and six foot three,
> Who used to write poetry by the yard,
>> And worked Geometry, no matter how hard.

Aunt Lizzie Bateman and the Bateman estate

Grammie Runnalls' mother was a McCracken, one of the family of ten children of Squire John McCracken who had emigrated from Ireland in 1846. Of all those sons and daughters, the longest lived, and the one who played the largest role in the lives of my grandparents, was Aunt Lizzie. She was Frances Elizabeth McCracken, and had been born in County Antrim in Ireland on 15 November 1843. She married a Bateman—Charles Edward, born in Caradoc Township in June 1849. They were married in 1873. The Bateman farm was next to the original McCracken farm on the Second Concession of Caradoc, and Aunt Lizzie and Uncle Charlie lived there until 1901, when they moved into Mount Brydges, to a white frame house on Bowan Street (where Grandad Runnalls would live during the last five years of his life). The Batemans had no children, but their household included a third family member, Aunt Lizzie's youngest sister, Matilda, who had been born in Ireland in 1846. During the 1890s, when the Batemans were still on the farm on the Second Concession, Matilda worked as a domestic for her brother-in-law, and she continued to live with him and her sister after they moved to Mount Brydges. She never married, and died of nephritis in November 1924.

Uncle Charlie died on 18 June 1922, of "apoplexy" (a stroke) suffered some days earlier. He had been attended by his brother, who was a doctor in Strathroy, and the official record of his death includes a curious fact. In answer to the question, "Did an operation precede death?" the response (as given by his brother) was "bloodlettry"—a surprising procedure to be used at this late date. The funeral was held on Tuesday 20 June; the brothers of St. John's Lodge, of which Uncle Charlie was a member, attended in a body; and he was buried in Strathroy Cemetery.

Uncle Charlie was well-to-do, making his money out of horses and land. He raced horses, and he owned properties both on the Second Concession and in Mount Brydges. He left an estate valued at $17,829, of which seven thousand dollars were in real estate; he also held promissory notes valued at $3368 and mortgages worth $5864. In his will he left everything to Aunt Lizzie "absolutely, during her lifetime," and he appointed Aunt Lizzie, Thomas Andrew McEvoy and Joseph Runnalls as his executors. McEvoy eventually withdrew from his responsibilities as executor, leaving Aunt Lizzie and my grandfather—but effectively my grandfather—as executors. In those days, executors not only oversaw the disposition of the will but also administered the estate, and those duties might carry on indefinitely. Grandad Runnalls had the care of the Bateman estate over the next twenty years, and it was not only a considerable amount of work, but also a source of worry and anxiety.

Aunt Lizzie was seventy-nine when her husband died. She was a member of St. Andrew's Church, a faithful worker in the Ladies' Aid and the Women's Missionary Society, and a frequent host of both organizations. At the January 1924 meeting, which was held at her home, she was presented with a life membership certificate, "in recognition of her faithful service to the society and to the church. Mrs. Wyatt read the address and Miss R. Waters made the presentation." Then Aunt Lizzie served lunch, "and a social time was spent" (*Age* 17 January 1924).

The first thing the executors did after Uncle Charlie's death was hold an auction sale, which disposed of his farm equipment and some of his lots in Mount Brydges and on the Second Concession. His cattle were sold privately. Ten years later—this is an indication of the length of time executors were expected to act—the executors filed a petition in Surrogate Court asking for an audit of the estate account, to fix their compensation "for care, pains, trouble and time expended." The judge granted three hundred dollars to my grandfather.

There are some interesting details in the audit. Among the disbursements from the estate account are various sums paid to Aunt Lizzie herself, for groceries and for redecorating the house, and there is a recurring payment to her of five hundred dollars, "for private use." The most interesting item is a payment of $560 to Strathroy Granite and Marble Works, for "monument." That was the Bateman stone in Strathroy cemetery, and it was the subject of much discussion by (and the disapproval of) my grandparents, who considered the monument an extravagance. It is an unusually large upright rectangular stone, and the price was about two-thirds the annual salary of a public school teacher at the time. Mixed up with this disbursement was some controversy over where my grandparents would be buried. Their preferred spot was Cook's cemetery, and I think there was already a plot there with spaces for them, but something happened, and Grandad went in to Strathroy and bought a plot in the cemetery there, with room for four graves.

Two matters in the Batemen estate were worries for my grandfather. One was the McEvoy mortgage. Thomas Andrew McEvoy had been named as one of the executors, but had withdrawn. The mortgage was for $550, and it went unpaid. In the audit of 1932 it was listed as one of the "assets unrealized and on hand." Helen McEvoy, who was a year older than my mother, was McEvoy's daughter, a year ahead of my mother in school and at Normal School. When Helen started teaching in Caradoc Township, the mortgage must have been on her mind, for she eventually paid it off in full. Just when she did this I do not know: in 1936 she had married a man named Coulter, who took over his father-in-law's farm. It was at the same corner of the Fourth Concesson and the Adelaide Road as St. Andrew's church, my mother told me, and it was half swamp. Helen's discharging of the mortgage from her school teacher's salary made up for Coulter's poor management of the land. Helen must have felt a great attachment to that farm, for she still owned it in the Centennial Year, 1967, when she had it designated as a "Century Farm."

The other great worry for my grandfather was a squatter on the Bateman farm. His name was Charles Gannon, "well-known in Caradoc Township as a hunter, trapper and handyman" (*Age* 7 March 1935), and he had lived in a shack on the Bateman farm since the turn of the century. Aunt Lizzie had held on to the farm after Uncle Charlie's death, renting it out for pasture, but in 1933 she decided to sell it. The sale fell through because Gannon refused to get out, claiming that Uncle Charlie had promised that he would always have a home on the property, and insisting on "squatter's rights." By March 1935, the dispute ended up in a London courtroom.

"His hair a grizzled gray and wearing high rubber boots, Gannon told Judge Wearing that shortly before Charles Bateman died in June, 1922, he said to him, "Charlie, you have a home here as long as you live and all the wood you need. I will give you a deed this Fall." Gannon added: "But, he died a little too soon; in June." "Gannon told the court he had made many improvements and did a lot of work about the farm. He said he put up a garage in 1923; helped plant grass, cut wood, kept fences in repair, planted trees and did many other odd jobs." "Gannon recalled one occasion when Mr. Runnalls came to see him about giving up the shack. 'I was cleaning a skunk when he came around. He accused me of cutting the trees and said if I didn't stop they would put me off. I wouldn't talk to him' " (*London Advertiser* 1 March 1935).

When Grandad took the stand, he said that "soon after Mr. Bateman died ... he went to see Gannon. At that time, the latter agreed to cut the weeds, look after the cattle and mend fences on the farm in return for being allowed to remain in the little cottage." At the time of the auction sale in 1922, Grandad paid Gannon twenty-five dollars for "work" (according to the later audit). When the cheque was produced at the trial, Gannon denied that he had endorsed it ("That's my name, but it wasn't my signature") and said he never got the money.

When Judge Wearing handed down his judgment, it was in favour of the executors. " 'In order to obtain what is known as squatters' rights,' his honor stated, 'it is necessary for a man to have exclusive, open, continuous and uninterrupted possession of the land for at least ten years.' Pointing out that the Batemans had paid the taxes on the property, used it as pasture for their own cattle, and took wood from it, Judge Wearing held that Gannon had not that 'exclusive' use of the property which might have established his claim" (*Age* 14 March 1935). So Gannon was evicted and the farm sold. Gannon himself died in 1937, at the age of seventy, and was buried in Mount Brydges cemetery.

In December 1932, at the age of eighty-eight, Aunt Lizzie had suffered a stroke, but by the time of her ninetieth birthday in October 1934 the paper reported that "despite her years she enjoys very good health and delights in seeing her friends" (*Age* 25 October 1934). By January 1936, however, when Aunt Lizzie was in her ninety-second year, she was "confined to her bed" (*Age* 23 January 1936) and was an invalid for the rest of her life. That spring she was interviewed by Myrtle Home, who wrote historical pieces on Caradoc Township for the *Age*; Aunt Lizzie was the last surviving member of the ten children of Squire John McCracken and the last to have experienced the family's early days. The interview, which appeared on May 14, provides us with an immigration narrative for the McCrackens and a brief account of their pioneer life (see Chapter Two).

Aunt Lizzie died on 1 February 1941, in her ninety-eighth year, and was buried beside Uncle Charlie in Strathroy Cemetery. Grandad Runnalls was now the sole surviving executor of the estate and, at the age of seventy-three, was thinking of retiring from farming. Aunt Lizzie's house on Bowan Street in Mount Brydges had been empty for some time, and needed updating, plus new paint and wallpaper, but my grandparents decided that it would suit them as a retirement home. They gained possession of the house and lot in July 1942 as part of the settlement of the estate. My grandfather had personally advanced some $2900 to the estate—why I do not know—and agreed to accept the house and lot (valued at $1400) as part payment of the amount due him.

Aunt Mary (Runnalls) Ringrose

Mary Ringrose was Grandad Runnalls' oldest sister, the second child in the family of Richard and Hannah Runnalls. I never met her. While my mother was alive, it never occurred to me to ask about Aunt Mary, and I heard about her only years later, from Aunt Ruth. She lived "out West," and when Ringrose died in 1918, Aunt Mary started to correspond with a Mount Brydges man named Gibbs, with whom she had gone to school when the Runnallses and the Gibbses were living in Dawn Township, and she eventually came east and married him. They lived on a little plot of land near St. Andrew's church, on the Fourth Concession of Caradoc—not far from my grandparents' farm. The marriage lasted only a short time, and Aunt Mary went back west. "I saw her only once in my life," Aunt Ruth said; "Dad always described her as 'flighty,' not a bit like the rest of the family."

The marriage was a surprise to my grandfather. He went into Steers' grocery store in Mount Brydges, and Gibbs's daughter, who worked there, said to him, "I guess you and I are related." And when Grandad looked puzzled, she said, "Your sister and my father stepped off the train last night. They're married." "Well!" Aunt Ruth said; "Dad just about collapsed on the spot."

Aunt Agnes Irvine

Aunt Agnes was Grammie Runnalls' younger sister. She was the third of the six children of John Thompson and Sarah Jane McCracken (Grammie was the first), and she had been born on 22 July 1872. As a young woman she taught in her home school, Cook's (S.S. No. 5 Caradoc), for two years (1895–7), and left (as I have already said) after the tragic death of one of her pupils, Emily Trott. She went to Orangeville, taught there, met Norman Irvine, married him in 1902, and moved to Toronto. Their home was in Rosedale, at 51 Castle Frank Road, and later they had a summer place at Erindale, overlooking the Credit River. They had one son, Bob, born in 1907.

Uncle Norm was a businessman. He opened a decorating business in Toronto in 1902, the year he and Aunt Agnes were married, and it eventually became the Thornton-Smith Company. The name was that of two young brothers who had come out from England and opened a furniture and antiques store in Toronto. It faltered; Uncle Norm was called in to manage it; and by 1920 he owned it outright. The company (which had grown out of the Arts and Crafts movement in England) manufactured reproductions of English antique furniture, with designs by Chippendale, Sheraton and Heppelwhite. Its retail store, built in 1922, was at 340 Yonge Street, in what is now a heritage building designed by the same man (John Lyle) who designed Union Station and the Royal Alexandra Theatre. The business flourished, with Toronto's well-to-do and fashionable people patronizing Thornton-Smith, and the company eventually became so well-known that it had contracts to decorate several famous interiors, including Rideau Hall in Ottawa and government houses in several provinces.

Uncle Norm was always going on buying trips for upholstery, drapes, carpets, fine fabrics and household furnishings such as vases and prints, and he travelled regularly to England and Italy. He would even buy up whole rooms of English oak panelling from estates in the U.K. and ship them back to Toronto. Aunt Agnes sometimes went with him. She did so in December 1912 and January 1913, when they were in London, Glasgow and Edinburgh, and she did so again in the summer of 1925, when they were in Italy. From Rome she sent a postcard to her sister: "Dear Tillie—Visited St. Peter's today—have had a wonderful two days sightseeing while here. Had a chance to be received by the Pope if we had had time. Agnes." And there were holidays, such as one to Bermuda in March of 1924: "Dear Tillie: Just arrived this a.m. after a two day trip from New York. It is lovely sunshine gleaming white houses flowers & palms. Agnes." Such destinations were far out of reach for the Runnallses, but nonetheless Aunt Ruth always maintained that they got around more than most. "Others got to go to Mount Brydges fair," Aunt Ruth once said, "but we got to Toronto." She remembered that, when the Prince of Wales visited the city in September 1919, she and Aunt Agnes were in the stands at the CNE, cheering him as he drove by in an open car.

For the Runnalls family, Aunt Agnes provided glimpses into a world of wealth and privilege, which she took delight in sharing with her nephews and nieces. Uncle Frank recalled that, when he was a student at Knox College, Aunt Agnes introduced him to "the proper social etiquette of the day." "She had a maid to do her housework and to serve the table at mealtime. Dinner was a formal occasion. ... Knives, forks, and spoons ... were set out to accommodate all the courses. ... I had to watch my aunt to see which knife and/or spoon should be used for each course. ... We also had to be properly dressed for dinner, the men with a coat or dinner jacket and the women with a dinner dress. The maid removed the dishes after each course, and served the next course. She did not eat with the family but had her meal alone in the kitchen" (*Memoirs* 38).

Aunt Agnes was an intrepid traveller, the result of her boundless curiosity about the world, her delight in its infinite variety, her sense of life as an adventure, and her readiness to have fun. She was always sending postcards home to Mount Brydges from (what must have then seemed) exotic destinations. There is a 1914 postcard to her sister, with a breezy message: "Dear Tillie—we ran down to Atlantic City for the weekend and this is the hotel we stayed at." That same April, she sent a card to her niece Ruth with the casual line, "Just down to New York for a few days." And that fall she was in New York again, and this time sent a card to her nephew Howard: "Am having a lovely time on Long Island near where Teddy Roosevelt lives. See the ocean and ships. Aunt Agnes." There is an October 1912 card from Winnipeg, on which Aunt Agnes tells her sister that she "had J.C. Elliott with me on the train this far." (John Campbell Elliott was from Melbourne, knew the Thompsons, and would become the M.P. for the West Middlesex riding in 1925, Minister of Labour in 1926, and Postmaster-General in 1935. He was the politician my grandparents knew best.) There are postcards from famous hotels: the Chateau Laurier in Ottawa, the Chateau Frontenac in Quebec City, the Blackstone Hotel in Chicago, the Biltmore in New York. And there are messages from more remote places: the Saguenay ("we are nearly to Tadoussac (find it in the geography) and we are going up the Saguenay river to the end"); and St. John's (where Aunt Agnes herself expresses wonder at being there: "It seems funny to think I am spending to-night in Newfoundland").

Aunt Ruth remembered being in Toronto during the war years, when matrons in Rosedale would hold teas to raise money for the Red Cross. Aunt Agnes would see the notice of a tea in the newspaper and propose that she and her niece go to it. "But do you know them?" Aunt Ruth would ask. "No," Aunt Agnes would say, "but let's go and see the house and have some fun."

Summer activities in the 1920s

My mother remembered excursions to Port Stanley, then as now a popular summertime destination, and what she remembered most was the dust of the unpaved roads that the convoy of cars took from Mount Brydges to that Lake Erie resort. The day was an adventure for the young people's society of St. Andrew's Church. They travelled in open cars, dust flying from one car in the lead because the driver said he knew "the back way to Port," and all the other cars following in the dust behind. There was the inevitable blow-out of a tire and, my mother said, it went off like a shot, because each three-inch tire had sixty-five pounds of pressure in it. The trip was an all-day affair. The group had lunch and dinner on Invererie Heights, reached by an incline railway, and they spent the afternoon on the beach, "while Old Sol smiled on the gay crowd" (*Age* 30 July 1925).

Alice at the Strathroy Collegiate Institute (1925–6)

The school in Mount Brydges was a continuation school, offering four years of high school but not the fifth year that Alice needed if she were to continue to Normal School and teacher training. At that time only the "collegiate institutes" offered a fifth year, and they were different from "high schools" because the teachers had to have university degrees. The nearest collegiate was in Strathroy, and Alice went there for her final year of high school, 1925–6.

She did well. At the end of the year, she had passed in ten papers, and stood second in a class of twenty-seven (her cousin, Neil Runnalls, stood first). She earned firsts in English Composition and Literature, History, Latin Authors and Composition, and French Authors, and seconds in Algebra, Geometry and Trigonometry, and French Composition. In the "teachers' remarks" part of her report cards there is just one word: "excellent."

In June of 1926, Alice wrote the Upper School Examinations, which were province-wide, and the results came out at the end of August. She earned firsts in History, Trigonometry, Latin Authors, Latin Composition, and French Composition; seconds in Algebra and French Authors; and a "C" in Geometry. Among my mother's papers is a congratulatory postcard from a Georgia Parr: "You did splendidly as usual, and now I wonder whither you are bound, Normal or University?" It was to be the London Normal School.

Good as Alice's marks were, they were overshadowed by those of her cousin Neil Runnalls, who was university-bound. He was at the head of his class, with eight firsts and three seconds, and won scholarships from Western. "Brilliant student" was the headline in the Strathroy paper. Neil would go on to earn a B.Sc. and an M.Sc. from Western, in geology. His master's thesis was on the rocks of the Timmins area, where both he and Uncle Howard would eventually teach.

Among Alice's other classmates at Strathroy were Eileen Sisson, her best friend, who would go on with her to the London Normal School and marry Archie Cameron, a farmer in Warwick Township; Marguerite Purdy, already an accomplished pianist and organist in the United Church, from whom my mother took music lessons (as would Marjorie and I years later)—and who married Nelson Johnson, who taught in the Strathroy Public School; Wilbert McKeen, who would become a scientist at Western; Ella Sexton, who went on to teach high school and became an inspector; Ernest Wright, one of the Wright family who manufactured pianos in Strathroy (Marguerite Purdy's father was the foreman of the factory's stringing and tuning department); Bill Willmott, who (like his father) became a dentist (and provided dental care to my sister and me when we were small); and Mabel Toles, who would board with my mother when they were both at Normal School, and who eventually married Neil Runnalls.

In addition to her academic work, Alice was a competitor in oratorical contests, and she was a member of the collegiate's basketball team. One of her fellow players from Mount Brydges—Bernice Wilcox—was also on the team; the others were Ella Sexton, Margaret Bolton, Alice Boyd, Mary McCabe, and Sara Bogue (*Age* 20 January 1927).)

Alice had to wait for the school's Commencement Exercises, which for her class were held on 14 January 1927, to formally receive her diploma, a shield awarded to the basketball team on which she played—and a gold medal for public speaking.

Alice wins a gold medal for public speaking

In January 1926 the Strathroy paper announced an oratorical contest at the collegiate, "when eight of the best speakers in the school will be heard" (*Age* 21 January 1926). A week later, the paper observed that, among "the many opportunities ... for self improvement" in the educational system, "the art of public speaking has become a regular feature of training in nearly every well conducted secondary school in our land" (*Age* 28 January 1926). In an earlier issue, however, the paper had been critical of some judges' verdicts: "Oratory does not consist in a feat of memory work, and a recitation, word for word, of what has not been original writing or composition"; instead, it should be "a fluent, rational, forceful speech," which springs from "natural enthusiasm" and is based on "a thorough knowledge" of the subject (*Age* 14 January 1926). I suspect that my mother's oratory involved memory work, perhaps even a word-for-word recitation of a text she had written in advance. On this occasion her subject was "Pauline Johnson." The speech is among her papers, written in the fine cursive script then taught in every school.

The contest was held on the evening of Friday, 22 January 1926, and the occasion was front-page news the following week: "Large Audience Delighted with Excellent Orations of Competitors at the Collegiate Institute." There were eight competitors that evening. "Miss Eleanor [an error for Alice] Runnalls, daughter of Mr. and Mrs. Jos. Runnalls, of Caradoc, who spoke on the Indian poetess, Pauline Johnson, was adjudged the best of the girls, and awarded the Dr. R. A. Willmott prize" (*Age* 28 January 1926).

I still have that gold medal (with gold chain, and a little red, white and blue ribbon), inscribed "Sr. Girls Oratory 1st A. Runnals [sic] donated by Dr. R. A. Wilmott 1925–26." The emblem on the front, a book resting on a crossed scroll and pen, and surmounted by a lamp, lit, sums up the character of those literary societies which had such great cultural significance in Ontario at the time.

Alice received a congratulatory message, an affectionate and chatty letter, from her former principal at the Mount Brydges Continuation School, Georgia Davidson, then teaching in Delaware. And she received a note from Aunt Agnes, who wrote in her characteristic scrawl and breathless style: "Dear Alice:—Congratulations just heard yesterday that you had won a medal (was it a medal) I think I'll have to get you to give that oration on Pauline Johnston for me the next time I come up—Ruth & Eva will have to visit her grave in Stanley Park when they go West this summer. Send me a paper with your picture. Agnes I."

Alice's success meant that she would represent Strathroy in the W.O.S.S.A. (Western Ontario Secondary School Association) competitions. The first was on Friday 12 February, and again it was front-page news in the *Age* (18 February 1926): "Before an audience that practically filled the spacious auditorium of the United Church, the W.O.S.S.A. speakers presented their masterful display of oratory on Friday evening last. For the first time in the final contests, Strathronians had the pleasure of listening to three splendid and well prepared speeches from young lady students from Western Ontario schools. Miss Alice Runnalls, the representative from the Strathroy Collegiate Institute, with her clean-cut delineation of her topic, 'Pauline Johnson,' vanquished her fair rivals, Misses Leslie and Billingsley, of Sarnia and St. Thomas, respectively. While Misses Leslie and Billingsley had more pretentious subjects for public speaking, they lacked power to convince their listeners, who, with the judges, were unanimous in showing their approval of the award. Our town and school may well feel proud of this young lady, who, when she competes in the finals at Woodstock, carries with her our very best wishes in her attempt to bring the gold medal to the old school on the hill."

The "finals" were not in Woodstock but in London, on Friday 5 March. The venue was Convocation Hall in the newly completed Arts Building on Western's campus, and the host was the university's "literary debating society," which (following the usual practice of literary societies) "will provide a program in addition to the splendid orations to be presented" (*Age* 4 March 1926). "When it is realized," the announcement said, "that five girls who will contest this event have already competed in their districts, a real appreciation of the event should be exhibited." Alice was not nearly so successful in the finals. The gold medal went to a girl from Windsor, the *London Advertiser* misspelled Alice's surname, and the Strathroy paper did not report the competition at all.

Alice's brothers and sisters in 1925–6

Grandad Runnalls, as I have already said, had little schooling himself, but was determined that his children would all have good educations. Howard, like Frank, went to university: he registered in mathematics and physics at Western in the fall of 1925, when the campus had only two main buildings, the "Arts Building" (now University College) and the "Science Building." He would complete two years of the program before returning to farming with his father, perhaps for lack of money, perhaps because he was unsure about what he wanted to do with his life. It wasn't farming, as a memory of my mother's clearly indicates: she remembered her brother ploughing—walking in a furrow behind a small plough pulled by a team of horses—and Uncle Howard holding a book between the implement's handles. After two years, and with a loan from my mother (who by that time was teaching school), Howard would be back at Western.

In the meantime, Ruth and Eva, who now had incomes of their own, were ready for travel and adventure, and in the summer of 1926 they went west, all the way to the coast. Their relatives who had preceded them in the western migration from Ontario were the focal points of their journey, and the railways which had been so important in opening up the country defined their route. They started on the CNR's "Continental Limited," which took them through Winnipeg and Saskatoon to Edmonton. There they visited their Griggs cousins, and then went to Stettler, for a family reunion with Aunt Mima and Uncle John Thompson. Then Jasper and Prince Rupert, and a two-day voyage down the "Inside Passage" to Vancouver. At this point in Aunt Ruth's photograph album there is a picture of Uncle Frank and Aunt Nellie, Frank holding his infant daughter Jean in his arms. Aunt Ruth's caption: "The ones we so gladly greeted at the Vancouver Docks."

Sightseeing in Vancouver included places that the travellers already knew about and wanted to see: the Harding monument in Stanley Park, for instance, "The last place he spoke publicly; the only time an AM president spoke in Can," when Aunt Nellie's father was the president's host; or Pauline Johnson's grave at Siwash Rock, "where [she] loved to look over the water and get inspiration for her poems"; or "The Great Hollow Tree," with Ruth and Eva and Frank and baby Jean standing inside it. All of them went on to Victoria, to Aunt Nellie's parents. Aunt Ruth took a photograph of the premier's home, a modest storey-and-a-half bungalow; and the premier himself drove them on the Malahat Mountain Drive, "40 miles," Aunt Ruth noted, "over which Mr. Oliver took us on a Saturday afternoon." A year later, Mr. Oliver would be dead, of cancer.

Ruth and Eva returned east on the CPR, on the route through the mountains that had been built at such cost and with such difficulties in the 1880s, to Banff and Lake Louise. There they stayed in the CPR's famous hotel, and "looking from the chateau," Aunt Ruth wrote, "one of the most beautiful sights seen on our trip was the awe-inspiring vision of the sunrise on Lake Louise." Then on to Calgary, and across the prairies to the lakehead, where the travellers took a boat through Lakes Superior and Huron to Sarnia. The boat was the Northern Navigation's *Noronic*, which would continue service on that route until it burned at its dock in Toronto in 1949.

CHAPTER FIVE
MY FATHER'S LIFE 1927–1935

Death of Grandad Hair: October 1927
Grandad Hair died on 25 October 1927 at the age of eighty-one, and Dad always talked about his grandfather's death as a desirable one: he died in his sleep. He had been active and in reasonably good health, apparently, for the day before his death he went to Arkona with his son James and his grandson Harold, to see the power station at Rock Glen. According to his obituary in the *Guide*, he "was found dead in his bed by members of the family when they went in to arouse him. Although Mr. Hair had not been in the best of health for the past year or so, he apparently slipped quietly away in his sleep without pain or suffering" (*Guide* 28 October 1927). He had lived on the Brooke Township farm for most of his life, but sometime after Grandmother Hair's death, his daughters Beccie and May had tried living in London, where May worked in a store. Grandad Hair went with them for the winter months, to their house at 356 Piccadilly Street, east of the CPR station in the city's "Old North." He was there in the winter of 1926-7, and often sat in a rocking chair in the front window, to watch what was going on on the street.

The accidental death of Uncle Jim Hair: March 1928
Only a few months after Grandad Hair's quiet death, his eldest son, John's Uncle Jim, was killed in an explosion. The *Guide-Advocate* carried a front-page story in its issue of March 16: "JAMES HAIR DEAD FROM CARBIDE EXPLOSION. DIES IN STRATH-ROY HOSPITAL FROM TERRIBLE INJURIES."

"The third tragic death in this vicinity within one week came to Mr. James A. Hair, wellknown farmer on 12th line Brooke, on Wednesday [14 March] when he passed away in Strathroy Hospital about 4 p.m. as a result of terrible injuries received shortly before noon when the tank of his acetylene lighting plant exploded. Mr. Hair was refilling the tank with carbide as he had done scores of times, when from some unknown cause, the tank exploded with such terrific force that the lid and the violence of the explosion caused a fracture of the skull, broke the jawbone, the loss of eyesight and terrible burns to his face and body. ("His right eye had been torn out and his left eye badly burned by the flaming gas, which flared up" according to the *Sarnia Canadian Observer*.) / With Mr. Hair when the accident occurred were his son, Harold, and his nephew, Horace Delmage. They were temporarily stunned, but pulled Mr. Hair away from the flaming tank. / Drs. Urie and Sawers of Watford were called and conveyed the injured man to Strathroy, where he succumbed later in the afternoon from the terrible injuries received. / Mrs. Hair was in Detroit at the time, having gone there on Monday on a short visit with relatives. The elder daughter, Miss Amy, is teacher in S. S. No. 5, 2nd line north, Warwick. / Mr. Hair, who was in his 56th year, was born and raised on a farm about a mile from his late residence. / He is survived by his wife and five children: Amy, Elsie, Harold, Clarence and James; five sisters and one brother also survive, they are Mrs. Angus Galbraith, of Appin; Mrs. John Mark in [Warman] Saskatchewan; Mrs. Louise Delmage of Watford, Misses Becky and May Hair of Strathroy, and Sherman, who lives on a nearby farm."

My father added a few details to this account. Carbide lamps, he said, provided light in the house, the gas being generated by water dripping on crystals in a tank outside the back door. Uncle Jim had just filled the tank and was reaching over it to turn the tap when it exploded, driving pieces of metal into his face, eyes, and head. The explosion, Dad said, could be heard from our farm. Elsie phoned the Hall family in Warwick Township, where her sister Amy was boarding while teaching (Bert Hall drove Amy home after she had dismissed her pupils), and she phoned my grandmother; my grandfather and Dad went up to Uncle Jim's immediately. Aunt Arabella was visiting her sister in Detroit and had been shopping at Hudson's. She came home to a shocked family and community. The funeral was held from the family residence on Friday—"there was an open casket and a handkerchief covered most of his face," Helen Clark told me—and burial was in Strathroy cemetery.

"I recall the gas lights attached to the walls and ceilings in the Hair home and I don't believe they were ever used again after the accident," Helen Clark wrote to me. Uncle Jim's death had serious consequences for his family. Aunt Arabella was devastated, and may have suffered subsequently from depression. Helen remembers only that her mother said of her grandmother that "she wasn't well." Harold, who was just sixteen at the time, had to quit high school to take care of the farm. "There was little money at the Hair farm and I know that mom lent Uncle Harold a large portion of her meagre teacher's salary, which he eventually paid back many years later."

Sherman Hair as Brooke Township councillor

My grandfather had been active in church and community events, judging cattle, giving talks on farming methods, occupying the chair when there was entertainment at social gatherings, and taking part in debates on the issues of the day, so it is not surprising that he entered municipal politics, perhaps at the urging of his neighbours. In 1927 he became a Brooke Township councillor.

Municipal elections were held annually. There would be a nomination meeting at the end of December, and the election would take place early in the new year. Councillors were elected for a one-year term, which ran from January to December. Sherman's entry into politics was a quiet one. In January 1927 the Watford paper reported that the Reeve of Brooke for 1927 was James H. Johnston, the Deputy-Reeve Jas. Wallis, and the councillors Harry Wilcox, Nevin McVicar, and Sherman Hair—"all by acclamation."

The first council meeting that my grandfather attended was in Code's Hall in Alvinston on January 10, when all members signed a "declaration of office." Then, in the minutes kept by the clerk, W. J. Weed, the first order of business was the appointment of an assessor. There were four applications. Sherman Hair, in his first act as councillor, moved that the application of Clayton King be accepted; the motion was seconded by Nevin McVicar, and carried. King had applied to do the job for $115.

The council met monthly. Councillors were paid $37.50 quarterly. In addition, each councillor had the responsibility of overseeing the construction or maintenance of one or more drains in the township, the role being described as "commissioner" and involving remuneration in addition to their regular stipend. For instance, at the November 1928 council meeting, "Mr. Sherman Hair, commissioner in charge of repairs to the Watt and 6-7 concession road drain reported the work completed with a balance due the drain of $62.70." Council approved a payment of forty dollars to my grandfather for this work.

There seem to have been no major issues in the township during Sherman's first term: the 1927 council was re-elected, by acclamation, for 1928.

The chief concerns of the council were roads and drains, and most of the motions recorded in the council minutes deal with those issues. But the council also had regular duties: each month it examined the accounts, which were itemized in the minutes, and authorized the clerk to pay them; it acted as a Court of Revision for appeals against assessments; and it had to decide on annual mill rates and on yearly expenditures. For example, at the February 1928 meeting, Sherman Hair moved a motion "to provide for expenditures on roads in 1928 be filled in as follows": four thousand dollars for road construction, two thousand dollars for bridge construction, five hundred dollars for machinery, eight hundred dollars for superintendance, and fifteen thousand dollars for maintenance and repairs. Among the men paid for work on the roads in that year was my father, for whom council, at its July 14 meeting in Alvinston, authorized a payment of $101.00. Townlines—the roads that were the boundary between two townships—were notorious for being neglected by both municipalities, but Sherman Hair tried to correct that situation on the east side of the township when, at the council's 16 June 1928 meeting in Inwood, he moved a motion "to have 24-25 sideroad and the Brooke and Mosa townline a good gravel road."

Sherman Hair's first two years on the township council—1927 and 1928—seem to have been largely without controversy. He had been elected by acclamation, and the council's work was praised by the *Alvinston Free Press* in December 1928: "The officials of the township for 1928 were of the highest calibre and very few criticisms of their work can be given. This year they even lowered the tax rate, in the face of increasing costs all around. There is such a thing as economy and neglect. The past council has reduced the rates, but can point with pride to the fact that every department has been kept up to standard and can compare with any township in Western Ontario." But in spite of that good report card, the Watford paper in its issue of 28 December 1928 was of the opinion that a "Contest in Brooke Township" was "probable." "The municipal pot has been bubbling in Brooke Township during the past few weeks," said the paper, "and according to rumors afloat along the concesssions may result in a merry battle of ballots for the honors of the council chairs for the coming year. According to these rumors, which appear to be quite general and for the most part authentic, the contest will be for both the Reeve and Deputy-Reeve chairs, which may be extended on nomination day to the Councillors." Then the paper did some speculating: councillors Harry

Wilcox and Nevin McVicar might "step up," while "Sherman Hair, the remaining councillor, will apparently be well satisfied to remain in the humbler chair as councillor and continue to give his individual attention to municipal work in his own ward."

The nomination meeting was held on Monday, 31 December, with the result that "Brooke township, for the first time in four years, is having a contest." Two men challenged the incumbent reeve, J. H. Johnston; two more challenged the incumbent deputy-reeve, James Wallis; and nine men were nominated for council, though only four— Sherman Hair, James Johnston, Archie McIntyre, and Henry Dundas—allowed their names to appear on the ballot. Uncle Harry Watson and Gilbert Woods had nominated my grandfather.

The date set for the election was Monday, 7 January, and in the paper the preceding Friday Sherman Hair inserted an "election card": "Township of Brooke. To the Electors: Having served on the Council Board of Brooke for the past two years and having the interests of the Township continually at heart, I take this means of soliciting your vote and influence for election as COUNCILLOR at the coming election on Monday next. Wishing you the compliments of the season. SHERMAN HAIR."

My grandfather's hard work paid off: "Sherman Hair Heads Poll for Councillor" was part of the *Guide*'s headline on 11 January 1929, when the paper was reporting on an election that stirred up a lot of interest. "There was a heavy vote polled in Brooke Township election on Monday, despite the prevailing 'flu' epidemic and the intense cold winds, 739 electors in the twelve divisions marking their ballots. / James E. Wallis, former Deputy-Reeve, defeated Reeve James H. Johnston for the presiding chair by a majority of 95, while Nevin McVicar bested Harry Wilcox in the race for the Deputy's chair by a majority of 48. In the Councillors' contest to eliminate one of four candidates Henry Dundas came within three votes of tie-ing Archie D. McIntyre for third place. Sherman Hair, seeking another term, headed the poll with 417 votes, and W. J. Johnston, a former municipal worker, polled second." (The township was divided into twelve polling divisions, numbered from south to north. Sherman had a majority in the northern and some of the middle divisions and a respectable number of votes in the south.) My grandfather must have been elated with the results, for he inserted a "Card of Thanks" in the Watford paper on 11 January: "Township of Brooke. To the Electors: Many thanks for the splendid vote polled for me in election as Councillor on Monday last. This indication of your approval of my past work will only be an incentive for even closer attention to the Township business during 1929. SHERMAN HAIR."

The first meeting of the new council was held in Code's Hall, Alvinston, on 14 January 1929, and the first motion, by McVicar and Hair, was to submit a petition to the Minister of Public Works and Highways for the statutory grant for expenditures on township roads during 1928, a grant which amounted to $22,036.27. A month later, Sherman Hair moved that council purchase two "No. 4 Sawyer-Massey road graders." Statute labour to maintain roads had been abandoned in Brooke in 1921, but still, in the late 1920s, nearly all the roads in the township, including the Nauvoo, the main north-south road, were gravel: dusty in summer, muddy in spring, and often blocked with snow in the winter. Spring thaws sometimes made the roads impassable as frost broke up the gravel surfaces, and the paper regularly carried items about bad road conditions. Even in the 1940s I remember great pits in the roads in the springtime, where mud and quicksand would heave and bubble and look like lava that had boiled up, ready to sink vehicles to the axle.

By January 1930, Sherman Hair had had three years' experience on council and had headed the polls in the last election, so his decision to run for deputy-reeve (and hence for a seat on the Lambton County Council) is not surprising. The concerns of voters had changed. "The rural taxpayer has come to realize in recent years," said the Watford paper on 3 January 1930, "that most of his increased taxation cannot be attributed to any particular increase in expenditure within the Township, but the yearly increases are generally caused by the public demand for better educational facilities [and] extensive good road systems…." That led to "keen contests" and "lively municipal elections" at the beginning of 1930. Brooke held its nomination meeting in Code's Hall in Alvinston on 30 December 1929. Sherman Hair was nominated for councillor by his neighbours Paul Kingston and George Bowie, but he withdrew, and he was subsequently nominated for Deputy-Reeve. His opponents were Dougald Campbell and Harry Wilcox.

As he had done the previous year, Sherman Hair placed an "Election Card" in the paper on 3 January 1930: "Township of Brooke. To the Electors: Ladies and Gentlemen: Having entered the contest for election as Deputy-Reeve of Brooke Township, I solicit the vote and influence of all my friends throughout the Township for my election as Deputy-Reeve for 1930. I have endeavored to serve you faithfully in the past as a member of the Council, and would appreciate your continued support. SHERMAN HAIR"

Sherman lost the election by one vote. Wilcox polled 394 votes, Hair 393, and Campbell 118. On Thursday 9 January the *Sarnia Canadian Observer* published a page-one story with the headline, "Seek Recounts in Two Townships," one of the two being Brooke. But on 17 January 17 the *Guide* denied that story. "Contrary to reports in the daily press, there was no suggestion made of a recount in Brooke Township, where Harry C. Wilcocks [sic] defeated Sherman Hair for the office of Deputy-Reeve by a majority of one. At the check-up of the ballot boxes by the clerk [W. J. Weed] a majority of one was disclosed, breaking the tie that had existed for a day."

So Sherman was out of municipal politics for 1930. His defeat can be attributed, I think, to the three-way race, Campbell being the spoiler and taking votes that would ordinarily have gone to either Hair or Wilcox.

A year later, Sherman determined to run again for deputy-reeve, and again the municipal elections stirred up considerable interest. "Lively election in Brooke," said the *Guide*'s headline on 2 January 1931, and there were two reasons for the intense interest: Leslie Oke, who for ten years had been the East Lambton member of the provincial legislature and had held the seat for the United Farmers of Ontario, challenged James Wallis, the reeve; and Sherman Hair and Harry Wilcox renewed their rivalry, this time with no third candidate in the running.

Nomination meetings were ordinarily held in Alvinston at the very end of December, but this time the meeting, which took place on 29 December 1930, was in the Masonic Hall in Inwood, "the largest ever held, in respect to ratepayers' attendance." The paper attributed the large turnout to the fact that "this nomination was the first held in the eighty odd years of the township's existence" in Inwood, where "many from the west end were able to be present, who would not otherwise have attended." The township clerk, W. J. Weed, chaired the meeting. The list of nominees included Sherman Hair, who was nominated for deputy-reeve by Archie McIntyre and Paul Kingston, one of Sherman's neighbours on the Twelfth Line. The paper gave an extended account of the statements of the candidates and a summary of the questions and discussion. Oke had the most to say. He focused on a recurring theme: the need for restraint at the county level, and hence the importance of strong representation on County Council: "He recognized that taxes were high, and also that the local council was unable to do much in keeping them down. The place to do that was at county council, and he thought the need was for two strong men to be sent this year to Sarnia and fight the high expenditures, in this a very strenuous financial time. Changes must be made." Wilcox made the same point: he talked about his work on county council, "not all fun," he asserted, and "the place to start cutting was on the county rate."

The views of my grandfather, who was by all accounts a quiet man, earned only one sentence in this account: "Sherman Hair, who was defeated by Wilcox last year, gave his theory of hard times, claiming that the cities will have to come down in their wages and commodities if they expect the farmer to buy."

Sherman placed an "Election Card" in the *Guide* on 2 January 1931: "TOWNSHIP OF BROOKE / To the Electors: Ladies and Gentlemen:—I am in the field again this year seeking election as Deputy-Reeve for the coming year: My defeat last year by one vote has persuaded me to again allow my name to go before you for your consideration and approval. If my past record in municipal service warrants your support I shall be grateful for your vote on Monday. SHERMAN HAIR."

The election was held on the first Monday in January, 1931, and my grandfather must have been gratified by the results: he was elected Deputy-Reeve by a majority of 173 votes over Wilcox, and so won a seat on County Council. The vote was 664 for Hair and 491 for Wilcox; Wilcox did well in the divisions in the south part of the township, while Hair prevailed in the north, his largest majority being in the twelfth division, where he polled 107 votes to Wilcox's three. In the contest for Reeve, Oke must have been highly disappointed: James Wallis was elected Reeve by a majority of 186. Councillors were Wm. J. Johnston, Henry Dundas, and Archie McIntyre. A week later the new council took the oath of office before the clerk.

Stockers

In addition to the crops and chickens and pigs my grandfather and father grew on the farm, they also made money from cattle. The ordinary practice at that time was to buy half-grown cattle (called "stockers") from the west, feed them over winter and pasture them over summer, and then sell them in the fall, for (one hoped) a profit. Dad himself usually, in later years, bought his through an agent in Winnipeg and had them shipped to Watford by rail, but he told me that his father went west himself to buy "stockers." Sherman Hair's last trip out west was in 1928, when he bought a carload of cattle (32 of them) in Winnipeg, and shipped them home. A day or so after they arrived, they began to fall ill. The veterinarian in Watford, Dr. McGillicuddy, recognized the illness as "shipping fever" (rather like a flu that develops into pneumonia) because he had seen it among horses being shipped to the Front in the First World War. There was a serum available, but it was expensive (two or three dollars a shot). Nonetheless, Dad drove the "vet" to London in the new Pontiac, and they brought back the necessary quantities. The serum—and mustard plasters—saved all but two of the cattle. Meanwhile, my grandfather had gone on to Regina, where he bought two more carloads of cattle. They were shipped home and remained healthy.

When the time came, in the fall of 1929, to ship those cattle, "things were beginning to get very bad," my father said, and they were lucky to sell the beasts for a price which just allowed them to break even. At that same time, their neighbour Jack King was offered twelve cents a pound for his cattle, and spurned it because, he claimed, his were in prime condition. In the spring of 1930, he accepted six cents a pound. The Great Depression had arrived.

Glimpses of farm life

Accidents, deaths, council meetings, church services and social gatherings were reported in the paper. Not reported was the daily and seasonal round of farm life: the chores that had to be done morning and evening to look after the livestock and poultry, the sowing and cultivating, the haying in late spring and the grain harvest in summer, the threshing, the cutting and stooking of corn in the fall, the fall ploughing, and the caring for horses and machinery. Only occasionally does one catch a glimpse of that life, mainly in the "For Sale" notices placed by my grandfather: "CHOICE HEIFERS about due to calve; also Fat Heifers suitable for beef ring"; "Bred-to-lay Barred Rock Baby Chicks $15.00 per 100"; "CUSTOM HATCHING 4¢ per egg. Also baby chicks for sale: Barred Rocks $15 per 100, White Leghorns $14 per 100. Also a Purebred Shorthorn Bull for sale"; "30 LITTLE PIGS, 6 weeks old for sale." My grandfather still had an apiary at this time, and in July 1931 gave notice of "FRESH HONEY for sale. 7¢ a pound. Bring your own containers."

The daily chores were the great burden of farm life. Cattle, horses, pigs, and poultry all had to be fed and watered, regardless of the weather or any other responsibilities. There were never any holidays from "doing the chores."

The closing of Salem Church: June 1929

The Brooke Circuit of the United Church was comprised of Bethesda, Walnut, and Salem, and the "Church Notices" published weekly in the *Guide* gave the usual time for Sunday services: Bethesda at 10:30 a.m., Walnut at 2:30 p.m., and Salem in the evening, at 7 p.m. The minister in the late 1920s was the Reverend Forbes Rutherford, and the parsonage was in Watford. The three churches were all country churches with small congregations. The circuit had come into being in 1883 with the union of the Methodist churches, but by the late 1920s it was no longer sustainable, and was disbanded in 1929. Walnut and Bethesda had congregations large enough to continue in new alliances with other churches; Salem did not, and closed for good.

On 31 May 1929 the paper reported that arrangements had been completed for Bethesda to join St. Andrew's United Church in Watford. (And I should say that there were two United churches in Watford, St. Andrew's, which had been Presbyterian, and Erie Street, which had been Methodist; church union in Watford was largely in name only.) Walnut was reported as seeking a union with Inwood and the Brooke-Enniskillen United Church; the parsonage in Watford was advertised "for sale or rent"; and the last services on the Brooke Circuit were on Sunday, 30 June 1929, with Walnut and Salem uniting for the day at Salem, when Mr. Rutherford, who had been called to Woodham near St. Marys, preached his farewell sermon. Attendance was "exceptionally large" (*Guide* 5 July 1929).

The Salem congregation was "left under the care of Erie St. Church, Watford" (*Guide* 28 June 1929), and my father and grandparents attended Erie Street at least for a time before settling on another country church, Walnut, as their home congregation. My father sang in the Erie Street choir, and my grandmother was active in the

Women's Association. Erie Street United Church at that time had a total membership of 212, with forty-four members received during 1929 (*Guide* 17 January 1930). My guess is that a goodly portion of the forty-four were from Salem. The Reverend T. W. Hazlewood was Erie Street's minister from the time of Salem's closing until 1931, when he was called to a congregation in Leamington. His successor was the Reverend Enos Hart. In 1933 Walnut became part of a three-point charge that included Erie Street in Watford and Zion in Warwick Township. That arrangement would continue all the time my sister and I were growing up.

During this time my father was in demand as a soloist at various churches in Brooke and Warwick. At the end of October 1928 Walnut had celebrated its fiftieth year, with services morning and evening, and my father was one of the featured soloists. "The church was beautifully decorated with autumn leaves, fruit and flowers, and every available space was occupied by members and former members…," the paper reported (*Guide* 2 November 1928). In October 1929 Erie Street held Thanksgiving services, when the choir "rendered" anthems (in the quaint diction of the day), and "Mr. Will Smith, John Hair and Gerald Robertson sang solos greatly enjoyed by all" (*Guide* 4 October 1929). On 17 November 1929, St. Andrew's United Church on the Brooke-Enniskillen townline had anniversary services, and my father was again soloist. His accompanist was Mrs. Howard Lett, and the choir's selections included "the old favourite gospel song 'The Old Rugged Cross'" (*Guide* 22 November 1929). Erie Street held anniversary services on 23 March 1930, with Rev. Dr. T. Albert Moore of Toronto, the secretary of the General Council, as guest minister. "The choir rendered excellent music and the anthems, the number by the male chorus and the solos by Messrs. John Hair, Wm. Smith and Gerald Robertson were all of a high order" (*Guide* 28 March 1930). In May 1930 Walnut held its anniversary services; in September Zion United Church in Warwick Township held theirs; and in October there was Erie Street's anniversary: my father sang at all three.

Edna Dolbear

My parents were always reticent about any romantic involvements they may have had before they met each other. Whom did they—in the mild and neutral diction of the day—"go with" before they themselves became "an item"? I could not answer that question about my mother until long after her death, but she was of course curious about my father, and told me that he had "gone with" Edna Dolbear. "She had the fine looks of all the Dolbears," my mother said.

Edna Dolbear was a name never mentioned at home, and never mentioned, my mother pointed out, when we passed her grave in Alvinston cemetery, so I do not know much about my father's relationship with her. But among my father's things are two mementoes. One is an undated photograph showing an unidentified couple. The young man in the photograph is my father, very much "the glass of fashion and the mould of form," the fashion being that of the late 1920s: he is wearing a smart gray fedora, and white shirt and tie show in the "v" at the neck of a dark tailored overcoat. Leather gloves cover his hands—for the time is winter, and he is standing in snow, in front of a dark evergreen—and he is not posing but about to rub his hands together and looking as if he might spring into action at any moment. Beside him, looking placid and happy, is a pretty young woman in a dark fur-trimmed hat and overcoat. Is she Edna Dolbear? My cousin Bill Dolbear could only say, when I sent him the photograph, "it might have been Aunt Edna but I am not sure." The other item is a funeral card announcing her death: "Edna Margaret Dolbear died Sunday, August 10, 1930, aged 20 years, 7 months, 5 days. Service at family residence, lot 17, con. 10, Brooke on Tuesday 2 p.m. Interment Alvinston Cemetery."

What happened?

Edna had gone to high school in Watford, left school in June 1929, and, like many young women of her time who did not want to be either a teacher or a nurse, went to Westervelt College in London, a long-established private "business school" where she could learn typing, shorthand, book-keeping, and office management. During the 1929–30 year, the "Brooke" columnist in the Watford paper noted Edna's visits to her parents: at Thanksgiving and Christmas 1929, and on weekends in March and May 1930. During that time there were social gatherings at Walnut—a St. Patrick's party, a box social—and John and Edna may have been at them.

Then, in August 1930, came the headline in the Watford paper: "MISS EDNA DOLBEAR DIES SUDDENLY." The obituary was an extended one: "One of the most tragic deaths ever recorded in Brooke Township occurred on Sunday when Miss Edna Margaret Dolbear, second daughter of Mr. and Mrs. William R. Dolbear, Nauvoo Road, died suddenly, in her 21st year. / Miss Dolbear, who was home on vacation from London, arose Sunday morning and complained of not feeling well, and later decided to lie down until the indisposition passed. When her mother went to her room a few hours later, she was horrified to discover her daughter dead. Drs. Sawers and Bunt, hastily summoned for a consultation, attributed her sudden death to a heart seizure" (*Guide* 15 August 1930).

Bill Dolbear could add little to that account. In a letter he told me that "My Grandmother Dolbear found her dead in bed on Sunday morning. What a shock to the whole family according to my Dad. It was a heart attack I believe. / The Dolbear family never really recovered from her untimely death. / She apparently was an attractive and capable lady" (letter dated 3 July 2007).

So the link-that-might-have-been between two Brooke Township families, the Hairs and the Dolbears, did not happen—until my father's first cousin, Dorothy Delmage, married Edna's brother Calvin. Dorothy and Cal were married on 19 August 1933, and lived on a farm on the southwest corner of the Nauvoo Road and the Twelfth Line. Dorothy had been at the London Normal School in the same year as my mother—1926-7—and she taught in Warwick Township and in Kerwood. She and Cal would have four sons and three daughters, all of whom Marjorie and I went to school with at S. S. No. 5; Paul was my age, and Mary was Marjorie's age.

Chester McLellan marries Ruth Runnalls: November 1930

While my father was "going with" Edna Dolbear, there was another courtship in progress: Chester McLellan, the youngest of the four McLellan brothers, courted, and married, my mother's oldest sister, Ruth. That marriage would have consequences: it led to my mother's meeting my father, and that in turn led to my father's first cousin Harold's meeting (and eventually marrying) my mother's first cousin, Honor Robinson.

How did Uncle Ches and Aunt Ruth meet? At that time nurses often worked with private patients in their own homes, living with the patient's family so long as expert help was needed. Aunt Ruth had nursed her first cousin, Bob Irvine, in Toronto when Bob contracted typhoid, and sometime after that she was hired to tend to a man on a farm in Warwick Township. Uncle Ches appeared to buy livestock, and so they met. The courtship was not a long one, for Aunt Ruth told me that she had never known Uncle Ches's parents. His widowed mother had died in February 1929; they were married on 8 November 1930.

The "write-up" in the paper focused on fashion: "The bride was charming in a silk flat crepe dress of autumn brown with alencon lace sleeves and yoke and wore a velvet hat, brown shoes and other accessories to match. She was attended by her sister, Alice M. Runnals [sic], wearing a dress of sanmarco blue georgette with lace trimmings and a blue velvet hat. Howard J. Runnalls, brother of the bride, acted as groomsman. Immediately after the ceremony Mr. and Mrs. McLellan and attendants motored to the home of the bride's parents, where the wedding breakfast was served. The diningroom was tastefully decorated with streamers and white wedding bells. After a wedding trip to Sarnia, Detroit and points west, Mr. and Mrs. McLellan will reside in Brooke" (*Guide* 14 November 1930).

Later that month, Uncle Ches's brother Sam and his wife hosted a family dinner for the newly-weds, and "later in the evening a few of the neighbors joined in an evening of cards and music" (*Guide* 21 November 1930). Where were all the McLellans in 1930? On their home farm, at the corner of the Twelfth Line and 27 Sideroad, Norm, one of the middle sons, was living alone in the white frame farmhouse fronting on the sideroad, in a stand of maples that gave the name to the property: "Maple Grove Farm." Norm had been born with a disability of some sort—I do not remember him and do not know exactly what limitation he suffered from—and he never married. Uncle Ches had built a new house on the next farm to the west—the original Hair farm—and on the other side, across the sideroad, was the farm of the oldest son, Sam. He was twice married. His first wife was a Pike from Metcalfe Township; they had married in 1913; she died in 1923, at the age of forty-one and after a lingering illness because, Aunt Ruth said, "no one knew much about cancer in those days." Sam's second wife was Ethel Newell, the daughter of a family living on the Warwick side of the Sixth Line; they were married in 1925. The other middle son, Herm, lived in Windsor, and in 1914 had married Ethel Brooks who was, I think, an American, for in 1915 they moved across the river to Detroit where Herm worked as a builder and contractor. It was he who built the new house that Uncle Ches and Aunt Ruth would live in. Uncle Ches had been preparing for the construction as early as 1925, when he was cutting lumber out of his own bush, but lost it all when fire destroyed his barn in August of that year. The paper said that the barn had been struck by lightning, but my parents always suspected that Uncle Ches had been careless with a cigarette. He himself was badly burned in trying to save what he could (*Guide* 7 August 1925).

Uncle Ches's mother, who was a Chittick, was one of a large family of three sons and six daughters, and two of her brothers, Christopher and Joseph, had moved to Michigan. They settled in Deckerville in the "thumb" area; there Uncle Ches's mother died on a visit to her brothers; and there one of Christopher's daughters married the man who owned the Ben Franklin store. The McLellans were always motoring over to Deckerville to visit their relatives, and they kept up with them until Uncle Ches's death in 1980.

Very soon after their marriage, Aunt Ruth became active in the McLellans' church—St. James Anglican Church on the Sixth Line—and in the Brooke Women's Institute. She hosted meetings of both the Institute and of the St. James Guild and W.A. And she once told me how she first met my father. "Not long after we were married," Aunt Ruth said, "your Dad and your grandfather walked over to our place after they had done the chores." "What was my grandfather like?" I asked her. "He was a small man, like Harold," Aunt Ruth said. "Everyone liked him."

Dessa Hair and the Brooke Women's Institute in the early 1930s

In the early 1930s my grandmother continued to be active in the Institute. In the spring of 1932 she hosted a meeting that was more literary than scientific: members answered the roll call with "Writings from Bliss Carman's Pen," and Mrs. Tom Woods gave a paper on Carman's life and works (*Guide* 25 March 1932). My grandmother was again hostess in May 1933, when the members returned to more usual activities: one paper was on "Preparing an Asparagus Bed," and at the end of the meeting there was "an exchange of roots, slips and seeds" (*Guide* 19 May 1933). After that, my grandmother's name disappears from accounts of Institute meetings, probably because of my grandfather's illness, and after his death Dessa seems to have withdrawn entirely from the organization.

The great project of the Brooke Women's Institute at this time was the preparation of a history of the township. The chief mover was Mrs. Mac Campbell. In April 1932 she gave a paper outlining the early history of Brooke, a paper that became the basis of the book that would eventually be published. It finally appeared in August 1936.

Sherman Hair as Deputy-Reeve of Brooke Township and as Lambton County councillor

By 1931, when Sherman Hair was back on the Brooke Township Council, the Great Depression was affecting everyone's lives, and my father summed up that era by saying, "Nobody had much money then." Farmers were lucky, he said: there was always enough to eat on a farm, and there was shelter over one's head. But paying taxes could be a problem (as could mortgage payments), and there was pressure on the township council to reduce expenditures, which they did in the fall of 1931. "BROOKE TAXES DOWN" was the headline in the Watford paper for 18 September 1931: "On Saturday the township council set the tax rate for 1931 at 17 and 6/10 mills. The 1930 rate was 21 and 3/10 mills.... This does not mean that township work is being neglected, but that more work is being done for less money. We believe the council deserves credit for these reductions."

My grandfather's thinking was not confined to the small world of Brooke Township. Earlier in 1931 he had moved a motion that council send a petition to the Department of Railways in Ottawa urging a reduction in freight rates. He pointed out that, while prices for farm products were now "considerably below pre-war prices," freight charges had remained the same, at a time when "the farmers of Ontario find it practically impossible to make a fair living on their farms" (*Strathroy Age* 23 April 1931). I do not know whether or not council received any response to this request.

The reduction in the mill rate made township residents satisfied with the existing council, and although there was an election in January 1932, former council members were returned over challengers. For Deputy-Reeve, Sherman Hair defeated his old rival, Harry Wilcox, with a majority of 298 (the vote was 704 for Hair, 424 for Wilcox). The nomination meeting had been held in Code's Hall, Alvinston, on 28 December 1931, and Sherman had been nominated again by Uncle Harry Watson and by another neighbour on the Twelfth Line, Howard Shirley.

Being deputy-reeve gave Sherman a seat on the Lambton County Council, along with Nevin McVicar, the reeve. County Council usually met three times a year, during the last week in January, the first week in June, and the first week in December. Sherman's first experience of County Council was at the January 1931 session. At that time Council met in the court house in Sarnia, then on Christina Street North, when the courtroom became the council chamber. The clerk of the county was John A. Huey, and the treasurer was John E. Leckie—two men who would figure prominently, much later, in my father's experience of county administration. Sessions began with a ritual dignity not known in the township meetings: "The warden took his place behind the massive oak desk on the platform at the north end of the council chamber, with all the formality that goes with the opening of the session. He was gowned in the long, black flowing robes and the three-cornered hat of office and as he entered the chamber his colleagues rose in their places while he proceeded to his chair" (*Sarnia Observer* 2 December 1931). The county clerk then called the roll.

The first order of business at the January session was always the election of a new warden, who held office for one year. Council had a number of standing committees, and a "Select Committee" provided a list of nominees to them. Sherman Hair was made a member of the Agricultural Committee and the Printing Committee. Some of the concerns of Council were the same as those of the township, "Good Roads" (the Council's label) being the most important, but others were different: council funded the "Administration of Justice" (the court system), the jail, registry office, the House of Refuge, and schools, and made grants to many societies, boards, and institutions. The particular concern of the Agricultural Committee was grants to the various agricultural fairs in the county and to school fair boards.

The makeup of the 1931 County Council seemed to mark a new direction in political response to the Depression. The *Sarnia Canadian Observer* for 28 January 1931 made much of the new members and "many changes in representation": "Out of a total of 29 representatives from the 20 municipalities in the county, 14 were members who were not in the 1930 county council." "Many of us were elected on platforms of economy," the reeve of Bosanquet said, and, not surprisingly, the new direction was mainly in the form of cuts to expenditures. There was also a suggestion that the salaries of county council, county officials, and the number of workmen be reduced, and that happened at the June session. Councillors had been paid seven dollars a day for attending sessions; that was cut to six (plus five cents—instead of six—for each mile necessarily travelled to get to council). The reduction of existing salaries became for many people one of the painful consequences of the Depression.

The January and December sessions of council typically began on a Tuesday and ended the following Saturday, but the June session always began on a Monday, and the Wednesday of that week was a break from council business—at least its formal business—when councillors attended the Warden's Picnic. It was usually held in Grand Bend, and while it was a day of socializing—at lunch, at a ball game, and at dinner—it was also a day of politicking, when members of council who aspired to be warden announced their intentions and explored the level of support they might expect from their colleagues. The day had its own traditions and rituals. The captains of the opposing ball teams were always new members of council, and the presentation of the trophy to the captain of the winning team at dinner that night was a source of ongoing amusement: the trophy, which came in an elaborately wrapped box, was a chamber pot.

The cutting of expenditures was a priority for both the township and county councils in 1932. At the January session, county council passed a resolution requesting the provincial government to do no paving in Lambton County that year, because "the county owes the province $72,000 which represents its share of 20 percent of the cost of highway construction in 1931 in Lambton," and it was unwilling to increase its debt in 1932. At the June session, county council cut the salaries of all county officials by ten percent. And in their own townships councillors themselves took a cut in pay. At its meeting in Inwood on 25 June 1932 Brooke council approved a payment of thirty dollars to each councillor, that amount being "six months salary." When Sherman Hair first became a councillor in 1927, the stipend for the same period had been seventy-five dollars. But tax revenues were down sharply in the township. In 1922 the township had collected $92,816.40 in taxes; in 1932 the total amounted to only $64,775 (*Guide* 28 October 1932).

When people had little money, the possibility of easing part of their tax burden with manual labour instead of cash became once more attractive. Brooke Township had abandoned the practice of Statute Labour for road maintenance in 1921, but as the annual municipal election time approached in December of 1932, there was a move afoot to return to the old system. Warwick Township had never abandoned it. Would it not be cheaper to reinstate it in Brooke? Sherman Hair, who intended to run again for Deputy-Reeve, was clear in his stand on the issue. He was firmly against Statute Labour, on the grounds that the savings would be minimal and the loss of the provincial grant (40% of the cost of all road work) a serious setback.

The matter was not left to Council. The question was to be put to all ratepayers in the township, and the decision to include the issue on the ballot sparked a debate in the last few weeks of 1932. Everyone needed information. The township clerk, W. J. Weed, was asked to provide a report, which the Watford paper printed on 9 December, and the issue was "thoroughly aired up and down the concessions" (23 December 1932). The nomination meeting in Inwood on the last Monday in December, "one of the best and most largely attended municipal meetings held in [Brooke] township for many years" (30 December 1932), narrowed the focus to two practices that provoked vigorous opposition: "a yearly salary for the road superintendent, and the hauling of gravel by trucks instead of farmers' teams" (*Guide* 30 December 1932). But everyone who spoke at the meeting agreed on "the farmers' plight in the present economic crisis and burdensome taxation."

My grandfather, who had been nominated for Deputy-Reeve by his neighbours Isaac Foster and Isaac Patterson, began his speech by saying that he was "pleased there was so much intelligent discussion of county and municipal affairs." Then he launched a vigorous defence of the township's present system of road maintenance: "The township could not afford to lose the 40% grant on all gravel and road drainage work. He reminded the ratepayers that Warwick township had reverted to statute labor and the township rate had been lowered only about 40¢ on a $4,000 assessment. The cost of hauling gravel during the past year had been 14¢ per yard per mile." That was presumably by truck; the paper did not report the cost if farmers' teams did the work.

My grandfather's arguments prevailed in the election of 2 January 1933, his key point being repeated by the *Guide* as the chief reason for the result. "Ratepayers Vote Emphatic 'No' Against Proposed Change of Road System" was the headline in the Watford paper on 6 January 1933. "It takes more," the paper said in its lead story, "than the hard wallops the farmer has endured in the past three years of depression to stampede the hard-headed, level-thinking Scots of Brooke township into a panic over high taxation, and a scheme to abandon the present system of road maintenance which receives a 40% refund from the Ontario Department of Highways." Nearly 1200 ratepayers went to the poll, and those "in favor of continuing the present government road system under the supervision of a road superintendent" were "a huge majority over 500."

The other headline for the story on the Brooke election was "Old Councillors Returned to Office," also by large majorities. Among them was my grandfather. "Sherman Hair, Deputy-reeve for the past year, was returned with a majority of over 250 above Archie D. McIntyre, of Alvinston, a member of last year's council."

So far as I can determine from the public record, Sherman Hair never missed a meeting of either the township or the county council. "Members all present" was a standard line in the minutes of the Brooke council, through June, July and August 1933. At the August meeting Sherman Hair moved, and Robert Luke seconded, "that Council do now adjourn to meet in Alvinston on Saturday the 6th day of September...." But on that day Sherman would be, for the first time, not in attendance, "absent through illness," according to the minutes. An item in the paper (published on the same day as the council meeting) made that phrase an ominous one: "Sherman Hair Improving / The condition of Mr. Sherman Hair, 12th line, who has been suffering from high blood pressure for the past few weeks, is indicated as a slight improvement this week, and he has been sitting up for short intervals the past few days. Friends throughout the district will hope for his speedy recovery" (*Guide* 6 September 1933). So the heart problem which would claim our grandfather's life made its first appearance.

Sherman had not recovered sufficiently to attend the council meeting on 14 October but he was present in Alvinston on 18 November. It was the last township council meeting he would ever attend. Sherman also missed the December 1933 session of county council. On the final day of the session council, in a generous gesture, passed a motion that "Messrs. Sproule and Hair, who have been unable to attend the session through illness, be paid their sessional allowances."

During that session of county council there was the usual election gossip, and the Sarnia paper was of the opinion that "Nevin McVicar and Sherman Hair will stand for re-election in Brooke township" (9 December 1933). They could well be unopposed. "Quiet in Brooke" was the *Guide*'s headline on 15 December: "Although Brooke township has the tradition of many stormy nomination meetings in the past, election talk so far has been very quiet. Taxes have been coming down to an appreciable extent, and although Reeve Nevin McVicar may be opposed by ex-Reeve James Wallis if he comes back for re-election, most of the present Council will probably be given an acclamation" (*Guide* 15 December 1933). There was as yet no indication that Sherman would not run again, but a week later the first published notice of that possibility appeared in the Watford paper: "In Brooke township, election talk is very quiet, and it is quite probable that Reeve Nevin McVicar will be given an acclamation for his third term. If ill health should cause Deputy-reeve Sherman Hair to resign, his probable successor may be Wm. J. Johnston" (*Guide* 22 December 1933). Sherman did resign a few days later, and there was an unexpected election for deputy-reeve.

Sherman Hair's last illness and death

I do not know a great deal about my grandfather's last months. They were a painful time for my grandmother and my father, and neither ever said much about them. The one fact that my father did tell me was that they arranged for a specialist to come out from London to examine my grandfather and determine what could be done for him. But in those days there was little knowledge about the treatment of a heart weakened by rheumatic fever, and the specialist told my grandmother and my father that he could recommend nothing.

I have tried to imagine my grandfather's thoughts and feelings when he knew that his death was imminent. One thing I do know: he acted responsibly, and in January 1934 made his will. It is dated 24 January and his signature was witnessed by Uncle Harry Watson and Uncle Pete Watson. The document is not a complicated one. In it he conveyed "to my wife Dessa, and my son John, equal shares in my farms, being E 1/2 of Lots 26 con 12 and 13 of Brooke," and he appointed them executrix and executor.

So far as I know, my grandfather did not go to a hospital. He was under the care of Dr. Sawers, the doctor in Watford, and he remained at home on the farm. He died there on 21 May 1934. As was the practice in those days, the funeral was held at home, burial was in a hastily purchased plot near Uncle Jim Hair's in Strathroy cemetery, and there was an extensive obituary in the *Guide-Advocate* on 25 May: "W. Sherman Hair, one of Brooke township's best known farmers, and for three years Deputy-Reeve of the township, until ill health forced him to retire last December, died at his home on the 12th line on Monday afternoon, in his 61st year. / Mr. Hair was born on the adjoining farm now owned by S. [an error for C.] McLellan and spent his lifetime in Brooke township. Of a quiet, unassuming nature, he was deeply interested in all activities of progress in the community, and his valued service in municipal affairs won him many friendships. / Surviving are his widow, who was formerly Dessa Watson, of Brooke, and an only son, John, associated with his father in the raising of purebred stock. There are also five sisters: Mrs. Angus Galbraith, of Appin; Mrs. John Mark, Saskatchewan; Mrs. Louise Delmage, Lake shore near Camlachie; Misses Beckie and May Hair, of Strathroy. A brother, James Hair, died of a tragic accident in March, 1928. / The funeral was held on Wednesday afternoon, with service at his late residence, lot 26, 12th line, conducted by Rev. E. W. Hart, of Erie St. United Church, with Rev. Norval Woods, of Louisville, assisting. Interment was in Strathroy cemetery, and six nephews served as pallbearers: Harold, James and Clarence Hair, Horace Delmage, John McNeil and Ward Zavitz. Two flower bearers were Calvin Dolbear and Harry Watson."

A week later there was a "Card of Thanks": "The Family of the late Sherman Hair wish to express their grateful appreciation to all the kind friends and neighbors for the many courtesies extended during their recent bereavement; also for the beautiful flower tokens; to Rev. E. W. Hart and Rev. Norval Woods and the assembled choir for their kind services."

So my grandmother was left a widow at the age of fifty-six, and my father, then thirty-one years old and not yet married, took over the operation of the farm. I have always thought of my grandfather as a quiet, intelligent, even-tempered man, with some endearing little peculiarities: "He had a sweet tooth," Dad said; "he never went into town without buying candy."

Family reunions

By the 1920s families were three or four generations away from their pioneering ancestors, and the number of one's relatives was becoming so great that even the Sunday visiting which was so common in those days was not enough for one to "keep up" with every aunt or uncle or cousin. So the family reunion—usually a summertime gathering with a picnic and a ball game—became an annual event.

The Hairs participated in the reunion of the descendants of Eliza England, the first of which was held in 1929. It brought together the relatives of Grandmother Hair, who had been a Carter before her marriage: Eliza England was her mother. The person mainly responsible for this grouping of relatives was William H. Johnston of Exeter, who was a son of Eliza England's first daughter, and he prepared and published a family history in 1940.

The England descendants held their annual gathering in Grand Bend, with a dinner at noon, a "social hour" and sports in the afternoon, a business meeting and addresses, and supper at six. At the 1933 reunion, Sherman Hair was made vice-president, and Dr. W.V. Johnston of Lucknow secretary-treasurer (years later, in 1972, Dr. Johnston would write about his experiences in *Before the Age of Miracles: Memoirs of a Country Doctor*). My grandfather did not live to attend the 1934 reunion, when a letter of sympathy was "to be sent to Mrs. Sherman Hair and her son, John, of Watford, on account of the death of her husband." Family members who gave speeches "recounted some of the old traditions of the family, many of them quite amusing" (*Guide* 20 July 1934)—for story-telling gave a sense of something in common among now widely-scattered relatives, and the published newspaper account usually included a few facts about the family's origins and immigration. For the 1935 reunion, W.H. Johnston read a poem of his own: "OUR FOLKS (Written for the England Picnic)," subsequently published in the paper (*Guide* 19 July 1935). It pays tribute to "earnest men" who toiled "with courage and with zeal," and especially to the pioneer women, "our mothers," and their "fortitude."

The Watsons held their first family reunion in 1923, and it was still being held in the 1950s, when I was a boy. I remember it being in Springbank Park in London, but in the 1920s and '30s it was held on a Watson farm. The fifth "family picnic" in 1927 was "on the old homestead on the 12th line of Brooke Township.…There were present about 80 of the 150 descendants now living of James and Mary (Smith) Watson, who came to Brooke from Chippewa in 1853" (*Guide* 23 June 1927). The next year the family gathered on the Metcalfe Township farm of Harry Watson (this Harry Watson was the son of the oldest of Grandad Watson's brothers, William), and in 1930 our Uncle Harry Watson was host at his farm on the Twelfth Line. In 1928 "the dinner tables were bountifully laden and prettily decorated with red and white peonies, blue iris and cream roses. The three-story anniversary cake was cut by Lloyd Eastabrook, whose birthday falls on the 23rd of June. The afternoon was spent in races for the children and softball for the grownups" (*Guide* 29 June 1928). Uncle Pete Watson was the host for the 1935 reunion, his farm being "the home of the grandparents, Mr. and Mrs. James Watson, in whose memory the reunion is held annually" (*Guide* 28 June 1935).

The search for oil and gas in Brooke Township

Our mother always hoped that we would find oil or gas on our farm, a discovery that would land us, as the metaphor was then, "on easy street." (The opposite destination was "the poor house.") In the early 1930s a company that called itself Brookfield Oil and

Gas Limited bought up the rights for exploration on the Twelfth Line. The agreement for Sherman Hair's two farms is dated 21 September 1933, and the company began exploratory drilling immediately. It was part of "that long search of geologists and oil drillers for an oil area in Brooke Township, believed to be somewhere between Mosa and Petrolia fields" (*Guide* 15 December 1933). In December the drillers struck crude oil on Fred Atchison's farm, 405 feet down, and "within 55 to 60 feet of the Petrolia and Oil Springs level": "they have every hope of bringing in a pumping well" (15 December 1933). But the well on Fred Atchisons's farm yielded only ten to twelve barrels a day. More drilling on other neighbourhood farms, including Uncle Harry Watson's, proceeded, the men "hoping to locate that expected gusher [that] will make the success of Brooke's oil field assured" (*Guide* 16 March 1934). None met such optimistic expectations, and the effort was eventually abandoned. The only well that produced a steady flow in our neighbourhood was on Davidson's farm on the Sixth Line, and even it produced only about twelve barrels per day. Nonetheless, it provided the Davidsons with a steady supplement to their farm income—no small thing during the Depression—and my mother always hoped that we might be lucky in the same way.

The courtship of John Hair and Alice Runnalls

I do not know exactly when our parents first met. Aunt Ruth and Uncle Ches McLellan had been married in November 1930, and it may have been the next year when Alice first came to Brooke to visit her sister. By 1932 she was accompanying her sister to meetings of the W.A. and the Women's Institute.

Alice's name first appears in the *Watford Guide-Advocate* on 13 April 1932 when she went with her sister Ruth to the March meeting of the St. James Guild and Women's Association, which was held at the home of Mrs. Russell Powell. The program included "a piano solo by Miss A. Runnals [sic]." In August 1932 Alice went to a meeting of the Brooke Women's Institute, held at the home of Mrs. Clarence Coke, "with a good attendance," the paper reported: "Miss Runnalls gave a very pleasing piano solo and the Misses Margaret and Dorothy Coke sang a duet" (*Guide* 26 August 1932).

What brought my parents together? Initially, it was music. Our father was frequently a soloist at church services and entertainments around the countryside, and he needed an accompanist. Our mother was the organist at the Presbyterian church in Mount Brydges, and she was an accomplished pianist.

Little as I know about their early days together, I do know something about their first date, though I do not know when it took place. The time must have been summer, for they went dancing "under the stars" at Kenwick-on-the-Lake in Bright's Grove. At that time, Bright's Grove, on the lakeshore east of Sarnia, was a fashionable place to spend a summer vacation or a week at the beach—fashionable enough that the Labatts from London had a summer home there. Kenwick attracted big bands and well-known musicians. The dance floor was in the open air, and there were gardens with fountains and coloured lights; it was a magic place, what with the lights and music, on a warm summer night.

My father continued to be invited to sing at special church services, some of them far beyond the bounds of Brooke Township. I remember his mentioning singing at the church in Cairngorm (southwest of Strathroy in Middlesex County), for instance, and at a church in Dresden, when my mother accompanied him. A typical appearance close to home was at the anniversary services in Chalmers Presbyterian Church on the

Nauvoo Road at the Tenth Line in Brooke Township, in late August of 1933. Churches would usually have two services on Sunday, and a church supper and entertainment on Monday or Tuesday, to raise money. My father was part of the entertainment on this occasion and, said the Watford paper, "the supper and concert on Tuesday evening was a marked success." There were solos, a quartet, and a choir. "John Hair delighted the audience with his appealing songs" (*Guide* 1 September 1933).

The first recorded public appearance of my parents together was in June of 1933, in Mount Brydges. Caradoc Township remembered its war dead not on 11 November but in June, and on Sunday 18 June 18 there was a memorial service—the township's thirteenth—at the Mount Brydges war memorial, on the grounds of the community hall. It was an elaborate and largely attended service: school children and their teachers paraded to the monument; so did the choirs of two Presbyterian churches, St. Andrew's and North Caradoc. Five ministers took part, the main address being delivered by Alice's minister at St. Andrew's, the Rev. W. R. Macodrum. And there was music. Among the selections were "solos by Mrs. E. Batemen, of London, and Mr. Hare [sic], of Watford" (*Age* 22 June 1933).

When Chalmer's Presbyterian Church in Brooke Township held their anniversary and fowl supper in September 1935, my father was again invited to sing. Guest soloists were named in the paper; accompanists were not. But by this time my mother was my father's only accompanist. They were married a few weeks later.

My parents had considered postponing their marriage, for the Depression was at its height and money was scarce. My father estimated his annual income at two thousand dollars, and the price for beef had dropped to three cents a pound. The farm had a mortgage of $6500, with interest at six or six and one-half per cent, and making the payments was difficult. But my father said again that they considered themselves lucky during the Depression: though they didn't have much money, on a farm there was always plenty to eat, and there was shelter over one's head, and there was fuel to keep one warm in winter. So they survived when people in cities often had a much more difficult time. Even so, going ahead with the wedding was an act of courage on the part of my parents, and an expression of faith in the future.

The notice of their engagement was published in the Watford paper on 27 September 1935: "Mr. and Mrs. Joseph Runnalls, Mt. Brydges, announce the engagement of their youngest daughter, Alice Maud, to Mr. John A. Hair, only son of Mrs. Hair and the late Mr. Sherman Hair, Brooke; the marriage to take place early in October." The date chosen was 5 October.

CHAPTER SIX
MY MOTHER'S EARLY LIFE 1926–1935

Alice at the London Normal School 1926-7

Alice had decided to become a primary school teacher, like her sister Eva, and for that she needed a year at the London Normal School. The School occupied a handsome building on Wortley Road in the "Old South," its tower being one of the city's landmarks at the time. She boarded nearby, at 62 Bruce Street, with a family named Black. The house, which is still standing in the twenty-first century, is an Ontario cottage, which looks small from the street but, like all Ontario cottages, would have had a surprising amount of room inside. Mabel Toles, who would marry Alice's cousin Neil Runnalls, boarded with her. Also in her year at Normal School were Bernice Wilcox and Helen Wilton from Mount Brydges; Eileen Sisson, her best friend in high school; and a number of young women from Watford, including Dorothy Delmage, my father's first cousin.

One document that has survived from Alice's year at Normal School is a little booklet which she must have created as a project for one of her courses. It is called "Nature Lore," and it is a beautifully designed piece in an art nouveau style, with drawings, lettering in various styles, and a text written in her perfect cursive hand. It reveals my mother's characteristic responses to nature, usually (but not always) joyful and uplifting, and it displays her tastes in poetry, which run to sentiment and to diction that now sounds stilted because of its many exclamations, imperatives, and apostrophes.

At the centre of the little booklet is a plan of the school property (a whole city block), in which my mother maps and labels every tree and shrub, and there is a pencilled note that she "worked with Miss Sisson in doing the Plan of the N[ormal] S[chool] Ground." The epigraph is from Robert Service: "The wild is / calling, / calling, / calling – / Let us go." This is followed by a piece Alice wrote titled "The Weather," which begins with a quotation from Tennyson and ends with an affirmation of faith: "It is the giver of all good and perfect gifts who gives the weather and whether man may choose to change the weather to suit his own particular desires, in spite of all his attempts, the weather will still remain—the weather." Then there is a section on "Our

Trees," which begins with Joyce Kilmer's "I think that I shall never see / A poem lovely as a tree...." There follows a diary of observations, with the name of the tree, "date of flowering," "date of leafing," and "remarks." Some of the "remarks" are a record of things seen in Caradoc and around Mount Brydges: ""How I joyed when I saw the elm on the 4th concession of Caradoc near my home covered with green on April 30"; "the horse chestnuts dotting Main Street in Mt. Brydges are indeed very beautiful in spring. First the pretty green leaves appear, then gradually and so unnoticed do the flowers appear that it seems almost as if a fairy's wand has been out at night when someday you see the pure white bell shapes nestling in a bed of green." Other "remarks" are about the "Old South" in London: "The beautiful magnolia tree on the corner of Duchess and Edward, which yearly attracts hundreds of visitors, presents to the spectator a massive array of pinkish blossoms. How sorry one feels to see the ground beneath the tree being covered with large delicate petals"; "as I was walking up Elmwood Ave with a girl friend I remarked, 'What a beautiful tree!' She informed me that it was an apricot tree. Seldom have I seen a tree so hidden from view by blossoms"; "it is very lovely to see a tree in blossom—it is more lovely to own one. That is why I take such pride in the plum tree at 62 Bruce Street—not that I own it but that I feel as if I do. And even as the bees visited this beautiful tree arrayed in its lovely spring garment, so I visited it very often that I might carry away some of the sweetness that it shed about"; and of the English cherry, "this tree in the yard at 62 Bruce St was a close rival of the plum at flowering." The last half of the booklet is devoted to birds, many of which Alice observed in a place she refers to as "the flats," and which I assume to be the area known now as "The Coves," a backwater of the Thames River just west of Wharncliffe Road. There she saw the redwinged blackbird, the Savannah sparrow, the American bittern, "greater yellow legs," and the white-breasted nuthatch.

Alice's longest entry in entitled "The Mourning Dove," and it is a little story of sad observation. The setting is the row of spruce trees that her father had planted along the lane of the farm on the Fourth Concession. The piece begins with its author watching a "glorious" sunset, which evokes a thought: "what proof have we that yonder sun so bright to-day will rise to-morrow or on days to come? This thought has dwelt with me since childhood and even as it returned I became sad." Then she hears the "sad call," the "prolonged, plaintive coo" of the dove, and wonders at the cause of its sadness: "longings, disappointments, cares and heartaches"? She searches for the bird's nest, and at last finds it, "merely a platform of loose, dry twigs and sticks," but with "two snowy white eggs." Eggs and bird disappear, leaving the writer to meditate on "a home ruined, a family lost." The sadness is not without a tentative note of consolation: "perhaps it was the Father's will—who knows?" For my mother's faith, always quiet and rarely expressed, was strong, and remained strong throughout her life.

By June 1927, Alice had earned an "interim first-class certificate" and was qualified to begin teaching in an elementary school. Two years of experience later, on 6 September 1929, she received her "permanent first-class" teaching certificate, plus a certificate of qualification to teach elementary agriculture and horticulture.

Grammie Runnalls and the Ladies' Aid

While her youngest daughter was at Normal School in 1926 and 1927, Grammie Runnalls was in charge of the Ladies' Aid at St. Andrew's Church: she was formally elected president for 1927, but in the fall of 1926 she had been "in the chair" when, at a meeting held at the manse, the ladies "made their final arrangements for the anniversary and fowl supper" (*Age* 16 September 1926). Aunt Lizzie Bateman was the hostess for the January 1927 meeting, when Grammie again "took the chair." "The treasurer's report was very gratifying, as it showed the receipts for the past year were four hundred dollars. It was decided to hold the oyster supper Feb. 16" (*Age* 20 January 1927). Then Grammie assisted Aunt Lizzie in serving lunch to the twenty-six women in attendance. "A large number of the congregation" were present at the April 1927 meeting, when Grammie not only presided over a decision "to hold a sale of home cooking at the home of Mrs. Bellamy" but also led the group in prayer (*Age* 21 April 1927).

Though her children were travelling widely by this time, and though Grandad had been out west several times, Grammie herself did not venture far from home. So far as I know, London and Port Stanley were her only destinations. But in September 1926, probably at the urging of Aunt Agnes, she went to Toronto for the Canadian National Exhibition. She travelled with a group of friends and relatives: her sister Aunt Liza McKee of Melbourne; Mr. and Mrs. Frank Davidson and family, and Mr. William Kincade.

Grammie presided at the July 1927 meeting of the W.M.S. and Ladies' Aid, when twenty members and fifteen visitors were present. They decided to hold a "ten-cent tea," and Grammie offered her home for the event. The paper reported on it as follows: "The August meeting of the W.M.S. and Ladies' Aid of St. Andrew's Presbyterian Church was held at the home of Mrs. Joseph Runnalls, with an attendance of over fifty members and visitors. The president, Mrs. Brown, presided, and Mrs. Harris led in prayer. Mrs. Frank Iles favored with a splendid reading, 'We Are Building Day By Day,' and Miss Eva Runnalls rendered a beautiful solo, 'One Sweetly Solemn Thought.' It was decided to hold the quilting the last Thursday in August. A letter with a generous donation was received from Mrs. Wilson, one of our old members, for W.M.S. supply work. Roll call was answered with the verse of a hymn. The meeting closed with prayer, after which Mrs. Wyatt conducted the Ladies' Aid meeting. It was decided to hold a bazaar this fall. A cup shower was held at this meeting, when over thirty cups were received. After the meeting, everyone adjourned to the lawn, where tables were set for a ten cent tea, the proceeds of which amounted to over five dollars. ..." (*Age* 18 August 1927). As for the bazaar, it was held in the Community Hall on 25 November and was, according to the paper, "very successful." "Fancy articles, home baking, candy and ice cream were sold, and afternoon tea was served. The proceeds amounted to over $45.00" (*Age* 1 December 1927).

Grammie continued to work in the Ladies' Aid all through the late 1920s and 1930s, and her name is occasionally mentioned in newspaper reports of the group's activities. In August 1934, for instance, she hosted a joint meeting of the W.M.S. and Ladies' Aid, when she led in prayer, and when my mother "favored with a piano solo." On that occasion the Ladies' Aid was "a purely routine meeting" (*Age* 23 August 1934). But in February 1935 they planned a crokinole party (*Age* 21 February 1935). There was no subsequent report on that activity.

Caradoc Township apples

The year 1926 was not a good one for potatoes: the fall was wet and the crop rotted in the fields. But apples were abundant and of good quality. They were handled by the Apple Growers' Association, whose head was Edward Bond, and the Bonds were members of St. Andrew's Church. The Association had a central packing house at the Caradoc C.P.R. station, which employed twenty-seven persons to pack the barrels. "With an average output of fifteen hundred barrels per week, the association expect to market about 50 carloads this year" (*Age* 4 November 1926). In fact, shipments exceeded estimates, and amounted to 54 carloads (*Age* 27 January 1927). The varieties were ones that have mostly disappeared from grocery store shelves: Greenings and Baldwins, Kings and Snows; only the Northern Spy continues to be available. We had all those varieties in our Brooke Township orchard: the Snows were a particular favourite of mine. They had a bright red skin and snow-white flesh, juicy and sweet. I remember that they did not keep very well, but eating them directly from the tree was one of the pleasures of fall.

Alice's first year of teaching at S.S. No. 7, Caradoc: 1927–8

The London Normal School took some responsibility for placing its graduates, and in June of 1927 the principal, William Prendergast, alerted Alice to a vacancy in Westminster Township. She did not follow up on his suggestion, perhaps because she already had a school in Caradoc. On 11 August 1927 the "North Caradoc" columnist for the Strathroy paper included this one sentence: "Miss Alice Runnalls, of Mt. Brydges, has been engaged as teacher at S.S. No. 7, Caradoc."

Her school was in the north-east part of the township, on the Eighth Concession (now Scotchmere Drive), at the intersection with a sideroad now called Aberdeen Road. The schoolhouse was an old one, having been built in 1867. It was thirty feet by twenty-four feet, with a twelve-foot ceiling. It had no electricity, and was lit by hanging lamps which had been bought by the Literary Society. Outside were a woodshed and flagpole and a small pony shed. Originally white, the school was painted red during the time my mother was teaching there, and it was surrounded by mature maple trees. Three of those trees have survived, long after the schoolhouse was torn down (in 1961) and replaced by a house. Then, when Highway 402 was built between London and Sarnia, its alignment in Caradoc Township was roughly parallel to Aberdeen Road. The highway, which is at the bottom of a slope below the original site of the school, obliterated the old intersection, which was where the Scotchmere Drive overpass now is. Only those maple trees make it possible to picture a school there.

Alice started teaching at the age of nineteen. She was small, slight, and fine-boned, with blue eyes and light brown wavy hair; she stood five feet six inches tall, and (as Aunt Eleanor once said of her) "she wouldn't weigh a hundred pounds soaking wet." Her inspector, J. H. Sexton, who wouldn't get away with such a remark nowadays, called her "little girl."

Alice taught in S.S. No. 7 for eight years, from September 1927 to June 1935—the longest tenure of any teacher in that school. Her annual salary? Only one of her contracts has survived, and it is for 1929–30, when she was paid one thousand dollars for the ten months of the school year. I remember that she told us that her starting salary in 1927 was $750, that it rose to $1050, but then dropped back to $850 during the Depression. Each rural school offered seven or eight years of education, from primer through four "forms," each with a junior and senior division, and Alice, like every other elementary school teacher of the time, taught all of them. The number of her pupils varied from nine to fifteen per year.

The school section in which Alice taught was very much like the one in which she had been brought up. The boys and girls attending her school all came from surrounding farms, and their surnames were predominantly Scotch. The church, which stood a mile or so to the west of the school, was the North Caradoc Presbyterian Church, and it was, at that time, half of the pastoral charge with St. Andrew's, Mount Brydges. Though the congregation had been formed much earlier, the church building itself, a plain yellow-brick structure, was relatively new, having been erected in 1913–14.

The Crawfords

Alice readily entered into the life of the North Caradoc church and of the school section, largely through the family with which she boarded. They were the Crawfords, John T. (for Thompson) and Jessie, and they lived on a farm on the north side of the Eighth Concession (officially Lot 19, Concession 9), close to the main line of C.N.R.; from there Alice walked every day to school. (Years later, our mother told Marjorie that one of the first purchases she made when she started teaching was a fur coat: it was a necessity for her walk on cold winter mornings.)

The Crawfords were a generation older than Alice, but had married late. Mr. Crawford had been born in 1883; Mrs. Crawford, who was Jessie Grant before her marriage, was six years younger than her husband, who was over forty years old when they married, on 23 August 1924, and by that time well known in the township for his involvement in council and in various agricultural organizations. He had been a township councillor in 1924 and 1925, became deputy-reeve in 1928, and reeve of the township in 1929. He was also an elder and Clerk of Session of the North Caradoc Presbyterian Church (he would serve in those capacities for forty-three years), and he was for twenty-six years Sunday School superintendent. Mrs. Crawford was a member of the Women's Missionary Society and of the Caradoc United Farm Women of Ontario.

Alice was very fond of the Crawfords, and for the rest of her life followed the fortunes of their only daughter, Margaret, who was born while Alice was on her summer break, on 22 July 1930.

Also living in the rambling old white-brick farmhouse at the time Alice was boarding there was Mr. Crawford's widowed mother, also named Margaret, and one story that "old Mrs. Crawford" told my mother became part of the lore surrounding the Donnelly plays that James Reaney wrote and staged in the 1970s: she was married in 1880, and her wedding night—3-4 February—coincided with the massacre in Biddulph Township. I have always thought of that as a Gothic coincidence. How, I once asked my mother, did the Donnellys get such a black reputation? "They had to be pretty bad," she said, "for their neighbours to do what they did to them."

The Christmas concert

A concert in mid-December was a regular part of the school year. It offered musical numbers, readings, and sometimes a short play, and it gave all the grades a chance to perform before an audience. Alice had been teaching a Sunday School class of teenage girls, and she had them prepare a number for the Christmas concert at the church, but in her first year of teaching she was anxious about much more extensive preparation. "Now that I was teaching school," she remembered, "I had to plan for a Christmas concert. … It was held on the afternoon on the last day of school before Christmas. There was a piano at the school so we always had a number of songs, motion songs and solos.

However I had not played very much in public and felt too nervous to do the accompaniment at the concert. Eva was home that fall so she came and helped me out that first year. She was a very accomplished pianist and also sang contralto solos."

The Christmas concert ended in a conventional way, as it did in 1930: "At the close Santa Claus arrived and unloaded the tree, well laden [with] gifts and candy for each pupil" (*Age* 23 December 1930).

"Except for one year I had a concert at school [every December] while I was teaching. That particular year there was a lot of snow and the day we would have had the concert the roads were blocked with snow and impassable. Dad came after me with the horse and cutter and on the way home when the horse was plunging through the snow the cutter turned over on its side and Dad and I went out in the snow."

My mother loved the sound of sleigh bells. When her parents moved from their Caradoc Township farm, she kept the ones that had been attached to the cutter, units of four bells on a metal strip, and the ones attached to the horse's harness; some were small round bells on the narrow strips of leather; others were larger bells on wider strips. Their jingling to the trotting of the horse and the movement of the sleigh evoked memories of frigid air and blowing snow, layers of heavy clothing, and one's breath visible in the cold. My mother loved all those associations.

The Young Women's Missionary Society

Missionaries and missionary work were always at the centre of my mother's thinking and of her understanding of the religious life, and that interest happened to coincide with a new organization within her church. Wynne Kincade, a couple of years older than Alice and a Normal School graduate, was also an energetic and enterprising young woman, and in the summer of 1927 she organized a Young Women's Missionary Society at St. Andrew's. It was a mirror image of the existing W.M.S., but for the young women of the congregation. Alice and Eva Runnalls were involved in it from the outset.

Winnie Kincade hosted the first meeting of the group on 21 July 1927. The program differed little from the older W.M.S.: a hymn, prayer, scripture reading, the first chapter of the study book ("Young Islam on Trek," "very capably delivered by Miss Eva Runnalls"), a vocal solo, another hymn. Then my mother's interest in missionaries came to the fore: "Miss Alice Runnalls ... gave a very interesting reading on David Livingstone." Finally, the Lord's Prayer, a social hour ("during which wash cloths and picture books were made for the bale") and lunch (*Age* 28 July 1927). The group met on the third Saturday of each month, and both Aunt Eva and my mother were regular participants in its programs. Aunt Eva contributed musical and literary numbers (she is reported as singing a solo and reading a paper on the "life history" of Bliss Carman); my mother is mentioned as reading the scripture lesson, and in November 1927, "Misses Eva and Alice Runnalls favored with a delightful piano duet" (*Age* 17 November 1927).

At the same time as Alice was taking part in activities in her home church, she was also active in the North Caradoc Presbyterian Church. On 1 December 1927, the W.M.S. served a "birthday banquet" in the basement of the church, and Mrs. Crawford, who was a member of the W.M.S., must have been responsible for Alice's participation. The Strathroy paper reported that "the tables, which were most artistically and fittingly decorated, were divided into twelve sections, each section representing a month of the year, the guests being seated in the division allotted to the month of their birth, the admission fee being a penny for each birthday celebrated."

After the fowl supper, there was a program which involved many of the people in the section whom my mother would come to know well. One of them was Hugh Turner, and he was a school trustee. "Mr. Hugh Turner, in the absence of the pastor, Rev. E. T. Kennedy, through illness, acted as toastmaster. Mr. Turner proposed the toast to 'The King,' which was responded to by all singing the National Anthem. J. T. Crawford proposed the toast to 'The W.M.S.' and Mrs. Duncan Campbell, president of the society, most ably responded. The toast to 'The Young People' was proposed by Mrs. D. M. McNeill and responded to by Allan McNeill. During the program solos were rendered by Miss Annie Limon, Mrs. T. Greene, Mr. Ellis Cutler of Coldstream, and John C. Henderson. Readings by Miss Dorothy Cutler and Miss Alice Runnalls were greatly appreciated. Short addresses were given by Mr. Peter Lamont, T. Greene and Neil P. McGugan...." (*Age* 8 December 1927).

I do not know what my mother chose to read. Years later she told me that one of the texts she often used was Leacock's "My Financial Career." But she also read poetry, and the *Age* reported that, at a February 1930 meeting of the Caradoc U.F.W.O., she "read two beautiful poems" (*Age* 13 February 1930). National feelings prevailed for such occasions and the poets chosen were usually Canadian, Carman and Lampman being mentioned frequently. I suspect that such poets figured in Alice's private reading as well. When the West Coast poet Audrey Alexandra Brown published her *A Dryad in Nanaimo* in 1931, Uncle Howard gave her that book for Christmas. One poem which she kept—and showed me many years later—was by Goldwin Smith. Four years younger than my mother, he was one of the best pupils to come out of the Mount Brydges Continuation School, and had a long career as an historian in the United States. Early in 1929 he entered a poem called "The Dreamer" in a contest sponsored by the Canadian Authors' Association, Montreal Branch. The national president at the time, Charles G.D. Roberts, announced the prizes: "The Dreamer" received honorable mention (*Age* 21 March 1929).

In June 1931, Alice and Wynne Kincade were both at a meeting of the North Caradoc Young Women's Association and gave readings. That meeting was notable for its featured guest, who was a returned missionary from Formosa, a Mrs. McKay of Toronto. Was she related to the most famous of the Presbyterian missionaries, George Leslie Mackay? I do not know, but no doubt she fed my mother's continuing interest in missions as the heroic life.

My mother never learned how to drive a car, but Wynne Kincade was bolder: in the summer of 1929 she "purchased a new Durant coach" (*Age* 18 July 1929), and she, Alma Bond, and Lenna Runnalls (Uncle Ed's oldest daughter) commuted to a summer course in Art at the London Normal School.

Eva Runnalls marries Lewis Harvey: 31 December 1927

I do not know a great deal about Aunt Eva's life before her marriage. Marjorie remembers our mother telling her that Aunt Eva had suffered a disappointment in love, and had been so upset by the failure of the relationship that she had stayed home for some considerable period of time. What I do know is that Aunt Eva was teaching at a rural school—S. S. No. 8, West Zorra—in Oxford County in 1926–7, and the successful year was noted by the Mount Brydges correspondent for the *Age*: "Miss Eva K. Runnalls, teacher for the past year in West Zorra, near Woodstock, was successful in having her entire class of five pupils pass in the recent entrance examinations, three obtaining honors, all of whom had taken the fourth class work in one year" (*Age* 28 July 1927).

This was the context in which Aunt Eva met Lewis Harvey, an Oxford County farmer, and they were married on New Year's Eve, 1927.

Three days before the wedding, there was a gathering at her parents' home: "A delightful trousseau tea was held on Wednesday evening, Dec. 28th, at the home of Mr. and Mrs. Joseph Runnalls, Mt. Brydges, for their daughter, Eva, a bride-elect of the week. About 30 girl friends of the bride called during the evening. The tea table was prettily decorated for the occasion with white narcissus and silver candlesticks. The lovely trousseau was shown by Misses Ruth and Alice Runnalls, sisters of the bride, while her mother, Mrs. Joseph Runnalls, presided at the tea table. Assisting to pour tea was Mrs. John McKee, of Melbourne, the bride's aunt, and tea was served by Mrs. Leslie Runnalls and Miss Wynne Kincade. Many beautiful gifts were also displayed during the evening" (*Age* 5 January 1928).

The Woodstock *Sentinel-Review* carried an account of the wedding in its issue of 7 January 1928: "A pretty wedding was solemnized on Saturday afternoon, Dec. 31 [1927], at Sprucedale Farm, the home of the bride's parents, Mr. and Mrs. [Joseph] Runnalls, Mount Brydges, when their second daughter, Eva Kathleen, was united in marriage to Lewis James Harvey, eldest son of Mr. and Mrs. Lonzo A. Harvey, Embro. The ceremony was performed by Rev. T. E. Kennedy of St. Andrew's Presbyterian Church. / Promptly at 1 o'clock the bride, leaning on the arm of her father, entered the drawing-room, to the strains of the 'Bridal Chorus' ('Lohengrin'), played by her sister, Miss Alice Runnalls, who also played softly throughout the ceremony. The bride was charming in a gown of ivory duchess satin trimmed with sequins, and wore a veil of embroidered silk net, prettily caught at the sides with orange blossoms. Silver slippers completed her bridal costume. She carried a shower bouquet of white carnations and fern. Her only ornament was an emerald pendant, the gift of the groom. ... The ceremony was performed under an evergreen arch trimmed with flowers. During the signing of the register, Miss Ruth Runnalls, sister of the bride, sang sweetly 'O Perfect Love.' / After congratulations were over, the guests repaired to the dining-room and partook of a wedding dinner. The room was prettily decorated with streamers of red and green and white wedding bells."

When my mother remembered that day, she also remembered that "I had come down with a bad case of tonsilitis which marred it for me."

Aunt Eva and Uncle Lewie would have six children, four of whom would survive childhood: Merle (born 2 May 1929); Phyllis (born 10 December 1930); Arlene Alice (born 25 June 1932); Joyce (born April 1934; died 22 July 1935); Louise (born 28 July 1936); and Keith (born 16 January 1940; died 19 August 1940). The farm the Harveys lived on was on Number 2 Highway, halfway between Ingersoll and Woodstock. When the cement company eventually bought the property, they changed the course of the river and obliterated both house and barn.

The Caradoc Literary Society and the Caradoc United Farm Women of Ontario

The schoolhouse of S.S. No. 7 Caradoc was, like other country schoolhouses of the day, the centre of the section's communal activities, and my mother was frequently involved in them. North Caradoc had a literary society called "Maple Grove," and in March 1928 it met in the school, with "splendid attendance" and an extensive and varied program: musical numbers, readings, addresses and a debate. In addition, "a bronze tablet, a souvenir of the jubilee of Confederation, was unveiled by our popular teacher, Miss Alice Runnalls" (*Age* 8 March 1928). In that same month, the Caradoc U.F.W.O. held a St. Patrick's Day concert in the school with a program very much like that of the literary society: music, a paper on St. Patrick, and a "reading by Miss Alice Runnalls" (*Age* 29 March 1928). My mother gave another reading at the U.F.W.O.'s first meeting in the fall, which Mrs. Crawford hosted.

In November 1928 the U.F.W.O. sponsored an oratorical contest. Pupils from four township schools took part, and three boys from S.S. No. 7—Elgin McDonald, Joe Pask, and Lloyd Thompson—were awarded prizes (Winnie Kincade was one of the judges). No doubt my mother, with her own experience of public speaking, coached them, and she may have promoted the contest itself through Mrs. Crawford.

At this time Canada's first (and only) female M.P. was Agnes Macphail, the member for Southeast Grey, and in January 1929 the U.F.W.O. brought her to Strathroy to speak. The paper reported that she was "a strong advocate of greater organization among farmers." The "co-operation" she argued for we would now call "supply management": she praised the wheat pools as "the biggest interest in Canada outside of the government" (*Age* 17 January 1929). I know that Mrs. Crawford was present because she moved the vote of thanks. Did my mother hear Agnes Macphail? I simply do not know.

The end of the 1928 school year

For many years it had been the practice for school reports to be published in the local paper, when student progress seemed to be a matter for the whole community's interest and concern. Alice's first report was published in the Strathroy *Age* in July 1928, and included not only student grades but promotion results as well (*Age* 12 July 1928). Three pupils were named for "perfect attendance since Christmas."

The school year wound up with the Caradoc Township picnic and the memorial service in Mount Brydges. The picnic was much more than the name would suggest, "opening with a grand procession of trades, decorated floats and calithumpians, followed by the public schools of Caradoc." Baseball games were played; there was an official opening of the main street, which had been paved at last; there was an evening program with "high-class artists" and "at 10 o'clock a street dance … on the new pavement." The memorial service was on Sunday, when "all Caradoc public school and Sunday School children [decorated] the monument" (*Age* 12 July 1928). The weekend attracted large crowds. Attendance set a record the following year, when five thousand people turned out for the event (*Age* 11 July 1929).

My mother faithfully provided school reports annually between 1928 and 1935. They give evidence of her concern with attendance, and occasionally with other matters, such as spelling and horticulture: in her report of June 1934 she noted that Earl Thompson had won the "prize for best-kept school garden" (*Age* 19 July 1934).

The St. Andrew's Dramatic Club in 1929–30

In addition to all her other activities, Alice acted in plays. The typical play for church and community groups was a romantic comedy with plenty of broad character types, and Alice acted in at least two of them. In April 1929, "the Young People of St. Andrew's Presbyterian Church presented their comedy, 'Brides from Eaton's,' in the Community Hall." At the time, the Eaton's catalogue was in virtually every household in the country, and it seemed that one could order almost anything from it. Why not brides? The *Age*'s account of the production tells us something about the various parts (all acted "exceptionally well," according to the paper): "those included C. Adams and H.[Howard] Runnalls, real cowboys, with W. [Bill] Courtis as ranch owner and his son and daughter, Alice Runnalls and Hugh Forbes. The brides from Eaton's were Mrs. F. Iles, a typical old maid, Mary Courtis, Mildred Davidson, and Marie Davidson. Mrs. C. Adams as Princess, the Indian house-keeper, kept everyone laughing. F. Iles, a representative of the T. Eaton Co., with his son and daughter, Winnie Kincaid [sic] and H. Pincombe, completed the caste [sic]. The proceeds amounted to $141, which will be applied on the payment of the Sunday School piano" (*Age* 18 April 1929). A week later, "Mr. and Mrs. H[ugh] Forbes, of the 4th concession, entertained on Friday evening the members of St. Andrew's Dramatic Club."

In April 1930, the Club mounted a production of *Peg O' My Heart*, described as "the most popular Irish play ever written." Its author was a now long-forgotten Anglo-Irish playwright, John Hartley Manners; he wrote it for his wife, actress Laurette Taylor, who starred in the Broadway production and made it a great hit. The play had long runs in both New York and London; it inspired a popular song of the same title (we had the sheet music at home); and it was made into a film in the early 1920s. The piece had plenty of popular elements: class conflict (a lower-class girl in an upper-class home), Anglo-Irish relations (an Irish girl in an English context), and a Cinderella story line. And Peg, who is a feisty independent woman, is yet another version of the new century's New Woman (the play dates from the 1910s). Winnie Kincade, herself the embodiment of that New Woman, played the lead. The Strathroy paper's review of the production identified the play's appeal.

"The brilliant playing of innocent Irish 'Peg' (a poor relation from New York) by Miss Kincaide [sic], was worthy of great praise. Miss Kincade easily captivated her audience, keeping them in tears and laughter as they entered into the life of poor Peg, when she was launched into the stately family of the English aristocrats, the Chichesters. / Alma Iles, as the haughty Mrs. Chichester, was the perfect representation of the cold-hearted, artificial society lady, and one wonders how an amateur could possibly present such a character so perfectly. / Clifford Adams, her son, was a perfect scream of amusement as he portrayed the ideal English gentleman, who simply does not accept situations as any other human being in like circumstances.... The rest of the cast were equally as good, although taking minor parts. / Indeed, there was not a dull moment in the whole evening, and the over-flowing crowd of the second night only went to prove the satisfaction and comments of the full house of the first performance; many were turned away who could not find seating capacity in the large Community Hall" (*Age* 1 May 1930). The production was so successful that the St. Andrew's Club presented it in the New Lyceum in Strathroy on May 17, with the Strathroy Concert Orchestra in attendance. There is a copy of the evening's program in my mother's scrapbook. On it she has written, "I think [the New Lyceum was] on Frank Street in Strathroy. I was the maid."

The part of Bennett, the maid, was not a large one, but it included a spirited scene in which Bennet conveys Mrs. Chichester's instructions to Peg, only to have them stoutly rejected. Bennett: "You'll only get me into trouble." Peg: "No, I won't. I wouldn't get you into trouble for the wurrld. I'll get all the trouble and I'll get it now"—and she calls out "at the top of her voice" to the household. Bennett: "They've all gone out." Peg: "Then what are ye makin' such a fuss about? You go out too."

At some point that spring—probably for the May production—Alice had her picture taken in her maid's costume. She is standing in her father's orchard, surrounded by fruit trees in bloom, the abundant white blossoms matching the frilly white maid's cap she is wearing. On the back of that photograph my mother has written, "Our church had a dramatic club. Wynne Kincade was the director. Another play I remember was *Mail Order Brides*. It was quite humorous." (I assume she was referring to *Brides from Eaton's*; I have been unable to locate the playscript under either title.)

The summer of 1929: Port Stanley, Toronto, and a public speaking contest

"Miss Alice Runnalls spent last week holidaying at the Stewart Glen cottage, Port Stanley, with the C.G.I.T. [Canadian Girls in Training] group of South Caradoc" (*Age* 18 July 1929). Alice's photograph album is full of snapshots taken at this camp, though none of the pictures is dated and none of the people identified. She had barely returned from camp when she was off again: "Miss Alice Runnalls has returned after a two weeks' visit with her aunt, Mrs. R. N. Irvine, in Toronto" (*Age* 8 August 1929). There is a photograph of Alice with her aunt and uncle, taken on the back lawn of 51 Castle Frank Road, probably during this visit.

Alice returned to take part in a public speaking contest under the auspices of the West Middlesex U.F.W.O. It was on Thursday afternoon, 8 August, and it was held in S.S. No. 9, Caradoc. "Miss Alice Runnalls spoke on 'Rural Education in Denmark,' while Mrs. Galbraith, of Melbourne, spoke on 'Agriculture.' Both delivered excellent addresses." A woman from Simcoe "gave a very instructive talk on U.F.O. work"; lunch was served on the school grounds; and it was "a very successful social afternoon" (*Age* 29 August 1929).

In my mother's bookcase is a handsome leather-bound volume with gold lettering and a gold cover design: Dickens' *David Copperfield*. A note enclosed reads: "Strathroy, Aug. 26th - 1929 / Dear Miss Runnalls - / The West Middlesex U.F.W.O. wish you to accept this book as a slight token of their appreciation of your effort to make the Public Speaking Contest held Aug 8th 1929 such a success." It is signed by Mrs. W. R. Ferguson, at that time the district president of the U.F.W.O.

Alice's topic on this occasion reflects her growing professional interest in teaching. There was at this time a long-established West Middlesex Teachers' Institute, and Alice took part in it, in what we would now call "professional development days." Among her papers is the program for two such days, 6 and 7 October—no year specified—with sessions in the Strathroy town hall and the London Normal School. Alice is listed as one of the teachers who discussed "Devices in School Work." Two others talked about "The Teacher's Place in the Life of the Community"—a topic about which Alice could also have talked with some authority.

Family reunions: The Runnallses and the Dykemans

The first Runnalls family reunion was held in the summer of 1926, but not until 1929 is there any record of it. In July and August of that year, Aunt Mima Thompson and her daughter Hazel had come east to visit friends and relatives, and they were among the seventy-five people who sat down to "the reunion supper" in Springbank Park on Saturday 13 July. Aunt Mima "was presented with a vase of lovely roses, a token of love" (*Age* 18 July 1929). There is a photograph of Grandad Runnalls with his siblings from that occasion: only Aunt Mary Ringrose is absent.

At the July 1931 picnic, when 43 family members were present, Uncle Howard was elected president while my mother was named to the sports committee. The sports usually included a baseball game, but they also included races of various kinds, and the 1932 gathering had many that were just for fun: there were races for young ladies and young men, married ladies and married men (Uncle Ches won that one), a "three-legged race," a "relay race," a "blind pig race," a "necktie race," and a "suitcase race" (won by my mother and her cousin, Kenneth Runnalls) (*Age* 14 July 1932).

The Dykemans held their first reunion in 1927, also in Springbank Park. Their seventh, in 1933, featured a softball game between "In-Laws" and "Out-Laws," and "a bountiful dinner." The sports program included a "needle and thread race," "women's potato race," "grandfather's time race," and "ladies' shoe kicking race." On display was a document I have never seen: "the family tree, consisting of 56 names, and compiled by Mr. Alfred Dykeman, Mr. Elmer Dykeman and Mrs. Robert Prentice." Among the officers elected for 1934 were my mother and Uncle Howard, who became joint secretary-treasurers (*Age* 6 July 1933).

The Caradoc U.F.W.O. in 1929–30

The Caradoc U.F.W.O. figures largely in Alice's community involvement during her third year of teaching, mainly because Mrs. Crawford was such an active member: she was the club's secretary-treasurer for 1929–30. She hosted the September 1929 meeting, and Alice was part of the program: she gave a reading. The agenda of the U.F.W.O. expanded when, in October, the club decided to co-operate with the Women's Christian Temperance Union "in the temperance cause and assist financially" (*Age* 10 October 1929). "The annual meeting of the United Farmers of West Middlesex, held on Wednesday, Nov. 13, was the best meeting in some years, both from the standpoint of members present, clubs represented, and for general enthusiasm and quality of program. Some eighty members, who had been present at the business sessions in the morning, sat down to lunch in Prangley's parlors." There was a public speaking contest on that occasion, and Alice was one of four contestants: she repeated her talk on "Danish Schools." And though "every speech merited a winner's placing," in the judgment of the *Age*, and though "for soundness of material, precision in arrangement, enunciation and manner, the speakers were to be congratulated," Alice was not the winner (*Age* 21 November 1929).

In spite of the optimistic tone of this report, the U.F.O. was in decline. The party held its convention in Toronto in December 1929, and the secretary-treasurer noted "the falling off in agricultural club membership and the apparent apathy of the farmers themselves towards the U.F.O" (*Age* 12 December 1929). In response, the Caradoc U.F.W.O. discussed ways of increasing their membership, but the movement had had its day, and the country's descent into the Great Depression changed everything.

Uncle Frank and Aunt Nellie come east: Summer 1930

The fourth General Council of the United Church met in London in September 1930, and Uncle Frank, who was Secretary of the Vancouver Presbytery, was elected as a delegate. He and Aunt Nellie decided to make the trip their summer holiday, and they brought their two children, Jean and Dorina, with them, to "get acquainted with their grandparents." "My father really enjoyed taking Jean, his first grandchild, with him to Mt. Brydges, and almost spoiled her with the candy and ice cream that he bought" (*Memoirs* 121). Dorina was a delicate child who had been diagnosed with celiac disease, and her illness flared up while the family was in Mount Brydges. Uncle Frank and Aunt Nellie had planned a car trip to Ottawa, but Aunt Nellie stayed to look after Dorina, and my mother went in her place. It was a trip she always remembered.

"My sister Alice and I went in Father's Model A Ford," Uncle Frank writes in his *Memoirs*. "On the way we travelled via Peterborough, and visited the area of my old mission field in North Hastings to renew contact with some of the people there. Then via Combermere, Arnprior and Renfrew to Ottawa for two days sightseeing, including the interesting features of parliament hill, and enjoying a concert programme on the new carillon in the Peace Tower. On our return journey we came via Kingston and had a short visit with Aunt Agnes in Toronto" (121–2). In my mother's photograph album are pictures of rural roads, country people, and an al fresco picnic, with a blanket spread out under a tree with water—probably the St. Lawrence—in the background. When the food had been laid out, she and Uncle Frank took photos of each other sitting on the ground.

Alice kept two souvenirs of the trip, both of them menus. One was from the Chateau Laurier in Ottawa, a printed menu dated Thursday, 28 August 1930, for a five-course table d'hôte dinner in the Grill Room (priced at $1.50). The other was a luncheon menu from the Royal York Hotel in Toronto, a printed document dated Tuesday, 2 September 1930. The Royal York had just opened at that time, and advertised itself as the largest hotel in the British Empire and Commonwealth. Aunt Agnes, always enthusiastic about everything new and exciting in the city, had taken her niece and nephew there. The menu was a memento of a happy occasion.

The marriage of Ruth Runnalls and Chester McLellan: 8 November 1930

Ruth had graduated as a nurse from the Strathroy Hospital School of Nursing in 1924, but of her years between then and her marriage I know only a few details. On 12 January 1927 she entered the United States at Niagara Falls, travelled on to New York, and nursed in a hospital there. It was the Polyclinic Hospital at 345 West 50th Street, across from Madison Square Garden (which was located, at that time, not at Madison Square at all but on Eighth Avenue between 49th and 50th Streets). The hospital was a famous one: it had been the scene of Rudolph Valentino's death five months earlier. I do not know how long Aunt Ruth worked in New York, but she did recall going to the top of (what was then) the world's tallest building, the Woolworth tower on lower Broadway.

The New York hospital was the only one, so far as I know, that Ruth ever worked in. At home, she was a private nurse, and that led to her meeting Uncle Ches. They were married on 8 November 1930, and Alice was her sister's attendant (see Chapter Five).

Alice as president of St. Andrew's Young People's Society 1930–1

"On Friday, the 14th of November, about 30 young people of St. Andrew's church gathered in the basement of the church for the purpose of organizing a Young People's Society. The meeting was opened by the singing of a hymn, followed by prayer by Rev. Mr. Williams. The following officers were elected: Hon. President, Rev. Mr. Williams; President, Alice Runnalls; Vice-President, Herman Pincombe; Treasurer, Jean Iles; Secretary, Marguerite Brown; Organist, Mrs. W. Nichols; Executive Bessie Snelgrove, Edna Arscott, Dick Williams and Earle Pincombe" (*Age* 20 November 1930).

Their inaugural meeting was a week later: "The Young People's Society of St. Andrew's met at the church on Friday, Nov. 28, the president, Alice Runnalls, presiding. The meeting was opened with the singing of a hymn, followed by a report of the last meeting. The president then spoke, stating that if we intend to have successful meetings we must be present, punctual, prepared. Norah Snelgrove then gave a solo, followed by a scripture reading by Miss Bessie Snelgrove. Rev. Mr. Williams then led in prayer. A splendid social topic on the life of Abraham Lincoln was given by Edna Arscott, followed by singing of a hymn. Dick Williams then gave a scripture reading. A religious topic was given by Mr. Williams on 'Secret of Success.' The offering was then taken by Herman Pincombe. The meeting closed by a hymn, followed by the benediction" (*Age* 4 December 1930).

My mother's injunction to be "present, punctual, prepared" makes her sound very school-marmish.

In the new year, the Young People's Society held joint meetings with the young people of the North Caradoc church, with St. Andrew's in charge of the program in early February and North Caradoc at the end of the month. At the March meeting, with forty-three members present, Alice gave the "social topic," whatever that was, and in April she gave a reading (at that same meeting, the literary topic was "Memorial of Archibald Lampman"). The final meeting of the year was in May, when "games were enjoyed and refreshments were served" (*Age* 21 May 1931).

The summer of 1931: A storm, and Kintail Camp

Storms with thunder, lightning, heavy rain and wind were common during the Souwesto summer, but one near the end of July 1931 was unusually severe: "This village [Mount Brydges] was right in the path of the destructive hail storm which swept over this district from the 6th concession of Caradoc, southward, on Friday afternoon last, inflicting heavy damage. Hail stones as large as eggs fell steadily for 15 or 20 minutes and could have been scooped up in tubfuls. Thousands of dollars' damage was done to fruit and grain crops. Apple orchards suffered badly. The heavy hail stones cut fruit to pieces. A large acreage of cucumbers grown for a pickling firm was badly battered. Oats and wheat were levelled to the ground and corn stripped. Seventeen panes of glass in the windows of the Anglican church were smashed by the hail, while every residence in the district suffered the loss of one or more panes. Heavy rushing winds uprooted trees throughout the district. A large ornamental tree on the property of Dr. Pardy was thrown across the lawn. It was one of the most destructive storms experienced by this district for many years" (*Age* 23 July 1931).

Alice was not at home when that storm blew through. She and Marion Stiltz, a friend from St. Andrew's church, were at the Presbyterian summer school for young people at Kintail on Lake Huron (*Age* 23 July 1931). The camp is on the lake shore about halfway between Goderich and Kincardine, and Alice took many photographs of her fellow campers. None has a name or date.

Alice's fifth year of teaching at S. S. No. 7 Caradoc: 1931–2

The trustees were obviously satisfied with Alice's teaching, for there was an announcement at the end of the 1931–2 school year: "Miss Runnalls, the efficient teacher at S. S.

No. 7, Caradoc, has been re-engaged for next year" (*Age* 23 June 1932). Not mentioned is the question of salary. The Depression had resulted in a cut in pay for many teachers, and I have a vague memory of my mother telling me that she nearly lost the school because Uncle Ches had let it be known that she wouldn't accept a reduction in her salary. Exactly how that difficulty was resolved I do not know, but my mother was well liked in the school section, and she wasn't very happy about Uncle Ches's interference.

Alice as organist of St. Andrew's Presbyterian Church, Mount Brydges

My mother told us that she played the organ in St. Andrew's for five years before she was married, from 1930 to 1935. The minister in 1930 was the Reverend H. B. Williams, whose charge also included the North Caradoc Presbyterian Church, and he was well liked. The Strathroy paper described him as "an excellent preacher, and popular throughout the district which he serves" (*Age* 23 July 1931). In the summer of 1931, he accepted a call from two Presbyterian churches near Peterborough, and his last service at Mount Brydges was at the end of August. There was a farewell gathering at the Runnalls home: "The choir of St. Andrew's Church met for practice at the home of the organist, Miss Alice Runnalls. During the evening Rev. and Mrs. J. B. Williams, who are leaving for a pastorate at Milbrooke [sic], were presented with a beautiful Hudson Bay blanket. A well worded address was read by Miss Runnalls and Mrs. Ed. Nicholls made the presentation.... Lunch was served and a social hour spent" (*Age* 3 September 1931).

It was not until November 1931, that the three Presbyterian churches—Mount Brydges, North Caradoc, and Komoka—extended a call to the Reverend W. B. Macodrum, who was at that time the minister at Cobden in Renfrew County. He too would be well liked, and in 1935 he was the man who married my parents.

The Caradoc Township Sunday School Association

The Sunday School Association was a large and flourishing organization: there were fourteen Sunday schools in the township, with more than 160 teachers and officers, and over 800 pupils. In June 1932 it held its annual convention—its 44th—in Mount Brydges, and the ladies of St. Andrew's provided two meals, dinner and supper.

The program for the convention indicates some of the religious and social concerns of the day: "In the afternoon, R. B. Ferris, of London, addressed the meeting on 'Teaching,' with special reference to the method and manner of the Great Master Teacher. In the evening, he spoke on 'The Importance of Childhood,' as the impressionable time of life. Rev. W. B. MacOdrum, pastor of the church, stressed the privileges, responsibilities and importance of the work of Sunday School teachers. The resolution committee reported in favor of memorializing the government, against the sale of intoxicants by the glass" (*Age* 16 June 1932).

On that last issue, I know that, for my mother, temperance meant abstinence. At the January 1932 meeting of the Young People's Society of North Caradoc, one of the young men "very capably" gave a paper on temperance. He "pointed out the evil of drink, how it ruins lives and happiness and brings sorrow to many a home" (*Age* 14 January 1932). My mother was present at that meeting: she gave a reading.

The Young People's Society of North Caradoc Presbyterian Church in 1932

Alice took part in many of the meetings, giving readings, organizing contests, and helping with anything that involved speaking in public. The society met every two weeks, and at each meeting a different group was in charge of the program. Contests were popular. In February 1932 my mother and Graham Bolton were captains in "an interesting contest" which the paper did not define (*Age* 11 February 1932). Later in the spring all the Young People's Societies in the Presbytery held a "model devotional contest," a competition which led to "semi-finals" at St. Andrew's between North Caradoc and Mount Brydges. The judges made North Caradoc the winner, and North Caradoc went on to the finals in London. How that story turned out the paper did not record.

A wiener roast in the summer was a popular activity, and at the end of August 1932 both the Young Women's Auxiliary of North Caradoc and the Young People's Society of St. Andrew's held one. The North Caradoc gathering was on the church grounds; the St. Andrew's get-together was at the home of Ed Bond, who lived on the 16th Sideroad. Seats were arranged around the fire, and "the evening was spent in telling stories and playing games and roasting corn" (*Age* 1 September 1932).

The Strathroy paper's reports do not often specify the subject of my mother's readings, but one for September 1932 is an exception: at a "social evening" sponsored by the Ladies' Aid of St. Andrew's, she read a paper entitled "St. Andrew's Father" (*Age* 6 September 1932).

Sir Harry Lauder at the Grand Theatre, London, October 1932

The Runnalls family had a gramophone. It was not one with a flaring horn on top (like that in the RCA Victor icon, where a dog, head cocked, is listening to "His Master's Voice"), but rather a later model, a wooden box with a top that flipped up to reveal the turntable, and a front with flaps that opened to let the sound out. The records were 78 r.p.m., heavy lead discs easily broken, and they were stored in slots in heavy binders. The needles that ran in the grooves were worn after a few plays and had to be replaced frequently. There was a crank to tighten the spring that turned the turntable, and a record might give the listener six or seven minutes of music.

Many of the records featured the songs of the Scotch comedian and entertainer, Sir Harry Lauder. When he came to the Grand Theatre on 11 October 1932, Alice was in the audience: she kept the program in her scrapbook. At all his performances he sang his own compositions, among them "Keep Right on to the End of the Road," "Roamin' in the Gloamin," and the comic song "I Hate to Get Up in the Morning." Those would later be songs my father sang while my mother accompanied him.

My mother as president of the St. Andrew's Young People's Society, 1933

Alice was deeply involved in Young People's societies: she was president of the St. Andrew's group in 1933; she took part in the meetings of the North Caradoc Society; and joint meetings with other societies brought together large numbers of young people and varied programs. In March 1933, for instance, Mount Brydges and Appin held a joint meeting where Alice was in charge. About seventy young people were present (*Age* 9 March 1933). A week earlier, Alice had given a "topic" entitled "Missionary

Call" at a regular meeting of the North Caradoc Young People (*Age* 9 March 1933)—yet more evidence of her abiding interest in missions. A year later, on 19 March 1934, Alice gave a paper to the same group. Its title: "The Pathfinder of Tomorrow—George Leslie McKay"—a "topic" the paper described as "well given and very interesting" (*Age* 22 March 1934).

Mackay (the correct spelling of the name, according to the *Dictionary of Canadian Biography*) was from Oxford County, as I have already said—in fact, from Zorra Township—and he, like Uncle Frank, had received his theological training at Knox College, Toronto. His work as a missionary was controversial, and I wonder now if my mother dealt with any of his practices that earned criticism. The *Dictionary of Canadian Biography* describes him as "educator, Presbyterian missionary, dentist, anthropologist, and author" (13: 653). Dentistry was one of his "peculiar" methods. "He and his helpers would take their stand in an open place and, after singing and preaching, offer to extract teeth loosened by tropical diseases. 'The Bible and the forceps went together,' Mackay later stated, claiming he had extracted 40,000 teeth in 30 years." His "explosive egomania" coloured his relations with his fellow missionaries, but that same energy helped him found schools and hospitals (one in Taipei is still named after him). "He proved that one missionary could run an educational, medical, and evangelistic mission on a 'shoe-string budget,' aided by an army of paid evangelists and female catechists (in his case, at 60 stations)" (*DCB* 13: 653-4). What were my mother's sources? I simply do not know. But if Marian Keith's 1912 biography was one, her label for McKay—"the black bearded barbarian"—might have made him a flawed hero in my mother's eyes.

I have often wondered about my mother's views on the position of women in the church at that time. She had been independent and had been earning her own salary since she was nineteen, but what would she have thought of a woman as minister? The possibility was in the air. In April 1934 the St. Andrew's Young People held a debate, "Resolved, that women should hold office in the church." Wynne Kincade and Mrs. Macodrum spoke for the affirmative, Mr. Macodrum and Hugh Forbes for the negative. The judges decided in favour of the affirmative side (*Age* 19 April 1934).

Courting

There was a usual pattern in the life of a young woman who had graduated from Normal School and had started teaching in a one-room country school: a young man from the section, almost always a farmer, would become interested in her; he would court her and they would eventually marry. Did Alice have young men from the section interested in her? I simply don't know. But long after my mother's death, Aunt Ruth was telling me about a group home in Lobo Township, just north of Hickory Corners "on Clarence Ward's farm." Then she said, "You don't know who Clarence Ward was, do you? I shouldn't be telling you, but—" The Ward brothers farmed on nine hundred acres in the township, Aunt Ruth said, and when my mother was teaching, Clarence Ward "took her out." The relationship lasted about two years. Clarence had a big car, and drove Alice everywhere. Uncle Ches was courting Aunt Ruth at the same time (1930), and Uncle Ches and Clarence would both be at my grandparents'. "We used to make quite an elaborate lunch," Aunt Ruth said, "and Mother made a cake with dates and raisins. Clarence Ward would say, 'That's awful good cake.'"

Aunt Ruth recalled a more recent incident, when Mum and Dad were visiting her and Uncle Ches, and something was said about the Napier garden party. "It was so cold," Aunt Ruth reported my mother as saying, "that we had to sit in the car." "I don't remember that," Dad said. "You do remember it, John," my mother said; "I wasn't there with anyone else." Aunt Ruth and Uncle Ches could scarcely suppress their amusement at this claim: "I guess she never told your Dad that she went out with Clarence Ward."

According to my aunt, Clarence Ward was a "dude." That meant that he was something of a dandy, and confident in manner; it also meant that, in her view, he was probably not the best kind of man to be a husband. Clarence was eleven years older than Alice; he farmed in Lobo Township until 1937, when he moved to Adelaide. He never married. He died in Strathroy in December 1956, and was buried in the Ward plot in Poplar Hill Cemetery.

Though my mother never mentioned Clarence Ward, she did have a courtship story from her teaching days, when she was boarding at Crawfords'. "Mr. Crawford had a young Englishman as a hired hand," my mother said, "and they used to have great arguments. One day it was raining and he came to the school in the buggy to drive me home, and on the way he asked me to marry him." My mother was so surprised that she laughed at him. Shortly after that, when everyone was away, he stole fifty dollars from the house and vanished, leaving a note saying that "since Alice would not marry him he was leaving."

I do not know exactly when my mother met my father. They would not have met at all had it not been for two circumstances: Aunt Ruth's November 1930 marriage to Uncle Ches McLellan and her move to Brooke Township, to a farm next to the Hairs'; and Aunt Ruth's getting to know my father, unattached since the death of Edna Dolbear in August 1930. I can only speculate that Aunt Ruth did not approve of Clarence Ward, and liked my father. So it was that, when my mother visited her sister, she met the man she would eventually marry.

The first documentary evidence of their relationship is in the Strathroy paper in June of 1933. I have already noted the unusual practice of Caradoc Township in honouring its war dead not in November but in late June or early July, and in 1933 the service, which was attended by more than one thousand people, was under the auspices of the St. Andrew's and North Caradoc Presbyterian churches, who also provided the music. Among the "appropriate solos" sung on that occasion was one by "Mr. Hare [sic] of Watford." I would like to think that my mother accompanied him, but in fact "Mrs. Duncan Campbell was at the piano" (*Age* 22 June 1933).

Perhaps by this time my mother was going to garden parties with my father, and they may have been at North Caradoc's in August 1933. It drew a huge crowd: "The weather was ideal and a record crowd from all parts of the county, and also adjoining counties, turned out to enjoy the splendid program provided. James Dymond, popular warden of Middlesex, fulfilled his duties as chairman most acceptably" (*Age* 17 August 1933). The entertainment, which by this time was mostly professional, included a "harmony duo of Toronto," a "comedy team," also of Toronto, a "ventriloquist and magician," a "comedian boy soprano ... with his lilting songs and Scotch brogue," and two more comedians, plus the Canadian Cowboys Old Tyme Orchestra. At the 1934 garden party, Mr. Macodrum occupied the chair; the Canadian Vaudeville Exchange provided the entertainment; and there were "musical clowns," a "black-face comedian," a piano accordianist, and a "silver-toned tenor" (*Age* 16 August 1934).

Howard Runnalls marries Eleanor McEwen: 4 November 1933

Uncle Howard had graduated from Western in May 1931, and in 1931-2 he attended the Ontario College of Education in Toronto. His first teaching job was in the high school in Wallaceburg, and he taught there for two years, from 1932 to 1934. He had met Aunt Eleanor at Western, and they were married at her parents' home, Lot 28, Concession 2, Stanley Township (near Clinton) on 4 November 1933. The *Age* carried an account of the wedding: "The bride, who was given in marriage by her father, wore a gown of white satin and lace made in princess lines with a short white satin jacket, and veil of net held in place by a wreath of orange blossoms. She carried a bouquet of Johanna Hill roses and yellow orchids. The wedding music was played by Miss Alice Runnalls, sister of the groom. During the signing of the register, Miss Elizabeth Cluff, of Seaforth, sang 'O Perfect Love.' After the ceremony an informal reception was held. Mrs. McEwen, mother of the bride, was gowned in navy blue flat crepe and she wore a shoulder bouquet of Talisman roses. Mrs. Runnalls, mother of the groom, was dressed in black crepe and she wore a corsage of Prentier Supreme roses. Later Mr. and Mrs. Runnalls left by motor for a short trip, the bride travelling in a gray rabbit's wool dress with a black coat and black accessories. They will reside in Wallaceburg, where the groom is a member of the staff of the High School. Both bride and groom are graduates of 1931, Western University, London" (*Age* 9 November 1933).

Uncle Howard and Aunt Eleanor would have two children: Marilyn (born 20 September 1934) and Sandy (born 7 July 1941).

Uncle Howard taught in the high school in Wallaceburg for two years, from 1932 to 1934, and during that time he and Aunt Eleanor entertained my parents, who were now a couple, to dinner. Then, in the summer of 1934, they left on a trip to "New Ontario," and Grandad Runnalls went with them. ("New Ontario" is a label which has long since fallen into disuse, but at that time it designated the vast territories north of Lake Nipissing and the Mattawa River which had been added to the province in a series of boundary adjustments from the time of Confederation onwards.) As a result of this trip, Uncle Howard took a teaching position at the Timmins High and Vocational School. He and Aunt Eleanor were not sure they would like living in the north, but they did, and Uncle Howard spent the rest of his teaching career there. He taught mathematics, and in 1945 he became vice-principal of the school. Every July and August, Uncle Howard and Aunt Eleanor came to southern Ontario, and stayed in Clinton and Mount Brydges.

Also teaching in the Timmins H. & V. S. was Howard's first cousin, Neil Runnalls. Neil had done post-graduate work in geology and, after an M.A. at Western and more work at Queen's, he taught mineralogy in Timmins, the area where he had done his research for his thesis. At Christmas time, 1934, he married Mabel Toles, whom he had known since their school days in Mount Brydges, and who had boarded with my mother when they were both at Normal School in London in 1926–7.

The wedding of Bob Irvine and Kay Avery: 8 September 1934

Bob was the only son of Aunt Agnes and Uncle Norm, and in September 1934 he married Kay Avery. They planned a wedding which would be "very quiet and informal," in the words of Kay's mother who, in a handwritten note invited Alice to the ceremony, which was to be in Waldemar (near Orangeville), on the lawn at the home of Kay's grandfather, Robert Hewitt. Alice did not go. Years later she told Marjorie that she felt she could not afford an outfit to attend a smart wedding: the time was the depths of the Great Depression, and she had taken a cut in her annual salary. One detail about the ceremony indicated for my mother just how "smart" the wedding was: "During the ceremony and while the register was being signed, Madame Françoise Cadieux played softly on the harp" (*Age* 13 September 1934).

Alice did send a wedding gift—blankets with white satin bows—and received a note from Kay: "I am awfully sorry that you were not able to get to our little wedding. However, I do hope that you will be in Toronto soon & that I will be able to meet you. I have often heard Bob speak of you."

Bob and Kay would have two daughters, Denise ("Dede"), born 19 April 1940, and Barbara, born 14 November 1947. In the late 1940s, when Aunt Agnes and Uncle Norm would come to Brooke Township to visit Aunt Ruth and us, they would bring Dede with them. I remember her as a pretty girl with long brown hair and ringlets.

The St. Andrew's Young People's Society 1934–5

In October 1934 the society held a preliminary meeting to organize its winter activities, and Alice was one of those present "to draw up a program, select topics, make suggestions, and nominate officers to fill vacancies," as well as plan for a Hallowe'en party (*Age* 25 October 1934). During that fall, my mother seems to have focused most of her activities on her home church, where she was organist, and where she and my father were now a recognized couple. When the Masonic Lodge in Mount Brydges held a special service in St. Andrew's, there was also special music, and my father sang a solo (*Age* 25 October 1934). But my mother did not withdraw entirely from North Caradoc. In January 1935, when the Young People there were organizing their spring program, my mother was made assistant organist. My father again sang a solo in St. Andrew's in May 1935, when the lodge was celebrating an anniversary. No doubt my mother was his accompanist.

Preparations for a wedding

My parents set their wedding date as 5 October 1935. They had hesitated and delayed, for the Great Depression was at its height, and money was scarce. Had our mother considered continuing to teach? She may have, but at that time there was a prejudice against married women having jobs, the view being that they were supported by their husbands. In the spring of 1935 Alice handed in her resignation to the trustees in her school section. Her final report on her Caradoc pupils appeared in the Strathroy paper at the beginning of July.

The school section bade farewell to Alice with a gathering in late June: "The people of S. S. No. 7 Caradoc, met at the school last week to honor Miss Alice Runnalls, teacher for the past eight years, who has resigned. Sides were chosen and a ball game was played, after which supper was served. After supper Hugh Turner, as chairman, presented a short program including speeches by the trustees, and Miss Runnalls was called forward and presented with a silver tea service and tray. Miss Jessie Thompson read the address, while Donalda McNeill made the presentation. Miss Bernice Frank, of Mt. Brydges, will succeed Miss Runnalls as teacher at S.S. No. 7" (*Age* 4 July 1935).

Alice was always proud of the address and the words said about her, and toward the end of her life she made a copy of them for each of her children. Here is the address:

Miss Runnalls

Can we forget one friend
    Can we forget one face,
Which cheered us toward our end,
    Which nerved us for our race?
Oh! sad to toil, and yet forego
    One presence which has made us know
To God-like souls how deep our debt!
    We would not, if we could, forget.

We, your pupils, ex-pupils, and friends in S.S. No. 7 Caradoc, could not let this opportune moment pass without assembling ourselves here to say 'Au Revoir' and Bon Voyage, as you depart from us after giving eight years of competent and faithful service.

You have proved yourself a true teacher of our boys and girls endeavouring as you have by precept and example, to open to them the way of knowledge, and to instil into their precious little minds the fundamental principles of living.

Your influence in intellectual development, moral training and character building must needs have been far-reaching and deeply imprinted in and through the young lives entrusted to your care, as they daily were instructed by you throughout these past eight years. - Time, only, can reveal the fruits of your labours.

In our various other activities of church, and community, you have always most graciously and cheerfully given of your time and talents, for all of which we desire you to accept our sincerest appreciation and gratitude. In tribute, we ask you to accept this small gift of remembrance, and through the vista of future years may it fill your cup with fond and happy memories of the days spent in S.S. No. 7.

We shall not wish you riches
    Nor the glare of greatness
But that where'er you go
    Some weary face may brighten at thy smile,
Some weary heart know sunshine for a while,
    And so thy years shall be a track of light;
Like angels' footsteps passing through the night.

Signed on behalf of the section: Hugh Turner, John McGugan, D.A. McNeill.

The summer of 1935

Alice was at home in July, August, and September 1935. During the two summer months, the three churches in Mount Brydges held joint services in the park, and at the first of them "Miss Alice Runnalls, of the Presbyterian church, was the pianist, and a choir from the various churches assisted with the hymns" (*Age* 18 July 1935). Both the Runnalls and McCracken families held reunions in Springbank Park in London. St. Andrew's had a farewell gathering for the Arscott family: Lorne Arscott was the agent at the C.P.R.'s Caradoc station, and he had been appointed to the same position at the London depot.

That same summer, the Union Gas Company built a pipeline from their Dawn field, "reputed to have almost an unlimited supply of gas," to London, and the line in Caradoc Township was along the Fourth Concession, "passing through at the Presbyterian Church corner just north of the village" (*Age* 15 August 1935). Mount Brydges was hooked up to the line. And so, when Grandad Runnalls was a widower and living in town, he cooked with natural gas. It seemed an exotic fuel when we were still burning wood at home. The sight of the blue flames and the odour of gas in Grandad's house are part of my memories from the late 1940s, and the lighting of the stove—with the spurt of flame from the pilot light—was fascinating to a child.

Death of Joyce Harvey: 22 July 1935

Joyce was the fourth child of Aunt Eva and Uncle Lewie Harvey, and she had been born in April 1934. She fell ill in the summer of 1935, and died. How it all happened caused grief and anxiety for my grandparents, and affected my mother deeply: she was living at home at the time, and witnessed everything. The loss of a child was common enough in those days, and this particular loss left our mother with a stoic and resigned attitude: one simply had to accept the fact that giving birth to a child made one vulnerable to losing that child.

Joyce "had been ill with the flu earlier in the summer from which she had not fully recovered and was taken to London last Sunday by her parents to see a specialist. Finding him away, they continued on to Mt. Brydges to the home of Mrs. Harvey's parents. Yesterday the child was seized with a choking spell and was taken to hospital for attention where she passed away. She was one year old last April ..." (*Woodstock Sentinel-Review* 23 July 1935). Joyce died in the War Memorial Children's Hospital in London; the official cause of death was "left lobar pneumonia." The next day she was buried in the North Embro Cemetery, where her father's people are all buried.

Grandad Runnalls, so our mother told us, either went out and bought a little coffin or made the coffin himself, and the funeral service was held at home, in the farmhouse on the Fourth Concession. All her life, our mother was haunted by the appearance of the sick infant, which she referred to as "a baby sleeping with her eyes open." It was her experience of "death's counterfeit" which turned out to be not "counterfeit" at all.

St. Andrew's Church honours Alice: 2 October 1935

Three days before our parents were married, the congregation of St. Andrew's gathered to honour our mother. "A delightful evening was spent at the home of Mr. and Mrs. Joseph Runnalls, 4th concession, recently, when the congregation of St. Andrew's Presbyterian Church gathered in a body to honor their daughter, Miss Alice Runnalls, prior to her marriage to John Hair, of Watford. Miss Runnalls has been organist of the church for several years and also active in all the organizations of the church. A short program of solos, readings and music was given by Hugh Forbes, Mrs. Herb Davidson, Walter Nichols, Harry Karl and Earl Pincombe. An address of appreciation was read by Mrs. W. B. Macodrum [the minister's wife] and the presentation to Miss Runnalls, a cabinet of flat silver, was made by H. Frank; a pair of silver pepper and salt shakers was presented by Laureen Nichols. The remainder of the evening was spent in games and contests and lunch was served." (My mother pasted this piece in her scrapbook without dating it or noting its source, which may have been one of the London papers.)

The address on that occasion was as follows: "Dear Alice, We, a number of your friends connected with St. Andrew's Church, come to-night on a mission that has both the aspects of sadness and joy. We are sorry that you will be breaking those bonds of association that have been so pleasant in the past. We rejoice because you are taking a step that leads to the best that is in life. And we are glad that you are not going far from your old home.

"Life is largely made up of comings and goings and it is friendship that one has for the other that makes us anticipate new departures and makes good bye hard to say. But our adieus are mingled with joy because we know that your new station will be one of happiness.

"We remember you as a faithful worker in St. Andrew's congregation. Particularly we will not soon forget your diligence and enthusiasm in leading the choir into a more beautiful conception of the Service of Praise. In the Sunday School you were a true and skilful teacher and as President of the Y.P.S. [Young People's Society] you brought your undoubted talents to the aid of this branch of church work. In fact, all the organizations of St. Andrew's will sorely miss you. And on behalf of those efforts, the members and friends wish to offer this little tribute, hoping it will serve to cement the ties already made and to express the feeling that you will not forget us when you go to your new home.

"Signed on behalf of Session. Rev. W. B. Macodrum. Board of Managers, Thomas Colvin. Sunday School, Wm. S. Curtis. W.M.S. [Women's Missionary Society], Mrs. Wyatt. Y.P.S. [Young People's Society], Annie Pincombe. Choir, Olive Nicholls. Ladies Aid, Pearl Veale."

My mother copied this in her own hand, and added this note: "Copy of address given to me with a gift from St. Andrew's Presbyterian Church, Mt. Brydges. I had played the organ there for 5 years before I was married. This meant a lot to me."

CHAPTER SEVEN
WEDDING AND EARLY MARRIED LIFE 1935–1939

Wedding day: 5 October 1935

Alice and John were married on Saturday, 5 October 1935. The day was a cold one, our parents told us long afterwards, and in fact there was an early season snowfall: my father wore his winter overcoat. Bride and groom and their attendants drove to the manse in Mount Brydges for the wedding. After the ceremony, there was a meal at the Runnalls farm. The *entrée* was "pressed chicken," our mother said many years later. There was also a wedding cake, a piece of which our mother attempted to preserve in a tin which she stored upstairs in our Brooke Township farmhouse. When she opened the tin on their tenth wedding anniversary, she found that the cake had spoiled, perhaps because she had set it on a block of wood at the bottom of the container.

The chief document from the wedding is a little booklet our mother kept in the linen drawer of her china cabinet: it contains our parents' wedding certificate, the order of service, and the autographs of guests. There were only eight, in addition to the bride and groom: Alice's attendant, her first cousin Honor Robinson; John's best man, his first cousin, Harold Hair; Alice's parents, who signed their names as "Joseph Runnalls" and "Mrs. Jos Runnalls"; John's mother. who signed as "Mrs. S. Hair"; Honor's mother, Aunt Edna, who signed her name as "Mrs. E. Robinson"; and the minister and his wife, "Rev. W. B. Macodrum" and "Mrs. Daisy Macodrum."

The "Hair-Runnalls" wedding was reported in the Watford paper: "A quiet wedding was solemnized at the Presbyterian manse, Mount Brydges, when Alice Maud, youngest daughter of Mr. and Mrs. Joseph Runnalls, was united in marriage to John A. Hair, only son of Mrs. Hair and the late Mr. Sherman Hair, of Brooke. Rev. W. B. Macodrum officiated. The bride chose a becoming gown of wood violet silk velvet, shirred at the shoulders and trimmed with buttons, with matching veiled turban. A shoulderette of briarcliffe roses and violets completed her attire. The bride was attended by her cousin, Miss Honor Robinson, of South Caradoc, smartly gowned in palmer green satin and wearing a shoulderette of talisman roses. The groom was attended by his cousin, Mr. Harold Hair, of Brooke. Following the ceremony, a wedding dinner was served at the home of the bride's parents. The groom's gift to the bridesmaid was a dainty compact prettily decorated with an old English scene and to the best man, a silver initialed tie holder. Later the bride and groom left on a motor trip to Montreal and Quebec, the bride travelling in a dress of autumn brown with a tweed coat in brown and green tones and accessories to match. On their return they will reside in Brooke township" (*Guide* 11 October 1935).

The wedding trip

Their wedding trip to Montreal and Quebec always seemed to us kids something of an epic journey. They travelled in John's 1926 Pontiac, on highways that were mostly two-lane, and they stayed in tourist homes or cabins, the usual accommodations for motorists in those days. The cost of such accommodation was $1.00 or $1.50. John had a total of fifty dollars with him.

They set off after the wedding dinner, east on Highways 2 and 5, and spent their first night in Cooksville. For one dollar they stayed in a cabin there. It was unheated, and the people who owned the place took them into their house for a while, to get warm, and then gave them a coal oil heater that gave off a strong odour all night. The next day they drove as far as Brockville where, for $1.50, they had bed and breakfast.

By the third day they were in Montreal, and Alice sent a postcard to her mother. It is dated 6 p.m., 7 October 1935: "Dear Mother. Monday. Arrived in Montreal at 2 o'clock. We are going right on to Quebec so will write more tonight. Everything has gone O.K. and we have seen some grand scenery. Alice." They drove along the north shore of the St. Lawrence, taking pictures (with John's box camera) of streets in Trois-Rivières and farmhouses along the Route du Roy. Beyond Quebec City they stayed in a cabin at Ste.-Anne de Beaupré. They saw Quebec and Montreal and, to their embarrassment, were given a ticket for parking illegally on Mount Royal. (The receipt for their fine, which was two dollars, and dated 11 October 1935, turned up among my mother's papers. The amount seems small now, but at the time that was more than the price of overnight accommodation.) They stayed in a tourist home in Ste.-Anne de Bellevue, just off the west end of the island, and discovered that the main line of the C.N.R. was directly behind the house: trains kept them awake all night. The principal road they travelled in Ontario was Number 2 Highway, which extended across the province from Windsor to the Quebec border: it took them through the centre of every town and village in eastern Ontario, and along the shores of the St. Lawrence River and of Lake Ontario. On the second-last day of their trip they drove from Montreal to Toronto, and on the final night of their honeymoon, they stayed with Aunt Agnes in Toronto. The traffic was exceptionally heavy as they approached the city from the east, for there was a federal election that day, which was Monday, 14 October. Aunt Agnes and Uncle Norm were their usual hospitable selves, but Alice always remembered Aunt Agnes' injunction to leave something for the maid.

The federal election of 1935

The federal election of 14 October 1935 brought to an end the Conservative government of R. B. Bennett, and the Liberals under Mackenzie King regained power. In our riding, which at that time was Lambton-Kent, the Liberal candidate, Hugh McKenzie, was first elected to parliament, and in Lambton West, Ross Gray, a Liberal and the sitting member, was re-elected. Gray's opponent in that election was my father's cousin,

Dr. Russell Woods, who at that time had his dental practice in Arkona. But 1935 was no time for a Conservative to hope to be elected, and Russell Woods's one-time foray into politics was unsuccessful. My father's political views at that time were Liberal. He supported Hugh McKenzie, who had been a fruit farmer in Warwick Township before he moved into Watford (where he lived in a large house on the main street), and McKenzie's victory was notable: he was the first Liberal to represent the riding in thirty-nine years. Ross Gray was a lawyer in Sarnia, and an able man: shortly after this election, he was appointed Liberal whip.

Social gatherings 1935-6

One of the earliest gatherings my parents attended after their wedding was a Hallowe'en party in the Walnut School on the Tenth Line. "A successful masquerade party was held by the W. A. of Walnut United Church, on Friday evening, 25 October. The schoolroom was suitably decorated for the occasion and a number of Hallowe'en games and contests were greatly enjoyed." Prizes for costumes were awarded: the prize for "gent" went to "Mrs. John Hair" (*Guide* 1 November 1935). There was also a gathering which I know about only through an undated newspaper item in my mother's scrapbook: "A pleasant evening was spent recently when the members of the choir of Chalmer's Presbyterian church gathered at the home of Mr. and Mrs. John Hair. The evening was spent in games and music, after which Mr. and Mrs. Hair were presented with a table mirror and silver pepper and salt shakers. Miss Alice McDonald read the address and Miss Minnie McLean made the presentation. A dainty lunch was then served, bringing the enjoyable evening to a close." In December 1935 the Brooke Women's Institute met in S.S. No. 10, where they "entertained their friends at a social evening." My father is mentioned as "assisting with the musical part of the program"—no doubt with my mother at the piano (*Guide* 20 December 1935).

My parents attended Walnut United Church on the Tenth Line—the rural church that the Hairs moved to after Salem closed in 1929. Soon after her marriage, my mother became active in the church's W.A.—the Women's Association—and she would remain active in it throughout the next two decades. Her name is first mentioned in a St. Patrick's Tea sponsored by the W.A. on 17 March 1937: on that occasion, "Mrs. John Hair gave a very amusing Irish reading." The roll call had been answered by Irish jokes; women my mother would come to know well, Margaret and Dorothy Coke played piano solos, and Maggie Shugg (my grandmother's first cousin) and Ileen Swartz played a piano duet. The Reverend E.W. Hart, who was the minister at the time, gave a talk on Louis Pasteur, and "the remainder of the evening was spent in the basement of the church where games and contests were enjoyed. The ladies of the church served delicious refreshments" (*Guide* 3 April 1936).

In the early days my mother's activities in the W.A. were often musical. At the April 1936 meeting, for instance, she "contributed music during the paying of fees" and in December 1936 she "played an instrumental" (*Guide* 18 December 1936). Not surprisingly, her first elected role in the organization was as pianist, though she was also made a member of the program committee for 1937. She had read the scripture lesson at the September meeting, and gave "an interesting paper on 'Friendship'" in November (*Guide* 4 December 1936). The October 1936 meeting was special: it was "held at the home of Mrs. Sherman and Mrs. John Hair," joint hostesses, when there were thirteen members and eight visitors present. The program was typical of the time: "The vice-president, Miss Jennie Edgar, took charge. Roll call was answered by a verse containing the word 'Thanks.' Mrs. Ernest Dolbear led in prayer, and Mrs. Clare Edgar read the scripture lesson. A committee was appointed to arrange for a play to be put on by the young people later. Mrs. Robert Dowling gave a reading on Thanksgiving and Mrs. Calvin Dolbear read a paper entitled 'Aunt Elmira's Thanksgiving Dinner.' The meeting closed with hymn and prayer. The hostess served a bountiful lunch and a pleasant hour was spent" (*Guide* 6 November 1936).

My parents played a large part in the life of Walnut United Church. Early every January there was a congregational meeting, always preceded by a supper in the church basement. The 1937 meeting was on January 13; Mr. Hart presided; my mother was elected one of three organists, and my father the choir leader (*Guide* 22 January 1937).

While my mother was entering enthusiastically into the life of her new church, Grammie Runnalls was gradually withdrawing from the life of hers. From the beginning of 1936 on, her name no longer appears in the reports of the meetings of the W.M.S. and Ladies' Aid. She was by this time in her late sixties, and had been a faithful worker in both organizations, but she must have been getting tired. Grandad, however, continued to hold office. At the annual congregational meeting in February 1936 he was one of four men elected a member of Session. He had in fact been clerk of the session since 1902, the year St. Andrew's separated from Cook's. My mother returned to St. Andrew's for the September 1936 anniversary service, when the soloist was "Mr. Hare, of Kerwood," and when a former minister, Mr. Williams, spoke to "capacity crowds." The church supper the next evening was "a huge success" (*Age* 17 September 1936).

Dad's "acrobatic hen"
Also from this period (I think) is an item I have been unable to trace: it is dated 4 October, but I do not know the year, nor do I know which newspaper it appeared in. It is a human-interest story headed "Acrobatic Hen Does Six-Mile Riding Stunt." The story: "John Hare [sic], Brooke Township farmer, has an acrobatic hen that balanced herself for six miles on the side of a trailer. About to start off with a load of grain to the grist mill here [Watford], Mr. Hare noticed the hen perched in a difficult and precarious position on the side of the trailer. He left her there, supposing she would fly off when he started his car. Stopping at Watford, he found the hen in the same position. He put her in a bag for the return trip to the farm. Mr. Hare was asked if he thought it possible that the hen had laid an egg on the trip, but he said that if he said 'yes' the people might think he was stretching the story a little too far." The story is possibly from 1936 or 1937, since my mother kept a postcard with a George V stamp on it, from the "Newspaper Clipping Bureau" in Toronto, promising to send "an interesting news item about you from a Canadian Daily Newspaper" upon receipt of 25 cents in "stamps or coin."

There were two mills in Watford, and my father divided his business between them. One was run by Dave Gribben, and was in a big black boxy structure facing the railway, across from the station; the other was owned by Herb Clark, and was at the rear of a main-street hardware store and next to the arena. Both were noisy, dusty places. The grain, when ground, was referred to as "chop," and Dad fed it to the pigs.

My father's early career in municipal politics
After my grandfather's death in May 1934 my father was urged to take his place on the township council, but he refused. He did, however, apply to be assessor of the

township for 1935, probably because he needed the money. He put in a bid of fifty dollars; his was the lowest of four bids; the Great Depression showed no signs of lessening; and the township council, conscious of the need to cut costs wherever possible, accepted the lowest bid. (As an indication of just how bad things were, the assessor in 1927 had been paid $115—more than double my father's stipend in 1935.) Still, there was a benefit of the work which extended beyond pay: my father came to have an intimate and comprehensive knowledge of the township. I always marvelled at his ability, when we were driving along any concession or sideroad, to name who lived in the farmhouses, who owned pastures and woodlots and floodplain land, who had cut timber out of a bush, who had put up a barn and when, who was related to whom or who had married whom, and who could be counted upon to purchase municipal bonds.

My father's appointment as assessor was for one year only. He applied for a renewal in 1936, and put in a bid of fifty-five dollars. Wesley Douglas tendered for fifty dollars, and Council again chose the lowest bidder.

But in 1936 my father became a township councillor, and it happened in an unexpected way. The Liquor Control Board of Ontario had a store in downtown Sarnia, on Christina Street North, and in the spring of 1936 one of our neighbours on the Twelfth Line, Donald McDonald (whom we knew as "Dan"), was appointed manager of it. The appointment was a political one by the Liberal government of the day; McDonald had been elected to the Brooke Township council only a few months earlier; and his resignation left a vacancy on council which made necessary a special nomination meeting, held on 22 June. The Watford paper was of the opinion that "no doubt the vacancy will be filled by acclamation for the remainder of the year's term" (*Guide* 12 June 1936). The paper was right. On 26 June it reported that "John Hair was elected by acclamation on Monday at the Brooke twp. nomination for councillor to fill a vacancy caused by the resignation of Donald A. McDonald.... Mr. Hair is a son of the late Sherman Hair, a former deputy-reeve of the Township of Brooke, and will be a good council representative for the north-east corner of the township." My father told me that he had not sought the nomination and had not even been at the meeting: Uncle Harry Watson brought the news to him afterwards.

My father's entry into municipal politics could not match the drama of "Dan" McDonald's first days as manager of the liquor store in Sarnia. On his third day on the job, Saturday 23 May, just before closing time at 6:00 p.m., there was an attempted hold-up at the store, and in the shoot-out which ensued, the two would-be robbers and a police officer were killed. It turned out that one of the robbers was the country's most famous criminal, Norman "Red" Ryan, a bank robber who had served time in Kingston penitentiary. He had been released as the poster boy for correction and rehabilitation, but in fact was leading a double life. The shoot-out, more typical of Chicago gangsterism than Canadian crime, was a sensational news story, and the Sarnia paper made the most of it, publishing an extra edition in the evening of 23 May. It included a photograph of McDonald who, because he was an eye-witness to most of the action, told his story, which took up half a column. In a macabre bow to the public's prurient interest, Ryan's bullet-riddled body was put on display and attracted great crowds. His career, with all its moral paradoxes and ambiguities, gave rise to one of the important novels in Canadian literature, Morley Callaghan's *More Joy in Heaven* (1937): Callaghan based his central figure, Kip Caley, on Ryan.

In stark contrast, my father's first council meeting in Alvinston on 6 July was quiet and uneventful. His name appears on two motions, one to approve the funding for a drain, and one to pay the township accounts as listed in the minutes. Other local issues emerged a month later. "Clarence Lewis complained that weeds on 27 sr [sideroad] south of con. 12 had not been cut, also a culvert was out of repair." This was the section of the sideroad which ran past Grandad Watson's farm, which Clarence (our next-door neighbour) now owned. The sideroad would eventually be abandoned by the township, but in 1936 Clarence's complaint was referred to the road superintendent. At that same 3 August meeting, accounts were examined and approved for payment: among the items was one for six dollars, payable to my father for "sheep killed."

As the time for the annual municipal elections approached in December 1936, there seemed to be little likelihood of a contest. "Acclamation in Brooke?" was the *Guide*'s question above its lead story: "Popular Opinion Indicates Brooke Council Will Be Returned by Acclamation / In Brooke township opinion, sounded among the council members and the ratepayers alike at the present time would indicate the entire 1936 Council would be returned by acclamation for another year. / Municipal affairs have gone along very smoothly for the past year in the southern township: the tax rate is agreed as very reasonable, the township council contains men of sound judgement and long experience – 'why change for 1937?' – seems to be the consensus of opinion. / Reeve James E. Wallis, Deputy-Reeve Stanley Graham, and Councillors Donald McLean, Duncan Turner and John Hair (the latter succeeded D. A. Macdonald [sic] in the northeast corner of the township when he resigned in July) may go before the ratepayers at the annual nomination meeting to be held in Inwood on Monday, December 28th, give their reports of the year's work, and anticipate a unanimous approval and return to office for 1937 without opposition. At least such is the anticipation, ten days in advance!" (*Guide* 18 December 1936). The expectation became reality. "At the annual nomination meeting in Brooke on Monday, the entire 1936 Council was returned by acclamation for another term. Municipal affairs are considered entirely satisfactory in the southern township, and even the proposed candidates considered an election unnecessary this year" (*Guide* 1 January 1937). The stipend for councillors in 1937 was set at fifty dollars.

The last council meeting of 1936 (it had been held on 15 December) had included an echo—a distant one—of world events: "Members of Council and Officials signed the Oath of Allegiance to King George VI" (*Guide* 1 January 1937).

Duncan Turner

Duncan Turner was first elected to the township council in January 1936, and in that election he headed the polls for councillors. He would play a significant role in my father's career in municipal politics, as my father's ally and steadfast friend on council, and he would go on to become warden of the county in 1944.

Dunc Turner was a bachelor. He lived with his sister Flora on a farm near Inwood, and my father once told me that, after I was born, Dunc Turner said to him, with a mixture of envy and regret, "you have a boy at home." (And when I was a bit older and Dad was buying me a little train set, Dunc Turner, who happened to be with him, said he wished he had a son to buy a train for.) Two other Turner sisters and a brother lived in a big old white-brick house on a farm just south of Alvinston, on what is now Highway 80 (the Courtright Line) and east of the Nauvoo Road; the Kingscourt-Glencoe branch line of the C.N.R. cut diagonally across their fields.

Years later, my father reminisced about the Turners: Dunc came from a large family, he said, but neither he, nor any of his brothers or sisters, ever married. Rumour had it that there was a family disease, because a sister had died suddenly at Christmas, halfway through her first year of teaching. The Turners whom my father remembered (aside from Dunc) were Mac, Alma and Flora. Alma had a boyfriend, he said, who for years came out to the farm every Sunday night with a brick of ice cream. I have always thought that that relationship, which went nowhere, sounded like something in an Alice Munro short story. But my father had yet another story, and this one dates from years later, when Dunc was dead and Dad was clerk-treasurer of the county, selling County of Lambton bonds. Bell Gouinlock, the Toronto investment firm which issued the bonds, sent a man up to Sarnia to help sell them, and he and my father drove to Alvinston, hoping the Turners would buy some. They found Mac, in overalls and a shapeless hat, in the pool room in the hotel. He looked down-and-out, Dad said—and then he astonished the man from Bell Gouinlock by buying $10,000 worth of bonds. There was yet another surprise: "My sisters are up at the church quilting," Mac said; "maybe they'll take some too." So Dad and the investment dealer went up to the Presbyterian church, and Alma and Flora came out. One took $7,000 and the other $8,000. They were not the only Brooke township people to buy bonds that day, but they were certainly the best sale.

Joseph Haire, centenarian

In 1936 the Watford paper began to carry stories about Joseph Haire of Edmonton. It did so because Joseph had reached his one hundredth birthday on St. Patrick's Day, 1936, because he had Watford connections, and because he was (according to the *Edmonton Bulletin*) a colourful character. On 10 April 1936 the *Guide-Advocate* reprinted a piece from the Edmonton paper, an interview with the centenarian which contains just about every cliché one might expect of a journalist getting an interesting story out of a man more than willing to play the part of the aged and "genial Irishman": "as fit and frisky as a young colt," "the young oldster," "the old gent's amazing vitality," "neither smoked nor become a devotee of the flowing bowl," "has read the Good Book seven times," "has never seen a motion picture and never intends to," and "believes that people eighty years ago were much more happy than today's citizens." But the story also gives information about Joseph's early life in the west: he "settled in Alberta in 1903, lived in a sod shack for years, cut his grain with a cradle, hauled it twenty-five miles and sold it for 30 cents a bushel." Joseph's wife Martha died in September 1936 at the age of eighty-seven. She had been a Hume from Watford, and she and Joseph had been married for almost sixty-five years. Joseph himself died in June 1941, at the age of 105.

How is Joseph Haire related to us? He was a son of Thomas Hair, brother of our great-great grandfather, James Hair.

Death of Aunt Jennie (Munro) Watson, February 1936

My grandmother's surviving brother, Oscar, had married a Munro from Mosa Township. When my father was growing up, Uncle Oscar and Aunt Jennie farmed in "the peak of Mosa," that part of the township which thrust up into the eastern boundary of Brooke, and their closest village was Alvinston, only a mile or so away on the west bank of the Sydenham River. The farm was on (what is now) Buttonwood Drive, close to Highway 80, and the nearest community was Kilmartin, also on that highway. There on one side of the road stands Burns Presbyterian Church; on the other is the Kilmartin cemetery.

But the Munros were not Presbyterians; they belonged to the Church of Christ Disciples. Mosa Township was one of the places where the disciples had made early inroads after their origins in the United States: a church was organized in Mosa about 1862, according to Reuben Butchart's history, *The Disciples of Christ in Canada since 1830*, and both a John Munro and a John B. Munro were deacons in that congregation. The Disciples were distinguished as a denomination because they avoided an explicit creed and relied on a reading of the scriptures unmediated by inherited doctrine. Their goal was the eliminating of denominational lines and the "striving for Christian unity through a single scriptural fellowship." Though Uncle Oscar had been raised in the Methodist Church, he became a Disciple when he married Aunt Jennie.

They were married on 20 April 1911, when Uncle Oscar was twenty-nine and Aunt Jennie forty, and started their married life by renting the farm next to ours on the Twelfth Line, but they moved around a good deal. In 1927 they left Mosa and moved to London, where Uncle Oscar had been appointed manager of the farm attached to (what was then called) the Ontario Hospital, later the London Psychiatric Hospital on the northeast corner of Dundas Street and Highbury Avenue, which was called at that time "the asylum sideroad." The hospital had been headed, in the last decades of the nineteenth century, by Dr. Richard Maurice Bucke, a psychiatrist with progressive and humane ideas about the treatment of the mentally ill, a friend of Walt Whitman and the author of *Cosmic Consciousness* (1901), which owes much to the transcendentalism of Carlyle and Emerson. Bucke was long dead by the time Uncle Oscar took up his post, but the farm was part of the therapy Bucke had championed, and patients who were able to do so worked in the fields or the barns under Uncle Oscar's supervision. His niece Catherine Watson recalled going with her mother and her uncle to the barns at milking time, and seeing a man walk around and around their car: "if anyone else came near, he chased that intruder away. We could see Uncle Oscar looking out of the barn door from time to time to see what was going on." The man, they realized, "was protecting us."

Uncle Oscar did not have to make the farm "pay" in the way my father and grandfather had to make a living out of their farm, and my father would speak with some envy about his uncle's ordering a carload of something or other and having it paid for out of the hospital's budget rather than from the return on crops or milk.

Uncle Oscar and Aunt Jennie lived at a number of different addresses in East London, but by 1935 and 1936 they were in a house at 385 Ashland Avenue, which runs south off Dundas Street East. The nearest church of the Disciples was on Elizabeth Street, a block or so north of the East London business district. The church, a square handsome red-brick structure with a white portico and pillars, was new—it had been built in 1925—and it had an able and energetic young minister by the name of Benjamin Eckhart, who started preaching there in 1927 and who, according to the church's historian, "led the way to a remarkable advance under his long leadership" (Butchart 566). His was, indeed, a "long leadership": he was still preaching there when I was an undergraduate at Western in the late 1950s. His name was frequently in the newspaper or on the radio, and I thought at the time that here was a public figure who had never met a controversy he didn't like. One issue was the religious training school he founded. It was called Philathea College, and it was chartered by the province and licensed to issue diplomas, but it granted B.A.s and Ph.D.s as well—to considerable controversy when newspaper stories exposed the lax requirements for those degrees.

Aunt Jennie had not been well during the early years of their marriage, and in 1936 she fell seriously ill. My grandmother went to London to help her brother and sister-in-law, and was there when Aunt Jennie died on 21 February 1936. My father and my mother, on separate occasions, told me a story about that time, my father's focused on Eckhart, my mother's on making the point that my grandmother was "headstrong."

"Bennie Eckhart" (as my father called him) was Uncle Oscar's and Aunt Jennie's minister, and when Aunt Jennie lay dying, he came to the house and joined Uncle Oscar and my grandmother at her bedside, where he knelt and prayed—and prayed—and prayed, going on and on about whether or not she was "saved," until Uncle Oscar was nearly hysterical. My grandmother, who had a temper, observed all this until finally, when she could put up with no more of it, took Eckhart by the seat of the pants and the scruff of the neck and ran him out of the house. In spite of that, Eckhart conducted both funeral services, one at the house on Ashland Avenue, one in Burns Presbyterian Church in Mosa, after which Aunt Jennie was buried in Kilmartin cemetery.

I do not know how long my grandmother remained in London before returning to the farm. Uncle Oscar seems to have left the Ashland Avenue house soon after Aunt Jennie's death, and boarded or roomed at various addresses in the late 1930s. Nor do I know when he moved to Woodstock to manage the farm for the Ontario Hospital there. But at some point he met Jean (Breckenridge) Stephens, and they were married on 26 May 1945. I remember my grandmother's consternation when she received a letter from her brother telling her that he was about to re-marry, and her conflicted feelings when she wrote her reply. For Aunt Jean was a divorcée, and in those days that carried with it a certain stigma. Memories of the King and Mrs. Simpson were still fresh. But Uncle Oscar and Aunt Jean seem to have had a happy relationship. They lived at 485 Vincent Street in Woodstock, a two-storey white-brick house with an extensive garden, and Uncle Oscar, who wanted to keep busy in retirement, worked in the laundry of the Woodstock Hospital, which was just across the street. He died on 24 July 1952, just short of his seventieth birthday. He and Aunt Jean had attended Central United Church in Woodstock, but Uncle Oscar was buried in the Anglican cemetery there. Aunt Jean, who was a good deal younger, lived on in Woodstock for another twenty-five years, until her death on 17 June 1977. She too is buried in the Anglican cemetery.

Deaths in the Woods family, 1937

Arthur Woods and Dr. W.H. (William Henry) Woods, first cousins of my grandfather, Sherman Hair, died in the same month, January 1937. Arthur Woods had owned and operated the general store in Kerwood for thirty years, and W.H. Woods had long been the family doctor in Mount Brydges. Both the obituaries reminded the reader of family connections and history. Arthur Woods "was born in Brooke Township, a son of the late William Woods and Jane Carter, natives of Ireland, and early settlers in the district" (*Age* 14 January 1937). The same information appeared in Dr. Woods's obituary, with more detail: his parents "came to Canada as young people, met in Toronto, married and moved to a bush farm in Lambton County" (*Guide* 29 January 1937). The brothers were buried in the chuchyard of St. James on the Sixth Line, a cemetery which, as I have already noted, is the final resting place of many Irish Protestant immigrants from Counties Tipperary and Monaghan.

A few months later, on 31 May 1937, Mrs. Gilbert Woods died. Her death took place at the family home on 27 Sideroad, where her funeral, which was a large one, was also held. My father sang at the funeral, and no doubt my mother accompanied him. The piece he chose was "Some Day I'll Understand," and when the Woods family placed a "card of thanks" in the Watford paper, they "especially" mentioned my father. Soon after his wife's death Gilbert Woods retired from farming and moved into Watford, where he died in November 1942. Present at his funeral were many "descendants of Eliza England," the common ancestor of the Woodses, the Johnstons, and the Hairs, but the death they mourned represented a loosening of family ties and a loss of family memories. For a few years the descendants would continue to hold their annual reunion in Grand Bend, and we would continue to have ties with three of Gilbert Woods's sons: Will, who was a cattle dealer and rented our farm for pasture after Dad took the job in Sarnia; Russell, who was the dentist in Watford from 1942 on; and Norval, the United Church minister who, in 1940, was stationed in Exeter.

Though the ties of family members would eventually dissolve, the memories that preserved them did not entirely disappear. One of Eliza England's grandsons, William Johnston of Exeter, who was by this time in his early eighties, had prepared a family history, mainly by getting in touch with all his grandmother's known descendants and asking them for information. He had the history printed in Exeter and distributed, free of charge, at the 1940 reunion in Grand Bend. The following year, a great-grandson of Eliza England, Dr. Victor Johnston of Lucknow, was elected in charge of the reunion. Years later, he would publish the story of his life, which he titled *Before the Age of Miracles: Memoirs of a Country Doctor* (Toronto, 1972).

The story of Allan Edgar's house and barn

The Allan Edgars—she had been Gertrude Lucas before her marriage but my parents always referred to her as "Mrs. Allan"—lived on a farm on the north side of the Tenth Line, west of Walnut, and they went to our church, so we knew them well (we were in fact distantly related to Allan through the Smiths). Their son Lorne would become reeve of Brooke Township and, in 1964, warden of the county. How the house and barn on their farm came to be there is a story worth telling. It begins with the Foster farm on 27 Sideroad.

The Fosters lived on the east side of 27 Sideroad, north of Gilbert Woods's farm, which was on the west side. When Marjorie and I were small, Leander and Mabel Foster lived there, but before that Leander's father, Isaac Foster, had lived in a second house on the farm, built in 1922. Mrs. Foster died in 1931 and Isaac in 1933. Four years after Isaac's death, Allan Edgar bought his house, with the intention of moving it to his farm on the Tenth Line, ten miles away. "The building," the Watford paper reported, "is a 1 1/2 storey structure, 30 x 34, and scores have been out to have a view of such a large building moving along the road mounted on trucks" (*Guide* 4 June 1937). What happened next was told by the paper in its issue of 11 June.

The house "crashed through the Nauvoo Road bridge at Rhymes' hill, four miles south of Watford, on Friday afternoon, without any appreciable damage to the house, but completely destroying the 33-year old bridge. / Thousands flocked to the scene on Saturday and Sunday from all sections of the country between London and Sarnia, and on Monday morning two veteran experienced movers … took charge of the difficult job of retrieving the house from its precarious position over a crumbled mass of steel and concrete and placing it high and level on the solid roadway to proceed on its journey. / So thorough and successful were their preparations, and assisted by scores of neighboring farmers who volunteered their services, once the house started to move forward on the rollers it was soon out of the danger spot." It "is an exceptionally heavy, well constructed house," the paper reported. "The abundance of heavy joists, rafters and bracing in its interior framework was no doubt a contributing factor in escaping damage while on the move." By mid-June the house had arrived at the Edgar farm, but the Nauvoo Road remained closed until March 1938, when the new bridge was opened to traffic.

The barn on the Edgar farm was a typical Ontario barn, and it was put up in the summer of 1945. Its erection was the only barn raising I ever witnessed. I had just started to school, and I remember going with my parents, walking down the lane with Dad, and watching, from a safe distance, the gangs of men as they swarmed over the crossbeams and roof rafters and ridge line. The structure, which the paper described as "huge"—it was 36 by 84 feet—was raised on an eight-foot wall which had been enlarged from the old barn, and the event attracted "150 or more men, women and children from near and far" (*Guide* 29 June 1945). The whole structure went up in one day.

Donald's birth: 24 November 1937

I was born in the old Strathroy Hospital (now long demolished) at 8:05 in the morning of Wednesday, 24 November 1937, and I was, my father once told me, "not long in coming" into this world. Dr. Sawers, our doctor in Watford, delivered me. As was the custom in those days, my mother and I were kept in hospital for two weeks following my birth. My parents announced the event in the Watford paper on December 3: "BORN / Hair - In Strathroy hospital, on Wednesday, November 24th, 1937, to Mr. and Mrs. John A Hair, nee Alice Runnalls, the gift of a son."

Winter weather had already set in, and it was severe. On the weekend before I was born, there was a storm which led to a headline in the Watford paper: "November Blizzard Blankets East Lambton / Twenty-Six Inches of Snow Blocks All Roads." The blizzard began on Saturday evening (20 November), and the snow continued until mid-afternoon on Sunday. The next week was milder, but that weather did not last. By early December the paper announced that the district was "SNOWBOUND!": "Recurring snowfalls that covered the district with fifteen inches of snow on Monday and Tuesday, followed by cold driving winds that drifted the snow across highways and back concessions, completely tied up the community on Thursday. / After scraping continually on the Nauvoo Road and 15 sideroad all day Wednesday, the roads filled in again during the night, and a horse and cutter is the only practical way of getting anywhere. / ... in late afternoon [Thursday], there was no sign of a let-up in the storm ..." (*Guide* 10 December 1937). The Brooke Council met in Inwood on 15 December, and the minutes noted attendance: "All members present but Mr. John Hair."

The weather was not the only reason for my father's absence. I had picked up an infection in the hospital and, on Dr. Sawers' instructions, my father went into Watford and brought home a nurse, a Miss Collins, who stayed at our place for a week. When Dad went to pick her up (it was a Saturday night), the snow made the roads impassable with a car, and he had to take a team of horses and the sleigh. The snow was so deep that the horses could only walk, not trot, and the journey between our farm and town (a distance of six miles or ten kilometres) took two hours each way. The night was bitterly cold. At that time every farmer had several large and bulky fur coats, wolf or raccoon or bearskin, and we had two, which hung in our granary. Dad wore one himself, and took the other for Miss Collins to wear. She put it on over all her other clothing, and was, he said, "warm as toast."

Most of the snow that winter came in November and December. In mid-January the Watford paper said the season was "just an old-fashioned winter with lots of snow and no January thaw—as yet." The rest of the season turned out to be relatively mild.

My birth was as much of an event for my grandmother as it was for my parents. When I was old enough to start taking notice of things, she often said that she wished my grandfather had lived to see me. And I gave her a new name. I was told that my earliest attempt to say her name had resulted in "Bappy," and so she became Bappy to both Marjorie and me. Uncle Gord McNeil teased her about it (and she later teased him when his grand-daughter, Marilynne, called him "Pie"). When Marjorie and I were both older, our mother made several ineffectual attempts to have us call our grandmother by a more dignified name, and I think those attempts might have succeeded had Bappy herself wanted us to drop our childhood name for her, but she didn't, and cherished it all her life. Marjorie and I were both in university when she died, but she was still "Bappy" to us and we were her "kiddies."

When my mother was reminiscing about Christmases past, she wrote about "the special year when Donald was a baby. I well remember John bringing home the little red teddy-bear rattle. That was his very first Christmas gift…."

John Hair as Brooke Township councillor (1938–9) and deputy reeve (1940)

In January 1938, for the second year in a row, the Brooke Council was returned by acclamation. James Wallis continued as reeve and Stanley Graham as deputy-reeve. The councillors were, in addition to my father, Dunc Turner and Donald McLean. But a year later, in December 1938, an election was looming in Brooke. The annual nomination meeting was held in Inwood on Christmas Monday afternoon and, said the Watford paper in announcing the event, "it is generally reported and confirmed that Stanley Graham, present Deputy, will find himself forced to step up and oppose Reeve Wallis, from pressure among ambitious councillors." That pressure did not come from my father, but from Dunc Turner, who "has expressed his readiness to stand for Deputy-Reeve," and from Donald McLean, aspiring to the same position. "This would leave John Hair the only remaining Councillor, and an excellent opportunity for new municipal material to get started" (*Guide* 16 December 1938). The election, which the paper described as "keen" and "lively," took some unexpected turns: James Wallis defeated Stanley Graham by a majority of three to one, while Dunc Turner became deputy-reeve by acclamation. And for my father the election was a triumph: in a vote which had been heavy throughout the twelve polling subdivisions, he headed the poll for councillors. "John Hair, one of last year's councillors, was returned with the high vote of the day, 548"; Clare Edgar, just starting his municipal career and a member of Walnut Church, came in second with 501 (*Guide* 6 January 1939).

In that same issue of the paper my father inserted a "Card of Thanks": "I wish to tender my appreciation and thanks to the electors of Brooke township for the splendid vote given, placing me at the head of the poll on Monday, in re-election as Councillor for 1939. As ever, I shall try to serve you faithfully during the coming year. JOHN HAIR."

Among the projects undertaken by the 1939 council was the repair of two bridges on the Twelfth Line, one of them over the creek just west of 24 Sideroad, at the end of the laneway leading up the hill into Harold Hair's farm. That project appeared in a news story as an example of "Brooke Taxes Well Spent." The *Alvinston Free Press* praised the township, "where the rates are kept at normal level consistent with the upkeep of all necessary work to keep the municipality in good condition. This has been done in a most satisfactory manner." Such approval must have pleased the council and my father, who was always reasonable and prudent in spending taxpayers' money.

My father's move up to deputy-reeve and member of Lambton County Council was a quiet one. The 1939 reeve, James Wallis, became ill and did not stand for re-election. And, as things turned out, there was no repetition of the "keen" and "lively" contest of a year earlier, and the 1940 council took their seats by acclamation. In addition to my father as deputy, Dunc Turner became reeve; Bob Tait and Clare Edgar retained their seats as councillors; and Lyle Johnston was the new man.

The attention of people was not on municipal politics anyway. The Second World War had started the previous September, and the war effort was on everyone's mind. My father, who had been too young to fight in the first war, was too old to fight in the second, but young men whom we knew, in our neighbourhood and in our church, signed up. Dalton King from the Twelfth Line was one; Raymond Swartz from Walnut Church was another; yet another was our hired man, Albert Laferriere. John McNeil, Dad's first cousin, was twenty-two years old in 1939, and he too would go off to war.

The Reverend Enos Hart

When the Hairs first started attending Walnut church after the closing of Salem, their minister was a Mr. Hazelwood. He left the Erie Street charge in 1931, and the church "called" the Rev. Enos Hart, who would be our minister through most of the 1930s. When Mr. Hart first came to Watford, he was "one of the younger men of the London Conference": he had "served overseas with the 70th Battalion for three years. Wounded in action and invalided home to Canada in 1918 he entered Toronto University as a student for the ministry and graduated in Arts and Theology in 1923" (*Guide* 20 March 1931). He came to Watford before he finished his B.D. degree, which he received from Emmanuel College in 1932. The Harts were well liked. When, in February 1936, the question of Mr. Hart's staying for a sixth year was considered by the board of managers, they did not hesitate to invite him to remain. The Harts, the paper said, had been "unusually successful in their church work" and had "a host of friends within and outside church families" (*Guide* 28 February 1936).

The annual congregational meeting of Walnut Church was always held in early January, and it began with a potluck supper served in the church basement. The 1938 meeting was held on 4 January; Mr. Hart chaired the gathering; and all groups within the congregation were reported to be "in a flourishing condition" (*Guide* 21 January 1938). Four months later, in April 1938, Mr. Hart accepted a call to Amherstburg, where he was to take up his duties on 1 July. There was genuine regret at his leaving. He had been "one of the most popular ministers in Watford in many years," and he had brought to the three churches on the charge "a sincere, vitalized program of activity" (*Guide* 29 April 1938). Under Mr. Hart, "the relationship between Erie Street, Zion and

Walnut has been most satisfactory and cordial" (*Guide* 20 May 1938). In the past five years, Walnut had attracted thirty-five new members. The building had been redecorated; chairs were placed in the basement for Sunday school classes and other activities; electric lights had been installed; and a piano had been purchased. When Walnut marked its sixtieth anniversary with afternoon and evening services on Sunday, 15 May 1938, the church had much to celebrate.

Mr. Hart was long remembered by my parents, and he was frequently invited back to the Watford charge to preach at anniversary services. My mother, whose faith was quiet but profound, always had a deep respect for ministers, and she considered Mr. Hart's life to be exemplary. When he returned, forty years later, to preach at the church's one hundredth anniversary, which was celebrated on 21 May 1978, she told me this story: "Mr. Hart was in the First World War," she said, "and prayed before one of the major battles that he would become a minister if he were spared. Ninety per cent of his fellows were killed, but he was unscathed, and he kept his word."

Just before Mr. Hart left Walnut, he baptized me. The date was 12 June 1938. The occasion must have been uneventful, and I must have behaved, for my parents told me nothing about it.

Mr. Hart's successor was the Reverend W.T. Eddy, who was preaching in West Lorne when he accepted the call to Watford. "The Erie street pastorate," the paper said, "is a heavy one, with two rural churches and a town church, necessitating four services each Sunday .... The salary is $2050 from all appointments and the manse is well equipped as a commodious, comfortable home." (The manse was at the north end of Watford's main street, next to Wallis's garage and across from the Carnegie Library.) The Eddys were Newfoundlanders, from "hardy, sturdy, British stock," and they had four young sons, Allan, Keith, Bryan, and Louis (*Guide* 13 May 1938). Many years later, Louis, a lawyer in Sarnia, would become a judge and live just down the street from my parents on Webster Drive.

Walnut Church's sixtieth anniversary: Sunday, 15 May 1938

Anniversary services were always the occasion for special music, and this anniversary featured a male choir. My father was choir leader. There were three basses, two tenors (George Mellis and Will Smith), one baritone (Orville Shugg), and four men designated as "sopranos": my father, Leonard and Calvin Annett, and Mr. Hart himself. Accompaniment was from both organ and piano: Mrs. Shugg was organist, and my mother "assisted at the piano" (*Guide* 27 May 1938).

The music was not all: "The anniversary celebration continued on Tuesday night with a hot supper served by the ladies to more than 300 people." The meal was followed by a play (*Guide* 20 May 1938).

The music in the church became an issue at the congregational meeting of January 1939. Mrs. Shugg said that she wished to be relieved of her duties as organist, a desire "acceded to with regret," and there was much discussion of new arrangements. I do not know the issues nor my parents' views, but Mrs. Clarence Coke was appointed organist. Mrs. Shugg agreed to be choir leader, "with John Hair as assistant" (*Guide* 20 January 1939).

The Women's Association in 1938 and 1939

My mother continued to be active in the Walnut Women's Association. At their September 1938 meeting she gave a reading; at the May 1939 meeting she "recited a pleasing poem." And she and my grandmother hosted the November 1938 gathering—"at the home of Mrs. John and Mrs. Sherman Hair," the paper reported, "with 22 members present." The program was typical of the time: "The president, Mrs. C. Brown, presided. The meeting opened with a hymn, followed by prayer with Mrs. Ward Zavitz. Mrs. B. McEachern read the scripture lesson. The roll call on 'Peace' was well responded to. The topic was taken by Mrs. Calvin Dolbear, a splendid paper on the history of Czechoslovakia. The business meeting followed. Discussion took place in reference to the Christmas tree. The annual meeting will be in the church on December 15th. Mrs. Coke then favored with a solo. Mrs. Brown closed the meeting with prayer. The hostess served a delicious lunch" (*Guide* 2 December 1938). A year later, my mother and grandmother were again hostesses for the group.

Selling Christmas turkeys

One of the things my parents did before Christmas to earn a bit of money was to take poultry to butcher shops in Toronto and sell the birds to meet the Christmas demand for fresh chickens and turkeys. This always involved a lot of work. Dad killed the birds by chopping off their heads with an axe; my grandmother would dip them in boiling water to loosen the feathers, and then pull them off in great wet handfuls. Next came evisceration, which involved knowing how to avoid spilling any of the contents of the intestines, and how to remove the crop without cutting it open and exposing undigested grain and feed. Heart, liver and gizzard were set aside. Once the birds were eviscerated, my grandmother held them over an open flame above our big old cookstove, and singed them so that no pin feathers were left, and the skin was perfectly clean. The birds were then packed in big baskets and loaded on a trailer behind the car. We had no refrigeration, but at that time of year none was needed. None was needed in Dad's 1927 Pontiac either, for it had no heater.

My parents would drive to Toronto and go to the butcher shops along Queen Street West. If they were lucky, Dad said, one shop would take all of their birds. Then came the long drive home. I remember Dad's telling about icy roads and the difficulty of getting up the escarpment on Highway 2 above Dundas, when their hired man had to jump out and turn the trailer sideways to keep the car from slipping back down the hill.

This whole process meant that we had no illusions about the way our food got from barn yard to dinner table. Certainly no sentimental or romanticised view: just a realistic one about doing what was necessary to earn money, and to eat. But I should add, from the twenty-first century point of view, that all of our poultry was "free range." We were a long way from being a factory farm.

Harold Hair's barns burn: February 1939

It was the front-page story in the *Guide* for 3 March 1939: "Brooke Barns Stock and Feed Burned / $5,000 LOSS FRIDAY AT MRS. JAMES HAIR'S / Fire of undetermined origin, last Friday afternoon completely destroyed the huge barns on Mrs. James Hair's farm, 12th line east, Brooke, together with 25 head of cattle, 4 horses and one brood sow; also tons of feed in mows and silo, and huge quantities of grain. / First discovered about four o'clock by Mrs. Hair, the alarm brought Watford fire pumper in a hurry, but within a few moments, the huge barns and adjoining buildings were a mass of flames, and neighbors and firemen, after getting out a few pigs and hens, could do nothing but protect the implement shed. / Included in the livestock tied in their stalls were a row of 14 milking cows, the sire of the herd just recently purchased, and four valuable horses. An additional team of horses was away in the bush with Harold Hair at the time of the disaster. About 30 young cattle were out around the straw stacks and escaped the fire. / The barns were among the finest in the district and represented three generations of work and progress on the James Annett homestead. About $5,000 of the loss is covered by insurance in the Lambton Mutual."

In afteryears my father said little about this disaster, but he once told me that the agonized cries of the trapped animals were terrible to hear, and I think he was haunted by those sounds for the rest of his life. On another occasion he told me how the fire started. It was not of "undetermined origin," as the paper said. Jim Hair, the youngest son in that family, had herded all the stock into the stable, and then set fire to the barn. His mother saw him coming out of the barn, and then she saw smoke. In those days no one said much about mental illness, but Jim, who was twenty-five years old at the time, had been suffering from it, and used to wake up Harold, his brother, at night, "in a terrible state of mind," as his niece told me years later. She remembered going to the farm that evening and "seeing the red glow of the burning barn in the darkness." Her Uncle Jim was, she said, "upstairs in bed."

In those days a family member who was mentally ill was usually committed to the Ontario Hospital in St. Thomas. That is what happened to Jim: he spent the rest of his life in institutions. He was, to me, a shadowy figure, rarely mentioned by anyone in the family, though occasionally people would refer to "St. Thomas" as code for mental illness. I never set eyes on this first cousin. He died in 1996 and was buried in his parents' plot in Strathroy Cemetery.

The Royal Visit, 1939

The King and Queen came to London on Wednesday 7 June. The day was declared a civic holiday; the C.N.R. laid on special trains to London; and arrangements were made to transport school children to see the royal couple. My parents wanted to see them too, and they drove to London to do so. They told me that I was left in the care of my great-grandfather at Aunt Eva's on Bellevue Avenue, while they took up positions opposite the C.N.R. station on York Street, to await the arrival of the royal train. Dad had his box camera with him, and took pictures of the crowds outside the station, of men in uniform and of banners and bunting. When the King and Queen were driven past in an open car, Dad snapped a picture, but it turned out blurry: the shutter speed was simply not fast enough to capture movement. Nonetheless, my parents saw the royal couple: she was usually described as "a vision in pink," he as "a tall, shy young man." At the May meeting of the Walnut Women's Association, the National Anthem had been sung "in honor of the King and Queen's visit to Canada" (*Guide* 19 May 1939). It was the great event of that summer. Less than three months later, the world was at war again.

My father's appendectomy: July 1939

In its issue of 14 July 1939 the Watford paper reported, in its regular "Brooke" column, that "After several attacks of what was thought to be indigestion, Councillor John Hair, 12th line Brooke, was stricken on Monday evening with appendicitis. He was removed immediately to Strathroy Hospital, where he underwent a successful operation. His neighbors, as well as the ratepayers of Brooke, will hope for a speedy recovery." A week later the paper reported that "Councillor John Hair … is expected to return home from Strathroy Hospital about the first of the week." On 28 July the paper confirmed his return home, where "he is well on the way to a speedy recovery."

Appendicitis was a serious matter in those days. An attack could be fatal. My father was operated on by a Dr. Berdan, who had to leave a tube in his side to drain off the fluid. His going into hospital was complicated by a summer storm which brought down trees and closed roads. My mother, who was at the hospital, had to phone Aunt Beck and Aunt May and arrange to stay overnight with them. They were living at the time in one-half of a double house on Front Street, just west of the town's business section, where Aunt May had her hair-dressing business.

CHAPTER EIGHT
THE WAR YEARS AND AFTER: 1940–1947

Wartime measures: rationing, maple syrup, and milkweed floss
In the summer of 1940 there was a national registration in progress, of all men and women over sixteen. Its purpose was to provide accurate records of "labor power" and to answer questions: "How many can be moved to more important war-time jobs? How many girls and women can take over war jobs or farm work?" After answering the questions on a "war resources questionnaire," each person was to receive a registration card, "which must be carried at all times."

Farming was considered essential work, so the registration did not affect my parents' lives; and later, when rationing of gasoline came into effect (on 1 April 1942), extra gas was allotted to farmers. We had a forty-five-gallon drum of it sitting under a maple tree alongside our garage, and it was never empty. I think my father may have used that gas not only for the tractor, but for the car as well. One coupon permitted the purchase of four gallons of gasoline, but some motorists were entitled to more, among them "farmers who do not possess a truck" (*Guide* 20 March 1942). My father was one of those. By 1943 gas rationing was more severe. Consumers were allotted forty coupons for the year, and the amount each consumer could buy with one coupon was reduced to three gallons. Farmers, however, were given a break. In June 1943 the province decided not to charge farmers the Ontario Gasoline Tax, and the gas they bought was "marked": it was coloured purple. Anyone not eligible for "marked" gasoline and found with some could be charged. Rationing brought to an end all but essential motoring. Going into town, going to church, and going to Mount Brydges to see my grandparents and to London to see Great-grandad Watson and Aunt Eva and Uncle Gord McNeil, were the extent of our travels.

Wartime restrictions affected us in other ways too. We still did not have electricity on the farm, and by the beginning of 1942 limits were placed on further expansion of rural lines. Materials and equipment, especially transformers, were simply not available. We would not have hydro until after the end of the war, when Roy Chapman of Inwood (who was the manager of the Brooke Municipal Telephone Company) wired our house and barn. That was late in 1945, I think.

By 1942 there was rationing not only of gasoline, but of foodstuffs: meat, butter, and sugar. On the farm we were not much affected by the restrictions on meat and butter, and always seemed to have enough, but sugar rationing was another matter. Sugar was essential for canning and preserving. There was no such rationing in the United States, and several times my father travelled to Port Huron, crossing the St. Clair River on the ferry from Sarnia, and returning with a fifty-pound bag of sugar. In those days nothing went to waste, and my mother and grandmother made the bags themselves into sheets. They bleached out the printing on them, but the red lettering and the word "Redpath" could still be faintly seen.

Sugar rationing led my parents to make maple sugar. When my Runnalls grandparents sold their farm, my parents bought their sugar-making equipment: pails, spiles (the circular metal tubes that were driven into the trees themselves), and the evaporation pans. Dad constructed an "arch" back in our bush; it was just a low structure with parallel sides on which the pans were placed over the fire, and there was a lean-to above the pans to shield them from rain and snow. He tapped many trees in our bush and collected the sap in barrels, hauled on a "stone boat"—a flatbed on skids—pulled by one of our big Clydesdales. The sap went into the evaporation pans, which sat over a wood fire kept burning twenty-four hours a day. I remember that my mother would stay back in the bush overnight to keep the fire going. Images of steam rising from the pans, and the glow of the fire underneath, and the smell of wood smoke, stay with me. The syrup, when it was ready, had to be filtered—bits of twigs and other debris always got into it—and then was put into Mason jars. Once my mother made us a maple syrup pie: she said she wanted us to remember what one tasted like.

The Red Cross was a prominent presence in our lives during the war: in my first year in public school (1944–5) even the primary school children were organized and held regular meetings, with elections for a slate of officers. I cannot remember anything that we actually did, except for one thing: we collected the pods from milkweed, which grew wild along the roadsides and in farmers' fields. The soft white fibres inside could be used, we were told, as insulation in airmen's bomber jackets and as material for buoyancy in life preservers. The milkweed floss replaced kapok fiber, native to the Dutch East Indies but no longer available when the Japanese occupied those islands. Milkweed floss proved to be a good substitute: as little as two pounds of it, buoyant and water-resilient, could keep a man afloat for hours. There had not been time enough to have milkweed grown commercially, and so school children were mobilized to collect the pods that grew wild everywhere in the countryside.

In our wider community, groups under the name of the Red Cross raised money; conducted blood donor clinics; sewed quilts; made clothing—skirts, blouses, dresses, shirts, and coats—for women and children; knit socks, scarves, sweaters, gloves and toques; shipped jam and honey; and packed boxes of food and clothing for the troops. The Watford paper regularly printed letters of gratitude "From Watford Boys on Active Service."

Canadians were urged to save all waste fats and bones: "Fats make glycerine and glycerine makes high explosives." And by 1943 a permit was required to slaughter hogs, "because of the urgent need of securing the quantities of bacon and other pork products necessary to meet the wartime requirements of the United Kingdom." Hence the regulating of slaughter for domestic use in Canada. This order, however, did not apply to farmers slaughtering hogs for consumption on their own farms. I recall my father and Uncle Ches killing one of our pigs, probably about this time. I remember only that the weather was cold. I was too small to be allowed to witness the slaughter, and my father took pains to make sure I didn't even know about it until well after the event. But we all—Aunt Ruth and Uncle Ches as well as our household—had fresh pork, an advantage farmers had over city people, for whom most meats were rationed.

By the end of May 1943 nation-wide food rationing came into effect, and of course gas rationing continued. Sugar, tea, coffee, butter and meat were all rationed, and books of coupons for each had to be collected in person at specified times in the basement of the public library in Watford. Housewives could fill out a special form to obtain extra sugar for canning. Beef, veal, pork, mutton and lamb were all rationed; poultry and fish were not. How much rationed meat was an individual permitted to buy? An average of two pounds per week per person. Meat rationing did not pose much of a hardship for people on farms: we always had chickens and pigs. The only concerns I can remember my parents having were for sugar and gas.

My father as Deputy-Reeve of Brooke and Lambton County Councillor

My father became deputy-reeve of Brooke in January 1940, by acclamation, as I have already said. In February, council dealt with an issue raised by the village of Inwood.

The province had announced a new regulation, to take effect on 1 March, that all milk sold in the township must be pasteurized. Dad, seconded by Bob Tait, sponsored a resolution urging an amendment to the order-in-council. "We the Council of Brooke Township," the resolution read, "go on record as being opposed to the Act as applied to rural municipalities and especially the Police Village of Inwood, which only uses about 35 quarts of milk daily, and which would make the product very expensive delivered from outside points. ... Therefore we, the members of Brooke Council, request the Act be amended or some means provided whereby police villages using only a small quantity of milk be served from T.B. tested herds and handled under strict sanitary conditions." The resolution was forwarded to the Department of Health and to the M.P.P. for Lambton East, Charles Fairbank from Petrolia. I do not know the outcome of this action.

Lying behind my father's thinking on this resolution was a practice common among farm families in those days, which was to drink unpasteurized milk. When Marjorie and I were small, our bedtime snack was "bread and milk." Dad would come in from the barn with a pail of fresh milk, still warm from the cow; Mum would fill mugs and break some pieces of white bread into it. We would use spoons to eat the mixture, always deliciously fresh, warm and frothy. In my memory the time for those snacks is always summer, when we would be outside in the stillness of a deepening purple twilight and warm humid air, sitting on the steps of our back porch, and making the treat last as long as possible.

Yet another issue was occasioned by the war in Europe. There was a great fear at the time of enemies operating secretly within Canadian society, and in June 1940 the Brooke and Alvinston councils arranged to work together "to prevent subversive movements." The Brooke Council "appointed two members of the Alvinston council committee for anti-sabotage," and also "decreed that it will be necessary for any group, clan or organisation to get a permit from the clerk and reeve before any gathering can be held in the township." The ruling did not apply "to patriotic Red Cross or municipal meetings" (*Guide* 14 June 1940). At its August 1940 meeting council approved the formation of a Township Home Guard.

In addition to these matters, Council dealt with its regular business. In January, it applied to the province for the grant on road expenditures for the previous year. It appointed a host of officials: medical officer of health, assessor, auditor, school attendance officer, tax collector, weed inspector, printer, fence viewers, sheep inspectors, pound keepers, drain inspector and ditch inspector. Each month it authorized the settling of accounts payable; it set the annual township tax levy, and acted as a Court of Revision for assessment rolls.

The chief ongoing responsibilities of council were the repair of drains and bridges and the maintenance of roads. In 1941 (when the entire Brooke Township council was returned by acclamation, this time for a two-year term mandated by the province), council undertook repairs to a drain in the twelfth concession, and my father and Clare Edgar were appointed the commissioners. The job is a good example of my father's fiscal responsibility. The estimated cost had been $1,829; the actual cost was $1,686; the balance was returned *pro rata* to the property owners who had been assessed. In the summer of 1943 council authorized repairs to the Hair Drain No. 2. I do not know exactly where that drain was, but my father was again appointed commissioner and oversaw the work, no doubt with his usual prudence.

As deputy-reeve of Brooke, my father had, for the first time, a seat on Lambton County Council, and that meant travelling to Sarnia for the five days each of the January, June and December sessions. On 18 January 1940 the Sarnia paper published a photograph of the "six 'colts'" on council, my father being one of them. The winter weather for the January session of council was invariably bad, and 1940 was no exception: that week brought a cold snap and a blizzard. The June session was just the opposite: the 1940 meetings were held in the midst of a heat wave. The Warden's Picnic was always on the Wednesday of the June session, and was held in Grand Bend, with dinner in the Imperial Hotel there. The chief activity of the afternoon was a baseball game, and new members of council were always made captains of the opposing teams. That was because they didn't know about an ongoing joke: the trophy was an elaborately packaged chamber pot. Though my father was one of the "colts," he was not one of the captains, and I do not know whether or not he played on the winning team.

My father, as a new member of council, was appointed to two of the least important of the ten standing committees, the Printing and Legislative committees. The first had responsibility for contracts to print minutes and other council documents, and the second was responsible for responding to resolutions passed by other municipalities and sent on for Lambton's support.

But council's business also introduced my father to concerns well beyond those of the township council, matters with which he would, much later, be deeply involved. They were the costs for the administration of justice, the maintenance of the jail and court house, and services such as the House of Refuge and the Children's Aid Society. One ongoing issue was the co-operation between the county and the City of Sarnia on the division of costs for those services.

The war effort led to a decision of county council which would have repercussions for decades to come. On 12 October 1940 council held a special session to consider turning over to the provincial government the county's reforestation land in Bosanquet Township for war purposes. The land was 637 acres facing Lake Huron, and the

Department of National Defence wanted it "for a training centre for artillery." Council agreed to the request, set the price at one dollar, and said the site was "to be used for war purposes only." The result of this motion was the establishment of Camp Ipperwash and then, for decades after the war had ended, the standoff between the First Nations of the area and the federal and provincial governments. It was the seed that grew to the occupation of Ipperwash Provincial Park and the shooting of Dudley George.

December sessions of council, like the January sessions, often took place during bad weather, and the December 1940 session was true to form. There was so much snow that the Reeve of Point Edward asked whether "the City of Sarnia should not be expected to remove the snow from in front of the court house so that the council members would not have to wade through snow up to their knees in getting from their cars to the building." John Huey, the county clerk, who had a sense of humour, informed the reeve "that he was wanted outside to remove his car so that a city plow could operate." "The episode caused hearty laughter" (*Observer* 6 December 1940).

Marjorie's birth (7 December 1940) and her first Christmas

The December 1940 session of county council ran from Tuesday 3 December 3 to Saturday 7 December. The session ended on Saturday at noon, and Dad drove home, but the weather had been bad all week, and the Sarnia paper reported "drifting snow and icy roads." There would have been a hired man at our place during the week, to do the chores, but on Saturday night Dad himself was out in the barn when Bappy (who must have been apprehensive at Dad's absence during the week, and who was alarmed that night) came to the stable and said that he had better get Mum to the hospital immediately.

Marjorie was born at five minutes before midnight, in the old Strathroy Hospital on Carrie Street. I had turned three in November, and was just old enough to start taking notice of things—or perhaps moments that are charged with emotion are those which imprint themselves on our memories. At any rate, I remember standing at my grandmother's knees, while she sat beside the old cookstove in our kitchen, and her telling me that I had a little sister. And I remember the day my parents brought Marjorie home from the hospital—or at least I remember one detail: she was in a laundry basket, which they set down carefully in the dining room: there I had my first look at my little sister.

My parents called her "Marjorie Jean." "Marjorie" was my mother's choice: she had first encountered it in a book she had read and loved as a girl, a Christmas gift from the Robertsons (he was the minister at St. Andrew's). "Jean" was my father's choice: when we were small and he was addressing my sister affectionately, he called her "Jeannie."

When my mother was reminiscing about Christmases past, she wrote about "the year when Marjorie was a baby": "I well remember Christmas Day. There was no snow on the ground and it was like summer. Mother and Dad came up to Ruth's for dinner and came over in the afternoon. Also Don (Powell) brought Anne over. She looked so much larger than Marjorie as she had been born in October. I think Catherine [Watson] and Aunt Mary [Catherine's mother] were with Don as well."

Death of my mother's sister Eva (Runnalls) Harvey: 1 July 1940

My mother's sister Eva died of cancer in the Woodstock General Hospital on 1 July 1940, at the age of thirty-seven. Not quite six months before her death, she had given birth to a son, whom she named Keith Howard. He did not long survive his mother, for he had been in poor health since birth, and he died on 19 August 1940. Mother and son were both buried in the Harvey plot in the Embro Cemetery.

Aunt Ruth and Uncle Ches, who had been married in 1930 and had no children, wanted to adopt Louise, who was my age and the youngest of Aunt Eva's three daughters, but Uncle Lewie would not hear of it and insisted the children stay together. But he did not stay with them. Keith's obituary noted that "his mother passed away a few weeks ago and the father recently signed up with the Elgin Regiment and is stationed at London" (*Ingersoll Tribune* 22 August 1940). He was then posted overseas; when he returned from England he remarried—his second wife was May Packard—and when the cement company took over his old property on Number 2 highway, he moved to a farm on the hilltop just north of Ingersoll, overlooking the town and the valley of the Thames, and there he lived for the rest of his life. He died in 1968, and Aunt Eva's first-born and only surviving son, Merle, took over the farm.

I remember Uncle Lewie chiefly from his visits to Mount Brydges in the 1940s, when he would appear in his solder's uniform, with the kids, one of whom he would usually send over to the general store for cigarettes.

Anniversary services and their music

Walnut Church celebrated its anniversary on the third Sunday in May, and the services were always the occasion for special music, which my parents helped to provide: my father "rendered" tenor solos (in the quaint diction of the day) and my mother "presided" at the piano. When the Watford paper reported on the anniversary of 19 May 1940, its story was mostly about the music. My father was, at the time, assistant choir leader, and must have helped choose the anthems, which were "O Be Joyful Unto the Lord" at the morning service and "At Sunset" in the evening. My father was one of a "mixed quartett," two men and two women, who "rendered" "MyTask," and he also sang a solo, "Face to Face." "Organ and piano voluntaries by Mrs. Shugg and Mrs. Hair were appreciated" (*Guide*). (The word "voluntary" seems to have disappeared; it was a piece of music played as part of a church service, and was usually performed on an organ rather than a piano.) There was a similar report for May 1942, when Mr. Hart returned to preach to a capacity crowd, and when "the inspiring choral music and solo numbers added much to the services" (*Guide* 15 May 1942). My father sang a solo in the evening, and my mother accompanied him. I think I remember that particular service. My grandmother stayed in the car to look after me and my little sister, but when the time came for my father's solo, she went to the door of the church and stood there in the semi-darkness, listening to the music.

Perhaps it was on this occasion that my father sang the solo that I remember best. The piece was a standard selection of his, a showy piece called "The Holy City." It had been composed in 1892 by Michael Maybrick (writing under the alias Stephen Adams), and I can still remember Frederic Weatherly's lyrics (a dream vision) and the sound of my father's voice at the quiet beginning:

> Last night I lay a-sleeping
> There came a dream so fair
> I stood in Old Jerusalem
> Beside the temple there

> I heard the children singing
> And ever as they sang
> Me thought the voice of angels
> From heaven in answer rang....

Then my father's voice would soar to the dramatic climax of the piece and my mother would sound the thunderous chords in quick succession:

> Jerusalem! Jerusalem!
> Sing for the night is o'er.
> Hosanna in the highest!
> Hosanna forevermore!

Chalmer's Presbyterian Church, a mile to the east of Walnut, had its anniversary services in September. My father was guest soloist there on at least two occasions in the early 1940s. And my father was often asked to sing at the funerals of relatives and neighbours: he was soloist at Aunt Arabella Hair's funeral. She died on 30 December 1940.

Will Woods's locker service

In August 1940 Dad's cousin, Will Woods, opened a locker service in Watford. People at that time did not own freezers, and the practice of keeping meats, poultry, fruit and vegetables by freezing them was new and unfamiliar. We did not yet have hydro on the farm, but the Watford paper noted that "locker storage service is rapidly being extended in every community in Canada and the United States" (*Guide* 17 May 1940), and it was supposed to replace the older method of preserving food: "No more hot stove canning," said the paper. Up until then, canning, with Mason jars and parafin wax as sealer, had been the technique housewives used to preserve fruits and vegetables, and every year my mother and grandmother "put down" great quantities of peaches, pears, plums, cherries, raspberries, and strawberries, plus jams (strawberry, raspberry, black currant) and jellies (crab apple, red currant) as well as tomatoes, chili sauce, relish, and various kinds of pickles (dills, "sweet" pickles, mustard pickles, and my favourite, beet pickles). I cannot remember our using the locker service for any fruits or vegetables, but only for cuts of beef and pork. Behind the small lobby which fronted on the main street was a large "chill room" where the temperature was zero, and where families rented lockers—they were just a rectangular wire cage—for five dollars a year. When my mother and grandmother wanted to cook a roast or any other cut of meat, Dad had to go into town to get it.

The hired man

The tramp, as I said in an earlier chapter, was one of two marginalized figures in rural life. The other was the hired man. Dad had a whole series of hired men, but I remember only three of them. One was Ray, who was at our place in the winter time, during the weeks when Dad was away at County Council. All I can remember about Ray was my being coaxed to go to him, when I was very small, and he and my mother and grandmother were all in the kitchen of our farmhouse, ready to eat supper in the darkness of a winter night, with light from the coal-oil lamp our only illumination. The second man I remember was "Old Jack." He came to our place from the House of Refuge in Strathroy, that rather grim institution west of the town, which everyone referred to as "the poor house." But men normally available for farm work had gone off to war, and the scarcity of farm labourers had even led municipal councils to appoint supervisors to "connect with farmers wanting help" (*Guide* 19 June 1942). Old Jack, however, was lazy and no help to my father. I can well remember Dad deciding to let him go, after much discussion with my mother. And I remember the scene when Dad told him he would not do. It was a cold and dark winter night, and the snow was drifting down in the pole light out in our farmyard—by that time we had electricity—and there, in the falling snow, Dad met with Old Jack, who had been in the barn. And I remember driving Old Jack back to Strathroy and the House of Refuge. He was, I think our last hired man. One of his predecessors was Albert Laferriere. He was a much younger man, and he was from Quebec, and said that, when he went home, it took a day or so to get used to speaking French again. He was the one who wrecked my father's binder when the team of horses (which he had begged to be allowed to drive) bolted and ran away on him. He enlisted in the army in the Second World War, and Watford has always claimed him as one of its "vets."

Harold Hair's hired man was named Neil Macmillan. He was a great hulking figure, big and silent, always in faded and dusty overalls, and always a few steps behind Harold. The curious thing about Neil is that I cannot remember his ever saying a word.

Gone With the Wind

The year 1939 saw the release of a number of significant Hollywood films (among them *The Wizard of Oz*), but the one that gained the most attention was *Gone With the Wind*. People commented on its length (nearly four hours, with intermission), its Technicolour and its sound track (with Max Steiner's soaring "Tara's Theme"), its stars (Clark Gable and Vivien Leigh), and its depiction of the American Civil War. It was the must-see film of the day, and my parents drove to London for a showing. Their journey home was something of an epic action in itself.

My parents told me that they went to see the film "when it first came to London." Its first showing in London was in Lowe's Theatre on Dundas Street on 31 January 1941; my parents saw it in an afternoon in March. When they came out of the matinee performance, freezing rain was beginning to fall. My mother told me that she held a lighted candle to the windshield to keep the rain from freezing on it. The townline hill at the east end of the Twelfth Line was so slippery that Mum had to get out and push. And when Dad got going, he had to keep on going right up the hill (for fear of sliding back again), leaving Mum to scramble up as best she could. And when they got home, they had to crawl on hands and knees up the slope of the lawn to the house.

My mother and the Walnut Women's Association

During the war years my mother was an active member of the W.A., and her contributions reflected her interests in literature and in missionary work. She often gave readings, and the readings were often poems. At the October 1942 meeting, for instance, she "gave a very interesting paper on 'Poetry for Children' and many poems were read" (*Guide* 30 October 1942). I can remember being sick in bed with one of the usual childhood diseases—measles or mumps or chicken pox—and she read Longfellow's

Evangeline to me. Her other chief interest was missionary work. In May 1942 she was the "leader in Missionary Study" and "conducted an inspiring devotional period with special emphasis on church" (*Guide* 29 May 1942).

In 1943 my mother became president of the Women's Association, and presided at the monthly meetings. She and my grandmother hosted the February 1943 gathering. On this occasion, "several letters were read from boys in the service thanking the Society for their Christmas boxes"; Mrs. Calvin Dolbear led the worship service and Mrs. Shugg "gave the life story of Anne Sullivan Macy, the 'other half' of Helen Keller" (*Guide* 19 February 1943). Now it was my grandmother's turn to provide the missionary part of the program: in November 1943 "Mrs. Sherman Hair was leader for the W. M. S. program" (*Guide* 19 November 1943).

My mother served a second year in 1944 as president of the W.A., and she and my grandmother hosted the February 1944 meeting. At that gathering the women presented my grandmother's cousin, Maggie Shugg, with a gift: the Shuggs were leaving their Walnut farm and moving into Alvinston. Their son Orville, who had been supervisor of farm broadcasts for the CBC, resigned from that post and took over the operation of his parents' farm. He and his family attended Walnut Church with us.

My mother's second year as president of the W.A. was a busy one. In June there were anniversaries to be noted (for Reverend and Mrs. Eddy and for Ward Zavitz's parents) and a new member to be welcomed. She was Mrs. Harold King. The Kings had run a florist's business in Detroit, but they moved the operation to the Tenth Line and built a greenhouse there. Their business motto: "King's Flowers—Fit for a Queen!" In September, the W.M.S. held a joint meeting with the W.M.S. of Erie Street and Zion, with over sixty women present. My mother "assisted in the varied program that was given," described at length in the *Guide* for 22 September 1944. The last meeting over which my mother presided was in December, and it was a Christmas candle-lighting service: "carols were sung as five ladies lighted candles of Friendship for those of other countries" (*Guide* 22 December 1944).

My father's first cousin, Catherine Watson

Catherine and her mother, Uncle Guy Watson's widow, lived in a large frame house on Metcalfe Street in Strathroy, south of the tracks and facing the canning factory (which has long since disappeared). They were members of St. Andrew's Presbyterian Church, which stood just north of the tracks: the rumble of trains and the long wail of their whistle at all the level crossings through town were a constant sound during services. Catherine went to the collegiate in Strathroy, Beal Technical School in London, and the London Normal School. In the fall of 1940 she started teaching in S. S. No. 5, the school section next to the west of ours. S. S. No. 10 had closed the previous year for lack of pupils, and I think Catherine had only one from our section, Ernie Lewis. She boarded at Alex Kelly's during the week. On weekends she stayed with her aunt and uncle, Ern and Annie Powell, who lived "back 24 sideroad," Annie Powell being a sister of her mother, who had been a Hay. Catherine attended Walnut Church with us: on Sundays she would walk south on the sideroad to the Twelfth Line to meet us at the corner and to be driven to the service, which was always at 1:30 in the afternoon.

Catherine's mother, Aunt Mary Watson, died of cancer on 21 January 1942, at the age of sixty-two. I have vague memories of the house on Metcalfe Street when it was being cleared out and readied for sale; and Catherine asked if she could store a trunk full of her belongings at our place. It sat in our back kitchen for several years.

Catherine taught at S. S. No. 5 for four years (September 1940 to June 1944). I started to school at Easter 1944, so she was my first teacher.

But Catherine had decided that she wanted to become a deaconess in the Presbyterian church, and she left teaching to enrol at (what was then called) the Missionary and Deaconess Training School (now Ewart College), an affiliate of Knox College (the Presbyterian theological school) in Toronto. My father, I remember—and this is a reflection of the times—took a dim view of this move, and thought that, because she was alone in the world, she ought to get married.

There were two gatherings in Catherine's honour in June 1944. One was organized by the ladies of the section, who met at the school: there was "a social hour of contests and music"; addresses were read and a "beautiful gold locket" presented. "Miss Watson made a suitable reply, and the committee in charge served delicious refreshments" (*Guide* 30 June 1944). The other was at the home of one of Catherine's pupils, Bill Dolbear, and it was for us kids. "The children enjoyed a ball game after which supper was served on the lawn. A short program of musical numbers followed. An address was read by Maxine Lucas and Ernest Lewis on behalf of the pupils presented a comb and brush set. Miss Watson made a gracious reply" (*Guide* 30 June 1944).

Catherine graduated as a deaconess in the spring of 1947, and there was a gathering in her honour at St. Andrew's Presbyterian Church in Strathroy, which I remember. In the following years she had positions all across the country, where her prime responsibility was usually the church nursery school: at the Children's Centre in Vancouver, at Tyndale House in Montreal, at the Chinese Presbyterian Church in Victoria, and finally in Toronto, where she was visitor at Riverdale Hospital. She retired on 31 March 1983 and moved to Watford, where she lived out her retirement years until her death in 2001. Her family in Watford centred on her cousin, Ann (Phair) Fisher, the grand-daughter of her Aunt Annie Powell. Ann had married Don Fisher from Brooke Township, and he worked for Moffatt and Powell, the lumber dealers and roof truss manufacturers. I think Don (who was a year ahead of me in high school) was in charge of the truss factory. It and the wire works were Watford's two major employers.

At Catherine's funeral, which was held in St. Andrew's Presbyterian Church in Watford (and at which I was a pallbearer), the minister concluded her eulogy by saying "Well done! thou good and faithful servant." I thought that was moving, and entirely appropriate.

The wedding of Honor Robinson and Harold Hair: 15 August 1942

Honor was a first cousin of my mother; Harold was a first cousin of my father. Honor had graduated from Western and was a high school mathematics teacher; Harold farmed on the same farm worked by his father and grandfather on the Twelfth Line. Honor was my mother's attendant when she married my father in 1935, and Harold was my father's best man. That is how Honor and Harold met, and they were married seven years later, on 15 August 1942 in Cook's Church (by that time the South Caradoc United Church) on the second concession of Caradoc Township. The Robinson farm was nearby, south of the Longwoods Road (Highway 2), at Muncey, and the reception was held there, outdoors on the lawn.

I was four and one-half years old when Honor and Harold were married. I remember sitting in the church with my mother and grandmother, waiting for the ceremony to begin, and seeing Grandad and Grammie Runnalls sitting across the aisle. I was encouraged to go to them, and I did so, hesitantly, because my young mind could not figure out why they were there with all my Hair relatives. And I remember the reception afterwards. The afternoon was bright and sunny and warm. People were scattered around in groups on the lawn outside the farmhouse, admiring the flowers that grew extravagantly around the foundation, and visiting and eating. The ice cream and cake impressed my young self more than anything else.

Honor and Harold would have three children: two girls—Jane (born 23 August 1943) and Judy (born 18 January 1946)—and one boy, Jim (born 26 January 1951). Like Marjorie and me, they grew up on the Twelfth Line, we went to school together, and we sometimes played together, though they were younger. I have always thought of them as "double cousins." And they were always special to Aunt Ruth as well. When Aunt Ruth was a little girl and before she started to school, she lived with her grandmother Thompson and her Aunt Edna, who would become Honor's mother. She always retained a great affection for them.

The wedding of John McNeil and Dora Dicks: 12 December 1942

John was my father's first cousin, and the only son of Aunt Eva and Uncle Gord McNeil. He graduated in law from Osgoode Hall and was called to the bar in 1940, but service with the R.C.A.F. in the war interrupted his career as a lawyer.

On 12 December 1942, John married Dora Dicks. Like John, she was from the "Old South" of London, where her father was a florist, and she and John had been in high school together. They were married in Wesley United Church, and the reception was at the Highland Golf Club. For years we had a photograph on a table in our living room, of bride and groom coming up the aisle of the church: John in his air force uniform, Dora in a slim white satin dress and carrying a bouquet of white orchids and gardenias.

My grandmother was invited to the wedding but my parents were not: John and Dora excluded first cousins because there were so many of them on the McNeil side. As things turned out, however, my grandmother did not go to the ceremony either; instead she offered to stay with Grandad Watson for the day. By this time he was unable to leave the house on Bellevue, and I am not sure that he was even able to come downstairs. I remember him as always being in an second-floor bedroom.

I do not know much about John's service in the air force. I know only that he trained in Texas and served in India. While he was away in such unimaginably distant places, my grandmother prepared parcels for him and sent them overseas. His thank-you letters were heavily censored, and took the form of glossy photographs of the originals. I remember chiefly the thick black lines drawn through many of his sentences.

When John returned to London after the war, he established a law practice in partnership with an older lawyer, E.M. (Mel) Winder, Q.C. Later, John and Dora would have two children, Marilynne (born 25 April 1949) and Grant (born 13 February 1952). When Marilynne was born, we had an early-morning phone call from Aunt Eva, who was excited about her first grandchild. I well remember Mum telling us that morning that we had a new little cousin.

Lambton County Council 1941–3 and the equalization controversy

At the January 1941 session of county council, my father was beginning his second year as councillor, and he was appointed a member of one of the more important standing committees, the Finance Committee. It undertook an initiative which was to provoke a great deal of debate, controversy, and opposition: the equalization of assessment in the various townships, towns and villages in the county. My father, who had had experience as assessor of Brooke Township, gave notice of a bylaw to that effect at the June 1941 session; when the bylaw was presented, Dunc Turner moved it and my father seconded it. It was carried. That was the beginning of a long process when equalization remained (in the common metaphor) a "bone of contention."

The chief opposition came from Point Edward, which appealed the county assessment and took the matter to court. The judge found in favour of the municipality; the county appealed. The matter dragged on for six months, and curtailed the June 1942 session of council, which was unable to strike the county rate for the year. In an effort to solve the impasse, council began to talk about a complete (but costly) valuation of the county, and finally approved such a move. The report of the evaluators was ready for the June 1943 session, when the issue was at long last settled. Two townships and one village saw their assessment reduced; thirteen saw theirs increase. Brooke Township was one of two to enjoy a lower rate.

When my father was reminiscing about the December and January sessions of council, he said that the beginning of December and the third week in January always seemed to bring the worst winter weather. In December 1942 there was a blizzard, which the Sarnia paper described as "the worst snowstorm of the season" (*Observer* 3 December 1942). The weather was even worse for the January 1943 session, when the *Observer* had the headline, "Worst Snowstorm in Years Ties Up County" (19 January 1943). And he told me about one January—perhaps it was 1943—when he set out for the council meetings, and struggled by car into Watford, being delayed so much by the snow that he thought he had missed the train. He left the car in the Ford garage, which was at the south end of Main Street, and there Roy Dick told him that the train was coming. Dad set out for the station "on the dead run," he said, and went over the bridge just as the train was passing underneath. But he made it.

Grandad Runnalls retires from farming: Fall 1943

Grandad Runnalls was seventy-five at this time, and he and Grammie decided to retire to Mount Brydges. They sold the farm and made plans to move into town, to the house where Aunt Lizzie Bateman had lived on Bowan Street. They had gained possession of the property in July 1942, as part of the settlement of the Bateman estate. The sale of the farm, which was registered in March 1944, yielded $5,800. That was the price paid by Grandad's youngest brother, Uncle Ed, and his son Ralph. They had been living on the Sullivan farm, the next one to the east of Grandad's, since 1938. Uncle Ed was a great talker, and had an opinion about everything. My grandfather, who was more reserved, came home one day, disgusted after seeing his brother, and said to my grandmother, "That Ed talks too much!"

In November 1943 Grandad had an auction sale, and the list of items he was letting go is a good indication of a time—then fast disappearing—when farmers relied on horse power. Here are some of those items: one "aged team"; binder; mower; manure spreader; hay rake; disks; iron harrows; two-horse cultivator; scuffler; walking plow; seed drill; scales; fanning mill; "good wagon"; sleighs; hay rack; buggy; cutter; cream separator; sap pans; forks, shovels, hoes .... "Everything will be sold as farm is sold"

(*Age* 11 November 1943). As I have already said, my parents bought the sap pans and all the rest of the maple-syrup-making equipment.

A last stay at the old home

When my grandparents were preparing to leave the farmhouse where they had lived all their married life and move into Mount Brydges, my mother decided she would like to stay one last time in the home where she had grown up. She took my sister and me with her. Marjorie was not yet three years old, and I was not yet six, but I do remember parts of that visit vividly.

We slept in an upstairs bedroom that had a skylight, and I thought it wonderful—as my mother clearly did too—to lie in bed and be able to look up at the stars. My mother pointed to the sky in the rectangle of glass above us, and named the constellations. And I remember the next morning, when the house was cold—the season, I think, must have been late fall, 1943—and being in the kitchen, the only warm room, with Grammie Runnalls tending to the big old cookstove while my mother dressed my little sister, who was standing on a couch. I remember a meal at the long table in that kitchen, sitting beside Grandad Runnalls, who broke a soft-boiled egg for me, and showed me how to put the yolk and the white over my fried potatoes. And I remember a long afternoon in that kitchen, when I was, for some reason, lying on the floor and listening to the big old clock on the wall slowly ticking: that was my first experience of boredom, and I thought the time would never pass.

I cannot remember any other part of the house except the living room, which was forbidden to me: I have a vague memory of standing at the door and looking in, like a little Adam shut out of paradise. There was a jardiniere with greenery there, sitting on top of a black pedestal table. I cannot remember anything else in the room, but one item in a kitchen drawer fascinated me. It was a white porcelain egg, which was placed in nests to encourage hens to lay.

What Marjorie remembers from that stay were the kewpie dolls. They were a popular kind of doll in the 1920s and 30s, and there were several sitting on top of the beds upstairs. One of them had a great round paper skirt, which flared out into a pleated circle when you set the doll down on the bed. Marjorie still has that doll.

Was it when we were returning from that visit that I had my first train ride? Grandad Runnalls drove us to the station in Strathroy—a large handsome brick station, now long gone—and from there we took the train to Watford, where my father met us. I remember only the beginning of that journey, when the train was crossing the Sydenham on the western edge of Strathroy, and smoke was drifting back from the steam engine, and my mother told me not to touch the window sill because it was covered with soot.

The 1944 Brooke Township Council

At Christmas 1943 the Watford paper carried a front-page story on municipal politics in neighbouring townships. The question posed for our municipality was "All quiet in Brooke?" Then there was an analysis of the political situation of which my father was part.

"South in Brooke Township all is quiet and unless a surprise storm breaks [at] a nomination meeting in Alvinston Monday afternoon, it is freely predicted the 1943 Council will go back by acclamation for another year. Reeve Duncan C. Turner, Brooke's shy bachelor representative on County Council, is one of the four township reeves out for the Wardenship for 1944, and there are no voters in all East Lambton who would oppose his successful elevation to the county cocked hat and gown if he wants it! Duncan would be a worthy successor to Nevin McVicar who was Brooke's last Warden of the county five years ago. As Deputy-Reeve John Hair has given thoughtful efficient service both in township work and at County Council, and while he developed ability to serve well as Reeve, he is content to wait his turn. Councillors Robert Tait, Clayton Johnson and Clare Edgar each represent different sections of the township and are apparently not too impatient to await another year as Councillors before seeking promotion to the Deputy's chair. Unless present signs fail, indications are for a quiet acclamation in Brooke township for this year."

The paper was right in its prediction: Brooke's 1943 council was acclaimed for 1944. And Dunc Turner was successful in his bid to become the county's 1944 warden. The township celebrated his elevation with a dinner in his honour in the Columbia Hotel, one of the two big railway hotels in Alvinston (both now long demolished).

Casualties of the war: Fred Taylor, Ernie Phair, Ray Hart

These three men all had a connection with our family: Fred Taylor was married to my father's cousin, Evelyn Eastabrook; Ernie Phair had married Don Powell, the daughter of Ern and Annie Powell on Twenty-four Sideroad; and Ray Hart was Mr. Hart's oldest son.

Fred Taylor had worked at Andrews Wire Works in Watford, which was, at that time, the only manufacturing facility in town; it made kitchen utensils. He went overseas on September 1943, and by early 1944 he was serving with the Perth Regiment in the Allied advance northwards through Italy. The Watford paper regularly printed letters from the "boys on active service," and there are several from Fred, to "give the readers some idea of what this country of Italy is like" (*Guide* 4 February 1944). He described "the sights in the Eternal City," and he thanked the Rotary Club for its "welcome carton of smokes": "They dropped in at a very good time," Fred wrote, "because I was almost out. Thanks very much. I really enjoy a good Canadian smoke." Fred survived the fighting through Cassina and Ortono, but on 20 December 1944 he was killed in action. He was just twenty-five years old. He was buried in a Canadian war cemetery near Ravenna on the Adriatic coast. Years afterwards, long after a second marriage and children, Evelyn travelled to Italy and visited Fred's grave.

Ernie Phair had been an instructor at training centres in Chatham and Stratford, and was posted overseas in February 1944. He was reported missing in action in France on 2 August 1944, but it was not until April 1945 that his next of kin were notified "that Lieut. Ernest Phair, missing since the terrific Canadian assault on Caen in France last August, must now be presumed dead" (*Guide* 20 April 1945). Ray Hart was an air force navigator. On 3 November 1944 the Watford paper reported that "the former Watford boy and his crew are all missing following an R.A.F. patrol action off the east coast of Scotland." He was just twenty years old.

One fellow member of Walnut Church survived. He was Ray Swartz, who came home in February 1945. The Swartz's pew was directly in front of ours in the church, and I can remember my grandmother having an animated conversation with Ray when he appeared for the first time after returning from overseas. He had been with the R.C.A.F., and was on the Continent "with the first ground crew forces following D-Day" (*Guide* 23 February 1945). The church welcomed Ray home with a supper and a program in the church basement.

Donald starts to school: Easter 1944

My parents had long discussions as to when I should start to school. In those days in rural Ontario there was no such thing as kindergarten, and children normally enrolled in Grade One at the age of six. But my parents waited until after my seventh birthday to send me off. My cousin, Paul Dolbear, was six months older than I, and his parents and my parents decided that the two of us would start school together. The agreed-upon date was Easter 1944.

The school in our section had been closed since 1939, and the few pupils were "transported" (that was the word) to the school section next to the west of ours, S.S. No. 5. The man who took us to school was our next-door neighbour, Clarence Lewis. My parents were always annoyed with him because he would drop me off on the road at our line fence instead of bringing me several hundred yards further to the end of our laneway. Later, another neighbour on the Twelfth Line, Andy Spalding, would drive us to school. He took pride in never missing a day and never being late. He always brought me all the way home, and he would often stop for a few minutes to chat with my grandmother, waiting for me on the porch.

My late start in formal education was hardly a drawback. I could already read, thanks to my mother's teaching at home. She used the phonetic method, and had me pronounce words syllable by syllable. I can remember stumbling over the single-syllable "church," but she wouldn't tell me what the word was, and ended the lesson by sending me outside to be with my father, where I eventually figured out the puzzling combination of letters.

The party line

While we were on the farm, our telephone was a weighty wooden box attached to the wall in a kitchen alcove. It had a heavy black receiver, which one took down from a hook and applied to one's ear; and a mouthpiece that looked like a metal daffodil, into which one spoke. At the bottom of the box was a little shelf; at the top were two bells, with the ringer between them; a crank on the side of the box activated the ringer. One turn of the crank would summon the operator in Watford; a combination of long and short rings would summon whatever neighbour we wanted to talk to (our ring was a long and two shorts). Ours was a party line, which meant that everyone could listen in on everyone else's calls, and no one seemed to have any scruples about eavesdropping on supposedly private conversations, though no one admitted to doing so. During the long winter months, my mother and grandmother, working together in the kitchen, would listen in on every call, and when one of them lifted the receiver, she could hear the discreet clicks of other receivers being taken down. I was small at the time, and just barely big enough to start using the telephone myself, but I was the proverbial little pitcher with big ears, and I listened with interest to retailed conversations; to the overheard gossip and opinion; and to the (seemingly endless, to my boyish ears) discussing and dissecting and judging of everything heard.

The Brooke system was part of Bell Telephone, and I can still see the icon on the cover of the telephone book at that time: Mercury as the "Spirit of Communication," with wings like those of an angel, standing on the globe, grasping a graceful coil of telephone wires in his right hand, and in his left holding aloft a handful of thunderbolts. He was the image of the telephone as universal communicator; our party line was the local system that held our section together, when everyone knew everyone else far better than neighbours do now.

Death of Grammie Runnalls: 3 May 1944

I return to my mother's narrative: "Time went on and Dad sold the farm and planned to move to Mt. Brydges. It was a very busy time for [Mother and Dad] and we helped them move on Apr. 1st. 1944. It was a very miserable day weather-wise with periods of snow. Dad had not been well and was in bed so Mother had quite a responsibility. They got settled quite well but they were only there a month when Mother took the flu. We went down and brought Dad to our place and Mother to Ruth's. She was only there a week when she passed away [at the age of seventy-five]. That was in 1944 [3 May] and was a very sad time for all of us. Dad stayed at our place for six weeks and made a remarkable recovery. He was able to go out on the front porch upstairs and the sunshine was like a miracle healer and he went back to live alone at his home in Mt. Brydges. He was able to drive up and spend Christmas Day at Ches's or our place."

Grammie's funeral was held at Denning's in Strathroy, and she was buried in Strathroy cemetery. The pallbearers were Harold Hair, Stanley Robinson, A. McCracken, Hugh Forbes, W. Nichols, and Leslie Runnalls. My mother thought I was too young to face the facts of death, and she had decided not to take me to the funeral, but she had last-minute second thoughts just as she was leaving the house, and asked if I wanted to go. I said no and stayed with my grandmother, but later I wished that I had known my own mind better. For Mum had taken Marjorie and me to see Grammie while she was at Aunt Ruth's, and I can remember going upstairs to the bedroom and standing peering over the footboard at a tiny figure in an enormous bed, and sensing that she was very sick. Perhaps it was that night that she died.

The only other memory I have of my grandmother's death is from months later. My mother and I were out in our garden picking peas, and I asked her where Grammie was. "She's in heaven," Mum said. I looked up at the blue blue summer sky, doubtfully.

The cyclone of June 1944

Southwestern Ontario is just close enough to the American mid-west to have occasional tornadoes. They were then called "cyclones," and on a Friday afternoon in late June 1944, one blew through Warwick and Adelaide townships and into Strathroy. It damaged houses and barns and downed trees along what we then called "the main road"—Highway 22 between Warwick Village and Hickory Corners—and I can remember going with my parents to see the damage: enormous trees uprooted and flattened; a corner torn out of a brick farmhouse; barn siding scattered across fields; and, on the northern edge of Strathroy, houses damaged and a row of ancient evergreens snapped off and left splintered and broken. The damage, the Strathroy paper estimated, was over one million dollars (*Age* 28 June 1944).

My father as reeve of Brooke Township, 1945

On 29 December 1944 the Watford paper reported that there would be an election in Brooke Township on New Year's Day, 1945. Dunc Turner, my father's longtime friend and political ally, was retiring from municipal politics, so my father decided (as the paper put it) "to step up to the reeve's chair." He was challenged by Stanley Graham from Inwood. Graham had been deputy-reeve for one year, and he was a long-time councillor. Clare Edgar and Bob Tait faced each other for the deputy-reeve's position, and three men were nominated for council: Lyle Johnston, Fred Braithwaite, and our Twelfth Line neighbour Melvin Powell.

Local politics were rough and ready in those days. I can remember only one nomination meeting, when I was seven or eight and went with Dad and Uncle Ches to the hall in Inwood. We drove down a long straight sideroad with flat snow-covered fields stretching to the far-off bush, and with a deep drain parallel to the road—a characteristic feature of that part of the township that had once been covered with the Great Brooke-Enniskillen Swamp. The hall was filled with men in bulky winter clothing, the noise level high, and the air thick with cigarette and pipe smoke. In the first hour or so, men gathered in little groups to make the actual nominations, and I can remember Sam McLellan and Leander Foster with their heads together, perhaps to nominate my father. The speeches that followed dealt with township issues, of course, but every speaker told jokes, and the jokes always seemed to involve people in hotels where one had to go down the hall to the toilet. I can remember being disgusted by one joke that made the often-used phrase, "the s— hitting the fan," literal rather than metaphorical. And I can remember one candidate who told the assembly that "you can vote for me or you can go to hell!"

These gatherings were an all-male affair. No woman ever appeared at a nomination meeting; certainly no woman was ever elected to council; and my mother was reluctant even to set foot in the council chamber. I can remember being in Alvinston and waiting in the car for my father, who was taking a long time at whatever meeting he was attending, and my mother, rather than going herself to ask after him, sent me into the meeting room, where a number of men were sitting around, chatting idly. My father wasn't there, but was off somewhere inspecting something or other. I was too small to come back with anything but a garbled message.

As usual, my father placed an "election card" in the Watford paper: "To the Brooke Township Electors: Ladies and Gentlemen: I have tried to serve you faithfully in the past as Deputy-Reeve and I now ask for your continued support for election as Reeve for 1945. We shall try to have all township roads open on Monday, and will appreciate your effort to get the votes out in your division. May the new year bring us Victory and Peace! —JOHN HAIR." Stanley Graham also placed a card, saying that, in view of his experience, "I think I am entitled to appeal for your support for election as Reeve." My father and Graham were from opposite ends of the township—Dad from the northeast, Graham from the southwest—and they were opposites in temperament as well. My father privately described Graham as "a little bantam rooster," and thought him a hothead.

Both my father and Clare Edgar were successful in their bids for office. The Watford paper reported on 5 January 1945 that "Brooke township voters had difficulty getting through the snowblocked roads on New Year's Day, and as a result only about 40% of the township vote was recorded in the municipal elections. While the three councillors were secured by acclamation there was a keen contest for Reeve and Deputy-Reeve. John Hair, last year's deputy, over-ran Stanley Graham, a former deputy-reeve for one term, 393 to 259, to become reeve for 1945." There were twelve polls in the township; my father won seven of them and was almost even with Graham in three more; his largest margin was in our own division, where he had sixty-one votes to Graham's three.

Dad placed a card of thanks in the Watford paper (5 January 1945): "To Brooke Twp. Electors: Please accept my sincere thanks for the splendid support you gave me in election as Reeve for 1945 on Monday. In spite of the snow-blocked roads a fairly representative vote was polled. I shall try to merit your support in my year's work."

The chief initiative that my father undertook as reeve was to provide grants to servicemen who were returning to the township. There was a citizens' committee which recommended such action, and in June "a group of representative Brooke taxpayers" accepted their recommendations "with minor additions and amendments" (*Guide* 29 June 1945). There was a proposal to hold a plebiscite in September "so that ratepayers may signify whether or not they are in favor of raising the necessary funds by taxation." In the meantime, council appointed Dunc Turner and Stanley McKellar "to work in conjunction with the Department of Veterans' Affairs re Rehabilitation of Returned Soldiers" (*Guide* 21 August 1945).

When council drafted the bylaw, it stipulated that "all members of the armed forces or Merchant Marine who were resident in Brooke twp. on September 3rd, 1939, would receive a cash grant of $100 on discharge"; "each member of the armed forces or merchant marine who served overseas or on the high seas and who returns to farming or engages in business in Brooke Twp. may be granted $100 per year for five years, and if totally disabled an additional $100 per year for five years." The Watford paper judged the plan "most extensive and generous" (*Guide* 7 December 1945). The by-law was read, and given a second reading, at the council meeting in December, when it was "provisionally adopted." It was published in the Watford paper on December 7, over the signatures of "John A. Hair, Reeve" and "W. J. Weed, Clerk."

The vote on this undertaking was not held in September, as initially proposed, but coincided with the municipal elections on 7 January 1946. The bylaw was approved by a vote of 337 to 219.

In my mother's scrapbook there is a newspaper photograph of my father, without a date or source noted, but it has an intriguing caption: "MR. JOHN HAIR / Pictured here is reeve of Brooke Township, Lambton County, which has become internationally known for its plan of cash grants to war veterans to help them in agriculture and business." "Internationally known"? I have often wondered what evidence lies behind that statement.

This local initiative for veterans was in addition to the federal programs that became known as the "Veterans Charter," and to understand those programs and the thinking behind them, one needs to go to Peter Neary's book, *On to Civvy Street: Canada's Rehabilitation Program for Veterans of the Second World War* (2011). The aim of this federal program was to put every man and woman discharged from the armed forces in a position to earn a living—in contrast to the provisions after the First World War, which focused on the disabled. Mackenzie King's government passed several key pieces of legislation, including the War Service Grants Act of 1944 and the Veterans Rehabilitation Act of 1945. The enormous growth of the post-war economy was due in part to such stimuli.

When my father spoke to the Watford Rotary Club in November 1945, he listed the "post-war advantages" of Lambton County, "one of the best farming counties in Ontario": "our returning service men and women will find abundant opportunity right here at home," thanks to the local and national rehabilitation programs. Dad reviewed the history of the county, noted that it would celebrate its centennial in 1949, and focused on Brooke Township because, as the paper noted, his "grandfather settled there almost 100 years ago" (*Guide* 16 November 1945). The reference was to Grandad Watson.

There was one other significant action my father undertook as reeve in 1945. In spite of the severe winters and the frequently blocked roads during the early 1940s, the township had no snow removal equipment and, in attempts to keep the roads open, had relied on a grader which was, of course, designed to spread gravel rather than plow snow. In October 1945 council ordered "a 6-ton truck, equipped with snow plow, ... through the General Motors dealer, Orville Wallis of Watford" (*Guide* 12 October 1945). It cost $9,600 but, because the plow could be removed, the truck could also be used for general township work. It did not arrive until February 1946, almost too late for that year's winter.

In January 1945, for the first time, my father attended Lambton County Council meetings as a reeve, and as such he was automatically a member of council's Equalization Committee, formed after all the upheaval over assessment in the previous two years.

The winter of 1944–5 and the 1945 growing season

The winter of 1944–5 was severe. November had brought the first blizzard to the Watford district, and there were more storms in December, with (in the paper's conventional wording) "howling winds and drifting snow." The weather affected most activities, including the municipal election which made my father reeve, and the January 1945 session of county council, when many of the county roads were blocked. I do not know how my father got to Sarnia, but Dunc Turner, who was in his last days as warden, had to walk several miles. He reported to the Sarnia paper that "the banks on either side of the road were so high that only blower-type plows could dispose of the snow.... In some instances ... the cuts through the high banks were so narrow that car fenders were scraped in getting through" (*Observer* 16 January 1945). I remember that we were shut in at home for some length of time. It got to the point where my parents needed bread and other supplies from town, so my father took down the old sleigh from the rafters of our granary and hitched it up to one of our horses. That's how he and Uncle Ches got to Watford. I remember looking westward out of our kitchen window, and seeing horse and sleigh plunge through drifts at our lot line until they disappeared in a flurry of white powder.

Then, as if to make up for such weather, spring came early. March 1945 was mild and sunny, and "with no frost beneath, the snow melted away into the earth for next summer's crops. No wonder they call an abundant snowfall the poor man's fertilizer" (*Guide* 2 March 1945). At the end of the month, the paper was exclaiming over "June Growth in March: Earliest Seeding Here in Forty Years."

But farmers know how fickle nature can be. My father was at this time growing white beans, which yielded well and were a "cash crop," but when the time came to harvest them in October 1945, wet weather ruined them throughout the district. Those beans had been one of my father's chief sources of farm income.

Another "cash crop" that my father tried was sweet corn for the canning factory in Strathroy. He contracted with Dominion Canners, who supplied the seed (the variety was jealously guarded), and he duly planted, cultivated, and harvested the corn, taking it by wagon to Strathroy. But the yield was (as I remember) small, many of the cobs had been damaged by racoons, and he made little money from it. I can remember my mother helping Dad pick the surviving ears of corn, and the two of them expressing disappointment at the meagre crop.

Chickens and crows

Most farmers at this time had chickens, usually hundreds of them, and sometimes thousands. Dad hatched little chicks in an incubator next to the furnace in our basement and put them out in a "colony house" when they were only little yellow balls of fluff. The "colony house" was some distance from our house, for fear of fire: it had a heater with a broad flange on it, under which the chicks were kept warm and fed and watered. When they were half grown, Dad transferred them to the hen house in our barnyard. The pullets ran free—in those days there was nothing but "free-range" poultry—and in the open they attracted predators: foxes, owls, and crows. Crows were a particular problem for us. Dad tried to get rid of them by setting out a dead chicken laced with poison. That led to one of those stories that farm people tell each other. One day when Dad was away, my mother saw a crow fly down to the hen house and gorge itself on the poisoned chicken, with the expected result. She was squeamish about disposing of the dead crow, and turned a pail upside down over it so Dad could look after it when he came home. But when, several hours later, he lifted the pail, the crow flew away. It had disgorged chicken and poison, and recovered.

Provincial and federal elections in June 1945: Hugh Mackenzie MP and Zeb Janes MLA

My father, who (like Dunc Turner) was a Liberal in politics, was at this time a member of the federal riding's Liberal association and actively worked for Hugh Mackenzie, a Warwick Township farmer who had been elected to the House of Commons in 1935, and was then living in a big house on the main street in Watford. In June of 1945 there was a federal election, and although the Liberals under Mackenzie King won, Hugh Mackenzie was defeated in our riding. In October of that year he was named a supervisor in China for UNRRA (the United Nations Relief and Rehabilitation Association). By May 1946 he was established in Shanghai and overseeing the provision of food, clothing, shelter, and other necessities to victims of war.

Among my father's papers is a postcard from Hugh Mackenzie, headed "Shanghai Aug 11th" but with no year. Internal evidence, however, indicates that he was writing in 1946: "Dear John, I often think of you and what a good friend you always have been. My Headquarters are still in Shanghai although I have seen a good deal of China. Conditions here are not good and I do not know where it will all end. Do not let any one tell you that the Chinese are dumb. I have met some very clever people here. Their system is all wrong. Many very wealthy, millions in terrible poverty. Civil war is economic. Great unrest all over the world. Hope your crops are good and also your health. Have had a grand experience. Will be glad to get home. Mrs. MacK. arrived here July 1st. We are quite well. Take good care of yourself. Kindest regards to Mrs. Hair and yourself. Hugh."

There was also a provincial election in June 1945, and Zeb Janes was the Conservative candidate in our riding, which was East Lambton. I think my father voted Liberal federally and Conservative provincially, mainly because he knew Zeb Janes, also a Warwick township farmer who was married to one of my father's former public school teachers, Hazel Dolbear. In the event, Zeb was elected, and George Drew's Conservatives formed the provincial government. The Ontario government had been shocked by the results of the election of 1943, when the CCF formed the official opposition and threatened the Conservative majority. The Watford paper could not resist commenting, on 8 June 1945, that the election results "emphatically told the C. C. F. Socialist party that solid thinking Ontario still stood for sound money, free enterprise, and stable government instead of unsound, untried theories and ideas that would lead to dictatorship to enforce."

The Mackenzies returned to Canada in January 1948, and Hugh again became an M.P. in the election of 1949. He was re-elected in 1953 but defeated in 1957, after which he retired from politics. He had been a delegate to the United Nations in 1950 and 1956, and he advocated the recognition of the Communist government of China—a stance far in advance of the thinking of the time.

Hydro comes to the farm: Fall 1945

We did not have electricity on the farm until after the war ended, but it was soon after, in the fall of 1945, I think. Roy Chapman from Inwood wired our house and barn. I well remember the first electric light we had, which was a single bulb hanging from the ceiling in our back kitchen. The house was at that point only partly wired, and the kitchen light was the only one operating. I look back on that moment now as proof that Marshall McLuhan was right about the message of the incandescent bulb. For its light was pervasive, in contrast to the light from the coal-oil lamps we had been using, which left dark shadows in the corners of rooms. Lamplight was yellow and flickered, while electric light was white and steady. It changed the way we did things and saw things.

We did not use the word "electricity." In Ontario, water was the principal source of electrical power: we knew about the enormous installations at Niagara, and they produced "hydro."

Our first electric appliance was a washing machine. Up until that point, my mother and grandmother washed clothes by hand, using tubs and a washboard; they wrung them out and hung them on lines in the back yard. But at Christmas 1945 my father surprised them with a wringer washing machine, which he brought home without their knowing it, and which my grandmother discovered on Christmas morning. Her cries of delight woke the whole household.

But we did not even have a radio at this time. Aunt Ruth and Uncle Ches had one, and I remember being at their place for Christmas and listening to the King's message to the Commonwealth and Empire on Christmas morning. What I heard was a faraway voice, halting and hesitant, coming to us across unimaginable distances, from a place I could barely visualize, and never expected to see.

My father's second term as reeve: 1946

In January 1946 my father fought yet another election, and his challenger was his old opponent, Stanley Graham of Inwood. This time the race was a three-way contest, with Lyle Johnston the third candidate. Clare Edgar and Bob Tait were running for deputy-reeve, and for the three council positions there were four candidates: Clayton Field, Bill McDougall, Lyle McLean, and our neighbour on the Twelfth Line, Melvin Powell.

As usual, my father placed an "election card" in the Watford paper: "After having served you as a Councillor, Deputy-Reeve and Reeve, I am again before you seeking re-election for another term. I have tried to represent you to the best of my ability.

Should I be returned to office, I will continue to give you that service, coupled with experience gained while in office. Thanking you for past favors. JOHN HAIR."

The people around Inwood had been more vocal in their criticism of council than any other part of the township, and had asked for more from council than any other division. (I can remember my father receiving telephone calls at home, calls of the "why isn't our road plowed?" kind.) They were determined to oust Dad and his deputy, Clare Edgar. Stanley Graham led the disaffected, and the possibility of my father being defeated was very real.

But my father had a good sense of what had to be done. Dunc Turner had advised him to concentrate on the Sutorville area on the Twelfth Line west, saying "they won't bother to vote, but they will if you go to them." And Elmer Moffatt, Dad's cousin in Warwick township and a member of that council, gave him the same advice for the Sixth Line west. It was the boundary between Brooke and Warwick, and the people there, in Brooke's fourteenth concession, felt closer to Warwick and to Watford than they did to Brooke. They rarely voted in township elections, but would vote for my father, Elmer said, if asked.

When the returns were coming in on election night, the race was a close one, and Dad was behind. The Sutorville poll (where the Sixth Line people also voted) was the last in, and it put Dad ahead.

So my father won the election, but it was a narrow victory. He received 372 votes to Stanley Graham's 333, and in fact the vote was split almost evenly three ways, with Lyle Johnston also having the support of 333 voters. My father had a plurality in only five of the township's twelve divisions, but in three of them his plurality was a large one: in division 12 (our own division in the northeast corner of the township), and in divisions ten and eleven, one of those—I don't know which one—encompassing Sutorville and the Sixth Line. In our own division Dad had 61 votes to Graham's 26 and Johnston's 5. In the tenth division he had 62 votes to Graham's five and Johnston's zero, and in eleven he had 58 votes to Graham's nine and Johnston's none. So his campaign strategy paid off. But the brevity of his card of thanks reflected his just squeaking by: "Electors of Brooke Twp.: My sincere thanks for the generous vote given me by Brooke voters for my election as Reeve for 1946 — JOHN HAIR" (*Guide* 11 January 1946).

As for the others, Clare Edgar was re-elected deputy reeve, and Bill McDougall (then just beginning his career in municipal politics), Clayton Field, and Lyle McLean were elected councillors. Our neighbour Melvin Powell came in fourth; he had been on council for one year only and did not run for office again.

Inwood people had expected Graham to win, my father told me many years later. It had been a bad winter, and Inwood had complained loudly about the roads. There were over three hundred voters there, Dad said, and he and Clare Edgar didn't get more than ten votes each from them. But the results silenced the opposition, and the upshot was that Inwood never asked council for a thing all year.

The first council meeting of the year was on Monday 14 January at 11 a.m. in the township office. "The Reeve congratulated the Board on their election to office and asked their co-operation in the transaction of the business during the year. Declarations of office were signed by each member before Clerk" (*Guide* 18 January 1946). Council then proceeded to business.

One item of business which would affect both Marjorie and me during our high school years was the establishment of high school districts in the county. The Department of Education wanted to reduce the number of high and continuation schools throughout the rural parts of the province and wanted to direct assessments from areas as a whole to the remaining schools, so that it would be possible to increase the number of subjects taught and otherwise improve the schools kept open. The proposal included a plan to transport pupils from outlying areas to high schools by bus. In March 1946 Brooke council responded by proposing the boundaries of a district which would include all of Brooke Township, the villages of Alvinston and Watford, and a portion of Warwick Township, and sent the recommendation to County Council. At that time there was a continuation school in Alvinston and a high school in Watford; the proposal would close the Alvinston school and direct assessment to the school in Watford.

On a Saturday in April, at a council meeting held in Inwood, council gave third reading to the Veterans' Bonus bylaw, and finally passed it. The bylaw had significance far beyond Brooke's boundaries for, as the Watford paper observed, "Brooke Twp. was one of the first municipalities in all Canada to come forward with such a proposal and the plan, which will cost the ratepayers of the township about $10,000 over the next five years, was heartily approved in the municipal voting last January" (*Guide* 19 April 1946).

Brooke made its first payments to veterans in the summer of 1946. Each received one hundred dollars, with further grants promised to those who remained in the township. The Watford paper published (on 9 August) a list of names of those receiving the first payments. There were sixty-five names on the list, including that of Raymond Swartz from our church.

In August 1946, W. J. Weed, longtime clerk and treasurer of the township, gave notice that he would retire at the end of the year. He had started his municipal service as tax collector forty years earlier, and then had succeeded W. G. Willoughby as clerk. Council reluctantly accepted his resignation and appointed Dunc Turner in his place. "He is a man who knows the township and county well" was the assessment of the Watford paper (16 August 1946).

In January 1947 Brooke honored its retiring clerk. "Brooke Twp. council, officers and business associates, about 25 in number, gathered at the Grand Central Hotel in Alvinston last week for an appetizing turkey dinner and social evening in honor or William J. Weed, who retired at the end of the year, after 40 years of municipal service, eight years as collector of taxes and 32 years as clerk and treasurer. John Hair, retiring reeve, expressed the Council's appreciation of Mr. Weed's long period of service and the generous co-operation and wise counsel given the many members of Council and officers during their successive terms, and wished him many more years of health and enjoyment. Deputy-Reeve Clare Edgar, who becomes reeve for 1947, presented Mr. Weed with a handsome chair. The balance of the evening was spent in reminiscing and comparisons of municipal work during the last 40 years" (*Guide* 17 January 1947).

My father's seventh year on Lambton County Council, 1946

As an experienced member of council, my father was on a number of standing committees. By virtue of his position as reeve, he was a member of the Equalization committee; and he was county representative on the Lambton County Home Committee, which included the warden and a City of Sarnia representative. Two positions confirmed his growing stature among councillors: he was elected a member of the Finance Committee, the most powerful of the standing committees, and he was elected a member of the Select Committee, which drew up the slate of nominees for all standing committees.

In addition to its regular concerns, council dealt with two matters that had a lasting effect: the establishment of high school districts, and of a county health unit.

The high school districts were the chief business at the June session, and one by-law dealt with the Watford district, the boundaries of which had already been proposed by the Brooke council in March. County Council accepted the boundaries as proposed, and added a portion of Euphemia Township. This became the "Watford District" in the Watford District High School which Marjorie and I attended, and one result was my being bussed to Watford when I was in Grades Nine and Ten. I came to know students my age not just from Watford but from a wide geographical area as well.

My father was deeply involved in the establishment of a county health unit. At its June session, council set up a special committee to look into the matter, and made my father chairman of it. The committee was asked to visit municipalities where such units were already functioning, and report on probable costs. At the December session of council, my father provided an oral report. The committee had visited Middlesex and Oxford counties (London and Woodstock), he said. "Middlesex county had started [its] unit in a small way by employing only five nurses and a supervisor," and he gave their salaries. "Oxford county had a complete unit, consisting of a medical officer," a sanitary inspector, six nurses and two secretaries, and he gave details of their budget. He "pointed out that the units were not only concerned with the health of children, but in the counties they visited the necessity for sanitary inspection was stressed. Inspectors had ordered restaurants cleaned up and in homes which were quarantined had shown how milk should be handled" (*Sarnia Canadian Observer* 6 December 1946). Council made no decision on the health unit at this session, and by the time it established a unit, my father had moved on to other things.

Donald's appendectomy and Grandad Watson's death: April 1946

In the spring of 1946 I was eight years old and in Grade Two at S.S. No. 5. Early in April I suffered from indigestion at school, and while I cannot now remember the details nor the exact time sequence, the diagnosis of a subsequent attack was appendicitis, and I needed to be operated on immediately.

The date was Saturday 13 April, and my father was presiding over the Brooke Township council, which was meeting in Inwood. That was the meeting at which council gave final approval to the veterans' bonus, but most of its time was occupied by more mundane matters. "Almost the entire day's session," the Watford paper reported, "was taken up with drainage problems, with appeals from ratepayers for repairs to drains and courts of revision held on assessments of drains already accepted for repairs" (*Guide* 19 April 1946). "During the session Reeve John Hair was called home by sickness in the family," the paper said, "and deputy-reeve Clare Edgar completed the session in the reeve's chair." I was the reason for my father's sudden departure.

My parents drove me to St. Joseph's Hospital in London, where I was operated on that night by Dr. Peever, a well-known surgeon in the city. I can remember little except being wheeled to the operating room on a stretcher and being anaesthetized with ether administered in drops on a little mask placed over my mouth and nose. When I came to, I was alone in a small dimly lit hospital room. The first persons who came to see me were John and Dora McNeil, who assured me that I would recover "before you can say 'Jack Robinson.'" Later I was moved to a ward with other boys my age, and my mother came to see me every day for a week, travelling back and forth from Watford on the train. But she told me that she could not come on Tuesday—in spite of my tearful protests—and she did not tell me why.

The reason was that Grandad Watson had died, and Tuesday was the day of his funeral. He passed away on the same night that I was operated on (before midnight, according to his obituary in the Watford paper; after midnight, according to Catherine Watson), and when Uncle Gord and Aunt Eva phoned my grandmother and parents and asked them to make arrangements with Harpers, Uncle Ches (who had heard the telephone ring and was listening in on the party line) thought that I had died and that the funeral arrangements were for me.

On 19 April the *Guide* published my great-grandfather's obituary, with the headline "Brooke Twp. Pioneer, R. D. Watson, Dies." "Roderick David Watson, 93, farmer pioneer in Brooke township, until his retirement in 1918, died Saturday at the home of his daughter, Mrs. W. G. McNeil in London. He had been in failing health for four years. Born in Chippewa, near Niagara Falls, he moved into Brooke twp. at the age of 18 months with his parents, who cut a road through heavy bush to establish a home. Following his retirement, he lived in Strathroy and Delaware before going to London in 1928. He was an elder in the Salem Methodist church, Brooke township, for many years. He was a staunch Liberal. Mr. Watson was twice married. His first wife was Catherine Campbell. His second wife, who died 14 years ago, was Ella Reid. A son, Guy, died a number of years ago. Surviving are one son, Oscar, of Woodstock, and two daughters, Mrs. W. S. Hair of Brooke township, and Mrs. W. G. McNeil of London; also three brothers, Harry and Peter Watson of Brooke, Ceilan of London. The body rested at the Harper Funeral Home, Watford, where service was conducted on Tuesday at 2:30 p.m., ... and interment was in Alvinston cemetery."

So the man I knew as "the old grandad in London" passed away. I was too small to comprehend the fact that he had been born in 1852, and too little aware of history to know that he had been a living link with Brooke's earliest settlement. All that remains are photographs. There is one taken on the front porch of our farmhouse, probably in the spring of 1938: my great-grandfather is holding me, his great-grandson, as a baby. And there is one taken on the front steps of the McNeil house on Bellevue Avenue in London, probably in 1939: four generations are sitting there, David Watson with white hair and white moustache, my grandmother, my father, and me on my father's knee.

My mother's appendectomy: June 1946

Only a couple of months passed after my appendicitis when my mother was stricken also. By that time our family doctor was Earl Clysdale, whose office was in Alvinston. He drove Mum to London, to St. Joseph's Hospital, where she was operated on by the same surgeon I had had, Dr. Peever, on Saturday 8 June. Complete bed rest was the usual prescription after such an operation, and Mum was confined to hospital for a week. Dad drove us kids to London to visit her, and we encountered a severe thunderstorm on the way home. The rain was so heavy that Dad pulled off the road at what we then called "Calamity Corners." That was the intersection of Highways 4 and 22 (now the Masonville corner of Richmond Street and Fanshawe Park Road), at that time far out of the city, which ended at Huron Street. There was a Supertest gas station on one corner and the Knotty Pine Restaurant on the other. Beyond was open farmland. On top of the moraine to the north, up sloping fields, were the great houses on the Ivey and Labatt estates, their imposing rooflines rising above the trees.

With two operations and two hospital stays, my father's medical expenses in 1946 were significant. I think the surgeon's fee for my appendectomy was one hundred dollars, and I suppose it was the same for my mother. Dad remembered Dr. Peever saying to him, "Young man, you should never marry a woman who still has her tonsils and her appendix." My father's 1946 income tax return shows that doctor and hospital expenses totalled $332.00, in a year in which his net income was $1520.94. The need for hospital insurance was already apparent.

The 1946 haying season
By this time my father no longer had a hired man, and my mother drove the tractor when he needed an extra hand on the farm, but her surgery kept her from helping him with haying in 1946, and he thought me old enough to take her place. I was eight, but I knew how to drive the tractor. Dad had already cut the hay and raked it into windrows—haying at that time was done in several steps, first with the mower and then with the side-delivery rake—and the next step was to pile it on the wagon, with the help of the loader at the back, which picked up the windrows, carried them up a conveyor, and dropped them on the flatbed, where they had to be distributed. Dad did that with a pitchfork; I simply drove the tractor. All I had to do was keep the front wheels positioned over the windrow, but on my first turn at the end of the field I thought I had to make a short arc inside the row instead of a wide one to the outside, and I can remember Dad yelling at me, and then having to hop down and pitch by hand the hay I had missed. But after that things went smoothly, and my mother came out to the field with a box camera to take a picture. It was the first time I had been of real help to my father on the farm, and had he stayed with farming, it certainly would not have been the last.

"Old Baddalacks"
My father never called my mother "Alice." It was always "Al." His nickname for her was "Old Battle Axe," but he called her that with such tenderness and affection that I thought, for all the years when I was growing up, that "Old Baddalacks" was an ancient Irish term of endearment. I did not then understand irony, nor make the connection with the prevailing metaphor at that time for the domineering wife. The type was on view every week in the "funny papers," in the comic strip "Maggie and Jiggs." Jiggs was short and stout, and was always sneaking off to Dinty Moore's pub for beer and corned beef and cabbage. Maggie was twice his height, and had social ambitions: she was always dragging Jiggs off to the opera. The symbol of her domineering ways: a rolling pin, which she wielded freely.

Watford's Reo Theatre 1946–55
Going to the movies was the major form of entertainment in those days, just after the war and before television, but (aside from early days at the Lyceum) Watford had no place where films were shown until 1946, when the Reo Theatre opened on the main street. Bruce McLeod (who would later build the house that Uncle Ches and Aunt Ruth bought on Drury Lane in Strathroy) renovated space in one of the business blocks. The new theatre, which could seat four hundred people, had been "planned with most modern innovations, with newest equipment in seating, sound reproduction and luxurious furnishings" (*Guide* 26 April 1946). It opened on 28 November 1946, and the first movie shown was *State Fair*, with Dick Haymes, Jeanne Crain and Dana Andrews,

"in glorious Technicolor." We must have gone shortly after the opening, for I remember that film. The next week, it was Bing Crosby and Ingrid Bergman in *Bells of St. Mary's*.

The coming of television brought about the widespread decline of movie-going, even though the quality of the early television picture was vastly inferior to the technical advances in film, in colour photography ("Technicolor") and in wide-screen projection ("Cinemascope"). In Watford, the Reo Theatre closed at the beginning of May 1955, even though the paper urged people to get out and "keep our theatre." It had lasted fewer than ten years.

My father's last full year of farming: 1946

My chief source of information on my father's last full year of farming is his 1946 income tax return, the first he ever filed. In June 1943 the Watford paper had reported that "thousands of Canadian farmers are filing income tax forms this month for the first time in their experience. This situation arises from the fact that farm incomes have increased generally and tax exemptions have been lowered." But the income on our farm must have remained below the threshold level, for on the 1946 form, in answer the question, "For what year did you last file a return?" my father wrote "Did not file previously as I was not liable."

His net profit from the farm in 1946 was only $1108.44. (That was supplemented by his income from his municipal work, which was $412, for a total income of $1520.94.) He paid only eight dollars in income tax.

On the "Farmers T1 Supplemental," he listed our home farm and declared that sixty-five acres of it were cultivated; he listed the farm across the road, and declared that he paid my grandmother $300 to rent it; and he listed Grandad Hair's farm and declared that he paid Aunt Beck and Aunt May $225 in rent. The chief sources of his farm receipts for 1946 were cattle and white beans. He grossed $3136 for his cattle and $1045 for the beans. There were lesser amounts for wheat ($80), mixed grain ($330), alfalfa and corn ($200), other livestock (pigs $196, poultry $277), and eggs ($300). There was a long list of expenses, the chief one being the purchase of cattle ($2290, so that he made $846 in pasturing "stockers" that year). Then came seed ($30), feed grain ($303), fertilizer ($67), gasoline ($262), and many smaller items (veterinary fees, binder twine, tools, hatching eggs and chicks, repairs to fences and wells—including the well on Grandad Hair's farm—trucking, insurance premiums, and a portion of the cost of electricity, telephone, and car.

By 1946 Dad had a tractor and a combine, two pieces of machinery which changed the way he farmed. Prior to them, he had relied on horses, hired men and threshers; afterwards, he could do most of the farm work—especially the harvesting—himself. I can remember only one threshing at our place, when I was very small, and it was the kind of bee which was then common in the country: a gang of neigbourhood men, a large and heavy steam engine with a long belt attached to a pulley on the threshing machine itself, and a hot dusty day. My mother and grandmother provided a big meal at noon, and they typically roasted beef and baked many pies: the men always had good appetites. All that came to an end when Dad bought the combine. He did so in 1942, and paid $625 for it. So the harvests I chiefly remember were those we called "combining," but Uncle Ches and Aunt Ruth continued to have "a threshing" for several more years in the 1940s, and my mother would go over to their place and help Aunt Ruth prepare the noon meal while my father joined the other threshers.

My father is appointed Treasurer of Lambton County 1947

Dad was a farmer, but he didn't want to farm all his life. He was tiring of the hard physical labour and the small returns. In 1947 he was forty-four years old, and he had two children to educate. Though he was attached to the land, he never made any suggestion that I was to undertake farming with him, as he had with his father. I was to go to university, and I think my parents both had, in the backs of their minds, the idea that I would become a high school teacher, like Uncle Gordon McNeil or Uncle Howard Runnalls. Marjorie was to go to university too—my parents were always conscientious about treating us both the same—and I think they thought that she too might teach.

It was my father's career in municipal politics which led to his break from farming, and the opportunity arose in 1946.

At that time the county's two chief administrative officers were John Huey, who had been county clerk since 1920, and John Leckie, who had been treasurer since 1921. By June 1946 John Leckie's health was failing, and he asked council for a salary increase which would enable him to pay for the help of his daughter, who was acting as his assistant. Council referred the request to the finance committee, of which my father was a member, and when council went to committee-of-the-whole, there was a motion (seconded by my father) that no action be taken on the request. But it had alerted my father to the possibility of the treasurer's position becoming open, and that seemed even more likely by December 1946, when council again discussed the matter. In those days when elected and appointed officials were all men, "sentiment in the council favoured the appointment of a male rather than a female assistant to the treasurer, who could be trained to succeed Mr. Leckie if and when he decided to retire from office" (*Observer* 24 January 1947). The finance committee recommended the appointment of an assistant county treasurer, but council did not act on the recommendation, and the whole matter was deferred until the January 1947 session. Still, my father must have had a good sense of council's mind on the matter, and was optimistic enough about his chances that he did not stand for re-election as reeve of Brooke township.

The January 1947 session of county council began on the afternoon of Tuesday 21 January and ended on the morning of Saturday 25 January. My father, though no longer a councillor, seems to have been present for most of the sessions. Bruce Scott, the reeve of Bosanquet Township, was elected warden, and my father was one of many speakers who "came within the bar and addressed the Council and congratulated the newly elected Warden" (Minutes January 1947). The matter of the County Treasurer did not come up until Thursday afternoon, when John Leckie presented his report. The previous year's warden, Howard Miskell, had been charged by council to ascertain Mr. Leckie's preferences, and reported that "Mr. Leckie did not wish to act as treasurer with an assistant as both would have to be bonded and it would not work out. He preferred that a treasurer be appointed and that he act as his assistant, without any book keeping to do, and to train the new official. Mr. Leckie suggested the change be made June 1 and that he be paid $100 monthly after that," as a pension. John Huey, the clerk, "suggested that a month before the opening of the June session would be a more appropriate time for the change" and "Mr. Hair said that would afford him sufficient time to rearrange his affairs" (*Observer* 24 January 1947).

But my father was not the only man seeking the position. There were two other candidates, Richard Wilson, former reeve of Arkona, and Angus McGillivray, clerk and former reeve of Euphemia Township. All three men had the same background in municipal politics as the man they were hoping to replace, for John Leckie had been a member of Moore Township council, and had been a farmer and stock raiser.

When council resumed sitting at 4:10 that Thursday afternoon, there was a motion "that Mr. Hair be invited within the bar and [he] addressed Council in regard to the treasurer's position." In fact, I think that all three candidates must have addressed council, and after that—on this crucial Thursday afternoon—council moved toward a decision. On the first ballot, Wilson was in third place and dropped out; on the second McGillivray was eliminated, and my father emerged as winner. He had the edge, I think, because he had personally called on every member of council, asking for his support. He knew them all. He had worked with them for seven years, and they knew him for the honest and competent man he was. Years later one of those men—and I regret that I cannot now remember whom—told me about Dad coming to see him, and said that Council had made a good choice. Dad was immensely pleased when I told him that.

After that crucial Thursday session came the formalities of the appointment. On Friday morning council gave first and second reading to a by-law to appoint a County Treasurer; on Friday afternoon, council went into committee-of-the-whole and determined salary and dates, filling in the blanks of By-Law number 863. It named "John Hair, of the Township of Brooke," as treasurer and bonded him in the amount of $20,000. The by-law's third clause set my father's annual salary at two thousand dollars. The fourth set the date of taking office, 1 May 1947. On Saturday morning the by-law was given third reading and final passage.

I do not know exactly when my father returned home from that January 1947 council session, but I well remember his appearing late on a dark cold night, coming up the stairs of our farmhouse, and saying to Mum, "Well, I got the job!" Marjorie remembers that night too, remembers hearing our parents down in the kitchen, talking excitedly, while we kids were supposed to be asleep upstairs. We could not envisage at that time how much "getting the job" would change our lives.

There were articles about the appointment in the *Watford Guide*, of course, and in the *Sarnia Observer*, the *Windsor Star*, and the *Strathroy Age-Dispatch*. My parents were amused by the last sentence in the *Guide*'s story: "Ultimately [Mr. Hair] is going to have to worry about finding a house in Sarnia." The Sarnia paper, which had a photograph of my father, judged him "youthful looking": "In appearance the new appointee is more like a treasurer than an agriculturalist. He looks younger than the 44 years he owns up to, is tall and lean and dresses after the fashion of a city dweller rather than one who was adept at handling the plow."

Transition from the farm to county administration: February, March and April 1947

My parents decided that they would, for the time being, continue to live on the farm, and my father would commute to Sarnia, a distance of some thirty-five miles (sixty kilometers) each way. For that he needed a new car. He had driven our 1926 Pontiac all through the Depression and the Second World War, and it had lasted for twenty years only because he had replaced the engine in it. But late in 1946, before his appointment, he bought a new Chevrolet from Orville Wallis in Watford. It was a silver-gray four-door sedan, he paid $1200 for it, and I well remember my first ride in it. The old car had had no heater, and I was so used to the cold in it that the new car felt stuffy and hot on a winter's day.

My parents and grandmother—they all owned the farm jointly—had long discussions about what to do with it, and decided that they would turn the land into pasture and rent it out for cattle raising. Will Woods, Dad's cousin, was a cattle dealer, as were the Moffatts, and Woodses and Moffatts regularly travelled west, usually to Maple Creek, Saskatchewan, where they had relatives, to buy stockers. I think it was chiefly Will Woods who rented our fields, but others did so also, for briefer periods of time.

Our farm across the road was already mostly pasture, but our home farm was not. For the 1947 season Dad rented it to a man from Ekfrid Township named Arthur Irwin, with the stipulation that after the harvest the land be seeded, and that the "north mow" be filled with straw. For Dad was keeping one horse and one cow, and he needed the straw for the stable.

The "clearing auction sale": 3 April 1947

Then came the business of disposing of "farmstock and implements." The usual way of doing so was a "clearing auction sale." Dad engaged Gord Hollingsworth, the auctioneer in Watford, and set the date for Thursday, 3 April at one o'clock. He had the *Guide* print up bills which he posted in Watford and Alvinston and around the townships, and he placed an ad in the paper. The list of items for sale gives a good idea of his farming practices at the time. The two main items were our "Farmall A Tractor [with] power take-off and pulley, A1 condition," and our International Harvester combine with "pick-up, bean and clover attachments." But he had not entirely abandoned older methods. He still had a team of horses—our big Clydesdales, Pat and Mike—and I can remember his using them to plough our garden, shouting "Gee!" or "Haw!" and pulling on the reins when he wanted them to turn left or right. The bill had a long list of implements, among them a cultivator, bean puller, plow, harrows, discs, fertilizer drill, corn binder, rakes (side-delivery and dump), mower, buzz saw, rubber-tired wagon, and hay loader, plus a fanning mill, scales, litter carrier with 110 ft. track (this carried manure from the stable to the barn yard), harness, windmill, and much more, plus livestock. At the bottom of the bill was this notice: "Everything to be sold as proprietor is giving up farming."

I can remember very little about the actual sale day, which was cool, gray and damp, but I do remember the evening afterwards, when we realized that our dog, Snap, was missing. He had always followed the tractor when Dad took it out, and we guessed that he had followed it after the sale. The man who bought it was Albert Rundle, who farmed on the Nauvoo Road just north of the Tenth Line, and when Dad phoned, Albert said yes, the dog was at their place. Dad and I drove over that evening, got Snap on the floor in the back seat, and brought him home.

Snap's following of the tractor everywhere had, on one occasion, been disastrous for him. Dad was mowing alfalfa in the front field of the farm across the road, when Snap started a rabbit. It ran close to the tractor, and Snap followed, running right across the mower itself. The teeth caught one of his back legs and nearly severed it. Dad brought the poor dog back to our driveshed, bandaged the leg as best he could, and set out old blankets for him to rest on. We kids were warned to leave Snap alone. The leg eventually healed, though it remained bent at an unnatural angle, and Snap ran with a limp for the rest of his days.

Snap had a habit which made him known to everyone in the neighbourhood. He liked to chase cars. At that time there was not much traffic on the Twelfth Line, and a car going by would be noted by everyone living along the road. When Snap heard a car coming, he raced out to our mailbox and then turned vigorously in circles while the car was approaching, as if to launch himself after it when it went by. People remarked on the dog who turned circles.

Witching for water

When Dad turned the farm across the road into pasture and rented it out to Will Woods, he needed to provide water for the cattle. The Roanes must have had a well on that farm, but it was probably only a dug well, and the cattle needed a much more reliable source of water, so Dad arranged to have a well drilled. I do not remember who did the work, but I well remember the man witching for water—the only time I ever witnessed that old practice. It involved cutting a supple branch with a fork in it, so that the resulting stick had a "Y" shape. Then the man grasped either branch of the "Y," his palms up and the end of the stick held straight out, and he walked about the pasture. When the straight part of the "Y" dipped, that was where the well was drilled. The belief was that the underground water attracted the wood. There is no scientific evidence that I am aware of to back up this practice, but the well that was drilled at that spot was a good one, with ample supply of water for the cattle.

Once the well was drilled, Dad set up a windmill and built a concrete tank (he hired Ches Edgar, a member of Walnut Church, to do the cement work). The whole system was designed to work on its own, by wind power. The mill was controlled by a float on top of the water; when the level dropped, that triggered the windmill; the vane would swing round and the blades would face into the wind; the turning wheel would engage the gears on the long rod that went down the well, and it in turn would bring up water from the depths, until the float was at the top of the tank, when it would switch off the pump. It was a simple mechanical system, and it worked well.

My father's first months as Treasurer of Lambton County

My father officially became treasurer on 1 May 1947, and he was understandably anxious about learning the job. I can remember little about those days except long conversations between my parents about getting "the balance" at month's end, in preparation for the auditors, one of whom was Bill Connolly, originally from Watford. (The other longtime auditor during my father's years in county administration was Gerry Herbert from Warwick township.)

The June 1947 session of council was the first at which my father presented his report as treasurer. He did so on the morning of Thursday 5 June, when a motion was passed inviting him "within the bar" to "read his report upon the financial standing of the County." Dad summarized receipts and expenditures for the first six months of the year, and provided separate summaries for the County Road system and the Suburban Roads. He also provided an estimate of the "amount required to be levied to meet the expenditures of the County of Lambton for the current year, 1947." The total came to $194,000.

At the December 1947 session, the warden, Bruce Scott, "informed the Council" in his opening remarks "that when the Treasurer reported, there would be a nice surplus to carry over to 1948. He felt that the County should be proud to show a surplus, when prices are soaring so high." The estimated surplus, as given by Dad in his report, was $35,421.17.

In June council raised the treasurer's salary to $2,500. This must have given my father great satisfaction, since it was one thousand dollars more than his net income in 1946. The certainty of a monthly pay cheque ended his long-endured anxieties about the fluctuation of prices for farm produce and the vagaries of the weather.

The county building in 1947
The building that housed the county offices was on the west side of Christina Street a few steps north of St. Andrew's Presbyterian church, and north of Sarnia's main business section. (The site is now occupied by the Drawbridge Inn.) The building was a large square handsome structure in an Italianate style: a low-pitched roof above the second floor, projecting eaves supported by corbels, pedimented windows, and a bay window facing the street on the first floor. It had been built in the nineteenth century—the cornerstone had the date 1857 on it—as the Bank of Upper Canada, at a time when the Italianate style was popular, and the bank's agent at that time was Alexander Vidal, after whom Sarnia named one of its streets; he and his family occupied the residential part of the building. After the Bank of Upper Canada, the Bank of Montreal occupied the building, and then sold it to Timothy Pardee, and it became a private residence. Two generations of the Pardee family served in the Ontario legislature, and Frederick Pardee, Timothy's son, became M.P. and Chief Government Whip in Laurier's administration. The county bought the Pardee residence in 1904 and remodelled it, but the servants' quarters remained in the attic, small empty rooms connected to the rest of the house by a back stairs.

The treasurer's office was on the first floor, just to the right of the main entrance, which was on the south side of the building—a formal portico with pillars. The office had a long and substantial counter, behind which were desks and tables and an ornate fireplace, and there was a large vault where records and money were stored. The clerk's office was on the second floor—the *piano nobile*—to which one ascended on a wide curving staircase. That office, with its high ceiling and tall windows, extended across the whole front of the building. At one end was Mr. Huey's desk, in front of a fireplace, and at the other was a long table where committee meetings were held. There was also a desk for his secretary, who at that time was Josie Smith.

The rest of the building had offices for the administration of justice: for the crown attorney, the court clerk, and the sheriff (the law library was in an addition at the back). The crown attorney was S.A.K. Logan, the son of a lawyer who had been born in Brooke Township. He was called "Sak" because his parents had been unwise enough to christen him "Shirley." I cannot remember my father ever using "Sak"; he referred to "Shirley Logan" without any hesitation, as if the name were a perfectly ordinary one for a man.

Council met in the court house, a few blocks north and on the other side of Christina Street, and behind the court house was the jail. It was commonly thought that Alexander Mackenzie, Canada's second prime minister, had helped lay the stonework for the court house. He had been a mason while he was a young man living in Sarnia, but the records of his work are scanty, and (so far as I know) there is no firm evidence that he helped build the place. Still, I liked the idea of his having a hand in it. In spite of Earle Birney's well-known complaint that Canadians are haunted by their lack of ghosts, Mackenzie's ghost, in its guise as a mason, hovers over several houses and public buildings in Sarnia, and my sense of his presence seemed even stronger when I found his burial place in Lakeview Cemetery.

The fox bounty

By 1945 foxes had become a major problem in the county. Dwight Zavitz, Ward's brother, raised pullets in lots of one thousand on his Tenth Line farm, and was losing up to fifty of them each night. At the June 1945 session of county council, my father proposed a remedy: the paying of a bounty. But council did not act on his suggestion until June 1947, when they passed a by-law authorizing the payment of five dollars per fox. "There has been considerable loss of hens, sheep, and other small animals in Lambton during the past year due to the ravages of wild foxes," the Watford paper reported. "In one den in Bosanquet a few weeks ago, a farmer found four dead hens and several squirrels." Council debated whether to pay the same amount for cubs as for fully grown foxes, but decided to do so, "so any hunter who turns up a den full of cubs will have a profitable day of it" (*Guide* 13 June 1947).

The paying of that bounty became the signature activity of my father's early days in office. Since the by-law specified that any person claiming the bounty "shall produce to the Treasurer ... the hide or whole body (with hide thereon)," farmers and hunters brought the dead animals directly to Dad, who cut a notch out of the ear of each one so a second claim could not be made. Some of the dead foxes were handsome creatures, with red coats and bushy tails, but the cubs were a sorry sight when they came tumbling out of burlap bags onto the floor of the treasurer's office.

Day-trips to "The Falls"

Such trips to Niagara were rare, given gas rationing during the war, but we must have undertaken one such excursion when Marjorie was small: there is an undated photograph of Dad in front of the Laura Secord monument, holding Marjorie in his arms. The first trip which I remember was in the summer of 1947, in our new Chevrolet. We went to Niagara-on-the-Lake and then followed the river upstream to the Falls—and we climbed Brock's monument at Queenston. While we were driving, my parents and grandmother talked about the Battle of Queenston Heights, and filled my mind with images—horrific images—of General Brock and his men pushing the Americans backwards over the cliff and far down into the rocky gorge. I heard the story of Laura Secord too. At that time her image as a rather grim old woman was on every box of chocolates produced under her name. So I started to learn Canadian history in the best possible way, as stories told by my parents in response to the actual location of the events.

Marjorie starts to school: September 1947

By September 1947 Marjorie was six years old and approaching her seventh birthday. She started in Grade One at S.S. No. 5 that fall. Her first teacher—and my third—was Mrs. Verna McCaw. Mrs. McCaw's husband, Lionel, was an operator of the township's heavy equipment, and also drove one of the high school buses. They had two boys, Douglas and Huey. Douglas was old enough to be in school himself, but Huey was still small, and when his mother could find no one to look after him, she brought him to school with her. Huey's presence always enlivened the school day, for he would inevitably become bored and cranky, and then obstreperous, and his mother would hustle him back to the girls' cloakroom and spank him.

In the fall of 1948 the McCaws bought a hardware business in Alvinston, and at Christmas Mrs. McCaw resigned her teaching post to help her husband. Our new teacher was Miss Sadie Johnson of Melbourne. She taught in our school for six months only, and to us kids she was old and strict, but she was in fact a good teacher, and our parents thought highly of her.

CHAPTER NINE
THE POST-WAR YEARS: 1948–1954

Road trips: Niagara Falls, Ottawa, Quebec City, Montreal

Travel for pleasure became possible again after the war when, as my father said, "things were picking up," and with a new car and financial security my parents' thoughts turned to vacation "trips." Dad was always ready to travel. And for the first time in his life he was free of the seasonal rhythms of farm life and had summer holidays.

We had had regular one-day excursions to "The Falls," and we went again in the summer of 1948, this time for a very specific reason. Grandad Runnalls, now eighty years old, had never seen "The Falls," and we took him with us. I sat between my father and my grandfather on the bench seat in the front of our Chevrolet—no seat belts in those days—and my mother, grandmother and sister were in the back. We ate a picnic lunch on the grounds of Brock's Monument on Queenston Heights, and we stood at the very edge of the Horseshoe Falls, watching from only a few feet away that enormous volume of water plunge into the gorge. Grandad said that he had always thought that the whirlpool was immediately below the falls, and he was surprised to see it several miles downstream.

Dad took his summer holidays in July, and he and my mother decided on a "trip" to Ottawa, where my mother had gone with Uncle Frank in 1930, and to Quebec City and Montreal, where my parents had gone on their wedding trip in 1935. My father planned the route. At that time, Number 7 highway crossed the whole southern part of the province, from Sarnia to Ottawa, and since my father drove to Sarnia every day on that road, he thought he would like to drive its whole length in the other direction. It was mostly two lanes, and went through the centre of every town and village. Two hundred and fifty miles were considered a good day's drive, and three hundred miles a long day's journey.

At that time, accommodation for travellers was in what were called "tourist cabins," usually a row of small frame structures next to a gas station or tourist home, some with toilets and showers but most without, and they were unheated, since they were for summer use only. We cooked our own meals and ate them in schoolyards or parks. Dad had bought a Coleman camp stove, which operated on a cylinder of naphtha gas, so we always had hot food, and ate all our meals in the open air. On our first day on the road, we got as far as a tiny village called Norwood, just east of Peterborough, and stayed in a cabin there. The date was July 21—Dad's forty-sixth birthday. That was the first of many times that my father would celebrate his birthday while we were on the road.

My mother thought of the trip as educational for us kids, and encouraged me to keep a journal, though I needed little encouragement, since Marjorie and I were excited about travelling and were eager observers. In Quebec, my mother suggested making a vocabulary list, and so I learned my first French words: *école* and *épicier*, *lait* and *àrrêt*, and a great many more. And we visited places of national or historic significance: the Parliament buildings in Ottawa; the Plains of Abraham in Quebec City. In those days one dressed up to go into a city, and when we were preparing to go into Ottawa and tour the Parliament buildings, my mother got me into a suit and Marjorie into a dress. There is a photograph of the two of us, looking rather stiff and formal, on the front steps of Parliament, under the Gothic arch at the foot of the Peace Tower.

The Quebec countryside was a revelation after the Ontario landscape with which we were familiar. There were the roadside shrines, the outdoor ovens, the big farmhouses and the covered bridges, and the large churches with their gleaming silver steeples. In Ste-Anne de Beaupré the theatricality of Catholic practices impressed me: there were the crutches of the cured, clustered on pillars in the great church; the faithful ascended steps on their knees, and scooped up holy water in pop bottles. In Quebec City itself we walked on Dufferin Terrace alongside the Château Frontenac, and admired that stupendous view downriver. There is a photograph of Marjorie and me with our grandmother, underneath the statue of Champlain.

My grandmother said she would treat us all to a restaurant meal in Quebec City—the first restaurant meal I remember having. It could not have been a fancy place—it was called the "Gerard Soda Fountain and Restaurant" on the Rue St. Paul—and it wasn't even French, but it was a new experience for all of us except Dad, who had been buying his noon meal at the Crystal Grill in Sarnia. The usual cost for any meal in a restaurant in those days was fifty cents.

The journey home from Quebec City took all of two days and part of a third. I cannot remember much of Montreal, except for the traffic on Sherbrooke Street, but I do remember Cornwall, where we toured the Howard Smith Paper Mill. One of the plant managers showed us round, amid much noise and strong chemical odours, and explained the whole production process. The paper they happened to be making at that moment was for Eaton's catalogue, which at that time was in every Canadian household.

Walnut United Church and the Walnut Women's Association in 1949 and 1950

The mood of Walnut United Church's annual meeting in January 1949 was unusually upbeat, as reflected in the headline in the Watford paper: "Walnut Church Thrives in Rural Community." The story continued by quoting the minister: "'Walnut United Church is unique, because it fits its congregation,' said Rev. E. Lacey at the conclusion of the annual supper and congregational meeting of that church held last week. There was more inspiration for the minister in a small church filled to capacity than there would be in a half-filled cathedral.… Mr. Lacey felt that the future for Walnut Church was bright with around 100 persons attending, many of whom were children just beginning their church experience" (*Guide* 14 January 1949).

"Children just beginning their church experience" were the focus of much of the work of the church in the late 1940s, work which led to the creation of a Baby Band, a Mission Band, and a Junior Choir. At the beginning of October 1949 Genevieve Powell and Amy Zavitz organized a "Mission Band" at Walnut. They enrolled twenty-eight members, and I was elected its first president. Our meetings were a mirror image of the older church organizations: a worship service, discussion of projects for raising money, a story time, and closing prayer. There was also a Baby Band, and children moved up from it to the Mission Band. That involved a little ceremony, when Mission Band members formed an arch and Baby Band members marched up the aisle and under the arch to receive pins from the Mission Band leader. In addition to these organizations, there was a Junior Choir with fifteen or more boys and girls. When the congregation purchased a new pulpit and communion table, they also bought white surplices for the choir. Marjorie and I were both part of it.

In January 1948 my father had been elected an elder of the church, and the following year he and Ches Edgar became Sunday School superintendents. Dad was also made Temperance Superintendent. At that time there was an annual temperance sermon, which I always found embarrassing. There would be a guest preacher, usually old and apparently hauled out of retirement, looking the worse for wear, and he would wave an empty liquor bottle around and fulminate against alcohol. In our church, temperance, as I have already said, really meant abstinence—a lingering manifestation of our Methodist roots.

My mother taught Sunday School. Her class was the Intermediate Girls, and she must have been good, because years later one of those girls remembered my mother writing out prayers and other texts for them, and recalled the little gifts she gave them at Christmas. My mother also continued to be active in the W.A. and in the W.M.S., leading the missionary program and taking part in the dramatization of a study book chapter titled "Literature for the Newly Literate." In November 1949 she and my grandmother hosted a meeting of the W.A., and since both Marjorie and I were taking music lessons by that time, they used the occasion to show us off. After the devotional program and the study book, "Donald Hair favored with a piano instrumental" and "Miss Marjorie Hair sang a delightful solo with Donald accompanying at the piano" (*Guide* 25 November 1949). The reports of those meetings invariably ended with a sentence about the refreshments served, and if the Watford paper was doing the reporting, there was just a hint of a put-down in its diction: "All enjoyed a social half hour over the teacups" (*Guide* 29 October 1949).

In the postwar period the church took an interest in Japan, which was reflected in the Women's Association study book for 1950, *Japan Begins Again*. My mother provided the introduction to it at the September 1950 meeting. She "stress[ed] the need in these crowded islands, only 30 air hours from Canada, of more missionaries as the time is ripe for a change with their 80 millions crowded into such small acreage" (*Guide* 29 September 1950). Two years later, my mother bought and read Mrs. Vining's *Windows for the Crown Prince*, urged me to read it, and reported on it to the W.A.: Mrs. Vining, an American, was writing about her experiences as tutor in English to Crown Prince Akihito.

Death of Uncle Pete Watson: February 1949
Uncle Pete, whose full name was Peter Oliver Watson, was the youngest brother of my great-grandfather, David Watson, and he had built his home on the spot where the first Watsons to settle in Brooke Township had built their house. He died at home on 22 February 1949 at the age of seventy-eight, after a year's illness. His funeral was held at home too, as was often the practice in those days, and I remember how the ceremony ended: Uncle Pete's open casket in the front room, Aunt Net sitting beside it, someone playing the piano softly, and friends and neighbours filing past for a last look before they got in their cars and joined the procession on muddy country roads to the cemetery in Strathroy.

Orville Wallis opens his new showroom and garage in Watford: March 1949
Orville Wallis's GM dealership was thriving in Watford, and in 1949 he built a new showroom and garage on Main Street, two blocks north of his original location. The opening, which was on 7 March 1949, attracted two thousand people, who came to hear the band concert, watch the entertainment, and participate in the dance afterwards. My parents and Marjorie and I were all there. That was the garage where Dad always had his cars serviced, and it was the showroom where he bought new cars, usually every two years. He would continue to deal there until the end of his life.

The *Noronic*
For many years there had been cruise ships on the Great Lakes, and they docked in Sarnia at the Northern Navigation dock on Front Street south of Cromwell. The dock was a large two-storey building extending for some distance along the riverbank, and one could walk out on a pedestrian bridge to an open area on the second floor of the building and watch the shipping on the river. The best known of the cruise ships at that time was the *Noronic*, which was owned by Canada Steamship Lines. It could carry 600 passengers and had a crew of 200. Her captain was a man named Taylor, whose house we always noted: it faced the river near Corunna.

In the late 1940s Catherine Watson was working in Vancouver, but she came home each summer, travelling east on the C.P.R., to visit her Aunt Annie and Uncle Ern Powell and to see other relatives, including us. In the summer of 1949, she decided to take the boat from Sarnia to the Lakehead and the train from there to the west coast. We drove her to Sarnia one day in August, and we had a tour of the *Noronic* while it lay at anchor in the river. The decks, I remember, were wood, and inside there was polished wood everywhere.

In September of that same year the *Noronic* was on a special cruise from Detroit to the Thousand Islands, and docked in Toronto on Friday 16 September. Early the next morning, fire broke out, spread quickly, and soon engulfed the whole ship. There were 750 passengers on board, and 138 of them died in the disaster. Louis Eddy, the son of our former minister at Walnut, who had just finished his second year in Arts at McGill, had been working on the ship for the summer season as a deck steward. He survived, and helped other passengers to safety.

Music lessons

Music was an important part of the lives of our parents, and they wanted their children to enjoy it as much as they did. I cannot remember just when we started to take piano lessons, but our mother enrolled us with her former teacher, Marguerite Purdy. By this time she was married to Nelson Johnson, who was vice-principal of the public school in Strathroy, and she not only taught music in the schools but gave lessons in her home, first in a house on Albert Street, and then in (what had been) the Purdy house at the west end of Front Street. We drove to Strathroy once a week, on Saturdays, for a half hour each with her.

I loved the piano, but not enough to practise as much as I should have, and my parents nagged me, no doubt with good reason. I can remember being moved just enough to resolve to practice for ten minutes every day. I thought this an enormous commitment on my part, and when I proudly told Mrs. Johnson about it, I couldn't understand why her response was so muted.

Every June, Mrs. Johnson's pupils gave a recital in the United Church in Strathroy, where she was organist, and Marjorie and I were always part of it.

Dutch immigrants on the Twelfth Line

The largest change in the demographics of the Twelfth Line after the war was the influx of Dutch immigrants. Canadian forces had been largely responsible for liberating the Netherlands in 1944–5, and a daughter of the royal family had been born in Ottawa during the war, so when Dutch thoughts turned to emigration, the destination was often this country. By 1949, one large family, and one couple just starting out, arrived in our section.

The large family was the Van den Broeks. They had emigrated in 1948, and in November 1949 bought the Gordon Bowie farm on the Twelfth Line. It was directly across the road from Harold Hair's, and had been rented out to a family by the name of Hayward before the Van den Broeks bought it. There were twelve children in the family (the father had been twice married). The ones we knew best, because they went to school with us, were Harry, Reika, Wilma, and Joe.

The young couple just starting out were Jo and Tina Jongsma. They came in the late spring of 1949, and they lived with Harold and Honor Hair, whose large old farmhouse could easily accommodate an extra couple: Jo started as their hired man. Harold and Honor were fond of them, and helped them on their way. They were an enterprising couple, and ten years later they built a motel in London, the Wellington Court Motel, on Wellington Road South, and still later would add a dining lounge and tavern. They borrowed heavily to undertake the whole complex, but Harold reported Jo as saying that they had started out with nothing, and they weren't afraid of losing everything.

In April 1953, Henry and Tina Van Dinther emigrated from Holland and bought Uncle Pete Watson's farm on the Twelfth Line, and Theo Verhoysen and his wife Anna bought Uncle Harry Watson's place. The Kingmas (Rimmer and Aantje) bought Jack King's farm across the road. Later arrivals were the Mintens and the Sanders (one of whom would eventually own our farm). Today almost every farm on the Twelfth Line—now the Lasalle Line—has a second- or third-generation Dutch family on it.

Death of Grandad Runnalls, 22 December 1949

Grandad Runnalls died just before Christmas 1949 and was buried in Strathroy Cemetery on Christmas Eve. It was our saddest Christmas ever.

Grandad had been determined not to be a burden to his children, and sometime during the last year of his life, he made arrangements for a family to move in with him, with the idea that they would look after him, probably in return for accommodation. Their name was Sparling. Grandad did this without consulting Aunt Ruth or my mother, both of whom were surprised and alarmed to find strangers living in his house, and they took a dim view of the situation. There were awkward moments when we visited in Mount Brydges.

On 1 August Aunt Jean and Uncle Oscar Watson had invited us to Woodstock for the day, but my mother did not go. Grandad had suddenly been taken ill, and we drove her to Mount Brydges while we went on to Woodstock. That evening, I can remember standing around and waiting outside Grandad's house, looking at the day lilies and hollyhocks that he had planted around the foundation, and not knowing what was happening. I cannot remember Uncle Howard being there, but he probably was. He and Aunt Eleanor and our cousins Lyn and Sandy spent part of every summer in Mount Brydges, the children living in a tent pitched in Grandad's garden. The Strathroy paper reported that they returned to Timmins at the beginning of September, after having "spent some time with their father, Mr. Joseph Runnalls, who has been ill" (*Age* 1 September 1949).

How Grandad was cared for in the fall of 1949 I do not know. One story survives: he was taken to Strathroy Hospital by ambulance, and it stalled on the railway tracks in Strathroy—a potentially tragic situation. Dennings, who owned the funeral home in Strathroy, ran the ambulance service and, in a macabre practice in those days, their hearse doubled as an ambulance.

I have few memories of the funeral, but more of the interment. Christmas Eve was gray and cold and damp. There was snow on the ground in the cemetery, and the light was dim—and made even dimmer by the enormous dark spruce trees that lined all the roadways. I remember the cold, the snow, and the polished wood of Grandad's coffin being lowered into the grave. It was a bleak, sad scene.

I remember my grandfather as a handsome man. He looked like Louis St. Laurent, the prime minister at the time, with his trim moustache and white hair and courtly manners, reflected in the simple courtesies he paid to my grandmother. He always washed hands and face and combed his hair before sitting down to a meal.

Our last teacher in S.S. No. 5: Mary Evelyn McLean

Mary Evelyn McLean came to teach in S.S. No. 5 in September 1949. She was fresh out of Normal School, and I suppose she was about nineteen at the time. The McLeans lived east of us, on the Sixth Line of Metcalfe Township, in a rambling old farmhouse surrounded by an overgrown orchard, and they were neighbours of the McNeils, Uncle Gord's family. Mary Evelyn was one of a new generation of teachers, not so strict about memory work and leaning more toward fostering creativity in children. I think my parents were a bit doubtful about her teaching. She was my teacher until I went to high school in the fall of 1951, and she was Marjorie's teacher until our own schoolhouse—S.S. No. 10—opened once again, in September 1952, after having been closed since 1939.

Round the Gaspé: August 1950

In the summer of 1949 we took only day trips, to Windsor and Jack Miner's bird sanctuary at Kingsville; and to Tyrconnell and the site of the Talbot settlement and Port Stanley. (The Sarnia paper published an account of this excursion on 30 July 1949: reporters from the *Observer* were always coming into Dad's office, sniffing around for news, and this one must have been hard up for a story.) But in the summer of 1950 we undertook a far more ambitious trip than any we had yet made: it involved long distances, the east coast and a first sight of the Atlantic, and hundreds of miles of unpaved roads in a remote part of the country: the Gaspé. I think now that my parents were courageous to undertake it.

The sight of Québec from Lévis is one of the iconic Canadian images, and on this trip we saw that view for the first time: the great river, the terrace high above the Lower Town, the towering bulk of the Chateau Frontenac, and the ramparts of the citadel.

Below Quebec City, we followed the south shore of the St. Lawrence, seeing lumber mills and pulpwood, outdoor ovens, stone houses and churches, an ever-broadening *fleuve* that was salt and tidal, and fish fillets hung on racks to dry. At the mouth of every river coming out of the mountainous interior was a picturesque village, with tidal flats, fishing boats, and clustered houses. On our fourth day on the road, beyond St-Joachim-de-Tourelle, the pavement came to an end, and from there on we were driving on gravel. Every bridge was a covered bridge, and though we counted, we lost track of the number we crossed. The road was narrow and winding, dipping at some points below cliffs and down to water level, climbing at others high above the river. Rain made the road muddy, and there was one point at which Dad was afraid of getting stuck. But we made it to Gaspé itself. The Jacques Cartier monument on the shores of the blue waters of the bay was the occasion of another history lesson.

Our first sight of Percé was a dramatic one: a descent down a hill, a sudden drop below the fog—and there was the rock, looking like an enormous dark ship moored out in the bay. We walked on the gravelly beach, in the gray wetness, with seagulls screaming around us, great green breakers foaming on shore, rolls of orange kelp strung along the strand, and the odour of decaying fish and salt water everywhere. The gulf was very rough. Beyond Percé the road was so close to the rocks on the shore that spray dashed up on the car.

The rest of the trip was not nearly so dramatic. We crossed Chaleur Bay on a ferry to Dalhousie, and had a long drive south through New Brunswick to Moncton and St. John. Our seventh day of travelling brought us to the American border at Calais, Maine, and to Route 1 heading south. The next day we saw the ocean for the first time. It was at Old Orchard Beach, south of Portland. We walked on the firm wet sand and stared at the green water and the foaming white breakers racing up the strand. There is a picture of my mother and my grandmother standing up just out of reach of the surf and looking out to sea.

Our final night on the road was in a village on Route 7 just east of Troy, New York, which is on the Hudson River. We had driven through two New England states, and Dad was amused, later, to be able to tell how we had crossed "the White Mountains in New Hampshire and the Green Mountains in Vermont." Our tenth and final day was a marathon drive. There was no New York State Thruway at the time, and travel was on Route 20, the main east-west highway across the upper part of the state. Dad wanted to be home that night. As usual, we made an early start, but darkness was falling by the time we reached Paris, Ontario, and we kids went to sleep in the back seat of the car. I remember waking up when Dad stopped for a cup of coffee at the Supertest gas station at Calamity Corners in London. It was eleven o'clock at night when we got home. We had travelled 2700 miles in all, and Dad, always interested in maps and distances and travel times and rather proud of our daring on this trip, would tell everyone that they could easily be at the ocean in two days.

Minstrel shows in Watford

The minstrel show is a form of entertainment which has totally disappeared, since it seems in retrospect to have been racist, but for several years from 1950 on there was an annual minstrel show in the Lyceum in Watford, and we saw most of them. They were popular, and attracted large crowds. They were organized by the minister of St. Andrew's United Church, the Reverend Clarence Beacom, and they always included musical and dance numbers, and sometimes a one-act play. But the defining feature of the show was the circle of men in black face around the interlocutor: he was the straight man, and the men in black face "cracked wise" and made people laugh. "Rev. C. E. Beacom ably handled the role of interlocutor," the paper reported, and around him were "wise-cracking, black-faced end-men in derby hats and cut-away coats...." (*Guide* 14 April 1950).

The sale of Grandad Runnalls's house and contents

Grandad had named my mother and Uncle Howard as his executors, and in March 1951 they sold the Mount Brydges house to Uncle Stanley Thompson. Earlier, on 11 November 1950, they had held an auction sale of the household furniture. The day was mild and damp, and my mother and Aunt Ruth worried about people tramping through the house with muddy boots and shoes, but the weather made it possible for them to set everything outside. The Runnalls siblings had agreed that, if anyone wanted a particular item, he or she would bid on it, like anyone else at the sale. Aunt Ruth and Uncle Ches wanted the good bedroom set, and bought it. One item that did not sell was the enormous brass bed that had been my grandparents'. In 1950 no one wanted such an old-fashioned piece of furniture, and after the sale it was left sitting forlornly in the open door of the little barn at the back of the property.

Marjorie's appendectomy: May 1951

On Monday 21 May Marjorie had an attack of appendicitis, and that evening our parents took her to St. Joseph's Hospital in Sarnia. She was given penicillin and operated on the next morning. It happened that Peggy Joyce, the daughter of Josie Smith, the county stenographer, also had an appendectomy at the same time, and the two of them shared a room in the hospital. Among the many cards and letters Marjorie received was one from Aunt Agnes, who was, as always, planning a trip: "I think maybe starting Aug 1st we may go to Montreal and Quebec and then on to Cape Cod something the same trip as you took only not so far. I think we will take DeeDee." "DeeDee" was Denise, her much-loved granddaughter.

The "chores"

I started to high school in September 1951, travelling to and from Watford on a school bus. I was among the first to be picked up in the morning, and had a long ride south to Alvinston and back into town, but that meant that I was (except for the Logan girls on the Sixth Line) the first off the bus in the afternoon. My early return gave me time to do the "chores" before Dad came home. By now we had only a horse, a cow, and some chickens, and my job, when I got home from school, was to let Pat (our Clydesdale) and Daisy Mae (our cow) out so that they could drink from the tank of water at the end of the barnyard: in the winter months, I had to chop a hole in the ice. While they were out I cleaned the manure out of the stable. Then I used a pitchfork to get down from the mow fresh straw, which I scattered about the stable floor, and fresh hay, which I loaded in the mangers. And, of course, Daisy Mae had to be milked. I did that by hand, sitting by her side on a little stool and pulling rhythmically at the thick teats while milk squirted into the pail at my feet. There was a knack to squeezing the teats in just the right way to get two steadily alternating streams of milk. Cows grow accustomed to the milker's hands, and Daisy Mae was certainly used to mine: she was quite content to stand quietly in her stall while I released the fullness in her udder.

My grandmother's pies
My grandmother always made her pie crusts with lard. She turned up her nose at shortening. "The Watsons were great ones for pies," my father once told me: "Uncle Pete Watson ate pie for breakfast every morning."

Nothing tasted better than my grandmother's apple pie when it had been warmed up in the oven before serving. I remember one time when Aunt Eva and Uncle Gord were at our place for a meal, and Uncle Gord suddenly put down his fork and asked abruptly, "Who made this pie?" My mother looked at my grandmother, who said, hesitantly, "I guess I did." Uncle Gord praised it extravagantly.

My favourite among all the fruit pies my grandmother made was elderberry pie. Elders grew in wild profusion along the ditch at the back of our farm, and they yielded abundant amounts of berries, though we had to pay close attention to the colour of the stems: green stems meant that the berries were bitter; purple stems indicated sweetness. The berries themselves were small and had tiny seeds in them, but their flavour could not be matched by any domesticated berry. If I was willing to pick the berries—and I certainly was—my grandmother was willing to make them into pies. Elderberry pies and pumpkin pies were our fall treats.

My parents' evolving relationship
Toward the end of the 1940s, with her children both in school, my mother started going to Sarnia each day with Dad. From the beginning of his appointment as county treasurer, she had helped him with the accounts and book-keeping, and I often went to sleep listening to their pillow-talk, which was gentle arguing over "the balance" or "the tax sale" or the permanently troubled "Beach o' Pines," that badly surveyed development in Grand Bend. I do not know exactly when the county started to pay my mother for book-keeping, but it eventually did, and so she had a small income of her own, and was part of the staff in (what they called) "the building"—a social network she shared with my father. It was a happy arrangement for everyone.

Uncle Harry Watson and his son Vern
Of all the brothers of my great-grandfather Watson, we were closest to Uncle Harry,

whose farm was at the very end of the Twelfth Line, on the easternmost part of the original Watson homestead.

Uncle Harry's personal life was a tragic one: his wife died after the birth of their first and only son, who was disabled. His wife was Mary Elizabeth Saunders, and they had been married on 11 January 1893, when Uncle Harry was not quite thirty years old. Seven years passed before the birth of their first child, on 19 May 1900, and eleven days later Mary died. She was just thirty-three years old. Mary's sister Ellen stayed with Uncle Harry to look after the baby, who was named Vern Aguelda, and she raised him.

Vern was deaf and dumb, and could make only inarticulate sounds, but he was not stupid, and when he was old enough, his father sent him to the "Ontario School" in Belleville. Officially it was the Ontario Institution for the Education of the Deaf and Dumb, and it had been established in 1870. It was the first provincial school of its kind, and it was widely recognized for its programs in special education. There Vern learned to read and write, and to communicate in sign language, which his father and his Aunt Net Watson both learned as well. And his Aunt Ellen, who (according to Catherine Watson) was "very particular" and wanted everything "just so," taught him how to cook and keep house.

Ellen Saunders continued in her role as surrogate mother to Vern and housekeeper to Uncle Harry for nearly thirty years. She died on 22 July 1929, at the age of sixty-seven. "Although never in robust health and having suffered failing health for many years, the end came suddenly on Monday morning after only a few hours' illness," the Watford paper reported in its obituary (2 August 1929). She was buried beside her sister, in Mount Carmel cemetery on the Twelfth Line.

Vern grew up into a man who was hunched over, and whose head looked as if someone had scrunched it down between his shoulders, leaving him with no neck. He always wore glasses. When I was small, I was, for no good reason, afraid of him, but he was in fact a gentle man with a ready smile. My grandmother would sometimes send me down to Uncle Harry's with baking or fresh vegetables, and if Uncle Harry were not there, Vern would appear, smiling and nodding, happy to receive the "goodies." I asked on one of these occasions where Uncle Harry was, and Vern must have read my lips: he replied by writing a note.

When Vern was a young man, he took to delivering mail to his neighbours. At that time, rural mail delivery went no farther on the Twelfth Line than 27 Sideroad, and at that corner there were mailboxes for all the families east of there. Every day (according to reminiscences passed down by Catherine Watson) Vern would wait at those boxes, take the mail when it arrived, and deliver the pieces to each farm, "even," Catherine said, "down that long lane to Kings.'"

In those days anyone with a disability was hidden away by his or her family, and Vern lived what must have been a rather lonely life with his father on the farm. I remember one time, in the summer of 1949, when my grandmother's brother, Uncle Oscar Watson, then living in Woodstock with his second wife, Aunt Jean, invited the Hairs and the Watsons to visit. But Uncle Harry told Vern he could not go, and Vern went in tears next door to his aunt and uncle, Net and Pete Watson. When we arrived, my grandmother—bless her heart!—said Vern was to go too, and he did. There is a photograph of the Watsons taken that day, in Uncle Oscar's garden at 485 Vincent Street. Vern is grinning broadly.

Vern was not expected to live long, but he survived for fifty-one years, and died at home on the farm on 7 December 1951, "after only a few days' illness" (*Guide* 7 December 1951). I well remember that day. Vern died about noon on a Friday, and Uncle Harry must have summoned help. My parents were both at work in Sarnia, but Uncle Ches McLellan drove my grandmother and me to Uncle Harry's. Vern was lying dead on the couch in the dining room. My grandmother did her best to comfort her uncle, but he was overcome with emotion, and walked away from the little group surrounding the body and stood by a window until he regained his composure.

Vern was buried three days later beside his mother and his Aunt Ellen in Mount Carmel cemetery. At the time of his death his father was eighty-seven years old, and he left the farm soon afterwards to live in Watford, with his nephew Lloyd Eastabrook and his wife Elsie. (Lloyd was the son of Uncle Harry's sister Elcie, who had married Joseph Eastabrook.) Uncle Harry and Vern had always come to our place for Christmas dinner, along with Sam McLellan and Aunt Ruth and Uncle Ches. Now Vern was gone; 1955, when we were living in Watford, turned out to be Uncle Harry's last Christmas with us; and when he died in 1957, at the age of ninety-four, he was the last surviving sibling of the eleven brothers and sisters in my great-grandfather Watson's family.

A death in the family always precipitated a flurry of food preparation and the coming and going of relatives. When Vern died, my grandmother and mother sent dinner down to Uncle Harry, and they prepared meals for visitors. The day before the funeral, Uncle Oscar and Aunt Jean were at our place, along with Uncle Ceil Watson's daughter Jane and her husband Earl Holme. And after the funeral the next day, Aunt Eva and John McNeil came for dinner.

"Keeping up" with relatives

Most of our relatives lived close by, and we saw them regularly at church or in town or in our neighbourhood, but others lived farther away, and visits to and from them were more memorable. Aunt Eva and Uncle Gordon McNeil visited us frequently, Aunt Eva saying that coming to the farm always felt like coming home, and we went often to London to see them and to have a meal with them. Aunt Eva was a more venturesome cook than my grandmother, and she served things we never had at home, which I thought delicious: roast lamb, for instance, or warm spiced apple juice. I remember also a rich seafood casserole, full of scallops and shrimp. Aunt Eva always set a gracious table, with crystal and silverware and linen serviettes on a lace cloth in the dining room at 3 Bellevue.

Uncle Gord was always good to us kids. When I was very small and he caught me staring at him, he would wink and smile an impish smile; when I was older, and he and Dad sat talking in his study, I had the run of his library, and I can remember reading large chunks of Toynbee and of Creighton's biography of Macdonald before Aunt Eva called us in to dinner. The odour of Uncle Gord's pipe tobacco, which I liked and found homey and comforting, pervaded his study. I also remember his sitting in our kitchen on the farm, wreathed in blue clouds of cigarette smoke. In those days most men smoked (though Dad did not), and no one thought anything of second-hand smoke.

Aunt Agnes and Uncle Norman Irvine came up from Toronto every spring to stay with Aunt Ruth, usually around the twenty-fourth of May, and brought fireworks, which we set off after dark on our front lawn. They also brought our little cousins, Denise (whose pet name was "Dee-Dee") and Barbara. In mid-summer, there was the much-anticipated visit of Uncle Howard and Aunt Eleanor, with our cousins Lyn and

Sandy. Playing with them was always the highlight of the season. Every summer Aunt Ruth had our cousins from Ingersoll for a week. I can remember the oldest, Merle, being there only once, shortly after his mother died, but the three girls—Phyllis, Arlene and Louise—were annual visitors, and occasionally one of them would stay at our place. Bruce Runnalls, Uncle Frank's son, was in the engineering program at Queen's in the early 1950s, and while he went home to British Columbia for the summer, he came to Aunt Ruth's for Christmas, and was at our place as much as he was at McLellans'. Mum always remembered the occasion when Bappy made doughnuts, and Bruce ate them as fast as she could deep-fry them. Visits from Bruce's parents were rarer, because they were so far away, but I remember one in particular, in the spring of 1951, when Uncle Frank bought a new car. He had discovered that he could save money by buying direct from the GM assembly plant in Oshawa and then driving the car west himself, and so he asked Dad to pick up the vehicle in Oshawa and store it until he and Aunt Nellie came East. They did so at the end of April. Any time that Uncle Frank visited, my mother always wanted him to hear our minister, and so my parents took Uncle Frank and Aunt Nellie to a service at Walnut. But Mum's plans did not always work out. Our minister, having been introduced to Uncle Frank, invited him into the pulpit, and so instead of hearing a sermon, Uncle Frank delivered an impromptu talk on the United Church in British Columbia. Perhaps he was already working on his history of the church in that province: it would appear twenty years later with the title *It's God's Country*.

The royal visit: Fall 1951

Princess Elizabeth and Prince Philip came to Canada in the fall of 1951, and we followed their progress across the country in the newspapers and on radio. They were in London on Sunday 14 October. When we heard on the live radio broadcast that the royal train was leaving London, we realized that we could see it at Glencoe, and we made a hurried trip south through Brooke and Mosa townships. No stop was scheduled in Glencoe, but everyone knew that there would likely be one, for the steam engines in those days had to take on water regularly, and there was a tank beside the tracks in that town. When we got to the station, we found a large crowd, probably about 1,500 people, all with the same expectations we had. The train duly arrived and passed by slowly, and when the last car came into view in the lights from the station, there, on the observation platform, were prince and princess, smiling and waving to the crowd. At first we thought that the train would only slow down, but it stopped five hundred yards down the track, and the crowd ran after it, surging forward and surrounding the platform where royalty stood. There were informal exchanges. Philip asked, "Is this Glen Cow?" and someone replied, "No, it's Glen Coe!" We also heard him say, "You kids should all be home in bed." Elizabeth peered anxiously forward around the end of the car when filling the boiler seemed to be taking longer than expected. Then a lone voice, strong and clear, started singing, "God Save Our Gracious King," the crowd took up the hymn with many voices, and the train moved slowly forward. Our last sight was of the couple waving and fading from view in the evening darkness. But we had seen them: we seemed to have had a glimpse of a much wider world than our little one, and the sense of excitement, the feeling of having participated in something much larger than ourselves, lingered for a long time.

Only a few months later, George VI died, and Elizabeth became queen.

We drive to Florida: July 1952

After the war, Florida became a popular destination for Canadians, and the many accounts we heard of it, from people we knew or from magazine and newspaper articles, made my parents want to see it for themselves. They were, of course, not free to go south in the wintertime, and could travel only during Dad's holidays, which were in July. It was a long drive. There was, at the time, no interstate highway system in the United States, and much of the journey was on busy two-lane roads. Dad, who loved to study maps, planned a route, and settled on Daytona Beach as our destination.

As on our earlier trips, we cooked our own meals on a Coleman camp stove and ate them at roadside tables or in parks. At that time the various states encouraged tourism by setting out picnic tables by the highway: we made good use of them. And while we still occasionally stayed in tourist homes, motels were replacing the cabins which were common in the 1930s and '40s. I do not know when the word "motel" entered the language, but after the war the motel became the commonest and most widespread accommodation for travellers in the States, and our first full experience of them was on this trip. But even then the word "motel" had downscale connotations: the ones we stayed in were often called "motor courts," which suggested superior accommodation. But they were motels: the rooms all opened directly to the outside, and one parked the car right at the door.

We set out on Monday, 14 July and were away for ten days. Driving as far as we could each day, getting to our destination, and getting home again, were Dad's main preoccupations; he was not much for staying in one place for any length of time. He was always calculating distances and driving times, and, of course, careful of the cost of gas and accommodation.

Getting to Daytona Beach took us four days. We went south through Ohio, Kentucky and Tennessee on a route roughly parallel to that of the future I-75. South of Lexington, the highway took us into hilly country and then the Cumberland Mountains. We were used to flat farmland in southwestern Ontario, so the sight of wooded hills and deep river gorges, rocky cliff faces, and wave upon wave of blue mountains, was new and exciting, but the driving tried my father's patience: there was hardly ever a straight stretch of road, and we were always going around curves and making long twisting ascents or descents, often behind slow-moving traffic, so that our progress was slow.

My father had decided that we would cross the Appalachians by going through the Great Smoky Mountains National Park, and so it was with a considerable sense of anticipation that we drove through Knoxville, east to Sevierville, and then started climbing, on a narrow twisting road that followed the Pigeon River, to Gatlinburg. That was the gateway to the national park, and the beginning of the ascent to Newfound Gap. The climb tested the car's engine; the descent on the North Carolina side tested its brakes. In the parking lot at the summit we saw cars whose engines had overheated and were steaming; and Dad worried about the brakes on the way down, so lengthy was the descent and so constant the need to slow down.

We thought—and hoped—that after we had crossed the Smokies, we would be out of the mountains, but we weren't, and something someone had said to us the day before—"you'll be in mountains all day"—turned out to be true. By this time Dad was feeling frustrated. He had studied a map of Georgia and had found a highway that ran down the whole length of the eastern side of the state, US 441, the "Uncle Remus Trail."

It ran pretty much in a straight line from north to south, and Dad hoped to make good time on it. And I think he was determined to be in Florida by nightfall on the fourth day: we left our motel in Athens shortly after six o'clock, when the morning was still dark.

The day was a day of steady driving through the rural parts of the state, though we did stop to pull up some peanut plants from the edge of a field. Farther south, palmetto began to appear, and Spanish moss; the air was hot and humid; and the land was low-lying and wet: we saw turtles and lizards when we stopped for dinner by the roadside. When we crossed the Florida state line, my mother threw up her hands and gave a cheer: we had made it! I was an adolescent at the time and thought her gesture embarrassing, but adolescents are always embarrassed by their parents, and I think now that her reaction was entirely understandable.

In Daytona Beach, my parents decided to splurge on an ocean-front cottage for two nights. The cost per night was fifteen dollars, double what Dad usually paid for a motel room or tourist home, but well worth it, in the view of us kids, for the cottage was directly above the beach, and the first thing we did was go down on the hard sand, take a dip in the ocean, gather shells, and watch the pelicans skimming the waves and the sandpipers running up and down ahead of the breakers flooding in foam up the beach. We could see the ocean from our window, smell the salt air, and hear the roar of the surf all night. And before we went to sleep, there was the sight of moonlight on the water. An enchanted place, I thought.

When we started for home, we visited an alligator farm in St. Augustine, and we followed the coast north as far as Jacksonville, but after that we turned inland, and everything seemed anticlimactic. And we no longer had the moderating effect of the ocean: in the Okefenokee Swamp and southern Georgia, the temperature was one hundred degrees, and the next day in Atlanta it was one hundred and twelve. Since this was a time before air conditioning was widely available, we were used to summer temperatures and minded the heat less than we would now, but still we were sticky and uncomfortable. We kids must have been getting on our parents' nerves, for when my mother and grandmother were settled in a motel in southern Georgia, Dad took us—just my sister and me—across the road to a restaurant and bought us hamburgers and fries, food we rarely ate, and iced tea, which I had never tasted before, and thought exotic.

Dad had been wrestling with the question of the best route home, and he wanted to avoid at least some of the mountain driving that had slowed us down so much on our way south. Someone had told him that, if he headed northwest in a diagonal line towards Chattanooga and then followed the valley in a north-easterly direction toward Knoxville, he would have a relatively easy time of it, and that is what he decided to do. But that route was decidedly less interesting. And once we reached Knoxville, we were back on the same highways that brought us south.

In all, we drove a little over 2,700 miles, and we came home laden with things from the south: tree-ripened oranges, pecans and pecan candy, green coconuts and conch shells, and (wilted) cotton and peanut plants. A little cactus I had dug up by the roadside in Georgia lived on for a couple of years, in a pot on the kitchen windowsill.

There is an aspect of our trip which I find, in retrospect, acutely problematic. That was our observation of the life of black people in the United States. The time was just before the civil rights movement, but we were largely unaware of segregation in the south: the blacks we saw were just part of the landscape. My own blindness was the result of my romanticising the south: I had grown up loving Henty's *With Lee in Virginia*, and my head was full of pictures of white-pillared plantation houses and ancient oaks covered with Spanish moss. What we actually saw in the south was very different: the black sections of towns and cities, invariably crowded and poor; unpainted wooden shacks in rural areas; blacks working in the cotton fields; a black couple in a wagon pulled by a mule. I cannot find in all that I wrote as we were travelling any hint of understanding of their plight.

Death of Uncle Oscar Watson: 24 July 1952

We arrived home from Florida on a Wednesday (23 July), and the next morning we had a telephone call from Woodstock: Uncle Oscar had died about 4:30 a.m. It was Gib Stephens who called—Uncle Oscar's stepson, who was a barber in Woodstock. I remember my grandmother taking the call, and then going into the dining room and sitting down by herself in a chair, unable to speak for a while. She had been close to her brother, and his death was a shock.

On Friday 25 July we went to the visitation in Woodstock, and took Uncle Harry with us. Aunt Eva and Uncle Gord had us all for supper that night back in London. The next day we returned to Woodstock for the funeral. When the time came to close the coffin, Aunt Jean and her family gathered round to say their goodbyes, and they stroked Uncle Oscar's brow and patted his cheek; my grandmother, much more reserved and not liking such demonstrations, refused to join them and sat firmly in her chair. Her grief was private, and she held herself aloof from Aunt Jean. "Something was not quite right": that is what Aunt Jean said about the night that Uncle Oscar died, and I think that casual comment rankled with my grandmother.

Uncle Oscar was buried in a new part of the Anglican cemetery in Woodstock, where there were no upright stones but only headstones laid flat in the ground. Neither at the service nor in the obituary was there any mention of his first wife, and I have always found it sad that Aunt Jenny lies alone in Kilmartin Cemetery. But the Munroes were from Mosa Township, and Aunt Jenny is still there, among her own people.

The search for a new minister at Walnut

Toward the end of August 1952 Edward Lacey, who had been our minister for the past seven years, accepted a call to a Toronto church. On a Sunday evening in mid-September, the Walnut congregation had a gathering to say farewell to the Laceys, and my father, representing the members of session, presented Mr. Lacey with a purse of money. There was no immediate call to a new minister, and a retired man by the name of Amos took the services for the next few months. In the meantime, our parents were members of the committee searching for a new minister, and travelled to services in Milverton, Lambeth, Lawrence Station, and Tupperville to hear prospective preachers.

It was not until February 1953 that a new man accepted a call from Watford. He was the Reverend Donald Cameron, and he was from Loring in the Lake Nipissing District. His induction service was in Central United Church on 2 July, and since Mum and Dad had been on the search committee, they were in the receiving line at the reception afterwards.

Mr. Cameron often gave what were called "cartoon talks," presentations which combined humour with a message. He stood beside an easel on which were large blank sheets of paper, and sketched rapidly on each sheet before flipping it over to the next, talking all the while, and timing his comments to his strokes on the paper. "Originally he intended to make cartooning his life's work, but changed his mind in favor of the church" (*London Free Press* 16 May 1958). He had served in the Royal Flying Corps in the First World War, and he had been padre of a bomber squadron in the Second. His experiences of war left him deeply scarred, but my parents liked the Camerons and became close friends with them.

Death of our neighbour Jack King: October 1952

Jack and Beccie King lived on a farm at the east end of the Twelfth Line, opposite Uncle Harry Watson. House and barn were not at the road but halfway back in the farm, and east of the farm buildings were open fields and floodplain land, to the townline and beyond, so their place seemed lonely and isolated. Jack was the same age as my grandfather Sherman Hair, but he had married much later, and he and Beccie, who had been a Pollock before her marriage, had no children. Their life on the farm had been unchanged for decades: when hydro came to the Twelfth Line, the Kings did not install it, and they continued to use coal-oil lamps for light and a wood-burning cookstove for heat. I remember that one time the Kings invited us all for a meal. We had long had hydro, and we kids were warned not to make any comments about anything being old-fashioned, for the season was mid-winter, the night was dark and cold, and we seemed to be stepping fifty years back in time. Beccie served a fine meal, and afterwards we sat down in the living room, where several coal-oil lamps provided light, and entertained ourselves with a stereoscope. This was a device popular in the late nineteenth century, and it presented the viewer with three-dimensional photographs. The photographs were in fact two, each taken from a slightly different angle, and printed side by side on a card. When one looked through the lens of the stereoscope, the photographs merged in one and gave the illusion of depth. Such was 3-D back then.

Beccie King was a dear kind soul; Jack was not nearly so outgoing, and was, I think, a bit of a skinflint. "Frugal" would describe their lifestyle.

Jack King's end was a tragic one. A fire had broken out around the chimney at the rear of the house, and Jack got up on the roof to throw bucketsful of water on it, which Beccie handed up to him. Just as he got the fire out, "he apparently suffered a heart seizure and fell" off the roof, "splitting his skull against a concrete cistern" (*Guide* 10 October 1952).

Dad collected money from the neighbours for flowers. Less than a month after the funeral, Beccie moved to Strathroy to live with her sister Adeline, and the farm was sold to a Dutch couple, the Kingmas. The school section had not had an opportunity to say farewell to Beccie, and so Dad again collected money from the neighbours and bought an end table and lamp, which he and my mother, and Aunt Ruth and Uncle Ches, took to Strathroy and presented. Beccie was much moved by this gesture from the people she had lived among for most of her life.

Our parents buy a house in Watford: November 1952

There was speculation, at the time Dad was appointed county treasurer, that we would move to Sarnia, but that did not happen, and I think our parents thought it better for Marjorie and me if we received our primary and secondary education in familiar surroundings rather than city schools. But there was no longer any reason to stay on the farm. Mum and Dad had had their eye on a house in Watford for some time, and in mid-December 1952 Dad signed an agreement to purchase the home of Dan and Mabel Steele, for possession on 15 March 1953. The agreed-upon price: eight thousand dollars.

The house was a substantial two-storey red-brick structure in the same style as our house on the farm, and had been built in the same year, 1922, and by the same builders, Johnny Hawes and George Stephenson. It stood right next to the high school, on (what was then called) Wall Street, and to the west was undeveloped land, open fields, across which we could see the back of the other United Church in Watford, St. Andrew's, which was built on a slight rise and had a high steeple. There were only two other houses on that short section of Wall Street, both of them cottages.

The original owners of our Watford house were James and Mary Coke. He was the son of a pioneer couple in Brooke Township, and she had been Mary Margaret Kingston before her marriage and was a daughter of Paul Kingston on the Twelfth Line. They had two daughters, Mary and Maud, and two sons, Clarence and Will. Will was a doctor and head of the Canadian Army Medical Corps, but we knew Clarence best. He farmed on the Tenth Line of Brooke, and he and Remalda went to Walnut Church.

James Coke died in November 1933, and his widow moved to Sarnia. She did not immediately sell the house but rented it to the priest in town, Father Glavin, for two years, when Dan Steele bought it. The Steeles were recent immigrants from Ireland; Dan was a machinist and worked at the wire works. When, two decades later, he got a job at the Canadair factory in Fort Erie, he put their house up for sale.

Such was the history of our Watford house. We did not know at the time that we would be its last occupants.

There was fine woodwork everywhere in the house, in doorframes and windows, staircase balustrade and fireplace mantel; and French doors between dining room and living room (as there had been in our house on the farm). There was a second structure on the property, a small hip-roofed barn, which served as a double garage, and which had a loft above. The lot was a large one—big enough for an extensive lawn at the front and a big garden at the back. The two were separated by a white lattice fence covered with climbing roses, and halfway along that fence was a gazebo. A row of grape vines produced great clusters of purple fruit in the fall.

The one part of the house which the Steeles had allowed to deteriorate was the street front. There was a closed-in porch there, but the front steps were crumbling and the landscaping badly in need of replacement. The first big project that Dad undertook after we moved in was new concrete steps with a wrought-iron railing, new sidewalk with an ornamental light on a pole, and—across the whole front and extending back a few feet on both sides of the house—a low brick wall enclosing raised beds for spirea, evergreens, and perennials of various kinds. All that gave the house a neat trim look.

Dad accepts an all-expenses paid trip to Florida: January 1953

My father was an ethical and honest man, but on this occasion he did something he should not have done: he accepted an all-expenses-paid trip to Florida from a company that did business with the county. The company was Fred A. Stonehouse & Son, Sarnia—the son was Don Stonehouse, by that time in charge of his father's business—and they did most of the road construction and paving for the county. The providing of such a "perk" to members of what was then called the Good Roads Committee and to a few other officials raised troubling questions. I do not know how the county handled tenders for its road work, but I do know that members of the road committee tried to keep the trip a secret: they must have felt that there were ethical questions that they would rather not answer. Dad was aware of those issues. He went anyway, but it was the one and only time he ever accepted such a gift.

The men travelled to Detroit, stayed overnight in the Statler hotel there, and the next morning flew out of what was then Detroit's main airport, Willow Run in Ypsilanti, to Miami. It was the only time in his life that my father ever flew. The plane was an Eastern Airlines Lockheed Super Constellation, an aircraft considered at the time to be the most up-to-date and luxurious of passenger airliners, propeller-driven (this was before the jet age), with four engines: the flight to Miami took four hours and fourteen minutes. Air travel at that time was glamorous and adventuresome, and every detail of the flight excited my father's wonder and admiration, as is evident in a letter he wrote to me: "Dear Donald, I am writing this on the plane. The stewardess brought pad and paper. This is a huge plane, 127 ft. wing spread and seats 88 passengers. We are flying at 15,500 ft. and are nearly three miles up. The sun is very bright as we are above the clouds. The captain had just announced that we are travelling 320 miles an hour and will reach Miami at 2:10 p.m. We have had dinner and I'm sure Marjorie would have been delighted with the tray. There was a place for everything and nothing could slide around.... There are two girls and a boy looking after the passengers. We landed at Cleveland and after we left there they put cushions at our backs and at dinnertime they put cushions on your knee and set the tray on them. The tickets cost $150.00 so we are travelling in luxury....I hope Mummy and Bappy and Marjorie are O.K. Will post this when we land. Love, Daddy."

The group stayed at the Columbus Hotel in Miami and had the use of two 1953 Pontiacs for the week. They went to the dog races, the horse races at Hialeah, and spent a day on a deep-sea fishing boat. Dad saw porpoises and a shark, and caught several fish that he described as "fair sized."

Meanwhile, at home, reporters who were always nosing about the county buildings got wind of the trip, and word must have spread, for on the Wednesday when Dad was away, W. C. Aylesworth, the editor of the *Watford Guide-Advocate*, telephoned. He told my mother that the story had come out in the *Windsor Star*, with the names of all eleven men who were travelling. My mother was discreet and gave out very little information, but Aylesworth published a piece in the Watford paper anyway, with the headline "Secret Mission...?" In it he named all the travellers (*Guide* 30 January 1953).

Dad did not like the whole situation, and he never again allowed himself to be subject to the questions that were implicit in the story. In December 1956 Don Stonehouse invited the warden, the road committee, and Dad, on a trip to Havana, and again tried to keep it secret. Dad turned down the invitation.

Selling the farm

In mid-February 1953, Dad placed an ad in the *Windsor Star*: "200 ACRE FARM FOR SALE, Brooke Township, Lambton County. Choice clay loam, 20 acres bush, balance all workable. Modern red brick house, bank barn, drive shed, other small buildings. Hydro, good water, near school. Close to sugar beet loader and canning factory. Price $25,000, terms. John A. Hair, R. R. 7, Watford, Ont."

Though Dad advertised the farm as a unit, he was in fact willing to sell the farm across the road separately—both Wellington Annett and the Moffatts had expressed an interest in it—and he would ask $10,000 for it. For our home farm, if sold separately, he wanted $18,000. At the beginning of April, Dad closed a deal with Lloyd Moffatt, who wanted the farm across the road to pasture cattle. The agreed-upon price: $9,000.

But in the summer of 1953 Dad had second thoughts about selling our home farm. He reconsidered because Elmer Moffatt told him that drillers had struck oil on Gord Hollingsworth's farm—"the biggest strike in Ontario," according to Elmer, who said that Imperial Oil was trying to lease his place because of its proximity to the strike. Watford will boom, he predicted. And Dad fantasized: if they struck oil on our farm, we would be rich. He considered our living in town in the winter and on the farm in the summer. But, as so often happened with the finding of oil in east Lambton, there was not enough for a profitable enterprise, and great expectations remained just that—great expectations.

We move into town and Dad finally sells our home farm: 1953-4

Steeles moved out on 16 March 1953, and we got the key the next day. A first walk-through left my parents rather depressed at the sight of how much needed to be done. The house was dirty; wallpaper and lighting fixtures needed to be replaced. And the Steeles had left a lot of junk. My parents immediately embarked on a cleanup, and then on redecorating. The next six or seven months were devoted to painting and wallpapering, sanding hardwood floors and varnishing, all of which my parents did themselves, with help from the rest of us. They redid every room in the house.

At the beginning of September 1953 I started in Grade 11 at Watford High School, and Marjorie started in Grade 8 at Watford Public School, all this in anticipation of our move into town. We did the actual move in several stages, taking boxes of dishes and other things with us when we went to work in the house. But at the beginning of October 1953 we started moving furniture, and on Thanksgiving Day we made quite a few trips with a loaded trailer, so that, as I noted in my diary, "home looks barer and barer and the house more and more like home." Our section had a farewell party for us in S.S. No.10 on Friday 6 November and the next day we made the final move: Aunt Ruth and Uncle Ches came and helped with the heavy things—the heaviest was the piano—and that Saturday night, for the first time, we slept in town. That year we had our first Christmas in the new house. Uncle Ches and Aunt Ruth were there, of course, and Uncle Harry Watson and Sam McLellan, and Bruce Runnalls, here for the holidays from Queen's.

In the "Brooke" news in the *Guide* for 20 November 1953 was a report headed "Community Honors John Hair Family." The story: "A very pleasant evening was enjoyed recently at S. S. No. 10 Brooke when the section and friends gathered to spend a social evening with the Hair family on the eve of their departure from the community. The early part of the evening was spent in playing cards, after which an address was read by Alex McLean, and Andrew Spalding presented a trilight lamp to Mr. and Mrs. John Hair and gifts to Mrs. Sherman Hair, Donald and Marjorie. The family expressed their sincere thanks and appreciation. All joined in singing For They Are Jolly Good Fellows. A delicious lunch brought the evening to a close."

The date of the gathering was, as I have said, Friday evening 6 November, and I remember all of us sitting on the platform at the front of the schoolroom while the gifts were presented. Dad expressed our thanks, though each one of us also did so, briefly. He talked about living in the section for fifty years, and when he said that, his voice broke. He had seemed to have no regrets about leaving the farm, but just at that moment his emotions betrayed him.

Dad had our home farm up for sale from the time we moved into town, and he was asking $16,000 for it. The property was listed with W. W. Taylor, the real estate agent in Watford. A provincial policeman looked at the property in February 1954 but did not buy. By the summertime, Dad had dropped the price to $13,500, and in mid-August Taylor reported that he had four prospects. One was a man from Windsor, but he had only three to four thousand dollars to put down, and Dad refused his offer. So all through the growing season of 1954 the farm was ours: we grew vegetables out there; we picked strawberries and raspberries and currants; and in the fall we harvested apples from the orchard.

At the end of September, a man from Belle River, Edward St. Pierre, agreed to Dad's price and offered six thousand dollars down, with Dad taking the remainder in a mortgage at 5%. Mr. St. Pierre, who had seven children (four boys and three girls), wanted possession immediately, and we had to scramble to pick the last of the apples and get the last of the furniture out of the house. The move raised the question of what to do with some things that had been stored in the attic for years, antique pieces such as two spinning wheels that had somehow survived from pioneer days. We took them with us to Watford.

On Sunday, 10 October 1954, we paid a last visit to the farm—to the barn and driveshed and granary and pumphouse—and we walked through all the rooms in the house. The next day the St. Pierres moved in, and Dad and I (along with Bruce Runnalls, who was visiting at the time) went out and gave them the house keys. It was with complex and mixed emotions that we drove away from the place that had been home to three generations of Hairs.

A trip around Lake Huron: July 1953

Our parents were too busy preparing for the move into Watford to take an extended trip this summer, but they did want to shop for clothing in the United States, where consumer goods were usually cheaper than in Canada, and if one wanted to avoid paying duty at that time, one had to stay across the border for forty-eight hours. They decided that we would shop in Flint, Michigan, and then travel north to Sault Ste. Marie, east to Sudbury and North Bay, and home by way of Schomberg, where Dad would show us the Kitchen house, Orangeville, where Aunt Agnes had met Uncle Norm, and Mitchell, where my mother would point out the Heath Funeral Home, run by one of her first cousins, a son of Grandad Runnalls' sister Lectie.

At that time there was no bridge across the Straits of Mackinac. There was a ferry every hour, and the trip took forty-five minutes. The ferry was a large vessel, and we kids thought the decks wonderful places to explore. There is a photograph of Marjorie and me on the top deck, with smoke belching from smokestacks behind us. "You're lucky the smoke was going the other way," Bruce Runnalls said when he saw that picture.

We stayed that night in Sault Ste. Marie, Michigan, to wait out our forty-eight hour absence from Canada, and the feeling in the air was one of alarm. The Cold War was then at its height, and the newspaper we bought had the ominous headline, "All-Out War Looms if Truce Talks Fail." The Sault seemed to be prepared for an attack. The canal and the locks were heavily guarded, and behind the high barbed wire fence we could see sandbags and gun placements and the barrels of anti-aircraft weapons pointing skywards. On the highway we had seen convoys of army trucks, and on the Mackinac ferry there had been instructions on what to do in case of an atomic blast. Fear of "the bomb" was pervasive in the 1950s.

So our feeling that night was anything but a comfortable one. But when we crossed to the Canadian side the next morning, we found no signs of alarm. All was quiet. No guards at canal or bridges or on the ferry across the river. Just the calm of the ordinary.

Outside North Bay we drove in to Callander. It is forever associated with the Dionne Quintuplets, and Aunt Ruth and Uncle Ches had actually seen them, when they were small and on display, under the care of the Ontario government. By 1953 the "quints" were young women and there were only buildings to be seen: the farmhouse outside Corbeil where they were born; the great stone house built for the family by the Ontario government; and the nursery where they had been made a spectacle for the public.

The Warden's Banquet 1953

The Warden's Banquet, held in late November, was an annual event for county councillors and officials, and my parents attended every one of them. The 1953 warden was W. S. "Duffy" Atkin, and in November of that year he and Mrs. Atkin entertained members of the Lambton County Council and their wives, and members of his own council and their wives, at a turkey banquet in the Community Hall in Oil Springs.

The guest list names the officials with whom Dad was working at the time: "Mr. John A. Huey, County Clerk; Mr. Bryan L. Cathcart, M. L. A. and Mrs. Cathcart; Mrs. C. E. Janes [wife of the M.L.A. for East Lambton, Zeb Janes] ; Mr. John A. Hair, county treasurer, and Mrs. Hair; Mr. Shirley Logan, Crown Attorney, and Mrs. Logan; Mr. William Connolly, County Auditor, and Mrs. Connolly; Mr. Gerald Herbert, County Auditor, and Mrs. Herbert; Mr. Brock Wellington, Sheriff, and Mrs. Wellington; Mrs. Josie Smith, County Stenographer; Mr. Douglas B. Gardner, County Engineer, and Mrs. Gardner...." (*Guide* 27 November 1953).

The newspaper account gives the typical proceedings at these banquets: "Following grace by Rev. R. E. Southcott, Warden Atkin proposed a toast to the Queen. After the guests were welcomed by their host, John Webb proposed a toast to the ladies, which was replied to by Mrs. Fred Gallie of Forest. T. A. Evoy, clerk of the village, then traced the history of Oil Springs and the oil industry from its beginning and showed a specimen of the gum beds at Oil Springs which led to the discovery of the first oil well on the North American continent and was the beginning of the great petroleum industry which has made Lambton County famous. Rev. R. E. Southcott, quoting from the Psalms, told how Canada at the time of Confederation secured its name 'Dominion' and also pointed out that we should follow the example of Jesus, who was a servant to all mankind. Mr. Herman Atkin, father of the Warden [then in his eighties], also spoke. The dinner was prepared and served by Group 2 of the Women's Association of the United Church of which Mrs. Atkin is a member. About 200 friends and neighbors joined the banquet guests to conclude the evening with dancing in the auditorium" (*Guide* 27 November 1953).

Walnut's Married Couples Club: The Jolly Twosomes

Though we moved into town late in 1953, we continued to attend Walnut church out in the country, and would do so as long as we were in Watford. At the end of October 1953 a Married Couples Club was formed at Walnut, and my parents were an enthusiastic part of it.

"An enjoyable evening was spent recently at the home of Mr. and Mrs. Dwight Zavitz when twelve couples from Walnut United Church met to organize a Married Couples Club. The meeting opened with a short devotional period conducted by Mr. and Mrs. Lorne Edgar. Following this, Mr. and Mrs. Harold Hair, co-presidents of the Happy Doubles Club of Central United Church, Watford, outlined the purpose of Couples Clubs and the working set-up of their own group. After discussing the desirability of forming a similar organization, those present came to an unanimous decision to do so, and Rev. P. D. Cameron presided for the election of officers. It was decided that there would be no age limit on membership and that all offices be held jointly by husband and wife. The officers elected were as follows: Presidents, Mr. and Mrs. Lorne Edgar; Vice-Presidents, Mr. and Mrs. Raymond Swartz; Treasurers, Mr. and Mrs. John Hair; Secretaries, Mr. and Mrs. Melvin Powell; Program Convenors, Mr. and Mrs. Jack Edgar. All members were divided into four groups, each group to be responsible for one part of the program for each meeting, with the groups to rotate, and the convenorship within the groups to alternate also. The convenors of groups for the December meeting are: Devotional, Mr. and Mrs. Ernest Dolbear; Intellectual, Mr. and Mrs. John Hair; Recreational, Mr. and Mrs. Eldon Edgar; Lunch, Mr. and Mrs. Calvin Annett. ... The December meeting is to take the form of a Christmas party to be held at the home of Mr. and Mrs. Calvin Annett on December 23rd" (*Guide* 4 November 1953).

My parents' activities in the Couples Club varied, and their names are mentioned in almost every report of the monthly meetings. For instance, at the January 1954 meeting, they led a sing song; at the March 1954 meeting (by which time the members had settled on a name, The Jolly Twosomes), Dad sang a solo. In April, Genevieve and Melvin Powell hosted the group, and Dad was the featured speaker, talking about his work as county treasurer (he repeated that speech the next night for the Rotary Club in Alvinston). At the May meeting, Zeb Janes, M. L. A. for East Lambton, was the guest speaker; Lorne and Evelyn Edgar hosted the meeting, and it was Dad who thanked them for the use of their home. The June meeting was a wiener roast at Rock Glen. The November meeting was at the manse in Watford: "Mr. John Hair read the scripture and Mrs. Melvin Powell led in prayer. The highlight of the meeting was a tour of the Andrews Wire Works plant" (*Guide* 10 December 1954).

My parents hosted the December 1954 gathering, and it was typical: Lorne Edgar led in prayer; Rilla Annett read the scripture; there were hymns and the treasurer's report. Then Mr. Cameron gave a talk on flying saucers. Christmas carols, games, lunch, and the exchange of little gifts—and afterwards, in a deliberate reversal of gender roles conventional at the time, the men washed the dishes while the women sat in the living room and watched our new television.

My mother's reading, and Christian Education

About this time my mother's work for the Women's Association began to reflect more and more her own interests, which were in books and music. At the January 1954 meeting of the W. A., she was elected pianist and "Literature Secretary," whose job it was to give oral reviews of books and suggest books to be read.

Our mother was still reading aloud to us kids in 1953 and 1954, and I have fond memories of those quiet times and the sound of her voice. When we were smaller she had read us Bible stories, out of *Hurlbut's Stories of the Bible*, and Joseph and his brethren, Samuel, Joshua, Moses, Daniel, Ruth and Naomi, David and Jonathan, and many other figures remain in my mind after all these years. When we were older she read to us Lloyd C. Douglas's *The Robe* and *The Big Fisherman*, and Lew Wallace's *Ben-Hur*, all of which left my imagination full of images of Biblical times—images reinforced by the movies based on those books.

In August 1954, three Watford churches—Central United, Trinity Anglican, and St. Andrew's United—held a vacation Bible school, daily morning classes for two weeks, with a total of 140 children. Our mother, who was well qualified in Christian education, was one of several teachers. In 1948 and 1949, under the direction of our minister, Mr. Lacey, she had taken two courses in Christian Leadership, one "The Personal Religious Life," the other "Getting acquainted with the New Testament." And when she was at Normal School in London, she had passed the examination in Religious Knowledge, for which she received a certificate from the Presbyterian Church. Now she had charge of the twenty-five boys and girls in the eleven- to thirteen-year old class, which met at St. Andrew's. The theme of the school was "a friendly church." The three ministers, of course, were all involved, but for reasons I can no longer remember, their relations were strained, perhaps because of the psychological scars Mr. Cameron had from his war experiences. Mum witnessed one day a scene between Mr. Cameron and the minister at St. Andrew's, a Mr. Watson, which ended with Mr. Cameron saying "this is not a friendly church."

A split in the Walnut Congregation

Church congregations are rarely the harmonious gatherings they ought to be. Too many egos too easily bruised; too many initiatives and too much effort not (apparently) sufficiently appreciated; too much offense taken at a careless word spoken; too much gossip and rumour. Congregations often split into factions, and that is what happened early in 1954 in Walnut. The issue was the music at the anniversary services. The church had both a senior choir (in which my parents were deeply involved) and a junior choir (for which Marjorie and I were now too old). Mr. Cameron, who had a good voice, led the senior choir, and they held weekly practices in various homes, including ours. From the beginning of the year they were practising not only for regular Sunday services but also for anniversary. But some thought the junior choir (led at the time by Esther Dowling) ought to sing at those special services. Mr. Cameron put his foot down: the senior choir had been faithfully singing all year, he said, and would sing at anniversary. He made this announcement at one of the weekly choir practices in early February, and in the car on the way home—the Camerons had gone with my parents—he said to his wife, "Myrtle! All those fathers and mothers of those kids in the junior choir will be against us now!" And that is roughly what happened. There was an anti-Cameron faction in the church and a pro-Cameron faction. My parents (who disliked any such split) remained loyal to the Camerons, whom they considered not only "the minister and his wife" but personal friends.

The senior choir did provide the music at the anniversary services that year, but at the morning service Esther Dowling sang a solo, with Mrs. Eldon Edgar as accompanist; in the evening, my father sang "Nearer, My God, to Thee," and my mother was the pianist.

Aunt Agnes's last visit and her death: 1954

Aunt Agnes was always sending things to our place or to Aunt Ruth's: a toboggan, a stack of *Life* magazines, a parcel full of clothes: a black velvet coat with white fur collar, dress, blouse, and so on, and her Golden Anniversary dress, which she said was "too youthful" for her. (She and Uncle Norm had celebrated their fiftieth anniversary on 26 November 1952.)

In mid-June 1954 Aunt Agnes herself, then over eighty years old, came for a visit with her nieces: Honor, Aunt Ruth, and our mother. She had always been a spirited woman, but this time there was a noticeable change in her: she looked old; she tired easily; and she dawdled over this and that, to the despair of Aunt Ruth, who thought they would miss the train when Aunt Agnes was returning to Toronto. Still, there was some of her old energy in her conversation, which was always entertaining. About her maid Susan, for instance: she has her "good points," Aunt Agnes said, but "you have to watch her all the time to make her cook something really good." And about her granddaughter, Barbie: "just as stubborn as her grandfather." She had been talking to Uncle Norm on the phone, who reported that he and Susan were having "a whale of a time." Marjorie wore the Golden Anniversary dress for the visit, and Aunt Agnes was delighted to see it on her, and to see how becoming it was.

Aunt Agnes was at our place for a meal, and a day or so later Aunt Ruth had a large family gathering: Honor and Harold Hair were there, with Jane, Judy and Jimmy; Honor's brother Stan Robinson and his wife Jean; and Uncle Stanley Thompson (Aunt Agnes's brother) and Aunt Sylvia. Aunt Agnes and Uncle Stanley sat at the head of the table and presided over the meal. I wanted to take a picture of the two of them, but Aunt Agnes said she took a terrible picture. I respected her wishes, but she and Uncle Stanley were the last remaining members of Grammie Runnalls's family, and I dearly wanted a visual record of them.

When we were leaving, I said goodbye to Aunt Agnes and shook her tiny thin hand. "Goodbye," she said; and then, as she must have said to two generations of nephews and nieces, "Come on down to Toronto this summer. I'll show you all around—the subway, etc.—and you won't miss a thing." Then Judy piped up: "You didn't get a picture, Donald." "The light wasn't good," I said. "Yes," Aunt Agnes agreed, "it wasn't, and I take a terrible picture. We'll just say the light wasn't good."

But the next morning I did take a photograph after all. Aunt Ruth and Uncle Ches brought Aunt Agnes into town, to the railway station, and while we were waiting on the platform for the train to arrive, Aunt Agnes, who was all dressed up—navy coat and hat, white shoes and white gloves—posed willingly with Marjorie. So I have a blurry photograph of her, taken on the last day I ever saw her: Saturday, 19 June 1954.

At the beginning of October 1954, Aunt Agnes was sick with pneumonia, and her nurse sent a letter to Aunt Ruth which alarmed her. But then Aunt Agnes herself wrote, saying she was better and also saying that she liked my photograph of her very much. On October 19, Uncle Norm called Aunt Ruth to say that the pneumonia had affected Aunt Agnes's heart, and she now had a special nurse. On November 12, Stan Robinson drove Uncle Stanley Thompson, Honor and Aunt Ruth to Toronto, to see her. She was being cared for at home, and knew them and talked to them, when they went in to see her one at a time. Aunt Ruth planned on going to Toronto again, by herself, on the train, but before she could act on that plan, Aunt Agnes died. The date was Tuesday 30 November.

My parents were preoccupied with events in Sarnia and did not go to the funeral, which was on Thursday 2 December, but Stan Robinson drove Uncle Stanley, Aunt Ruth and Honor to Toronto, and after the service and committal, they all had dinner with Uncle Norm. He did not outlive Aunt Agnes for very long. He died at home (51 Castle Frank Road, Toronto) on 15 May 1955, at the age of seventy-seven, and was buried beside Aunt Agnes in Mount Pleasant Cemetery.

When Aunt Agnes died, my mother wrote a heartfelt letter of condolence to Uncle Norm, but it was Kay, Bob's wife, who replied: "My dear Alice, Just a note to say thank you for the many kind thoughts.... It was most comforting to Bob & his father to have so many messages from the family she loved so well. She was so fond of Marjorie and Donald and it was so nice that she had her visit with Ruth and Ches this summer while she was well enough to enjoy it all.... Grandpa is standing up very well considering the anxious time he has had for the past ten weeks—he is very busy at the factory and it does help tire him so he hasn't too much time on his hands to brood. Again many thanks for your kind sympathy. Love, Kay."

Our 1954 motor trip: Virginia and Washington, D.C.

Dad's initial plan was to motor to Winnipeg, and in May he was studying maps and planning our route. Though neighbours and relatives often motored "out west," the prairie provinces and British Columbia did not seem to appeal to Dad as much as destinations in the United States, and by July we had settled on Virginia and Washington, D.C. There are always worries, of course, and one of them was the chronic ulcer on my grandmother's leg. It had healed sufficiently for her to travel, and she was determined to go, but she had been in and out of bed all spring, under Dr. Clysdale's care, and the ulcer might well open up again.

We drove in a southeasterly direction through Ohio, seeing sights we had not seen before—Harding's tomb in Marion, the state capital in Columbus—and on across the Ohio River into West Virginia, when the hilly country of southern Ohio changed to mountain scenery. We ate an evening meal in the Hawk's Nest State Park, which had a magnificent view of a river far below, dam, bridge, and railway tracks, framed by the steep timbered slopes of the Appalachians. We saw the Shenandoah Valley and the Blue Ridge Mountains; we paid to see the "natural bridge," a natural arch of limestone high above a creek; and we drove around Richmond, admiring the neoclassical architecture and the gleaming white columns of the government buildings. Our easternmost destination was Virginia Beach, where a salesgirl in a souvenir shop told us we didn't speak like most Canadians—with a British accent, I assume she meant—but sounded French!

The Tidewater region of Virginia has such a long history, and so much of it preserved in buildings and monuments, that we could absorb only bits and pieces of it. And Dad was not much for stopping and going into houses and churches and historic government buildings: a look at them from the outside, a photograph or two, and we were on our way. That was how we saw Yorktown, Colonial Williamsburg, and Fredericksburg, but we did walk through Mount Vernon. Washington we saw mostly through our car's windows. Our only stop was at the Lincoln Memorial, where we walked up the steps to stand before the great brooding statue there. That night we stayed in a cabin on the Gettysburg battlefield. It was the one area that we did explore thoroughly, both that evening and the next morning. Markers, monuments and statues, stone soldiers and stone generals on horseback making heroic gestures, guns, cannon balls, shot and shell were everywhere along the narrow roads twisting through the rough and rocky terrain. Though we got out and read many of the inscriptions, we didn't do much walking. A sign at Devil's Den read "Beware of poisonous snakes among the rocks."

On our last night on the road, we stayed in a motel in East Avon not far from Buffalo, New York. There was a television in the room, and for the first time in our lives we sat down and watched. The set was, of course, black-and-white, and reception was uncertain: every time a transport truck went by on the highway outside, there was a snowstorm on the screen. But we watched with fascination the news, a game show ("Twenty Questions") and a situation comedy ("Meet Millie")—the kind of programming that was then typical of this new technology.

Our first television set

We did not have television of our own until late in 1954. In October Dad bought an Admiral from Tanton's furniture store in Strathroy. He paid $379 for it, quite a large price at that time. It was, of course, a black-and-white set, and was a substantial piece of furniture, which he installed in the corner of our living room. There were only four channels available. Three were American, out of Detroit: channel 2, the CBS station; channel 4, NBC; and channel 7, ABC. The only Canadian station we could get was channel 10, CFPL-TV in London. Occasionally, if weather conditions were favourable, we could access channel 13, CKCO-TV in Kitchener. To receive any of the signals, we had to have an aerial. It was a tall metal structure which stuck up high above the corner of the roof of our Watford house, and on top was an antenna, which had to be directed toward the signals. There was a small motor up there to turn it, and a control box on top of the television set, to shift the antenna toward the southwest, for the Detroit channels, or to the east, for London. In the 1950s, television aerials poked up into the sky from almost every rooftop—a feature of both the rural and urban landscapes which has long since disappeared.

Having a television was wonderful for us kids—wonderful in the root sense of the word "television," seeing from afar. We marvelled that we could sit at home and watch something happening hundreds or even thousands of miles away. We watched constantly, and quickly became familiar with the various programs. Newscasts, of course, and Mickey Mouse, Liberace (whose piano playing we much admired), Arthur Godfrey and Jackie Gleason, Jack Benny, Laurel and Hardy, Abbott and Costello, and Jimmy Durante. Groucho Marx hosted a game show called "You Bet Your Life," in which the chief interest was Groucho's wit. Our favourite situation comedies were "Our Miss Brooks," "Ozzie and Harriet," and "I Love Lucy"; our favourite variety show was Ed Sullivan's "Toast of the Town," broadcast every Sunday night from New York. The wonder of television came home to us especially in the summer of 1956, which was an election year in the United States: we watched hours and hours of the Democratic convention in Chicago, when Adlai Stevenson became his party's nominee.

Marjorie recalls our grandmother's response to our early experience of television. She and Bappy were watching Liberace, and Bappy turned to her and asked, "Can he see us too?"

The accidental death of Captain Glen McLachlan: November 1954

Souwesto's rather peculiar geographical location, between Lakes Huron and Erie, meant that our sense of place was always bounded by shorelines and beaches and water, which we saw occasionally, usually on summer excursions. But the proximity of the lakes also meant a working life for fresh-water sailors, and in our section the McLachlans were the family associated with the water.

Several generations of the McLachlan men in Brooke were ships' masters on the Great Lakes, and Glen McLachlan, who married our neighbour Jessie Saunders, carried on that tradition. He and Jessie lived in her parents' house on the Twelfth Line, partly because Glen was away all through the shipping season, and at home only during the winter freeze-up. During those winter months, he was studying for his captain's papers, and he sometimes rode to Sarnia with Dad to receive training and write exams. By the summer of 1953 he was First Mate on the S.S. *Outard*, and when the ship travelled to Anticosti Island for a load of pulpwood, Jessie sailed with him. At the beginning of the shipping season in 1954, he was appointed captain of his own ship.

His ship was called the *Shelter Bay*, and it was owned by the Ontario Pulp and Paper Company. It had a crew of twenty, and its route extended from Killarney and the north shore of Manitoulin Island to Montreal. Toward the end of April 1954 Glen left the Twelfth Line to take up his appointment.

Glen's career as captain ended tragically. His ship had an accident in one of the canals near Montreal, which resulted in damage to its side; workmen began repairs immediately. Glen, anxious to get through the canal, was standing by an open hatch with the foreman, watching the workers. The ship was carrying flax, and the snow-covered deck was slushy and slippery. Somehow Glen lost his footing and plunged through the open hatch to his death. He was thirty-nine years old, and left behind three young children—Ray, Lois, and Roy—whom we had gone to school with. And Glen and Jessie were members of Walnut Church.

My mother was pianist at the funeral, and Mrs. Bill Miller (who lived in town and worked in McLaren's Drug Store) was soloist; Jessie mentioned both in her card of thanks (*Guide* 19 November 1954).

John Huey's death: November 1954

John Huey was the longtime clerk of the county—by 1954 he had held that position for thirty-four years—and his life was Lambton and its administration. He had no interests outside the clerkship, and though he was now seventy-two years old, he had no intention of ever retiring. His long service had given him an unmatched understanding and knowledge of municipal affairs, and his advice to warden and councillors was authoritative. He was to me a quiet, kindly man, always in a gray suit, with a bit of a paunch, and with a sense of humour. One day while I was helping Dad with some routine job or other, he came down the stairs and into Dad's office with a cheque which he gave to Dad and said "Give me ten dollars." Then he looked at me with a twinkle in his eye and said, "I bet *you* can't get money that easy!"

By the end of the summer of 1954, Mr. Huey was failing, and on November 17 he had a heart attack. He was in St. Joseph's Hospital for only a little more than a week when he died, on 26 November. His daughter Lillian phoned our place that night, and it was I who answered, since my parents were in Oil Springs at a wedding celebration. The next day, Dad helped make the funeral arrangements. For Mr. Huey had come more and more to rely upon my father, and had been asking for him in the hospital, when he was still doing county business from his sickbed.

The funeral was on Monday, 29 November, and was, according to the paper, "one of the largest in the history of Sarnia." More than seven hundred people had filed past the bier at the Robb Funeral Home, and 150 cars followed the hearse to Lakeview Cemetery, where Mr. Huey was entombed in the mausoleum. My father was one of the pallbearers, along with the crown attorney, the sheriff, and Sarnia's chief of police.

My father is appointed Clerk-Treasurer of Lambton County: December 1954

With John Huey's death, County Council had the task of appointing his successor. Council acted quickly. According to an *Observer* story, Bill MacDougall, who was the 1954 warden, announced that council would meet on Tuesday December 7, "at which time a clerk will be appointed temporarily to act during the Council meeting and until such time as a permanent appointment can be made. It will also be necessary, Mr. MacDougall said, to arrange for someone to sign cheques in place of the late John Huey. It is probable that the temporary appointee will be the County Treasurer, Mr. John Hair." The paper was right. On the first day of council's December session, my father was appointed clerk *pro tempore* at a salary of $270 per month.

There was then a discussion among council members: should they appoint a clerk, or should they combine the offices of clerk and treasurer? On Wednesday the 8th, "Reeve John McNally, of Sarnia Township, ... suggested to County Council that County Treasurer John Hair be appointed clerk-treasurer, and that he be permitted to hire necessary assistants to help him cope with the job. ... The suggestion met with mixed feelings among county councillors. Several supported Mr. McNally, stating that in several townships the clerk-treasurer scheme has proven successful" (*London Free Press* 9 December 1954). But the *Windsor Star* (10 December 1954) quoted two council members—Elton Freer, the reeve of Petrolia, and Jack Hayward, the reeve of Moore Township—as saying that "the job of clerk was big enough in itself." My father's opinion was also sought. "Asked what he thought of combining the two offices, Mr. Hair said, 'I wouldn't like to hog the works, but I would be happy to take the job if council decides that is the best solution.' Mr. Hair stated he would not want to give up the office of treasurer for the clerk's job" (*London Free Press* 9 December 1954).

The matter came to a head on Thursday morning when Duffy Atkin, the reeve of Oil Springs, and John McNally, the reeve of Sarnia Township, moved that council "hold an open vote whether we will have a Clerk-Treasurer, or a Clerk." The motion passed, and there was a "standing vote" on the issue. The result is not recorded in the official minutes, but the *Windsor Star* noted that the vote was in favour of a clerk-treasurer. Then, in what the paper called "a surprise move," council took "swift action" and immediately appointed my father to the newly created post. The appointment was moved by Ralph Burr, the reeve of Point Edward, and seconded by Dad's cousin Elmer Moffatt, the reeve of Warwick Township. The Windsor paper explained why the move was a surprise: "Although Mr. Hair was most frequently mentioned as leading candidate for the clerk's seat, it had been expected that council would appoint a committee to go into the advisability of having the job of clerk and county treasurer combined in one, or leave them separated as before."

The by-law was read a first and second time; final passage was on Friday morning, 10 December. It set my father's annual salary at $4,500 "and 8 cents per mile travelling expenses." The Windsor paper recorded my father's reaction: "The new official said he was 'a little overcome' but he appreciated the confidence which was placed in him. He said he would need a good assistant. One of the first jobs would be to reorganize the clerk's and treasurer's departments. A new filing system would be an immediate necessity, he pointed out, since records were getting in a chaotic state." Alongside this story was a photograph of my father being congratulated by Bill MacDougall. The Watford paper reprinted the photograph and said in its caption that "Brooke Twp. is proud of both native sons, and both are graduates of Watford High School" (*Guide* 17 December 1954).

By way of saying thanks, my father provided a dinner for the entire County Council at noon on Friday, 10 December.

Just as council had moved swiftly to appoint my father, it moved with the same speed to appoint a deputy clerk-treasurer. My father was hoping that Gerry Herbert, one of the county auditors, would take the job, but while Gerry said he would help out for a couple of months, he was not willing to give up his various roles in Warwick Township. Council met in a special session on 22 December 1954, and out of a field of fifty applicants chose Currie McVicar. My parents knew Currie, because he had married Doris Foster, the only daughter of our neighbours on 27 Sideroad, Leander and Mabel Foster. Currie and Doris farmed on the Fourth Line east of Watford, in Warwick Township, and they had three small children: two boys and a girl.

A year later, in December 1955, the county held its annual banquet in the Guildwood Inn in Point Edward, and the proceedings included an address to my father which indicates the success of his first year on the job: the council thanked him "for the splendid services you have rendered the County of Lambton during this past year." "None of us here could ever hope in the short space of one year to acquire the vast knowledge of county affairs that your predecessor had: but I am quite certain that you, Mr. Hair, have fulfilled the duties of County Clerk better than any other Lambton County resident could have done."

As clerk-treasurer, my father had no vote on county council. His role was to advise and implement. The speaker characterized his assistance as "friendly, courteous and ever willing." He might have added "knowledgeable."

CHAPTER TEN
THE WATFORD YEARS: 1954–1960

My father's duties: presiding over the election of the warden

At the January 1955 session of county council my father presided, for the first time, over the election of the warden. What did "presiding" involve? I quote Council's minutes. First, "The County Clerk-Treasurer called the meeting to order and called the roll. All members present. / The Clerk-Treasurer then invited Rev. Donald P. Cameron of Watford to open the Session with the reading of the Scripture and Prayer. / It was then announced by the Clerk-Treasurer that the first order of business during this our initial session of the year 1955 was to elect a Warden for the current year and that five minutes would be allowed for receiving nominations. He explained the provisions of the Act relating to the election of a Warden." Orville Cox was nominated by Lorne Henderson (then reeve of Enniskillen) and Elton Freer (reeve of Petrolia). "There being no further nominations within the time limit the Clerk-Treasurer declared Mr. Orval Cox, Reeve of Euphemia Township, duly elected Warden by acclamation for the year 1955, and requested him to take the chair." This procedure did not vary from year to year. The minutes, however, do not tell the whole story: they do not name other candidates, and they do not record the results of the ballots. For those one has to go to the Sarnia paper. On this occasion there were six candidates for warden, and six ballots before Cox emerged as winner. Among the candidates was Lorne Henderson, at that time the reeve of Enniskillen, who would go on to a long career in municipal and provincial politics, and become Ontario's Minister of Agriculture.

In my eyes about this time, my father's life was taking on a new glamour. At the very end of January 1955, Dad went to a convention in Toronto, and on his return we all went down to the C.N.R. station to meet him. There was the excitement of the Toronto-Chicago train itself—a long, sleek and gleaming train with many coaches, and a fast steam engine (they had not yet disappeared from the railways)—and then the excitement of seeing Dad step down off the train, with the warden (Orval Cox), the past warden (Bill MacDougall), the county assessor (Bert Oakes), and our local member of the legislature (Zeb Janes). They had stayed at the King Edward Hotel; they had been on the new subway in Toronto; and they had been at meetings in the provincial parliament buildings. Dad was a long way from the farm on the Twelfth Line.

On 14 February 1958, Dad again travelled to Toronto by train, his business being the county's turning over to the province the land which would become the Pinery Provincial Park. He met the premier, who at the time was Leslie Frost, and he was a guest of Zeb Janes in the legislature. Frost would later introduce a provincial sales tax, which Dad always referred to (with an impish grin) as "the Frost bite."

My father's duties as clerk-treasurer

One of the reporters for the Sarnia *Observer* at this time was a man named E. G. Ahern, who had a regular column in the paper. In May 1957 he wrote a profile of my father, and in April of 1958 he published a series on local government administrators and their duties. No doubt it was my father who listed his responsibilities for Ahern. They provide a snapshot of county administration at the time.

"As secretary, Mr. Hair must attend all meetings of County Council and also all committee meetings (usually in the evenings), to take minutes. Before Council meetings he must prepare all bylaws and have them passed by Council. Then he must have the bylaws registered when required, and have them approved by the various provincial departments. / He must act as secretary of the Lambton Twilight Haven Committee and check all hospital indigent patients to ascertain if they are entitled to assistance. Also transfer patients from Hospitals to Nursing Homes. / Orders for office supplies for all county offices pass through Mr. Hair's hands. He must also advertise all tenders for county equipment. / … Assessment returns for all municipalities in the county are collected in Mr. Hair's office and listed for use by the County Assessor. / There are many reports required by the different Provincial Government Departments. These must be completed and forwarded through the Clerk-Treasurer's office. He must also administer and carry out all resolutions, bylaws, etc. passed by County Council. / As treasurer, Mr. Hair has to supervise the payment of all county accounts, grants and salaries, also fees for witnesses in court cases. He must estimate the amount of money required to be raised by county levy, and submit this estimate to County Council for their approval. / Then the treasurer must arrange for bank loans to carry on the county's business until county rates are collected. He must hold the three-year tax arrear roll and carry out all the requirements in connection with tax sales. Also he has to supervise collections of tax arrears and remit these to the various municipalities in the county. / All ledgers, cash books, journals etc. in connection with receipts and disbursements of monies are in the care of the Treasurer. And in connection with the County Home, Jail, Court House, Administration of Justice, Registry Office and other offices, the treasurer must submit figures to the City of Sarnia so that the city may be able to pay its share of operations. / And, in his dual capacity, the Clerk-Treasurer must prepare and have published all minutes of council and an itemized financial statement …" (*Observer* 24 April 1958).

There were no such profiles of my mother, who at this time was working regularly as a book-keeper for the county, and instead she got her name in the paper in a conventional role for an administrator's wife: she poured tea at official functions. There was one at Twilight Haven in May 1957, for instance, when four hundred people appeared. "Pouring tea" was considered an honour, and my mother got "all dolled up," as she said, to preside over a silver tea service, ranks of tea cups, and gleaming containers of cream and sugar. She had no objection to the gender role she played.

How my father handled sensitive issues

I never had a chance to observe my father at work, and it was only long after his death that I came across an item in the minutes of council that showed how he handled difficult issues.

In 1957 the School of Nursing at Sarnia General Hospital had been threatened with closure. At the December session that year, a Mrs. Ruth Foster "came within the bar and addressed" council, ostensibly about the regulation of margarine, but in fact about her campaign to save the nursing school, and about her dealings with my father. "The County received a great deal of adverse criticism in those days so my next step was to call on Mr. Hair to hear the County side. I would not have blamed Mr. Hair if he had refused to see me; many unkind and unjust things had been said by some. I am thankful to say Mr. Hair was very courteous, patient and intelligent when I met with him. I have great respect for his calm and sensible handling of our affairs. With each discussion in 1956 and 1957 this respect has grown." She goes on to tell how Dad arranged a meeting of county and city men, the result being "good sound planning, understanding and co-operation"—and the continuing operation of the School of Nursing.

The building of Twilight Haven in Petrolia 1954–6

In the first few years after my father became clerk-treasurer, the county undertook two major construction projects. He was deeply involved in both.

"House of Refuge" was the official name given to the municipal institution which housed indigent men and women. It was popularly known as "the poorhouse," but after the war it began to provide care that would later be typical of homes for the aged and infirm. There was a House of Refuge in Strathroy which would later become Middlesex County's Strathmere Lodge, and there was a House of Refuge in Sarnia, with which my father had a great deal to do. It was on East Street south of St. Joseph's Hospital, had been built in 1896, and sat on sixty acres of land: many of the county homes originally had farms that provided food for the institution and employment for those who could work. In 1952 the county wound down the farming operation and sold fifty acres of land to the City of Sarnia, for a park. The building that remained was fifty-six years old, and it housed sixty residents, with separate quarters for men and women. It was becoming inadequate and outdated, and there were discussions about building a new county home.

Bill MacDougall, reeve of Brooke Township, was elected Lambton County warden for 1954, and the chief initiative during his year as warden was the building of a new home for the aged. There was a special session of council in April 1954, when members decided on a site in the middle of the county for the new home. They bought seven and one-half acres on the western outskirts of Petrolia, and estimated the cost of the new home at $600,000. The story continues in my father's words: "Construction of the new Home commenced in 1954 and Mr. W. S. Atkin turned the first sod on November 10th. The corner stone was laid on May 1st, 1955, by Mr. William MacDougall. The home had 117 beds and was completely equipped with dining-rooms, kitchens, and a large auditorium, as well as offices, staff quarters and doctors' examining rooms. On February 4th, 1956, the residents were moved from the Sarnia home to their new quarters. On May 16th, 1956, the Home was officially opened" (*History of Lambton County Officials* 97). The county enlarged the home to 180 beds in 1964, when Lorne Edgar was warden; a new chapel was built at the front; and there was another official opening on 22 September 1965. Dad was a member of the construction committees both for the original home and the addition, and was involved in every detail of the process.

A major part of his participation was the selling of the municipal bonds which financed the construction of the home. At a special session on 21 September 1956, county council approved the issuing of $400,000 worth of bonds with an interest rate of 5%. There was a motion to place the sale of the debentures in the hands of a bond company, but it was lost, and the task was delegated to my father. Two and one-half months later, on the opening day of the December 1956 session, the warden, Gordon Branton (reeve of Sombra Township), said in his opening remarks, "With regard to the debentures issued on the Lambton Twilight Haven, I wish to comment on your excellent choice in the selling of the debentures privately. This was carried out by our worthy Clerk-Treasurer, John A. Hair, and he should be congratulated on his efforts which was a job well done for the County of Lambton."

Council's gratitude took a concrete form at the annual warden's banquet in 1956, which happened to fall on Marjorie's birthday, 7 December. In addition to the usual gifts, council gave my parents one hundred dollars each, for their work in selling the bonds. Their efforts had saved the county sixteen thousand dollars.

The new county administration buildings, court house, and gaol

The second large project the county undertook in the 1950s was the construction of a new administrative building, court house and gaol.

By the mid-1950s the buildings on Christina Street in which the county carried on its business—not only the administration building and the registry office but the court house and the adjoining gaol—were no longer adequate. They had all been built in the late nineteenth and early twentieth centuries, and were outdated. All needed replacing. The first step toward doing so was taken when Lorne Henderson was warden, in 1957, when there was a formal meeting involving officials from the county, the city, and the province, since all three governments would share the cost. By the 1959 Municipal Act, the County had the responsibility of providing facilities for the administration of justice—the court house, the gaol—and the registry office. The Act also required the city to pay its just share of those expenses, and Dad was involved in a great number of meetings with city officials, until city and county signed a cost-sharing agreement in April 1959. The co-operation of county and city was exemplary: Alderman Ralph Knox, with whom Dad worked closely, praised the working relationship at the 1959 warden's banquet, and the "key-note" that he struck was echoed by my father, who also spoke (*London Free Press* 7 December 1959).

The whole project took about three years, and occupied a great deal of my father's time and attention. The first step was to settle on a location. The county owned ten acres of land on East Street in Sarnia—the site of the old House of Refuge—but some thought the buildings should be in the centre of the county, like Twilight Haven. City and provincial officials favoured a site in Sarnia, arguing for accessibility and convenience in the administration of justice. In October 1958 the *London Free Press* published a photograph of the building committee at the East Street site: my father is at the end of a line of councillors and architects, and is quoted as saying that a decision "shouldn't be long now" (29 October 1958). But council did not come to a decision until 1959. The site they selected was indeed in Sarnia, but not on East Street: it was a parcel of open land called Dufferin Park, on the northeast corner of Christina Street and Highway 402. It was owned by the city, and purchased by the county.

The next question was the design of the buildings themselves. The building committee gathered information and visited a number of new buildings in Hamilton, Toronto and Windsor, mainly to gain a sense of the work of various architectural firms, and they ultimately chose a Windsor firm, Giffels and Vallet, as architects. Giffels and Vallet proceeded to draw up plans and specifications; county council examined them and called for tenders; and of the eight tenders received, chose that of Eastern Construction Company, also of Windsor. The price: two and one-quarter million dollars.

For its share of the cost, the county approved a bond issue of one million dollars, and one day, toward the end of January 1960, my parents brought the bonds themselves home from Sarnia, to take them to Toronto to be registered. They were wrapped up in a brown paper parcel, and Dad stowed it away under the bed overnight. The next morning—Monday, 25 January—the 1960 warden, Esli Dodge, and Dad and I all went down to the station in Watford, I to return to classes at Western, Dad and the warden to go on to Toronto. The bonds sat on a bench in the station and in an overhead rack in the train. We wondered what people would have said had they known that we were travelling with a million dollars in negotiable bonds.

Kelso Roberts, Ontario's Attorney-General at the time, turned the first sod on 19 November 1959, and construction began immediately. The project manager and consulting engineer for Eastern Construction was a man named James Walmsley, and Dad worked closely with him throughout the following year.

There were three main buildings in the new complex, all connected with each other: the county administration building, the court house, and the gaol. The first became Dad's workplace. It contained the council chamber—for the first time, county council had a space designed specifically for their purposes—plus Dad's office, offices for the warden, deputy clerk-treasurer, county engineer and assessor, and the registry office, plus a large walk-in vault. There were two committee rooms and, in the basement, a staff lunch room and many square feet of storage space. From Highway 402, the buildings presented a modern and up-to-date appearance in a park-like setting. The court house, three floors high, was a rectangular box, with the dark vertical lines of the windows contrasting with the white horizontal thrust of the building itself. A covered plaza connected it with the county building, which was one floor, and featured a series of barrel vaults as its roofline. Those vaults not only gave the building a striking appearance when viewed from the highway, but were visible in the interior design as well: the offices were all high-ceilinged, with the barrel vaults above softly lit by indirect fluorescent lighting, the whole giving a sense of airy spaciousness. The gaol was a separate building to the north of the courthouse, and connected to it by a tunnel.

Construction took about a year—much of 1960—and although the official opening of the buildings was not until 1961, the county administration building was far enough along that council was able to hold its December 1960 session in its new quarters, even though one wall was not yet finished, and workmen had been cleaning up at four o'clock that morning. One item which was very much in evidence in the new quarters was the Lambton County crest, which up until then was to be seen only in council's minutes and on the county's official stationery. There was a large one, in full colour, on the wall above the warden's chair, and my father, who was wearing a navy blazer, had the crest sewn on his breast pocket.

The official opening of the county buildings did not take place until 18 August 1961, and it was a red-letter day for my parents: the prime minister, Mr. Diefenbaker, had accepted the county's invitation and would cut the ribbon. At 10:30 on a fine summer's day, we drove out to the airport where, a half hour later, a silver DC-3 touched down, and the Prime Minister and Mrs. Diefenbaker stepped smiling from the plane, to be greeted by J. W. Murphy, MP (Lambton West), who introduced the warden (Jim Dalton of Grand Bend) and the mayor (Iven Walker). City and county hosted a luncheon at the Sarnia Golf Club, to which Mum and Dad were of course invited, and both were presented to the Diefenbakers. When Warden Dalton introduced Dad as clerk-treasurer, the P.M. said, "Ah yes, your office does all the work." Dad told him how honoured the county was to have him present.

The official opening ceremonies took place at three o'clock that afternoon, under the canopy at the main entrance to the county building. Diefenbaker spoke for twenty minutes and sounded again the "keynote," saying the buildings were "a splendid example of that co-operation which is essential to a strong Canada." Then he cut the ribbon. Immediately after the ceremonies, the prime minister mingled with the crowd and shook many hands, including mine and Marjorie's.

There remained the question of what to do with the old county building, court house and gaol. In his remarks, the prime minister waded into the controversy surrounding them: all had been sold to developers, but historians and others wanted to preserve them. Mr. Diefenbaker, apparently on the side of the historians, "paid a glowing tribute to the work of Canada's second prime minister, the late Alexander MacKenzie, who as a stone mason took part in the construction of the old county buildings now in process of demolition. He voiced regret at the tearing down of the old county court house and said such monuments of our past greatness should be preserved wherever possible" (*Petrolia Advertiser-Topic* 24 August 1961). Demolition of the county building, like that of the courthouse, was also under way: mantels and woodwork had been removed, and windows taken out, leaving gaping black holes in the façade; the structure was already an empty shell. In spite of the prime minister's remarks, neither it nor the courthouse survived: both were replaced by "motor hotels."

The county records, which went back to the middle of the nineteenth century, had been stored in the attic of the old building on Christina Street, and since records could not be destroyed or discarded without the written consent of the Ontario Municipal Board in Toronto, most were moved into storage in the new building. No one looked at them for several years, until Ed Phelps, a Sarnia librarian and trained historian, began inquiring about them, and then ultimately made an inventory of them. There were minute books, tax book records, a letter book containing the correspondence of long-time county clerk John Dalziel (clerk from 1894 to 1920), and probated wills. The most important item Phelps discovered was a minute book—a beautifully hand-written leather-bound volume—of council meetings from 1850 to 1857, from the time Lambton had been combined in an administrative unit with Kent and Essex, through the division of the counties in 1853. In a newspaper story, my father is quoted as saying "he didn't even know about the book until the fire marshall ordered the county to clean the huge mound of papers out of the attic of the old building on Christina Street. ... It took five or six men a week to clean them all up and this book was found lying in the pile. It is the only known record of the splitting of the three counties" (*Windsor Star* 17 July 1965).

My father's relations with the wardens

My father prided himself on getting along with every warden he worked with during his many years as clerk-treasurer. That he did so is a tribute to his character, his tact and his even temper. The wardens were a varied lot, differing greatly in makeup and temperament and in their preferred ways of doing things, and on occasion some of them tried Dad's patience. Of all those men, the most colourful was Lorne Henderson.

Henderson was reeve of Enniskillen Township when he was elected warden in 1957, and later, when he entered the Ontario legislature, he came to be considered the type of the rural Conservative politician. He knew everyone in Petrolia and in the township, and had an unusual knack of remembering everyone's name, even after only one meeting. And he went to every gathering, was aware of every move affecting the township and of every shade of opinion there, and knew how to coalesce all that into political support. As a result, he was unusually successful in getting himself elected and re-elected, first in municipal politics and then to the provincial legislature. Years later (in October 1969) the Sarnia *Gazette* ran an unflattering portrait of him, saying that he rose to political prominence "by attending every wake, wedding and dog fight over twenty years—typical of the Conservative, rural 'back bench' which controls Ontario." Henderson was not quite literate enough to frame motions for county council. His grammatical errors (and the occasional malapropism) were notorious, and one pronouncement of his has remained stuck to his name. When in 1975 the province gave money to the hospital in Petrolia, Henderson made the official announcement at the presentation ceremony by saying "Me and the premier brung you this cheque!" And when he was arguing that OHIP be supplemented by fees that would in part serve as a deterrent to abuse of the health care system, he was reported as saying "I'm in favour of detergent fees."

It was with amused tolerance that my father observed Henderson in action. You could always tell when he was lying, Dad said, because he chopped the air with his hand. And when he was caught out in a lie, he just shrugged it off, saying "That's politics!"

The Ontario Municipal Association

The Ontario Municipal Association (O.M.A.), which by the 1950s had been in existence for half a century, promoted strong and effective municipal government in Ontario, and it created a forum for the discussion of mutual concerns at an annual conference, usually in late June. I do not know when my father started attending those conferences, but from the mid-1950s on, county council authorized my parents, and the warden and his wife, to attend, with all expenses paid. The conference was held in a different city each year, and as a result my parents got to see much of the province. I remember their going to Windsor, St. Catharines, Ottawa, North Bay, Sudbury, and Niagara Falls (several times). The 1956 meeting was at Honey Harbour on Georgian Bay. On that occasion, we all went, and stayed in a cottage while Dad attended the sessions, which were at the Delawana Inn, a luxury resort at that time. In 1958 the meetings were in Ottawa. My parents thought they had a grand time: they stayed in the Chateau Laurier and saw Parliament in session (Mr. Diefenbaker was in his first year as prime minister, and faced Mr. Pearson across the aisle).

My father earns an A.M.C.T. from Queen's University: 1958–62

In the 1950s, administrators usually had a background in municipal politics like Dad's, but by the middle of the decade the provincial Association of Municipal Clerks and Treasurers was promoting a more professional approach in its members, and established, through Queen's University, a training course (by correspondence) for them. It was a three-year program, and Dad started it in the fall of 1958, reading course materials, preparing and typing regular assignments and mailing them to Kingston, and writing examinations in the spring. Completing the course (which he did in May 1962) gave him the privilege of appending the letters A.M.C.T. to his name, as it appeared on the letterheads of the county's official stationery.

Weddings of our first cousins, 1954–6

Most of our Runnalls cousins were older than Marjorie and me, and married a decade earlier than we did. We were not at the wedding of Merle Harvey, the oldest of our Harvey cousins, who farmed with his father on a hilltop overlooking the valley of the Thames at Ingersoll, but we were invited to the weddings of all three Harvey girls. Phyllis, who had trained as a nurse, married a man who worked for Purina in Woodstock, Bob Smith, in October 1954. Louise married Michael De Paulo, who was of Italian descent and a steelworker in Hamilton, in February 1955. Arlene, who had become a public school teacher, married Jim Bond, who worked for the Ingersoll post office, in July 1955.

There were two weddings in the summer of 1956: one was eight hundred miles away, in Timmins; the other was close by, in Brooke Township. In May 1956 Marilyn, Uncle Howard's daughter, graduated from Western with a B.Sc. and a gold medal. She was engaged to another science graduate, George Grant, and both were working for the Dominion Research Board in Ottawa. They couldn't say much about their work: it was on atomic energy. We drove to the wedding, fifteen and one-half hours each way. On the day itself, rain fell steadily, so much of it that when we were returning to southern Ontario the next day, there were places where the shoulders of the highway had washed away. At the reception, which was in the McIntyre Centre in Schumacher, the minister got a laugh with the line, "never had the heavens wept such tears of joy!" In September that year, Bruce Runnalls, Uncle Frank's only son, married Grace Lovell, who was from Brooke Township. Bruce had graduated in engineering from Queen's and was working for the steel company in Hamilton. They were married in Ebenezer United Church, and Bruce's parents came east for the occasion and stayed with us. It was the last time all four surviving members of my mother's family—Uncle Frank, Uncle Howard, Aunt Ruth, and Mum herself—were all together, and I took a photo of them in front of the church.

Walnut Church 1954–60

Though we were now living in town, we continued to attend church in the country, and both my parents were active in it. In its music, of course: Dad sang in the choir; my mother was pianist. They were part of the Jolly Twosomes and joint presidents of the group in 1958, hosting meetings and planning and providing programs: a bowling party in Petrolia, a tour of the new Twilight Haven, and an evening of "progressive crokinole" that the paper described as "exciting and enjoyable": "Mrs. John Hair and Rev. Don Cameron held high scores" (*Guide* 1 May 1958). Dad himself spoke about stamps. He already had an extensive collection of Canadian stamps, and maintaining and expanding it would be a major activity in his retirement years.

In 1957, the congregation undertook a major renovation to the church: the original front door was replaced by a white frame addition to the side, giving better access to both auditorium and basement; woodwork and walls were redecorated in a new and warmer colour scheme, and a thick green carpet was laid in the centre aisle. There were special morning and evening services to celebrate the re-opening, at one of which "Mr. John Hair sang in fine voice 'Jesus, Lover of My Soul'" (*Guide* 1 November 1957). My mother accompanied him.

My mother was by this time a longtime member of the W.A., and the role into which she gradually moved was specially suited to her interests. She was "literature secretary," and that involved reviewing current books she had read and recommending current books to the other women. At the first meeting of 1956, she "gave a gratifying report on the book reading of last year" (*Guide* 27 January 1956), and later that spring she was guest speaker for the Afternoon Group of Central United in town: "Mrs. Cameron in her very lovely manner introduced" my mother, "who gave us a most interesting and informative talk on reading books and discussing some of the better ones she had read" (*Guide* 27 April 1956). Her usual choices were ministers' lives, and accounts of the religious life and of missionary work: Catherine Marshall's biography of her husband, *A Man Called Peter*; Sholem Asch's *Salvation*; Olin Stockwell's *With God in Red China*; Albert Schweitzer's *On the Edge of the Primeval Forest*; and the letters of Egerton Ryerson to his daugher (*My Dearest Sophie*), which the Ryerson Press—at that time the United Church's publishing house—had issued in 1955.

In 1959-60 I was in my fourth year at Western and was just discovering Canadian literature. I was bowled over by Sinclair Ross's *As for Me and My House*, for its compelling evocation of the Depression years on the prairies, and I recommended it to my mother. That was a mistake. She did not like the portrayal of the flawed minister who is at the centre of Ross's story; reading about him upset her, a response I shrugged off at the time, but one that I would afterwards regret causing.

The Camerons leave Walnut Church
Much as my parents liked the Camerons, they also knew that his time as minister of the Watford-Walnut-Zion charge had been a troubled one. Walnut church was divided, with some members wanting to get rid of him, and others, like my parents, supporting him. I do not remember the issues, but I do remember that much was said on both sides, with people threatening to leave the church if this or that were done or not done. I also remember that my parents did indeed talk about leaving Walnut and going to church in town. But that did not happen. In March 1958 Mr. Cameron resigned, effective at the end of June; in April, he received a call to Thamesville; and in the meantime Watford issued a call to the Reverend Ewart Madden, then at Madoc and Marmora.

In mid-June, my parents invited the Camerons to our place for a meal and the evening. Mr. Cameron was in fine form and enjoyed himself, while my parents showed slides of our trips and I showed off the record player that I was proud of: I had bought it with my own money from working in the A&P supermarket. At the end of June, there was a farewell gathering in Walnut, and Mum and Dad drove the Camerons out from Watford to it. Since my parents were presidents of the Jolly Twosomes, they had charge of the program, which began with a worship service and ended with hot dogs, marshmallows and ice cream bars. The paper records that Marjorie sang a solo, and "Mrs. Hair spoke on the value of Tolerance in our everyday life and in the teaching of our children" (*Guide* 3 July 1958). The paper does not record the fact that my mother wrote the farewell address to the Camerons, and she was the one who read it at this gathering. I thought it a fine and moving piece of work, especially her opening sentence, in which she echoed the address read to her twenty-three years earlier, when she was leaving St. Andrew's church in Mount Brydges: "Life is largely made up of comings and goings and it is friendship that one has for the other that makes us anticipate new departures and makes good bye hard to say." And I think that her choice of tolerance as her subject was by no means a haphazard one. Mrs. Cameron had confided in her and repeated a great deal that was being said about her husband, hurtful things, and he resigned to keep the church together.

Mr. Cameron preached his farewell sermon in Walnut on Sunday, 29 June, and Mr. Madden's first Sunday was 6 July. He had been inducted the previous Friday night, and it was Dad who made the speech of welcome to Walnut church. But my parents did not care for their new minister: they thought that Mr. Madden had half the intellect of Mr. Cameron, and twice the evangelical zeal. Privately, they punned on his name, saying they found him "maddening." But a major change was coming very shortly to the Watford charge: in the summer of 1960 the two United Churches in town at last decided to become one. The ministers at both St. Andrew's and Central accepted calls elsewhere, and a new man, the Reverend Ross Cumming, took over the reorganized charge. As part of that reorganization, Walnut decided to go with the Alvinston and Ebenezer churches in Brooke Township. The change did not affect my parents: before it came into effect, they moved to Sarnia, and their thirty-year-long relationship with Walnut—a relationship into which they had put so much time and effort—came to an end.

My father as a Rotarian 1956–60

Dad had never belonged to any service club or fraternal organization, and I think he considered that he had missed an experience he would like to have had when he decided to become a Rotarian in the spring of 1956. The Rotary Club in Watford had been founded in 1939, with Harold Newell, who ran Andrews Wire Works, as its first president. By 1956 Orville Wallis, who had the GM dealership in town, was president, and he inducted Dad and our neighbour Melvin Powell, who was now partner with Keith Moffat in a lumber business. Dad was introduced by his cousin Hiram Moffat; "Rev. Don Cameron outlined the aims and objects of Rotary and Four-Way Test. President Orville Wallis presented the members' attendance buttons, and treasurer Ken Pope [who was the manager of the Bank of Montreal] explained the privileges and responsibilities of membership" (*Guide* 13 April 1956). Dad was made the club's secretary.

One of the Rotary meetings which made a profound impression on Dad was the one at which Sam Handelman spoke. The Handelmans were the only Jews in Watford, and owned and operated Imperial Poultry Company, which processed chickens and turkeys for market. Sam spoke of his boyhood in the Ukraine and of the persecution of Jews there; he talked about coming to Watford in 1936 and starting to buy poultry, along with his brother Benny, when they knew nothing about either the birds or the business, and he told amusing stories about his ignorance on getting started. Then, as the paper reported, "their adherence to fair dealing and good business practices steadily expanded their business until last year they completed the construction of one of Ontario's most modern poultry processing plants with Government inspection of graded fast frozen poultry, that operates throughout the year, and provides a steady market for all types of poultry gathered from producers throughout a large area" (*Guide* 11 May 1956).

In 1957–8, my father's cousin, Dr. Russell Woods (who was the dentist in Watford) became president of the club, which the district governor praised as "one of the most active ... he has so far visited" (*Guide* 20 September 1957). My father, who seems to have been both secretary and treasurer, was often called upon to speak: to thank the church women for a dinner in Central United, when the club honored Sunday School teachers and superintendents; to introduce the head table at the annual five-dollar banquet, also in Central United; to welcome Ray Morningstar into Rotary membership. The total membership in 1957–8 was thirty-seven.

At this time Rotary membership was restricted to men, and their wives became involved as "Rotary Anns." My mother, who was my father's partner in everything he did, was one. The Rotary Anns occasionally had their own gatherings: when Dad was away in Toronto and Mrs. Arthur Brown hosted a supper for the Rotary Anns, my mother went on her own. But she also sometimes went to the regular meetings, and when the district governor visited in the fall of 1958, there was a sing-along for which my mother was "an appreciated assistant" (she was pianist: *Guide* 23 October 1958).

The district governorship, which began on 1 July of each year, alternated between Michigan and Ontario, and since the governor for 1959–60 was to be from Ontario, the Watford club endorsed Dr. Russell Woods for the post. In mid-April, at the district assembly in Port Huron, Woods was elected, and would go on to a training course in Lake Placid, formal induction in New York City, and a busy year of visiting the thirty-five Ontario clubs and seventeen Michigan clubs in his district. But at the same time my father's years as a Rotarian were coming to an end. In October 1960 he "announced that pressure of county business forces him to resign as club secretary, which was accepted with regret" (*Guide* 13 October 1960). This was just at the time when our Watford house was being expropriated and my parents were moving to Sarnia: Dad did not continue his association with Rotary after that.

The Royal Visit: Summer 1959

The St. Lawrence Seaway was officially opened at the end of June 1959, and the Queen and the Duke of Edinburgh sailed into the Great Lakes on the Royal Yacht *Britannia*, visiting all the major ports that were now open to ocean-going vessels. They came to Sarnia on Friday, 3 July.

Christina Street was gloriously decorated for the visit, and the old county building—the new one had not yet been constructed—was decked out in flags and bunting. It was evening when the royal couple arrived. Thousands of people lined Christina Street, from the Imperial Oil dock to Canatara Park, where the official welcoming ceremonies were held. We stationed ourselves on the curb outside the county building, and waited. Darkness was falling by the time the procession was approaching—we could hear the waves of cheering coming toward us up Christina Street and see the popping of flashbulbs—and at last there was the Cadillac, with the Queen and Prince Philip. Only a moment, and they were gone. Then we settled down to wait for their return, after all the introductions and handshakes in the park. The time was almost eleven o'clock when they went past again. After that, we walked over to Front Street and down to the riverfront. From there we could see *Britannia* at the Imperial Oil dock to the south; see its gleaming royal blue hull, its three masts, and the royal standard. The ship was brilliantly lit. We watched it slip away from the dock, proceed upriver past us, and disappear under the Bluewater Bridge, in the warm soft air of a luminous summer night.

Among those presented to the royal couple in Canatara Park was "Pat" Johnson, the county's 1959 warden, along with his wife Flossie. Pat told Dad afterwards that he (Pat) said, when presented to Prince Philip, "They tell me I look like you." Both the Queen and Philip laughed heartily, Pat said, and the Queen's hand was the "softest little thing you'd ever wish for."

Our travels between 1955 and 1960

Dad's holidays were always in July, and each year now we went on a trip, always to the United States. And each year, when Dad celebrated his birthday, we were on the road in some far-distant place. He had never lost his interest in photography, and before we set out in the summer of 1955, he bought an expensive camera, a Zeiss Eikon, for which he paid $175. It took 35 mm film and produced colour slides. Later he would buy a projector, slide trays and screen, plus a light meter—all part of the photographic technology of that time. His first roll of film he shot from the Bluewater Bridge.

In 1955 we returned to Florida; in 1956, we undertook the longest of our trips, to Salt Lake City and the Grand Canyon; in 1957, we drove to New England and Boston, and in 1958 to New Orleans. The next year we were in Atlantic City and New York, and in 1960 we made for Charleston, South Carolina, though we never got there: our abbreviated journey took us back to Washington, D.C.

In Kentucky, on our second trip to Florida, we sought Abraham Lincoln's birthplace, and found a huge granite and marble temple containing the log cabin in which he was (purportedly) born—an American myth enshrined. We walked the grounds of the state capital in Nashville, and we toured Andrew Jackson's home, The Hermitage. In Florida, we drove down the Gulf coast, miles of it at that time not much developed, just thin pine forest with palmetto undergrowth. And we drove the Overseas Highway to Key West. The highway was then a series of narrow two-lane bridges—one of them, the Bahia Honda bridge, built on top of the old railway bridge, and humped and rickety—and Dad had to be constantly on the alert to avoid scraping the sides of the car, so narrow were the traffic lanes. Miami Beach, lined for miles with luxury hotels, was an impressive sight. In the Indian River area, one morning when we were having breakfast by the roadside, flanked by a grove of citrus trees, we found grapefruit lying on the ground. We had never before had tree-ripened citrus fruit, and it was sweet and juicy beyond any we had ever had imported back home. We spent a leisurely two days driving up Florida's east coast, and then another four days to get home. One of those days was a return to the Great Smoky Mountains National Park.

For our mid-day meal, our usual practice was to stop at a grocery store just before noon and buy fresh hamburger, which Dad cooked on our Coleman stove; then he added to it a can of spaghetti or corn or potatoes or some other vegetable. The combination made a good meal.

I do not know why Dad wanted to see the American west rather than the Canadian prairies. His father and his aunts had gone west, and his cousins the Woodses and the Moffatts went to buy cattle; there were Annetts from Brooke Township in Maple

Creek, Saskatchewan; and my mother had an aunt and cousins in Stettler, Alberta, and a brother and his family in British Columbia. But Dad wanted to see Salt Lake City and the Grand Canyon. And our grandmother, caught up in the new world of television, wanted to see California. She once said something to me about "persuading Daddy" to drive to Los Angeles, but that was five hundred miles farther than Dad wanted to go, and my grandmother never did realize her wish.

But we had plenty to see: Lincoln's home and tomb in Springfield, Illinois; Mark Twain's home in Hannibal, Missouri, on the banks of the Mississippi; President Truman's house in Independence, Missouri; and then the great plains of Kansas, sunburnt and treeless, where one could see for miles, under the great stretch of dazzling blue sky. In the east the sky is always obscured by trees or buildings; in Kansas it stretches unbroken from horizon to horizon. The further west we drove, the drier the land: there was dry grass, of course, but also sage brush and tumbleweed. Beyond Denver, we began climbing into the Rockies, and marvelled at snow-capped mountains and the sharp switch-backs on the road up to the Berthoud Pass. In Salt Lake City, we walked on the grounds of the Mormon Temple, and Mum told us that the reach of Uncle Norm's Thornton-Smith company had extended all the way here: he had decorated one of the buildings in the temple complex. In Arizona we saw the browns and reds of true desert for the first time, and we stood on the rim of the Grand Canyon, "a most fascinating, most magnificent sight," my mother wrote in the journal she was keeping. Then we started for home, on Route 66, that celebrated highway that runs all the way from Chicago to Los Angeles. It took us across New Mexico and Texas, Oklahoma and Missouri, until we left it somewhere in Illinois. By the time we reached home, we had driven nearly 4,800 miles—our longest trip ever.

Our 1957 trip was not nearly so long or demanding. It was to New England and Boston. By this time, the construction of interstate highways was well under way in the United States, and in Ontario the 400-series highways were being built in segments. Some of those finished portions speeded up our drive to Kingston and the Thousand Islands. At this time, too, the St. Lawrence Seaway was under construction. The riverside towns had not yet been flooded, but the move to higher ground was well under way. Upriver from Cornwall, we had a tour of the dam being built there by Ontario Hydro and the New York State Power Authority. In New England, I remember the maple syrup museum in St. Johnsbury, Vermont; an ascent in a cable car at Franconia Notch, New Hampshire; and the Battle Green in Lexington, Massachusetts. We read all the inscriptions on the monuments there with a limited sense of history (my phrase modifies both our reading and the inscriptions themselves). They presented the Revolution as a battle against an external force—"British tyranny and oppression"—and glorified the actions of "patriots." Nothing that we saw suggested a more balanced view: that the Revolution was also a civil war; and that "loyalists" were just as much a part of it, and just as heroic, as "patriots," who were really rebels. Nor did we know at that time much about our own Loyalist ancestors. My mother's grandmother had been a Dykeman, and she had come of a Loyalist family, but my mother knew no details about her forebears and thought they had come from Pennsylvania: our Loyalist connection had faded in the Runnalls family into the vaguest of memories.

So, in Boston, we were immersed in the dominant American view of the revolutionary war: Bunker Hill, Old North Church, Paul Revere's house. In Quincy, we toured the Adams house, home to two presidents (father and son); and we saw Plymouth

Rock, which glorifies the voyage of the Mayflower; and Cape Cod, though we drove only half its length. Providence and Hartford, and then the valley of the Hudson River and Hyde Park, where we walked through both the Roosevelts' home and the Vanderbilt mansion. The Roosevelts' was very much a family home; the Vanderbilts' was a show of wealth and opulence. We had no mental images of the Vanderbilt home before we saw it, but we came to the Roosevelts' already knowing a good deal about it. That was because we had at home a copy of Eleanor Roosevelt's *This I Remember,* with its amusing account of entertaining the King and Queen in 1939, and we had her stories in mind when we looked into the bedrooms where the royal couple had slept, when we saw the short flight of stairs down which the butler fell with a tray of drinks, and when we saw the pool deck where the King and Queen were served hot dogs and hamburgers. In 1957, Mrs. Roosevelt was still active in American politics and in American public life, and the Hyde Park house seemed not so much a museum as the home to which she might return at any time.

By the summer of 1958, Marjorie and I were very much aware of movie stars and pop musicians. James Dean, whom we had seen in all three of his major films—*Rebel Without a Cause, East of Eden,* and *Giant*—had been killed in a car crash in 1955, and had a cult following. We knew that he was buried in Marion, Indiana, and we persuaded Dad to take us there on our way to New Orleans, and into the cemetery to see his grave, with its trampled grass, picked-apart wreaths, and chipped letters on the stone. And whatever else Memphis was—it billed itself as the cotton capital of the world—it was for us the home of Elvis Presley. We had to ask for directions to Graceland, his home, and recognised it by the front gates, which were ironwork with musical staves and notes. The property was surrounded by a stone wall seven feet high, but the lot next door was vacant and mostly woods. Marjorie and I walked back along the wall until we judged that we were opposite the house, and then took turns hoisting each other up to have a look. A white board fence still farther back was covered with graffiti: those declaring "Elvis, I love you" were written in lipstick.

From Memphis, we followed the line of the Mississippi River all the way to New Orleans. That meant that we saw the Civil War battlefield at Vicksburg, the wonderful antebellum homes in Natchez, and two great houses in the Feliciana Parish of Lousiana, Afton Villa and Greenwood—the latter, in my romanticised view, the perfect example of the southern plantation house. In New Orleans, we walked about Jackson Square and the French Quarter, and Marjorie and I rode down the middle of Canal Street in an open-air streetcar, where we witnessed segregation: whites sat at the front, blacks at the back. We saw more signs of segregation in the city's suburbs: barber shops marked "white" and "colored," rest rooms designated the same way.

On most of our trips, Dad was always anxious to keep going, to drive as far as possible each day, but on this one our parents decided to spend some time on the Gulf coast, shopping and exploring the area. We stayed for two nights in a motel near Gulfport, shopped there and in Biloxi, and relaxed on the beach and in the motel's pool.

When we headed north through Alabama, we became even more conscious of the need for the civil rights movement then agitating the United States. North of Montgomery, we saw a gas station with the sign "We serve white customers only," and everywhere we saw black people living in crowded and wretched conditions. We were aware of Rosa Parks's refusal to give up her seat on a Montgomery Alabama bus two and one-half years earlier, and we knew about the troubles at the high school in Little

Rock, Arkansas the previous September. It was not possible to maintain the simple, uncomplicated, romantic view of the American South that I had long held. (And still less possible had we known about lynchings.)

Our 1959 trip took us to Pennsylvania Dutch country, Philadelphia, Atlantic City, and New York. When we were approaching Lancaster, Pennsylvania, the heart of the Amish community, my grandmother said that her grandmother had lived there. I didn't follow up on that comment, and regret not doing so. What more did she know? I assume she was referring to Mary Elizabeth Smith, the wife of James Watson, and the Smiths were originally Schmids. But I knew none of this family history in 1959, and I suspect that my grandmother knew only that *her* grandmother was "Pennsylvania Dutch," a common-enough label for ancestors of people in Ontario: it was usually all that remained of a more detailed family history.

We toured the usual tourist sites in Philadelphia—Independence Hall, Christ Church Burying Ground, the Friends Meeting House and the Betsy Ross house—and in Atlantic City we walked the boardwalk, both in the afternoon and at night, with its dazzling lights, its crowded shops and restaurants and theatres, its constant assaults on the senses, and people, people everywhere. New York we saw entirely from the windows of our car, on Broadway and Fifth Avenue. But our first sight of the city was a dramatic one. We drove north on Staten Island and took the ferry across the Upper Bay; the day was hot and humid, and we watched the skycrapers of lower Manhattan and the outline of the Brooklyn Bridge slowly take shape out of the thick haze. To our left the Statue of Liberty gradually appeared, and I pointed it out to my grandmother. She seemed excited about it and happy that I had pointed it out to her—and that moment became one which has remained in my memory ever since: my sitting in the open air beside my grandmother on the upper deck of the Staten Island ferry, and sharing with her our first sight of a famous landmark.

My grandmother had always been an intrepid traveller and had always enjoyed being on the road and seeing everything she could, but in 1960 she was eighty-three years old, and her health was beginning to fail. That summer we had intended to go to Charleston, South Carolina, but we got only as far as Asheville: we were into our third day of driving when she developed an upset stomach and was feeling miserable. Dad was worried: he knew we had to give her a chance to rest. He found a housekeeping cottage set on a wooded mountainside six miles north of Asheville: it had two bedrooms, and my grandmother could have one all to herself. We did not know how long we would be there.

We put in the time by shopping, and by visiting the Biltmore estate and the Thomas Wolfe house. The next day, my grandmother was no better: she was lying in bed in a darkened room, and we were hundreds of miles from home. And then car trouble compounded my father's worries. When I was driving our Pontiac, I kept hearing a clank when I changed gears. It turned out that the driveshaft bearings were gone. At the garage, we encountered yet another difficulty: our Pontiac was Canadian-made, and American parts did not fit. But the mechanic was resourceful: he disappeared for an hour or so, and when he came back, he had Chevrolet parts with him, hoping they would work on our car. We were in luck: they did.

By the time we got back to the cottage that day, Bappy was feeling better, and we set off again. There was no question of going on to Charleston; instead, we headed in a northeasterly direction toward the coast. Why we did not make for home I do not know: my grandmother had been hospitalized with an infected leg and nausea two years earlier, and this episode seemed similar. But she herself had always been strong physically and mentally and did not like to be the cause of a cancelled trip. So we saw Richmond for a second time, and walked through the state capitol building and the Poe museum. And we saw Washington for a second time, and not just from the windows of our car. We walked through the White House, took a guided tour of the Capitol, looked at the Declaration of Independence in the National Archives, ascended to the top of the Washington Monument, and explored the nave and side aisles of the Washington Cathedral. My mother, who had reviewed Catherine Marshall's biography of her husband, *A Man Called Peter*, for the Walnut W.A., wanted to see the New York Avenue Presbyterian Church where he had ministered, and we walked to it from the White House. Through all of this, my grandmother remained in the back seat of the car. Dad warned us kids that we were to say very little about all that we had seen.

The expropriation of our Watford house

Our house was next to the high school, and even before we moved into town in 1953 there was talk of the need for the school to expand. It could not go to the north: the town's water tower and water works were there. On its south side there were three properties to the corner of Simcoe Street: ours, Caleys', and Mrs. Rapson's. Ours was a substantial two-story red-brick house; the other two were cottages.

But the school owned enough land on its south side to build the first of its additions: a two-story wing with three classrooms (one of them a chemistry lab) and quarters for school administration. Construction was delayed because the five municipalities affected—the townships of Brooke, Warwick, and Euphemia, and the villages of Watford and Alvinston—could not agree on sharing the costs. The holdout was the Watford council. In February 1954 a delegation to Watford urged an end to the stalemate and compromise on the issue, and in that same month the dispute was finally settled. Actual construction started in April 1955, and so, during our second year in the Watford house, we watched as the addition took shape and reached out toward our lot line. What had once been a broad green lawn disappeared under steel and brick, concrete and glass. Also gone was the handsome south entrance to the old school, with its red brick and stone Gothic arch above double doors.

It was not long until the school board was talking about further expansion to the south. At commencement in November 1957 Harold Newell, then chairman of the board, outlined the need for more space because of increased enrolment: it was to be another four-room addition, and the board wanted it ready for the 1959–60 school year. Cost-sharing remained an issue (even though the province was paying eighty per cent), and getting agreement would probably delay construction, but in the meantime my parents, worrying that they might be forced to move at short notice, started looking at houses in Sarnia.

The whole situation was one of uncertainty and anxiety for Mum and Dad. They knew that the high school would eventually force us out of our Watford house, and they followed stories in the *Guide* to try to gain some sense of when that would happen. The first few months of 1959 were particularly worrying, since the paper kept making references to "next September," only a few months off. But costs had risen, and among the additional costs was (the paper reported) "the gradual acquisition of three residential properties, with a frontage of 193 feet south of the school property to the Simcoe St.

boundary." That involved the "ultimate removal of the three homes now owned by John A. Hair, Roy Caley and Mrs. Rapson" (*Guide* 11 June 1959).

Harold Newell started putting pressure on Dad to set a price on our house, and at the end of May Dad said he was asking $19,500. Early in June, Newell telephoned Dad to say that the board had agreed to buy our place at that price, but he cautioned Dad that the municipal councils in the school district would have to agree also.

In the meantime, my parents engaged a realtor in Sarnia, Jack Dudley of D.B. White & Sons, who showed them various properties. The one they liked best was a new house, a split-level, on Cathcart Boulevard. The initial asking price was $18,500. In early June, when the school board confirmed that they would buy our Watford house, my parents put in an offer on the Cathcart Boulevard house. But by then the price had risen to $19,500, and the builder wanted an additional eight hundred dollars to put up a garage. My parents balked; they had long conversations with the realtor; and in mid-June they finally put in an offer for $19,200. It had a crucial proviso: if there was no "binding agreement" with the school board on the Watford house by July 15, their deposit of five hundred dollars was to be returned and the agreement considered "null and void."

By the 15th of July Dad had heard nothing from the school board. This time the Warwick Township council was responsible for the delay, and laid the matter over without coming to a decision. Harold Newell must have been frustrated, and my parents were both relieved by and resigned to being in Watford for another year. But there was a problem with the realtor: Dad had to start legal proceedings to get his deposit back. The lawyer he hired was Bud Cullen, whom Dad knew well because he was the county solicitor, along with his law partner Jim Bullbrook. Cullen would later become a Liberal M.P. and a member of Pierre Trudeau's cabinet as Minister of National Revenue. The realtor, D.B. White, kept stalling but finally paid up when Cullen set a deadline of August 5.

By mid-August, and because of the local councils balking at the cost, it seemed likely that the school board would not simply purchase our house but would rather expropriate it. But school had to open that September without the additional classrooms, and the building was "overly crowded," according to stories in the *Guide*, which described the makeshift measures to accommodate students (3 September, 10 September 1959). That was when Harold Newell told Dad that the school board had been "forced" into expropriation. But there was no movement on the issue until the beginning of April 1960, when Newell, without any warning, told Dad that we might be forced out of our house at the end of the month: the board wanted to rush construction through the summer to have the new space ready for students in September. Dad's response was to hire a lawyer. He was Ralph Steele from Chatham, and he was a well-known criminal lawyer in Southwestern Ontario: he would later be appointed head of Legal Aid in the province. The board's lawyer was a Mr. Slater, and the whole expropriation process was now in his hands and those of Steele.

April came and went, and nothing happened.

The delay was a fortuitous one for Marjorie. My parents had been hoping that she would be able to finish high school in Watford rather than in Sarnia, but time lost to illness had pushed back her fifth year, and she did not write the Grade XIII exams until June 1960. She did well: she wrote nine papers and passed all of them. She decided to register in the Honours Music program at University College, Toronto. Meanwhile, I had completed four years at Western and had won a Queen Elizabeth II Ontario scholarship, which would pay for my M.A. year in English, also at the University of Toronto. Marjorie and I were excited about being in Toronto together: we ended up living close to each other on St. George Street, Marjorie in Whitney Hall, the UC women's residence, and I in Knox College, where Uncle Frank had prepared for the ministry forty-five years earlier.

The board, in the meantime, had had to abandon its plan to have the new addition ready for September, but it moved decisively to have it built for the following school year. At the end of August, two real estate men from London appeared at our door, saying they had been retained by the board to appraise the house: our parents were away, and Marjorie would not let them in. That same evening, Billy Taylor, the real estate man in Watford, also came round: he didn't get in either. At the beginning of October 1960, the *Guide* published photographs of our house and Caleys', under the headline "To Demolish Home in 30 Days for High School Building Space." Of our house the story said "The Board has already called for tenders on its demolition" (*Guide* 6 October 1960).

Marjorie and I came home on the train for Thanksgiving (which was on Monday 10 October), and Mum and Dad and Bappy all met us at the station in Watford with the news that they had bought a house in Sarnia. It was a new house at 1267 Webster Drive, not in the city but in Sarnia Township, one block south of the Lakeshore Road and two blocks east of Murphy Road, which at that time was the city boundary. The builders were two Dutchmen, Cornelius Van Reenan and Theunes Braaksma, and the property was officially part of lots 25 and 26, Plan 320. The asking price was $21,000; Dad got it for $19,000. The lawyer who handled the deal was Louis Eddy, the son of our old minister, who also lived on Webster Drive. No mortgage was involved: Dad wrote out a cheque for the full amount.

He was able to do so because the board was willing to release $12,700 from court and pay it out "without prejudice to the rights of any person." Ralph Steele advised Dad that "this appears to us to be very desirable," and he was slowly moving toward a final settlement. "In the meantime," he wrote, "the valuators will want to see the inside of the house and you might give them every co-operation, as the Solicitor for the Board at least seems to be quite reasonable and possibly co-operation may bring the entire Board around to a somewhat better frame of mind than has been displayed so far." That was in October. Negotiations dragged on over the next two months, and Dad began to expect that he would have to go to court when, on 20 December, Steele reported that he had reached a settlement with the board, which had agreed to pay $15,300 for the house. Dad must have written a letter accepting that amount, for Steele wrote on 21 December that "we have your letter of the 20th and now enclose a Deed to be signed by all three owners of the property" (my parents and grandmother were the "three owners"). One of those signatures was problematic. My grandmother was in hospital with a broken hip and a wandering mind, but Dad held her hand and she managed to write her name. Steele said that "we should be able to close this transaction very shortly," but in fact it was not until the end of April 1961 that he sent Dad a cheque for $2,600, the remainder of the sale price after adjustments and legal costs. Even then the whole transaction was not quite complete, but Steele wrote that he thought it best "to send this cheque immediately so as to reduce the amount of inconvenience you have had to put up with since the deal was arranged."

The new house was built of gray brick and stone, with white siding on the top level and pale green trim. The arrangement of the rooms was typical of the split-level design popular at the time. On the highest level were three bedrooms and the main bath; on the next level down—the main level—were the living room (with fireplace), dining room, kitchen, and front hall; a short flight of stairs led down from the kitchen to a den beside the garage, and behind the garage a laundry room and half-bath; and in the basement, another flight down, there was a finished recreation room plus the furnace room. The house sat on a good-sized lot, without any landscaping at that time, and while there was city water, there were no sanitary sewers: instead, there was a septic tank and drain field in the sandy soil of the back yard.

In October 1960 Walnut Church had a farewell gathering, with generous gifts for all of us. Our parents had already started moving things to Sarnia, smaller items that they could pack in the car, but they hired professional movers for the furniture and all the bigger things. I do not know exactly which day was moving day, but when I went home on Friday, 4 November, I went, for the first time, all the way to Sarnia, where my parents met me at the station. A month later, on 4 December, we were in Watford, and went round to see our house. It was gone. Bricks and cement, lathe and plaster, shingles and rafters and joists, lay in a great heap; the two beautiful French doors that had been between the living room and dining room were leaning up against a wall in the little barn that had been our garage. It too would be torn down. We did not linger.

Our grandmother's last illness and death

After her sickness on the road during the summer of 1960, Bappy, though just a bit frailer, kept up with her usual activities, and she coped well with the move to Sarnia. When on 18 November my parents were invited to a banquet in London, she said she would spend the evening with Aunt Eva and Uncle Gord. I met her at their place after coming on the train from Toronto—by this time they were living in a smaller one-floor house on Janes Street—and Aunt Eva served coffee and dessert while she and my grandmother had a good visit.

A week later, on 23 November 1960, Aunt Min Watson died, at the age of ninety. She was the widow of Uncle Ceil Watson and the last of my great-grandfather Watson's siblings and in-laws. My grandmother said she would not go to the funeral, which was in London on 26 November, but she would like to go to Strathroy cemetery where Aunt Min was to be buried: she could see the family there. She was getting ready to go, and was in the bathtub when she fell and broke her hip.

Marjorie and I did not know anything about this until the following week, when our mother wrote to say that our grandmother was in the General Hospital in Sarnia and would have a pin put in her hip. But it was not until we went home for the high school commencement on 2 December, when Marjorie received her honours graduation diploma, that we realized just how serious her condition was. The surgery on 30 November had been successful, but her mind was wandering, and she did not recognize Dad. Dr. Hill, our family doctor, confirmed that she had had two little strokes, one when she fell, and one the night before the surgery. He said her age was against her, and he did not hold out any false hopes: if she did recover physically, he said, she would need long-term care.

When we walked into Bappy's room at the hospital on the following weekend she was immediately alert, and said "Oh, my kiddies!" But she was very sick; waves of nausea swept over her; and she was agitated and anxious, saying "don't leave me." When

Marjorie and I returned to Toronto that Sunday night, we went thinking we might never see our grandmother alive again.

But she hung on, all through December, when Marjorie and I were home for the holidays, and we saw her almost every day. On most of those visits she knew us, in the midst of confusion: she kept saying she was "very tired." On 20 December, Dad went up to the hospital after work and found her much worse. He came home, upset: I had never in my life seen him cry. But the next day we found Bappy the brighest and clearest in mind that she had been since her fall. While we were with her, she sat up, ate a good supper, and chatted with us. She knew that she had been confused, and said that she seemed to be living in a dream world.

Two weekends into the university's second term, Marjorie and I went home on the train to Sarnia, on a cold snowy January night (Friday the 13th). Mum and Dad met us at the station, and while we were driving north on Murphy Road in the darkness of a winter night, Dad looking straight ahead and concentrating on the road, Mum told us that Bappy had died that morning.

She passed away about 10 a.m. Two days earlier, Dad had gone to Toronto with county council for a meeting at Queen's Park with the Minister of Highways, Fred Cass, a meeting which would eventually lead to the construction of a new Highway 40 south along the river. On that same day, Dr. Hill had warned Mum and Dad that the end was near, and that Bappy would pass away in her sleep, as she did. Dad saw her about 8:30 that Friday morning; at ten he had a phone call saying she was gone.

Visitation was at Harper's in Watford on the weekend, when my parents received the sympathy of a large number of relatives, neighbours, friends, and people from Walnut Church and county council. Between the afternoon and evening visitations, Aunt Ruth said we were to come out to the farm for supper—a welcome respite for my parents, who had been standing and talking all afternoon. The day of the funeral was bright and cool. Mr. Cumming, the new minister at the United Church in Watford, took the service. Our neighbours, Winston Sifton, Uncle Ches, George Reid, Clarence Lewis, Alex McLean and Melvin Powell, were pallbearers. Then the long procession of funeral cars to the cemetery in Strathroy where, under the great spruce tree at the edge of the Hair plot, Bappy's coffin was lowered into the ground. So the much-loved grandmother Marjorie and I had grown up with, the one we knew so well, was buried beside the grandfather we had never known.

Many years later, when I had gained some perspective on my grandmother's life, I thought that the circumstances after my parents' marriage—mother-in-law and daughter-in-law living together in the same household—must not have been an easy one for either woman, and it is a tribute to the character of both that they got along so well, respected each other, and cared for each other deeply. Among the many expressions of sympathy my parents received, my mother kept only one. It was from Pat and Flossie Johnston. Pat had been warden in 1959, and he and Flossie had travelled with my parents to the municipal convention in Sudbury that summer. Flossie wrote: "Dear Alice & John, We were so sorry to hear of your loss. You will miss your mother a great deal. We marvelled at the harmony in your home with your mother. Her wishes certainly had preference. Not many daughter-in-laws are so thoughtful and considerate as you were, Alice. But I know you will never regret it. You will only have pleasant memories of your mother-in-law. You and John, as well as your children, must have made her later years very happy. She was a wonderful woman. I can remember her saying Good-bye to all of us as we left for Sudbury.... We are so sorry we did not know of her death so one of us at least could have gone to the funeral.... To you and your family our deepest sympathy."

CHAPTER ELEVEN
THE 1960s and EARLY '70s

Living in Sarnia

In 1961, for the first time since he had been appointed county treasurer, my father did not have a thirty-five mile commute to work, but could be at his office in ten or fifteen minutes. But my parents had left behind two social contexts—one, our school section, the other Walnut Church—and now, aside from relatives, the staff at "the office" and the members of county council were the people they socialized with. But they also joined the nearest United Church. It was Grace United, on the northeast corner of Cathcart Boulevard and Indian Road, a new church with a young congregation from the expanding northeast parts of the city. It had been formed in 1956 and the church itself built in 1959–60. Its minister was the Reverend Glen Eagle. In 1964 he was succeeded by Dr. James Mackenzie, who stayed for the next sixteen years, until his retirement in 1980, when the Reverend Douglas Greenough became minister. My parents attended Sunday services, but they were not nearly so active as they had been at Walnut: they no longer took part in the music, and my mother no longer taught Sunday School. They were among people who were mostly strangers to them, and their sense of a closely-knit community was much diminished.

So they remained nostalgic for Walnut. One Sunday in April 1963 they drove to Watford, intending to see Aunt Ruth and Uncle Ches, but they weren't home. "We came back by Walnut," my mother wrote in a letter to me; "church was just out so we stopped for a while. Nearly everyone was there," and they had a good visit with all the people they had known so well.

The disappearance of the "school section"

By the 1960s the one-room country schools were disappearing, to be replaced by central schools to which students were bused. In Brooke Township that change happened in 1961, when the township constructed a ten-room school on Highway 79 just north of Alvinston. It opened in September 1961; our cousin, Jack Dolbear, was the first vice-principal, and Kate McEachern, whom we knew well from Walnut Church, was one of the teachers.

In that same month, the Board sold the thirteen existing rural schools in the township. So our school—S.S. No. 10, which three generations of Hairs had attended—and S.S. No. 5, which Marjorie and I had both attended, disappeared. The latter, which was a frame building, was moved to a farm on the Fourth Line east of Watford, to serve as a storage shed for machinery; and the former, which was brick, was torn down to make room for a new house on the property. But the people who built the house incorporated into the foundation the stone that had been over the entranceway, with the school's name and date. That too was gone at the beginning of the twenty-first century, when that first house was demolished and another new one erected in its place. As for S.S. No. 5, not a trace of it remains. The land has become part of a farmer's field.

The creation of the central school affected our sense of identity. People had always referred to their community as "our section," but when "sections" no longer existed, ties to a well-defined rural area loosened.

Our last two family trips: the Gaspé and Halifax (1961) and Mexico (1962)

Early in the summer of 1961, my parents talked about driving west to see Uncle Frank, but the distance was daunting, and they decided against it. My mother would dearly have loved to go, and in later years I was hoping that she and Dad might go west on the train, as Aunt Ruth and Uncle Ches did. I can remember my mother, toward the end of her life, saying sadly about Uncle Frank, "I'll never see him again."

Instead of the west coast in 1961, we went to the east coast. It was in part a nostalgic trip, to see places we had already been, and it was our first without our grandmother. We did a boat tour of the Thousand Islands; we toured the dam and powerhouse at Cornwall, which we had seen under construction in 1957; we drove the Route du Roy on the north shore of the St. Lawrence, and we saw again the sights in Québec City and Ste-Anne de Beaupré. By this time the highway around the Gaspé was paved and the covered bridges had all disappeared. In spite of the wonderful scenery, there was not quite the same sense of adventure. But Gaspé and Percé, though now commercialized, still seemed remote and picturesque. A boat tour that circled Bonaventure Island was new to us: great rocks and sheer cliff faces above the dark water, and every ledge covered with thousands of sea birds, gannets, petrels, cormorants, puffins and gulls.

The south shore of the Gaspé peninsula is not so bleak as the north: grassy fields run down to Chaleur Bay; some towns had English-speaking populations and little white Anglican churches. But we had trouble finding a place to stay. All the motels were full in village after village, and we ended up driving after dark, as far as Port Daniel, where the Sea View Lodge had one room. Mum and Marjorie stayed in it; Dad and I had a makeshift arrangement, in a pretty private home (that of the son of the lodge's owners) just across the road. The next morning, Dad and I woke up in a bright little room, with the sun shining in through frilly curtains. Our window looked out on grassy fields and the sea.

The drive south through New Brunswick was not new, but beyond Sackville we were seeing landscapes we had not seen before: the Tantramar Marshes (one of the defining settings in the Canadian literary imagination, thanks to Roberts' poem "Tantramar Revisited"), and the highway across Nova Scotia to Halifax. There we walked around the Citadel, went into museums and St. Paul's church and the legislative building, and drove out to Peggy's Cove, which was as picturesque as it was reputed to be, with its lighthouse and the Atlantic surf pounding the great humped boulders and throwing up massive jets of spray. The day was very much an east coast day: gray light, damp air, and fog rolling in. Back in New Brunswick, we stayed overnight in Moncton and ate breakfast the next morning in a city park beside a massive steam locomotive. While we were eating, a car with the CN logo on the door drove up, and a large jovial man got out. He was curious to know where we were from, and he told us that the locomotive had been moved to the park only a month earlier, to commemorate the city's role as a rail centre. When he was leaving, he surprised us by saying, "When you go back, you can tell 'em you met the mayor."

Though we drove across southern New Brunswick to St. John, we knew at that time nothing about our Loyalist ancestors, the Dykemans. Had we known, we would have visited the graves of the earliest Canadian Dykemans, Gerritt and Eunice (Hatfield), in the churchyard of St. John's Anglican church, Gagetown, and we would have looked with a strong personal interest at St. George's Street in St. John, where Gerrit Dyckman (as the spelling was then) had been granted a lot in 1783, and at King's Square and the Loyalist House, a handsome white frame building in the Georgian style.

I persuaded Dad to avoid the "long way around" to the border crossing at St. Stephen, and to travel "as the crow flies," by ferry through the islands in Passamaquoddy Bay to Eastport, Maine. That was a mistake. There was a long wait at the dock in Letete; there had been a fatal accident on Deer Island and emergency vehicles took precedence on a narrow winding road; there was another long wait for the second ferry, which turned out to be only a scow pulled by a tug: its captain was sleeping when we arrived, but woke up to say he would sail in twenty-five minutes. Customs and immigration in Eastport were no more than a uniformed officer by the side of the street as we drove uphill from the water. We had lost a lot of time, and Dad was justly annoyed with me.

In Maine, we saw Bar Harbor; we took a northern route across New Hampshire and Vermont and a ferry from Burlington across Lake Champlain. Then on to Lake Placid, up Whiteface Mountain in a chairlift, and into Watertown, New York, where my parents shopped.

In all our travels, we had never been to a non-English-speaking country, but in 1962 I suggested driving to Mexico. Highways were good enough by then; others that we knew had gone there; and it would be a great adventure for us, in what turned out to be our last extended motor trip as a family. We had never had passports before; and we had never had smallpox vaccinations. Now we had both.

Five days of driving brought us to the Mexican border. We went south through Illinois to the vast low-lying and flood-prone area where the Ohio and Mississippi Rivers meet; we saw the sights in Little Rock, in Dallas and in San Antonio (including the Alamo and the San Jose Mission); and we stayed overnight in Laredo. There we exchanged forty American dollars for 496 pesos.

Saturday, 21 July was Dad's sixtieth birthday, and it was the day we drove across the Rio Grande into Mexico, and as far as Monterrey, one hundred and fifty miles to the south. The border crossing took nearly two hours, with long waits in a series of rooms: in one, an officer examined our passports and issued our tourist cards; in another, we obtained the permit for the car. It was an unhurried operation: for each permit, the officer had to walk off to some other office and have papers stamped. At the car, our suitcases were inspected and sealed, the seals not to be broken until we reached the last federal inspection point north of Monterrey.

The Pan-American Highway was the chief north-south route at that time, safe then but not to be attempted at the beginning of the twenty-first century: the illegal drug trade has made both that road and the border towns very dangerous. South of Nuevo Laredo the road ran in a straight line through grazing land and desert, dotted with sage and mesquite and cacti and spiky trees I could not identify. We carried our own food and water, and south of a small village called Vallecillo we stopped by the roadside and ate dinner under the meager shade of a clump of trees. While we were eating, a man passed by on the other side of the road, leading a flock of sheep and carrying a lamb in his arms, and for a long time we could hear the distant clank-clank of sheep bells carried to us on the wind. A timeless pastoral sight and sound.

South of Sabinas Hidalgo, the only town of any size between Laredo and Monterrey, we left the plain on which we had been travelling ever since we had crossed the Rio Grande, and started climbing the arid hills to the mesa on which Monterrey is built. Signs warned us of a *camino sinuoso*, and the road was indeed winding, around dead-end canyons and along the sides of dry dusty hills. Monterrey, Mexico's leading industrial city, lies in a great valley surrounded by mountains, including the one which is the city's icon, the *Cerro de la Silla* (Saddle Mountain). It is a setting of great beauty. The best vantage point is El Obispado, the Bishop's Palace, an eighteenth-century domed structure still scarred from the Mexican-American conflict in the 1840s; from that height, west of the downtown and up a steep road, we could look down on the whole city spread out below us.

In the city centre, the Plaza Zaragoza, we parked, and were immediately besieged by hordes of ragged olive-skinned little boys and girls, who would (1) watch your car for a peso an hour; (2) clean your shoes for a peso; (3) sell you gum or hats (one little girl, very determined, threw packages of gum in Marjorie's lap). While I was struggling with the parking meter and Mexican coins, one little kid assured me that I had "mucho tempo, mucho tempo, señor!" We found that, if we paused in the street, we were likely to find some little kid at our feet, polishing our shoes. Dad finally gave in to one of the shoe-shine boys, and I took a picture—a sixtieth birthday picture—of him with the kids. More disturbing were the women begging. One poor woman came up to us, carrying a thin baby and wordlessly holding out a cup.

We stayed overnight in a motel on the north edge of the city. It cost ninety pesos (eleven dollars) and might have been anywhere in the United States, except for one feature: it was surrounded by a high wall, in the top of which broken glass had been fixed. Who was being kept out? we wondered; what danger did that wall keep at bay?

We knew there were bull fights in Mexico, usually on a Sunday and usually at five o'clock in the afternoon. There was a bull ring in Monterrey, but the late afternoon start would give us too little time to get back to Laredo that night; instead, we went to the Plaza de Toros in Nuevo Laredo. We knew that the *corrida* would be not only ritualistic but gory, and we had mixed feelings as we heard the stirring music, saw the procession of *matador*, *banderilleros* and *picadores*, and then the sudden dash of the bull into the ring, to a great roar from the crowd. It was indeed a bloody spectacle, right down to the final thrusting of the sword and the collapse of the bull in the dust. We came away thinking we had seen enough.

Our return journey took us along the low-lying Gulf coast of Texas and Lousiana and into Mississippi. The days were hot and steamy; the air was so wet that it obscured everything in a thick haze. We saw Natchez again, and there Marjorie bought a book of Natchez recipes, one of which began, "Take two fat hens, or eight squirrels, and…." And since I was attracted to romantic ruins, I wanted to see the remains of Windsor plantation, near Port Gibson—once the grandest of plantation houses but since 1890 a burnt-out ruin. All that remains are twenty-two tall fluted columns with Corinthian capitals, some joined by a wrought-iron balustrade, mouldering and threatened by encroaching vegetation. All around them was a barnyard, where pigs grunted in the dirt, chickens scratched the dry soil, and cattle stood in the shade, flicking away flies with their tails. The place smelled of manure and decay and dust. So much for the actualization of my romantic imagination.

In the northern part of the state we came to Lafayette County—William Faulkner's Yoknapatawpha—and Oxford, the county seat (Jefferson in the novels). Two of Faulkner's novels had been on the fourth-year curriculum at Western, and I had liked them so much that I went on to read as much Faulkner as I could lay my hands on. Faulkner had made most of his fiction out of this small county, and I remembered the end papers of the Modern Library editions of the novels, with a fictional map of Jefferson and Yoknapatawpha County and the inscription "William Faulkner, Sole Owner and Proprietor." The white courthouse, the square around it, the old stores with pickup trucks outside, angle-parked against the curb, a few farmers and housewives moving slowly along the sidewalk—all was just as Faulkner had described it. One man I saw might have been a Faulkner character: he was wearing a grocer's apron and was carrying a broomstick that he pretended was a shotgun, aiming it playfully at someone he knew in a passing car. When he saw me, he asked, "Y'all want a taxi?" and grinned a wide-mouthed grin.

As it happened, Faulkner had died just three weeks earlier. I wanted to see where he had lived and where he was buried, but I was a bit ashamed of my curiosity since his death had been so recent. But when I asked for directions, I got a ready response. And so we were able to look down a lane curving between trees to his house, without going any closer, and in the cemetery we found his grave, on a hillside between two oak trees. No marker or stone yet; just a mound of red soil, partly eroded by the recent rain. On top of the mound, a basket of faded flowers with a yellow ribbon, and a green glass bowl filled with dead zinnias.

In Louisville, Kentucky, we found an unexpected connection with our Mexican adventure. Zachary Taylor, the twelfth president, is buried in a military cemetery there. He had been a general in the Mexican wars of the 1840s, and it was he who led the forces that invaded and captured Monterrey.

Why search out such an obscure connection? As kids, we organized our knowledge of the United States in an old-fashioned way, by lists which we memorized: state capitals, presidents, presidential homes and graves, writers and their homes (just as we organized our knowledge of English history with the reigns and dates of kings and queens). My father was an indulgent and generous parent. When his children wanted to see something or do something, he was always ready to satisfy them, and while he must have said "No" on occasion, my chief memories of childhood are of his saying "Yes." Even when Marjorie and I were very small, we soon knew enough, when we wanted to go beyond what we thought was allowed, to "Ask Dad."

My mother's letters 1962–3

When I was in graduate school at the University of Toronto, I went home to Sarnia every other weekend, to see my parents and to spend Saturday night with Arlene, who was by that time teaching at the collegiate institute in Strathroy. On alternate weekends, I stayed in residence, for the social activities there, and often for dinner and a movie with my best friend from undergraduate days, Duncan Johnson, who was working in the re-insurance division at Manufacturers' Life. On those weekends, my mother wrote me a letter, and those letters give glimpses of my parents' daily life and their concerns during this time.

"I have been to the office every day," my mother wrote on 27 September 1962. Dad's office collected overdue taxes on behalf of every municipality in the county and, if taxes were not paid after a specified period of time (three years), sold the properties at the annual tax sale. The "rolls" of tax arrears sent in by the municipalities had to be checked, names and property descriptions and amounts recorded, and penalty and interest calculated. My mother did that work, sometimes with help, as in February 1963: "Pat Smith [who was, I think, the court stenographer] is helping this week. She is a whiz to type. She makes Josie sound like I sound beside Josie" (Josie was Josie Smith, Dad's secretary—no relation to Pat). And in April 1963: "Pat & I are working on the Sombra roll. It is our longest roll. We are half done but will not likely finish it to-morrow since we have to send out the 3 months taxes. Brooke roll is also in & likely more will be right along. Pat is certainly good to work with on them. We can make good time in most of them." The tax sale that year was on 11 January 1963. "There are 38 properties still on the list. I hope some more are paid off in the morning [of the sale itself—last-minute "redemptions"]. They all mean more work when they go through." And there was a "little incident": "A man bought a property—it was an old store in Camlachie. He ran it up to $1350 & when he came up he said he thought it was the one on the other side of the street & refused to take it. There were 3 properties not sold which would go to the adjourned sale...."

In the meantime, my father had frequent meetings to attend, and many of them were in the evening, so being in Sarnia made things easier for him. "Daddy has to go to a meeting at City Hall at 7," my mother wrote on 10 October, "to plan for the centenary & one at 9 at the County Bldgs. to meet with the tennis club," who were in a dispute with the county over the use of courts on the Dufferin Park property. The weeks were even busier in January 1963: "There is something on every night but Mon.," my mother wrote. "Tues. night the Chamber of Commerce is having a dinner & speaker at the Holiday. Wed. is the card party at Twilight Haven. Daddy has to take money at the door. It will be late. Thurs. & Fri. are committee meetings." In March: "They phoned from Pt. Edward for Daddy to take part in a panel discussion at the Home & School meeting. Daddy has to answer questions on County Government."

There was a municipal conference in Kitchener at the end of October, and as she often did my mother went along with Dad. She wrote her letter to me on the stationery of the Walper Hotel: "We left home about 7:30 & picked up Bert Logan [the reeve of Sarnia Township] and Ken [Gray, reeve of Moore Township and the 1962 warden]. It rained all the way so was not nice driving. However Ken keeps up a continual chatter so is quite entertaining.... I don't know how he can keep it all up & actually not say too much.... There are 7 or 8 ladies registered & they took them on a 3 hr. bus trip of the County this afternoon. However I thought I would rather explore by myself. It was drizzling a bit but not so much but what I could get around. Eaton's is about 3 blocks away and I got a brown skirt and blouse. It is not nearly as nice for shopping as London but there are more stores than in Sarnia.... Daddy is at the banquet but I ate in the dining-room—snazzy, price wise too."

There were so many municipal gatherings that my father occasionally forgot one. On a Saturday in April 1963 County Home Committees from several counties were meeting in Leamington, and Dad did not remember it until that morning, when Shep McCallum asked him about it. "Then we wondered if we should go. So we got ready and left about 9. It was a quarter to twelve when we got there.... It was at the new Essex County Home. They put on a lovely luncheon at noon cafeteria style." My parents were glad they had gone: fourteen people from Lambton, all associated in one way or another with Twilight Haven, were there. "It was after 4 when we left for home so we had supper in Wallaceburg & got home about 8:30."

The warden's banquet in late November or early December had become a tradition in Lambton County, and the neighbouring counties all had similar gatherings. My parents, and the warden and his wife, were routinely invited to banquets in Essex, Kent, Middlesex and Huron counties. The November 1962 event in Goderich was typical. My mother reported that "we had a nice time.... they have a new hall at the church & had a lovely dinner (turkey with all the trimmings). The speaker was Reverend Stewart from Kitchener, a Presbyterian minister, and he was good but the acoustics were not very good so you had to listen carefully to get it all. They had a dance after in the hall & we went over for a little while. So it was about 1 when we got home." They were even later in returning from the Kent banquet in Chatham. "We picked up the Grays & were invited to the Warden's Alan Cousins in Wallaceburg afterwards. They have a lovely place. It was 2 o'clock when we got home...." Lambton's own banquet was at the end of November. There were 210 people present, my mother reported. "Everyone thought they had a nice time. None of the speeches were too long. Zeb Janes was the only M.P. there and he never talks too long."

The new warden was always elected at the January session of county council, and my father always had to adjust to the new man's ways of doing things. In 1963 the reeve of Sombra Township, "Shep" McCallum, was elected, and my mother described the period of adjustment: "Well we received Call No. 2 from the Warden 6:30 Mon. night. However we were not in bed [as they had been for Call No. 1, made much later in the evening]. He has called a committee meeting for this Sat. night. So I guess it will be a year of irregularities. However there is one whole week gone by & since we have survived it I guess we will survive the rest." McCallum never worried about scheduling meetings on holidays, and in April "he phoned about 8 this morning to know if the office would be open Mon. It is a holiday." So "you can be thinking of our trials and tribulations," Mum said ruefully. She expected more. McCallum had wanted something from the fire insurance company in Watford, and on a Sunday night had picked up the company's administrative assistant and took her to the office to get it for him. "If we do not have some unscheduled visits before the year is over I miss my guess."

In the spring of 1963 the Fairbank House, a Petrolia landmark on a bank high above Bear Creek, was being set up as an Adult Education Centre, and the opening was on Sunday, 21 April. "I guess we will be going," my mother wrote, "as I had a letter inviting me to pour tea from 4 to 5." Some six thousand people toured the house, the crowd "the largest to converge on Petrolia for more than a decade. Main St. was lined with cars for nearly one-half mile and waiting lines to enter the house were more than 200 yards long" (*Windsor Star* 22 April 1963). My mother got her picture in the Windsor paper.

In the year or so after they moved to Sarnia, my parents did a lot of entertaining, of relatives, and of friends from Walnut church, and many of those occasions involved a private tour of the new buildings, to all of which Dad had a master key. (He even had a key for the gaol before it was occupied.) In June 1961, he showed the buildings to Aunt May and Aunt Beck, Alice Cavanaugh, and Horace and Ferne Delmage, and afterwards Mum had everyone back to our place for a roast beef dinner. A week or so later Uncle Howard and Aunt Eleanor were in Sarnia, and they too were given the tour and dinner. So were Harold and Honor Hair, Jane, Judy and Jimmy in December 1961. The next fall my mother was entertaining people from Walnut church: "I called up Clare Edgars & invited them to come next Sun.," she wrote on 10 October 1962. "But they could not come any Sunday in Oct. so they suggested a Sat night so we settled on the 27th.... So I am writing letters to Allan Edgars, Lornes [Lorne and Evelyn Edgar] & Dorothy & Cal [Dolbear] & will plan on having some more entertained." Two weeks later, "I have been getting ready for Sat. night. I asked Calla [Brown-Lucas] to come & she seemed pleased." Then, on 29 October, "We had our company last night & everything went off fine. I tried to get some news. The one thing they were worrying about was that at the end of the year they just have Nettie Lou [Dolbear] to play since Fishers intend to change to Alvinston. Also Mabel [Edgar] has given up the Junior choir for lack of numbers...."

My mother was always hoping for a windfall. She had come to maturity during the Great Depression, when money was scarce, and she was attracted to stories of people striking oil or getting a big price for something that had just been lying around the house, such as glass sealers that had been used for canning, or old coins, or stamps. Her response was to start collecting things she thought might be valuable by the time Marjorie and I inherited them. "Aunt Ruth said a man came to Marion's before their sale & wanted to know if they had old envelopes. He would pay 5¢ for every one before 1926. So now I am getting Daddy to save the envelopes that have special stamps on them."

The Cuban missile crisis of October 1962 is mostly forgotten now, but at the time the world seemed to be on the brink of nuclear war, and people expected the worst. "I have been listening to the radio all day," my mother wrote on 25 October , "to see if there were new developments. If you have to go to shelter take the warmest things you have sweaters & overcoat & a wool blanket. What else would you sleep on? It may turn out there is no heat. Let's hope it doesn't come. Daddy thinks Russia will back down but they are so cunning no one knows." In the meantime, I and many of the residents of Knox College were in the common room, listening to the radio. On Monday 22 October 22 President Kennedy announced a naval blockade of the island. Tuesday the 23rd was, I wrote in my diary, "a strange edgy day, waiting for the first encounter ... as the Russian ships steam closer to Cuba. Everyone jokes about today being the end, but underneath the bantering there is a strange fatalistic attitude. We feel so helpless." The showdown was to come on Wednesday the 24th, "and yet we set out for our classes as usual." By evening, the Russian ships had altered course, and by the weekend the crisis was over.

Death of Sam McLellan
Aunt Ruth and Uncle Ches McLellan were still living on the farm on the Twelfth Line

in 1962–3, but they were thinking of retiring, and events precipitated that decision. One was an accident that put Uncle Ches in the hospital. He had been good to help the Dutch immigrants on our road (though he was driven by curiosity and a love of gossip as much as neighbourliness), and when Deena Van Dinther had an emergency while Henry was at work, she phoned McLellans, at 1:30 on a Sunday morning. Deena, Aunt Ruth reported, "said she was trying to get Henry at the wire works and had to go to the hospital right away. Henry didn't answer, and she wanted Ches to go and get him." Uncle Ches said he would drive her to the hospital (was she about to give birth? I don't remember), but "she said she wanted Henry so Ches went to the wire works for him. But the front door was locked," Aunt Ruth continued, "and he did everything to try & make [Henry] hear. He finally decided to go around to the back door … when he fell over something in the dark. He broke his right arm at the elbow also fell on his face and broke his glasses also hit his mouth & broke his teeth in two. He was really a wreck when he came home and covered with blood.… We took him to the hospital Sunday.… Since this happened Sam is upset and I have the two of them not well.…"

Aunt Ruth had planned to have Christmas, but my mother cooked the turkey and the pudding and we took all that food with us out to the farm on the Twelfth Line. It was a very cold night. After the meal, we sat around the coal-burning stove in the living room, watching the glowing fire through the little glass in the stovefront, listening to the wind whistling in the windows and seeing the snow drifting in the darkness outside. Uncle Ches said that they would not likely be on the farm for another winter, and Sam said, as we were leaving, that he hoped we would all be spared to meet again next year.

That was not to be. On 21 March 1963 the Watford paper printed a piece that went well beyond the conventional obituary: "SAM McLELLAN DIES ALONE AT HOME / Samuel McLellan, 83, lifelong resident of lot 28, con. 13, Brooke twp., passed away some time last Wednesday evening [March 13]. His brother, Chester, on a nearby farm found his body Thursday morning. Despite the urging of relatives and friends he should seek care in a home, he refused to leave his home of a lifetime, insisting he preferred to die there." Many years later, Aunt Ruth told me that Uncle Ches was "awful mad" at W.C. Aylesworth, the editor and publisher of the *Guide*, for this piece. "Sam wasn't dead when Ches found him that morning," Aunt Ruth said; "he was still alive."

My parents ordered flowers—"a dozen large yellow mums, 4 white carnations and 3 mauve iris with a yellow bow," my mother wrote. "Ruth got Mrs. Duffy to help at the house. I took a cake down Fri. night & others brought in cakes & cookies. She had invited quite a few back afterwards & they had sandwiches, pickles, cake, cookies & tea.… It was not too good parking at Ches's. We got stuck & Ches had to pull us out with the tractor."

Sam was buried beside his first wife in Strathroy cemetery. His second wife, Ethel Newell, had left him in 1935, but Sam never sought a divorce and, when he died, he was still legally married to her. She had a claim on his estate, and did receive her legal entitlement, but she outlived Sam by only two years.

In June of 1964, Aunt Ruth and Uncle Ches bought a house in Strathroy, a new house in a new area on the west side of town, at 316 Drury Lane. They had not yet sold the farm—in fact, we celebrated Christmas 1964 there—and they would not move until the next year. Up until this time, the house and barn on the original McLellan farm— the one at the corner of the Twelfth Line and 27 Sideroad—were still standing, though empty. Uncle Ches's brother Norm had lived there after their mother's death in 1929, and Uncle Ches had been born there. One day toward the end of July 1965, house and barn both burned to the ground, and my parents and I drove out to see what remained. Timbers were still smouldering, and an acrid odour hung in the air about the ruined foundations. All around lay quiet green fields, and the line of maples along the sideroad threw long shadows in the evening sun. Now, in the twenty-first century, not a trace of buildings or trees remains. Only flat ploughed fields, with no fences, and dark clay stretching from the edge of the sideroad all the way back to the distant bush.

The summer of 1963

Marjorie had completed her third year in Toronto, and for the summer was working at the Ontario government tourist bureau at the foot of the Bluewater Bridge. I had passed "the generals" at Toronto in the spring of 1962, and had been writing my doctoral dissertation in 1962–3. For the next year (1963–4) I was lucky enough to be granted a Canada Council Fellowship, which would pay for my travel and living expenses for research in the British Museum (which at that time housed the British Library), and I planned to be away for nine months, from the end of July 1963 to April 1964.

On 25 July 1963 the *Watford Guide* published a front-page story with information that could only have been supplied by my parents: "Donald Hair, Watford native and son of Lambton clerk-treasurer John Hair and Mrs. Hair, of Sarnia, sails from Montreal this Friday on S.S. *Franconia* to do research in English in the British Museum in London for the next eight months. This will attain his final qualifications for his Ph. D. and open the door for university appointments as specialist in English. / His parents and sister, Marjorie, are seeing him off at dockside. / All Watford district friends wish him a most interesting and successful year of study in London town."

While I was in England, my mother wrote me weekly letters, on the light blue air mail stationery the post office had at that time, and the service was very good: Mum would post the letter in the box close to our house on Webster Drive on Sunday afternoon, and it would be in my mail box in Mecklenburgh Square on Tuesday morning. I wish I had all those letters now, but when my parents were clearing things out of the Sarnia house, they burned all that correspondence. They shared the Souwesto view that the revelation of anything personal was in some vague way shameful, and once letters had served their purpose, they were to be destroyed.

I defended my dissertation in Toronto at the beginning of May 1964, and in June both Marjorie and I received our degrees at convocation, Marjorie her honours B.A. and I my Ph.D. Marjorie would have one more year, to earn her B.L.S. at Library School, and then she started working in the Music Library at St. Clair and Avenue Road; by that time I had completed my first year of teaching at Western. Our parents must have been relieved: they had been determined that both my sister and I would have good educations, and they had been more than willing to help us financially. We were very lucky to have grown up enveloped by such care and love.

Resignations and appointments in 1964

In mid-May 1964 Dad's life at the office became a little easier: Josie Smith, the secretary whom he had inherited from John Huey some ten years earlier, threw a tantrum and resigned. Every time county council met, she had lobbied for a raise, and Dad had supported her requests until, in a fit of ingratitude, she had criticised him for not doing enough, and he said that was the last time he would go to bat for her. Her replacement was Mrs. Verna Stewart. She was very different from Josie: even-tempered, efficient, and capable. Both my parents thought a great deal of her, and she would remain with Dad until he retired.

Five months after Josie resigned, Currie McVicar also resigned, to take up an appointment as clerk-treasurer of Mitchell. He had been Dad's deputy for nine years, and he had been an amiable man to work with, but there had been occasions when Currie had been censured (off the record) for the way he handled cash, and Dad had never been entirely comfortable with some of his practices. Once again, Dad tried to persuade Gerry Herbert to take the job. Gerry had been one of the county auditors since 1949, and Dad liked him for his efficiency, intelligence, even temper, and quiet ways. But Gerry was happy with his current responsibilities in Warwick Township—he was clerk-treasurer there—and, as it happened, council chose another man from Warwick, Bill McRorie. He had been a councillor and reeve for many years, was a director of the Wanstead Farmers' Co-op, and had been the co-op's accountant. He was a capable and honest man. Like Dad, Bill completed the course for municipal administrators from Queen's, and when Dad retired in 1970, Bill was appointed as his successor.

There was another resignation at the end of 1964. Bill Connolly, who had been one of the two county auditors for thirty-three years, notified County Council that he wished to retire at the end of December. Gerry Herbert carried on as the county's sole auditor.

My father as secretary of the St. Clair Parkway Commission

The St. Clair Parkway had been the original Highway 40, and it ran southwards along the river from Sarnia to Wallaceburg, through Corunna, Courtright and Sombra. The commission was set up in 1966 to oversee parks and develop a golf course along the route, and Dad was appointed its first secretary. One Sunday in September 1966, a man named Kennedy invited members of the commission for a cruise on the river aboard his yacht, and my parents were included, as was the minister of highways at that time, Charles MacNaughton, the MLA for Huron.

Death of Ward Zavitz: July 1966

Ward, who was married to my father's first cousin, Amy Hair, died at the age of sixty-eight, and his funeral was in Walnut Church. Dad was soloist at the service, and I accompanied him on the piano. It was the last occasion on which my father sang in public. For it he chose a very old hymn, "No Night There." The phrase is from the Book of Revelation, and "there" is the Heavenly City, with its streets of gold and buildings of precious stones. "Very old-fashioned," my mother said, having in mind a recent article she had read on the subject in the *United Church Observer*.

Family weddings: Arlene and Don (20 August 1966) and Marjorie and Michael (9 September 1967)

By the mid-sixties our parents could take some pride in the results of their raising my sister and me. We both had a good education, and we both had good jobs. Marjorie had graduated from the University of Toronto with a B.A. and B.L.S., and was head of the Music Library of the Toronto Public Library system. Through undergraduate friends she had met Michael Hale, a graduate of McGill, who was on his way to becoming an actuary, and they were married in 1967. I had finished my doctorate at Toronto in 1964 and was on the faculty in the Department of English at Western. I had met Arlene MacVicar from Strathroy when we were both in our first year at UWO, and she was now teaching in the collegiate in Strathroy. We were married in the summer of 1966.

Our wedding was in St. Andrew's Presbyterian Church in Strathroy on a warm sunny Saturday in August. Bill Mercer, the Anglican minister in Watford, married us, in the absence of the Presbyterian minister (Mr. Marshall, who was away on holidays) and the United Church minister (Mr. Pollock, who had had a heart attack). The reception was in the church, and afterwards the MacVicars had everyone back to their house on Maria Street, to see the gifts, have punch and wander around the back yard, where Arlene's Dad cultivated roses.

Before our wedding, my parents and Arlene's parents started getting to know each other. One Sunday in mid-June, Mum and Dad invited the MacVicars to Sarnia, and my mother prepared a big meal, since she included not only Arlene and me, but also my best man, Duncan Johnson, who was visiting from Toronto. A few weeks later, on a Sunday in July, the MacVicars invited my parents to Strathroy for a barbecue. They included Marjorie, who was home for a month's holiday. Arlene's parents had a "rec room" in the basement of their house, and there they had set up a display of our wedding gifts.

There were only four people from our grandparents' generation at our wedding: Aunt Eva and Uncle Gordon McNeil; Uncle Ed Runnalls, Grandad Runnalls's last surviving brother; and Aunt Beck, sister of my Grandfather Hair. We were told afterwards that she had gone around saying to everyone, "I'm the great aunt!" Both my Hair and Runnalls grandparents were long dead by this time, and Arlene's last surviving grandparent—her Grandmother MacVicar—had died the previous February.

Marjorie and Michael were married in St. Paul's Anglican Church on Bloor Street in Toronto. Marjorie was a member of the choir there; the organist, Dr. Charles Peaker, provided the music; and the minister was Canon Robert Dann. The reception was in The Four Seasons hotel. It just so happened that Uncle Frank and Aunt Nellie had come east at that time, and were able to be at the wedding.

Christmas 1967 in Sarnia was the first occasion on which our family was all together again after the weddings. Eight of us sat down to roast turkey: our parents, Aunt Ruth and Uncle Ches, Marjorie and Michael, and Arlene and I.

1967, the Centennial Year; 1968 and Prime Minister Trudeau

In the mid-sixties my parents did a good deal of travelling around the province, mainly to attend the meetings of the Ontario Municipal Association. But when the convention was held in Port Arthur (as half of Thunder Bay was then called), my mother did not go, and Dad went west by himself on the C.P.R.'s "Canadian," at that time the luxury transcontinental passenger train. He also went by himself to Expo 67, the world's fair in Montreal. Our mother had decided she did not want to go, and instead stayed with Marj and Mike in Toronto at the end of September, while Dad went overnight on the train to Montreal, spent a day at Expo, and came back to Toronto in sleeping car accommodation. Next month, both our parents were at the convention in Niagara Falls, and in the next spring and summer they travelled to gatherings in Windsor, Peterborough, and Stratford.

But Ottawa in July 1968 brought them a surprise encounter. There was a federal election that year; Trudeaumania swept the country; Trudeau himself had called an election immediately after he won the Liberal leadership; and on 25 June he won a majority government. In May my parents had been excited about the Liberal nomination meeting in Sarnia, mainly because Bud Cullen, the lawyer who was the county solicitor and with whom Dad had worked for years, got the nomination, and he was subsequently elected to the House of Commons. On 9 July, my parents were in Ottawa, driving around, and Dad was taking pictures of the sights. They turned into Parliament Hill and, ignoring for a moment the "No Parking" signs, stopped beside the East Block, only to see a large Cadillac flying a Canadian flag come in behind them and park by the curb. The Prime Minister got out of it, to the astonishment of my parents, who did nothing but stare while he headed for his office—until my mother called out after him, "Sir! Sir! We voted for you!" At that Mr. Trudeau turned around, greeted my parents, and posed so that Dad could take his picture. "We think you're doing a good job," my parents said, and he said, "Well, I don't know how long it will last."

Dad's photograph of the Prime Minister is excellent: Trudeau in a light summer suit, white shirt and tie, posed casually, one hand in a pocket, on the sidewalk outside the East Block.

The Lieutenant-Governor regularly entertained delegates to various conventions in Toronto, and my parents were regularly invited to the Lieutenant-Governor's Suite in Queen's Park. In my father's collection of newspaper clippings, programs, and other memorabilia, there are several such invitations. There is one for 5 April 1967, in honour of the delegates to the spring conference of the Association of Ontario Counties. The Lieutenant-Governor at the time was Earl Rowe, and he was succeeded by W. Ross Macdonald, who issued an invitation two years later to delegates of the 1969 spring conference. During this time, Dorothy Johnson, the mother of my best man, Duncan Johnson, was private secretary to the lieutenant-governor, and I was delighted when she and my parents met at one of those gatherings.

Health problems

My mother had never been strong physically, and she never enjoyed robust good health—perhaps the lingering effects of her premature birth. Like Grammie Runnalls, she was a thin small woman and for most of her life weighed no more than a hundred pounds, but in the late 1950s she started to put on weight and became quite plump. That weight gain had its consequences: by the spring of 1960 she was feeling ill. She was diagnosed with a "virus"—that catch-all diagnosis—but subsequent tests showed that she had Type 2 diabetes. There were more tests to determine the amount of insulin she had to take, and how to administer it. As things turned out, she could control the disease with a strict diet, 1800 calories a day, and pills, but at that time there was no device by which she could measure her blood sugar, and she had to rely simply on how she felt. The diet had its effect: she returned to her normal weight. And though, in later years, she had to inject the insulin with a needle, and always had to watch what she ate, she was able to lead a more-or-less ordinary life. But there were occasional upsets: in January 1968 Dad took her to emergency when her blood sugar level was dangerously high, and she was in Sarnia's General Hospital for a week to restore the balance of her blood sugar and the insulin.

On that same occasion my mother was coughing up blood, the result of her other long-term health problem, chronic bronchitis. It had been diagnosed also in 1960, after she had been in Victoria Hospital, London, under the care of a specialist.

My father, unlike my mother, had always been strong and healthy, but toward the end of November 1968 he woke up in the middle of the night, unable to get his breath. He walked around for a little while and the pain and tightness in his chest eased, and the spell passed off, but he was, of course, alarmed, and wondered what kind of attack he had had. The same thing happened again the next morning, and was much worse. He called the doctor, who told him to come in at 5 p.m. Dad had meetings to attend that day—one of them, I remember, was to make up lists of potential jurors—and he went to them before keeping his medical appointment. When the doctor examined him, he told him that his heart was enlarged, and put him on digitalis immediately. He also advised him to stay off work for two weeks.

At this point Dad was sixty-six years old, and this episode was the first sign of the heart disease that would eventually take his life. But at the time the doctor was reassuring: whatever was wrong with the valve or muscle that caused the pain was "nothing serious," the doctor said, and "certainly nothing to shorten his life." Dad expected that his heart would never return to normal, but in fact with regular exercise (walking) it did shrink, nearly to normal, the doctor told him. "The Watsons all had strong hearts," Dad said to me years later, "but it was all that heavy lifting on the farm that hurt me." He blamed it especially on the bags of white beans, which were far heavier than bags of grain.

Dad determined to start taking things easy—he was instructed not to shovel snow or do any heavy lifting—and, for the first time, he started talking about retirement. The next spring he bought a little garden tractor. In May my mother reported that "Dad mowed the lawn Monday & I have not seen anyone happier than he is to have the tractor. I imagine he will be just as glad to have it for snow." In the meantime, both my parents started paying a lot of attention to diet and exercise.

The summer of 1969

During the 1968–9 academic year, I applied to the Canada Council for a research grant, and the application was successful: it was for my next scholarly project, which was on Tennyson's poetry, and it paid for research in the British Museum and at the Tennyson Research Centre in Lincoln. Arlene and I decided that we would combine my work with a tour of Europe. Our plan was that I would fly to England in mid-May, and work until the end of June, when Arlene would be finished teaching; she would join me in England at the beginning of July, we would drive around Europe, and when she returned to Canada in mid-August, I would carry on with my research until the middle of September, just before classes started again at Western. The fifteenth of May and of September were my end dates.

We left with our parents copies of our itinerary, and my mother wrote regularly to us. (So did Aunt Ruth, who always began her letters with "Just a line today" and ended with "Lovingly, Aunt Ruth.") My mother's letters give a picture of their activities during that summer.

Much that she reported was about family: visits to Aunt Beck in Watford; visits from Aunt Ruth and Uncle Ches; a visit to Aunt Eva, who seemed frail (Uncle Gord had died suddenly the previous summer); Uncle Howard's flying down from Timmins to be a delegate at the General Assembly of the Presbyterian Church; he and Aunt Eleanor driving to the west coast. But "the big news is that Marjorie & Mike have bought a house." It was at 3 Glenrose Avenue, "just below St. Clair off Inglewood Drive," Marjorie herself reported, "a very small little house, English Tudor style with small little windows—beige stucco with brown slats, and trimmed with stone." It needed work, and Marj and Mike did extensive renovations and redecorating. They were enthusiastic about the place, and so were our parents when they came to stay overnight at the end of August: "we fell in love with their house," my mother wrote.

When we were on the farm, having a vegetable garden, and canning fruits and vegetables for the winter, were always major summer activities. By the time my parents were living in Sarnia, canning had long been superseded by freezing, but my parents still "put down" fruit when it was in season, and they still had an extensive vegetable garden. At the beginning of July, my mother wrote that "our garden is growing really well now and we have all the onions, radishes & lettuce we can use. The beans & carrots are coming along too." Later that month, she wrote that "on Tues. afternoon we drove to Arkona & got our cherries so we had those to do yesterday. To-day I am waiting for Mr. Winiger to call saying the berries are ready." Then, at the end of August, "we are getting green corn, tomatoes & peaches in abundance now. Make you hungry?"

My mother had by then given up her job as book-keeper and no longer worked on the tax sale. "Bill [McRorie] and Mrs. Hunt are busy" with it, she wrote at the end of August. "It is a relief not to have to prepare the list as I did for so many years."

My father's chief responsibility that summer was the building of the new county home for the aged in Forest. It was Lambton's second such home, after Twilight Haven in Petrolia, and it was to be called the North Lambton Rest Home. On 4 July my mother reported that "Wed. was council meeting and to-day is the deadline for tenders for the new rest home.... Mrs. Stewart reminds Dad when they built the C.A.S. [Children's Aid Society] building he said that was his last & now there is another one on the go." It meant "extra work" for my father during the summer, and he was so busy that he could not take his holidays as a single unit of time. "Friday night was the turning of the sod for the new rest home in Forest," my mother wrote on 10 August. "We drove out for that. It is quite a nice site. There were about half the council there." Construction proceeded through the fall and winter and into the next year; the official opening would be in November 1970.

By this time county council was meeting more frequently. "Council meeting is Wed.," my mother wrote on 31 August; "it does come around in a hurry." And its deliberations were not always models of parliamentary procedure. "There are some in now who like a good time more than business," my mother wrote, "& Dad and Bill [McRorie] get pretty upset by times. They argue over small issues & put big things through without much thought." For that particular September meeting, the warden "arranged for council to go to Don Stonehouse's for lunch (he had opened a motel & restaurant on East Street). Dad was not too happy about it. Last time they couldn't even get them back to start the afternoon sesssion."

In the meantime, my parents travelled, as usual but now for the last times, to the municipal conventions around the province. "We are at Niagara," my mother wrote on 19 August, "on the 12th floor at Sheraton-Brock & the view is magnificent. It is quite a thing to see the American Falls dried up and the crowds are terrific.... The dinner last night was good & they had an excellent program after although it lasted until 11 o'clock. There is another dinner to-night...." Their last convention before Dad's planned retirement was in Belleville at the end of September. On that occasion, my parents spent a weekend in Prince Edward County, and on their return they came through Port Hope. They wanted to find Vincent Massey's grave in St. Mark's churchyard there, but while Dad was searching the cemetery, a dog appeared, and it bit him. The bite was severe, so much so that he had to have tetanus shots, and he faced possible shots for rabies. The dog was placed under observation and, fortunately, proved not to be rabid.

My father's retirement: May 1970

By the late 1960s my father was making definite plans for his retirement, and he had settled on a date: 1 May 1970, after twenty-three years as a county administrator, when he would be in his sixty-eighth year.

Major changes were coming in municipal government in Ontario. When, in November 1968, the Petrolia paper ran a photograph of my father working at his desk, and praised him as "probably the most knowledgeable man on county administration in Lambton," the caption also noted that "his retirement comes in 18 months, just about the time regional government is expected to alter drastically the role of county councils in Ontario." My mother's letters in the summer of 1969 were full of rumours and gossip about the coming of regional government, about new boundaries and "land grabs," about who would gain and who would lose. "The big issue now," my mother wrote on 31 July, "is Paul Blundy [the mayor of Sarnia] wants to grab Sarnia Twp. Moore & Pt. Edward for Sarnia & let the rest of the County go & it looks as if he may very well succeed." In her next letter, she says "it seems Toronto sort of agrees with him so just about anything could happen." The next day Dad had a meeting in Wallaceburg over regional government—one of many—and on 19 August my mother reported yet another meeting: "Lambton & Kent to talk about regional gov't & if it goes through it would also become one riding for prov. elections. Now they have 3 members McKeough & Bullbrook & Henderson & now we know why Lorne Henderson is fighting against regional gov't. It begins to add up. There would just be 1 member."

How my parents would finance retirement was, of course, a topic they discussed at length. Dad would have a pension from OMERS (the Ontario Municipal Employees Retirement System), but it was not quite as much as he would like, and he wanted to work part-time for two more years, as secretary-treasurer of Twilight Haven and North Lambton rest homes. He was already managing a $700,000 trust fund for them, and to a reporter he described the position as "a full-time job but without the responsibility and pressure of the clerkship." (Privately, he was also worried about having something to do when he retired.) Council considered his request in March but did not give its final approval until the June session.

On Saturday, 25 April the County gave a retirement dinner for my parents. It was in the Village Inn in Point Edward, a large hotel-dining-conference complex on Christina Street North, just over the 402 and opposite the county buildings in Dufferin Park. The whole evening was beautifully organized, thanks to Dad's secretary, Mrs. Stewart, who looked after every detail, from the excellent meal itself to the guest book and an orchid corsage for my mother; and thanks too to Bill McRorie, whom council had appointed as the new clerk-treasurer on Dad's recommendation. Over two hundred guests sat down to dinner.

They included the office staff from the county buildings and various county officials such as the county engineer and the plumbing and building inspector; present and past members of county council and township councils; past wardens; Mrs. Eva Cox, the deputy-reeve of Petrolia and the first woman ever to sit on Lambton County Council; clerks and administrators from other nearby counties; the mayor of Sarnia, some of his council, and the city manager; Judge and Mrs. Carscallen; Louis Eddy, at that time the county solicitor who would become a judge himself; the caretaker of the county buildings; two M.L.A.s (Lorne Henderson and Jim Bullbrook) and one M.P. (Bud Cullen).

Guests were seated at round tables in groups of eight. The head table (colourful with flowers and candles) included, besides my parents, the warden Alvin Perritt and his wife (they were from Watford); past warden Stan Campbell and Mrs. Campbell; the minister at Grace United Church, Dr. Mackenzie and Mrs. Mackenzie; Marjorie and Michael, and Arlene and me. The speeches were brief, and glowing in praise of Dad. Lorne Edgar, who was from Brooke Township and Walnut Church, spoke on behalf of wardens past and present and Mike Fraser (the governor of the jail) on behalf of county employees. They were followed by the mayor, members of parliament, other clerk-treasurers, and finally Bill McRorie. Mentioned again and again were Dad's courtesy and tact, his thorough knowledge of municipal politics and of municipal law, his skill in applying his knowledge to every situation, and his efficient handling of county business. My mother was praised too, for her courtesy and her efficiency as a book-keeper.

Dad had been thinking about his reply for some time, and he had discussed it with me. He chose not to give a conventional list of achievements over the course of a long administration (he had, after all, presided over every major building project the county undertook during that time), but instead talked about the great snowstorm of January 1943 and his adventures in getting to sessions of county council; he talked about the county's centennial in 1949 and the rarity of Victor Lauriston's book on the county's first one hundred years; and he talked about the warden's pictures in the halls of the county buildings. A nice sense of history, I thought, especially since my grandfather's career in municipal politics had been mentioned. But Dad also said that "he had reaped the value of many wonderful experiences during his years of service for the county and had made many enduring friendships. 'I would like to thank all the past and present county councils, and all the other officials that I worked with'" (*Guide* 30 April 1970). A month earlier the *Sarnia Gazette* had interviewed my father, and his comments then anticipated his remarks at the dinner. About the county councillors Dad had said, "They have always treated me wonderfully well. I have made many staunch friends from the long list of men who have served our county over these years and, too, I have got to know and to like the elected and administrative people in the city and in all our municipalities. Unless you, yourself, have served on a Council you cannot realize how much the elected people do. It is a heavy load and it is the job of municipal administration to make it easier. This I have tried conscientiously to do over the years."

A long line of people came up to speak to my parents afterwards and, according to the *Windsor Star*, there was "almost an hour of handshaking by well-wishers." That was a trial of my mother's physical strength and stamina. From the beginning of the year she had been having problems with her blood sugar count and finally, in February, she had gone into hospital to have it monitored and corrected. Up until then she had been controlling her diabetes with pills; now she had to take insulin by a needle, and she was shown how to give herself injections. She practised by injecting water into an orange. But getting things just right was not easy: early in April she had a severe reaction to the insulin and was back in hospital for another week or so. She was released only ten days before the retirement dinner, and was worried about being able to hold up for the whole affair. In the event, she did, but after that hour of handshaking Aunt Ruth took her off to the room she and Uncle Ches had taken for the night, and there Mum broke down, for she was very excited: "Just think: all those nice things said about your Dad," she said to me through tears.

My parents kept the guest book, of course, and also the many cards and letters they received. But the note which, I think, most pleased my parents was from Mrs. Stewart: "April 30th. 1970. Dear Mr. Hair: First of all - I'm writing this rather than saying it - as I'm afraid I might burst into tears! So many people were able to say wonderful things about you - but I find myself groping for words trying to express what I really feel! Maybe I'll just say - what a pleasant six years I've had working for you! I know it must have been pretty hectic for you - but I have enjoyed the relationship so much! And deep down inside I guess I really hoped this day would never come - but to quote an old cliché … 'all good things come to an end'! I do want to thank you for your patience, your understanding, your loyalty to me - believe me, I needed it all! I like to think that maybe I helped you a wee bit! I know that in the years to come, the memory of working with you will always be a delight to me. The very best of good health and much happiness always, to you and to Alice! Yours most sincerely, Verna Stewart."

My father's duties as secretary-treasurer of Lambton's rest homes

Just before his official retirement on 1 May 1970, my father was interviewed by a reporter for the *Sarnia Observer*, and the subsequent story focused on his post-retirement appointment:

"Retirement for John Alexander Hair, 65 [an error], at the end of the month will simply mean moving from one office in the Lambton county building to another. He will step down as clerk-treasurer after 23 years and devote himself full-time to the duties of secretary-treasurer of the county's two homes, Twilight Haven and North Lambton Rest Home. Two days a month he'll be visiting each home. One day will be taken up with distributing $15 a month from their old age pensions to the residents; the other he'll spend at a board meeting. In between, the official will be busy administering the homes' trust funds. Before a resident enters the home, he must turn over his assets as collateral against care to be received, Mr. Hair confirmed. 'This doesn't end his claim on his own funds, however,' he added. Residents may draw on them within reason, he indicated. One man has been given permission to purchase a new car, for example. The county official also gratuitously performs other services such as paying operating expenses on existing properties and even helping sell houses on request. 'Any residue in the account after the resident dies is turned over to the estate,' Mr. Hair explained. A bank auditor checks the fund periodically as required by the Provincial Homes for Aged Act. While the city of Sarnia has the right to put one-third of the residents in Twilight Haven (the county has the remaining two-thirds) the charge against the city isn't automatically that amount, Mr. Hair explained. 'They pay for the patient hours only,' he said. In addition, those who can't pay their own way receive treatment equal to those who can, he pointed out. Charge for ambulatory patients at Twilight Haven is $7.75 a day; bed care, $9.25. Rates are reviewed each year by the Department of Family Services, home for the aged branch. Rates for North Lambton have not yet been established. Tenders are out for furnishings and equipment for the $1,200,000 home in Forest. It is slated to be completed and ready for occupancy in August" ("Hair's Retirement Doesn't Mean Stop," *Sarnia Observer* 27 April 1970).

Deaths of the Hair sisters: Aunt Mary Galbraith, Aunt Lou Delmage, Aunt Beccie Hair

Aunt Mary, Aunt Lou and Aunt Beck were the last remaining sisters of my grandfather Hair, and they died within a few months of each other, in September and November 1970 and in February 1971. Aunt Mary was the first to go, on 30 September 1970, and she was buried in the cemetery in Appin. Aunt Lou died a few weeks later, on 20 November 1970. She had gone into the new North Lambton Rest Home in Forest, but was there only three weeks before her death. She was buried in Beechwood Cemetery in Forest, beside Uncle Disney, after having been a widow for nearly fifty years. Aunt Beck died on 24 February 1971. "Interment in St. James Cemetery, where she was laid to rest near her parents and grandparents, James and Nancy Hair" (*Guide* 4 March 1971). The Hair sisters lived long lives. Aunt Mary was ninety-five when she died; Aunt Lou was ninety-one (she was just a week short of her ninety-second birthday); and Aunt Beck was ninety-one.

Aunt May Hair had died years earlier, on 18 April 1962, after a heart attack, in her eightieth year. Dad was soloist at her funeral, which was on Good Friday, and she was buried in the Hair plot in St. James.

Governor-General Roland Michener comes to Sarnia: 4–5 March 1971

The vice-regal visit was the first to Sarnia since 1946, when Earl Alexander of Tunis had been in the city. He was the last of our British-born Governors-General, and I remember his visit, because he proclaimed a holiday for all school children in Lambton County. The occasion of this visit, a quarter century later, was the opening of Lambton College of Applied Arts and Technology. There was a formal reception, dinner and dance in the Village Inn, Point Edward, to which my parents were invited, and since the invitation specified "Black Tie and Decorations or Dark Business Suit," Dad rented a tuxedo for the occasion. Mum wore a long formal gown that she borrowed from Marjorie. They reported that Michener looked hale and hearty, and was "not at all stuffy": his speech was full of wit and humour. Mrs. Michener they described as "frail": she apparently had Parkinson's disease, for her head shook continuously.

The next day, the Governor-General came to County Council, and Dad was presented to him there. Eldon Brown, the 1971 warden, was his guide on a tour of the buildings.

My father's heart problems

About the time of the vice-regal visit, my father had not been feeling well: he couldn't sleep at night, and he was short of breath. On Sunday, 7 March, Dr. Murphy admitted him to hospital. My mother, who was terrified of staying alone and said that she had never stayed alone for a night in her life, arranged for a neighbour from Cathcart Boulevard to stay with her. But the woman was a South African who lectured my mother on the natural inferiority of blacks, and my mother would not put up with much of that. But she held her tongue: she needed the company at night. In the meantime, Dad was having a series of tests: his heart was enlarged, but his cardiogram showed nothing, and his blood pressure and other vital signs were good. Dr. Murphy doubled his dosage of digitalis, and when I was in Sarnia a week after his admission to hospital, I was happy to find that he was being discharged, and I could drive him home, to his considerable relief.

During the summer of 1971, Dad exercised (mainly by walking) and watched his diet. When, in late November, he had a checkup, Dr. Murphy told him that his heart had returned to its normal size.

My father retires fully: 30 June 1972

Dad retired as secretary-treasurer of the county homes on 30 June 1972. He might have continued working, and in fact in April was offered the job of court clerk, but he refused it, saying he was both happy and relieved to be retiring. The Social Club at the county buildings—it was everyone who worked there—had a party for my parents on the afternoon of 30 June, and presented them with two chaise longues. A large cake said "Happy Days, Alice and John."

Dad celebrated his seventieth birthday on 21 July 1972, and our whole family was in Sarnia for the event. Our mother prepared a big meal, and baked a cake. The day was a hot July day, and we ate in the back yard of 1267 Webster Drive, under the shade of the willow tree which Dad had planted more than ten years earlier, and which had grown far too rapidly.

CHAPTER TWELVE
THE FINAL DECADE: 1972–1983

1267 Webster Drive, Sarnia

My parents had moved to Sarnia in the fall of 1960, and they lived there for the next twenty-one years, until my mother went into hospital in the late summer of 1981. Their home, at 1267 Webster Drive, was actually in Sarnia Township, northeast of the city limits and close to the lakeshore. Webster Drive runs in an easterly direction off Murphy Road, at that time the city boundary, and the house itself stood at the south end of Carl Street, which runs north into the Lakeshore Road. Next door to my parents, on the west, were Glenn and Merlene (Matthews) Moffatt; Glenn was a cousin of my father. On the east were people by the name of Jennings. Down the street to the west were the Adamses, whom Dad came to know, and still further down was Louis Eddy, the son of our old minister at Walnut, a lawyer (and afterwards a judge). But there were also many neighbours whom my parents did not know, or whom they knew only slightly. There was not the same sense of community as there had been on the Twelfth Line or in Watford.

My father's retirement hobbies: Stamps, coins, model windmills

My father had collected stamps as a boy, and he continued to be interested in philately, especially when he retired and had time for it. He collected Canadian stamps. He had a standing order with Canada Post for all new issues, not only for individual stamps but also for corner blocks and first-day covers, and he mounted everything in albums, for which he bought printed pages from a philatelic company in the United States. His collection was almost complete, from the country's earliest postage stamps to the present, but it lacked a few of the rarest (and hence most expensive) issues, such as the "twelve-penny black" from 1851. That stamp was selling for far more than Dad was willing to pay.

Dad also collected Canadian coins. Each year he bought mint sets of that year's issue, and he also bought up silver dollars, thinking that they would eventually be worth much more than their face value. In addition to his stamp and coin collections, Dad had a basement workshop, where he built model windmills. One of them was for our garden in London, and like everything Dad made, it was so sturdy that it would take a tornado to blow it apart.

Going out in the car

My parents loved going out in the car. They constantly made little trips out of Sarnia: "down the river" to Wallaceburg and Walpole Island; out to Forest and Arkona, to pick berries which they froze; to Port Lambton to pick apples; "down" the Twelfth Line and "down" to Mount Brydges and around Brooke and Caradoc Townships; to Napier and Port Stanley; and to Dawn Township to see Mawlams' farm. They ventured as far afield as Port Dover and Kitchener, where they visited Mackenzie King's boyhood home, Woodside. An example of their exploring: my parents spent some time trying to locate the grave of J. C. Elliott, once Postmaster-General of Canada, M.P. for West Middlesex, and a friend of the Runnallses: my mother claimed he was a distant relative. They finally found his burial place in the Baptist Church cemetery on Highway 2 west of Melbourne.

When an excursion involved a lot of walking, Dad went on his own, to Brigden Fair, for instance, and to the ploughing match. The International Ploughing Match was held in Lambton County in 1973, for the first time in fifty years, and while the earlier match had been held on the Goodison farm just east of Sarnia (a farm my grandfather, Sherman Hair, once considered buying, my father told me), the 1973 match was in Brooke Township, on J.D. McGugan's farm on 15 Sideroad (now Old Walnut Road). The site included neighbouring farms, six hundred acres in all, and Dad spent a day there.

My parents motored regularly to Strathroy to see Aunt Ruth and Uncle Ches, and they came to London on various occasions, and always for birthdays. When Arlene and I started to build our house, in (what was at that time) London Township, my parents made regular trips to see the progress being made by our contractor, Carl Bice. And they drove to Toronto, to stay with Marjorie while Mike was away on business. Dad took long walks in the St. Clair–Yonge Street area; Marj drove them around the city; and they both found great happiness in the grandson who had arrived a few months earlier.

The first grandchild

Shortly after ten in the evening of 5 June 1973, my mother telephoned to tell us that Marjorie had had a baby boy—my parents' first grandchild. The next evening Marj and Mike themselves phoned, from Marjorie's room in Women's College Hospital. The baby, who weighed eight pounds thirteen ounces at birth, had arrived about ten the previous night, a fine healthy boy. They named him Robert Bradford.

Later that month my parents drove to Toronto to see the baby, and in early September they went again, for Robert's christening. Canon Dann performed the ceremony in the chapel of St. Paul's church on Bloor Street, and could not resist saying, by way of greeting to Mike's parents, "Are we all hale and hearty today?" Arlene and I became godparents. The baby, I noted, was very good indeed: an alert little fellow, sturdy and strong, and able (even at three months) to hold his head up. He smiled and gurgled whenever anyone talked to him. Sleep deprivation is the usual fate of new parents, but Marj said he was sleeping through the whole night. At Christmas, which we celebrated in Sarnia, the baby was the centre of attention, and my parents loved having their grandson in the house.

Western University honours my father: 13 June 1973

Every year, usually in June, Western entertained the councils from the surrounding counties by way of saying thanks for the annual grants from those municipalities. I had known for some time that, at the June 1973 gathering, there would be some kind of presentation to Dad, for I had been talking to Bill Baldwin, a member of the Board of Governors, at one of the president's post-convocation receptions at Gibbons Lodge in early June. He had known Dad for several years, and characterized him as "a good man, a gentle man." I had said to Baldwin that I wanted to "sneak in" to the Great Hall in Somerville House and stand at the back for the presentation, but Bill must have put in a word on my behalf, for Mr. Way, the secretary of the Board, called to invite me to the reception and dinner. I was delighted to go. Dad introduced me to most of the councillors from Lambton, and I in turn introduced him to the university people I knew. The chairman of the Board made the presentation. He was Captain Joseph Jeffrey, who was also the head of London Life, and he presented Dad, Len Coles from Oxford, and Bud Blowes from Perth each with a round copper tray bearing the university crest and the words "The University of Western Ontario." Dad's was engraved: "Presented to / JOHN A. HAIR / Clerk-Treasurer of Lambton County 1947–1970 / and a / Good Friend of Western / 13 June 1970." Dad was pleased, and I was pleased for him. I still have that tray.

A glimpse of Dad's daily routine

Marceil Saddy, who would be the mayor of Sarnia but who was in the early 1970s editor of the *Sarnia Gazette*, lived in Bright's Grove and drove into the city each day on the Lakeshore Road. He had an "Editor's Corner" in the paper, and one day, probably in the summer of 1973, he wrote about the sights on his daily commute. One was "John Hair the past County Clerk-Treasurer, in Bermudas and golf hat, jauntily strolling back from a corner store … the *Globe and Mail* under his arm."

My father's continuing involvement in Liberal politics

There was a provincial election in the fall of 1975. Jim Bullbrook, who had been the county solicitor since 1958 and who had held the Sarnia riding for the Liberals since 1967, was seeking re-election, and he invited Dad to a luncheon with Robert Nixon, who was the provincial Liberal leader at the time. Both my parents voted Liberal on September 18, but the Conservatives (under Bill Davis) formed the government and the NDP the official opposition, while the Liberals dropped to third place. Bullbrook, however, held on to his seat. In the Lambton riding Lorne Henderson was re-elected and entered cabinet as minister without portfolio.

Our parents' fortieth wedding anniversary: 5 October 1975

In August 1975 Marj and Mike sold their house on Glenrose and bought a larger one with a private drive, a garage, and a yard. It was at 95 Bessborough Drive in Leaside. Mum and Dad helped with the move. On 5 October, Arlene and I drove to Toronto, and we all had dinner with our parents at the Granite Club. Mum and Dad stayed on in Toronto until the end of October, since Mike had been sent to England by Imperial Life, and when they returned to Sarnia, Marjorie and Robert went with them. Rob was at the stage where he was imitating everything and everyone. My father loved taking his grandson around, holding him by the hand, and showing him things. He took him for walks in his stroller, and he carved a pumpkin for him, for Hallowe'en.

A new Buick

Late in November 1976 Arlene and I arrived in Sarnia one Sunday and were surprised to discover that our parents had a new car, a '77 Buick. It was, we found out, a necessary purchase. On Tuesday, 16 November, Dad had been driving along Exmouth Street, and at Capel a car ran through a red light and slammed into the side of Dad's car, spinning it around completely and damaging it badly. Dad, fortunately, was wearing a seat belt and was not hurt. The other driver claimed the light was green, but there were two witnesses who backed up Dad's story, and the police charged the other driver. Dad simply went down to Wallis's in Watford and bought a new car.

History of Lambton County Officials / 125 Years / 1850–1975

In 1917 Judge McWatt had published a history of Lambton County officials from the time that Lambton had been established in 1849, and when the county celebrated its centenary in 1949, County Council commissioned John Huey to bring the history up to date. His work, compiled, as he said, from records "of which I have been the guardian for over a quarter of a century," was published in 1950. Twenty-five years later, the Ex-Wardens Association decided to extend the history, and asked Dad to do the job. He worked happily on this project throughout 1975 and 1976, and was the logical person to do it: he knew every elected and appointed official personally, and had been involved in every one of the county's major construction projects in the 1950s and 1960s: the new county buildings and the Children's Aid building in Sarnia, Twilight Haven in Petrolia, the North Lambton Rest Home in Forest, the County Library in Wyoming, and the Oil Museum in Oil Springs. And he had the support of two ex-wardens who had a strong interest in municipal history—Bert Logan of Sarnia Township and "Duffy" Atkin of Oil Springs—plus the help of his successor as Clerk-Treasurer, Bill McRorie.

Each time Arlene and I visited—and we went to Sarnia every two weeks, weather and circumstances permitting—Dad and I discussed the history and his handling of it. John Huey had written his sketches of officials to a formula, giving the politics and religion of each. I suggested to Dad that, in addition to the details of an individual's career in municipal politics, he give an account of the major events during the term of office of each, and that is what he did. And he described fully each major building project. By the end of February 1976 he had the text almost finished, and had been conferring with the photographer and the printer. His work was interrupted in April, when he had the flu and was slow to recover. I contributed time as a copy editor, adding a comma here or changing the tense of a verb there; in May, I spent a long afternoon with Dad going over the whole typescript; and in November, when the page proofs had arrived, I did the proofreading for him.

The book was published early in 1977, and it became, unfortunately, the centre of a controversy. The Ex-Wardens' Association (which had commissioned the history and paid Dad one thousand dollars for his work) had applied for, and received, a one-thousand-dollar grant from Wintario, the provincial lottery. Jim Bullbrook, lawyer and M.P.P. for Sarnia, whom Dad had known for years, attacked the grant, saying that Wintario money should go to health care and education. Bullbrook did not mention Dad's name, but the news stories in the *Sarnia Gazette* and the *London Free Press* both used the book as an example of government money foolishly spent. Dad said nothing in public; if anyone responds, he said, it must be the Ex-Wardens' Association. So far as I know, no one responded, and the issue simply faded as no longer newsworthy.

A second grandson
On Friday, 16 April 1976 Marjorie went into Women's College Hospital just after lunch, and Derek was born at 5:15 that afternoon. He weighed eight pounds, ten ounces. His parents named him Derek John: Derek because they liked the name, John after his two grandfathers. In early June Mum and Dad went to Toronto to see their new grandson, and on Sunday, 18 June they and the Hales were present in St. Paul's when he was baptized. Arlene and I again became godparents.

Uncle Ches's declining health
In 1976 Uncle Ches was in his mid-eighties. Though he had always worried about straining his heart by over-exertion, he was a healthy and vigorous man, "never sick a day in his life" (according to my father), constantly "on the go" and always interested—to the point of being nosy—in what others were doing, and far too fond of gossip. He heard a lot of it from Clare Eastabrook, who had farmed on the Sixth Line and had moved into Watford when he retired. On a Saturday night in January 1976 Clare was visiting Uncle Ches and Aunt Ruth. They watched television (the hockey game, I suspect), and afterwards Aunt Ruth made lunch. A little later, Uncle Ches felt pains in his chest; they came on suddenly and were intense. A neighbour took him to the hospital, and a day or so later his doctor confirmed that he had had a heart attack. He was in hospital for some time, but was home by the end of February. He no longer smoked; he could no longer drive a car; and he had spells when he would black out. But he survived.

That year—1976—our mother determined to hold our family Christmas early, and she settled on 5 December, when she had a turkey dinner with all the trimmings ready at noon. Marj and Mike and the two boys came up from Toronto the day before; Arlene and I drove to Sarnia on that Sunday, and took Aunt Ruth and Uncle Ches with us. A couple of weeks later, just before Christmas, Uncle Ches had another heart attack. It happened on Tuesday, 21 December, and there was a second "spell" on Friday. He was once again in Strathroy hospital. On Boxing Day Aunt Ruth told Mum that the prognosis was "not too good," and he was sleeping much of the time. The doctor gave him three or four days. Would Mum and Dad come down to Strathroy and stay with her, Aunt Ruth asked—not because she was afraid of staying alone, but because she needed their support, she said. So they went to Strathroy, prepared to stay for as long as needed. And they did stay, until New Year's Eve. Each day seemed to be critical. On the 29th Dad told me that Uncle Ches was "sinking slowly" and was not expected to last the night. Dad had been in to see him, and Uncle Ches had grasped his hand, though Dad was not sure that he knew him. Aunt Ruth was exhausted. And Mum, in the meantime, had phoned Uncle Howard and Aunt Eleanor, and they planned to drive down from Timmins; and she had been talking to Uncle Frank, who was so weak that Aunt Nellie had to help him to the phone. Arlene and I expected a phone call at any time. But none came.

New Year's Eve came and went. By the beginning of January 1977, my parents reported that Uncle Ches was better, that he was eating, and that he was likely to come home. "He's a tough old bird," Dad said. He gradually regained his strength, but he was cantankerous, demanding this and refusing to do that: "ugly as sin," Aunt Ruth said of him. In the meantime, Uncle Howard and Aunt Eleanor were staying with her, and that was a great relief to my parents, who had found their time in Strathroy trying: Dad had nothing to do, and little habits of Aunt Ruth (like thawing frozen fish sticks and re-freezing those not eaten) had irritated Mum. Aunt Ruth had told Mum that she would have to make the lunch to be served after the funeral: "I'm counting on you."

Uncle Ches was discharged from the hospital on 20 January 1977, which just happened to be the day when I drove to Strathroy to see him. Knowing he had "a sweet tooth," I brought him a box of chocolates, which he took with shaky hands. He had always loved company, and he loved to talk, and he did so on that day with all his old gusto. His speech patterns will always remain with me: "Why, Donald, I mind when ..." (he said "I mind" when he meant "I remember"); the verbal tic at the end of his sentences, as in "the snow was three feet deep, yeah"; and "awful" as an intensifier—"he was awful upset about that" (this last said with relish and a malicious chuckle).

But Uncle Ches was soon back in hospital, this time with the flu. There was a morbid streak in him, and it showed up when Aunt Ruth wanted to lower his bed and he wouldn't let her: "I'll be lowered a lot farther pretty soon."

Death of Aunt Eva McNeil and of John McNeil

Since Uncle Gord's death in 1968 Aunt Eva had been living in an apartment at 95 Ridout Street South, in that part of London where she had spent most of her life, but eventually she needed long-term care, and went into Marian Villa. She died on 17 May 1976, at the age of eighty-six. The funeral service was the next day, at the Millard George Funeral Home on Ridout Street South, and Dad and I went. It was a sad affair. John was already seriously ill, and looked very thin and frail—so frail that he would begin panting at the slightest exertion, then catch his breath and go on. He died six months later, at the end of October. He was only fifty-nine. Dora telephoned to ask me to be a pall-bearer, and Dad came down to London to go with me to the funeral, which was in Wesley-Knox United Church. The pall-bearers were cousins from both the Watson and McNeil families. The day was bleak and cold, and a strong wind drove gusts of rain into our faces as we stood at the gravesite in Forest Lawn for the committal service. Afterwards, there was a gathering in the church parlour, when ladies of the congregation served lunch and Dad and I had a chance to chat with Dora, with Marilynne, and with Dora's mother, Mrs. Dicks.

London Normal School's Fifty-Year Reunion: June 1977

My mother had attended the London Normal School in 1926-7, and fifty years later, in June 1977, her class held a reunion. It was organized by one of her classmates, Gordon Duffin, who had gone on to become Deputy Minister of Education, and he had spent three years searching for the 250 graduates. He was able to account for 246 of them. Two hundred people were at the reunion; 135 of them were fifty-year graduates. The dinner was held in the University Community Centre on Western's campus; the speaker was Dr. Finlay Stewart of Kitchener, a former moderator of the Presbyterian Church; and it was "a great success," my mother reported. She had been looking forward to it for months. Among those present were Eileen (Sisson) Cameron, my mother's best friend and "teaching partner"; Dorothy (Delmage) Dolbear, first cousin of my father; Ruby (Atchison) Douglas from the Twelfth Line of Brooke; and Mabel (Trott) Runnalls, with whom my mother had boarded on Bruce Street, and who married her first cousin, Neil Runnalls.

Death of Aunt Jean Watson: June 1977

She was Uncle Oscar's second wife and the last surviving spouse in our grandmother's family. She died in a nursing home, Woodingford Lodge in Woodstock, on 17 June 1977, at the age of seventy-eight, and was buried beside Uncle Oscar in the Anglican Cemetery in Woodstock. Dad went to the funeral. Aunt Jean had two sons from her first marriage, and one of them, Gib Stephens (who was a barber in Woodstock), told Dad that his mother had been in Woodingford Lodge for nine years, and for more than half that time had not known anyone.

My mother's retirement projects

She started by collecting letterheads. She sent out requests to every city and county and regional government in Ontario, and looked forward every day to the arrival of the mail. Dad mounted the flood of paper in albums. Then, about 1978, she started collecting letters from political figures, to whom she wrote asking for a letterhead and an autograph: the premiers and lieutenant-governors of all the provinces; the prime minister and leader of the opposition; mayors of some of the larger cities; and a few international figures. The post each day brought something of interest: an autograph letter from Lily Schreyer, wife of the governor-general; a single sheet with the signature of Pierre Elliott Trudeau scrawled across it; a colour photograph of Bud Cullen, M.P., inscribed "To my loyal & dear friends John & Alice." And, from abroad, an autograph letter from Margaret Thatcher, on 10 Downing Street stationery; and from Rosalyn Carter, on White House stationery. All of those letters are now in the collection of the Lambton County Library in Wyoming.

Walnut Church's 100th Anniverary: 21 May 1978

The congregation made plans for a special centennial service, and invited the eighty-two-year-old Mr. Hart to return to the pulpit. He had been a well-liked minister at Walnut forty years earlier, from 1933 to 1938, and it was he who baptized me. "The small church on the 10th line of Brooke Township was filled beyond capacity," the Watford paper reported, and "the overflow crowd sat in cars listening to the service over loud speakers" (*Guide* 24 May 1978). Afterwards there was a reception and dinner in the Brooke Central School, attended by some three hundred people. Marjorie and Michael and the boys came up from Toronto to go with our parents, who were proud to show off their family.

But the days when small country churches could continue to be viable were coming to an end, and Walnut survived for only a few years beyond its centennial. It closed in June 1982; most of the congregation transferred to Hope United Church in Alvinston; and the building itself was demolished. In September of that year Dad and I ran into Raymond and Florence Swartz in Sarnia, and they told us that the church had been torn down; and when Dad and I drove along the Tenth Line in November we saw that the building had indeed disappeared. The site might have reverted to farm land (it was on a corner of Ralph Ferguson's farm), but it remains set apart at that crossroads, where spruce trees surround a patch of green grass. A bronze plaque set into fieldstone explains (and gives a later date for the closing). It reads: "This plaque commemorates WALNUT UNITED CHURCH built on this site in 1878 and served until 1983 and the community of Walnut settled about 1850." And 15 Sideroad, on the west side of this little patch of ground, was renamed Old Walnut Road.

Uncle Ches McLellan's decline and death

After his heart attack, Uncle Ches could no longer drive a car. But when, in the fall of 1978, one of their neighbours on Drury Lane in Strathroy, Simon McLeod, came over and offered to take them for a drive one Sunday in September, he asked where they would like to go, and they said, without hesitating, "Sarnia!" So they went, and Arlene and I just happened to be there that same day, and everyone stayed for dinner. But Uncle Ches was failing. His voice had grown thin, and he couldn't get rid of a gargling sound in his throat. When he stood, he took a long time to straighten up and get steady on his feet. But his mind was as alert as ever, and he still loved to talk and gossip.

It was Aunt Ruth who was feeling the strain of his declining health. When I delivered our gifts to them in Strathroy a few days before Christmas, she was worried and apprehensive: "we've been having a terrible time around here," she said, her fingers twisting the edge of her apron. For Uncle Ches was frequently dizzy, was afflicted with gout, and got around only with a walker. Two days before Christmas 1979, I was again delivering gifts in Strathroy. Uncle Ches had had a fall that morning, and was in bed. Aunt Ruth took me in to see him, and he got up, very slowly, and with great concentration put a slipper on each foot, and managed to get out to the living room, with the help of his walker and with Aunt Ruth holding on to his shirt tail. "I'm stiff, Donald," he said; "he's so unsteady on his feet," Aunt Ruth said.

In January 1980 Uncle Ches was back in the hospital with the flu, and by February he was no longer certain about controlling his bowels and bladder. Aunt Ruth was firm about not being able to look after him any longer at home, and wanted him to go into Strathmere Lodge. At first he resisted angrily; by mid-March he was in a more reasonable frame of mind, and made the move.

One day in June I went out to Strathroy and drove Aunt Ruth to the Lodge. Uncle Ches's room was like a hospital room, clean and bright, with four beds. Uncle Ches was asleep in one; there were two other old men in the room, both neatly dressed, but senile, staring into space. An orderly helped Uncle Ches up into a chair. "If you want to know what hell is like, Donald," he said to me, "this is it." He was "mad at everything," as Aunt Ruth said: he criticized the food, the service, and all the arrangements at the Lodge. And his morbidity surfaced again. "The only place anyone goes from here," he said to me, "is Dennings." Dennings' was the funeral home in Strathroy.

Aunt Ruth and Uncle Ches had been married on 8 November 1930, a cold day with four inches of snow, my mother told me. Their anniversary fifty years later fell on a Saturday, and it was a very different kind of day, with warm air, pale sunshine, and blue sky. Mum wanted to mark the anniversary: she had Dad get fifty silver dollars from the bank, and she arranged a family gathering at Strathmere Lodge that included not only Arlene and me but Aunt Eleanor and Uncle Howard as well (my mother had been Aunt Ruth's attendant, and Uncle Howard had been Uncle Ches's). It was not a success. Uncle Ches was in such physical and mental decline that he didn't know what was going on, and may have thought (as Arlene speculated) that we were gathered at his deathbed. An orderly got him up in a chair; he had trouble hearing us and seeing us; and almost immediately he put his head down in his hands. Dad and Uncle Howard and Arlene went out into the hall; Aunt Ruth and Mum and I stayed a little longer, and then we all left.

Two and one-half weeks later, he was dead. For days there had been no change in his condition. Then, about eleven o'clock in the morning of 19 December, Aunt Ruth received a phone call. He was in his 90th year.

Though my parents had had their bags packed all fall, ready to come and stay with Aunt Ruth and help her as best they could, they did not in fact go to Strathroy when the time came: Dad had bronchitis, and a persistent cough was keeping him awake at night; my mother had a dizzy spell and had fallen, without breaking anything, fortunately. So Arlene and I went to the visitation, and next day Marjorie came up on the train from Toronto and we went to the funeral together. It was at Dennings'. I looked around and thought that not much had changed since Grandad Runnalls' funeral there in 1949: the same brown woodwork, the same flowered wallpaper, the same heavy drapes. Outside, snow was falling steadily. At the cemetery, it was falling thickly on the little group of dark figures gathered at the grave, in a white and gray landscape—falling thickly on the flowers and on the polished wood of the casket. Then the cold gave way to the family gathering afterwards: a warm house, crowded with people, smelling of tea and coffee, and alive with the buzz of conversations. Uncle Howard and Aunt Eleanor, who were staying with Aunt Ruth, were there. All of our cousins from Woodstock and Ingersoll were there, and Harold and Honor Hair, and Helen Ferguson (Uncle Ed Runnalls' daughter). Aunt Ruth was focusing on arrangements, and after nearly everyone had left, she asked me, "Was everything all right?" I assured her that it was.

It was not until weeks later that Aunt Ruth talked about the funeral, when she was obviously going over everything in her mind, and it was then that she told me about Uncle Ches's final days: how for a long time there had been no change in him, so that when the Lodge phoned and said they had "bad news," she thought he had broken his hip. She had been to the Lodge every day that week. Uncle Ches always asked her if she had brought an apple, and she had always peeled one for him to eat. He would eat a chocolate bar as well, and she would go round to the shop and buy him one. When she left him on that last Thursday, he said, "All you've done today is feed me." Those were the last words he said to her. In telling me all this, Aunt Ruth also seemed to be coping with feelings of guilt, which everyone in her situation is bound to feel. "I might have tried to look after him if he hadn't been so demanding and impatient," she said. He would wake her in the middle of the night and want a drink "right now." When he was complaining about the Lodge and Aunt Ruth would try to reason with him, he would say, "You're supposed to be on my side."

Aunt Ruth gave me Uncle Ches's ring—a ruby set in yellow gold—and the gold pocket watch he had when they were married. "He always thought that you and Marjorie were closest to him," she said, "and I think he would have liked you to have them."

Death of Uncle Ed Runnalls

Uncle Ed died on 27 January 1980, two months short of his one hundredth birthday. He was the youngest of Grandad Runnalls' brothers and sisters and the last surviving member of that family. He lived with Ralph and Jean (Ralph was his son) on their Warwick Township farm, on Number 7 Highway about halfway between the Nauvoo Road and Warwick Village, and Ralph's sons, Ian and Wayne and their families, both had houses on that same farm. They were a close-knit family. Uncle Ed lived life with gusto, and his death was quick and easy: a stroke at home, a second stroke a few hours later in hospital, and he was gone. His sense of humour is evident in a verse written down by his daughter-in-law, Jean, who heard Uncle Ed repeat it to ladies at the Presbyterian Church:

> Hurrah! Hurrah! for bachelor's hall!
> The Queen is away and I'm monarch of all;
> I don't have to hang up my coat or my hat,
> And when I get lonely, I talk to the cat.

Stories from my parents

My parents' stories now were often darker and more sensational that they had been when my sister and I were small: accidents and crimes and family scandals never talked about in front of us kids, though all were from the distant past. About "Jim Kelly [Nina's father] running off with his sister-in-law"; about "Dr. Hicks getting the Harper girl in trouble"; the sad story of a neigbour "whose child had just died of diphtheria, going in to Watford to fetch the undertaker, and returning to find another child dead"; about a woman in a horse and buggy coming so close to being hit by a train that the horse had to turn its head; about Orville Wallis's lucky escape when he was a boy and was offered a ride home by "the Bowie girl," who had just put her mother on the train: at a country crossing she drove her car right into the side of the train and was killed. Orville was thrown free. Dad told me about running over our dog when I was very small. Our neighbour Clarence Lewis's cattle had got out, and Dad was driving down the road with our dog and Clarence's running alongside the car; our dog swerved, right into the path of our Pontiac. Apparently I cried and cried; now I wonder why I have no memory of that event.

But there were comic stories too. Dad told about a young Englishman he knew, who came out to Canada and worked on a farm near ours. He started going with a girl from the neighbourhood, and was walking her home one night when a skunk crossed the road in front of them. He didn't know what it was, and gave it a kick. Well, Dad said, he never saw the girl again. He himself ran and jumped into a pond, and he had to burn all his clothes.

When I was putting up shutters that Dad had made, I said that I was a coward when it came to climbing ladders to high places, and that got Dad reminiscing about men of his generation up on the roofs of barns and thinking nothing of it. He told me about getting up on our barn at home, when it was to be re-roofed, and putting on the first two rows of cedar shingles, moving along the edge of the roof with nothing but his "creeper" and one foot in the eavestrough. And he talked about going up on Uncle Harry Watson's forty-foot windmill, which was as high as he wanted to go. But other men, he said, seemed to have no fear of heights, and would walk upright along the peak of a barn roof or—even scarier—along the edge just above the eavestrough.

When my mother and my aunt were together, they often reminisced about people in Mount Brydges: about Annie Courtis, for instance, brisk and aggressive and mannish, who never hesitated to ask people how much money they made, and who taught in the Adelaide School and tolerated no misbehaviour from her pupils; and about her sister Allie, the giantess, who remembered everyone's birthdate and talked about nothing else at quilting bees; about their mother, who boasted to Grammie Runnalls about Allie's size and good health when she was a baby, in contrast to Uncle Frank, who was the same age and sickly as a child. At church Mrs. Courtis would ask, "Well, Mrs. Runnalls, and how many pounds does *your* baby weigh?" "But when Allie kept on growing," Aunt Ruth said, "she shut up." Then there was their brother Bill, who had Parkinson's. "They were a queer family," said Aunt Ruth; "there was something strange about every one of them."

Our parents' deteriorating health

Except for the brief period in her life before she was diagnosed with diabetes, our mother had never weighed more than one hundred pounds, but by the fall of 1979 she was down to seventy-five pounds, and was feeling very weak. Once again she needed an adjustment of the amount of insulin she was taking. Dr. Murphy also told her that she had osteoporosis, so that she had to be very careful walking or going up and down stairs: a fall could easily result in broken bones.

Though my parents made an effort not to talk about their aches and pains when we were visiting, their symptoms became increasingly hard to ignore. One Sunday in February 1981, we found Dad with one leg painfully swollen. Mum was trying to persuade him to see the doctor. He finally did, the next day, and Mum telephoned, almost in tears, with the diagnosis: "Dad has congestive heart failure," she said. Dr. Murphy admitted him to hospital the following day, and I picked up Aunt Ruth in Strathroy and drove her to Sarnia: she had offered to stay with Mum, and that relieved me immensely. Dad's condition on admittance was alarming: his legs and feet and belly were all seriously swollen; his breathing was quick and shallow; and he was out of breath just walking to the bathroom. When Dad was settled, I was able to have a private conversation with Dr. Murphy. He said that Dad had probably had heart disease for twenty years, but it did not become apparent until 1968; he has been doing very well since then; and his present condition was the usual development in a man seventy-eight years old. "He should be out of hospital in three or four days," Dr. Murphy said, and he was—now with four kinds of pills and with the promise of a V.O.N. checking on him every few days.

When I was taking Aunt Ruth back to Strathroy, I asked her if Mum had fussed a lot. "She always was a fusser," Aunt Ruth said, "but now she's ten times worse." But Aunt Ruth was level-headed and didn't mind. "Ches always got mad if I fussed," she said, "so I soon got over that."

My mother's fall and hospitalization

It was a Saturday night, 29 August 1981, just before supper: my mother was in the kitchen, reached for something, missed, and went down on the floor. She knew she had a broken bone, and thought it was her hip. She had just been ready for her insulin and the food she ate immediately after the injection and, worried about not being able to keep to her schedule, she insisted on having both before they called an ambulance, which took her to St. Joseph's Hospital. X-rays revealed that she did not have a broken hip, but a cracked pelvis: cracked on both sides, with a crack in her hip as well. A broken hip would have required surgery, but a cracked pelvis did not. She was told that she would be in hospital for four to six weeks, and physiotherapy would be a major part of her treatment.

But my mother, who was only too well aware that a fall of the sort she had had was a harbinger of death, had resigned herself to what she regarded as the inevitable, and did not expect to be able to return home. Though her rehabilitation was progressing, she would likely have to use a walker, and would not be able to cope with stairs. That made a return to 1267 Webster Drive problematic: the house was a split level, and four floors meant always having to go up or down flights of stairs. She thought that she and my father ought to go into Strathmere Lodge. A better idea, I thought, was one of the senior citizens' apartments attached to the North Lambton Rest Home in Forest. Dad had been on the Home's building committee; the administrator, George Maybury, had known my parents since his first appointment there in 1970; and George told Dad that an apartment would be ready any time he wanted one.

But Dad came to realize that Mum was going to need long-term care, and he knew that he could not provide it. He was also determined to stay with her, wherever she ended up: one gets married for companionship, he said to me, and he took seriously his wedding vows, "to love and to cherish, till death us do part": that meant, in Dad's practical way of looking at things, "looking after her" (his words) as long as they were alive. He did not like living on his own in the house on Webster Drive, and while he cooked for himself, he was, he said "awful lonesome." Meanwhile, my mother told me that she was trying to answer the question, "What did I ever do to deserve this?" She seemed to think she was being punished for sins, and I got angry with her.

Going into a Home together seemed the best option. But my mother complicated matters by insisting she was not ready to leave the hospital: she would be quite happy to be looked after there for the rest of her life; and she kept telling me about another woman who had been there for two years because "they won't let her go home." But in fact St. Joseph's was not prepared to keep my mother for much longer, and had been phoning Dad to ask about his plans.

His plans were to go into the North Lambton Rest Home, and he was anxious to make the move "before the snow flies." In mid-November my father secured a double room in the Home. There was a waiting list for accommodation, but George Maybury credited my father with getting him the job as chief administrator, and he gave my parents preference—a decision for which my father was profoundly grateful. Dad could then go ahead and make preparations for the move: he got clothing together; he decided on the three pieces of furniture they could take—a chair, a chest of drawers, and the television set—and got them ready for the truck the Home would send to Sarnia to pick them up. My mother would be taken to Forest by ambulance. The actual move was on Thursday, 19 November, a gray day with a cold drizzle in the air.

The move was a major change for both our parents. I helped them unpack, hang up clothes in closets, and put things away. The housekeeper came in and introduced herself. Others came and marked each item of clothing for the laundry. As I was leaving in the late afternoon, I could smell the odours of supper being cooked, and there was a warm and cosy feeling about the place. Mum had wanted to go into Strathmere but, Dad said, "this is much nicer." And Dad himself was immensely relieved: "now," he said, "if one of us goes, the other will be looked after."

Two weeks after the move, my father had a stroke. It was not a major one, but he blacked out and slumped down; his left arm and leg and the left side of his face were numb: numb, but not paralysed. Mrs. Boomer, the head nurse in the Home, said the timing of the stroke fell into a pattern they were familiar with: when Dad was in Sarnia he couldn't allow himself to get sick, but once settled in Forest all the tension and anxiety within him could finally manifest itself. Aunt Eleanor's note with their Christmas card said it best: "Ruth phoned us on Sunday to tell us about your Dad. We were really sorry. We didn't think he looked good when we saw him in Sarnia in November—he was really worn out looking after himself and going to the hospital every day."

The stroke was a blow to my father's independence. He could no longer drive the car—he had been going downtown in Forest and back and forth to Sarnia—and one of the first things he did after the stroke was to sell the Buick back to Wallis's. He got around now with a walker, and at the end of the month felt well enough to go with me to Sarnia and look after various pieces of business he had been worrying about. But getting around was not easy: our driveway on Webster Drive was clogged with snow, and he had to negotiate snow banks and icy sidewalks to reach the Bank of Commerce downtown.

The last days

Toward the end of January 1982, my mother's condition was deteriorating: fluid was accumulating in her limbs and around her heart, and she was panting. On the morning of Tuesday, 26 January, the doctor saw her and hospitalized her immediately. I offered to drive Dad to Sarnia, but he said a nurse from the Home was going that evening, and would take him. Later in the week, Dad and I did go to Sarnia, and we planned to go again on Sunday the 31st, with Marjorie, who would come up on the train from Toronto.

But on Sunday morning Arlene stuck her head in the dressing room while I was shaving. "They're predicting a bad storm," she said, "and saying it could be the worst this winter." I cursed the weather, thought about how anxious Dad was to get to Sarnia, and cursed myself for not going in the few hours when the sky had been clear the previous afternoon. Arlene phoned Marjorie, and got her just as she was leaving for Union Station. And I phoned Dad. He said it was already snowing heavily in Forest. In London, things got steadily worse throughout the day. A high wind from the east drove snow before it; all day the whiteness streamed past our windows and swirled around the house; all day we could hear the hiss and sough of the wind.

So it was not until Monday evening that I could get to Forest and go on to Sarnia with Dad. Mum was hooked up to tubes and monitors and oxygen, and though her breathing was shallow, she did brighten up a bit while we were there and talked to us.

What I did not tell Dad (and I think now I ought to have) was that Mrs. Boomer had telephoned that afternoon to say that the hospital had called her about Mum, with the message that "her condition is deteriorating." Because the next day—Tuesday, 2 February—we were awakened by the telephone about 3:30 in the morning. It was St. Joseph's Hospital. I heard only "Mrs. Alice Hair" and "she passed away a few minutes ago."

I telephoned Marjorie, but I didn't want to waken Dad: he needed his sleep. Instead I shaved and dressed and got in the car and drove through the sub-zero darkness of a winter morning to Forest. There I went quietly into Dad's room several times. Finally, about 6:30, he wakened and saw me. "What are you doing here, Don?" I sat on the edge of his bed and said, "Mum died this morning."

The next two and one-half days were difficult ones, and they were complicated by bad weather. Marjorie arrived from Toronto about mid-afternoon on the 2nd, and we drove with Dad to Watford to make the arrangements at Harper's. Visitation was on Wednesday afternoon. Snow was already falling when I left London, and the weather worsened as the afternoon wore on. Still, many people came: neigbours from Watford and the Twelfth Line, people from Walnut Church, relatives and friends and many who had worked with Dad and Mum at the county buildings. I was worried about getting back to Forest, but it was late afternoon by the time we got away from Harper's. Visibility was poor out on the highway; there was a whiteout that left me shaken; but on Highway 21 we were heading directly into the north wind, so there were no drifts to cut through and visibility was better. Though we had scheduled a visitation for the evening as well, there was no question of our getting back to Watford. Marjorie and I both stayed in the Home overnight.

In the meantime, Mike and the boys were coming on the train from Toronto, and Marjorie had intended to meet them in Strathroy. In desperation, she telephoned the town police, who picked them up and took them to a motel. The station in Strathroy had been closed, and the three of them had been standing in the lee of one end of it, as much as possible out of the wind and the snow.

The next morning—the day of the funeral—was bitterly cold and frosty, but it was clear and calm. I drove Marjorie over to Watford and dug her car out of the snow. Then I returned to Forest and, a few hours later, brought Dad to Watford. When we pulled up outside the funeral home, he saw the hearse parked on the side street, and had to sit for a few minutes to control his grief.

The minister was our parents' minister from Grace United Church in Sarnia, Douglas Greenough. The pallbearers—Mum herself had picked them out—were Harold Hair, Stan Robinson, Bill McRorie, Ralph Runnalls, Lorne Edgar, and Gerry Herbert. The cemetery in Strathroy was covered with deep snow. We watched the coffin carried to the grave and set on the straps that would lower it into the ground. The air was bitterly cold. So we stood, Marjorie and I on either side of Dad, and Arlene and Mike and the boys with us, staring at the polished wood and the pink-and-white flowers of Dad's arrangement on top, while the minister said the words of committal. When Dad and I were at last out of the cold and in my car, he said to me, "We'll never see her again." It was difficult to get away. The minister's car got stuck in the snow, and the rest of us had to turn around. That meant having to pass the grave again, with the coffin still above the ground and no one, apparently, around. "I hate to leave her there," Dad said.

I had arranged for a gathering in the United Church in Strathroy, and about thirty-five people sat down there for sandwiches and coffee. My chief worry was Aunt Ruth. She had not been at the funeral nor the reception, and I said we had better drive round to the house. There we could see her sitting in the front window. "Donald," she said when we went in, "everything's gone wrong today, just everything!" Our cousins Jim and Arlene Bond were to drive up from Woodstock and take Aunt Ruth to the funeral, but their car broke down. Then Aunt Ruth thought she would call a taxi and go to the church—but the snow plough came along her street and filled in the end of her driveway to such a depth that she could not climb over it. A couple of weeks later Aunt Ruth told me that she "just wasn't thinking on the day of the funeral." She wanted to know how Mum looked. "Like Grammie Runnalls," I said. "She always did," she said.

That night I stayed in the Home with Dad. He wanted to talk, and told me story after story, about neighbours and relatives, deaths and births, prices for wheat and cars. Most of the stories I had heard before, but I listened again, thinking I must remember everything. He wasn't ready to sleep, and he was still talking long after lights out.

A difficult few months

My mother's death affected my father both physically and psychologically. At the end of February he picked up a virus; his high temperature brought on heart failure; and he was taken to the cardiac unit of the hospital in Sarnia. I asked Dr. Bartlett—he was the doctor in Forest whose practice included the Home—if Dad would pull out of this latest assault on his heart, and Bartlett said, "He's on the edge and could go either way." This time he did pull out of it and was back in the Home at the beginning of March. But he was "not as good as we would like him to be," Mrs. Boomer said. "Should I take him out today?" I asked her on one of my visits. "Yes, if he wants to go," she said; "sometimes people say of old people, 'Oh, he's too sick to go out,' but I say, 'What are you saving them for?'"

But there was a problem in addition to his heart. "He is very depressed," Mrs. Boomer told me; "he gets teary, and says he wishes it were all over, that he wants to 'be with Al.'" One of the other nurses urged me to get another medical opinion, preferably from a heart specialist: "He may tell you that there is nothing to be done," she said, "but at least you will know that you have done everything you can do." So I talked to Dr. Bartlett. He said that he couldn't treat depression, and his treatment of Dad's heart was pretty standard, but he did agree to refer Dad to a cardiologist at University Hospital in London. I drove him to the hospital on the 5th of May; there he was seen by a Dr. Jablonsky and had an echo-cardiograph, which Dad described as "making a movie of my heart." The test, Dr. Jablonsky told me privately, showed that all the muscles of Dad's heart were very weak and were functioning in an irregular way; his "nerves" were a symptom of heart failure. "How much longer has he got?" I asked. "I wouldn't like to say," Jablonsky replied; "if I did, I would be wrong." But Dad could go on for some time yet, Jablonsky said, and he would be discharged from hospital in a few days—though a psychiatrist might want to try some further treatment for his depression. Dad had already been started on an anti-anxiety drug called maprotiline, and a psychiatrist, a Dr. Morrison, said he would like to monitor the effects of the drug over a two-week period: would I agree? I talked this over with Dad and he said he was willing: "what else is there to do?" But I had misgivings about that decision: for Dad was moved to the psychiatric unit on the tenth floor; the move, which put him among patients with various mental problems, increased his anxiety; and too much of the drug left him groggy and indifferent. Marjorie saw him and was appalled at his appearance and upset by his surroundings. We conferred; I talked to Morrison, told him that Dad was "intensely unhappy" in the hospital, and said I was taking him back to the Home. That was against the doctor's advice: I had to sign legal forms absolving the hospital of responsibility.

So I drove Dad back to Forest on a warm sunny morning in May. He looked at the fields and commented on the seeding in progress. He insisted on walking into the Home, though he had to lean on my arm, and when the residents and staff greeted him, he said "I'm awful weak." I had been aware of a fact that I didn't want to admit fully to myself: that Dad had expected to die in University Hospital, so his return to the Home was as if he were coming back from the dead. Mrs. Boomer said to me that the hospital experience was probably good for him: he might realize the Home was not such a bad place. And so it proved to be.

Alice Cavanaugh, Dad's first cousin, had driven Aunt Ruth to London, and the two of them had gone up to the 10th floor and were upset at Dad's appearance and his drugged responses. "Well really, Donald," Aunt Ruth said, "this is the worst mess you've ever got into." "There's nothing wrong with his head," she went on; "he's just old."

Clearing out and selling the house in Sarnia

Long before my parents fell seriously ill, they were thinking about our having to clear out the house after they were gone. Their concern was with things: "I hope you and Marjorie won't quarrel over our things," my mother said to me on a number of occasions. Marjorie was to have the good dishes and the piano; I was to have the organ and the stamp collection. They destroyed letters, assuming (as did many people in Souwesto) that the personal revelation was to be avoided as somehow shameful; and they started giving us things: a Toby jug that came from Aunt Agnes and sat on the buffet at Grandad Runnalls'; a bowl that had been a gift from Uncle Oscar and Aunt Jenny (they had been very good to her, my mother said, when she was first married). It was the well-known willow pattern, blue and white, with the date 1795 on the bottom. The things all had some kind of tie or association: on one visit my mother took me round cabinets and showed me various pieces and told me where they came from: old dinner plates from Aunt Lizzie Bateman; Grammie Runnalls' sugar bowl; Grandad's shaving mug; antique egg cups.

Our mother kept practically everything. When my sister and I started going through the house after our mother's death, we discovered notes on almost every item, telling us who was to have it and where it came from. Every dish and quilt and blanket had a note, Marjorie said, and there were notes in books as well. A typical one was in Grandad Runnalls's Bible, and it was addressed to me: "Grandad's Bible. It is well worn. He used to read it every Sunday morning. I liked the part at the back where you could look up almost anything. I wanted you to have it." And in my mother's copy of a childhood favourite, *Alice in Wonderland*, was a little slip on which she had written "This book for Don / Mom."

Marjorie and Arlene spend several tiring days in Sarnia sorting and packing and discarding, and I cleared Dad's tools out of the basement. By mid-June everything was ready; we made arrangements with Bowley's, whose business in London was the auctioning of estates, to take everything out of the house—a job that took two men four hours to do—and truck it back to London. Bowley's held regular auction sales, but I did not go on 21 July when our parents' things were disposed of: the associations were more than I wanted to cope with. In the meantime, Marjorie and Arlene cleaned the now-empty house and readied it for sale. Various real estate agents in Sarnia had written to ask about listing the house, and Dad and I, after looking over those letters, decided to go with a woman from Royal Trust named Stella Milway. She went through the house with us, said it had obviously been well looked after, and listed it for $76,900. That was at the end of June. A couple of weeks later Milway held an open house, to which only four couples came. For the economy in 1982 was bad; inflation and unemployment were worrying; high interest rates on mortgages kept houses from selling. Milway advised us about dropping the price. In mid-September a couple from Bright's Grove made an offer of $60,000, conditional on their selling their own house. Dad agreed, but nothing happened, and the situation dragged on into October. On the 20th Milway phoned to say she had another offer, this one from a man named Saaman, for $61,000 cash, with no conditions. Milway suggested we counter with $62,000; Saaman agreed; Milway gave the Bright's Grove couple forty-eight hours to match the offer; and they didn't respond. So the house was sold; Dad signed the papers on 22 October, for a closing on 2 November. We were in Sarnia on the 22nd, sitting in my Volvo in the driveway of the Webster Drive house, with my father and Milway in the front seat and I in the back. Dad balanced the forms on Stella's purse and signed them; Stella posted a "SOLD" sign over the "For Sale" sign on the front lawn, and shook hands with Dad, who was a bit teary. Stella said something about this having been a happy house.

The plot in Strathroy Cemetery

One day in early June, Dad and I drove to Strathroy to see Aunt Ruth, and when we left Drury Lane Dad said that perhaps we should go to the cemetery. He talked about seeding the plot and having the date carved on the stone, and I had come prepared. I raked away the evergreen needles, scattered grass seed, and pulled the light soil over it. Dad walked around a bit and didn't say much, but he was teary when we got back in the car and said, "I didn't think it would be so hard."

Being with Dad

After his stay in University Hospital, Dad's outlook and interest in life slowly improved, and he looked forward keenly to the visits from Marjorie and me. Marjorie made the three-hour drive from Toronto to Sarnia every week, and I went to Forest every Thursday. He knew that I usually telephoned on Tuesday nights, but one Tuesday he phoned Arlene and me, because he thought he had heard his telephone ringing and had missed our call. There was a Thursday when he phoned Arlene to see if I was coming, only to see me drive into the parking lot at the Home while he was talking.

My Thursday visits started to fall into a predictable pattern: I would arrive in Forest in the early afternoon; Dad and I would go out in the car, and drive some distance east or south or north—to Watford and Alvinston and Petrolia, along the Twelfth Line and the Tenth Line, to Napier and Inwood, Wallaceburg and Chatham, to Point Edward and Grand Bend, Bayfield and Goderich—and then have dinner at some restaurant along our route. We had a couple of good meals in the Fireside Inn in Thedford, surprisingly good for a small village, but his favourite place to eat was Swiss Chalet on the London Road in Sarnia. He always ordered the same thing, the barbecued chicken dinner, and he always had in his wallet the exact amount of money to pay for our meal and a tip. When we returned to the Home (where Dad now had a private room), I would stay for the evening, until the staff served tea and toast and cookies; then he would turn in for the night and I would go back to London. I had always loved my father, but I think he and I were closer during this time than we had been at any other period in our lives.

Dad's eightieth birthday fell on 21 July 1982, and I brought him into London for a fine meal that Arlene had prepared. She put a lighted candle in Dad's piece of lemon torte.

More stories from my father

One was a funny story about getting tipsy on dandelion wine. During a threshing on a hot day, he drank a tumblerful straight down, because it tasted so good and refreshing. And he had stories about young men just out from England, who knew nothing about farming. Aunt Arabella Hair (Uncle Jim's wife) had a hired man who was English, and she sent him out into the garden to get a saucepanful of potatoes. He came back after some time and said, "Mrs. Hair, I've looked everywhere, and there are no potatoes on any plant in that garden." He told me again the story of harvesting oats and the runaway team and the wrecked binder: in this telling the culprit was not Albert Laferriere but a young Englishman. Dad was resourceful after the accident: he bought an old binder at a sale, used its frame and the gears from the wrecked binder, and put together one good machine. For like many men of his generation, he was practically- and mechanically-minded, and did repairs and maintenance on his machinery himself.

Dad had a slightly risqué story about a Watford family named Chambers, who ran a mill. When the husband died, the wife carried on the business. She kept her money in a petticoat pocket, and when she made change, she would pull up two or three layers of outer skirts to get at the pocket. There was much joking around town about Mrs. Chambers hauling up her skirts.

Dad had more stories about early days in Watford. Before the Hairs had a car, going to Watford meant driving a team of horses into town, where, for about twenty-five cents, they would be fed and watered at a livery stable. In Watford, Dad said, he always left the team in "Roches' shed" (the Roches had a hotel on the main street). On one occasion, Dad left the team outside a store without tying them up. When he came out, the team was gone. He went down the street and found them where they always went, at Roches'. "You never had to touch the reins for the team to turn off the Nauvoo onto the 12th line," Dad said; "they always turned themselves."

On one of my Thursday visits, we drove as far as Chatham, and on the return came through Kent Bridge and Louisville, and Dad told me a story about the days when he was "going with" Mum. Dad's cousin Norval Woods, who was a United Church minister, had a church just south of Dresden as part of his pastoral charge. The church had a fowl supper, and asked Dad to sing at it. He and Mum were not yet married, but Mum was playing the piano for him on such occasions. She came up from Caradoc on the bus; Dad met her at "the Fourth Line corner," drove her to Dresden, and then brought her back to Uncle Ches and Aunt Ruth's farm, where she stayed overnight.

The 1982 Warden's Banquet

In the fall of 1982 my father began to take a great interest in activities at the Home and in Forest, running the tuck shop from time to time, going on an expedition to Simpson-Sears in Sarnia, and speaking to children at the public school in Forest about Christmases he remembered. He was delighted to receive an invitation to the Warden's Banquet—he and my mother had probably not missed one in forty years—and I said that I would take him. It was on a Friday night, the 12th of November.

The 1982 warden, Donald Elliott, was from Euphemia, a township in the far southeast corner of the county, so the banquet was in the Community Hall in Florence. The village is only four miles from the Mawlam farm where Grandad Runnalls worked as a young man, and the area had never lost its rural character; Florence itself seemed not to have changed much from the 1880s, when Grandad gave the place as his address. Nor had the arrangements for the banquet changed much either.

George Maybury, the administrator of the North Lambton Home, met us at the door and escorted us past a crowd of people into the hall, and to our places. We were seated across from Ronn and Vicki Dodge (he was the mayor of Forest at the time) and

Marceil Saddy (the mayor of Sarnia). A great many people came up to speak to Dad, including Lorne and Rita Henderson—he was now a cabinet minister and was there with his Toronto staff and his chauffeur, all of whom he introduced. The Warden and the head table were piped into the hall, and the pipers and drummers turned out to be the warden's sons—a nice touch, I thought. The ladies of nearby Shetland United Church served the meal—it was roast turkey and plum pudding—and it was good. The turkey was passed on great platters, and the potatoes and vegetables and stuffing in steaming bowls. Afterwards, there were a series of toasts, introductions, and speeches; mayors, members of parliament, Lorne Henderson, visiting officials, and those aspiring to be warden all had to have their say. Dad was pleased that he was introduced, and asked to "stand and be recognized." When all this was over, there was a general clatter as the tables were cleared away for dancing. Dad chatted with a great many people; George Maybury looked after him while I got the car; and so we drove, through darkness and snow squalls, back to Forest. Dad was tired, but he had enjoyed himself tremendously.

Ontario Gothic

One day in late December, after Dad and I had been to Sarnia and the Swiss Chalet, I stayed on at the Home during the evening to chat with Dad and to have tea before going back to London. That was when one of the nurses' aides sat down with us. She was a good-hearted soul, but loud and talkative, cheerfully telling us all sorts of depressing things about the other residents: who had cancer, and who had Alzheimer's, and whose wife died. Then the weather (December had been mild and wet): "They say a green Christmas means a full cemetery in the spring." She turned to Dad and repeated the saying in a loud voice: "Have you ever heard that?" she asked. Dad shook his head. She talked about last winter and all the snow, "like when your Mum died." "It'll soon be a year," she said. Thank goodness Dad's hearing was poor enough that he could make out less than half of what she said.

When Dad and I had finished our tea, an old couple who rarely said a word—I don't even know their names—got up to return to their room. One of the residents, a Mrs. Lougheed, who was sitting across from me, said of the husband, "He has a beautiful voice" and asked him to sing. And this old man burst into a funny song about a man and a maid, courtship and mothers-in-law, with comic rhymes and witty wordplay.

Bill McRorie retires

Bill was Dad's successor as clerk-treasurer; he retired at the beginning of January 1983; and Dad was invited to the retirement gathering, which was in the Legion Hall in Petrolia. As he had at the Warden's Banquet, Dad enjoyed himself: he had long talks with ex-wardens like Cecil Tinney, Duffy Atkin, and Stan Campbell. In his speech Bill mentioned Dad, and Lorne Edgar, who also spoke, said Bill had had a good teacher "from Brooke Township." Dad was too hard of hearing to pick up these remarks, but he was pleased when I repeated them to him. Dad said it was "quite something" that Bill's predecessor should be at his retirement party.

Bill's successor was Wayne Kloske, and he, as I pointed out to Dad, was the first clerk-treasurer not to have served as a county councillor. He had worked in a bank and then in the Regional Assessment Office, and had a more professional preparation for the job than his predecessors.

The first few months of 1983

By the end of January 1983 Dad was not quite as good as he had been. The sight in his left eye was blurry; he wouldn't get new teeth "because I am old"; his hearing was getting worse; and when asked if he wanted to go for a drive, he would agree but say "Not too far." He tired easily.

At the beginning of April, Dad was invited to the banquet of the Lambton County Municipal Association. It was in the Legion in Petrolia, and I said that I would take him. The Association had been founded by W. R. Stephenson, who ran the business school in Sarnia, and Dad had a funny story about him: he forgot to order the dinner for an earlier banquet and made a frantic appeal to a Sarnia hotel, which managed to produce a meal in an hour and a half. Dad—and this was something I didn't know—was honorary president of the Association, so he was introduced, and mentioned by several speakers. After the roast beef, Lorne Henderson presented plaques to various worthy people; officers and guests were introduced; and Claude Bennett, MLA for Ottawa and Minister of Municipal Affairs and Housing in Bill Davis's cabinet, spoke. I cringed at the joke he made about a sign he had seen on his way to Petrolia ("Sheep manure for sale"), and I wondered about a politician who prefaced his statements with the assurance that "I have to say to you very honestly and very sincerely...."

In mid-April, Dad was back in the hospital in Sarnia, with a suspected "deep vein thrombosis"—a blood clot—in his right leg; it turned out that he was suffering from gout. But on two of the days when he was in hospital and having a series of tests, Dr. Bartlett told me, he was "in and out of heart failure." Once again he pulled through, and once again he was back in the Home. We resumed our weekly drives, though we did not go far, and Dad brightened a bit when he was out in the car. On the Thursday before the Victoria Day weekend, he had a birthday card ready for Arlene. "Don't lose it," he said to me; "it's got cash in it."

The last weeks and days

On Victoria Day (Monday 23 May) Marjorie called from Sarnia: Dad was in the Intensive Care Unit of St. Joseph's Hospital, and the news was not good: the doctor—a Dr. Dunleavy—said that he had had "a massive heart attack" and would not survive for more than twenty-four hours. I got in the car and drove immediately to Sarnia, where I found Dad with an oxygen mask over mouth and nose, tubes in both arms, a catheter, and a monitor above his head where numbers flashed his blood pressure and squiggly lines traced his heartbeat. He was intensely restless. My sister and I stayed with him until well after midnight, when nurses suggested we go to the little waiting room down the hall. But all we could do there was doze fitfully, and I was awake every time I heard footsteps in the corridor. In the early morning we returned to Dad's bedside. He had had a rough night, but he was quiet now and talked to us a bit. "I'm dying, aren't I?" he asked me. I hesitated for just a couple of seconds before saying, as gently as I could, "Yes, Dad."

But he was better, and quieter, and stable. Marjorie decided to return to Toronto, and I went back to London. The next day—Wednesday—the hospital telephoned to say that Dad was going downhill, and I had another anxiety-filled drive to Sarnia, through rain and under gray skies. But by the time I reached his room, he was rallying. I talked to Dr. Dunleavy on the phone. He said that the electrocardiogram showed old damage that had gradually worsened, and I said, "What can you tell me?" "I know what you are asking," he said; "he will not leave the hospital alive. But I don't know why the nurses phoned you. He came through Monday, and it will be a much slower process than I at first expected."

Dr. Dunleavy was right. In spite of occasional alarms and setbacks, Dad was eating again; and in spite of confusion, he responded to the sound of my voice, though his conversation often did not make sense. He wanted me to look after "that business," to watch out for "the Wyoming bunch," and to "go to the desk and sign in." "I'm not dead yet," he said. And indeed he did go on, from day to day and week to week.

A month after the Victoria Day when Dad had been admitted to hospital, one of the nurses asked me to stay in the evening: the palliative care group wanted to talk to me. They were three: nursing supervisor Nancy Major, Dr. Linda Bowring, and nurse Carol Power. I didn't even know that the hospital had a palliative care unit, but it turned out to be wonderful, not only in dealing with and relieving Dad's discomforts and anxieties, but in working with me and Marjorie in determining the care he was to receive: his likes and dislikes in food, the handling of his incontinence, the hiring of a private nurse to be with him during the night; the administering of small doses of morphine to relieve the suffering I thought he was feeling; and things he would like in his room, such as the clock-radio Marj and Mike had given him, with its easy-to-read numbers, and the Arlene Lundgren painting of our family that had been at the foot of his bed in the Home.

On the first of July, the university held a special convocation to give Prince Philip an honorary degree, and I was Chief Usher for the ceremony. Though I had made arrangements in case I was called to Sarnia, I worried anyway, and was mightily relieved when the day went off without a conflict of responsibilities.

On Wednesday, 6 July the hospital called again: Nancy Major wanted me alerted to Dad's worsening condition. I packed a bag and left at once for Sarnia, intending to be with him for as long as necessary. I found him not visibly worse, but Nancy Major said his vital signs could hardly be detected: "I cannot tell you how much time," she said. "How much time" turned out to be several days, on each of which we thought he would not survive the following night. Marjorie came on Thursday and brought the boys with her. While they were having lunch in the cafeteria and listening to doctors being paged, Derek said, "Grandad can't be as sick as those people. They haven't called his number yet." Marjorie came again on Saturday morning (9 July) and we sat talking by Dad's bedside. He was breathing gently now, drawing one quiet breath after another, when the breaths stopped altogether. Nurses came in and one took his blood pressure. "He's gone," she said. The time was ten minutes after eleven.

I have always found some comfort in the fact that Dad died peacefully, and if he could still hear anything, the last thing he heard was the sound of his children's voices. "The processes of the earth"—that was the phrase Dr. Bowring used when she confirmed the death. Yes, I thought, and July, when the orange lilies were in bloom, was Dad's month: the month of his birth and the month of his death. He was two weeks short of his eighty-first birthday.

We had one visitation, in the evening of Monday 11 July, and for three and one-half hours Marjorie and I, and Arlene and Mike, greeted people and heard their expressions of sympathy. Friends of ours from London appeared, but most of the crowd came because of their links with Dad: old neighbours from the Twelfth Line, former members of Walnut Church, members of council and former wardens, county officials and staff, our cousins from Woodstock, and Nancy Major from palliative care. The funeral was the next afternoon. Mr. Greenough, our parents' minister, was away; the service was taken by Earl Burr from Parker Street United Church in Sarnia. He didn't know Dad, and could only read and preach from the usual texts. "Impersonal," Marjorie said.

Arlene and I followed the hearse, with Marj and Mike and the boys in the car behind us, and Aunt Ruth and Alice Cavanaugh in the third car. We set out slowly through the streets of Watford, and then went a little faster as we turned east on the Fourth Line. And so across the hot summer landscape, the trees and the fields of grain shimmering in the heat, the orange lilies in full bloom by the roadside, the sky a pale expanse of blue. At the cemetery in Strathroy, the procession entered the gates and passed slowly under the massive evergreens and back to the family plot. We stood and watched the pallbearers carry the coffin to the grave (the bearers were Lorne Edgar, Bill McRorie, Jim Clarke, Harold Hair, George Maybury, and Lloyd Pole); flowers were set about; and we gathered round for the committal service.

Back at the Strathroy United Church, the ladies had set out plates of fresh sandwiches, and cakes and squares of various kinds, and tea and coffee. The gathering was a large one, and I tried to speak to everyone there. But that evening, a sense of emptiness overwhelmed me. So many of my thoughts had been bound up with Dad's care over the past two years—and now I did not have him to look after any more.

Epilogue

Weeks later, in mid-August, Aunt Ruth asked me to drive her out to the cemetery. She wanted to visit Uncle Ches's grave, and she pointed out nearby graves: the Frys, and Siftons, Alex McNeils and Uncle Ches's brother Sam and his first wife, who had died of cancer sixty years earlier. Then we went to look at my parents' graves, and stood talking there for a while. She reminded me of Dad's old disappointment with that plot: it is too near the caretaker's building, and the spruce trees are so big that no grass will grow. Dad apparently thought of moving his father's grave, but there was no outer covering for the coffin—and I remember a caretaker silently shaking his head when Dad asked him about a removal.

I asked Aunt Ruth what she remembered about my Grandfather Hair's death. Dad told me little about it, and I didn't ask him because I thought the recollection would be painful. Aunt Ruth began by telling me about meeting Dad and his father for the first time, just after she was married in 1930, when the two of them walked over to McLellans' after chores. "Your grandfather was not a big man," she said; "he was more like Harold, not tall. Everyone liked him." He was into cattle in a big way, and showed them in Toronto. "What happened at the end?" I asked. "He had a spell," she said, "and went wrong in his head. I don't think he was sick more than a week before he died." Anyway, Aunt Ruth continued, "In those days, you could have a specialist come out from London for twenty dollars. So this man came out. Ches and I went over and sat in the back kitchen. The doctor came out, and your Dad paid him the twenty dollars—a lot of money in those days—and Ches asked, 'What is the news?' 'Not good,' your Dad said; 'there's not much hope for Dad.' And your Dad sat down in a chair and cried."

So I and my aunt, white-haired and slightly stooped, wandered among the gravestones, on the dry grass, the sky overcast with August haze and the air hot and humid, and she said, "It's sad, Donald; it's awful sad."

Nearly thirty years after that summer scene, I was listening to CBC's Radio One, which was re-broadcasting a BBC program, and I heard this sentence: "Perhaps, when we die, we all become a story, told and retold by those who love us." And I thought, yes, for my parents, this is that story.

REFERENCES AND SOURCES

Akenson, Donald Harman. "Foreword." *Irish Migrants in the Canadas: A New Approach*, by Bruce S. Elliott. Kingston and Montreal: McGill-Queen's University Press, 1988. xiii-xiv.
Allen, Thomas B. *Tories: Fighting for the King in America's First Civil War.* 2010. New York: Harper, 2011.
Anderson, Clara E. A Character Sketch Entertainment for Young People's Societies, Bible Classes and Other Church Organizations entitled *The Minister's Bride*. 1913. Ottawa: Printed by James Hope & Sons, [no date].
Atwood, Margaret. *The Journals of Susanna Moodie*. Toronto: Oxford University Press, 1970.
Austin, Alvyn J. "Mackay, George Leslie." *Dictionary of Canadian Biography* 13: 653-5.
Badgley, Kerry A. *Ringing in the Common Love of Good: The United Farmers of Ontario, 1914-1926*. Montreal and Kingston: McGill-Queen's University Press, 2000.
Bartlett, Reverend L[eonard]. *"Uncle Joe Little": Life and Memoirs of Joseph Russell Little*. Toronto: William Briggs, 1903.
Bateman, Charles Edward. Estate file G.B. Folio 51, Register 1922-515, microfilm number 15941, Archives of Ontario.
Beattie, Kim. *48th Highlanders of Canada 1891-1923*. [Toronto:] 48th Highlanders of Canada, 1932.
Beers, J.H., and Co. *Commemorative Biographical Record of the County of Lambton, Ontario: containing biographical sketches of prominent and representative citizens and many of the early settled families*. Compiled by J.H. Beers & Co. Toronto, 1906.
Belden's illustrated historical atlas of the County of Lambton, Ontario 1880. Edited and published with additions by Edward Phelps. Sarnia, Ontario: E. Phelps, 1973.
Berger, Carl. *The Sense of Power : Studies in the Ideas of Canadian Imperialism, 1867-1914*. Toronto : University of Toronto Press, 1970.
Berton, Pierre. *Vimy,* Toronto: McClelland & Stewart, 1986.
Bird, Kym. *Redressing the Past: The Politics of Early English-Canadian Women's Drama, 1880-1920*. Montreal & Kingston: McGill-Queen's University Press, 2004.
Black, George F. *The Surnames of Scotland: their origin, meaning and history*. New York: New York Public Library, 1946.
Brouwer, Ruth Compton. *New Women for God: Canadian Presbyterian Women and India Missions 1876-1914*. Toronto: University of Toronto Press, 1990.
Butchart, Reuben. *The Disciples of Christ in Canada since 1830*. Toronto: Churches of Christ (Disciples), 1949.

Cahill, Barry. "Clarence Dunlop Mackinnon." *Dictionary of Canadian Biography* 16 (1931-1940).
Callaghan, Morley. *More Joy in Heaven*. 1937. Introduction by Hugo McPherson. New Canadian Library 17. Toronto: McClelland & Stewart, 1960.
Campbell, D. J. "The Settlers of Lobo Township," *London and Middlesex Historical Society* 8 (1917): 36-42. Campbell presented this paper to the society on 19 April 1904. See also "The Highland Pioneers of the County of Middlesex," *Ontario Historical Society Papers and Records*, 9 (Toronto 1910): 26-32. This paper may be by H. McColl of Strathroy.
Campbell, Reverend Ken. *The descendants of Duncan "the Laird" Campbell and his wife Euphemia "Fish" Campbell from Kilmichael-Glassary, Argyllshire, Scotland, 1831-1981*. Glencoe, Ontario, 1981.
Campbell, Sara L. *Brooke Township History 1833-1933*. Alvinston, Ontario: Brooke Women's Institute, 1936.
Clark, Helen Annett Zavitz. *HAIR(E): A Story about James and Nancy (Latham) Hair(e) and their family*. 155 pp. plus index. Parkhill, Ontario: Hearts and Crafts (Lorraine E. Hodgins), 1988.
———. "England-Searson-Carter Family." Typescript. 58 single-spaced pages. May 2015.
Clark, Mona. "Fifty Years With a Twinkle in His Eye" [Norman Irvine]. *Gossip!* 27 May 1954.
Clifford, N. Keith. *The Resistance to Church Union in Canada 1904-1939*. Vancouver: University of British Columbia Press, 1985.
Cole, Nan, and Todd Braisted. On-Line Institute for Advanced Loyalist Studies. www.royalprovince.com
[Cook's Cemetery, Caradoc Township - transcriptions] "A series of cemeteries in Middlesex County, Province of Ontario, Canada. Caradoc Township." London, Ont.: London & Middlesex Co. Branch of O[ntario] G[enealogical] S[ociety], [1978-1984]. Archives and Research Collections Centre, Western University.
Cook's United Church, Caradoc. One Hundredth Anniversary 1867-1967. Booklet.
Coulter, Helen (McEvoy). "Manuscript entitled 'The History of the Schools of Caradoc Township' c. 1830-1960. Written between 1970 and 1984, it 'briefly describes the history of school sections 1 through 16.'" Archives and Research Collections Centre, Western University.
Creighton, Donald. *John A. Macdonald: The Old Chieftain*. Toronto: Macmillan, 1955.
Davis, Charles Henry Stanley. *History of Wallingford, Conn. from its Settlement in 1670 to the Present Time*. Meriden, Conn.: The Author, 1870.
[Dawn Township.] Souvenir Booklet of Oakdale 1879-1939. Prepared for Diamond Jubilee Reunion. Lambton County Archives, Wyoming, Ontario.
Delmage, Horace. "Our Bonnie Doon - A Wee Drap o' Scotland." *Gazette* (Sarnia) 12 September 1973: 34.
DesRivières, Dennis. "The Great Enniskillen Swamp: Speculation, Drainage and Settlement." *Western Ontario Historical Notes* 26 (1972): 25-35.
Drury, E.C. [Ernest Charles]. *Farmer Premier: Memoirs of the Honourable E.C. Drury*. Toronto: McClelland & Stewart, 1966.
Elliott, Bruce S. *Irish Migrants in the Canadas: A New Approach*. Kingston and Montreal: McGill-Queen's University Press; and The Institute of Irish Studies, The Queen's University of Belfast, 1988.
Foster, Reverend J. L. "Salem Church Celebrates Diamond Jubilee." *Watford Guide-Advocate*, 19 September 1924.
Frye, Northrop. *The Bush Garden: Essays on the Canadian Imagination*. Toronto: Anansi, 1971.
[Grogan, Gordon.] "Quarter Cord of Wood Paid Year's Tuition at Caradoc School Section 87 Years Ago" [A history of S.S. No. 7 Caradoc] *Strathroy Age-Dispatch* 20 April 1939.
Gurney, Lieut.Colonel Russell. *The History of the Northamptonshire Regiment, 1742-1934*. Aldershot: Gale & Polden, 1935.
Gwynne-Timothy, John R.W. *Western's First Century*. London, Ontario: The University of Western Ontario, 1978.
Hair, Alice (Runnalls). "Christmas Times Past as I Remember." Autograph MS. 11 pages. March 1979.

———. "My Home and School Years." Autograph MS, c. 1978. 12 pages.

———. The Family of Joseph Runnalls (1868-1949) and Matilda Thompson (1868-1944). [Family tree compiled by Alice (Runnalls) Hair] December 1978; updated by Donald Hair to 1995.

———. "Reminiscences of the Mt. Brydges High School during Miss Davidson's Teaching Term." *Strathroy Age-Dispatch* 13 August 1925.

[Hair family Bible.] *New Devotional and Practical Pictorial Family Bible, containing the Old and New Testaments, Apocrypha, Concordance, and Psalms in Metre ... together with Dr. Wm. Smith's Complete Dictionary of the Bible* ... Paris, Ontario: John S. Brown, 1875. Includes the marriage certificate of John Hair and Ann Carter, and "Births" listing their children.

Hair, John. "Our Neighbours." Autograph manuscript, 41 pages, typescript, 12 pages. 1979-80.

———. "Looking Back." Typescript, 5 pages. 1979-80.

———. "Some of the events and happenings in my early years." Autograph manuscript. 1978-9.

———. *History of Lambton County Officials / 125 Years / 1850 - 1975*. By Judge D. F. McWatt, John A. Huey, and John A. Hair. Sarnia, Ontario, 1975.

———. "Lambton County Buildings Opened." *Municipal World*, June 1961.

Halliday, Hugh A. *Wreck! Canada's Worst Railway Accidents*. Toronto: Robin Brass, 1997.

Hare, William. Reference number WO 97/624/55. WO [War Office] 97 Series, Soldiers Service Documents, 1760-1854. The National Archives, Kew, England.

Hatfield, Abraham. *The Hatfields of Westchester: a genealogy of the descendants of Thomas Hatfield of New Amsterdam and Mamaroneck, whose sons settled in White Plains, Westchester County, New York*. New York: New York Genealogical and Biographical Society, 1935.

Home, Myrtle E. "Historical Review of St. Andrew's Church." *Strathroy Age-Dispatch* 17 September 1936.

Irving, Washington. *The Sketch Book of Geoffrey Crayon, Gent.* Ed. Haskell Springer. *The Complete Works of Washington Irving*, vol 8. Boston: Twayne, 1978.

Jasanoff, Maya. *Liberty's Exiles: American Loyalists in the Revolutionary World*. New York: Knopf, 2011.

Johnston, William H. *A Brief History of the Descendants of the late Eliza England of Mountrath, Queen's County, Ireland*, compiled from reports made by many members of various branches of the England family, 1763-1940. Exeter, Ontario: Times-Advocate Press, 27 May 1940.

Johnston, William Victor. *Before the Age of Miracles: Memoirs of a Country Doctor*. 1972. Paperjacks. Don Mills: General Publishing, 1975.

[Lambton County.] Minutes, Reports and By-Laws of the County Council, County of Lambton.

[Lobo Township] *The Heritage of Lobo 1820-1990*. Ilderton: Lobo Township Heritage Group, 1990.

MacLysaght, Edward. *The Surnames of Ireland*. Shannon, Ireland: Irish University Press, 1969.

Manners, J[ohn] Hartley. *Peg o' my heart: a comedy in three acts*. [Canada:] 1916.

March, David. Third Avenue Methodist Church (Saskatoon) Quilt, A Canadian Red Cross Quilt. 2014. crcq.webplus.net

McCormick, Charles Howard. *Leisler's Rebellion*. New York: Garland, 1989.

[McCracken, Samuel and Maria.] "An Account of the Family History and Descendants of Samuel and Maria McCracken," [compiled by Mrs. Mamie Beattie]. Typescript, seven pages. Prepared for Family Reunion, Springbank Park, London, Ontario, 20 July 1963.

[McLellan family Bible] *New Devotional and Explanatory Pictorial Family Bible, containing the Old and New Testaments ... together with Dr. William Smith's Dictionary of the Bible* .... Paris, Ontario: John S. Brown, 1870 (?).

McLellan, Samuel. Reference number RG 9 IIA5. Medals, Honours and Awards, Military and Peacekeeping, Library and Archives Canada.

McSherry, Peter. *Red Ryan. The Big Red Fox*. Toronto: Dundurn, 1999.

Middleton, C.W. *St. Andrew's; Knox - Komoka; North Caradoc*. [A History of the Presbyterian Churches in Caradoc Township] 1978.

Morton, W. L. "The Relevance of Canadian History." *Contexts of Canadian Criticism*, ed. Eli Mandel. Chicago: University of Chicago Press, 1971. 48-70.

Murray, Heather. *Come, Bright Improvement! : The Literary Societies of Nineteenth-Century Ontario*. Toronto: University of Toronto Press, 2002.

Neary, Peter. *On To Civvy Street: Canada's Rehabilitation Program for Veterans of the Second World War*. Montreal & Kingston: McGill-Queen's University Press, 2011.

New Brunswick Genealogical Society. First Families. www.nbgs.ca/firstfamilies

Palmer, Gregory. *Biographical Sketches of Loyalists of the American Revolution*. [a revision of Lorenzo Sabine's 1864 book of the same title.] Westport, CT.: Meckler, 1984.

Prendergast, John P. *The Cromwellian Settlement of Ireland*. "Second edition, enlarged." Dublin: McGlashan & Gill, 1875.

Reaney, James. *The Box Social and Other Stories*. Erin, Ontario: Porcupine's Quill, 1996.

Riker, James. *Harlem (city of New York): its origin and early annals*. New York: The Author, 1881.

———. *Revised History of Harlem*. Rev. by Henry Pennington Toler. New York: New Harlem Publishing Company, 1904.

"Roane, Thomas." *Commemorative biographical record of the county of Lambton, Ontario: containing biographical sketches of prominent and representative citizens and many of the early settled families*. Toronto: compiled by J.H. Beers & Co., 1906. 41-2.

Roberts, Kenneth. *Oliver Wiswell*. Toronto: McClelland & Stewart; New York: Doubleday, 1940.

Romer, H. Dorothea, and Helen B. Hartman. *Jan Dyckman of Harlem and his Descendants*. New York: J.A. Thompson, 1981.

[Runnalls family] "The Family of Richard Thomas Runnalls (1835 - May 10, 1915) who in 1862 married Hannah Elizabeth Dykeman (1845 - April 3, 1891)." Typescript, 31 pages. No date.

Runnalls, Francis Edwin. *Memoirs and Reflections*. Published by his daughter, Dr. Donna Ruth Runnalls, 1999.

Runnalls, Jean (Mrs. Ralph). "Runnalls Family History." Manuscript, 22 pages. December 1987.

Runnalls, John Lawrence, compiler. "The Runnalls Clan." [Family tree] 1941.

Runnalls, Richard Roy. Regimental number 802908. File: RG 150, Accession 1992-93/166, Box 8544-48. Library and Archives Canada.

Ryerson, Egerton. *Canadian Methodism: Its Epochs and Characteristics*. Toronto: William Briggs, 1882.

Sargent, Clem. *The Colonial Garrison 1817-1824: The 48th Foot, The Northamptonshire Regiment in the Colony of New South Wales*. Canberra: TCS Publications, 1996.

Scarf, J. Thomas. *History of Westchester County, New York. Including Morrisania, Kings Bridge, and West Farms, which have been annexed to New York City*. 2 vols. Philadelphia: L.E. Preston, 1886.

Semple, Neil. *The Lord's Dominion: The History of Canadian Methodism*. Montreal & Kingston: McGill-Queen's University Press, 1996.

Stapleford, L. M. "Walnut, in Brooke Twp., Centred in Nut Groves, Thrived Ninety Years Ago." *Watford Guide-Advocate*, 27 August 1948. Reprinted from the *London Free Press*.

Strathroy Age-Dispatch [weekly newspaper], Strathroy, Ontario, 1866- .

Thompson, Jemima (Runnalls). "Memories of My Dawn Home." Typescript, 1973.

Thompson, Wilbert and Doreen. "Robert Thompson Family Tree." Typescript. Mount Brydges, Ontario, August 1977.

Todd, Sandra Vermilyea. *The Vermilyea Family (Vermilya, Vermilye, Vermilyea, Vermilyer) Descendants of Johannes Vermilje, New York, 1662-2009*. www.vermilyeafamilyreunion.com

Toler, Henry Pennington. *The New Harlem Register. A Genealogy of the descendants of the twenty-three original Patentees of the Town of New Harlem*. New York: New Harlem Publishing Company, 1903.

Turnure, Robert F., and Joan D. Turnure. *Tourneur Family History*. Various websites.

[United Farmers of Ontario] Minute Book and Treasurers' Accounts of the Lambton East United Farmers of Ontario 1919-1932. Copied from the original owned by Rey Werden, Alvinston, Ontario. Archives and Research Collections Centre, University of Western Ontario, London, Ontario.

University of Toronto. *University of Toronto Roll of Service 1914-1918*. Ed. G. Oswald Smith.

[Toronto:] University of Toronto Press, 1921.

Vance, Jonathan F. *Death So Noble: Memory, Meaning, and the First World War.* Vancouver: University of British Columbia Press, 1997.

[Walnut United Church, Brooke Township.] "Walnut United Church 1878-1964." Typescript, 16 pages.

———. "One Hundredth Anniversary 1878-1978. Walnut United Church, Concession 11, Lot 16, Brooke Township, Lambton County, Ontario." [Includes a history of the church.]

War Diaries. 15th Canadian Infantry Battalion 48th Highlanders of Canada, 1916/05/01 to 1917/12/31. www.canadaatwar.ca

War Diaries. 6th Brigade, Canadian Field Artillery 1917/08/01 - 1918/07/31. Canadian Great War Project. www.canadiangreatwarproject.com

[Watford, Ontario] *Watford Centennial 1873-1973.* Published for the Centennial Committee by Progressive Printing, London, Ontario.

Watford Guide-Advocate [weekly newspaper], 1875–.

[Watson] "Londoner Has Marriage Certificate Issued to His Great Grandparents." *London Free Press* (2 August 1961): 23.

Watson, Catherine. "The Campbells," Five pages. Undated typescript.

———. "The Children of James and Mary Watson." Eight pages plus one photograph of the Watson family. Undated typescript.

———. "The Children of Peter and Mary Smith." Four pages, Undated typescript.

———. "The Family of John and Margaret Smith" (five pages); "The Family of David and Catherine (Kate) Watson" (one page); "The Family of Duncan Jr. and Nancy Campbell" (two pages); "The Family of Alfred and Mary Ann Clothier" (one page); "The Family of John and Sarah Bowlby" (five pages); "The Family of John and Mary Graham (Minnie) Campbell" (one page); "The Family of James (Jim) and Jauneta Christina (Min) Edgar" (three pages). Undated typescript.

———. "The Family of Duncan 'Hedley' and Margaret Campbell." Undated typescript, two pages. "The Family of Duncan and Sarah Campbell." Undated typescript, four pages.

———. "Roderick David Watson and His Family." Ten pages plus three pages of photographs. Typescript dated 22 November 1999.

———. "The Smith Family." Sixty-six pages. Undated typescript.

———. "The Watson Story." Eighteen pages. Undated typescript.

Watts, C.A.H. Review of *Before the Age of Miracles. Journal of the Royal College of General Practitioners* 24 (1974): 540.

Webb, Todd. *Transatlantic Methodists: British Wesleyanism and the Formation of an Evangelical Culture in Nineteenth-Century Ontario and Quebec.* Montreal & Kingston: McGill-Queen's University Press, 2013.

Whyte, Donald. *A Dictionary of Scottish Emigrants to Canada Before Confederation.* Toronto: Ontario Genealogical Society, 1986.

Wilson, William Tully. Regimental number 89141. File: RG 150, Accession 1992-93/166, Box 10485-52. Library and Archives Canada.

Wright, Esther Clark. *The Loyalists of New Brunswick.* Fredericton, 1955.

Wright, Mary. *Zestful Lives: The Unusual Wrights of Strathroy 1865-1995.* London, Ontario, 1997.

INDEX

Anderson, Clara E., *The Minister's Bride*, 80-1

Annett, Ross (author of "Babe" stories), 72

automobiles: the Hairs' first car (1918), 83-4; their 1926 Pontiac, 95-6; Mr. Rutherford's Star car, 96; Alice Runnalls's first car ride, 101; our 1947 Chevrolet, 212-13; new Buick after accident, 291

"Barnardo boys": Norm Wilson, Clarence Lewis, 62-3

Bateman, Frances Elizabeth (McCracken) ("Aunt Lizzie"): immigration narrative, 49; marriage to Charles Bateman, 117-18; his death, 118; the Bateman estate, 118-20; last years and death, 120

Beck, Sir Adam, 80

"boodlers," 14

box social ("basket sociable"), 26

Brides from Eaton's (Mail Order Brides), 152-3

Brooke Township: topography and survey 2-3, 21; immigrants from Monaghan and North Tipperary, 10-12; "a howling wilderness," 18; draining the swamp, 21; the lumber industry, 22; woodcutting as a competitive sport, 22-3; maintenance of drains, 23; pathmasters and poundkeepers, 27-8; remuneration for animals killed by dogs, 28; elections for councillor, 127; duties of council, 128; search for oil and gas, 141-2; annual elections, 127; wartime measures of council, 186-7; nomination meeting in Inwood, 200; rehabilitation of returned servicemen, 201, 206; Dutch immigrants on the Twelfth Line, 222; disappearance of school sections, 268-9; International Ploughing Match (1973), 289

"bush": "bush farm," 13; in Dawn Township, 43; "back at the bush," 13, 23

"Calamity Corners" (London, Ontario), 208, 225

Cameron, Reverend Donald, 233-4, 240, 247, 254, 255-6

Camp family ("Tories," Loyalists), 56-7; Satira Camp (wife of Jacob Dykeman), 51

Campbells of Lobo Township, 19-21; clan gathering at Poplar Hill, 19-21

Campbell, Duncan and Sarah (McLellan) (great-great-grandparents), 20

Caradoc Township: its topography and survey, 36-7; railways, 37; its war memorial and annual service, 110, 151-2, 161, 164; its potatoes, 114, and apples, 146-7; literary society, 115-16; natural gas line, 165

Caradoc Township Sunday School Association, 158-9

Carter, William (great-great grandfather): emigration, 10, 12; second marriage, 12-13

Cavanaugh, Alice (Galbraith) (first cousin), 15, 275, 303, 309

Chalmers Presbyterian Church, Brooke Township, 24-5, 95, 142

childbirth, deaths of young women in, and infant mortality: 2, 20-1

Church of Christ Disciples, 174

cisterns, 76

Clark, Helen Annett Zavitz, xiv, 12-13, 14, 21, 127

Cook's Church, Caradoc Township: its establishment as a Presbyterian Church, 47-8; its cemetery, 47; description of services, 47-8; first meeting of Joseph Runnalls and Tillie Thompson, 46, 48; its garden parties, 48, 110; wedding of Honor Robinson and Har-

318 • Donald S. Hair

old Hair, 193-4
"co-op": *see* United Farmers of Ontario
corporal punishment in elementary schools: in Dawn Township, 43-4; in S.S. No. 10, Brooke, 62-3
Crawford, John T. and Jessie, 148
creamery and cheese factory: at Kerwood, 73-4; at Walnut, 24
crokinole, 146, 254-5
Cuban missile crisis, 275
cyclone, 199
Dawn Township, Lambton County: pioneer experiences of the Runnalls family, 41, 42-5; of the Dykemans, 50
Delmage, Horace: my father's story about his birth, 72; "Bonnie Doon," 91
Depression (the 1930s): its effects in Brooke Township, 128, 131, 143; Lambton County Council's cuts in expenditures and salaries, 137-8; reduction of my mother's salary, 147, 157-8; the farm in 1935, 143
Diefenbaker, John, Prime Minister, 252, 253
dogs: running wild, 28; our dog Snap, 213-14
Dolbear, Edna Margaret, 133-4
Donnellys: my father at the St. Nicholas Hotel, Appin, 74; the story of "old Mrs. Crawford," 148; their reputation, 148
Drury, E. C. (Ernest Charles, premier of Ontario), 87-8
"dumb waiter," 93
Dumbells, 80
Dykeman family history, 49-58, 270: our seventeenth-century forebears in Manhattan, 51-3; our Dykeman line of descent, 57-8
Dykeman (Dyckman), Garrit (Loyalist ancestor), 53-6
Dykeman, George Joseph Hatfield (great-great grandfather), 50
Eckhart, Reverend Benjamin, 174-5
Eddy, Louis (lawyer and judge), 221, 288
Eddy, Reverend W.T., 180
Edgar, Allan: the story of his house and barn, 176-7
Edgar, Lorne, 239, 249, 284, 301, 306, 309
Elliott, Bruce, xv, 7, 10
Elliott, John Campbell (M.P. for West Middlesex and Postmaster General), 122, 289
England, Eliza (great-great grandmother), 10-13, 141, 176
family reunions: descendants of Eliza England, 141, 176; the Watsons, 141; the Runnallses, 154-5, 164; the Dykemans, 49-50, 155
farm, Sherman Hair's, 1, 3; new house, 92-3; description of house, barn, and other buildings, 92-4

farm, Joseph Runnalls's, 36
farming practices: cradle, 1-2; binders, 2; haying, 94, 209; threshing, 2, 23, 132, 210; "stockers," 131-2; "chores," 132, 225-6; seasons, 132, 195-6; white beans and sweet corn, 202-3; chickens and crows, 203; tractor and combine, 210; farm income (1946), 210; items at Grandad Runnalls's auction sale, 195-6; items at Dad's auction sale, 213
Faulkner, William, 272
Foster family (neighbours), 8, 176, 220, 246
Frye, Northrop, x-xi, 13
garden party: at Cook's Church, Caradoc, 48; at St. Andrew's, Mount Brydges, 110; at Cook's and North Caradoc, 110;
Gone With the Wind, 191
gramophone, 159
Green, George W. ("George Watson"), 70-1
Hair, Alice Maud (Runnalls) (our mother): *see* Runnalls, Alice Maud
Hair, Ann (Carter) ("Grandmother Hair"): emigration, 10; marriage to John Hair, 12; as *accoucheur*, 14; her death, 86
Hair, Dessa (our grandmother): *see* Watson, Mary Fedicia Catherine
Hair, Donald Sherman: birth, 177; starts to school, 198; appendectomy, 207; haying, 209; doing the "chores," 225-6; University of Toronto, 263-4; England, 277; marries Arlene MacVicar, 278-9; Europe, 281
Hair, Elizabeth Jane ("Aunt Liza"), 15, 70
Hair, Floranna May ("Aunt May"), 15; in Saskatoon, 70-1; in London, 126; as hairdresser in Strathroy, 183
Hair, Harold (first cousin): as my father's best man, 167; barns burn, 181-2; his hired man, 191; marries Honor Robinson, 193-4; family, 194; the Jongsmas, 222; Happy Doubles Club, 239; with Aunt Agnes, 241
Hair, James (great-great grandfather): emigration, 4; baptismal record of son Thomas, 5; his farm and its produce, 9; selling wood to the railway, 8-9; retirement and death, 9
Hair, James Alexander ("Uncle Jim"): marriage, 71; move to Annett farm, 67; accidental death, 126-7
Hair, John Alexander ("my father"): birth, 1; "my early years," 59-60; at S.S. No. 10, Brooke, 60-2; "our neighbours," 64-8; his reading, 72; teaches cat to open door, 72; music lessons, 75-6; first solo in public, 78; "Daily War Puzzle," 78-9; plays wedding march, 82; at Watford High School, 83; Harrison's dog, 89; card-playing and dancing, 89-90; "driving Mr. Fortner," 90; as tenor

soloist, 94-5; United Church Conference of 1926, 95-6; work in Detroit, 96-7; as guest soloist at anniversary services, 133; Edna Dolbear, 133-4; courtship of Alice Runnalls, 142-3; marriage and wedding trip, 167-8; social gatherings, 169; as choir leader at Walnut, 170; "acrobatic hen," 170; assessor of Brooke Township, 170-1; township councillor, 171-2, 178-9; Donald's birth, 177-8; as deputy-reeve, 179, 186-7; selling Christmas turkeys, 181; appendectomy, 182-3; as Lambton County councillor, 187-8; music at anniversary services, 189; "The Holy City," 189-90; as reeve of Brooke Township, 199-202, 204-6; Liberal politics, 203, 290; "Old Baddalacks," 209; last year of farming, 210; appointed Treasurer of Lambton County, 211-12, 214-15; as elder and Sunday School superintendent, 220; buys house in Watford, 233-4; all-expenses-paid trip to Florida, 234-5; sells the farm, 235-7; appointed Clerk-Treasurer of Lambton County, 245-6; his duties, 248; handling sensitive issues, 249; Twilight Haven, 249-50; new county building, courthouse and gaol, 250-2; Prime Minister Diefenbaker, 252; relations with the wardens, 253, 273-4; A.M.C.T. from Queen's, 254-5; as a Rotarian, 256-7; expropriation of Watford house, 262-4; 1267 Webster Drive, Sarnia, 264; Grace United Church, 268; "ask Dad," 272; St. Clair Parkway, 278; Prime Minister Trudeau, 280; lieutenant-governor's receptions, 280; onset of heart disease, 281, 286-7; North Lambton Rest Home, 282; retirement, 283-5, 287; secretary-treasurer of Lambton's rest homes, 283, 285-6; Governor-General Roland Michener, 286; stamps, coins, model windmills, 288-9; first grandchild, 289-90; honour from Western University, 290; history of Lambton County officials, 291-2; second grandson, 292; heart problems, 298; University Hospital, London, 302-3; selling the Sarnia house, 303-4; "being with Dad," 304; more stories, 297, 304-5; the 1982 warden's banquet, 305-7; Lambton County Municipal Association banquet, 307; last days and death, 307-9

Hair, John ("Grandad Hair"): emigration, 4-5; marriage to Ann Carter, 12; their seven children, 13-14, 15-16; purchase of Chittick house and farm, 14; description of house, 15; barn raising, 14-15; travel "out West," 70; his use of wind power, 85-6; death, 126

Hair, Marjorie Jean: birth, 188; starts to school, 216-17; appendectomy, 225; University of Toronto, 263-4, 277; marries Michael Hale, 278-9; their first house, 282; Rob's birth, 289-90; Derek's birth, 292

Hair, Mary Ann (Galbraith) ("Aunt Mary"), 15, 72, 286

Hair, Nancy ("Ann") (Leathem) (great-great grandmother), 4

Hair, Rebecca ("Aunt Beck"), 15; in Chelsea, Michigan, 71; as care-giver, 126; death, 286

Hair, Sarah Louise (Delmage) ("Aunt Lou"), 15; education, marriage and family, 72; death of Disney Delmage, 91; her death, 286

Hair, William Sherman ("my grandfather"): baptism, 13; walk to Napier for whisky, 14-15; his early life and education, 29-30; harvest excursion, 70; Ontario Agricultural College, 87-8; as judge of livestock at fall fairs, 59-60; his character, 30, 34, 136, 140, 309; marriage to Dessa Watson, 34; as chair at an oyster supper, 77; as debater, 77; as bee-keeper, 77-8, 132; hosts meal for soldiers, 79; new house on the farm, 92-4; as Brooke Township councillor, 127-31; heads poll in election of 1929, 129; loses bid for deputy-reeve by one vote, 130; as deputy-reeve, 131; opposes reintroduction of statute labour, 138; illness and death, 139-40, 309

Hair (Hare, Haire), William, 6-7
Haire, Joseph (centenarian), 173
Hale, Robert, 289-90, 291
Hale, Derek, 292
Harrison, Ivy and Mary: rural mail delivery, 73; the Harrisons' dog, 89
Hart, Reverend Enos W., 133, 140, 169, 170, 179-80, 294
Harvey cousins, 229, 254
Hatfield (Loyalist family, Westchester County, New York), 53-4; Eunice Hatfield Dykeman, 55-6
Henderson, Lorne, M.L.A., 247, 253, 283, 284, 290, 306
Herbert, Gerry (county auditor), 214, 238, 246, 278, 301
hired man: Ray, "Old Jack," Albert Laferriere, 190-1
high school districts, 205-6, 207
"Holy City, The" (tenor solo), 189-90
Huey, John (clerk of Lambton County), 137, 211, 244-5, 291
hydro comes to the farm, 204
Ireland: Clontibret, 5; Roscrea 10-11
Irvine, Agnes (Thompson) ("Aunt Agnes"): tragic death of Emily Trott, 101-02; "always sending clothing," 98; marriage and the

Thornton-Smith Company, 121; her travels, 122; life in Rosedale, 121; congratulatory letter, 124; Alice's visit, 154; lunch at the Royal York, 156; wedding of Bob Irvine and Kay Avery, 162-3; visits to the farm, 228-9; last visit and death, 241-2

Irving, Washington: Reformed Dutch Church in Sleepy Hollow, 53

Janes, Charles Eusebius ("Zeb") (M.L.A for East Lambton), 61, 203-04, 239, 247-8, 274

Johnson, Marguerite (Purdy) (Mrs. Nelson Johnson), music teacher, 123, 222

Johnston, William H. (family historian), xiv, 12-13, 30, 141, 176

Johnston, Dr. William Victor, 141, 176

Jones, Jeddie (O'More), my father's music teacher, 75-6

Kelly family, 7-8

King, Jack and Beccie (neigbours), 66, 68, 81, 233

Kitchen family, Schomberg, 60

Lambton County Council: in 1931, 137; election of warden, 137, 247; effects of the Depression, 137-8; the June session, 137-8; January, June and December sessions in 1940, 187-8; the equalization controversy, 194-5; bad weather for sessions, 195; establishment of health unit, 207; the "old" county buildings, 215-16, 252; the fox bounty, 216; the warden's banquet, 238, 274, 305-06

Lauder, Sir Harry, 94, 159

Leckie, John (treasurer of Lambton County), 211-12

Lewis, Clarence (neighbour), 62-3, 95, 172, 198, 266

Lightfoot, Joe (neighbour, "a cranky old customer"), 66-7

literary and debating societies: in north Brooke, 76-7; and the United Farmers of Ontario, 88; Caradoc Literary Society, 115-16; emblem, 124; public speaking contest, 154

locker service in Watford, 190

Loyalists: see Dykeman, Camp

Mackay, George Leslie (Presbyterian missionary), 112, 160

Mackenzie, Hugh, M.P.: election of 1935, 168-9; letter from China, 203-04

Macphail, Agnes, M.P., 152

mail, rural delivery, 73

"Maple Leaf Forever," 77-8, 110

maple syrup and sugar making: in Dawn Township, 42; on our farm, 185

Mawlam family in Dawn Township, 45-6

McCracken family, 39: emigration and pioneer life in Caradoc, 49

McEvoy, Helen (Coulter): history of the schools of Caradoc Township

McLachlan family: ships' masters on the Great Lakes, 67; Captain Glen McLachlan, 68; his accidental death, 68, 243-4

McLean, Mary Evelyn (teacher), 223

McLellan, Chester ("Uncle Ches"): marries Ruth Runnalls, 134-5, 156; accident, 276; heart attack, 292-3; decline and death, 295-6

McLellan, Ruth (Runnalls): see Runnalls, Ruth Muriel

McLellan, Samuel ("Uncle Ches's father"), 1, 8, 64-5; dances an Irish jig, 12; "never shaved in his life," 64; Fenian Raid medal, 64-5

McLellan, Samuel ("Uncle Ches's brother"): McLellan family in 1930, 135; death, 275-6

McLuhan, Marshall, 204

McNeil, Ada Margaret Evelyn (Watson) ("Aunt Eva"): Brooke Women's Institute, 78; as lead in *The Minister's Bride*, 80-1; marriage to Gordon McNeil, 82-3; birth of son John, 83; visits, 228; her death, 293

McNeil, Gordon: as teacher in S.S. No. 10, Brooke, 61; education, 82; marriage to Eva Watson, 82; as teacher in a collegiate institute, 82, 211; praises my grandmother's pies, 226; visits, 228

McNeil, John Grant: birth, 83; marries Dora Dicks, 194; their family, 194; death, 293

McRorie, Bill (clerk-treasurer), 278, 283-4, 301, 306, 309

McVicar, Currie (assistant clerk-treasurer), 246, 278

Methodism: conversion of James Watson, 17-18; deathbed confession of faith of "Kate" (Campbell) Watson, 33; "the most Canadian of all the churches," 32; their beliefs, 32; centrality of the Word, 32-3; social and cultural attitudes, 33-4; church services in Dawn Township, 44; "Free Methodist" camp meetings at Shetland, 44; card playing and dancing, 89-90

milk, unpastureurized, 186

Mount Carmel Methodist Church, Brooke Township, 19, 24

Murray, Heather, 76, 116

Neary, Peter, 201

Niagara Falls, excursions to: 69, 216, 218, 282

Noronic (passenger ship, Northern Navigation Company) 125: tour of, 221; burns, 221

North Caradoc Presbyterian Church, 113, 148-50, 158-9; the 1933 garden party, 161

"Northwest Fever," 46, 69-71

Oke, Leslie Warner (M.L.A for East Lambton), 86, 88, 130
Ontario Gothic, 3, 102, 306; *see also* Donnellys
Ontario Municipal Association, 253, 273-4, 279-80, 282-3
Orange Lodge: in Mount Brydges; the "Glorious Twelfth," 114
oyster suppers: "one of the greatest benefits to the social life of the community," 77; Sherman and Dessa Hair as hosts, 84; at St. Andrew's Presbyterian Church, Mount Brydges, 111
Peg O' My Heart (John Hartley Manners), 153-4
ploughing match, 289
Port Stanley, 122, 154
Powell family, Brooke Township, 33, 68-9
Powell, Melvin (neighbour), 65, 200, 204-05, 239, 256, 266
Presbyterian Church in Canada: services, 44, 47-8; the 1911 General Assembly, 99-100; overseas missions, 111-12; church union and the "continuing Presbyterians," 112-13
prohibition in Ontario: referendum of 1919, 87
railways: Great Western's London-to-Sarnia line, 8; railways across Caradoc Township, 37; Grand Trunk line across Brooke Township, 60; excursions to London, Niagara and Sarnia, 69; Sherman Hair's petition on freight rates, 136; *see also* Wanstead railway wreck
Reaney, James, xiii-xiv, 3, 26, 74, 148
Reid family, Brooke Township, 66
Reid, George (neighbour), 62, 66, 266; service in First World War, 79-80
Reo Theatre, Watford, 209-10
Roane family, 3, 11-12
Roberts, Kenneth, *Oliver Wiswell*, 55
Robertson, Reverend Duncan (minister at St. Andrew's, Mount Brydges), 104
Robinson, Honor (Hair; first cousin), 40, 112, 134, 167; marries Harold Hair, 193-4; their family, 194
Royal Visits: 1939, 182; 1951, 229; 1959, 257-8
Runnalls, Alice Maud (Hair) (our mother): her birth, 36; her cautionary tales (the Buchanan boy, Emily Trott), 101-02; "My Home and School years," 98; childhood on farm, 100-01; neighbours (Buchanans, Sullivans), 102-03; elementary school, 103; Christmases, the Christmas concert, 104-05; Mount Brydges Continuation School, 114-15; basketball team, 115; oratorical contests, 115-16; excursions to Port Stanley, 122; at Strathroy Collegiate Institute, 122-3; gold medal for public speaking, 123-5; interest in poetry, 150; at London Normal School, 144; "Nature Lore," 144-5; as teacher at S.S. No. 7, Caradoc, 147-8; her love of sleigh bells, 149; missionaries and the Young Women's Missionary Society, 149; her readings, 150, 159; trip to Ottawa with Uncle Frank, 155-6; St. Andrew's Dramatic Club, 152-3; as President of the Young People's Society, 156-7; Camp Kintail, 157; as church organist, 158; Young People's Society of North Caradoc, 159-60, 163; papers on missions and missionaries, 160; Clarence Ward, 160-1; a courtship story, 161; "going with" John Hair, 142-3, 161; resignation, farewells and addresses, 163-4, 165-6; wedding, 167; wedding trip, 168; Walnut Women's Association, 169; hosts meetings of W.A., 180-1; president of the W.A., 191-2; a last stay in her old home, 196; appendectomy, 208; as Sunday School teacher, 220; reading aloud, 239-40; as "literature secretary" for the W.A., 220, 239, 255; as county book-keeper, 226, 273; courses in Christian Leadership, 240; vacation Bible school, 240; pouring tea, 248, 274; as a Rotary Ann, 257; meetings and conventions, 273-4; entertaining friends and relatives, 275; onset of diabetes and chronic bronchitis, 280-1; letters (1969), 281-3; first grandchild, 289-90; retirement projects, 294; second grandson, 292; Normal School's fifty-year reunion, 293-4; fall, last days, and death, 298-302
Runnalls cousins (Marilyn Grant, Bruce Runnalls), 229, 254
Runnalls, Edwin ("Uncle Ed"): buys Grandad Runnalls' farm, 101; moves to Warwick, 40; death, 296-7
Runnalls, Eva Kathleen (Harvey) ("Aunt Eva"): as public school teacher, 117; travel to west coast, 125-6; marries Lewis Harvey, 150-1; their family, 151; death of Joyce Harvey, 165; Aunt Eva's death, 188-9
Runnalls, Reverend Francis Edwin ("Uncle Frank"): at Strathroy high school, 105; rejection for military service, 109; on church union, 113; ministry in British Columbia, marriage to Nellie Oliver, their family, 116-17; visits to Ontario, 155-6, 229
Runnalls family: Grandad Runnalls's siblings, 39-40; his forebears in Cornwall, 38, 40-1; "the old house," 40; move to Dawn Township, 41; return to Caradoc, 45
Runnalls, Hannah (Dykeman) (great-grand-

mother), 38, 41-2: in her daughter Jemima's memories, 42-3; her birth at Sheffield, 50, 58; marries Richard Runnalls, 41, 50; Loyalist 49

Runnalls, Howard Joseph ("Uncle Howard"): at Mount Brydges Continuation School, 117-18; University of Western Ontario, 125; marries Eleanor McEwen, 162; their children, 162; move to Timmins, 162; visits to the farm 228-9

Runnalls, Joseph ("Grandad Runnalls"): birth 42; as elder in the Presbyterian Church, 38; boyhood in Dawn Township, 42; shoots deer, 43; as farm labourer, 45; as singer and choir leader, 44; buys a farm in Caradoc, 46; marries Tillie Thompson, 46; as delegate to the General Assembly of the Presbyterian Church, 99-100; in Stettler, Alberta, 100; as member of the Orange Lodge, 114; as executor of the Bateman estate, 118-20; a squatter on the Bateman farm, 119-20; retires from farming, 195-6; excursion to Niagara, 218; death, 222-3; sale of house and contents, 225

Runnalls, Matilda ("Tillie") (Thompson) ("Grammie Runnalls"), 40; marries Joseph Runnalls, 46; domestic help, 100; Ladies' Aid and Women's Missionary Society, 110, 145-6, 170; a typical meeting of the W.M.S., 112; president of the Ladies' Aid, 112; withdrawal from church groups, 170; death, 199

Runnalls, Mary (Ringrose; Gibbs) ("Aunt Mary"), 39, 120, 155

Runnalls, Neil Dykeman (first cousin): at Strathroy Collegiate Institute, 123; teacher in Timmins, 123, 162; marries Mabel Toles, 144, 294

Runnalls, Richard Thomas (great-grandfather), 40-1; emigration to Canada, 38; as devout Methodist, 38; death, 42

Runnalls, Roy (first cousin): military service, letter home, death, 105-08

Runnalls, Ruth Muriel ("Aunt Ruth"): at Strathroy Hospital School of Nursing, 117; travel to west coast, 125-6; as nurse in New York, 156; marries Chester McLellan, 134-5, 156; as member of St. James Anglican Church, 135; move to Strathroy, 209, 276; caring for Uncle Ches, 195-6

rural mail delivery: its coming to the Twelfth Line, 73

Ryan, Norman "Red," criminal, 171

Ryerson, Egerton, 32

St. Andrew's Presbyterian Church, Mount Brydges: its history, 37-8; and the First World War, 109-10; socials, garden parties, and church suppers, 110-11; "anniversary," 111; vote against church union, 112-13

Salem Methodist Episcopal Church: its history, 25; as "Watson's Meeting House," 63; social gatherings and fund raisers, 25-7, 74-5; its ministers, 64, 90; garden party at Sherman Hair's, 75; sixtieth anniversary, 95; Mr. Rutherford and his Star car, 96; Christmas bazaar, 96; closing, 132-3; subsequent use of building, 63-4. *See also* tea meeting, box social

School Section No. 5, Brooke Township, 27; sale 269

School Section No. 10, Brooke Township, 27, 29, 60; its heating and ventilation, 61; its teachers, 61; sale 269

School Section No. 7, Caradoc Township, 147

School Section No. 10 ("McEvoy's School"), Caradoc Township, 37; its teachers, 103; the Christmas concert, 104-5

Searson family, 11, 12

Semple, Neil, 32-3

Smith (Schmid) family, 17-18

Spanish flu epidemic, 85

statute labour (maintenance of roads): defined, 27-8; Brooke Township's referendum of 1933, 129, 138-9

Stewart, Mrs. Verna, 278, 285

storm of November 1913, 69

tea meeting: at Salem Methodist Church, 25-6; at the Presbyterian Church at Oakdale, 44; revival at St. Andrew's Presbyterian Church, Mount Brydges, 111

telephone: its coming to the Twelfth Line, 72; the party line, 198-9

television: our first set, 243

temperance: elided with abstinence, 87, 155, 158; annual temperance sermon, 220

Thompson family history: in County Down, Ireland, 47; in Nelson Township, Ontario, 47; move to Caradoc Township, 47

Thompson, Jemima (Runnalls) ("Aunt Mima"), 39-40: "Memories of my Dawn home," 42-5

Thompson, John Hamilton (great-grandfather), 38-9: his move to Caradoc Township, 47; pioneer life in Caradoc, 47; his two wives and his thirteen children, 40; his death, 48

Thompson, Sarah Jane (McCracken) (great-grandmother), 48-9

Thornton-Smith Company, Toronto: *see* Irvine, Agnes

threshing: *see* farm practices

tramps, 34-5, 45

trips by car: Niagara, 218; Ottawa and Québec,

218-19; "round the Gaspé," 224-5; Florida, 230-2, 258; around Lake Huron, 237-8; Virginia and Washington, D.C., 242-3; Grand Canyon, 258-9; New England, 259-60; New Orleans, 260-1; Atlantic City and New York, 261; Washington, D.C., 261-2; Halifax, 269-70; Mexico, 270-2

Trudeau, Pierre Elliott, Prime Minister, 280

Turner, Duncan, and the Turner family, 172-3, 178, 196-7, 202, 205

United Farmers of Ontario: in Brooke Township, 86-9; the "co-op," 88-9; the Farmers' Store in Watford, 88-9; decline of the movement, 155

United Farm Women of Ontario, 88, 151-2, 154, 155

Wallis, Orville (GM dealer in Watford), 202, 212, 256; survives railway accident, 297; new showroom, 221

Walnut Methodist Church (afterwards United Church), Brooke Township: its founding, 24; exorcism, 24; anniversary services, 95, 189; as part of three-point charge, 133; its sixtieth anniversary, 180; anniversary services in 1940 and 1942, 189; Mission band and Junior Choir, 220; The Jolly Twosomes, 238-9; a split in the congregation, 240; renovations, 255; its one-hundredth anniversary, 294-5; its closing, 294-5

Wanstead railway wreck, 69

Watson, Catherine ("Kate" Campbell) (great-grandmother), 19; her obituary, 31

Watson, Catherine (first cousin), 68, 188, 174: teacher at S.S. No. 5 Brooke, 192-3; deaconess in Presbyterian Church, 193

Watson, Guy Bernard ("Uncle Guy"): his birth, 31; "out West," 70; his early death, 90-1

Watson, Henry ("Uncle Harry"): as a lumberman, 22-3; as thresher, 23; hosts Watson reunion, 141; his marriage and his son Vern 226-8; Verhoysens buy his farm, 222

Watson, James David (great-great-grandfather): journey of Watson family from Chippewa to Brooke, 16-18; the eleven children of James and Mary Watson, 18-19; his death 16-18

Watson, Jennie (Munro) ("Aunt Jennie"), 173-4, 232

Watson, Mary Catherine Fedicia ("Dessa," our grandmother, "Bappy"): her early life, 30-1; marriage to Sherman Hair, 34; her character, 34; early married life, 34-5; the Brooke Women's Institute, 35, 77-8; papers for the Institute, 92; activities of the Institute, 136; origin of "Bappy," 178; hosts meetings of W.A., 169-70, 181, 192; her pies, 226; as traveller, 261; illness in Asheville, North Carolina, 261-2; last illness and death, 265-6; letter from Flossie Johnson, 266-7

Watson, Oscar Alexander ("Uncle Oscar"): his birth, 19, 31; marriage to Jennie Munro, 174; her death, 175; as manager of Ontario Hospital farms, 174; marriage to Jean Breckenridge, 175; in Woodstock, 223; his death, 232; Aunt Jean's death, 175, 294

Watson, Peter ("Uncle Pete"): his "chickens," 18; "pie for breakfast," 226; death, 221; Van Dinthers buy his farm, 222

Watson, Roderick David ("Grandad Watson"): arrival in Brooke as "a babe in arms," 18; his family, 19, 31; second marriage to Ella Reid, 4, 31-2; house destroyed by fire, 85; death, 208

Wilson, William Tully ("Billy"): military service, death at Passchendaele, 108-09

wind power: Grandad Hair's, 85-6; water for cattle, 214

witching for water, 214

women, status of: *The Minister's Bride*, 80-1; first vote in a provincial election, 87; in literary and debating societies, 88, 115-16; "little girl," 147; *Peg O' My Heart*, 153-4; debate on women as ministers, 160; United Farm Women of Ontario, 88; no women in municipal politics, 200; "sentiment in the council favoured the appointment of a male," 211; pouring tea, 248, 274; "Rotary Anns," 257; *see also* Women's Association; Women's Institute, Women's Missionary Society

Women's Association ("the W.A."), Walnut United Church: typical meetings, 169-70

Women's Institute, Brooke Township, 35, 84, 92, 136, 142; and First World War, 80; Dessa Hair's papers, 78

Women's Missionary Society: in St. Andrew's Presbyterian Church, Mount Brydges, 111-12

Woods family: Will (father of Gilbert), 11; Gilbert Woods (son), 65; Will (son of Gilbert), 65, 213; his locker service, 190; Dr. W.H. Woods of Mount Brydges, 48, 65; Dr. John T. Woods of Chelsea, Michigan, 65, 84, 175; Arthur Woods of Kerwood, 65, 175; deaths of Mrs. Gilbert Woods, 176, and Gilbert Woods, 176

Woods, Reverend Norval, 65, 96, 140, 305

Woods, Dr. Russell, 65; as entertainer, 75, 81; as district governor of Rotary, 257

World War One: "Daily War Puzzle" 78-9; Lambton's battalion and its training, 79;

military funeral in Strathroy, 79; changing attitudes, 80
World War Two: rationing, 184-6; maple syrup, 185; milkweed floss, 185; the Red Cross, 185; Camp Ipperwash, 187-8; Fred Taylor, Ernie Phair, Ray Hart, and Ray Swartz, 197; rehabilitation of returning soldiers, 201

Zavitz, Amy (Hair), 127, 220
Zavitz, Ward: in First World War, 80; death, 278

www.ingramcontent.com/pod-product-compliance
Lightning Source LLC
Chambersburg PA
CBHW020135130526
44590CB00039B/176